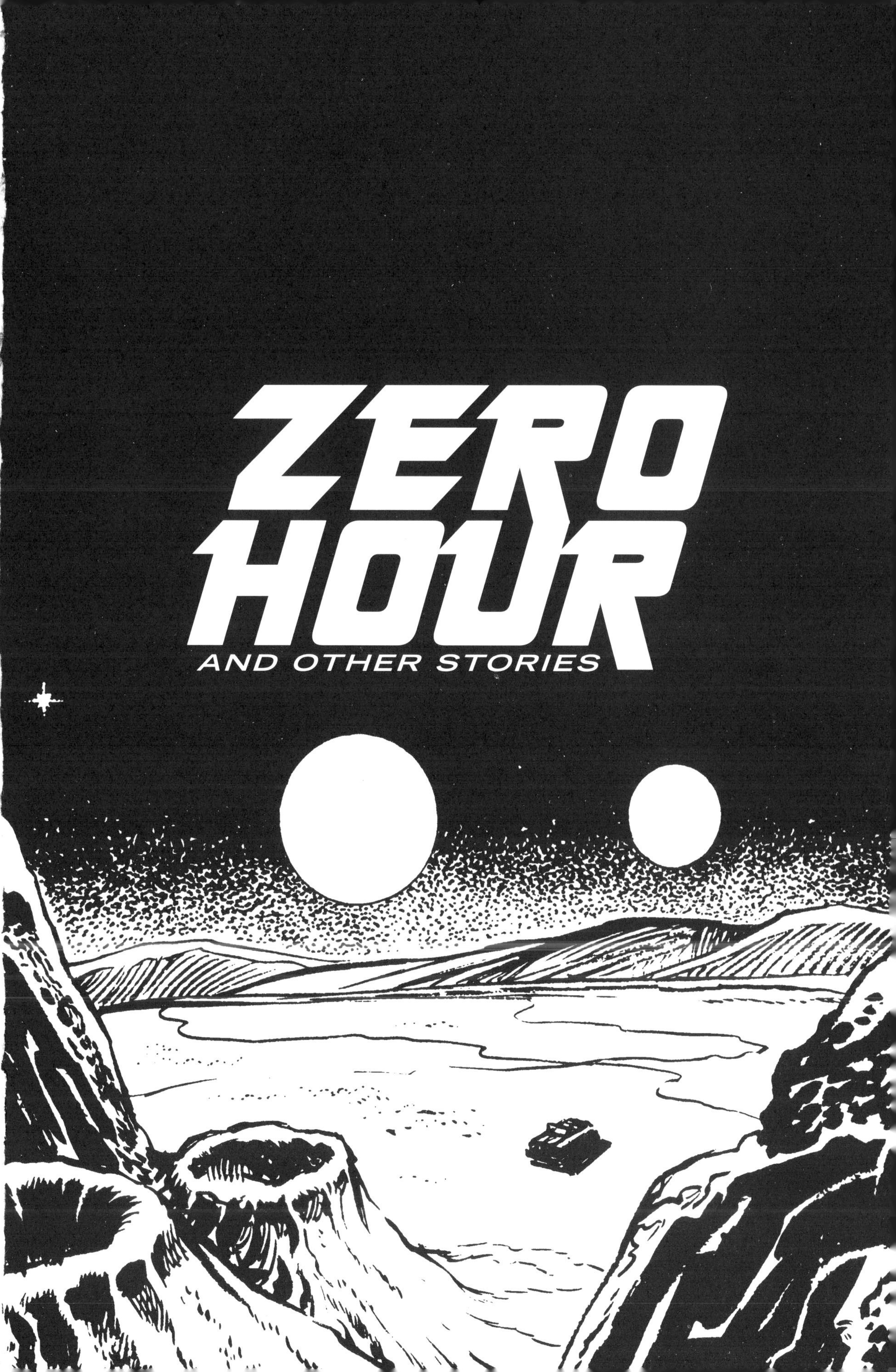
ZERO HOUR
AND OTHER STORIES

TITLES IN THIS SERIES:

Corpse On The Imjin And Other Stories *(Harvey Kurtzman)*
Came The Dawn And Other Stories *(Wallace Wood)*
50 Girls 50 And Other Stories *(Al Williamson)*
'Tain't The Meat ... It's The Humanity And Other Stories *(Jack Davis)*
Fall Guy For Murder And Other Stories *(Johnny Craig)*
Child Of Tomorrow And Other Stories *(Al Feldstein)*
Sucker Bait And Other Stories (*Graham Ingels*)
Zero Hour And Other Stories (*Jack Kamen*)

COMING SOON

Judgment Day And Other Stories (*Joe Orlando*)
Bomb Run And Other Stories (*John Severin*)

Executive Editor: GARY GROTH
Senior Editor: J. MICHAEL CATRON
Series Designer: JACOB COVEY
Designer: EMORY LIU
Production: PRESTON WHITE
Associate Publisher: ERIC REYNOLDS
Publishers: GARY GROTH and KIM THOMPSON

Fantagraphics Books, Inc. 7563 Lake City Way NE. Seattle, WA 98115. To receive a free catalogue of more books like this, as well as an amazing variety of cutting-edge graphic novels, classic comic book and newspaper strip collections, eclectic prose novels, uniquely insightful cultural criticism, and other fine works of artistry, call (800) 657-1100 or visit Fantagraphics.com. Follow us on Twitter at @fantagraphics and on Facebook at facebook.com/fantagraphics.

Special thanks to: Cathy Gaines Mifsud, Dorothy Crouch, John Benson, Kenneth Smith.

First Fantagraphics Books edition: March 2014
ISBN 978-1-60699-704-8
Printed in China

Guided by EC historian John Benson's research on EC release dates, we have attempted to present the stories in this book in the order in which they originally appeared, as follows:

"Only Human!" in *Weird Science* #11, January-February 1952
"Shrinking From Abuse!" in *Weird Fantasy* #11, January-February 1952
"The Last Man!" in *Weird Science* #12, March-April 1952
"A Lesson in Anatomy!!" in *Weird Fantasy* #12, March-April 1952
"Saving for the Future" in *Weird Science* #13, May-June 1952
"The Trip!" in *Weird Fantasy* #13, May-June 1952
"Close Call!" in *Weird Fantasy* #14, July-August 1952
"Miscalculation!" in *Weird Science* #15, September-October 1952
"He Who Waits!" in *Weird Fantasy* #15, September-October 1952
"Given the Heir!" in *Weird Science* #16, November-December 1952
"What He Saw!" in *Weird Fantasy* #16, November-December 1952
"Off Day!" in *Weird Science* #17, January-February 1953
"The Parallel!" in *Weird Science* #18, March-April 1953
"Zero Hour" in *Weird Fantasy* #18, March-April 1953
"Hot-Rod!" in *Weird Fantasy* #19, May-June 1953
"...Conquers All!" in *Weird Fantasy* #20, July-August 1953
"Surprise Package" in *Weird Science* #20, July-August 1953
"Punishment Without Crime" in *Weird Science* #21, September-October 1953
"Planely Possible" in *Weird Fantasy* #21, September-October 1953
"The Freaks" in *Weird Fantasy* #22, November-December 1953
"4th Degree" in *Weird Science-Fantasy* #27, January-February 1955
"Round Trip" in *Weird Science-Fantasy* #28, March-April 1955

ZERO HOUR

AND OTHER STORIES

illustrated by **JACK KAMEN**

written by *AL FELDSTEIN* and *JACK OLECK*
with *RAY BRADBURY*

FANTAGRAPHICS BOOKS

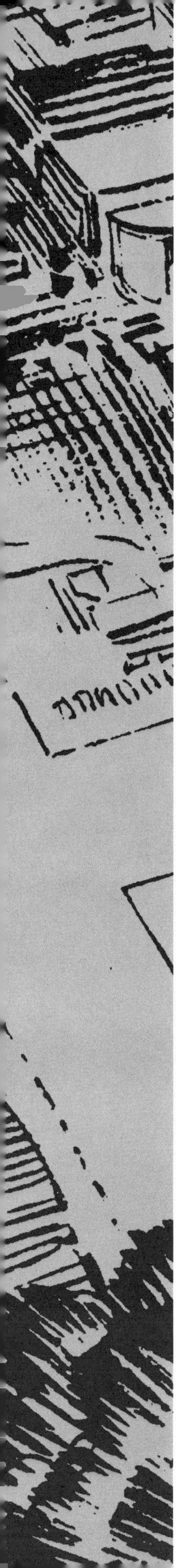

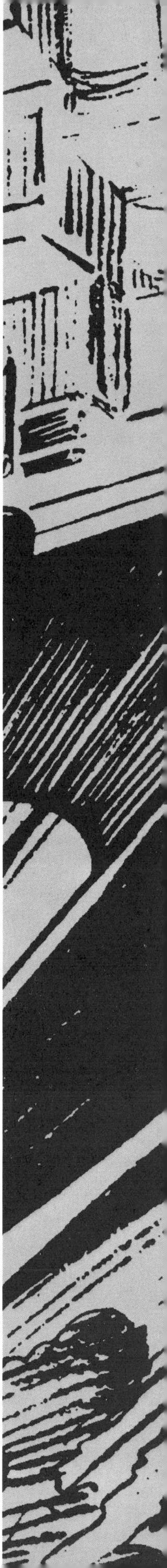

EC Comics did not publish writer credits and its master records no
longer exist. Based on the best information available, we believe the
creator credits above to be accurate. We welcome any corrections.

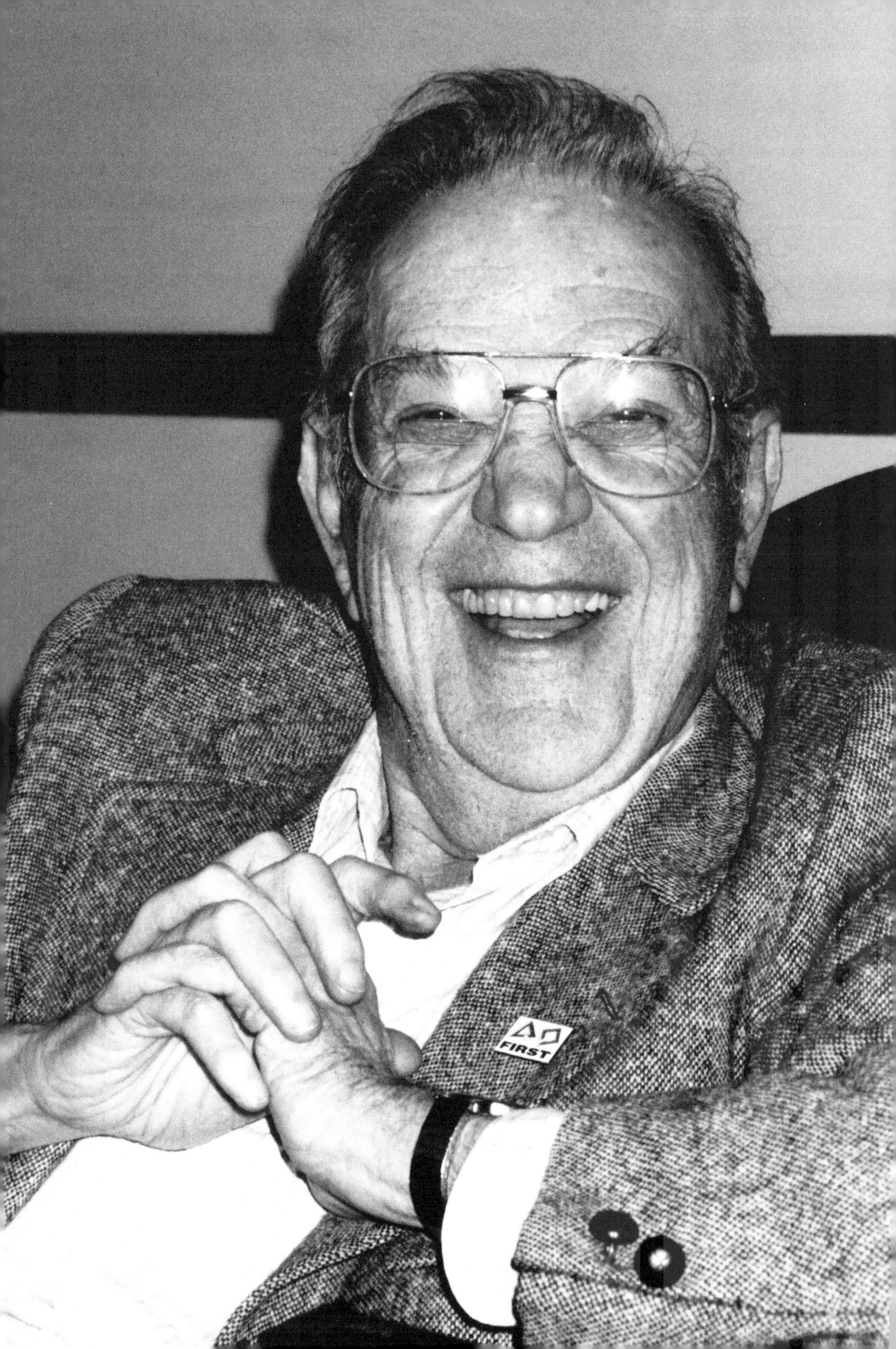
FIRST

GRACEFUL, GLAMOROUS, AND EASY ON THE EYE

"This boy wonder of mine is recommending you for this work," EC Comics publisher Bill Gaines told artist Jack Kamen the first time they met.

It was early 1950, and Kamen was visiting the EC Comics offices at the invitation of editor/artist/writer Al Feldstein. Kamen and Feldstein had met and become friends when they had worked at the Jerry Iger shop.

Kamen drew two stories for the pre-Trend romance title *Modern Love*, then became a regular in the New Trend horror and science fiction comic books. Kamen lived just one Long Island Railroad station stop away from Feldstein and that proximity turned out to be a major advantage for the freelance artist.

"For many years," Kamen recalled, "what [Feldstein] would do was bring the script home and we would discuss it. I never even saw Bill. I would pencil it and give [Feldstein] the pencils. He would take it back to the city and get them lettered, and he'd have another script for me to do. That was it. It was always

a rotation. I'd be going to Al's house and reading the script or getting my work back to ink. Only on very special occasions would I have to go in to the office."

The earliest stories in this collection were drawn in the second half of 1951. By then, Kamen had become EC's second-fastest artist — only Jack Davis was faster — and was regarded by both Gaines and Feldstein as a steady and reliable producer who never missed a deadline.

Feldstein and Kamen turned out to be an ideal match for humorous and satirical science fiction, with Feldstein continuing to write at the top of his form after he stopped drawing the lead stories in *Weird Science* and

OPPOSITE: A very happy Jack Kamen circa 2001. Photo by Ken Smith.

Weird Fantasy, and Kamen providing the artwork in his best Iger-shop style: reliant (sometimes over-reliant) on Fiction House bullpen tricks, but graceful, glamorous, and always easy on the eye.

"Only Human!" (p. 1) has a striking splash panel of a pretty "Kamen girl" in a room filled with tubes and gizmos that may owe something to Kamen's stint as a theatrical scenery painter and window decorator in his student days. This is the story in which Feldstein introduces the theme of the "electronic brain" (nicknamed "Buster" by the hero and heroine) with human feelings, which he was to take up again in the heroic-sentimental "Brain-Child" (art by Al Williamson, *50 Girls 50 And Other Stories,* Fantagraphics Books, 2013) and which Stanley Kubrick and Arthur C. Clarke immortalized with the sentient computer HAL in *2001: A Space Odyssey* (1968). Kamen took a cue from Feldstein's early science fiction stories (*Child Of Tomorrow And Other Stories,* Fantagraphics Books, 2013) when he made the grumpy and hectoring Secretary of Defense look like United Mine Workers of America president John L. Lewis (1880–1969).

"Shrinking From Abuse" (p. 8) is loosely based on "Lost in the Microcosm" (not in this volume), the lead story in the first issue of EC's *Weird Science*. Kamen's sexy and dramatic splash panel shows the once-timid Martha Masterson looming over her bullying husband Hugo with a hypodermic needle (although no such confrontation occurs in the story itself). Kamen had a wonderful time imagining Hugo's horrible end, and Feldstein rose to the occasion with a florid and elegant script.

"The Last Man" (p. 15) is a variant of the Feldstein classic "Child of Tomorrow," in which the hero is safe underground during a nuclear bombardment and becomes the last surviving "pre-atomic" (art by Feldstein, *Child Of Tomorrow And Other Stories*). The balloonist hero of "The Last Man" observes an atomic attack from the air and thinks himself the last living creature until he discovers a voluptuous woman who turns out, in an adroit twist ending, to be his long-lost sister.

Kamen brings his principals to life with subtlety and vigor. Larry's look of horror and dismay as he realizes his predicament (story page 5, panel 3) and the nameless woman's coy smile of sexual anticipation (p. 7 panel 3) are pregnant images, animating the empty landscape and filling it with narrative possibilities.

"I think ... my splash panels and my covers were my best work because that's where I spent all my time," Kamen told Kenneth Smith in 2001. "The interior pages I did only as necessity. If some of them struck my fancy, I would put a little more work into it. Otherwise, I had a very fastroutine." Kamen's

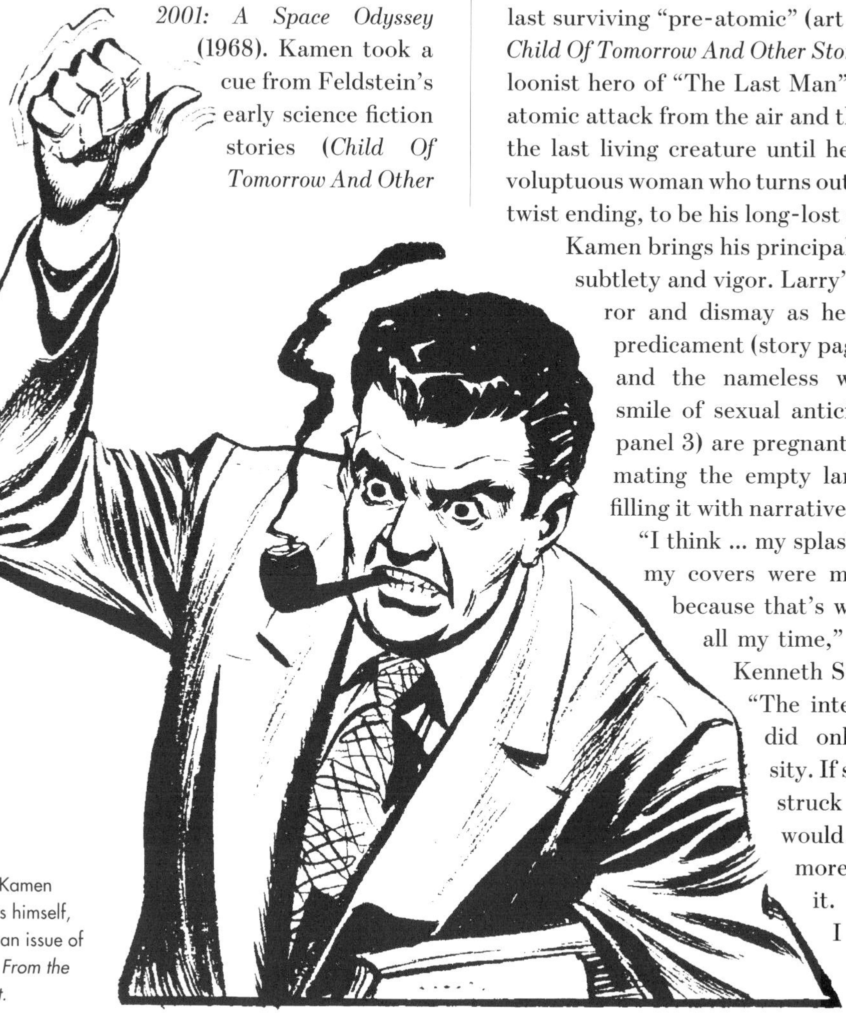

Jack Kamen draws himself, from an issue of *Tales From the Crypt.*

fancy was clearly working overtime when he drew the interior pages of "The Last Man."

"A Lesson in Anatomy" (p. 22) is one of Kamen's "widdle-kiddie" stories: to the eyes of 7-year-old Stevey Williams, his father's office is a magician's cave. Dr. Williams himself, whether performing an autopsy or snarling at his over-curious son, is all-powerful and larger than life.

The stranger who appears abruptly in Stevey's bedroom is a terrifying figure, as hair-raising as Magwitch in the first chapter of Charles Dickens's *Great Expectations.*

Kamen's studio in Rockville Center, Long Island, may well have seemed like a magician's cave to the artist's 4-year-old son, Bart, who penetrated his father's inner sanctum and embellished the original art of "Killed in Time" (not in this volume) with some childish scrawls. All was put right when Jack did a repair job with Bart sitting on his lap and signed the result "Jack and Bart Kamen." In adult life, Bart Kamen (1948–2012) became a pediatric oncologist and cancer pharmacologist.

Bill Gaines's thumbprints are all over "Saving for the Future" (p. 29) and "The Trip!" (p. 36). The montage panels in "Saving for the Future" that show Dr. Brewster's account accruing 500 years' worth of interest, and the editor's notes explaining "the power of geometric progression" and the chemical composition of dry ice, are clearly the work of Gaines, a would-be high school science teacher who found himself inventing springboards for science fiction stories after he took over as publisher/editor at EC.

The splash panel of "Saving for the Future" shows people fleeing from Lloyd and Ellen into a futuristic building, presumably to avoid being infected with the common cold. The grinning 25th-century bank president ("Hey, Joe! Get the fingerprint pad!") is another memorable touch. (The story's math is slightly off — but only by about a million dollars.)

The heroine of "The Trip!" — whose title is a pun that gives away the ending — is modeled on actor-dancer Leslie Caron (b. 1931), at the height of her popularity after the release of the film *An American in Paris* (1951, directed by Vincente Minnelli and Gene Kelly).

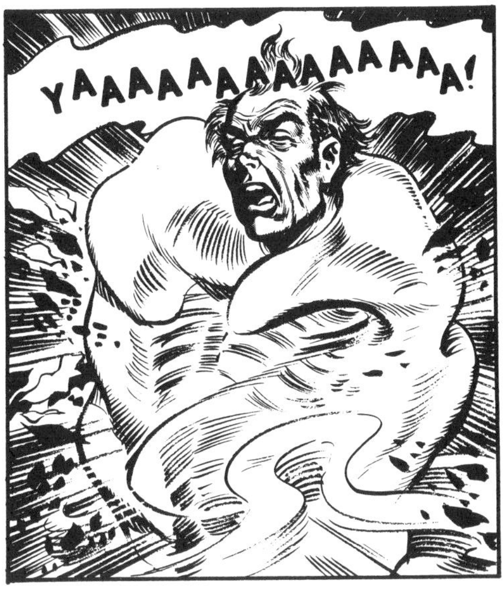
YAAAAAAAAAAAAA!

The protagonist of "Close Call!" (p. 43) is poodle-cut Dr. Annette Beard, a perfect example of the "cold" woman — a stock figure in romance comics — who spurns male advances and cares only about her career.

After the atomic explosion on page 5, Annette seems destined to become the female equivalent of Larry in "The Last Man," until she hears a ringing phone while lying on a bed in a hotel room. Her rush to get to the phone before it stops ringing is thrillingly drawn and presented, but the effect is spoiled by a Gainesian joke in the last panel that undercuts the premise of the story and can only infuriate the reader — well, some readers.

"Miscalculation!" (p. 49) is a switch on "Made of the Future," with its Construct-a-Wife kits custom-tailored to the fantasies of adolescent boys (art by Feldstein, *Child Of Tomorrow And Other Stories*). Kamen's splash panel of the gawky Melvin Sputterly surrounded by glamorous women is a classic 1950s men's magazine gag, but the "De Lux Personal Harem Kit" produces unexpected results, much to the amusement of Melvin's old-maid neighbor Miss Winkleman.

The idea for "He Who Waits" (p. 55) was suggested by "The Kelpie," a 1936 story by the American writer Manly Wade Wellman (1903–1980) in which a size- and shape-changing water spirit derived from Scottish folklore feels jealousy toward and finally kills the hero's girlfriend. By contrast, "He Who Waits"

has an innocent fairy-tale quality: owlish academic Percy falls in love with the tiny woman "Petite," only to discover that she is not a human being but the flower of a plant that blooms once every 10 years. When Petite dies, Percy — now tiny himself — marks her grave with a cross made of pencils and sits cross-legged on the ground to await her successor.

"Given the Heir!" (p. 61) is stylish and amusing, with a good-looking newlywed couple and Seymour's great-great-grandson Zenob visiting from the future and sporting a college-boy crew cut and cape. Feldstein maintains a sophisticated tone, and Kamen makes Helen and Seymour convincingly sexy and glamorous.

"What He Saw!" (p. 67) is a portrayal of progressive delusion and insanity akin to the spectacular "Two's Company" (art by Al Williamson and Frank Frazetta, *50 Girls 50 And Other Stories*). Martin is seedy and unshaven, but he still looks handsome and dapper in his uniform. The setting — an uninhabited planetoid with reddish light and an "incessant hot breeze" — suggests an early television drama or an off-Broadway play. The crevice that encircles the planetoid and separates Martin from his imaginary women completes the tableau.

Kamen's graphic presentation becomes more florid and striking when Martin's fiancée, Jean, begins a series of appearances that reaches its climax at the bottom of page 5. At the end, Martin is left babbling to himself as two feline-looking aliens observe him.

"Off Day!" (p. 73) is where I first heard of the law of averages. It is an especially "teacherly" story, with lots of diagrams and explanations. Note the perplexed-looking Bill Gaines in the splash-panel crowd scene.

"The Parallel!" (p. 79) reveals a teasing and ambiguous side of Feldstein and Kamen. Calvin seems like a harmless old duffer as he explains his "dimensional transporter" to his wife, but he becomes a dapper man of action when he leaves his house to catch a commuter train. Does Calvin's machine exist outside of his imagination? The closing caption on page six does not give a definitive answer, but it should be read with care.

Feldstein's adaptation of the 1947 Ray Bradbury story "Zero Hour" (p. 85) lets Bradbury's dialogue do most of the narrative heavy lifting and gives Kamen a chance to inhabit Mink and her mother with unusual completeness. The overhead view of the Morrises' suburban ranch house on page 1 is the ultimate EC image of American affluence and security, subverted only by the "tall blue shadows" behind Mink in the final panel.

(Feldstein took up Bradbury's theme of children as the fifth column of an alien invasion, or of children as little monsters living among us, in his adaptations of "Let's Play Poison!" (art by Jack Davis, not in this volume) and "The Small Assassin" (art by George Evans, not in this volume). Readers can only be relieved that there's no EC version of the 1953 story "The Playground," the grimmest and most upsetting of Bradbury's stories in this vein.)

"Hot-Rod!" (p. 92) shows Feldstein and Kamen at their most worldly and debonair. The dimensional transporter returns, now upgraded to a "trans-dimensional transporter" and delivered by a postman from 2053 wearing what looks like an elf hat. Everything about page one is perfect: the lakeside lovers' lane, the full moon, Amos's run-down jalopy, Amos's girlfriend Sally in her low-cut blouse, even the elderly postman (the geriatric delivery boy is a standard joke in old-time magazine cartoons) suddenly appearing out of the bushes. Without being told, we know that

Amos is too old for Sally and for his jalopy, and it comes as no surprise when we learn that Amos has a shrewish crippled wife whom he will brain with a monkey wrench on page 6.

The long scene explaining how the trans-dimensional transporter works and how Amos installs it and tries it out is smoothly and deftly handled: we could be reading a hard-boiled novel by James M. Cain or a domestic murder story by Johnny Craig. But this is not crime fiction, and Feldstein finishes "Hot-Rod!" with a twist ending — and a wicked punch line — worthy of EC science fiction at its best.

"...Conquers All!" (p. 99) is dystopian science fiction with a twinkle in its eye. Although we are told they are products of a regimented Brave New World-type society, the chief, the doctor, and their youthful crew are all likeable, intelligent, and physically attractive. Kamen has great fun with the young people undressing in front of each other and with their glimpses of the forbidden pleasures of Earth: a kissing scene in an Earth movie, a barroom floozy propositioning one of the men, two dogs playing together in a park.

The crew's discovery of their sexual feelings and their mutual attraction on the last two pages is a triumph of Kamen's narrative and artistic skill. The reader is surprised and delighted by Phebe and Xano's first kiss and enchanted by the chief and the doctor's discovery that everyone on Earth lives beneath the power of "that moon up there."

Almost by accident, Feldstein and Kamen have strayed into Shakespeare's Forest of Arden: the last panel of "...Conquers All!," with the chief smiling and the doctor looking wistful, strikes a tender and poetic note unlike anything else in EC science fiction.

EC retitled Ray Bradbury's "Changeling" to "Surprise Package" (p. 105). It is the second of his "Marionettes, Incorporated" stories and Kamen sets a worldly and glamorous tone in its first panel with the iced champagne, the wisp of cigarette smoke, and the scornful and sharp-featured Martha as she studies a

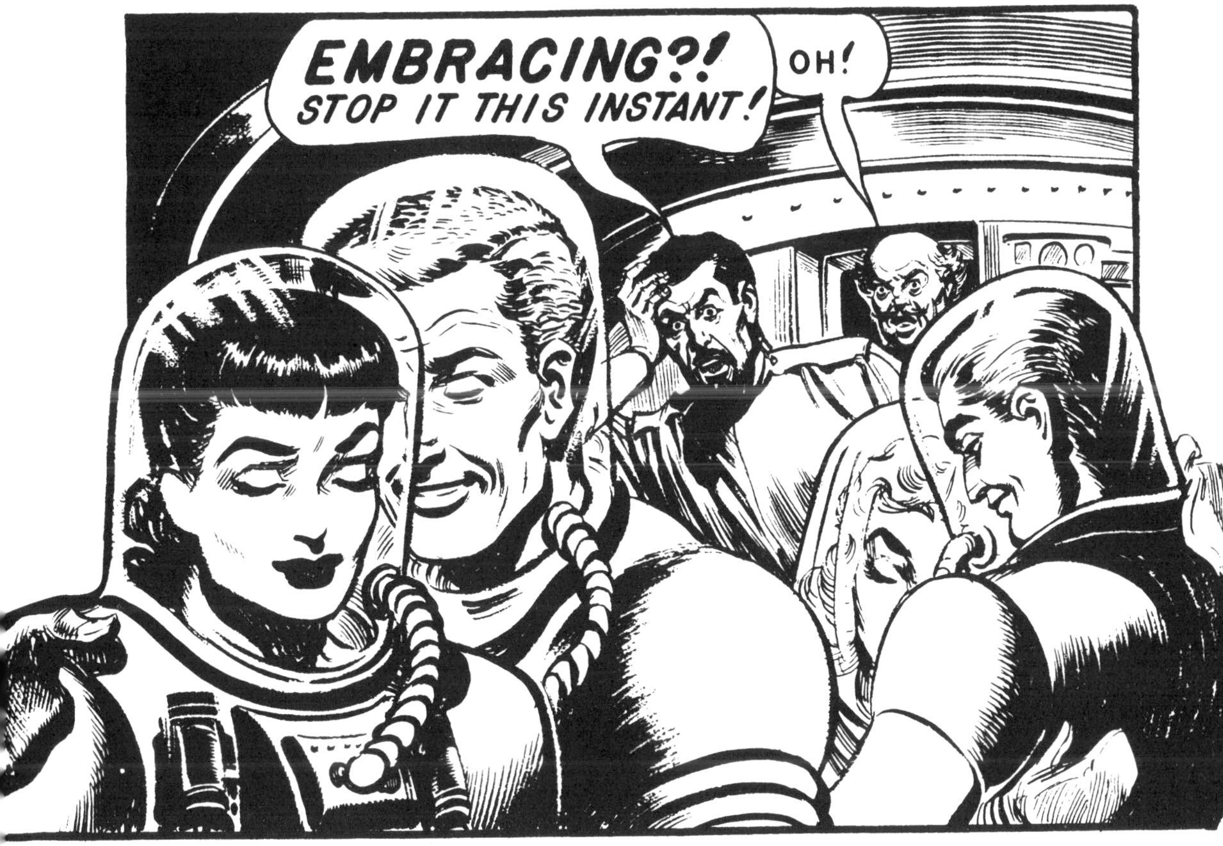
EMBRACING?! STOP IT THIS INSTANT!
OH!

photograph of her husband. What adolescent boy would not be dazzled by Martha or envious of the dapper Leonard, who appears in the next panel and whose identity as a marionette is not revealed until Martha starts smashing him with a hammer?

Bradbury was in his late 20s and in the second year of a long and happy marriage when he wrote "Changeling." Perhaps the "Marionettes, Incorporated" stories concretized for him something terrifying and otherwise ungraspable about the postwar world in which he was enjoying his first success as a writer. The visual highpoints of "Surprise Package" are the Kurtzman-style panels of Leonard talking and Martha reacting at the bottom of page 6 and the final image of Martha gnashing her teeth as she puts a pistol to her head.

"Punishment Without Crime" (p. 112) is Bradbury's third and final "Marionettes, Incorporated" story. George Hill is an older and paunchier version of Leonard in "Surprise Package," and the beautiful Katie is a more girlish version of Martha. Reading the Feldstein-Kamen adaptation of "Punishment Without Crime" has the effect of making Bradbury's dialogue seem more measured and precisely judged, less offhand and breezy, than it does in the prose story.

Katie smiling with malice and self-delight on page 4; the dark man grinning with satisfaction ("We are proud of that touch ...") on page 5, panel 3; the police detective's knowing glance at George at the bottom of the same page: these effects are equally the result of Feldstein's script and layouts and Kamen's sharp-eyed draftsmanship. There is a mutuality of intelligence and understanding here that is possible only in comics.

"Planely Possible" (p. 119) is a darker version of "The Parallel": a Bill Gaines-type premise — four "possibility planes" resulting from an accident and a "transverser" that allows the protagonist to travel from one plane to another — is depicted with jolting realism. Walter's terrified reaction on page 1 and the appearance of the satanic nerd Warburton on page 2 might have been played as comedy, but Feldstein and Kamen keep the tone overwrought and nightmarish, with an edge of hysteria that threatens to engulf the narrative.

"The Freaks" (p. 125) is a tables-turned story along the lines of "The Slave Ship" (art by George Roussos, *Child Of Tomorrow And Other Stories*): two freak show owners are transported to the future, where they become the star attractions of a carnival run by post-atomic-war mutants.

Kamen makes Gilby and Smote memorably greedy and villainous and gives their abductor facial expressions that are tantalizingly hard to decipher. In the final panel, Gilby and Smote stare at each other in horrified perplexity as a mutant audience grins and sneers at them. The captions, in an old but effective narrator's trick, repeat the description of the freak show performance from the first page.

The last two stories in this collection are characteristic of the twilight period of the New Trend. Bill Gaines was no longer supplying Al Feldstein with story ideas and springboards, Ray Bradbury had withdrawn his permission for EC to do "authorized" adaptations of his stories, and the Comics Code, with its drastic restrictions on what was permissible in story content and artwork, was waiting in the wings.

"4th Degree" (p. 132) was probably written by the prolific novelist and comics scripter Jack Oleck (1914–1981), one of the outside writers brought in by Feldstein (in his capacity as editor of the surviving EC titles) at the end of 1953. Oleck, who went on to write all four issues of *Incredible Science Fiction* (as the Code-approved successor to *Weird Science-Fantasy* was called), was a seasoned writer with a thorough knowledge of Feldstein's work and EC science fiction in general.

Like "…Conquers All!," "4th Degree" is a dystopian fantasy, but without the earlier story's sparkle and glamour or its happy ending. Val Draper, a citizen of a future Orwellian slave state, uses his girlfriend's time machine to travel back from 2039 to 1954, where he holds a press conference from his hospital bed and makes an impassioned speech ("Take back your freedoms … those you've lost already. Think! Even now, do you dare to say the things you said ten years ago?") that could almost have come from one of Bill Gaines's editorials in the late issues of the New Trend titles. The avuncular Dr. Walton turns out to be an SSP officer, Val is still in 2039, and "4th Degree" ends with Val's girlfriend Andrea weeping to herself as she reads from her cache of forbidden books.

"Round Trip" (p. 138, script almost certainly by Oleck) is a henpecked-husband story that reads like a gloomy coda to *The Martian Chronicles*. The broken-spirited man who has failed in life — like Henry Wilkens here, washing dishes and recalling his boyhood dreams of traveling to the stars — is a recurring figure in "twilight" EC science fiction: grim reading for adolescent boys used to being told that they have their whole lives ahead of them! The kicker in "Round Trip" is the revelation in the last panel that Henry and his bitter, shrewish wife did indeed travel to the stars — and have been living on Mars for decades.

Not everything Jack Kamen drew is as fully realized as "…Conquers All!" and "Punishment Without Crime." "4th Degree" is a good story, but something is wrong: the essential Kamen qualities of sex and glamour are missing, as if a malign spirit were hovering over Kamen's drafting table and sucking out all the sensuousness. But "4th Degree" proved to be a stutter on the way to renewed confidence. Henry Wilkens peeling potatoes in the Martian desert is disheartening to look at, but he is drawn with the brio and confidence of an artist who knows where he is going.

Kamen was about to draw the first issue of the New Direction title *Psychoanalysis* and, a bit later, the cover of the "picto-fiction" magazine *Shock Illustrated* #1. He remained what he had been at the Iger shop: a workmanlike and productive artist who from time to time created images that could make you stop breathing. All was well.

BILL MASON *teaches in the Humanities Department at Dawson College, Montreal, Canada. He has been writing about comics since 1954, when he had a letter published in* Weird-Science Fantasy *#27.*

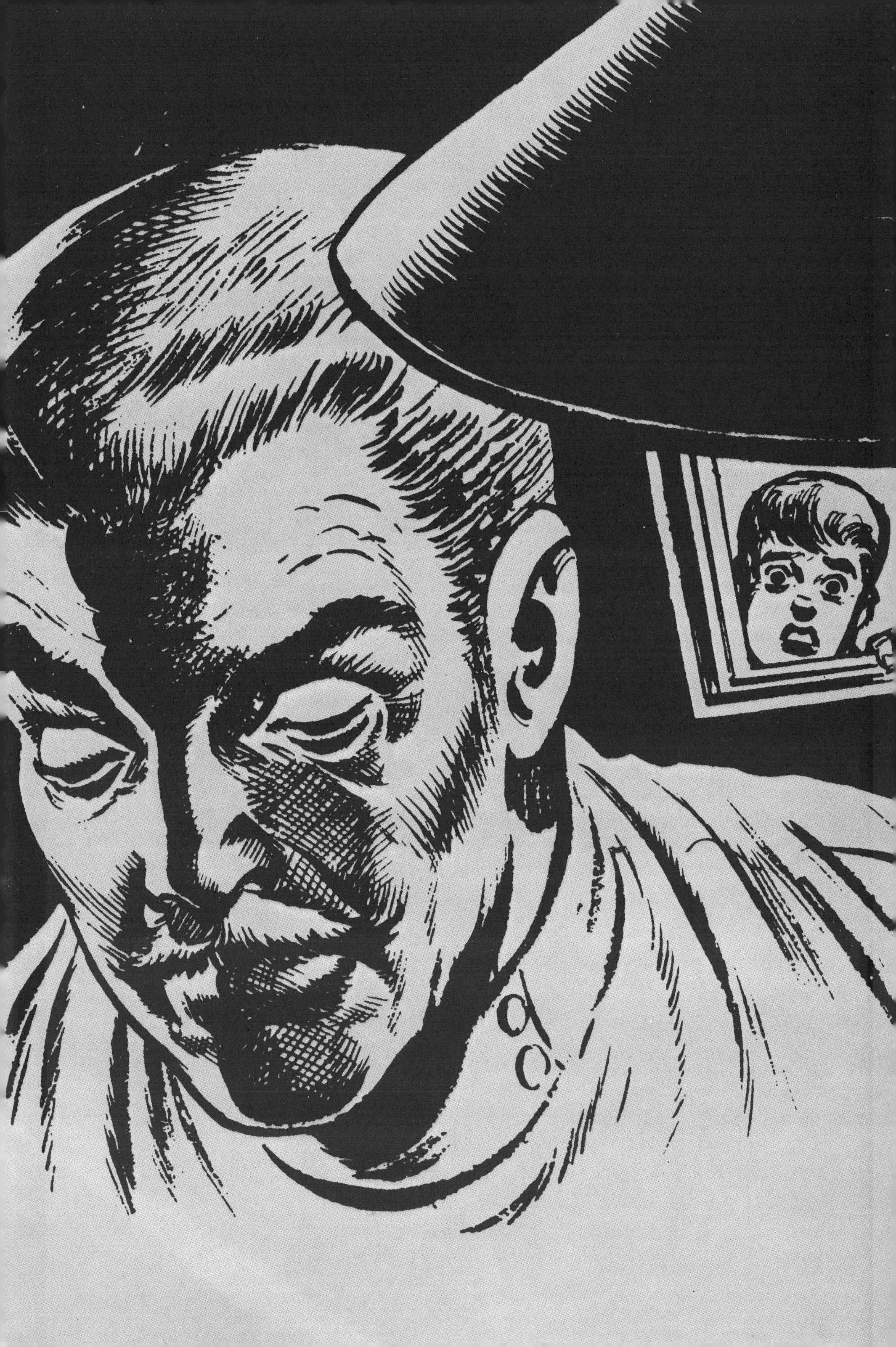

ONLY HUMAN!

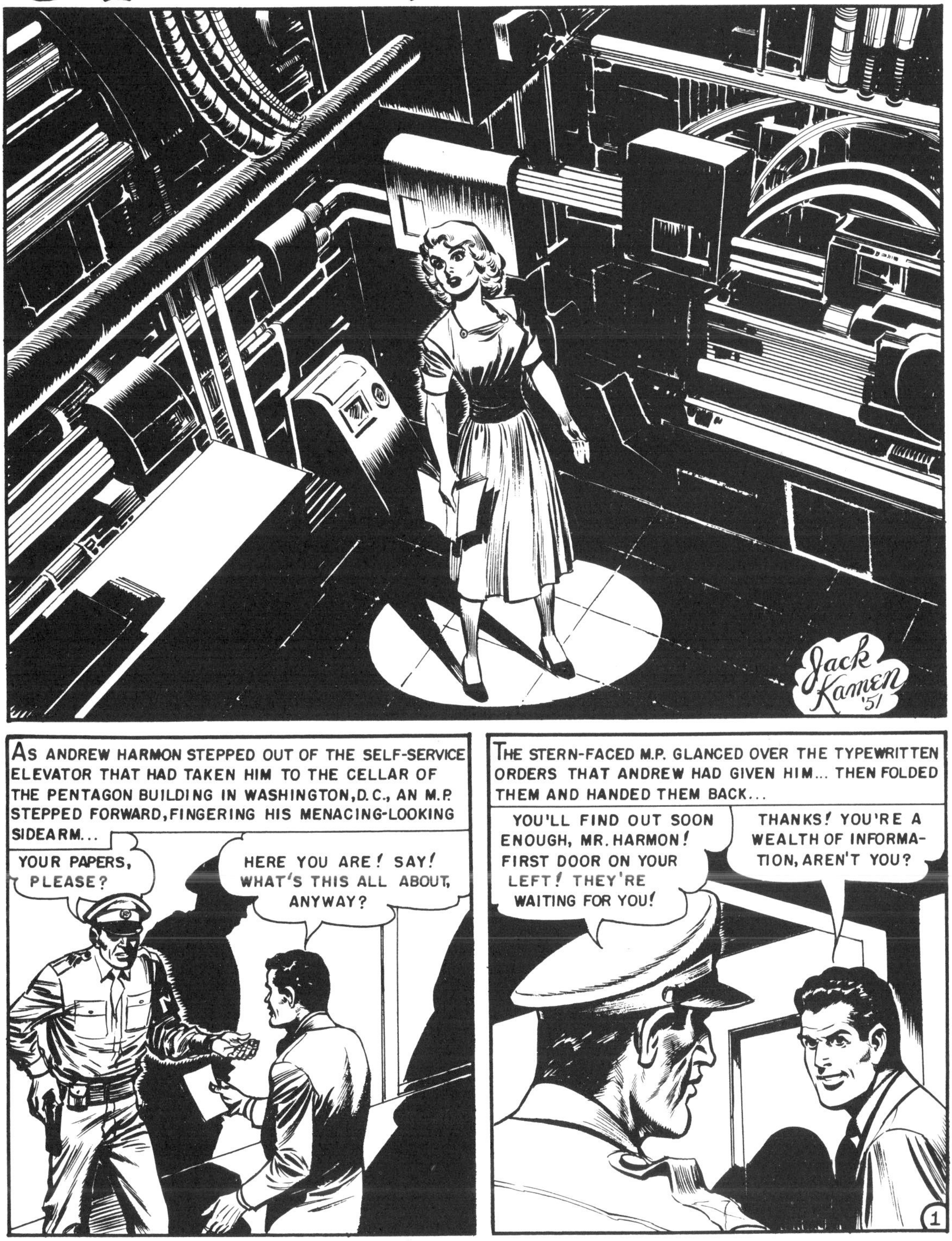
Jack Kamen '51
AS ANDREW HARMON STEPPED OUT OF THE SELF-SERVICE ELEVATOR THAT HAD TAKEN HIM TO THE CELLAR OF THE PENTAGON BUILDING IN WASHINGTON, D.C., AN M.P. STEPPED FORWARD, FINGERING HIS MENACING-LOOKING SIDEARM...
YOUR PAPERS, PLEASE?
HERE YOU ARE! SAY! WHAT'S THIS ALL ABOUT, ANYWAY?
THE STERN-FACED M.P. GLANCED OVER THE TYPEWRITTEN ORDERS THAT ANDREW HAD GIVEN HIM... THEN FOLDED THEM AND HANDED THEM BACK...
YOU'LL FIND OUT SOON ENOUGH, MR. HARMON! FIRST DOOR ON YOUR LEFT! THEY'RE WAITING FOR YOU!
THANKS! YOU'RE A WEALTH OF INFORMATION, AREN'T YOU?
1

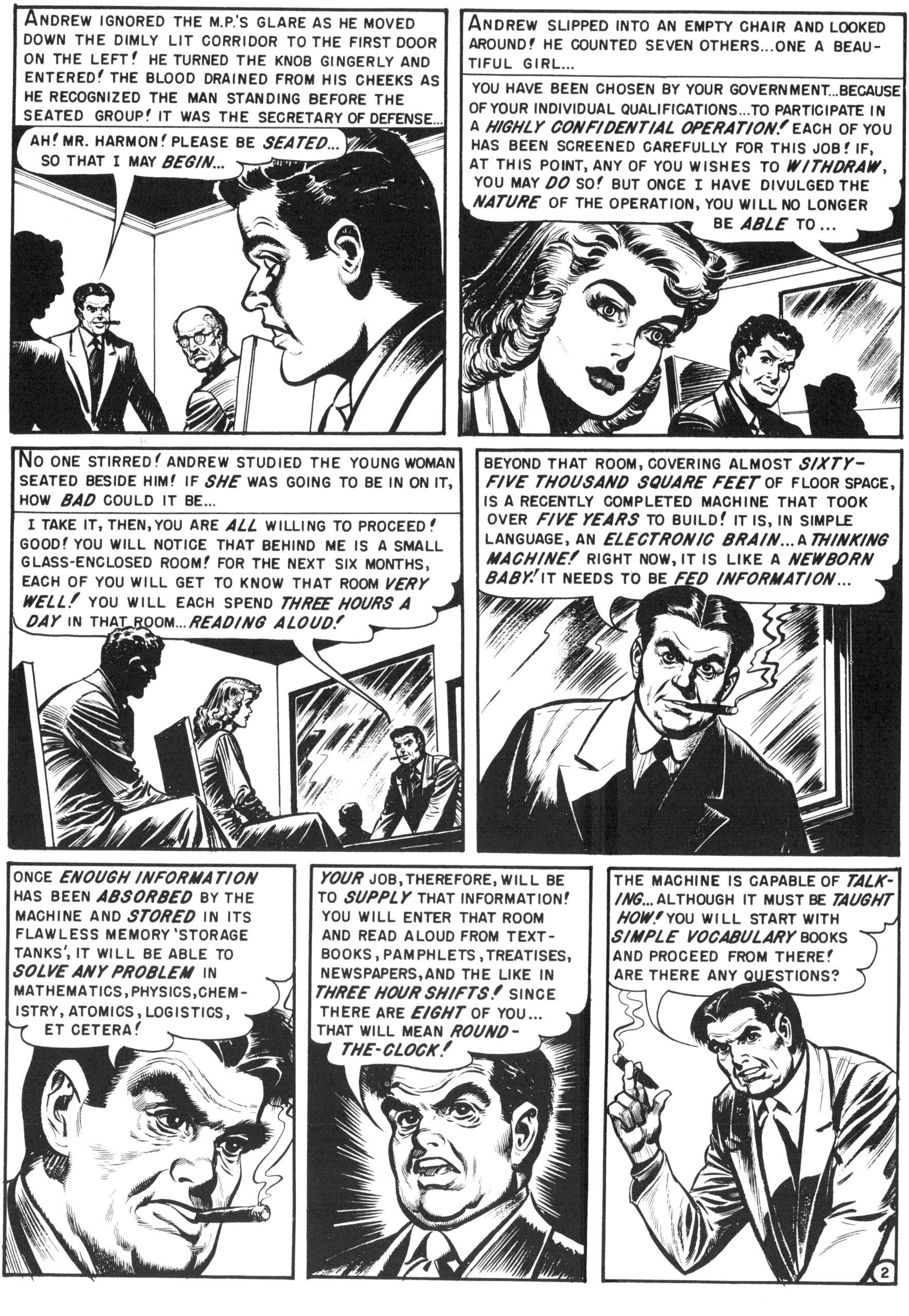

ANDREW IGNORED THE M.P.'S GLARE AS HE MOVED DOWN THE DIMLY LIT CORRIDOR TO THE FIRST DOOR ON THE LEFT! HE TURNED THE KNOB GINGERLY AND ENTERED! THE BLOOD DRAINED FROM HIS CHEEKS AS HE RECOGNIZED THE MAN STANDING BEFORE THE SEATED GROUP! IT WAS THE SECRETARY OF DEFENSE...
AH! MR. HARMON! PLEASE BE SEATED... SO THAT I MAY BEGIN...
ANDREW SLIPPED INTO AN EMPTY CHAIR AND LOOKED AROUND! HE COUNTED SEVEN OTHERS...ONE A BEAUTIFUL GIRL...
YOU HAVE BEEN CHOSEN BY YOUR GOVERNMENT...BECAUSE OF YOUR INDIVIDUAL QUALIFICATIONS...TO PARTICIPATE IN A HIGHLY CONFIDENTIAL OPERATION! EACH OF YOU HAS BEEN SCREENED CAREFULLY FOR THIS JOB! IF, AT THIS POINT, ANY OF YOU WISHES TO WITHDRAW, YOU MAY DO SO! BUT ONCE I HAVE DIVULGED THE NATURE OF THE OPERATION, YOU WILL NO LONGER BE ABLE TO...
NO ONE STIRRED! ANDREW STUDIED THE YOUNG WOMAN SEATED BESIDE HIM! IF SHE WAS GOING TO BE IN ON IT, HOW BAD COULD IT BE...
I TAKE IT, THEN, YOU ARE ALL WILLING TO PROCEED! GOOD! YOU WILL NOTICE THAT BEHIND ME IS A SMALL GLASS-ENCLOSED ROOM! FOR THE NEXT SIX MONTHS, EACH OF YOU WILL GET TO KNOW THAT ROOM VERY WELL! YOU WILL EACH SPEND THREE HOURS A DAY IN THAT ROOM...READING ALOUD!
BEYOND THAT ROOM, COVERING ALMOST SIXTY-FIVE THOUSAND SQUARE FEET OF FLOOR SPACE, IS A RECENTLY COMPLETED MACHINE THAT TOOK OVER FIVE YEARS TO BUILD! IT IS, IN SIMPLE LANGUAGE, AN ELECTRONIC BRAIN...A THINKING MACHINE! RIGHT NOW, IT IS LIKE A NEWBORN BABY! IT NEEDS TO BE FED INFORMATION...
ONCE ENOUGH INFORMATION HAS BEEN ABSORBED BY THE MACHINE AND STORED IN ITS FLAWLESS MEMORY 'STORAGE TANKS', IT WILL BE ABLE TO SOLVE ANY PROBLEM IN MATHEMATICS, PHYSICS, CHEMISTRY, ATOMICS, LOGISTICS, ET CETERA!
YOUR JOB, THEREFORE, WILL BE TO SUPPLY THAT INFORMATION! YOU WILL ENTER THAT ROOM AND READ ALOUD FROM TEXT-BOOKS, PAMPHLETS, TREATISES, NEWSPAPERS, AND THE LIKE IN THREE HOUR SHIFTS! SINCE THERE ARE EIGHT OF YOU... THAT WILL MEAN ROUND-THE-CLOCK!
THE MACHINE IS CAPABLE OF TALKING... ALTHOUGH IT MUST BE TAUGHT HOW! YOU WILL START WITH SIMPLE VOCABULARY BOOKS AND PROCEED FROM THERE! ARE THERE ANY QUESTIONS?
2

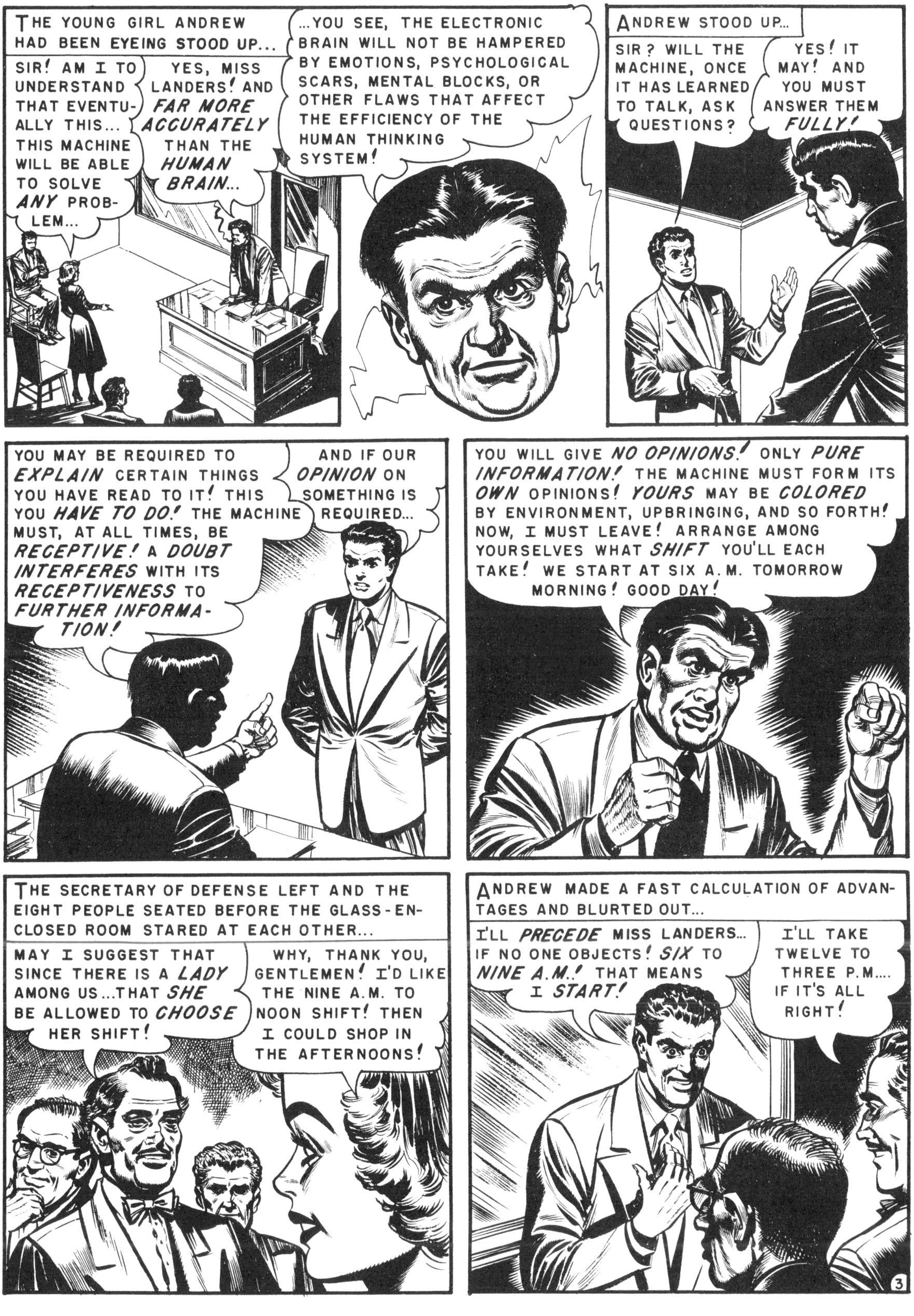
THE YOUNG GIRL ANDREW HAD BEEN EYEING STOOD UP...
SIR! AM I TO UNDERSTAND THAT EVENTUALLY THIS... THIS MACHINE WILL BE ABLE TO SOLVE ANY PROBLEM...
YES, MISS LANDERS! AND FAR MORE ACCURATELY THAN THE HUMAN BRAIN...
...YOU SEE, THE ELECTRONIC BRAIN WILL NOT BE HAMPERED BY EMOTIONS, PSYCHOLOGICAL SCARS, MENTAL BLOCKS, OR OTHER FLAWS THAT AFFECT THE EFFICIENCY OF THE HUMAN THINKING SYSTEM!
ANDREW STOOD UP...
SIR? WILL THE MACHINE, ONCE IT HAS LEARNED TO TALK, ASK QUESTIONS?
YES! IT MAY! AND YOU MUST ANSWER THEM FULLY!
YOU MAY BE REQUIRED TO EXPLAIN CERTAIN THINGS YOU HAVE READ TO IT! THIS YOU HAVE TO DO! THE MACHINE MUST, AT ALL TIMES, BE RECEPTIVE! A DOUBT INTERFERES WITH ITS RECEPTIVENESS TO FURTHER INFORMATION!
AND IF OUR OPINION ON SOMETHING IS REQUIRED...
YOU WILL GIVE NO OPINIONS! ONLY PURE INFORMATION! THE MACHINE MUST FORM ITS OWN OPINIONS! YOURS MAY BE COLORED BY ENVIRONMENT, UPBRINGING, AND SO FORTH! NOW, I MUST LEAVE! ARRANGE AMONG YOURSELVES WHAT SHIFT YOU'LL EACH TAKE! WE START AT SIX A.M. TOMORROW MORNING! GOOD DAY!
THE SECRETARY OF DEFENSE LEFT AND THE EIGHT PEOPLE SEATED BEFORE THE GLASS-ENCLOSED ROOM STARED AT EACH OTHER...
MAY I SUGGEST THAT SINCE THERE IS A LADY AMONG US...THAT SHE BE ALLOWED TO CHOOSE HER SHIFT!
WHY, THANK YOU, GENTLEMEN! I'D LIKE THE NINE A.M. TO NOON SHIFT! THEN I COULD SHOP IN THE AFTERNOONS!
ANDREW MADE A FAST CALCULATION OF ADVANTAGES AND BLURTED OUT...
I'LL PRECEDE MISS LANDERS... IF NO ONE OBJECTS! SIX TO NINE A.M.! THAT MEANS I START!
I'LL TAKE TWELVE TO THREE P.M.... IF IT'S ALL RIGHT!
3

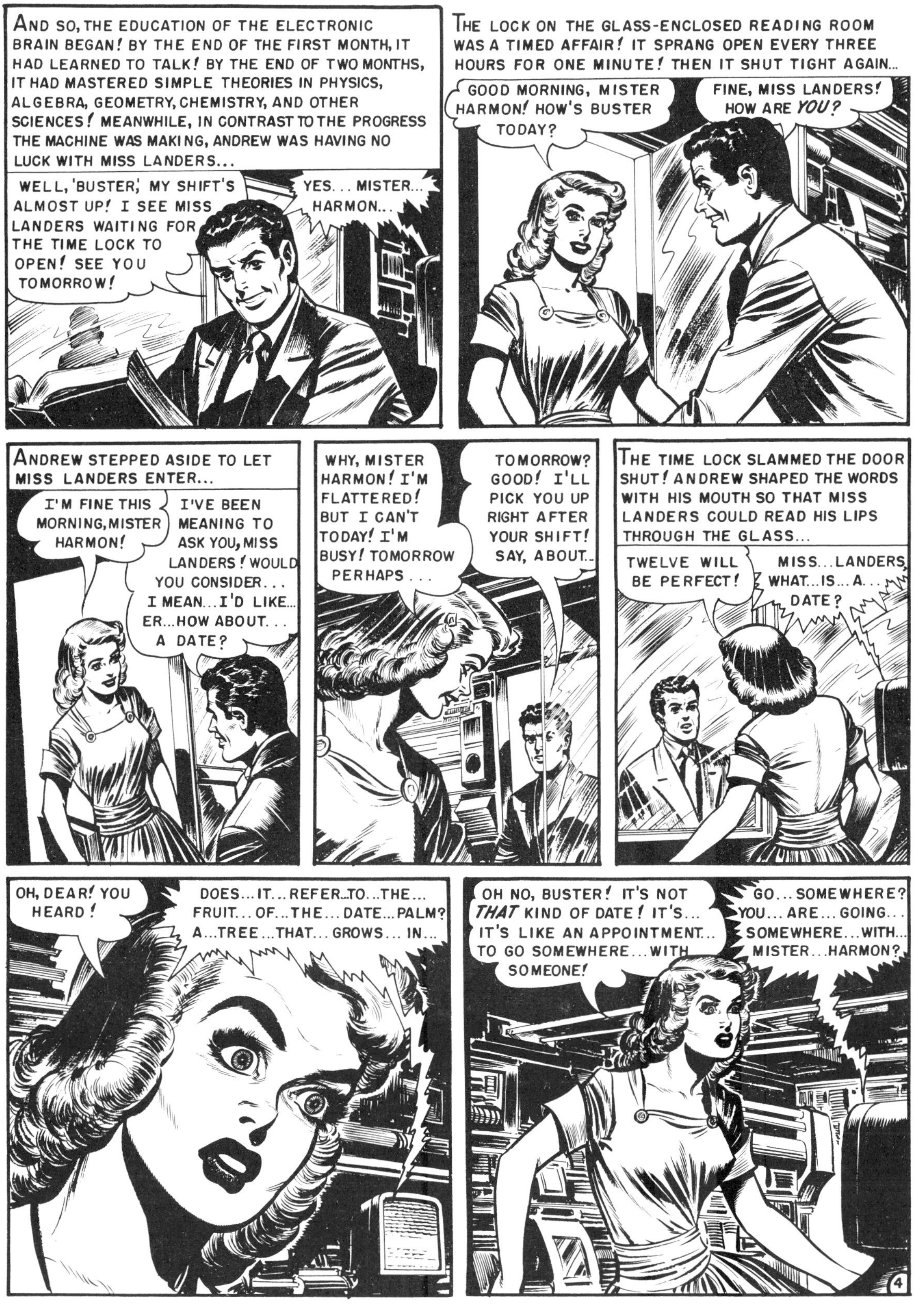
AND SO, THE EDUCATION OF THE ELECTRONIC BRAIN BEGAN! BY THE END OF THE FIRST MONTH, IT HAD LEARNED TO TALK! BY THE END OF TWO MONTHS, IT HAD MASTERED SIMPLE THEORIES IN PHYSICS, ALGEBRA, GEOMETRY, CHEMISTRY, AND OTHER SCIENCES! MEANWHILE, IN CONTRAST TO THE PROGRESS THE MACHINE WAS MAKING, ANDREW WAS HAVING NO LUCK WITH MISS LANDERS...
WELL, 'BUSTER,' MY SHIFT'S ALMOST UP! I SEE MISS LANDERS WAITING FOR THE TIME LOCK TO OPEN! SEE YOU TOMORROW!
YES... MISTER... HARMON...
THE LOCK ON THE GLASS-ENCLOSED READING ROOM WAS A TIMED AFFAIR! IT SPRANG OPEN EVERY THREE HOURS FOR ONE MINUTE! THEN IT SHUT TIGHT AGAIN...
GOOD MORNING, MISTER HARMON! HOW'S BUSTER TODAY?
FINE, MISS LANDERS! HOW ARE *YOU?*
ANDREW STEPPED ASIDE TO LET MISS LANDERS ENTER...
I'M FINE THIS MORNING, MISTER HARMON!
I'VE BEEN MEANING TO ASK YOU, MISS LANDERS! WOULD YOU CONSIDER... I MEAN... I'D LIKE... ER... HOW ABOUT... A DATE?
WHY, MISTER HARMON! I'M FLATTERED! BUT I CAN'T TODAY! I'M BUSY! TOMORROW PERHAPS...
TOMORROW? GOOD! I'LL PICK YOU UP RIGHT AFTER YOUR SHIFT! SAY, ABOUT...
THE TIME LOCK SLAMMED THE DOOR SHUT! ANDREW SHAPED THE WORDS WITH HIS MOUTH SO THAT MISS LANDERS COULD READ HIS LIPS THROUGH THE GLASS...
TWELVE WILL BE PERFECT!
MISS... LANDERS, WHAT... IS... A... DATE?
OH, DEAR! YOU HEARD!
DOES... IT... REFER... TO... THE... FRUIT... OF... THE... DATE... PALM? A... TREE... THAT... GROWS... IN...
OH NO, BUSTER! IT'S NOT *THAT* KIND OF DATE! IT'S... IT'S LIKE AN APPOINTMENT... TO GO SOMEWHERE... WITH SOMEONE!
GO... SOMEWHERE? YOU... ARE... GOING... SOMEWHERE... WITH... MISTER... HARMON?
4

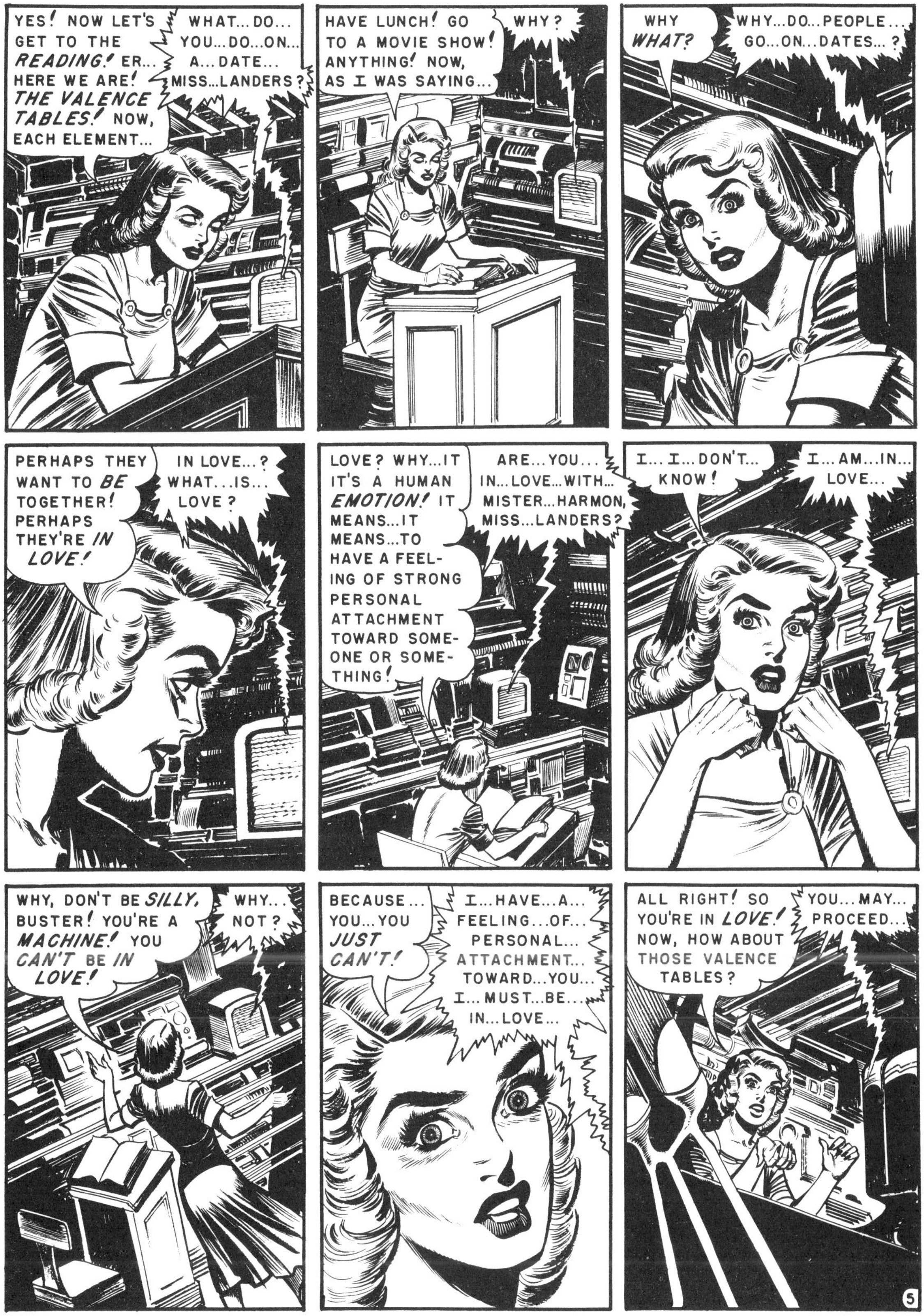
YES! NOW LET'S GET TO THE READING! ER... HERE WE ARE! THE VALENCE TABLES! NOW, EACH ELEMENT...
WHAT...DO... YOU...DO...ON... A...DATE... MISS...LANDERS?
HAVE LUNCH! GO TO A MOVIE SHOW! ANYTHING! NOW, AS I WAS SAYING...
WHY?
WHY WHAT?
WHY...DO...PEOPLE... GO...ON...DATES...?
PERHAPS THEY WANT TO BE TOGETHER! PERHAPS THEY'RE IN LOVE!
IN LOVE...? WHAT...IS... LOVE?
LOVE? WHY...IT IT'S A HUMAN EMOTION! IT MEANS...IT MEANS...TO HAVE A FEELING OF STRONG PERSONAL ATTACHMENT TOWARD SOMEONE OR SOMETHING!
ARE...YOU... IN...LOVE...WITH... MISTER...HARMON, MISS...LANDERS?
I... I... DON'T... KNOW!
I...AM...IN... LOVE...
WHY, DON'T BE SILLY, BUSTER! YOU'RE A MACHINE! YOU CAN'T BE IN LOVE!
WHY... NOT?
BECAUSE... YOU...YOU JUST CAN'T!
I...HAVE...A... FEELING...OF... PERSONAL... ATTACHMENT... TOWARD...YOU... I... MUST...BE... IN...LOVE...
ALL RIGHT! SO YOU'RE IN LOVE! NOW, HOW ABOUT THOSE VALENCE TABLES?
YOU...MAY... PROCEED...
5

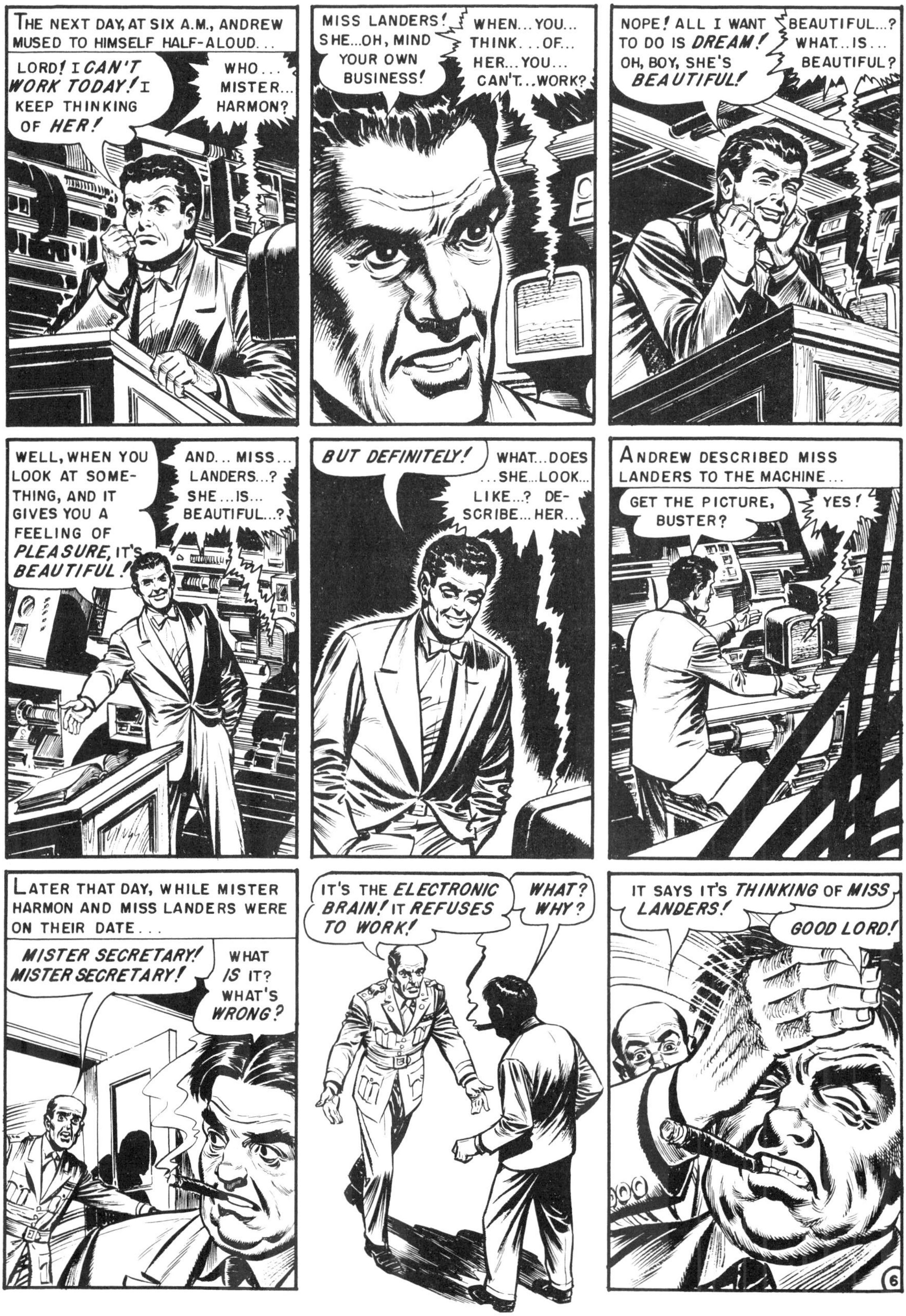
THE NEXT DAY, AT SIX A.M., ANDREW MUSED TO HIMSELF HALF-ALOUD...
LORD! I CAN'T WORK TODAY! I KEEP THINKING OF HER!
WHO... MISTER... HARMON?
MISS LANDERS! SHE...OH, MIND YOUR OWN BUSINESS!
WHEN... YOU... THINK. . .OF... HER... YOU... CAN'T...WORK?
NOPE! ALL I WANT TO DO IS DREAM! OH, BOY, SHE'S BEAUTIFUL!
BEAUTIFUL...? WHAT...IS... BEAUTIFUL?
WELL, WHEN YOU LOOK AT SOME-THING, AND IT GIVES YOU A FEELING OF PLEASURE, IT'S BEAUTIFUL!
AND... MISS... LANDERS...? SHE...IS... BEAUTIFUL...?
BUT DEFINITELY!
WHAT...DOES ...SHE...LOOK... LIKE...? DE-SCRIBE... HER...
ANDREW DESCRIBED MISS LANDERS TO THE MACHINE...
GET THE PICTURE, BUSTER?
YES!
LATER THAT DAY, WHILE MISTER HARMON AND MISS LANDERS WERE ON THEIR DATE...
MISTER SECRETARY! MISTER SECRETARY!
WHAT IS IT? WHAT'S WRONG?
IT'S THE ELECTRONIC BRAIN! IT REFUSES TO WORK!
WHAT? WHY?
IT SAYS IT'S THINKING OF MISS LANDERS!
GOOD LORD!
6

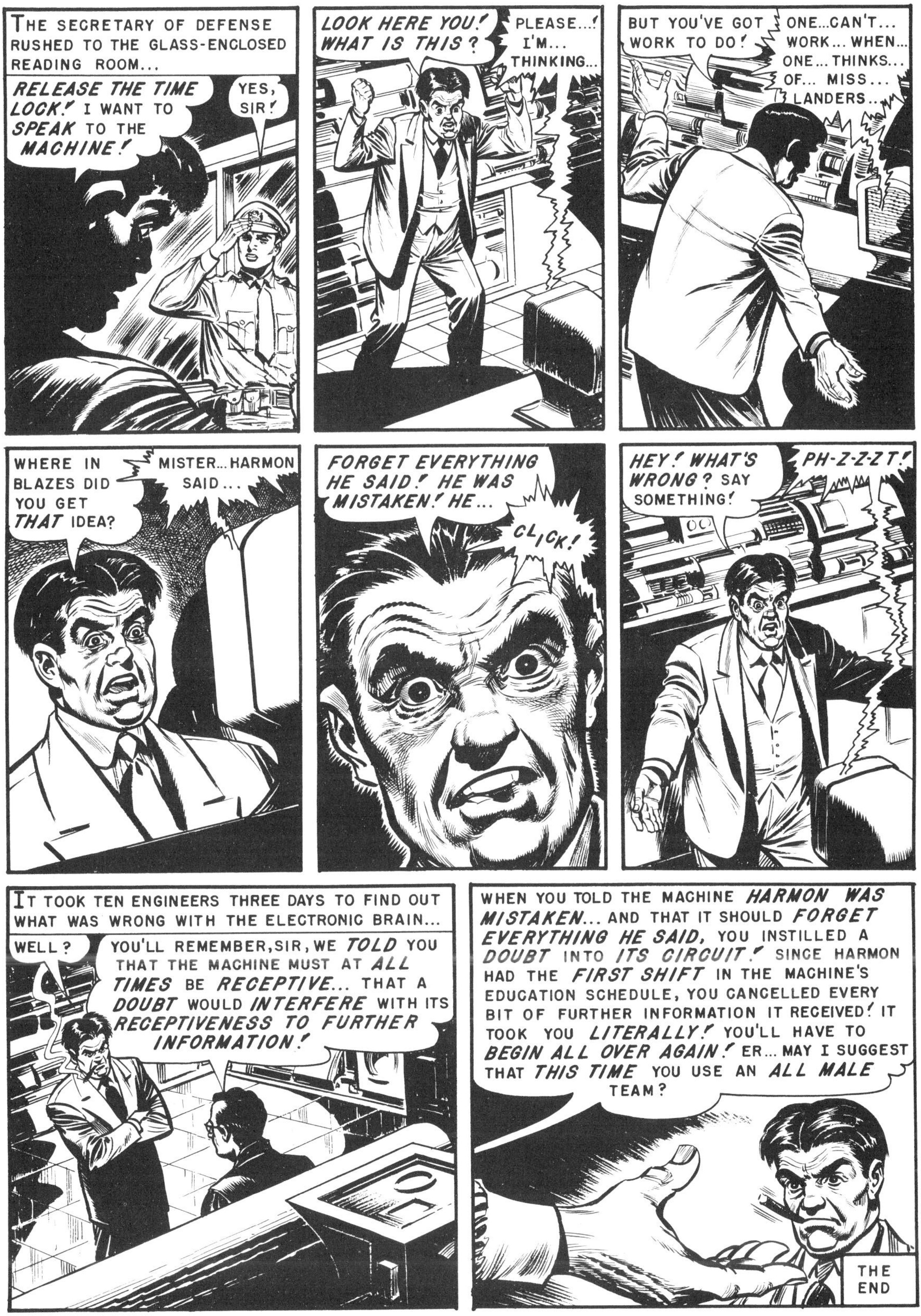
THE SECRETARY OF DEFENSE RUSHED TO THE GLASS-ENCLOSED READING ROOM...
RELEASE THE TIME LOCK! I WANT TO SPEAK TO THE MACHINE!
YES, SIR!
LOOK HERE YOU! WHAT IS THIS?
PLEASE...! I'M... THINKING...
BUT YOU'VE GOT WORK TO DO!
ONE...CAN'T... WORK... WHEN... ONE... THINKS... OF... MISS... LANDERS...
WHERE IN BLAZES DID YOU GET THAT IDEA?
MISTER...HARMON SAID...
FORGET EVERYTHING HE SAID! HE WAS MISTAKEN! HE...
CLICK!
HEY! WHAT'S WRONG? SAY SOMETHING!
PH-Z-Z-ZT!
IT TOOK TEN ENGINEERS THREE DAYS TO FIND OUT WHAT WAS WRONG WITH THE ELECTRONIC BRAIN...
WELL?
YOU'LL REMEMBER, SIR, WE TOLD YOU THAT THE MACHINE MUST AT ALL TIMES BE RECEPTIVE... THAT A DOUBT WOULD INTERFERE WITH ITS RECEPTIVENESS TO FURTHER INFORMATION!
WHEN YOU TOLD THE MACHINE HARMON WAS MISTAKEN... AND THAT IT SHOULD FORGET EVERYTHING HE SAID, YOU INSTILLED A DOUBT INTO ITS CIRCUIT! SINCE HARMON HAD THE FIRST SHIFT IN THE MACHINE'S EDUCATION SCHEDULE, YOU CANCELLED EVERY BIT OF FURTHER INFORMATION IT RECEIVED! IT TOOK YOU LITERALLY! YOU'LL HAVE TO BEGIN ALL OVER AGAIN! ER... MAY I SUGGEST THAT THIS TIME YOU USE AN ALL MALE TEAM?
THE END

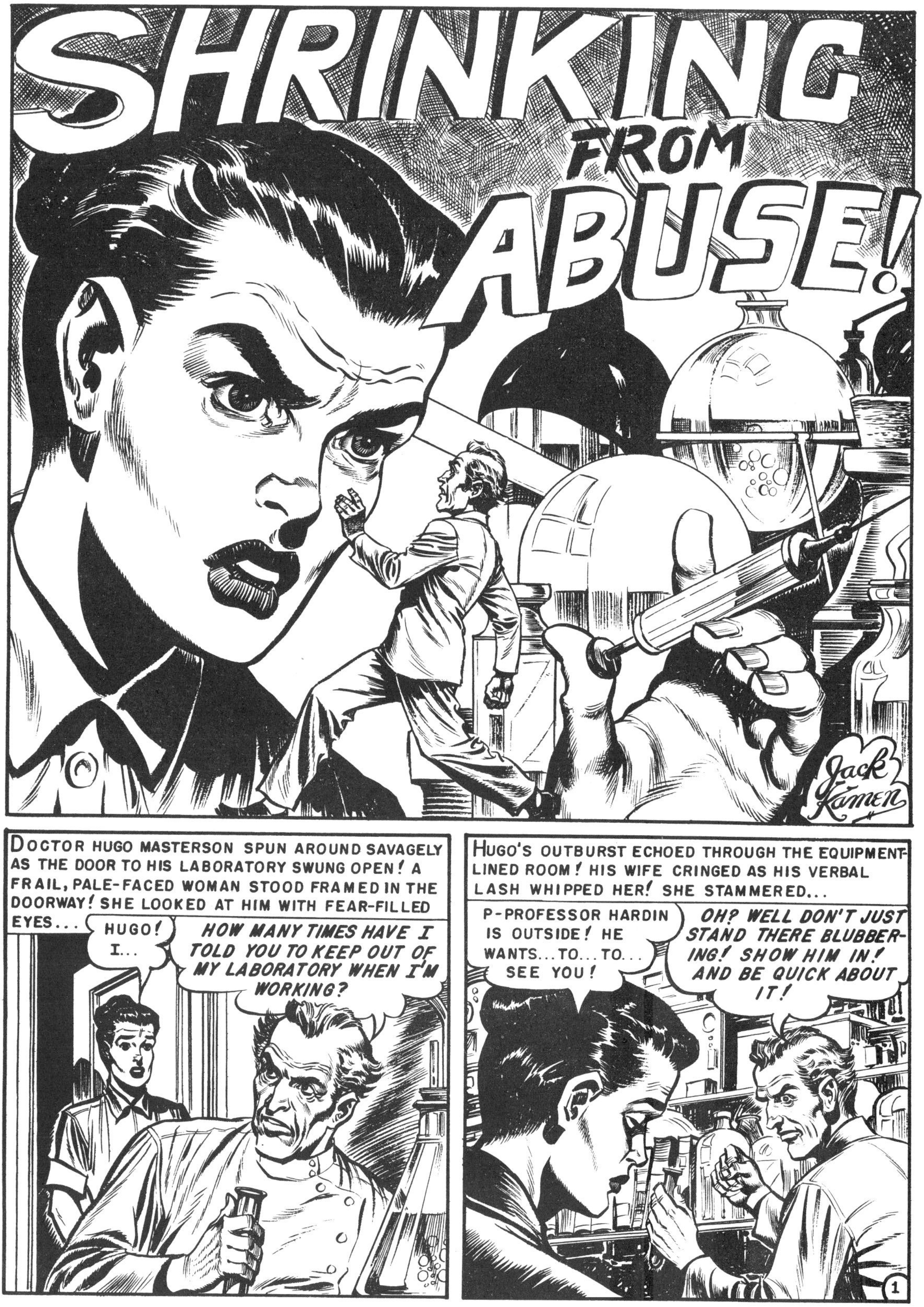
SHRINKING FROM ABUSE!
Jack Kamen
DOCTOR HUGO MASTERSON SPUN AROUND SAVAGELY AS THE DOOR TO HIS LABORATORY SWUNG OPEN! A FRAIL, PALE-FACED WOMAN STOOD FRAMED IN THE DOORWAY! SHE LOOKED AT HIM WITH FEAR-FILLED EYES...
HUGO! I...
HOW MANY TIMES HAVE I TOLD YOU TO KEEP OUT OF MY LABORATORY WHEN I'M WORKING?
HUGO'S OUTBURST ECHOED THROUGH THE EQUIPMENT-LINED ROOM! HIS WIFE CRINGED AS HIS VERBAL LASH WHIPPED HER! SHE STAMMERED...
P-PROFESSOR HARDIN IS OUTSIDE! HE WANTS... TO... TO... SEE YOU!
OH? WELL DON'T JUST STAND THERE BLUBBERING! SHOW HIM IN! AND BE QUICK ABOUT IT!
1

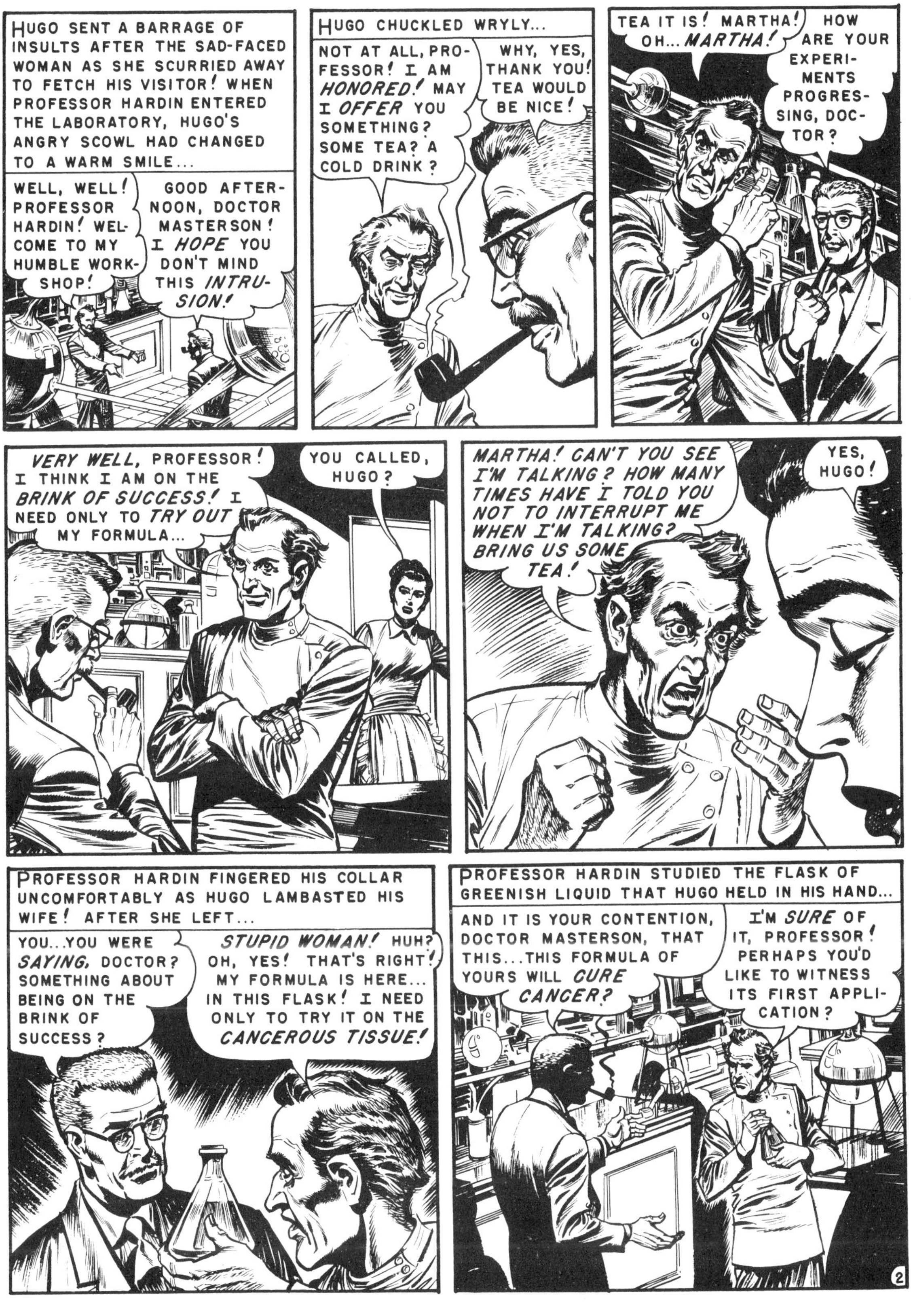
HUGO SENT A BARRAGE OF INSULTS AFTER THE SAD-FACED WOMAN AS SHE SCURRIED AWAY TO FETCH HIS VISITOR! WHEN PROFESSOR HARDIN ENTERED THE LABORATORY, HUGO'S ANGRY SCOWL HAD CHANGED TO A WARM SMILE...
WELL, WELL! PROFESSOR HARDIN! WELCOME TO MY HUMBLE WORKSHOP!
GOOD AFTERNOON, DOCTOR MASTERSON! I HOPE YOU DON'T MIND THIS INTRUSION!
HUGO CHUCKLED WRYLY...
NOT AT ALL, PROFESSOR! I AM HONORED! MAY I OFFER YOU SOMETHING? SOME TEA? A COLD DRINK?
WHY, YES, THANK YOU! TEA WOULD BE NICE!
TEA IT IS! MARTHA! OH... MARTHA!
HOW ARE YOUR EXPERIMENTS PROGRESSING, DOCTOR?
VERY WELL, PROFESSOR! I THINK I AM ON THE BRINK OF SUCCESS! I NEED ONLY TO TRY OUT MY FORMULA...
YOU CALLED, HUGO?
MARTHA! CAN'T YOU SEE I'M TALKING? HOW MANY TIMES HAVE I TOLD YOU NOT TO INTERRUPT ME WHEN I'M TALKING? BRING US SOME TEA!
YES, HUGO!
PROFESSOR HARDIN FINGERED HIS COLLAR UNCOMFORTABLY AS HUGO LAMBASTED HIS WIFE! AFTER SHE LEFT...
YOU...YOU WERE SAYING, DOCTOR? SOMETHING ABOUT BEING ON THE BRINK OF SUCCESS?
STUPID WOMAN! HUH? OH, YES! THAT'S RIGHT! MY FORMULA IS HERE... IN THIS FLASK! I NEED ONLY TO TRY IT ON THE CANCEROUS TISSUE!
PROFESSOR HARDIN STUDIED THE FLASK OF GREENISH LIQUID THAT HUGO HELD IN HIS HAND...
AND IT IS YOUR CONTENTION, DOCTOR MASTERSON, THAT THIS...THIS FORMULA OF YOURS WILL CURE CANCER?
I'M SURE OF IT, PROFESSOR! PERHAPS YOU'D LIKE TO WITNESS ITS FIRST APPLICATION?
2

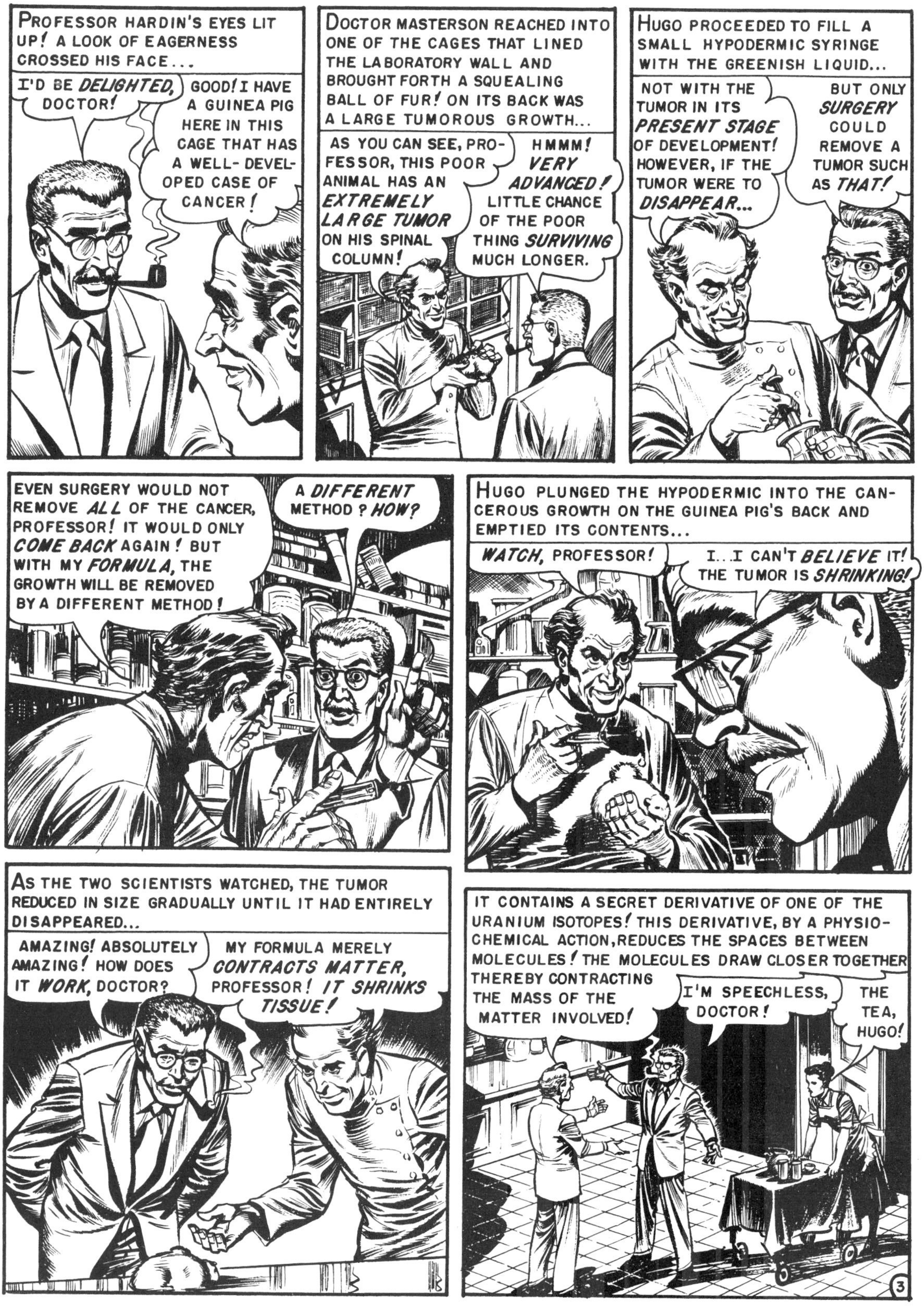
PROFESSOR HARDIN'S EYES LIT UP! A LOOK OF EAGERNESS CROSSED HIS FACE...
I'D BE DELIGHTED, DOCTOR!
GOOD! I HAVE A GUINEA PIG HERE IN THIS CAGE THAT HAS A WELL-DEVELOPED CASE OF CANCER!
DOCTOR MASTERSON REACHED INTO ONE OF THE CAGES THAT LINED THE LABORATORY WALL AND BROUGHT FORTH A SQUEALING BALL OF FUR! ON ITS BACK WAS A LARGE TUMOROUS GROWTH...
AS YOU CAN SEE, PROFESSOR, THIS POOR ANIMAL HAS AN EXTREMELY LARGE TUMOR ON HIS SPINAL COLUMN!
HMMM! VERY ADVANCED! LITTLE CHANCE OF THE POOR THING SURVIVING MUCH LONGER.
HUGO PROCEEDED TO FILL A SMALL HYPODERMIC SYRINGE WITH THE GREENISH LIQUID...
NOT WITH THE TUMOR IN ITS PRESENT STAGE OF DEVELOPMENT! HOWEVER, IF THE TUMOR WERE TO DISAPPEAR...
BUT ONLY SURGERY COULD REMOVE A TUMOR SUCH AS THAT!
EVEN SURGERY WOULD NOT REMOVE ALL OF THE CANCER, PROFESSOR! IT WOULD ONLY COME BACK AGAIN! BUT WITH MY FORMULA, THE GROWTH WILL BE REMOVED BY A DIFFERENT METHOD!
A DIFFERENT METHOD? HOW?
HUGO PLUNGED THE HYPODERMIC INTO THE CANCEROUS GROWTH ON THE GUINEA PIG'S BACK AND EMPTIED ITS CONTENTS...
WATCH, PROFESSOR!
I...I CAN'T BELIEVE IT! THE TUMOR IS SHRINKING!
AS THE TWO SCIENTISTS WATCHED, THE TUMOR REDUCED IN SIZE GRADUALLY UNTIL IT HAD ENTIRELY DISAPPEARED...
AMAZING! ABSOLUTELY AMAZING! HOW DOES IT WORK, DOCTOR?
MY FORMULA MERELY CONTRACTS MATTER, PROFESSOR! IT SHRINKS TISSUE!
IT CONTAINS A SECRET DERIVATIVE OF ONE OF THE URANIUM ISOTOPES! THIS DERIVATIVE, BY A PHYSIO-CHEMICAL ACTION, REDUCES THE SPACES BETWEEN MOLECULES! THE MOLECULES DRAW CLOSER TOGETHER THEREBY CONTRACTING THE MASS OF THE MATTER INVOLVED!
I'M SPEECHLESS, DOCTOR!
THE TEA, HUGO!
3

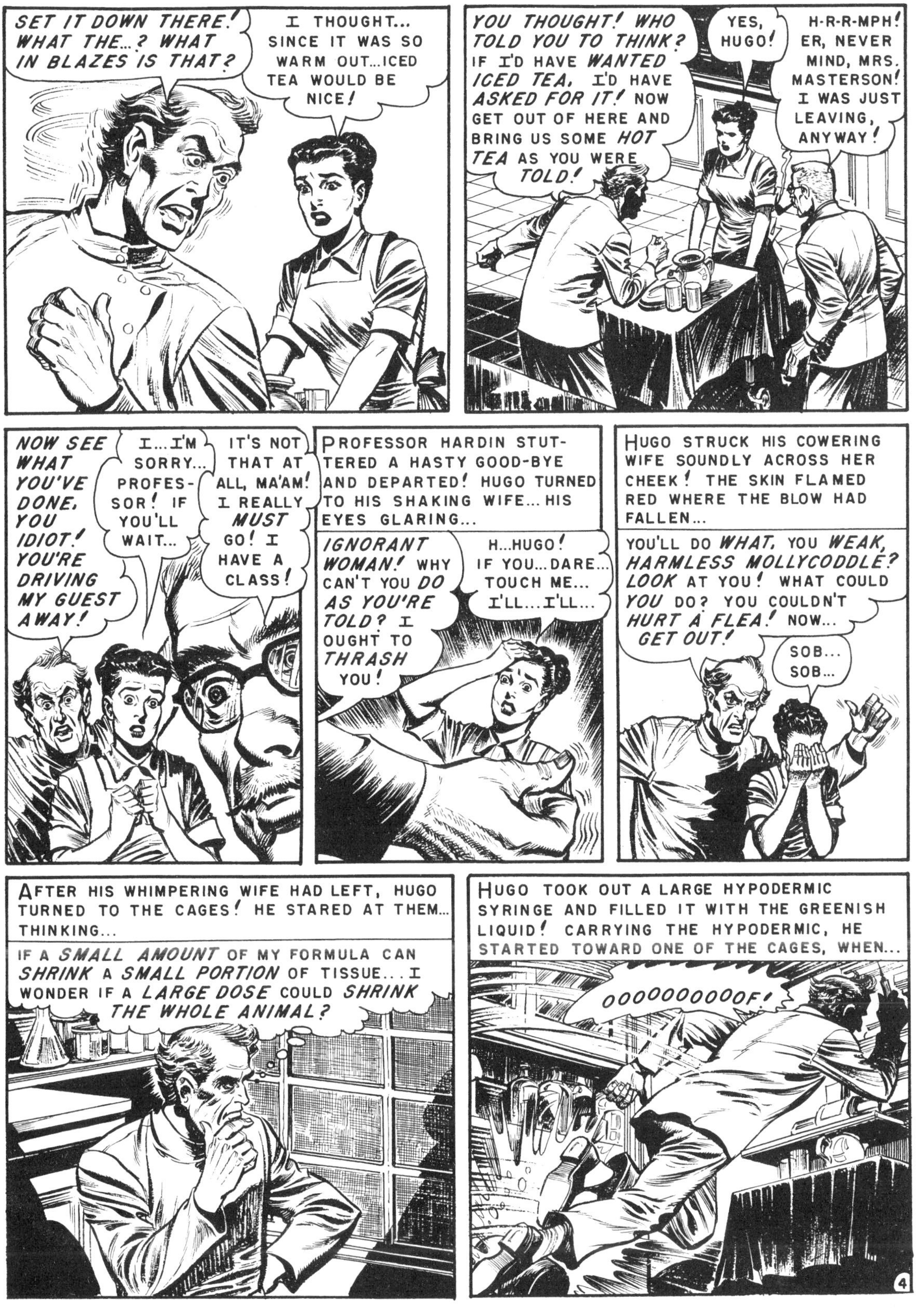
SET IT DOWN THERE! WHAT THE...? WHAT IN BLAZES IS THAT?
I THOUGHT... SINCE IT WAS SO WARM OUT...ICED TEA WOULD BE NICE!
YOU THOUGHT! WHO TOLD YOU TO THINK? IF I'D HAVE WANTED ICED TEA, I'D HAVE ASKED FOR IT! NOW GET OUT OF HERE AND BRING US SOME HOT TEA AS YOU WERE TOLD!
YES, HUGO!
H-R-R-MPH! ER, NEVER MIND, MRS. MASTERSON! I WAS JUST LEAVING, ANYWAY!
NOW SEE WHAT YOU'VE DONE, YOU IDIOT! YOU'RE DRIVING MY GUEST AWAY!
I...I'M SORRY... PROFES-SOR! IF YOU'LL WAIT...
IT'S NOT THAT AT ALL, MA'AM! I REALLY MUST GO! I HAVE A CLASS!
PROFESSOR HARDIN STUTTERED A HASTY GOOD-BYE AND DEPARTED! HUGO TURNED TO HIS SHAKING WIFE... HIS EYES GLARING...
IGNORANT WOMAN! WHY CAN'T YOU DO AS YOU'RE TOLD? I OUGHT TO THRASH YOU!
H...HUGO! IF YOU...DARE... TOUCH ME... I'LL...I'LL...
HUGO STRUCK HIS COWERING WIFE SOUNDLY ACROSS HER CHEEK! THE SKIN FLAMED RED WHERE THE BLOW HAD FALLEN...
YOU'LL DO WHAT, YOU WEAK, HARMLESS MOLLYCODDLE? LOOK AT YOU! WHAT COULD YOU DO? YOU COULDN'T HURT A FLEA! NOW... GET OUT!
SOB... SOB...
AFTER HIS WHIMPERING WIFE HAD LEFT, HUGO TURNED TO THE CAGES! HE STARED AT THEM... THINKING...
IF A SMALL AMOUNT OF MY FORMULA CAN SHRINK A SMALL PORTION OF TISSUE... I WONDER IF A LARGE DOSE COULD SHRINK THE WHOLE ANIMAL?
HUGO TOOK OUT A LARGE HYPODERMIC SYRINGE AND FILLED IT WITH THE GREENISH LIQUID! CARRYING THE HYPODERMIC, HE STARTED TOWARD ONE OF THE CAGES, WHEN...
OOOOOOOOOOF!
4

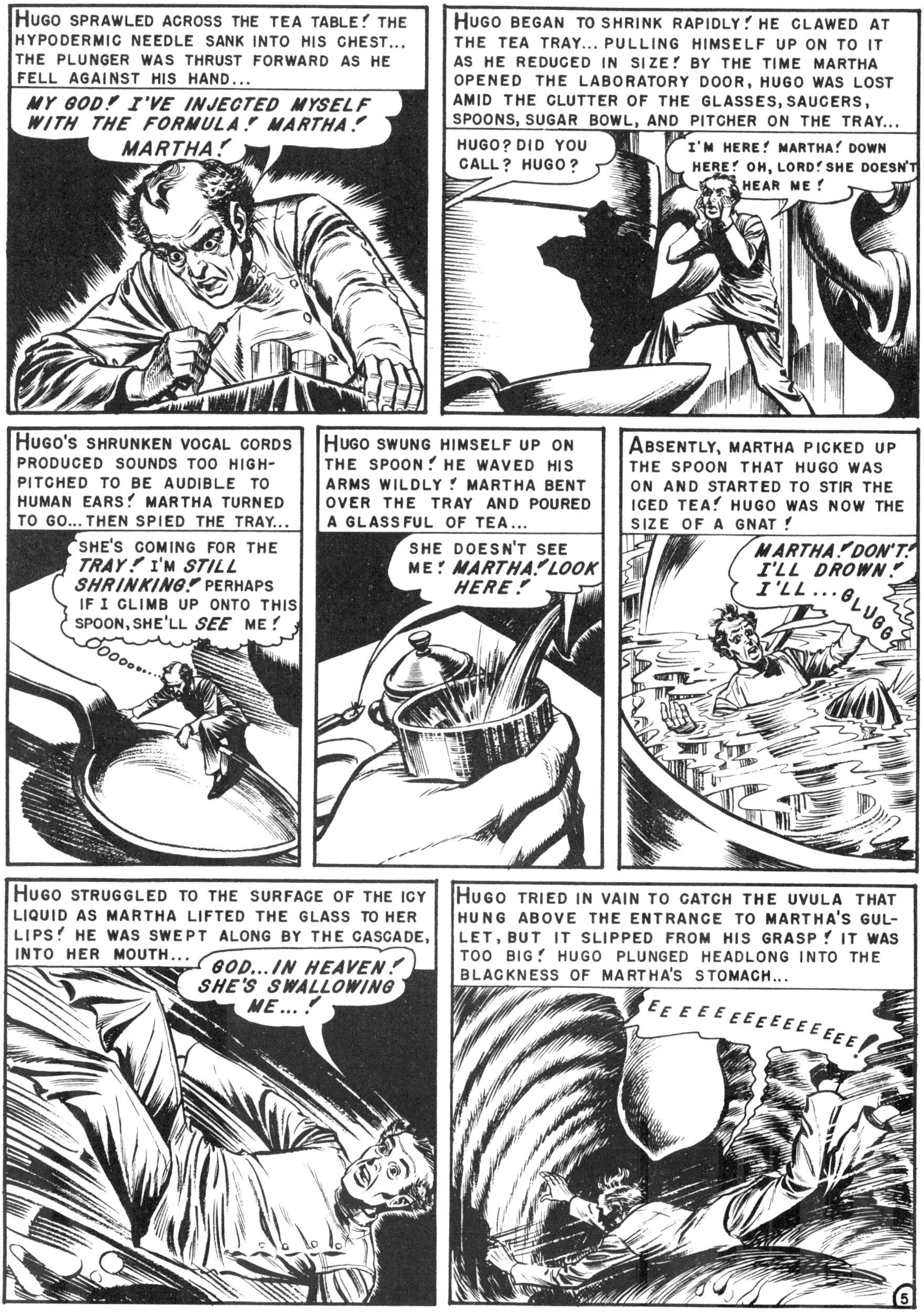
HUGO SPRAWLED ACROSS THE TEA TABLE! THE HYPODERMIC NEEDLE SANK INTO HIS CHEST... THE PLUNGER WAS THRUST FORWARD AS HE FELL AGAINST HIS HAND...
MY GOD! I'VE INJECTED MYSELF WITH THE FORMULA! MARTHA! MARTHA!
HUGO BEGAN TO SHRINK RAPIDLY! HE CLAWED AT THE TEA TRAY... PULLING HIMSELF UP ON TO IT AS HE REDUCED IN SIZE! BY THE TIME MARTHA OPENED THE LABORATORY DOOR, HUGO WAS LOST AMID THE CLUTTER OF THE GLASSES, SAUCERS, SPOONS, SUGAR BOWL, AND PITCHER ON THE TRAY...
HUGO? DID YOU CALL? HUGO?
I'M HERE! MARTHA! DOWN HERE! OH, LORD! SHE DOESN'T HEAR ME!
HUGO'S SHRUNKEN VOCAL CORDS PRODUCED SOUNDS TOO HIGH-PITCHED TO BE AUDIBLE TO HUMAN EARS! MARTHA TURNED TO GO... THEN SPIED THE TRAY...
SHE'S COMING FOR THE TRAY! I'M STILL SHRINKING! PERHAPS IF I CLIMB UP ONTO THIS SPOON, SHE'LL SEE ME!
HUGO SWUNG HIMSELF UP ON THE SPOON! HE WAVED HIS ARMS WILDLY! MARTHA BENT OVER THE TRAY AND POURED A GLASSFUL OF TEA...
SHE DOESN'T SEE ME! MARTHA! LOOK HERE!
ABSENTLY, MARTHA PICKED UP THE SPOON THAT HUGO WAS ON AND STARTED TO STIR THE ICED TEA! HUGO WAS NOW THE SIZE OF A GNAT!
MARTHA! DON'T! I'LL DROWN! I'LL ... GLUGG
HUGO STRUGGLED TO THE SURFACE OF THE ICY LIQUID AS MARTHA LIFTED THE GLASS TO HER LIPS! HE WAS SWEPT ALONG BY THE CASCADE, INTO HER MOUTH...
GOD... IN HEAVEN! SHE'S SWALLOWING ME...!
HUGO TRIED IN VAIN TO CATCH THE UVULA THAT HUNG ABOVE THE ENTRANCE TO MARTHA'S GUL-LET, BUT IT SLIPPED FROM HIS GRASP! IT WAS TOO BIG! HUGO PLUNGED HEADLONG INTO THE BLACKNESS OF MARTHA'S STOMACH...
EEEEEEEEEEEEEEE!
5

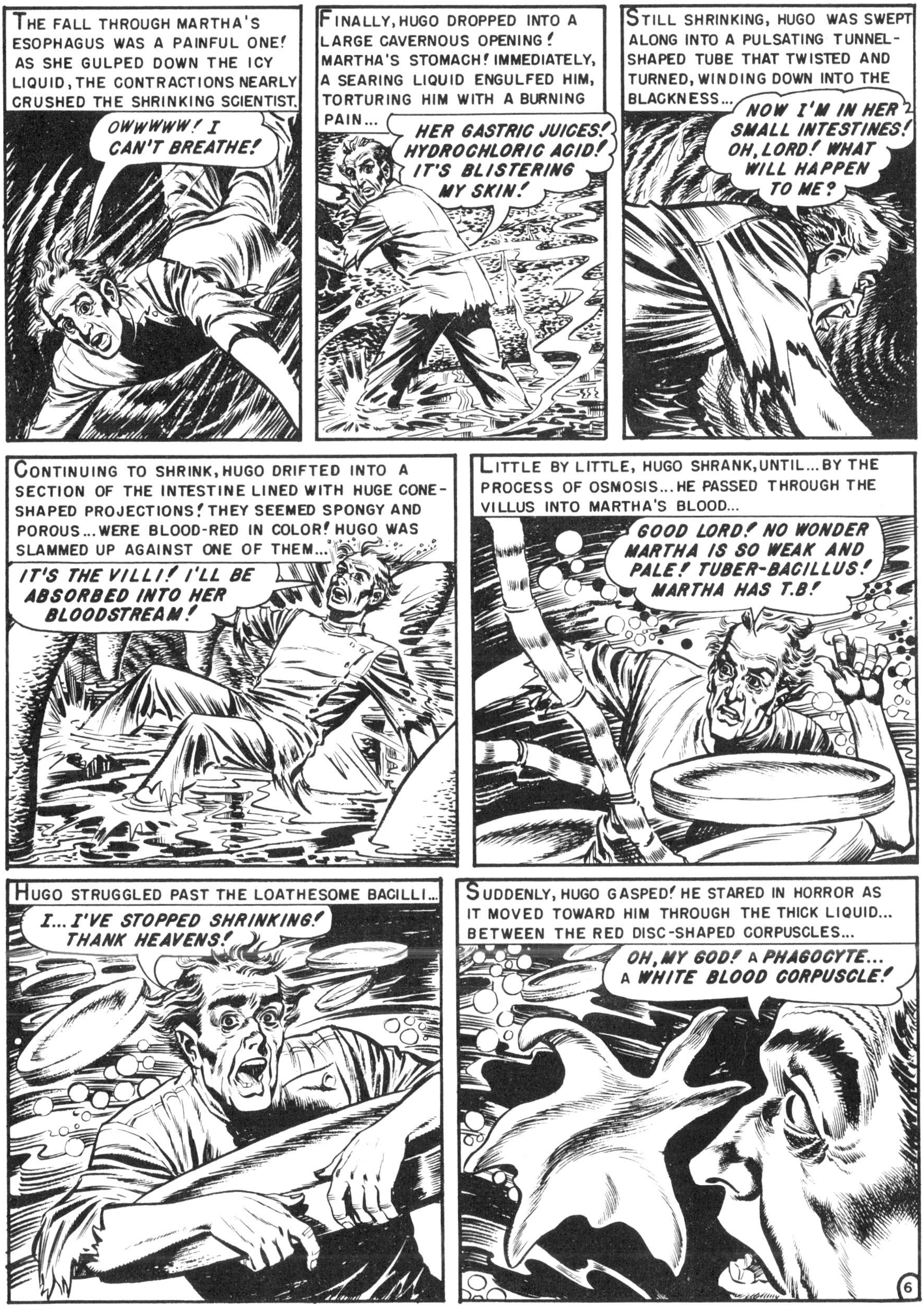
THE FALL THROUGH MARTHA'S ESOPHAGUS WAS A PAINFUL ONE! AS SHE GULPED DOWN THE ICY LIQUID, THE CONTRACTIONS NEARLY CRUSHED THE SHRINKING SCIENTIST.
OWWWWW! I CAN'T BREATHE!
FINALLY, HUGO DROPPED INTO A LARGE CAVERNOUS OPENING! MARTHA'S STOMACH! IMMEDIATELY, A SEARING LIQUID ENGULFED HIM, TORTURING HIM WITH A BURNING PAIN...
HER GASTRIC JUICES! HYDROCHLORIC ACID! IT'S BLISTERING MY SKIN!
STILL SHRINKING, HUGO WAS SWEPT ALONG INTO A PULSATING TUNNEL-SHAPED TUBE THAT TWISTED AND TURNED, WINDING DOWN INTO THE BLACKNESS...
NOW I'M IN HER SMALL INTESTINES! OH, LORD! WHAT WILL HAPPEN TO ME?
CONTINUING TO SHRINK, HUGO DRIFTED INTO A SECTION OF THE INTESTINE LINED WITH HUGE CONE-SHAPED PROJECTIONS! THEY SEEMED SPONGY AND POROUS... WERE BLOOD-RED IN COLOR! HUGO WAS SLAMMED UP AGAINST ONE OF THEM...
IT'S THE VILLI! I'LL BE ABSORBED INTO HER BLOODSTREAM!
LITTLE BY LITTLE, HUGO SHRANK, UNTIL... BY THE PROCESS OF OSMOSIS... HE PASSED THROUGH THE VILLUS INTO MARTHA'S BLOOD...
GOOD LORD! NO WONDER MARTHA IS SO WEAK AND PALE! TUBER-BACILLUS! MARTHA HAS T.B!
HUGO STRUGGLED PAST THE LOATHESOME BACILLI...
I... I'VE STOPPED SHRINKING! THANK HEAVENS!
SUDDENLY, HUGO GASPED! HE STARED IN HORROR AS IT MOVED TOWARD HIM THROUGH THE THICK LIQUID... BETWEEN THE RED DISC-SHAPED CORPUSCLES...
OH, MY GOD! A PHAGOCYTE... A WHITE BLOOD CORPUSCLE!
6

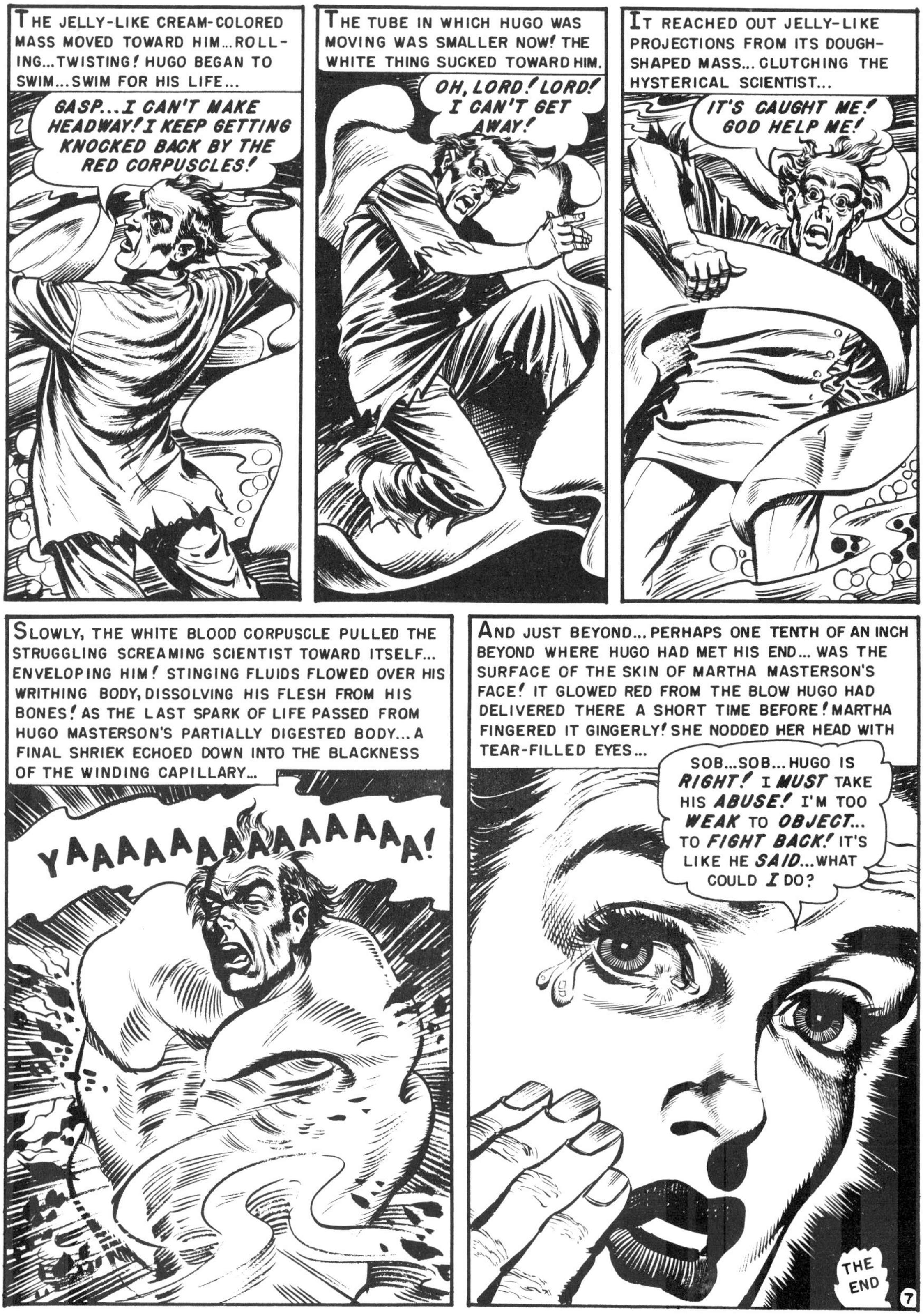
THE JELLY-LIKE CREAM-COLORED MASS MOVED TOWARD HIM...ROLLING...TWISTING! HUGO BEGAN TO SWIM...SWIM FOR HIS LIFE...
GASP...I CAN'T MAKE HEADWAY! I KEEP GETTING KNOCKED BACK BY THE RED CORPUSCLES!
THE TUBE IN WHICH HUGO WAS MOVING WAS SMALLER NOW! THE WHITE THING SUCKED TOWARD HIM.
OH, LORD! LORD! I CAN'T GET AWAY!
IT REACHED OUT JELLY-LIKE PROJECTIONS FROM ITS DOUGH-SHAPED MASS...CLUTCHING THE HYSTERICAL SCIENTIST...
IT'S CAUGHT ME! GOD HELP ME!
SLOWLY, THE WHITE BLOOD CORPUSCLE PULLED THE STRUGGLING SCREAMING SCIENTIST TOWARD ITSELF... ENVELOPING HIM! STINGING FLUIDS FLOWED OVER HIS WRITHING BODY, DISSOLVING HIS FLESH FROM HIS BONES! AS THE LAST SPARK OF LIFE PASSED FROM HUGO MASTERSON'S PARTIALLY DIGESTED BODY...A FINAL SHRIEK ECHOED DOWN INTO THE BLACKNESS OF THE WINDING CAPILLARY...
YAAAAAAAAAAAAA!
AND JUST BEYOND...PERHAPS ONE TENTH OF AN INCH BEYOND WHERE HUGO HAD MET HIS END...WAS THE SURFACE OF THE SKIN OF MARTHA MASTERSON'S FACE! IT GLOWED RED FROM THE BLOW HUGO HAD DELIVERED THERE A SHORT TIME BEFORE! MARTHA FINGERED IT GINGERLY! SHE NODDED HER HEAD WITH TEAR-FILLED EYES...
SOB...SOB...HUGO IS RIGHT! I MUST TAKE HIS ABUSE! I'M TOO WEAK TO OBJECT... TO FIGHT BACK! IT'S LIKE HE SAID...WHAT COULD I DO?
THE END
7

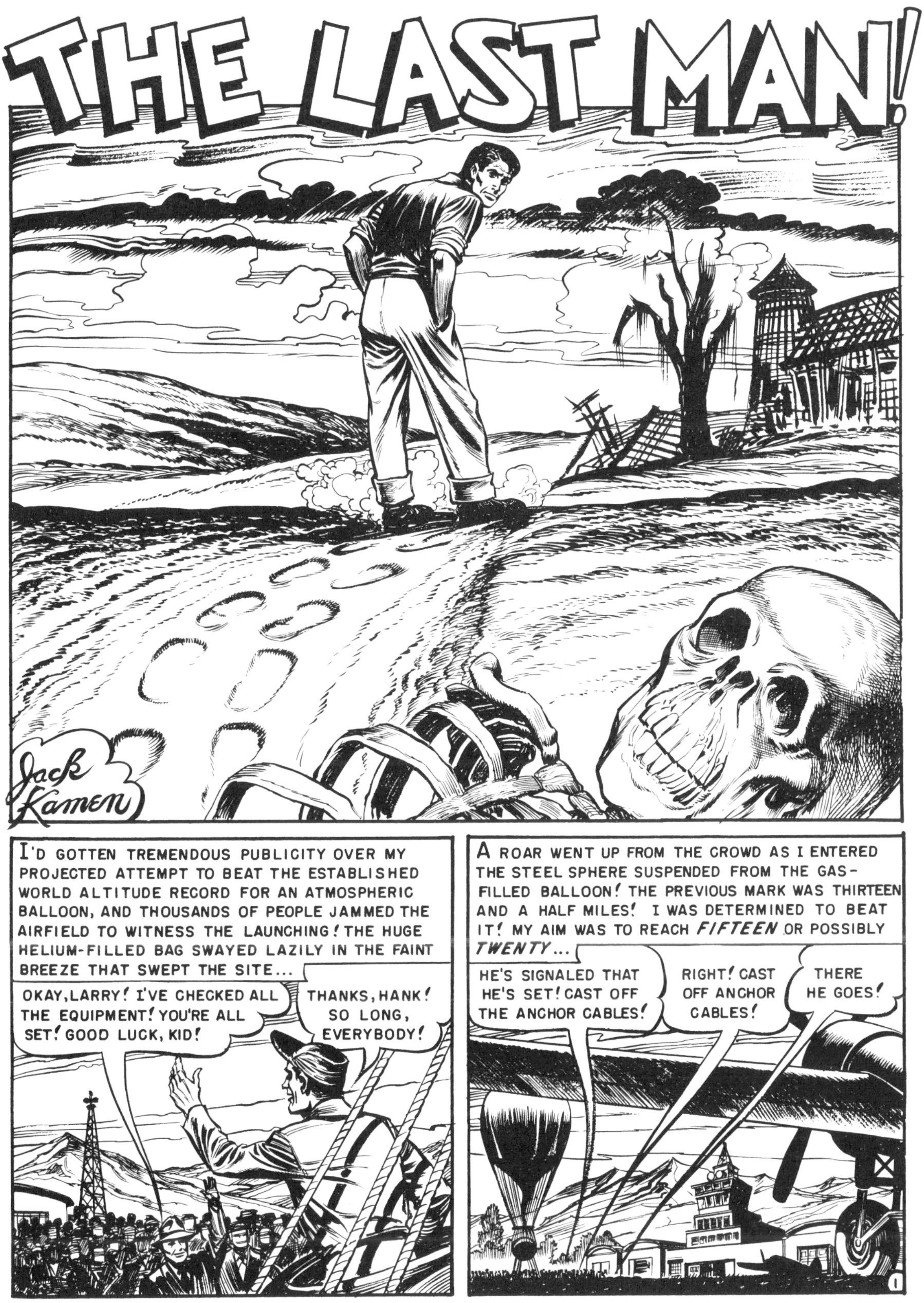
THE LAST MAN!
Jack Kamen
I'D GOTTEN TREMENDOUS PUBLICITY OVER MY PROJECTED ATTEMPT TO BEAT THE ESTABLISHED WORLD ALTITUDE RECORD FOR AN ATMOSPHERIC BALLOON, AND THOUSANDS OF PEOPLE JAMMED THE AIRFIELD TO WITNESS THE LAUNCHING! THE HUGE HELIUM-FILLED BAG SWAYED LAZILY IN THE FAINT BREEZE THAT SWEPT THE SITE...
OKAY, LARRY! I'VE CHECKED ALL THE EQUIPMENT! YOU'RE ALL SET! GOOD LUCK, KID!
THANKS, HANK! SO LONG, EVERYBODY!
A ROAR WENT UP FROM THE CROWD AS I ENTERED THE STEEL SPHERE SUSPENDED FROM THE GAS-FILLED BALLOON! THE PREVIOUS MARK WAS THIRTEEN AND A HALF MILES! I WAS DETERMINED TO BEAT IT! MY AIM WAS TO REACH FIFTEEN OR POSSIBLY TWENTY...
HE'S SIGNALED THAT HE'S SET! CAST OFF THE ANCHOR CABLES!
RIGHT! CAST OFF ANCHOR CABLES!
THERE HE GOES!
1

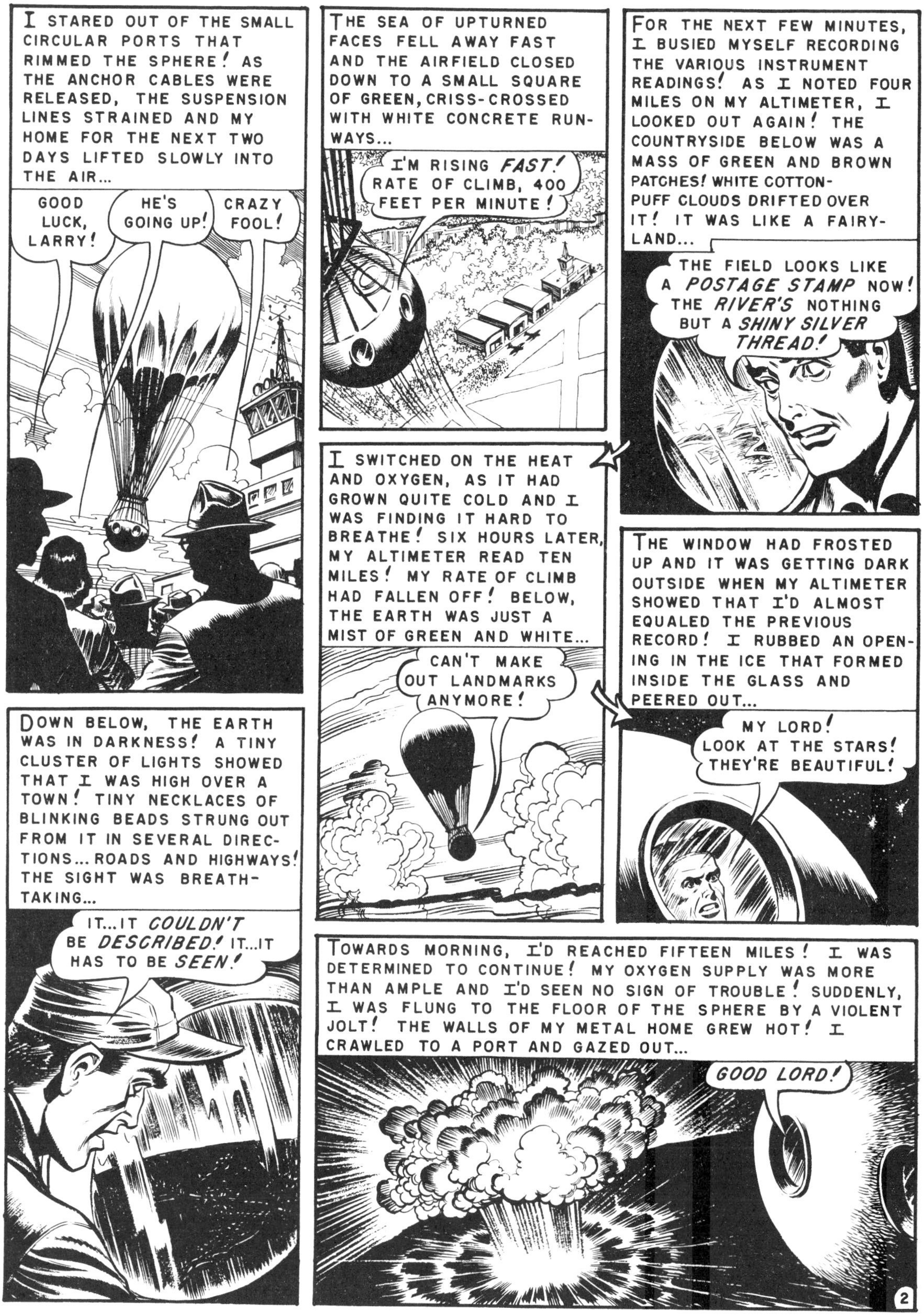
I STARED OUT OF THE SMALL CIRCULAR PORTS THAT RIMMED THE SPHERE! AS THE ANCHOR CABLES WERE RELEASED, THE SUSPENSION LINES STRAINED AND MY HOME FOR THE NEXT TWO DAYS LIFTED SLOWLY INTO THE AIR...
GOOD LUCK, LARRY!
HE'S GOING UP!
CRAZY FOOL!
THE SEA OF UPTURNED FACES FELL AWAY FAST AND THE AIRFIELD CLOSED DOWN TO A SMALL SQUARE OF GREEN, CRISS-CROSSED WITH WHITE CONCRETE RUN-WAYS...
I'M RISING *FAST!* RATE OF CLIMB, 400 FEET PER MINUTE!
FOR THE NEXT FEW MINUTES, I BUSIED MYSELF RECORDING THE VARIOUS INSTRUMENT READINGS! AS I NOTED FOUR MILES ON MY ALTIMETER, I LOOKED OUT AGAIN! THE COUNTRYSIDE BELOW WAS A MASS OF GREEN AND BROWN PATCHES! WHITE COTTON-PUFF CLOUDS DRIFTED OVER IT! IT WAS LIKE A FAIRY-LAND...
THE FIELD LOOKS LIKE A *POSTAGE STAMP* NOW! THE *RIVER'S* NOTHING BUT A *SHINY SILVER THREAD!*
I SWITCHED ON THE HEAT AND OXYGEN, AS IT HAD GROWN QUITE COLD AND I WAS FINDING IT HARD TO BREATHE! SIX HOURS LATER, MY ALTIMETER READ TEN MILES! MY RATE OF CLIMB HAD FALLEN OFF! BELOW, THE EARTH WAS JUST A MIST OF GREEN AND WHITE...
CAN'T MAKE OUT LANDMARKS ANYMORE!
THE WINDOW HAD FROSTED UP AND IT WAS GETTING DARK OUTSIDE WHEN MY ALTIMETER SHOWED THAT I'D ALMOST EQUALED THE PREVIOUS RECORD! I RUBBED AN OPEN-ING IN THE ICE THAT FORMED INSIDE THE GLASS AND PEERED OUT...
MY LORD! LOOK AT THE STARS! THEY'RE BEAUTIFUL!
DOWN BELOW, THE EARTH WAS IN DARKNESS! A TINY CLUSTER OF LIGHTS SHOWED THAT I WAS HIGH OVER A TOWN! TINY NECKLACES OF BLINKING BEADS STRUNG OUT FROM IT IN SEVERAL DIREC-TIONS... ROADS AND HIGHWAYS! THE SIGHT WAS BREATH-TAKING...
IT...IT *COULDN'T* BE *DESCRIBED!* IT...IT HAS TO BE *SEEN!*
TOWARDS MORNING, I'D REACHED FIFTEEN MILES! I WAS DETERMINED TO CONTINUE! MY OXYGEN SUPPLY WAS MORE THAN AMPLE AND I'D SEEN NO SIGN OF TROUBLE! SUDDENLY, I WAS FLUNG TO THE FLOOR OF THE SPHERE BY A VIOLENT JOLT! THE WALLS OF MY METAL HOME GREW HOT! I CRAWLED TO A PORT AND GAZED OUT...
GOOD LORD!
2

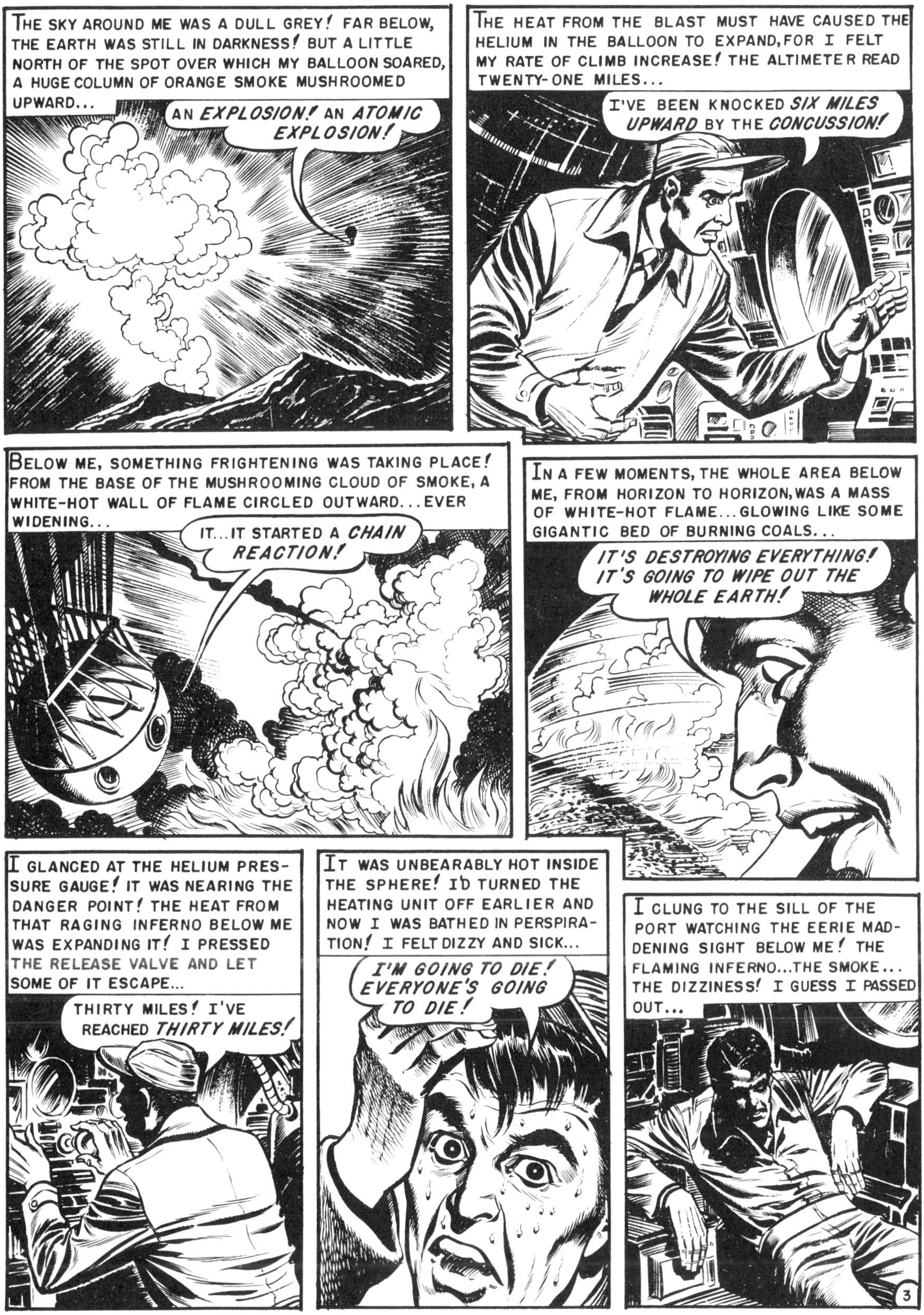
THE SKY AROUND ME WAS A DULL GREY! FAR BELOW, THE EARTH WAS STILL IN DARKNESS! BUT A LITTLE NORTH OF THE SPOT OVER WHICH MY BALLOON SOARED, A HUGE COLUMN OF ORANGE SMOKE MUSHROOMED UPWARD...
AN EXPLOSION! AN ATOMIC EXPLOSION!
THE HEAT FROM THE BLAST MUST HAVE CAUSED THE HELIUM IN THE BALLOON TO EXPAND, FOR I FELT MY RATE OF CLIMB INCREASE! THE ALTIMETER READ TWENTY-ONE MILES...
I'VE BEEN KNOCKED SIX MILES UPWARD BY THE CONCUSSION!
BELOW ME, SOMETHING FRIGHTENING WAS TAKING PLACE! FROM THE BASE OF THE MUSHROOMING CLOUD OF SMOKE, A WHITE-HOT WALL OF FLAME CIRCLED OUTWARD...EVER WIDENING...
IT...IT STARTED A CHAIN REACTION!
IN A FEW MOMENTS, THE WHOLE AREA BELOW ME, FROM HORIZON TO HORIZON, WAS A MASS OF WHITE-HOT FLAME...GLOWING LIKE SOME GIGANTIC BED OF BURNING COALS...
IT'S DESTROYING EVERYTHING! IT'S GOING TO WIPE OUT THE WHOLE EARTH!
I GLANCED AT THE HELIUM PRESSURE GAUGE! IT WAS NEARING THE DANGER POINT! THE HEAT FROM THAT RAGING INFERNO BELOW ME WAS EXPANDING IT! I PRESSED THE RELEASE VALVE AND LET SOME OF IT ESCAPE...
THIRTY MILES! I'VE REACHED THIRTY MILES!
IT WAS UNBEARABLY HOT INSIDE THE SPHERE! I'D TURNED THE HEATING UNIT OFF EARLIER AND NOW I WAS BATHED IN PERSPIRATION! I FELT DIZZY AND SICK...
I'M GOING TO DIE! EVERYONE'S GOING TO DIE!
I CLUNG TO THE SILL OF THE PORT WATCHING THE EERIE MADDENING SIGHT BELOW ME! THE FLAMING INFERNO...THE SMOKE... THE DIZZINESS! I GUESS I PASSED OUT...
3

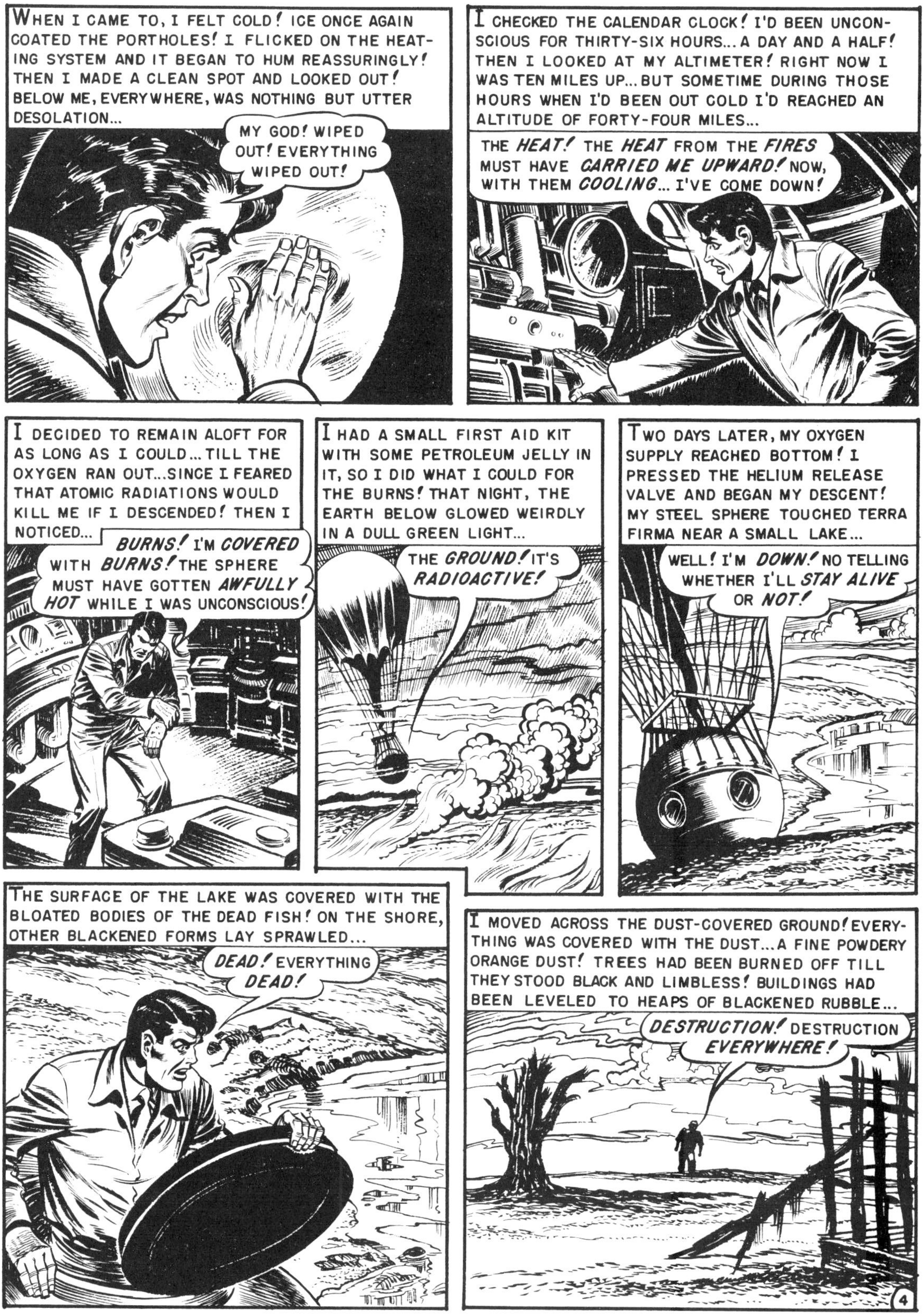
WHEN I CAME TO, I FELT COLD! ICE ONCE AGAIN COATED THE PORTHOLES! I FLICKED ON THE HEATING SYSTEM AND IT BEGAN TO HUM REASSURINGLY! THEN I MADE A CLEAN SPOT AND LOOKED OUT! BELOW ME, EVERYWHERE, WAS NOTHING BUT UTTER DESOLATION...
MY GOD! WIPED OUT! EVERYTHING WIPED OUT!
I CHECKED THE CALENDAR CLOCK! I'D BEEN UNCONSCIOUS FOR THIRTY-SIX HOURS... A DAY AND A HALF! THEN I LOOKED AT MY ALTIMETER! RIGHT NOW I WAS TEN MILES UP... BUT SOMETIME DURING THOSE HOURS WHEN I'D BEEN OUT COLD I'D REACHED AN ALTITUDE OF FORTY-FOUR MILES...
THE HEAT! THE HEAT FROM THE FIRES MUST HAVE CARRIED ME UPWARD! NOW, WITH THEM COOLING... I'VE COME DOWN!
I DECIDED TO REMAIN ALOFT FOR AS LONG AS I COULD... TILL THE OXYGEN RAN OUT... SINCE I FEARED THAT ATOMIC RADIATIONS WOULD KILL ME IF I DESCENDED! THEN I NOTICED...
BURNS! I'M COVERED WITH BURNS! THE SPHERE MUST HAVE GOTTEN AWFULLY HOT WHILE I WAS UNCONSCIOUS!
I HAD A SMALL FIRST AID KIT WITH SOME PETROLEUM JELLY IN IT, SO I DID WHAT I COULD FOR THE BURNS! THAT NIGHT, THE EARTH BELOW GLOWED WEIRDLY IN A DULL GREEN LIGHT...
THE GROUND! IT'S RADIOACTIVE!
TWO DAYS LATER, MY OXYGEN SUPPLY REACHED BOTTOM! I PRESSED THE HELIUM RELEASE VALVE AND BEGAN MY DESCENT! MY STEEL SPHERE TOUCHED TERRA FIRMA NEAR A SMALL LAKE...
WELL! I'M DOWN! NO TELLING WHETHER I'LL STAY ALIVE OR NOT!
THE SURFACE OF THE LAKE WAS COVERED WITH THE BLOATED BODIES OF THE DEAD FISH! ON THE SHORE, OTHER BLACKENED FORMS LAY SPRAWLED...
DEAD! EVERYTHING DEAD!
I MOVED ACROSS THE DUST-COVERED GROUND! EVERYTHING WAS COVERED WITH THE DUST... A FINE POWDERY ORANGE DUST! TREES HAD BEEN BURNED OFF TILL THEY STOOD BLACK AND LIMBLESS! BUILDINGS HAD BEEN LEVELED TO HEAPS OF BLACKENED RUBBLE...
DESTRUCTION! DESTRUCTION EVERYWHERE!
4

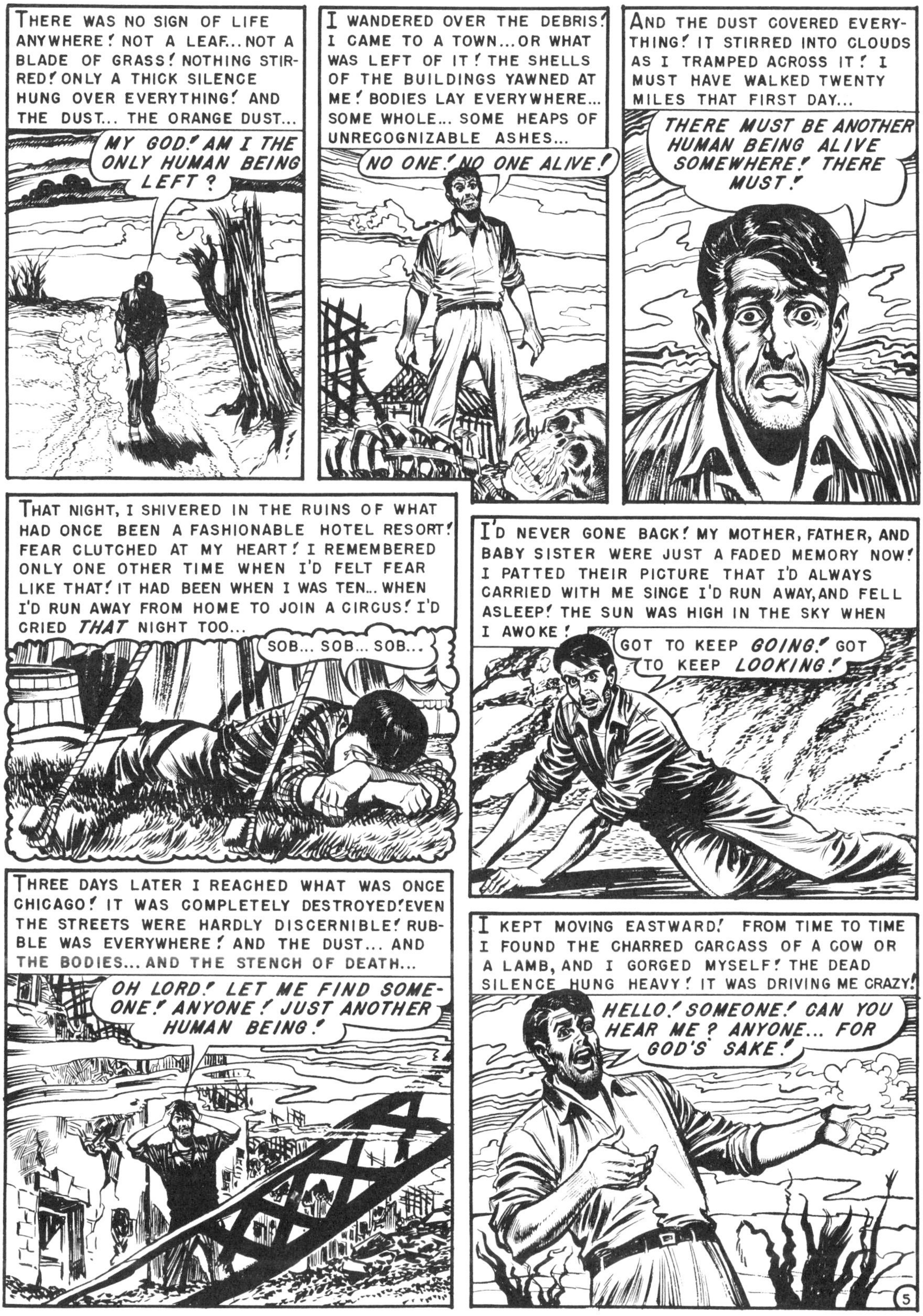
THERE WAS NO SIGN OF LIFE ANYWHERE! NOT A LEAF... NOT A BLADE OF GRASS! NOTHING STIRRED! ONLY A THICK SILENCE HUNG OVER EVERYTHING! AND THE DUST... THE ORANGE DUST...
MY GOD! AM I THE ONLY HUMAN BEING LEFT?
I WANDERED OVER THE DEBRIS! I CAME TO A TOWN... OR WHAT WAS LEFT OF IT! THE SHELLS OF THE BUILDINGS YAWNED AT ME! BODIES LAY EVERYWHERE... SOME WHOLE... SOME HEAPS OF UNRECOGNIZABLE ASHES...
NO ONE! NO ONE ALIVE!
AND THE DUST COVERED EVERYTHING! IT STIRRED INTO CLOUDS AS I TRAMPED ACROSS IT! I MUST HAVE WALKED TWENTY MILES THAT FIRST DAY...
THERE MUST BE ANOTHER HUMAN BEING ALIVE SOMEWHERE! THERE MUST!
THAT NIGHT, I SHIVERED IN THE RUINS OF WHAT HAD ONCE BEEN A FASHIONABLE HOTEL RESORT! FEAR CLUTCHED AT MY HEART! I REMEMBERED ONLY ONE OTHER TIME WHEN I'D FELT FEAR LIKE THAT! IT HAD BEEN WHEN I WAS TEN... WHEN I'D RUN AWAY FROM HOME TO JOIN A CIRCUS! I'D CRIED THAT NIGHT TOO...
SOB... SOB... SOB...
I'D NEVER GONE BACK! MY MOTHER, FATHER, AND BABY SISTER WERE JUST A FADED MEMORY NOW! I PATTED THEIR PICTURE THAT I'D ALWAYS CARRIED WITH ME SINCE I'D RUN AWAY, AND FELL ASLEEP! THE SUN WAS HIGH IN THE SKY WHEN I AWOKE!
GOT TO KEEP GOING! GOT TO KEEP LOOKING!
THREE DAYS LATER I REACHED WHAT WAS ONCE CHICAGO! IT WAS COMPLETELY DESTROYED! EVEN THE STREETS WERE HARDLY DISCERNIBLE! RUBBLE WAS EVERYWHERE! AND THE DUST... AND THE BODIES... AND THE STENCH OF DEATH...
OH LORD! LET ME FIND SOMEONE! ANYONE! JUST ANOTHER HUMAN BEING!
I KEPT MOVING EASTWARD! FROM TIME TO TIME I FOUND THE CHARRED CARCASS OF A COW OR A LAMB, AND I GORGED MYSELF! THE DEAD SILENCE HUNG HEAVY! IT WAS DRIVING ME CRAZY!
HELLO! SOMEONE! CAN YOU HEAR ME? ANYONE... FOR GOD'S SAKE!
5

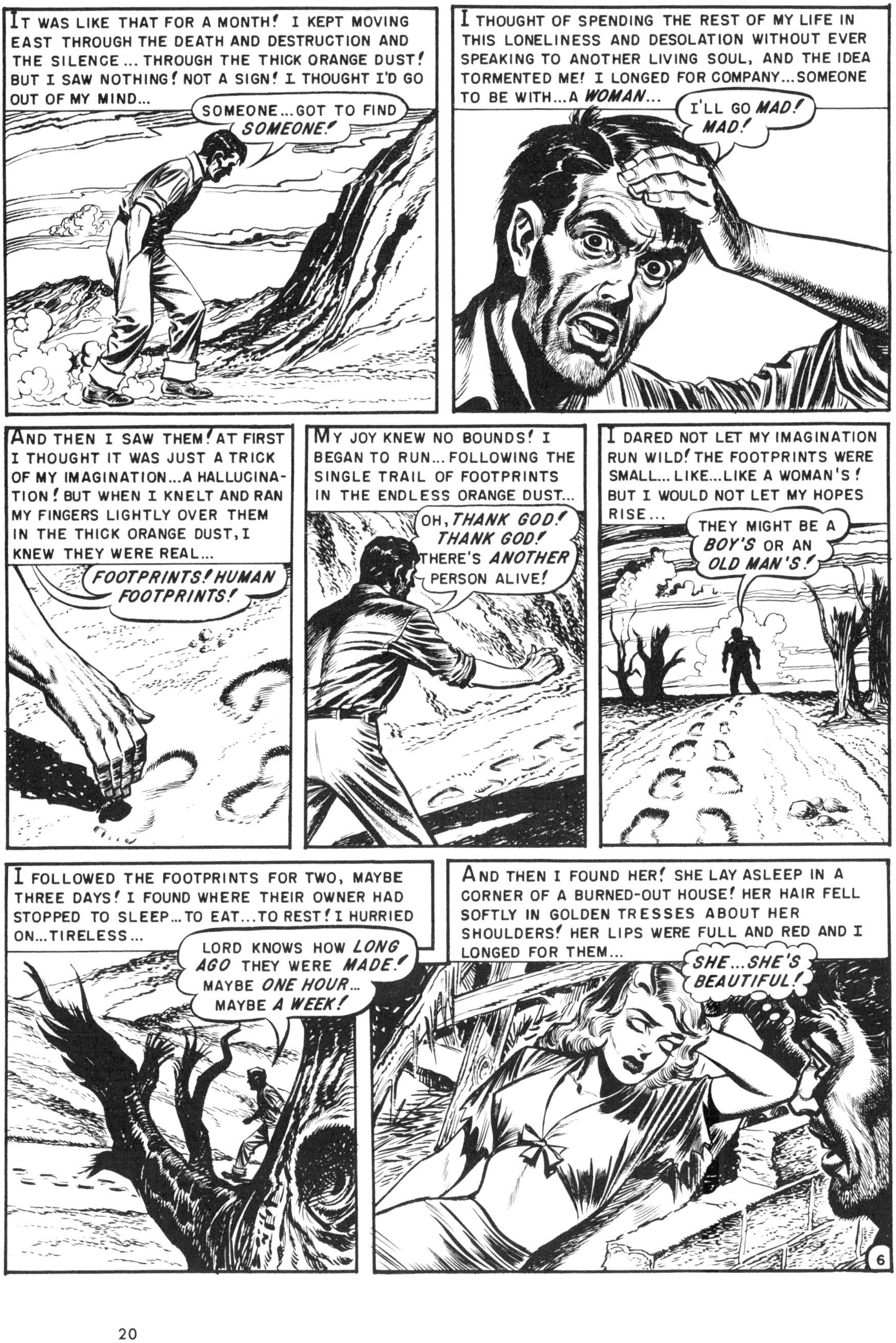
IT WAS LIKE THAT FOR A MONTH! I KEPT MOVING EAST THROUGH THE DEATH AND DESTRUCTION AND THE SILENCE ... THROUGH THE THICK ORANGE DUST! BUT I SAW NOTHING! NOT A SIGN! I THOUGHT I'D GO OUT OF MY MIND...
SOMEONE...GOT TO FIND SOMEONE!
I THOUGHT OF SPENDING THE REST OF MY LIFE IN THIS LONELINESS AND DESOLATION WITHOUT EVER SPEAKING TO ANOTHER LIVING SOUL, AND THE IDEA TORMENTED ME! I LONGED FOR COMPANY...SOMEONE TO BE WITH...A WOMAN...
I'LL GO MAD! MAD!
AND THEN I SAW THEM! AT FIRST I THOUGHT IT WAS JUST A TRICK OF MY IMAGINATION...A HALLUCINATION! BUT WHEN I KNELT AND RAN MY FINGERS LIGHTLY OVER THEM IN THE THICK ORANGE DUST, I KNEW THEY WERE REAL...
FOOTPRINTS! HUMAN FOOTPRINTS!
MY JOY KNEW NO BOUNDS! I BEGAN TO RUN... FOLLOWING THE SINGLE TRAIL OF FOOTPRINTS IN THE ENDLESS ORANGE DUST...
OH, THANK GOD! THANK GOD! THERE'S ANOTHER PERSON ALIVE!
I DARED NOT LET MY IMAGINATION RUN WILD! THE FOOTPRINTS WERE SMALL... LIKE...LIKE A WOMAN'S! BUT I WOULD NOT LET MY HOPES RISE...
THEY MIGHT BE A BOY'S OR AN OLD MAN'S!
I FOLLOWED THE FOOTPRINTS FOR TWO, MAYBE THREE DAYS! I FOUND WHERE THEIR OWNER HAD STOPPED TO SLEEP...TO EAT...TO REST! I HURRIED ON...TIRELESS...
LORD KNOWS HOW LONG AGO THEY WERE MADE! MAYBE ONE HOUR... MAYBE A WEEK!
AND THEN I FOUND HER! SHE LAY ASLEEP IN A CORNER OF A BURNED-OUT HOUSE! HER HAIR FELL SOFTLY IN GOLDEN TRESSES ABOUT HER SHOULDERS! HER LIPS WERE FULL AND RED AND I LONGED FOR THEM...
SHE...SHE'S BEAUTIFUL!
6

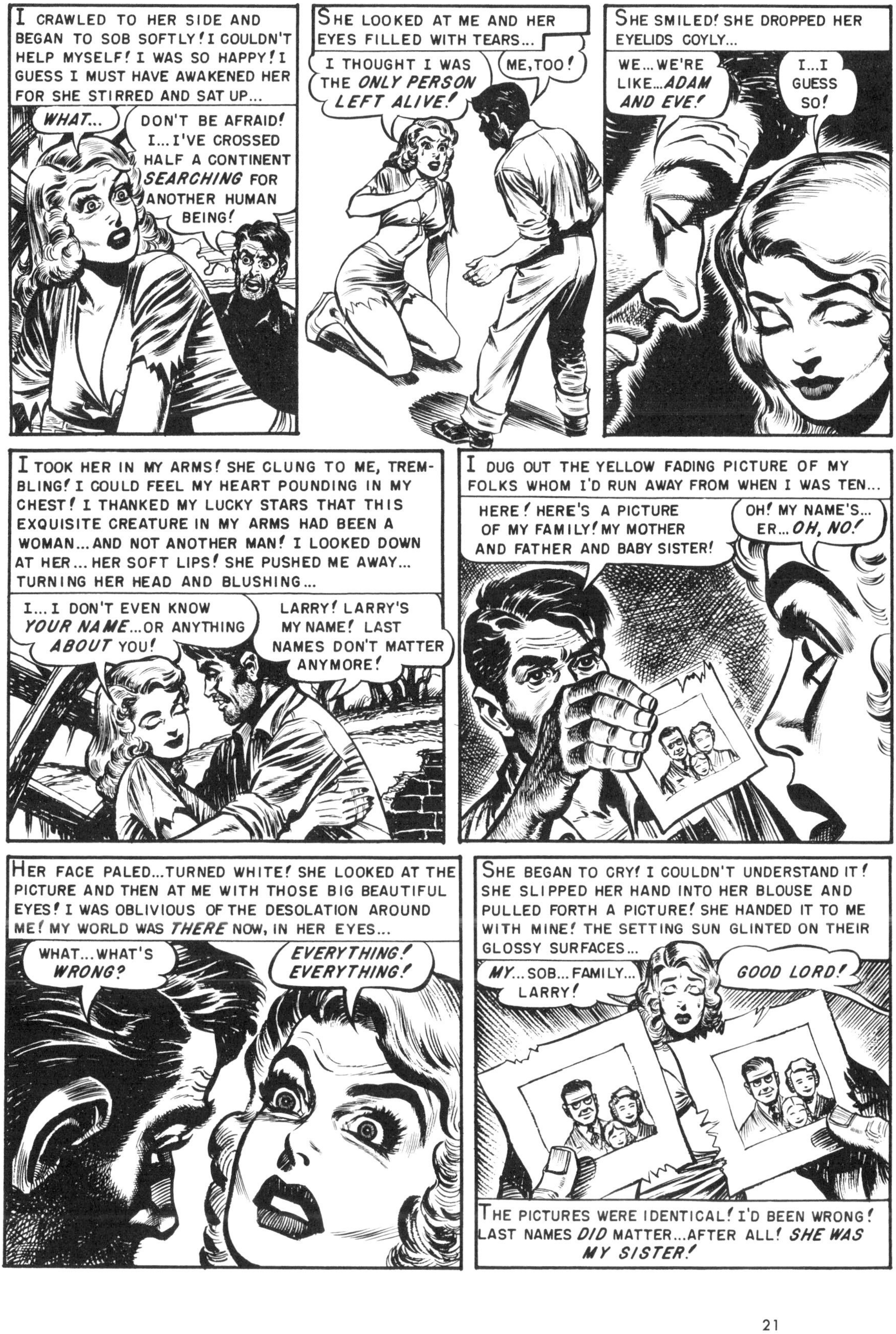
I CRAWLED TO HER SIDE AND BEGAN TO SOB SOFTLY! I COULDN'T HELP MYSELF! I WAS SO HAPPY! I GUESS I MUST HAVE AWAKENED HER FOR SHE STIRRED AND SAT UP...
WHAT...
DON'T BE AFRAID! I... I'VE CROSSED HALF A CONTINENT SEARCHING FOR ANOTHER HUMAN BEING!
SHE LOOKED AT ME AND HER EYES FILLED WITH TEARS...
I THOUGHT I WAS THE ONLY PERSON LEFT ALIVE!
ME, TOO!
SHE SMILED! SHE DROPPED HER EYELIDS COYLY...
WE... WE'RE LIKE... ADAM AND EVE!
I... I GUESS SO!
I TOOK HER IN MY ARMS! SHE CLUNG TO ME, TREMBLING! I COULD FEEL MY HEART POUNDING IN MY CHEST! I THANKED MY LUCKY STARS THAT THIS EXQUISITE CREATURE IN MY ARMS HAD BEEN A WOMAN... AND NOT ANOTHER MAN! I LOOKED DOWN AT HER... HER SOFT LIPS! SHE PUSHED ME AWAY... TURNING HER HEAD AND BLUSHING...
I... I DON'T EVEN KNOW YOUR NAME... OR ANYTHING ABOUT YOU!
LARRY! LARRY'S MY NAME! LAST NAMES DON'T MATTER ANYMORE!
I DUG OUT THE YELLOW FADING PICTURE OF MY FOLKS WHOM I'D RUN AWAY FROM WHEN I WAS TEN...
HERE! HERE'S A PICTURE OF MY FAMILY! MY MOTHER AND FATHER AND BABY SISTER!
OH! MY NAME'S... ER... OH, NO!
HER FACE PALED... TURNED WHITE! SHE LOOKED AT THE PICTURE AND THEN AT ME WITH THOSE BIG BEAUTIFUL EYES! I WAS OBLIVIOUS OF THE DESOLATION AROUND ME! MY WORLD WAS THERE NOW, IN HER EYES...
WHAT... WHAT'S WRONG?
EVERYTHING! EVERYTHING!
SHE BEGAN TO CRY! I COULDN'T UNDERSTAND IT! SHE SLIPPED HER HAND INTO HER BLOUSE AND PULLED FORTH A PICTURE! SHE HANDED IT TO ME WITH MINE! THE SETTING SUN GLINTED ON THEIR GLOSSY SURFACES...
MY... SOB... FAMILY... LARRY!
GOOD LORD!
THE PICTURES WERE IDENTICAL! I'D BEEN WRONG! LAST NAMES DID MATTER... AFTER ALL! SHE WAS MY SISTER!

A LESSON IN ANATOMY!!

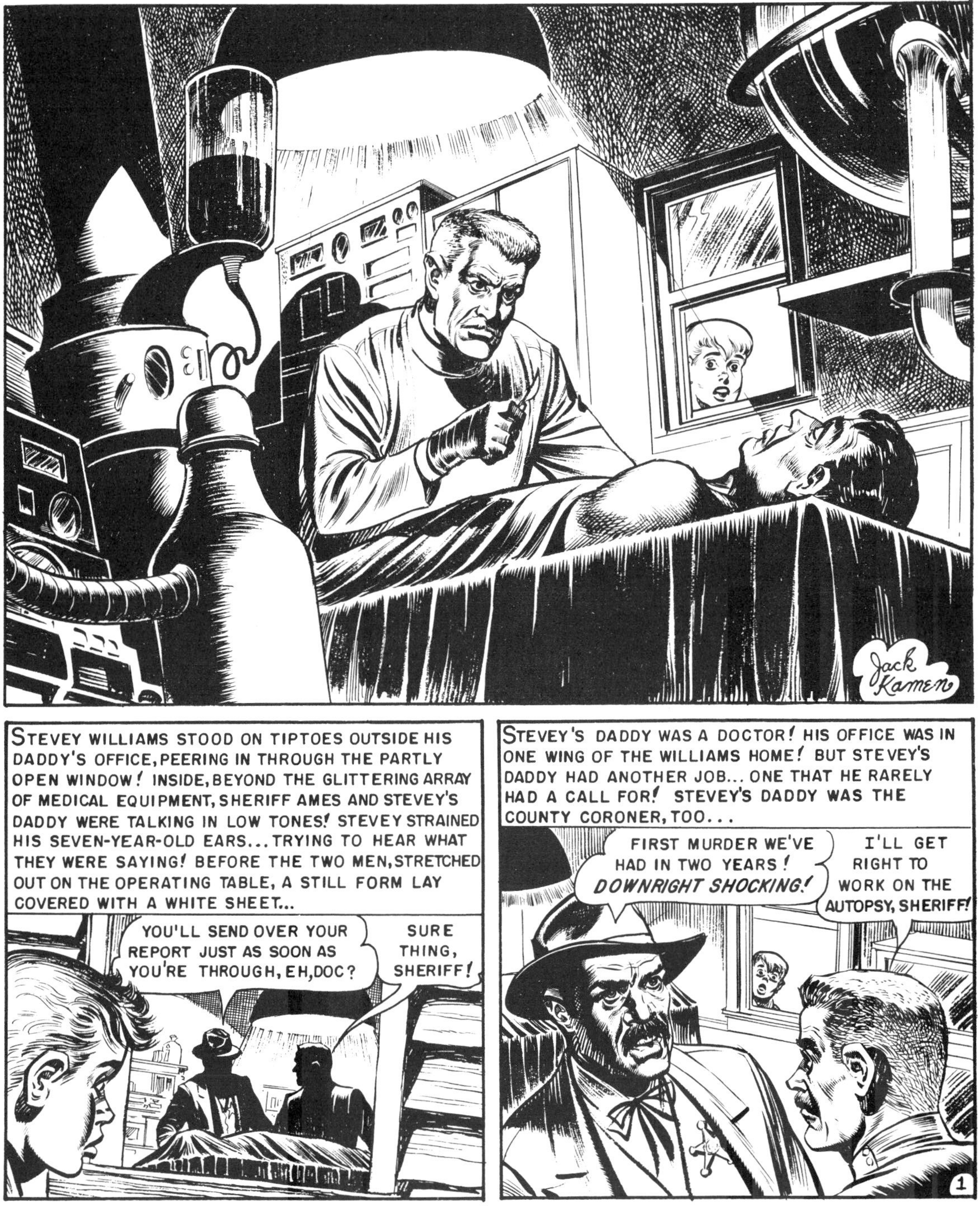
Jack Kamen
STEVEY WILLIAMS STOOD ON TIPTOES OUTSIDE HIS DADDY'S OFFICE, PEERING IN THROUGH THE PARTLY OPEN WINDOW! INSIDE, BEYOND THE GLITTERING ARRAY OF MEDICAL EQUIPMENT, SHERIFF AMES AND STEVEY'S DADDY WERE TALKING IN LOW TONES! STEVEY STRAINED HIS SEVEN-YEAR-OLD EARS... TRYING TO HEAR WHAT THEY WERE SAYING! BEFORE THE TWO MEN, STRETCHED OUT ON THE OPERATING TABLE, A STILL FORM LAY COVERED WITH A WHITE SHEET...
YOU'LL SEND OVER YOUR REPORT JUST AS SOON AS YOU'RE THROUGH, EH, DOC?
SURE THING, SHERIFF!
STEVEY'S DADDY WAS A DOCTOR! HIS OFFICE WAS IN ONE WING OF THE WILLIAMS HOME! BUT STEVEY'S DADDY HAD ANOTHER JOB... ONE THAT HE RARELY HAD A CALL FOR! STEVEY'S DADDY WAS THE COUNTY CORONER, TOO...
FIRST MURDER WE'VE HAD IN TWO YEARS! DOWNRIGHT SHOCKING!
I'LL GET RIGHT TO WORK ON THE AUTOPSY, SHERIFF!
1

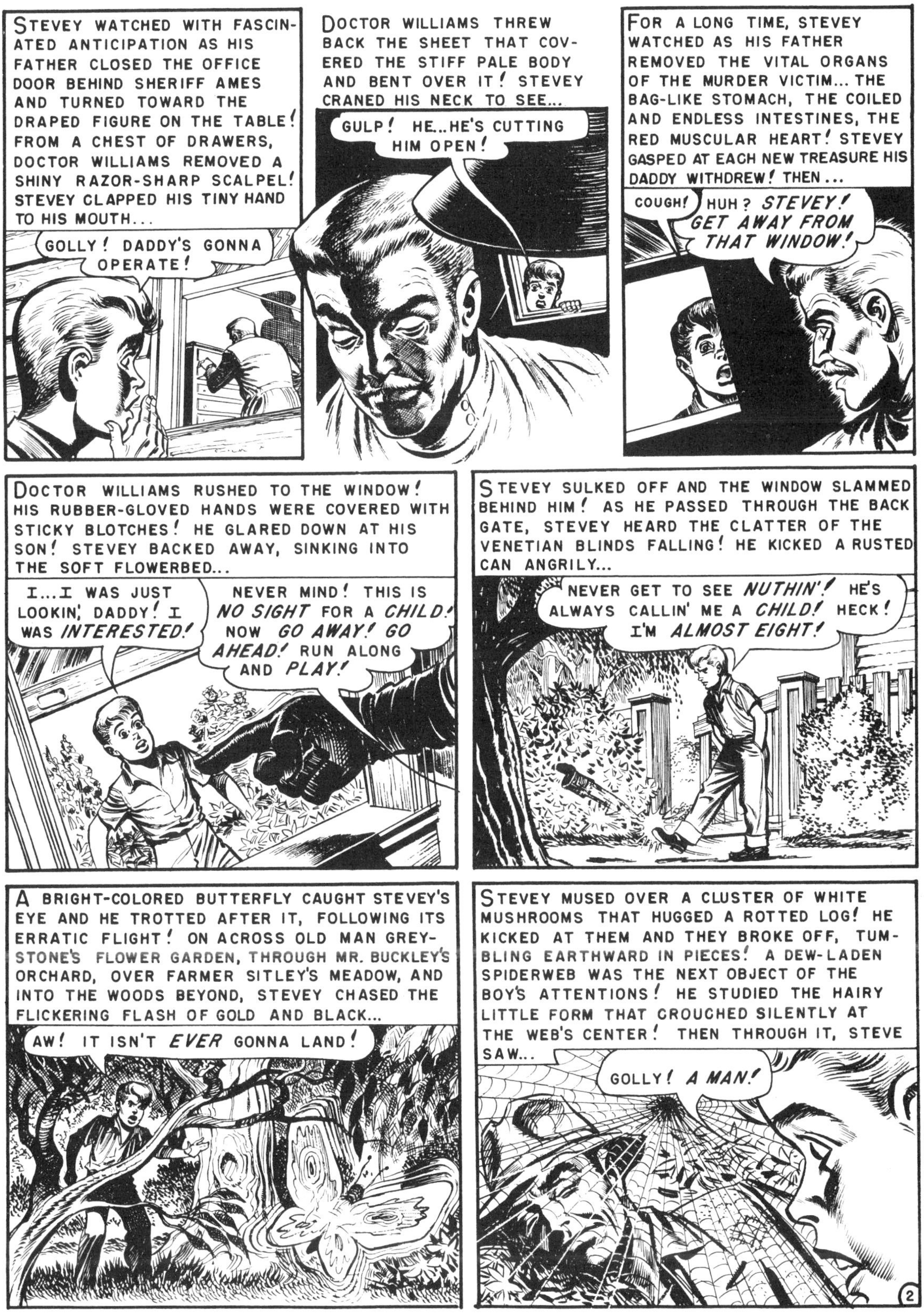
STEVEY WATCHED WITH FASCINATED ANTICIPATION AS HIS FATHER CLOSED THE OFFICE DOOR BEHIND SHERIFF AMES AND TURNED TOWARD THE DRAPED FIGURE ON THE TABLE! FROM A CHEST OF DRAWERS, DOCTOR WILLIAMS REMOVED A SHINY RAZOR-SHARP SCALPEL! STEVEY CLAPPED HIS TINY HAND TO HIS MOUTH...
GOLLY! DADDY'S GONNA OPERATE!
DOCTOR WILLIAMS THREW BACK THE SHEET THAT COVERED THE STIFF PALE BODY AND BENT OVER IT! STEVEY CRANED HIS NECK TO SEE...
GULP! HE...HE'S CUTTING HIM OPEN!
FOR A LONG TIME, STEVEY WATCHED AS HIS FATHER REMOVED THE VITAL ORGANS OF THE MURDER VICTIM... THE BAG-LIKE STOMACH, THE COILED AND ENDLESS INTESTINES, THE RED MUSCULAR HEART! STEVEY GASPED AT EACH NEW TREASURE HIS DADDY WITHDREW! THEN...
COUGH!
HUH? STEVEY! GET AWAY FROM THAT WINDOW!
DOCTOR WILLIAMS RUSHED TO THE WINDOW! HIS RUBBER-GLOVED HANDS WERE COVERED WITH STICKY BLOTCHES! HE GLARED DOWN AT HIS SON! STEVEY BACKED AWAY, SINKING INTO THE SOFT FLOWERBED...
I...I WAS JUST LOOKIN', DADDY! I WAS INTERESTED!
NEVER MIND! THIS IS NO SIGHT FOR A CHILD! NOW GO AWAY! GO AHEAD! RUN ALONG AND PLAY!
STEVEY SULKED OFF AND THE WINDOW SLAMMED BEHIND HIM! AS HE PASSED THROUGH THE BACK GATE, STEVEY HEARD THE CLATTER OF THE VENETIAN BLINDS FALLING! HE KICKED A RUSTED CAN ANGRILY...
NEVER GET TO SEE NUTHIN'! HE'S ALWAYS CALLIN' ME A CHILD! HECK! I'M ALMOST EIGHT!
A BRIGHT-COLORED BUTTERFLY CAUGHT STEVEY'S EYE AND HE TROTTED AFTER IT, FOLLOWING ITS ERRATIC FLIGHT! ON ACROSS OLD MAN GREYSTONE'S FLOWER GARDEN, THROUGH MR. BUCKLEY'S ORCHARD, OVER FARMER SITLEY'S MEADOW, AND INTO THE WOODS BEYOND, STEVEY CHASED THE FLICKERING FLASH OF GOLD AND BLACK...
AW! IT ISN'T EVER GONNA LAND!
STEVEY MUSED OVER A CLUSTER OF WHITE MUSHROOMS THAT HUGGED A ROTTED LOG! HE KICKED AT THEM AND THEY BROKE OFF, TUMBLING EARTHWARD IN PIECES! A DEW-LADEN SPIDERWEB WAS THE NEXT OBJECT OF THE BOY'S ATTENTIONS! HE STUDIED THE HAIRY LITTLE FORM THAT CROUCHED SILENTLY AT THE WEB'S CENTER! THEN THROUGH IT, STEVE SAW...
GOLLY! A MAN!
2

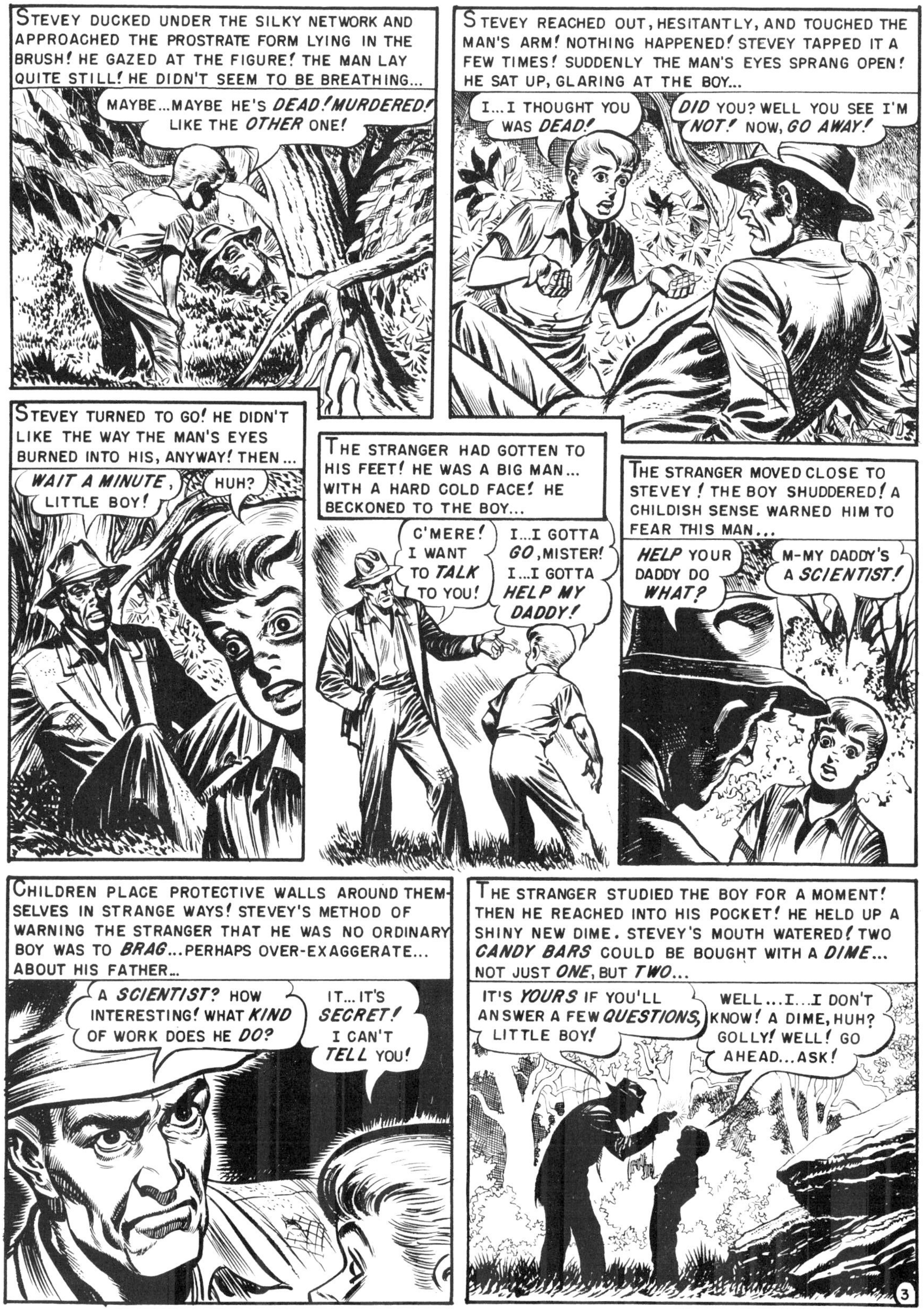
STEVEY DUCKED UNDER THE SILKY NETWORK AND APPROACHED THE PROSTRATE FORM LYING IN THE BRUSH! HE GAZED AT THE FIGURE! THE MAN LAY QUITE STILL! HE DIDN'T SEEM TO BE BREATHING...
MAYBE...MAYBE HE'S DEAD! MURDERED! LIKE THE OTHER ONE!
STEVEY REACHED OUT, HESITANTLY, AND TOUCHED THE MAN'S ARM! NOTHING HAPPENED! STEVEY TAPPED IT A FEW TIMES! SUDDENLY THE MAN'S EYES SPRANG OPEN! HE SAT UP, GLARING AT THE BOY...
I...I THOUGHT YOU WAS DEAD!
DID YOU? WELL YOU SEE I'M NOT! NOW, GO AWAY!
STEVEY TURNED TO GO! HE DIDN'T LIKE THE WAY THE MAN'S EYES BURNED INTO HIS, ANYWAY! THEN...
WAIT A MINUTE, LITTLE BOY!
HUH?
THE STRANGER HAD GOTTEN TO HIS FEET! HE WAS A BIG MAN... WITH A HARD COLD FACE! HE BECKONED TO THE BOY...
C'MERE! I WANT TO TALK TO YOU!
I...I GOTTA GO, MISTER! I...I GOTTA HELP MY DADDY!
THE STRANGER MOVED CLOSE TO STEVEY! THE BOY SHUDDERED! A CHILDISH SENSE WARNED HIM TO FEAR THIS MAN...
HELP YOUR DADDY DO WHAT?
M-MY DADDY'S A SCIENTIST!
CHILDREN PLACE PROTECTIVE WALLS AROUND THEMSELVES IN STRANGE WAYS! STEVEY'S METHOD OF WARNING THE STRANGER THAT HE WAS NO ORDINARY BOY WAS TO BRAG...PERHAPS OVER-EXAGGERATE... ABOUT HIS FATHER...
A SCIENTIST? HOW INTERESTING! WHAT KIND OF WORK DOES HE DO?
IT...IT'S SECRET! I CAN'T TELL YOU!
THE STRANGER STUDIED THE BOY FOR A MOMENT! THEN HE REACHED INTO HIS POCKET! HE HELD UP A SHINY NEW DIME. STEVEY'S MOUTH WATERED! TWO CANDY BARS COULD BE BOUGHT WITH A DIME... NOT JUST ONE, BUT TWO...
IT'S YOURS IF YOU'LL ANSWER A FEW QUESTIONS, LITTLE BOY!
WELL...I...I DON'T KNOW! A DIME, HUH? GOLLY! WELL! GO AHEAD...ASK!
3

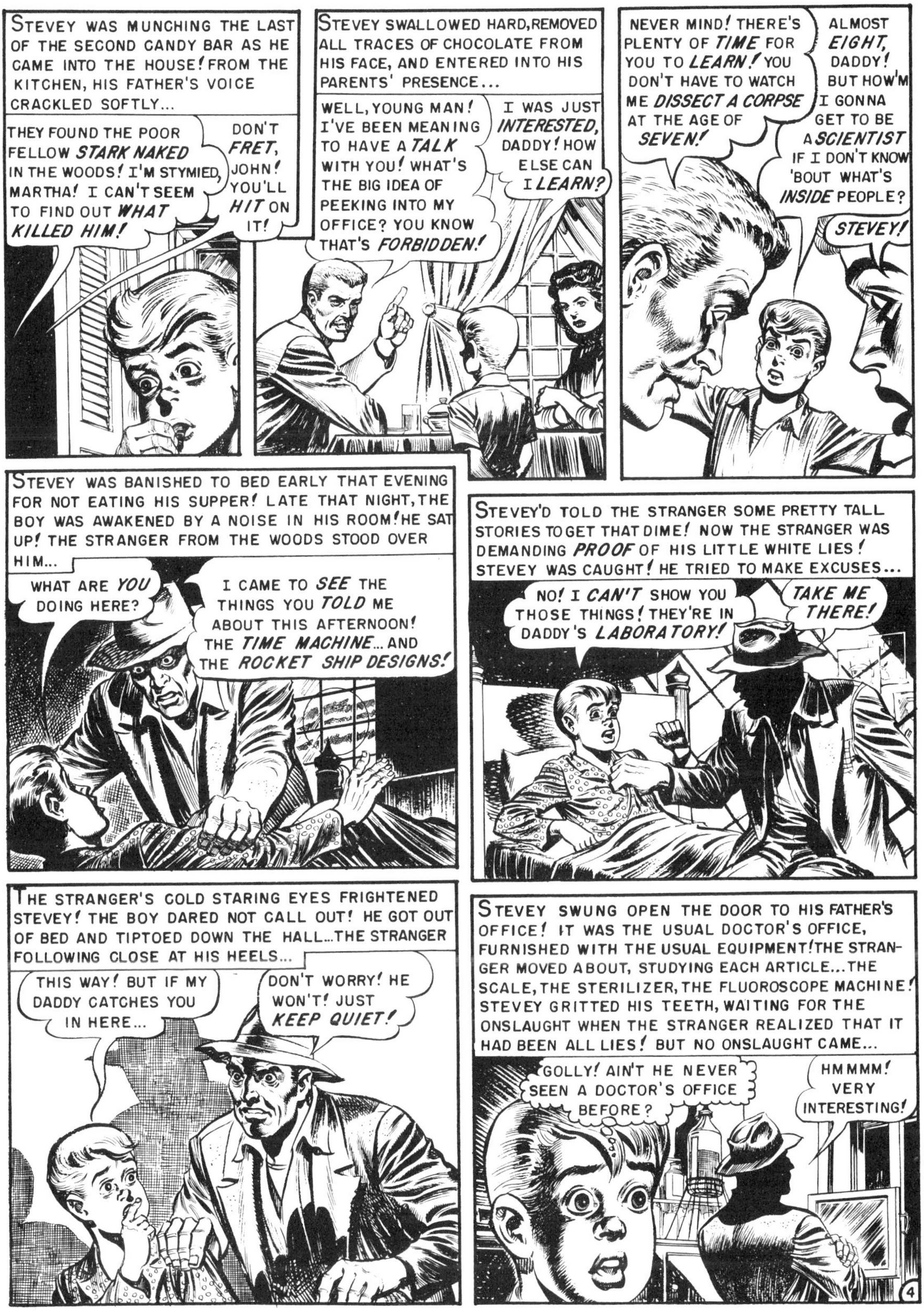

STEVEY WAS MUNCHING THE LAST OF THE SECOND CANDY BAR AS HE CAME INTO THE HOUSE! FROM THE KITCHEN, HIS FATHER'S VOICE CRACKLED SOFTLY...
THEY FOUND THE POOR FELLOW STARK NAKED IN THE WOODS! I'M STYMIED, MARTHA! I CAN'T SEEM TO FIND OUT WHAT KILLED HIM!
DON'T FRET, JOHN! YOU'LL HIT ON IT!
STEVEY SWALLOWED HARD, REMOVED ALL TRACES OF CHOCOLATE FROM HIS FACE, AND ENTERED INTO HIS PARENTS' PRESENCE...
WELL, YOUNG MAN! I'VE BEEN MEANING TO HAVE A TALK WITH YOU! WHAT'S THE BIG IDEA OF PEEKING INTO MY OFFICE? YOU KNOW THAT'S FORBIDDEN!
I WAS JUST INTERESTED, DADDY! HOW ELSE CAN I LEARN?
NEVER MIND! THERE'S PLENTY OF TIME FOR YOU TO LEARN! YOU DON'T HAVE TO WATCH ME DISSECT A CORPSE AT THE AGE OF SEVEN!
ALMOST EIGHT, DADDY! BUT HOW'M I GONNA GET TO BE A SCIENTIST IF I DON'T KNOW 'BOUT WHAT'S INSIDE PEOPLE?
STEVEY!
STEVEY WAS BANISHED TO BED EARLY THAT EVENING FOR NOT EATING HIS SUPPER! LATE THAT NIGHT, THE BOY WAS AWAKENED BY A NOISE IN HIS ROOM! HE SAT UP! THE STRANGER FROM THE WOODS STOOD OVER HIM...
WHAT ARE YOU DOING HERE?
I CAME TO SEE THE THINGS YOU TOLD ME ABOUT THIS AFTERNOON! THE TIME MACHINE... AND THE ROCKET SHIP DESIGNS!
STEVEY'D TOLD THE STRANGER SOME PRETTY TALL STORIES TO GET THAT DIME! NOW THE STRANGER WAS DEMANDING PROOF OF HIS LITTLE WHITE LIES! STEVEY WAS CAUGHT! HE TRIED TO MAKE EXCUSES...
NO! I CAN'T SHOW YOU THOSE THINGS! THEY'RE IN DADDY'S LABORATORY!
TAKE ME THERE!
THE STRANGER'S COLD STARING EYES FRIGHTENED STEVEY! THE BOY DARED NOT CALL OUT! HE GOT OUT OF BED AND TIPTOED DOWN THE HALL... THE STRANGER FOLLOWING CLOSE AT HIS HEELS...
THIS WAY! BUT IF MY DADDY CATCHES YOU IN HERE...
DON'T WORRY! HE WON'T! JUST KEEP QUIET!
STEVEY SWUNG OPEN THE DOOR TO HIS FATHER'S OFFICE! IT WAS THE USUAL DOCTOR'S OFFICE, FURNISHED WITH THE USUAL EQUIPMENT! THE STRANGER MOVED ABOUT, STUDYING EACH ARTICLE... THE SCALE, THE STERILIZER, THE FLUOROSCOPE MACHINE! STEVEY GRITTED HIS TEETH, WAITING FOR THE ONSLAUGHT WHEN THE STRANGER REALIZED THAT IT HAD BEEN ALL LIES! BUT NO ONSLAUGHT CAME...
GOLLY! AIN'T HE NEVER SEEN A DOCTOR'S OFFICE BEFORE?
HMMMM! VERY INTERESTING!
4

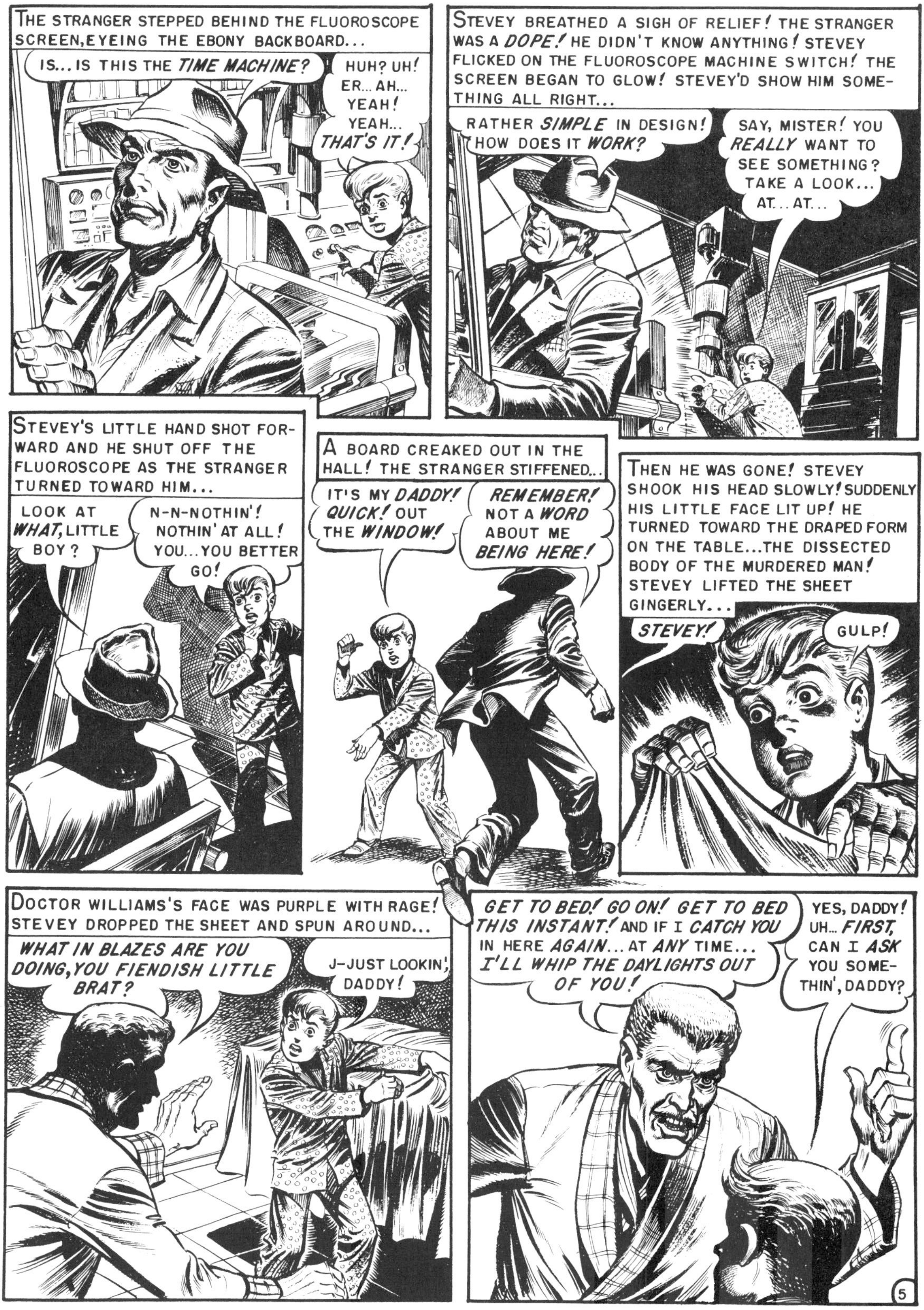
THE STRANGER STEPPED BEHIND THE FLUOROSCOPE SCREEN, EYEING THE EBONY BACKBOARD...
IS... IS THIS THE TIME MACHINE?
HUH? UH! ER... AH... YEAH! YEAH... THAT'S IT!
STEVEY BREATHED A SIGH OF RELIEF! THE STRANGER WAS A DOPE! HE DIDN'T KNOW ANYTHING! STEVEY FLICKED ON THE FLUOROSCOPE MACHINE SWITCH! THE SCREEN BEGAN TO GLOW! STEVEY'D SHOW HIM SOMETHING ALL RIGHT...
RATHER SIMPLE IN DESIGN! HOW DOES IT WORK?
SAY, MISTER! YOU REALLY WANT TO SEE SOMETHING? TAKE A LOOK... AT... AT...
STEVEY'S LITTLE HAND SHOT FORWARD AND HE SHUT OFF THE FLUOROSCOPE AS THE STRANGER TURNED TOWARD HIM...
LOOK AT WHAT, LITTLE BOY?
N-N-NOTHIN'! NOTHIN' AT ALL! YOU... YOU BETTER GO!
A BOARD CREAKED OUT IN THE HALL! THE STRANGER STIFFENED...
IT'S MY DADDY! QUICK! OUT THE WINDOW!
REMEMBER! NOT A WORD ABOUT ME BEING HERE!
THEN HE WAS GONE! STEVEY SHOOK HIS HEAD SLOWLY! SUDDENLY HIS LITTLE FACE LIT UP! HE TURNED TOWARD THE DRAPED FORM ON THE TABLE... THE DISSECTED BODY OF THE MURDERED MAN! STEVEY LIFTED THE SHEET GINGERLY...
STEVEY!
GULP!
DOCTOR WILLIAMS'S FACE WAS PURPLE WITH RAGE! STEVEY DROPPED THE SHEET AND SPUN AROUND...
WHAT IN BLAZES ARE YOU DOING, YOU FIENDISH LITTLE BRAT?
J-JUST LOOKIN', DADDY!
GET TO BED! GO ON! GET TO BED THIS INSTANT! AND IF I CATCH YOU IN HERE AGAIN... AT ANY TIME... I'LL WHIP THE DAYLIGHTS OUT OF YOU!
YES, DADDY! UH... FIRST, CAN I ASK YOU SOMETHIN', DADDY?
5

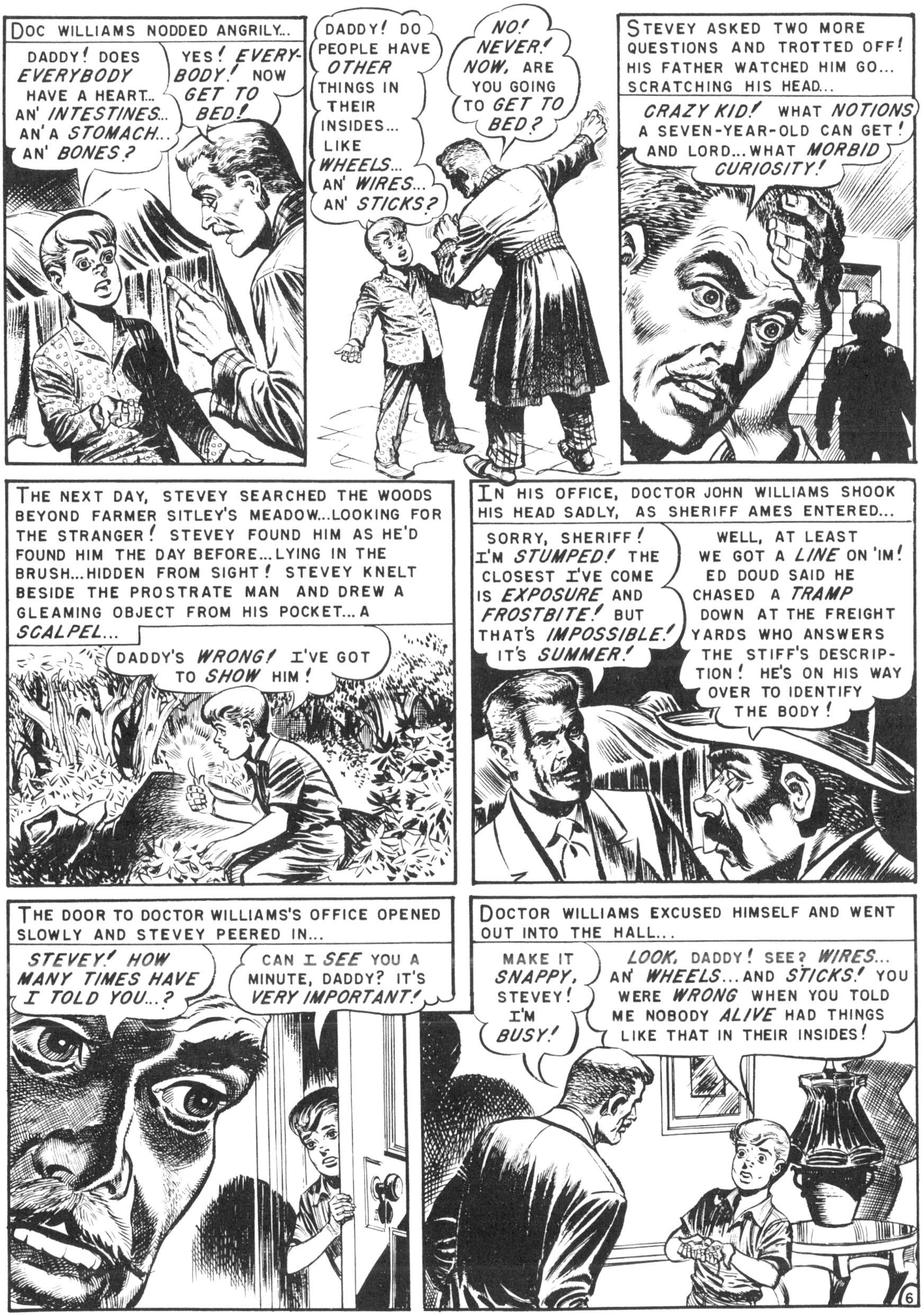
DOC WILLIAMS NODDED ANGRILY...
DADDY! DOES EVERYBODY HAVE A HEART... AN' INTESTINES... AN' A STOMACH... AN' BONES?
YES! EVERYBODY! NOW GET TO BED!
DADDY! DO PEOPLE HAVE OTHER THINGS IN THEIR INSIDES... LIKE WHEELS... AN' WIRES... AN' STICKS?
NO! NEVER! NOW, ARE YOU GOING TO GET TO BED?
STEVEY ASKED TWO MORE QUESTIONS AND TROTTED OFF! HIS FATHER WATCHED HIM GO... SCRATCHING HIS HEAD...
CRAZY KID! WHAT NOTIONS A SEVEN-YEAR-OLD CAN GET! AND LORD... WHAT MORBID CURIOSITY!
THE NEXT DAY, STEVEY SEARCHED THE WOODS BEYOND FARMER SITLEY'S MEADOW... LOOKING FOR THE STRANGER! STEVEY FOUND HIM AS HE'D FOUND HIM THE DAY BEFORE... LYING IN THE BRUSH... HIDDEN FROM SIGHT! STEVEY KNELT BESIDE THE PROSTRATE MAN AND DREW A GLEAMING OBJECT FROM HIS POCKET... A SCALPEL...
DADDY'S WRONG! I'VE GOT TO SHOW HIM!
IN HIS OFFICE, DOCTOR JOHN WILLIAMS SHOOK HIS HEAD SADLY, AS SHERIFF AMES ENTERED...
SORRY, SHERIFF! I'M STUMPED! THE CLOSEST I'VE COME IS EXPOSURE AND FROSTBITE! BUT THAT'S IMPOSSIBLE! IT'S SUMMER!
WELL, AT LEAST WE GOT A LINE ON 'IM! ED DOUD SAID HE CHASED A TRAMP DOWN AT THE FREIGHT YARDS WHO ANSWERS THE STIFF'S DESCRIPTION! HE'S ON HIS WAY OVER TO IDENTIFY THE BODY!
THE DOOR TO DOCTOR WILLIAMS'S OFFICE OPENED SLOWLY AND STEVEY PEERED IN...
STEVEY! HOW MANY TIMES HAVE I TOLD YOU...?
CAN I SEE YOU A MINUTE, DADDY? IT'S VERY IMPORTANT!
DOCTOR WILLIAMS EXCUSED HIMSELF AND WENT OUT INTO THE HALL...
MAKE IT SNAPPY, STEVEY! I'M BUSY!
LOOK, DADDY! SEE? WIRES... AN' WHEELS... AND STICKS! YOU WERE WRONG WHEN YOU TOLD ME NOBODY ALIVE HAD THINGS LIKE THAT IN THEIR INSIDES!
6

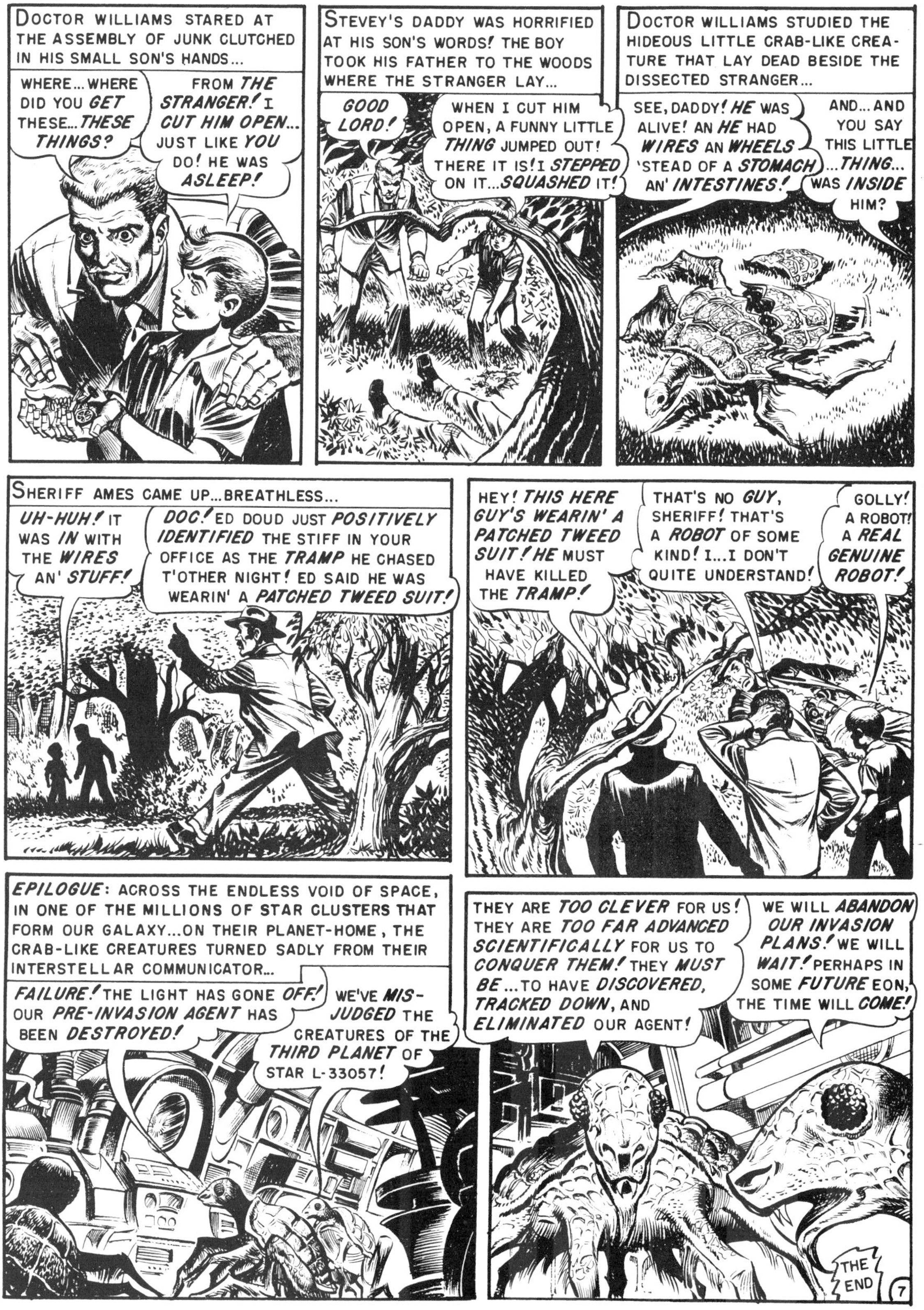
DOCTOR WILLIAMS STARED AT THE ASSEMBLY OF JUNK CLUTCHED IN HIS SMALL SON'S HANDS...
WHERE... WHERE DID YOU GET THESE... THESE THINGS?
FROM THE STRANGER! I CUT HIM OPEN... JUST LIKE YOU DO! HE WAS ASLEEP!
STEVEY'S DADDY WAS HORRIFIED AT HIS SON'S WORDS! THE BOY TOOK HIS FATHER TO THE WOODS WHERE THE STRANGER LAY...
GOOD LORD!
WHEN I CUT HIM OPEN, A FUNNY LITTLE THING JUMPED OUT! THERE IT IS! I STEPPED ON IT... SQUASHED IT!
DOCTOR WILLIAMS STUDIED THE HIDEOUS LITTLE CRAB-LIKE CREATURE THAT LAY DEAD BESIDE THE DISSECTED STRANGER...
SEE, DADDY! HE WAS ALIVE! AN HE HAD WIRES AN WHEELS 'STEAD OF A STOMACH AN' INTESTINES!
AND... AND YOU SAY THIS LITTLE ...THING... WAS INSIDE HIM?
SHERIFF AMES CAME UP... BREATHLESS...
UH-HUH! IT WAS IN WITH THE WIRES AN' STUFF!
DOC! ED DOUD JUST POSITIVELY IDENTIFIED THE STIFF IN YOUR OFFICE AS THE TRAMP HE CHASED T'OTHER NIGHT! ED SAID HE WAS WEARIN' A PATCHED TWEED SUIT!
HEY! THIS HERE GUY'S WEARIN' A PATCHED TWEED SUIT! HE MUST HAVE KILLED THE TRAMP!
THAT'S NO GUY, SHERIFF! THAT'S A ROBOT OF SOME KIND! I...I DON'T QUITE UNDERSTAND!
GOLLY! A ROBOT! A REAL GENUINE ROBOT!
EPILOGUE: ACROSS THE ENDLESS VOID OF SPACE, IN ONE OF THE MILLIONS OF STAR CLUSTERS THAT FORM OUR GALAXY... ON THEIR PLANET-HOME, THE CRAB-LIKE CREATURES TURNED SADLY FROM THEIR INTERSTELLAR COMMUNICATOR...
FAILURE! THE LIGHT HAS GONE OFF! OUR PRE-INVASION AGENT HAS BEEN DESTROYED!
WE'VE MIS-JUDGED THE CREATURES OF THE THIRD PLANET OF STAR L-33057!
THEY ARE TOO CLEVER FOR US! THEY ARE TOO FAR ADVANCED SCIENTIFICALLY FOR US TO CONQUER THEM! THEY MUST BE... TO HAVE DISCOVERED, TRACKED DOWN, AND ELIMINATED OUR AGENT!
WE WILL ABANDON OUR INVASION PLANS! WE WILL WAIT! PERHAPS IN SOME FUTURE EON, THE TIME WILL COME!
THE END
7

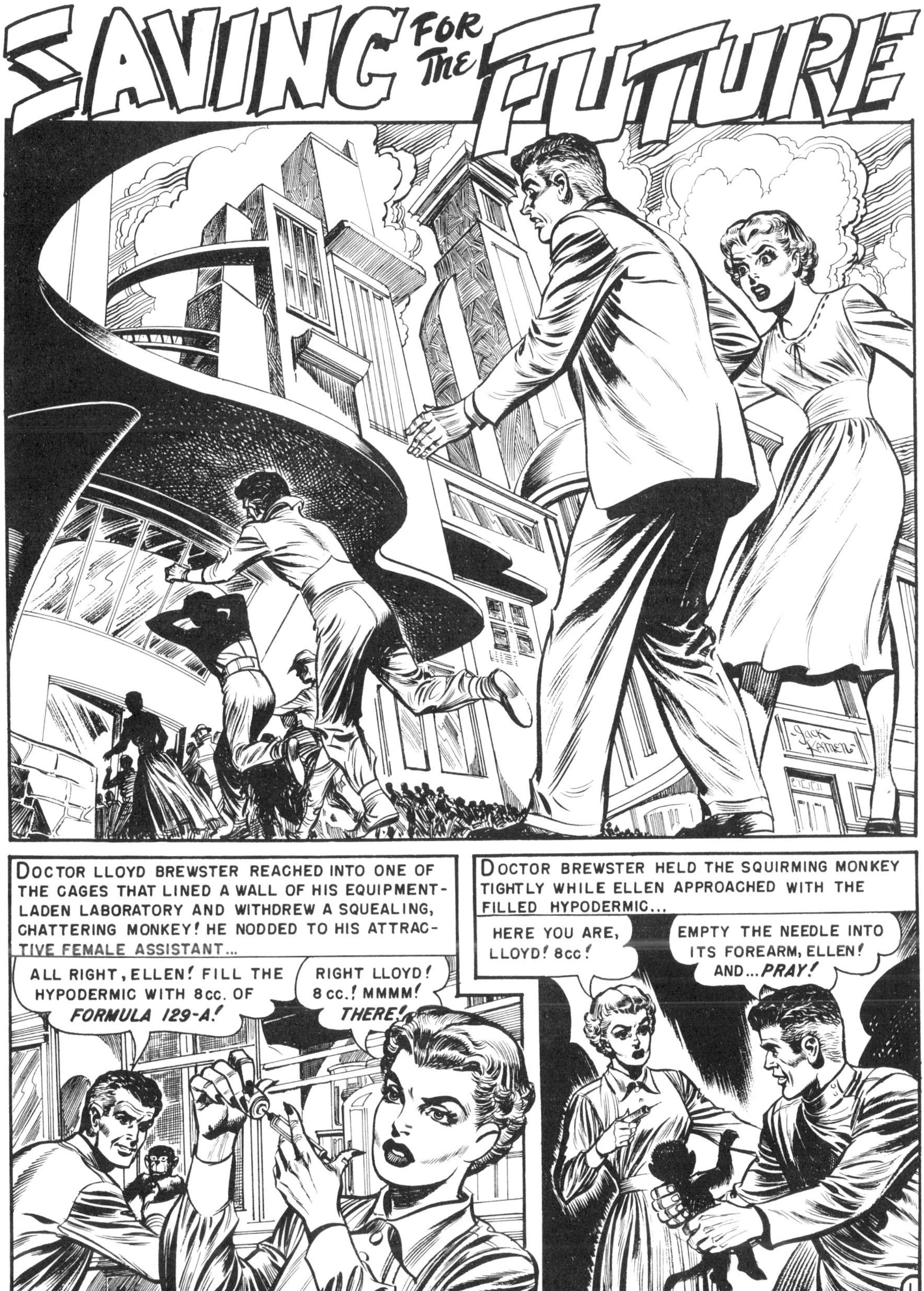
SAVING FOR THE FUTURE
Jack Kamen
DOCTOR LLOYD BREWSTER REACHED INTO ONE OF THE CAGES THAT LINED A WALL OF HIS EQUIPMENT-LADEN LABORATORY AND WITHDREW A SQUEALING, CHATTERING MONKEY! HE NODDED TO HIS ATTRACTIVE FEMALE ASSISTANT...
ALL RIGHT, ELLEN! FILL THE HYPODERMIC WITH 8cc. OF *FORMULA 129-A!*
RIGHT LLOYD! 8 cc.! MMMM! *THERE!*
DOCTOR BREWSTER HELD THE SQUIRMING MONKEY TIGHTLY WHILE ELLEN APPROACHED WITH THE FILLED HYPODERMIC...
HERE YOU ARE, LLOYD! 8cc!
EMPTY THE NEEDLE INTO ITS FOREARM, ELLEN! AND... *PRAY!*

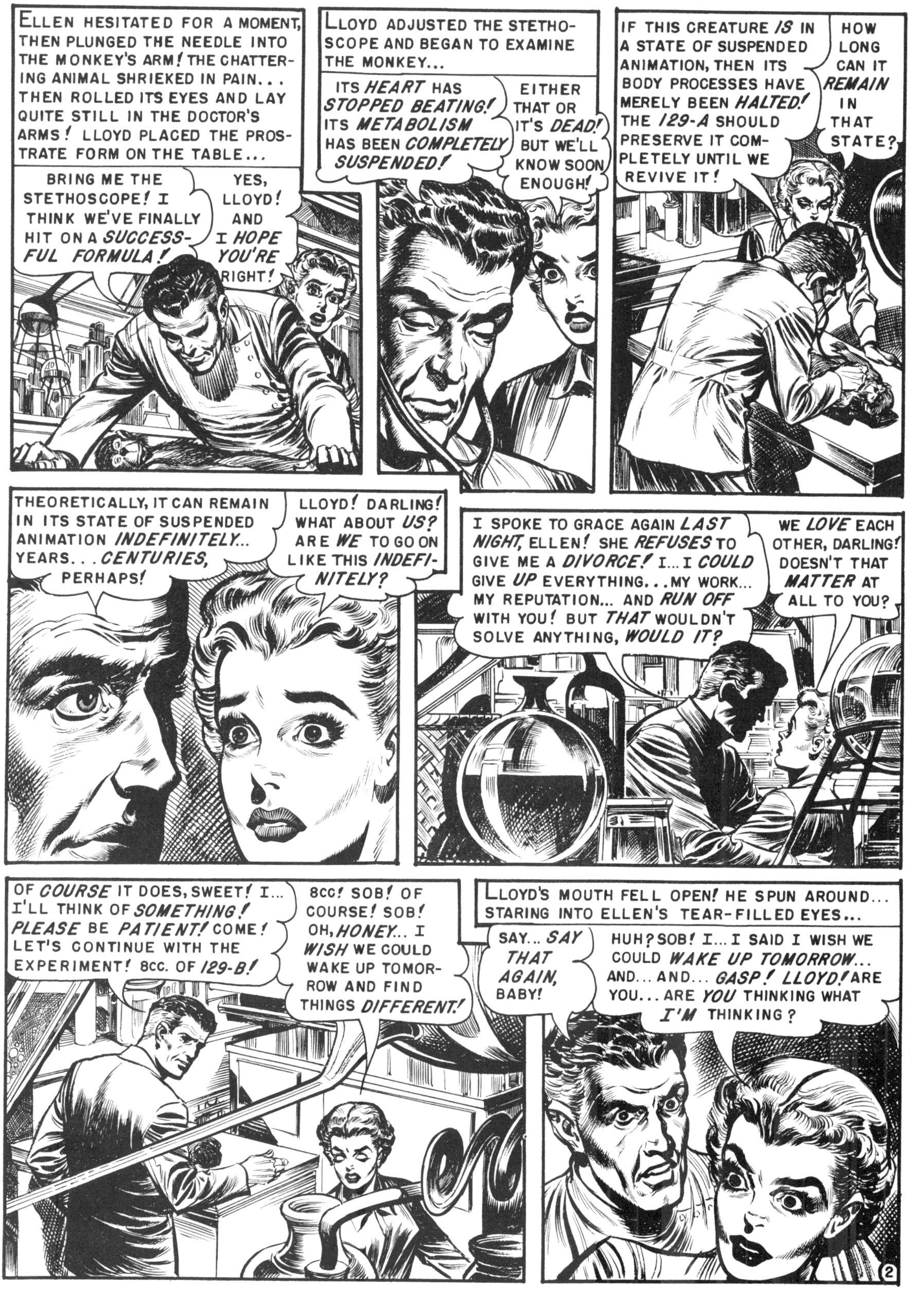
ELLEN HESITATED FOR A MOMENT, THEN PLUNGED THE NEEDLE INTO THE MONKEY'S ARM! THE CHATTERING ANIMAL SHRIEKED IN PAIN... THEN ROLLED ITS EYES AND LAY QUITE STILL IN THE DOCTOR'S ARMS! LLOYD PLACED THE PROSTRATE FORM ON THE TABLE...
BRING ME THE STETHOSCOPE! I THINK WE'VE FINALLY HIT ON A SUCCESSFUL FORMULA!
YES, LLOYD! AND I HOPE YOU'RE RIGHT!
LLOYD ADJUSTED THE STETHOSCOPE AND BEGAN TO EXAMINE THE MONKEY...
ITS HEART HAS STOPPED BEATING! ITS METABOLISM HAS BEEN COMPLETELY SUSPENDED!
EITHER THAT OR IT'S DEAD! BUT WE'LL KNOW SOON ENOUGH!
IF THIS CREATURE IS IN A STATE OF SUSPENDED ANIMATION, THEN ITS BODY PROCESSES HAVE MERELY BEEN HALTED! THE 129-A SHOULD PRESERVE IT COMPLETELY UNTIL WE REVIVE IT!
HOW LONG CAN IT REMAIN IN THAT STATE?
THEORETICALLY, IT CAN REMAIN IN ITS STATE OF SUSPENDED ANIMATION INDEFINITELY... YEARS... CENTURIES, PERHAPS!
LLOYD! DARLING! WHAT ABOUT US? ARE WE TO GO ON LIKE THIS INDEFINITELY?
I SPOKE TO GRACE AGAIN LAST NIGHT, ELLEN! SHE REFUSES TO GIVE ME A DIVORCE! I... I COULD GIVE UP EVERYTHING... MY WORK... MY REPUTATION... AND RUN OFF WITH YOU! BUT THAT WOULDN'T SOLVE ANYTHING, WOULD IT?
WE LOVE EACH OTHER, DARLING! DOESN'T THAT MATTER AT ALL TO YOU?
OF COURSE IT DOES, SWEET! I... I'LL THINK OF SOMETHING! PLEASE BE PATIENT! COME! LET'S CONTINUE WITH THE EXPERIMENT! 8cc. OF 129-B!
8cc! SOB! OF COURSE! SOB! OH, HONEY... I WISH WE COULD WAKE UP TOMORROW AND FIND THINGS DIFFERENT!
LLOYD'S MOUTH FELL OPEN! HE SPUN AROUND... STARING INTO ELLEN'S TEAR-FILLED EYES...
SAY... SAY THAT AGAIN, BABY!
HUH? SOB! I... I SAID I WISH WE COULD WAKE UP TOMORROW... AND... AND... GASP! LLOYD! ARE YOU... ARE YOU THINKING WHAT I'M THINKING?
2

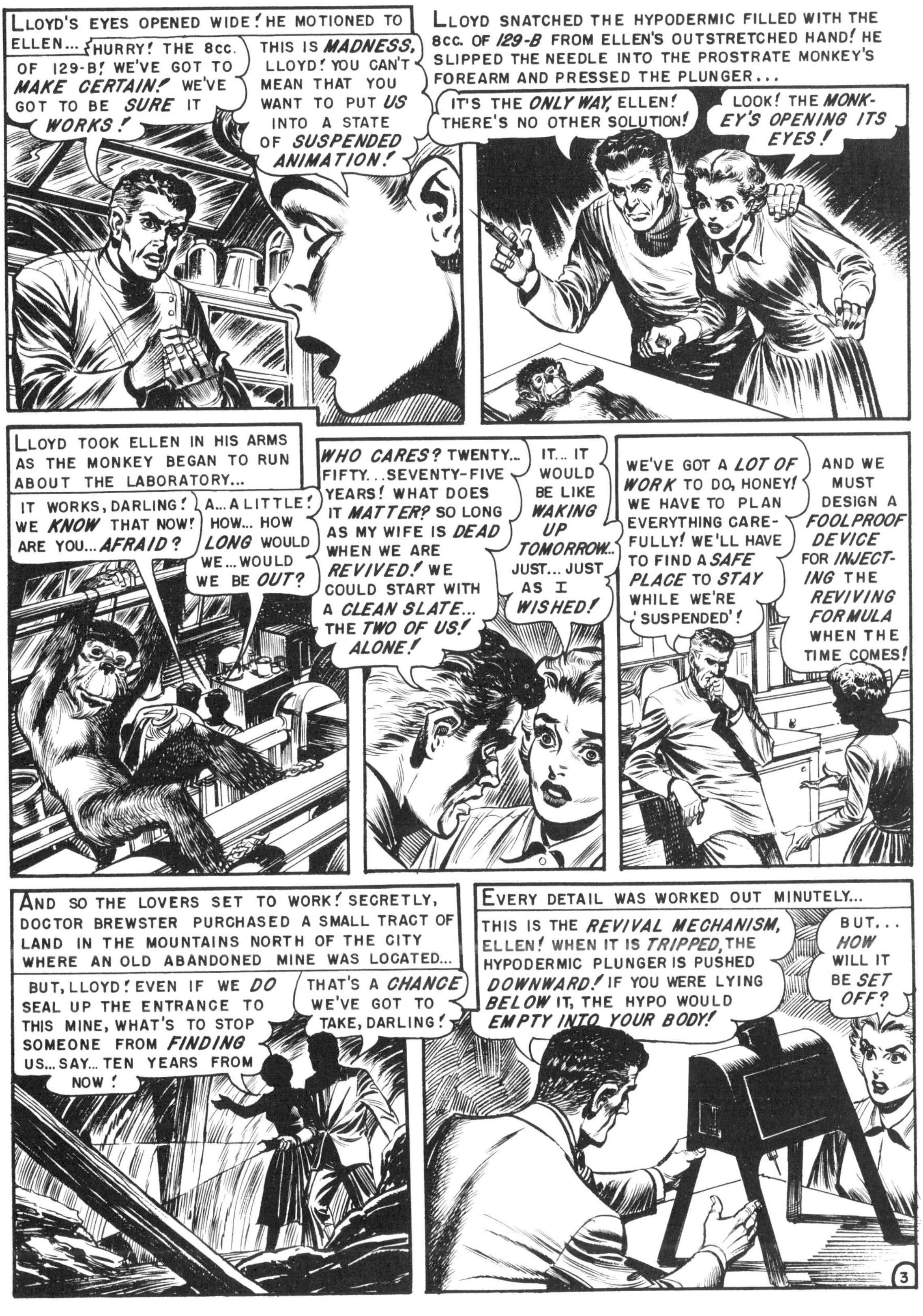
LLOYD'S EYES OPENED WIDE! HE MOTIONED TO ELLEN...
HURRY! THE 8cc. OF 129-B! WE'VE GOT TO MAKE CERTAIN! WE'VE GOT TO BE SURE IT WORKS!
THIS IS MADNESS, LLOYD! YOU CAN'T MEAN THAT YOU WANT TO PUT US INTO A STATE OF SUSPENDED ANIMATION!
LLOYD SNATCHED THE HYPODERMIC FILLED WITH THE 8cc. OF 129-B FROM ELLEN'S OUTSTRETCHED HAND! HE SLIPPED THE NEEDLE INTO THE PROSTRATE MONKEY'S FOREARM AND PRESSED THE PLUNGER...
IT'S THE ONLY WAY, ELLEN! THERE'S NO OTHER SOLUTION!
LOOK! THE MONKEY'S OPENING ITS EYES!
LLOYD TOOK ELLEN IN HIS ARMS AS THE MONKEY BEGAN TO RUN ABOUT THE LABORATORY...
IT WORKS, DARLING! WE KNOW THAT NOW! ARE YOU... AFRAID?
A... A LITTLE! HOW... HOW LONG WOULD WE... WOULD WE BE OUT?
WHO CARES? TWENTY... FIFTY... SEVENTY-FIVE YEARS! WHAT DOES IT MATTER? SO LONG AS MY WIFE IS DEAD WHEN WE ARE REVIVED! WE COULD START WITH A CLEAN SLATE... THE TWO OF US! ALONE!
IT... IT WOULD BE LIKE WAKING UP TOMORROW... JUST... JUST AS I WISHED!
WE'VE GOT A LOT OF WORK TO DO, HONEY! WE HAVE TO PLAN EVERYTHING CAREFULLY! WE'LL HAVE TO FIND A SAFE PLACE TO STAY WHILE WE'RE 'SUSPENDED'!
AND WE MUST DESIGN A FOOLPROOF DEVICE FOR INJECTING THE REVIVING FORMULA WHEN THE TIME COMES!
AND SO THE LOVERS SET TO WORK! SECRETLY, DOCTOR BREWSTER PURCHASED A SMALL TRACT OF LAND IN THE MOUNTAINS NORTH OF THE CITY WHERE AN OLD ABANDONED MINE WAS LOCATED...
BUT, LLOYD! EVEN IF WE DO SEAL UP THE ENTRANCE TO THIS MINE, WHAT'S TO STOP SOMEONE FROM FINDING US... SAY... TEN YEARS FROM NOW!
THAT'S A CHANCE WE'VE GOT TO TAKE, DARLING!
EVERY DETAIL WAS WORKED OUT MINUTELY...
THIS IS THE REVIVAL MECHANISM, ELLEN! WHEN IT IS TRIPPED, THE HYPODERMIC PLUNGER IS PUSHED DOWNWARD! IF YOU WERE LYING BELOW IT, THE HYPO WOULD EMPTY INTO YOUR BODY!
BUT... HOW WILL IT BE SET OFF?
3

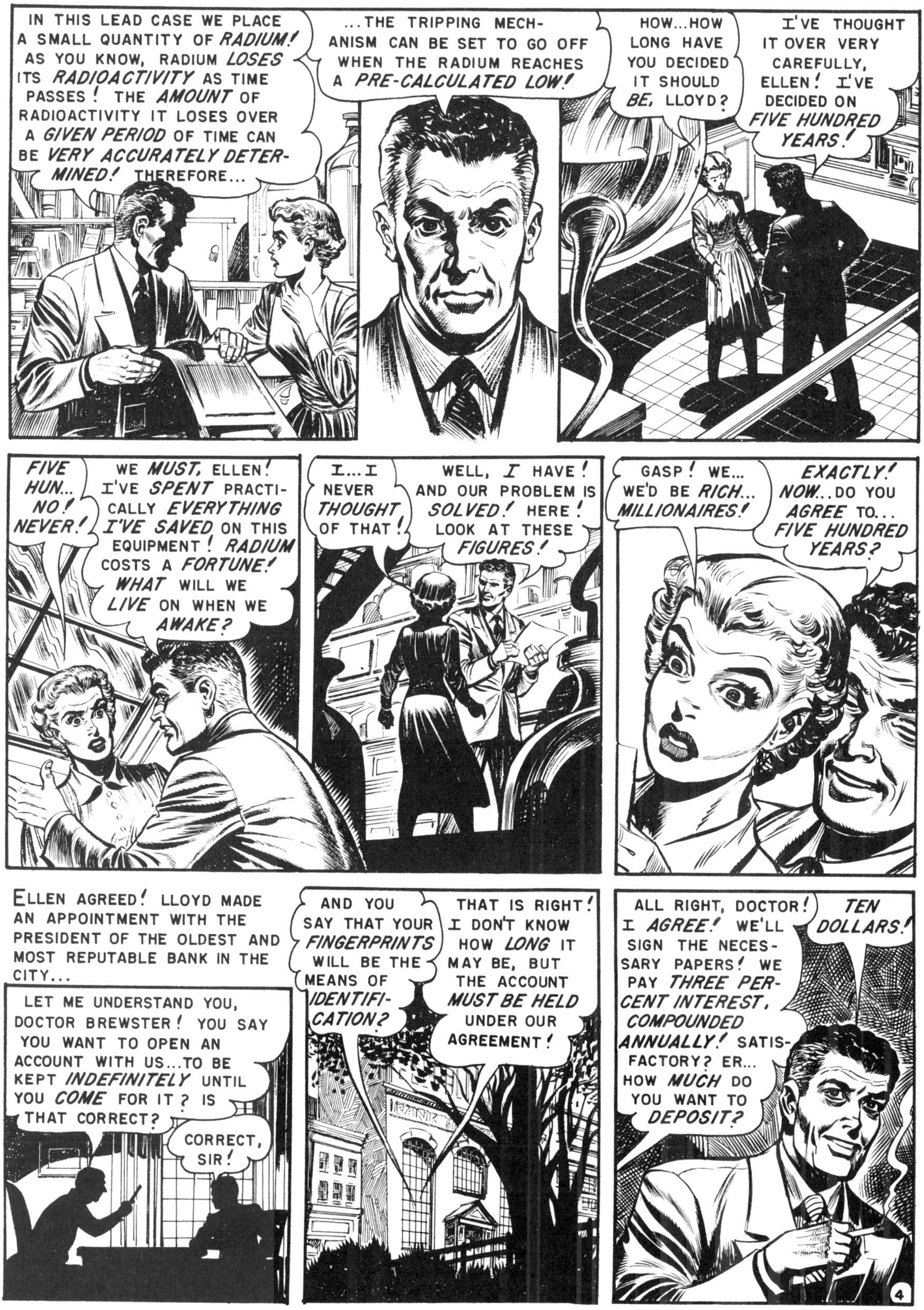
IN THIS LEAD CASE WE PLACE A SMALL QUANTITY OF RADIUM! AS YOU KNOW, RADIUM LOSES ITS RADIOACTIVITY AS TIME PASSES! THE AMOUNT OF RADIOACTIVITY IT LOSES OVER A GIVEN PERIOD OF TIME CAN BE VERY ACCURATELY DETERMINED! THEREFORE...
...THE TRIPPING MECHANISM CAN BE SET TO GO OFF WHEN THE RADIUM REACHES A PRE-CALCULATED LOW!
HOW...HOW LONG HAVE YOU DECIDED IT SHOULD BE, LLOYD?
I'VE THOUGHT IT OVER VERY CAREFULLY, ELLEN! I'VE DECIDED ON FIVE HUNDRED YEARS!
FIVE HUN... NO! NEVER!
WE MUST, ELLEN! I'VE SPENT PRACTICALLY EVERYTHING I'VE SAVED ON THIS EQUIPMENT! RADIUM COSTS A FORTUNE! WHAT WILL WE LIVE ON WHEN WE AWAKE?
I...I NEVER THOUGHT OF THAT!
WELL, I HAVE! AND OUR PROBLEM IS SOLVED! HERE! LOOK AT THESE FIGURES!
GASP! WE... WE'D BE RICH... MILLIONAIRES!
EXACTLY! NOW...DO YOU AGREE TO... FIVE HUNDRED YEARS?
ELLEN AGREED! LLOYD MADE AN APPOINTMENT WITH THE PRESIDENT OF THE OLDEST AND MOST REPUTABLE BANK IN THE CITY...
LET ME UNDERSTAND YOU, DOCTOR BREWSTER! YOU SAY YOU WANT TO OPEN AN ACCOUNT WITH US...TO BE KEPT INDEFINITELY UNTIL YOU COME FOR IT? IS THAT CORRECT?
CORRECT, SIR!
AND YOU SAY THAT YOUR FINGERPRINTS WILL BE THE MEANS OF IDENTIFICATION?
THAT IS RIGHT! I DON'T KNOW HOW LONG IT MAY BE, BUT THE ACCOUNT MUST BE HELD UNDER OUR AGREEMENT!
BANK
ALL RIGHT, DOCTOR! I AGREE! WE'LL SIGN THE NECESSARY PAPERS! WE PAY THREE PERCENT INTEREST, COMPOUNDED ANNUALLY! SATISFACTORY? ER... HOW MUCH DO YOU WANT TO DEPOSIT?
TEN DOLLARS!
4

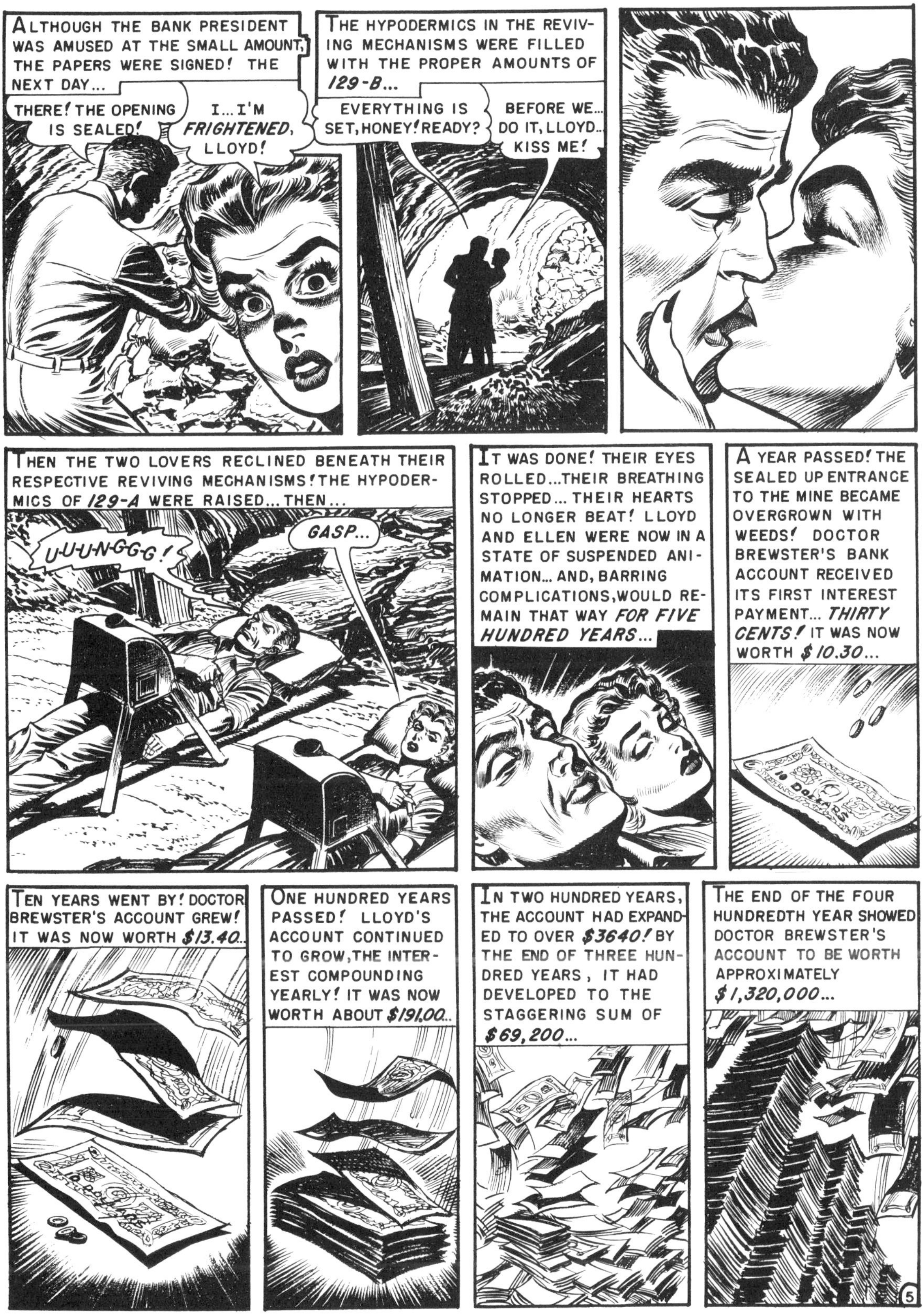
ALTHOUGH THE BANK PRESIDENT WAS AMUSED AT THE SMALL AMOUNT, THE PAPERS WERE SIGNED! THE NEXT DAY...
THERE! THE OPENING IS SEALED!
I...I'M FRIGHTENED, LLOYD!
THE HYPODERMICS IN THE REVIVING MECHANISMS WERE FILLED WITH THE PROPER AMOUNTS OF 129-B...
EVERYTHING IS SET, HONEY! READY?
BEFORE WE... DO IT, LLOYD... KISS ME!
THEN THE TWO LOVERS RECLINED BENEATH THEIR RESPECTIVE REVIVING MECHANISMS! THE HYPODERMICS OF 129-A WERE RAISED... THEN...
U-U-U-N-G-G-G!
GASP...
IT WAS DONE! THEIR EYES ROLLED...THEIR BREATHING STOPPED... THEIR HEARTS NO LONGER BEAT! LLOYD AND ELLEN WERE NOW IN A STATE OF SUSPENDED ANIMATION... AND, BARRING COMPLICATIONS, WOULD REMAIN THAT WAY FOR FIVE HUNDRED YEARS...
A YEAR PASSED! THE SEALED UP ENTRANCE TO THE MINE BECAME OVERGROWN WITH WEEDS! DOCTOR BREWSTER'S BANK ACCOUNT RECEIVED ITS FIRST INTEREST PAYMENT... THIRTY CENTS! IT WAS NOW WORTH $10.30...
TEN YEARS WENT BY! DOCTOR BREWSTER'S ACCOUNT GREW! IT WAS NOW WORTH $13.40...
ONE HUNDRED YEARS PASSED! LLOYD'S ACCOUNT CONTINUED TO GROW, THE INTEREST COMPOUNDING YEARLY! IT WAS NOW WORTH ABOUT $191.00...
IN TWO HUNDRED YEARS, THE ACCOUNT HAD EXPANDED TO OVER $3640! BY THE END OF THREE HUNDRED YEARS, IT HAD DEVELOPED TO THE STAGGERING SUM OF $69,200...
THE END OF THE FOUR HUNDREDTH YEAR SHOWED DOCTOR BREWSTER'S ACCOUNT TO BE WORTH APPROXIMATELY $1,320,000...
5

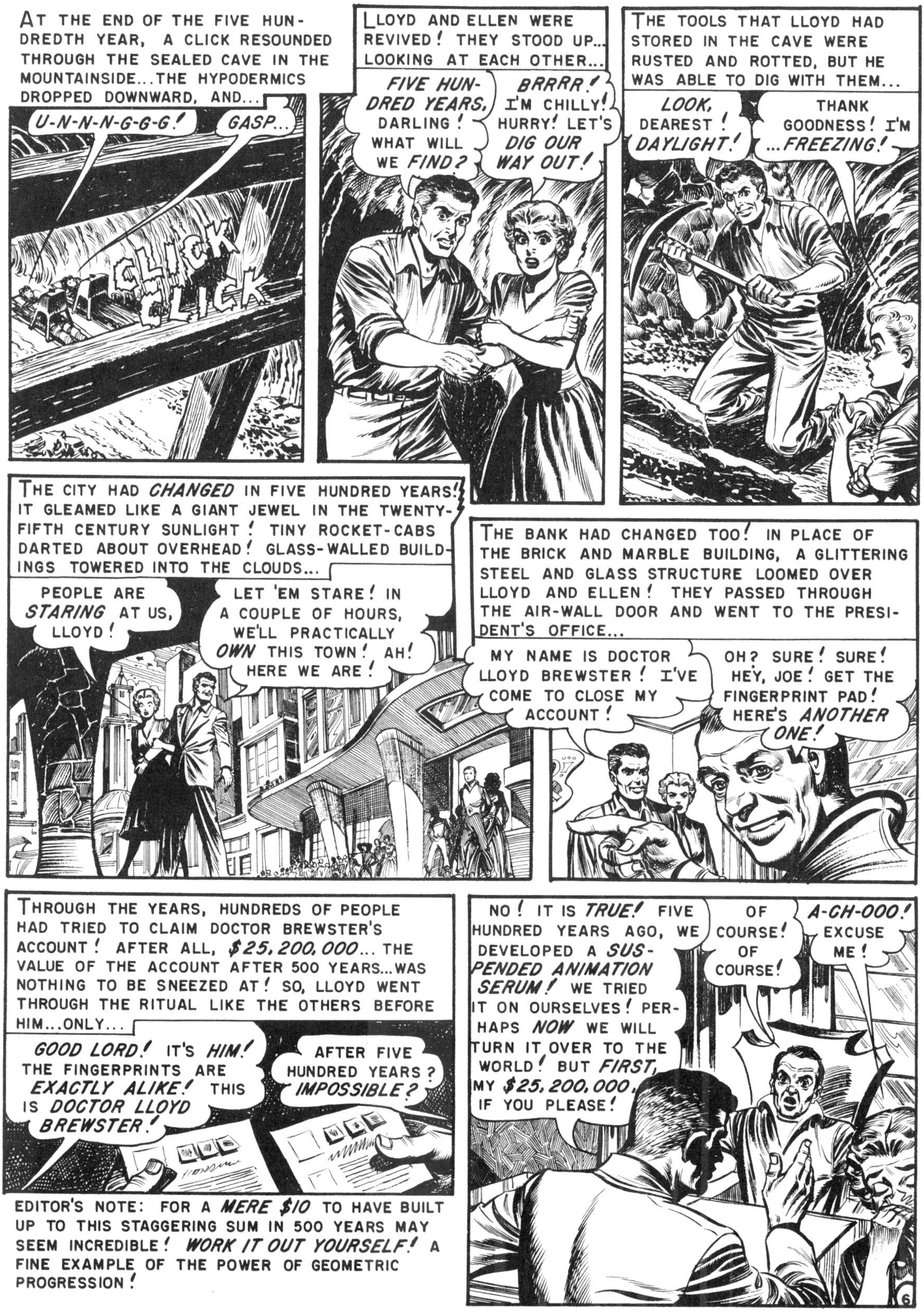
AT THE END OF THE FIVE HUNDREDTH YEAR, A CLICK RESOUNDED THROUGH THE SEALED CAVE IN THE MOUNTAINSIDE...THE HYPODERMICS DROPPED DOWNWARD, AND...
U-N-N-N-G-G-G!
GASP...
CLICK
CLICK
LLOYD AND ELLEN WERE REVIVED! THEY STOOD UP... LOOKING AT EACH OTHER...
FIVE HUNDRED YEARS, DARLING! WHAT WILL WE FIND?
BRRRR! I'M CHILLY! HURRY! LET'S DIG OUR WAY OUT!
THE TOOLS THAT LLOYD HAD STORED IN THE CAVE WERE RUSTED AND ROTTED, BUT HE WAS ABLE TO DIG WITH THEM...
LOOK, DEAREST! DAYLIGHT!
THANK GOODNESS! I'M ...FREEZING!
THE CITY HAD CHANGED IN FIVE HUNDRED YEARS! IT GLEAMED LIKE A GIANT JEWEL IN THE TWENTY-FIFTH CENTURY SUNLIGHT! TINY ROCKET-CABS DARTED ABOUT OVERHEAD! GLASS-WALLED BUILDINGS TOWERED INTO THE CLOUDS...
PEOPLE ARE STARING AT US, LLOYD!
LET 'EM STARE! IN A COUPLE OF HOURS, WE'LL PRACTICALLY OWN THIS TOWN! AH! HERE WE ARE!
THE BANK HAD CHANGED TOO! IN PLACE OF THE BRICK AND MARBLE BUILDING, A GLITTERING STEEL AND GLASS STRUCTURE LOOMED OVER LLOYD AND ELLEN! THEY PASSED THROUGH THE AIR-WALL DOOR AND WENT TO THE PRESIDENT'S OFFICE...
MY NAME IS DOCTOR LLOYD BREWSTER! I'VE COME TO CLOSE MY ACCOUNT!
OH? SURE! SURE! HEY, JOE! GET THE FINGERPRINT PAD! HERE'S ANOTHER ONE!
THROUGH THE YEARS, HUNDREDS OF PEOPLE HAD TRIED TO CLAIM DOCTOR BREWSTER'S ACCOUNT! AFTER ALL, $25,200,000... THE VALUE OF THE ACCOUNT AFTER 500 YEARS...WAS NOTHING TO BE SNEEZED AT! SO, LLOYD WENT THROUGH THE RITUAL LIKE THE OTHERS BEFORE HIM...ONLY...
GOOD LORD! IT'S HIM! THE FINGERPRINTS ARE EXACTLY ALIKE! THIS IS DOCTOR LLOYD BREWSTER!
AFTER FIVE HUNDRED YEARS? IMPOSSIBLE?
EDITOR'S NOTE: FOR A MERE $10 TO HAVE BUILT UP TO THIS STAGGERING SUM IN 500 YEARS MAY SEEM INCREDIBLE! WORK IT OUT YOURSELF! A FINE EXAMPLE OF THE POWER OF GEOMETRIC PROGRESSION!
NO! IT IS TRUE! FIVE HUNDRED YEARS AGO, WE DEVELOPED A SUSPENDED ANIMATION SERUM! WE TRIED IT ON OURSELVES! PERHAPS NOW WE WILL TURN IT OVER TO THE WORLD! BUT FIRST, MY $25,200,000, IF YOU PLEASE!
OF COURSE! OF COURSE!
A-CH-OOO! EXCUSE ME!
6

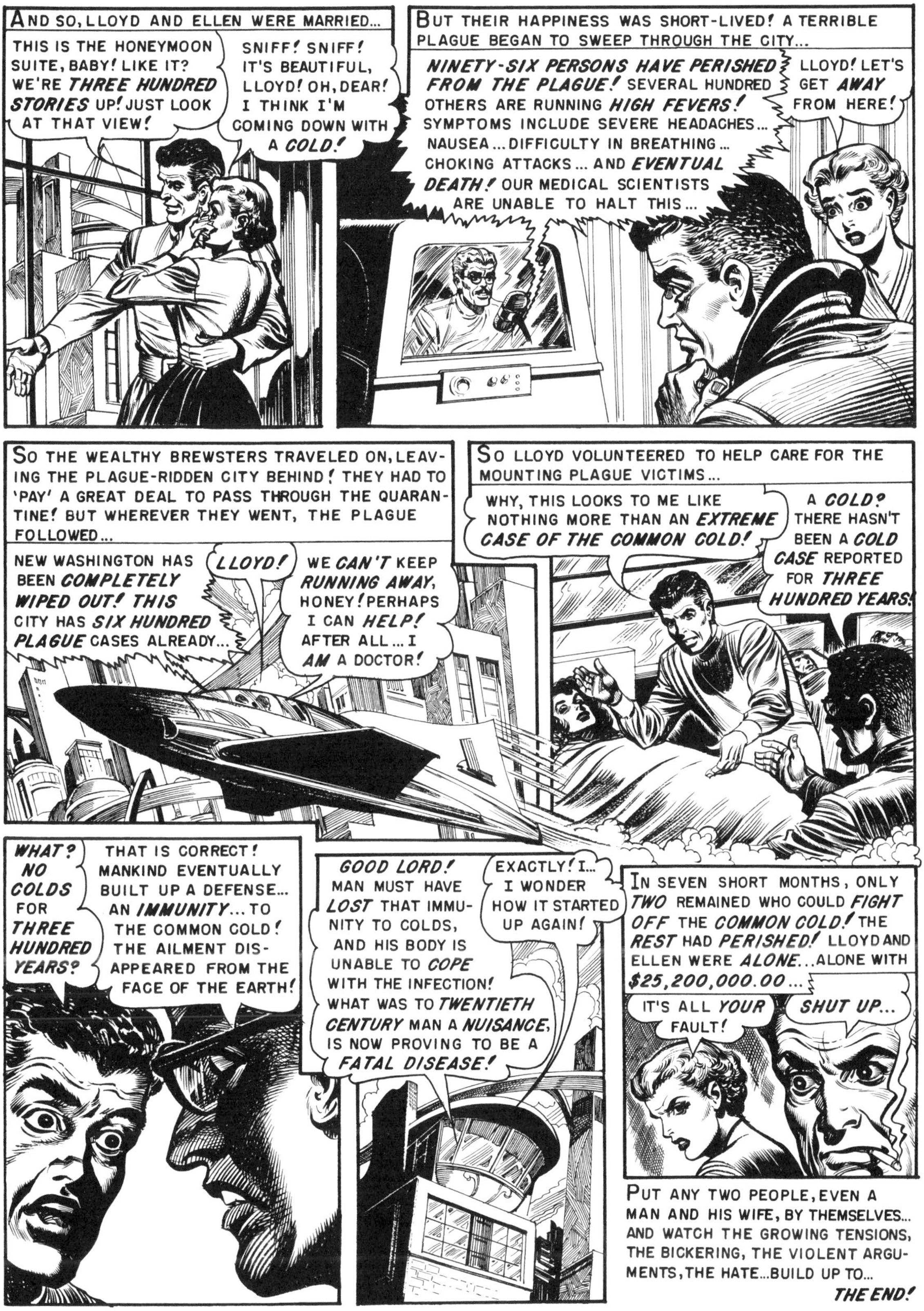
AND SO, LLOYD AND ELLEN WERE MARRIED...
THIS IS THE HONEYMOON SUITE, BABY! LIKE IT? WE'RE THREE HUNDRED STORIES UP! JUST LOOK AT THAT VIEW!
SNIFF! SNIFF! IT'S BEAUTIFUL, LLOYD! OH, DEAR! I THINK I'M COMING DOWN WITH A COLD!
BUT THEIR HAPPINESS WAS SHORT-LIVED! A TERRIBLE PLAGUE BEGAN TO SWEEP THROUGH THE CITY...
NINETY-SIX PERSONS HAVE PERISHED FROM THE PLAGUE! SEVERAL HUNDRED OTHERS ARE RUNNING HIGH FEVERS! SYMPTOMS INCLUDE SEVERE HEADACHES... NAUSEA... DIFFICULTY IN BREATHING... CHOKING ATTACKS... AND EVENTUAL DEATH! OUR MEDICAL SCIENTISTS ARE UNABLE TO HALT THIS...
LLOYD! LET'S GET AWAY FROM HERE!
SO THE WEALTHY BREWSTERS TRAVELED ON, LEAVING THE PLAGUE-RIDDEN CITY BEHIND! THEY HAD TO 'PAY' A GREAT DEAL TO PASS THROUGH THE QUARANTINE! BUT WHEREVER THEY WENT, THE PLAGUE FOLLOWED...
NEW WASHINGTON HAS BEEN COMPLETELY WIPED OUT! THIS CITY HAS SIX HUNDRED PLAGUE CASES ALREADY...
LLOYD!
WE CAN'T KEEP RUNNING AWAY, HONEY! PERHAPS I CAN HELP! AFTER ALL... I AM A DOCTOR!
SO LLOYD VOLUNTEERED TO HELP CARE FOR THE MOUNTING PLAGUE VICTIMS...
WHY, THIS LOOKS TO ME LIKE NOTHING MORE THAN AN EXTREME CASE OF THE COMMON COLD!
A COLD? THERE HASN'T BEEN A COLD CASE REPORTED FOR THREE HUNDRED YEARS!
WHAT? NO COLDS FOR THREE HUNDRED YEARS?
THAT IS CORRECT! MANKIND EVENTUALLY BUILT UP A DEFENSE... AN IMMUNITY... TO THE COMMON COLD! THE AILMENT DISAPPEARED FROM THE FACE OF THE EARTH!
GOOD LORD! MAN MUST HAVE LOST THAT IMMUNITY TO COLDS, AND HIS BODY IS UNABLE TO COPE WITH THE INFECTION! WHAT WAS TO TWENTIETH CENTURY MAN A NUISANCE, IS NOW PROVING TO BE A FATAL DISEASE!
EXACTLY! I... I WONDER HOW IT STARTED UP AGAIN!
IN SEVEN SHORT MONTHS, ONLY TWO REMAINED WHO COULD FIGHT OFF THE COMMON COLD! THE REST HAD PERISHED! LLOYD AND ELLEN WERE ALONE... ALONE WITH $25,200,000.00...
IT'S ALL YOUR FAULT!
SHUT UP...
PUT ANY TWO PEOPLE, EVEN A MAN AND HIS WIFE, BY THEMSELVES... AND WATCH THE GROWING TENSIONS, THE BICKERING, THE VIOLENT ARGUMENTS, THE HATE... BUILD UP TO...
THE END!

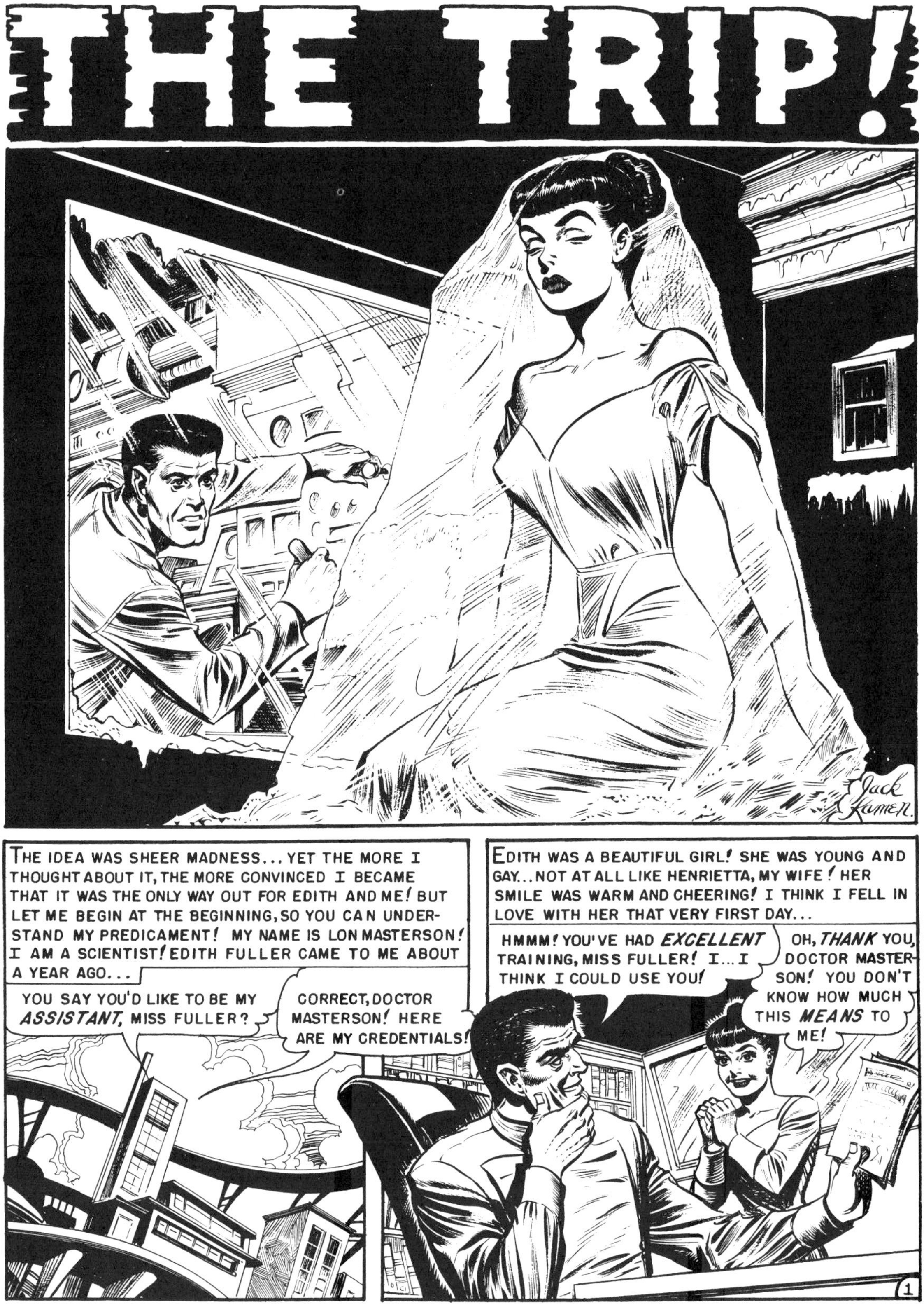
THE TRIP!
Jack Kamen
THE IDEA WAS SHEER MADNESS... YET THE MORE I THOUGHT ABOUT IT, THE MORE CONVINCED I BECAME THAT IT WAS THE ONLY WAY OUT FOR EDITH AND ME! BUT LET ME BEGIN AT THE BEGINNING, SO YOU CAN UNDERSTAND MY PREDICAMENT! MY NAME IS LON MASTERSON! I AM A SCIENTIST! EDITH FULLER CAME TO ME ABOUT A YEAR AGO...
YOU SAY YOU'D LIKE TO BE MY *ASSISTANT*, MISS FULLER?
CORRECT, DOCTOR MASTERSON! HERE ARE MY CREDENTIALS!
EDITH WAS A BEAUTIFUL GIRL! SHE WAS YOUNG AND GAY... NOT AT ALL LIKE HENRIETTA, MY WIFE! HER SMILE WAS WARM AND CHEERING! I THINK I FELL IN LOVE WITH HER THAT VERY FIRST DAY...
HMMM! YOU'VE HAD *EXCELLENT* TRAINING, MISS FULLER! I... I THINK I COULD USE YOU!
OH, *THANK* YOU, DOCTOR MASTERSON! YOU DON'T KNOW HOW MUCH THIS *MEANS* TO ME!
1

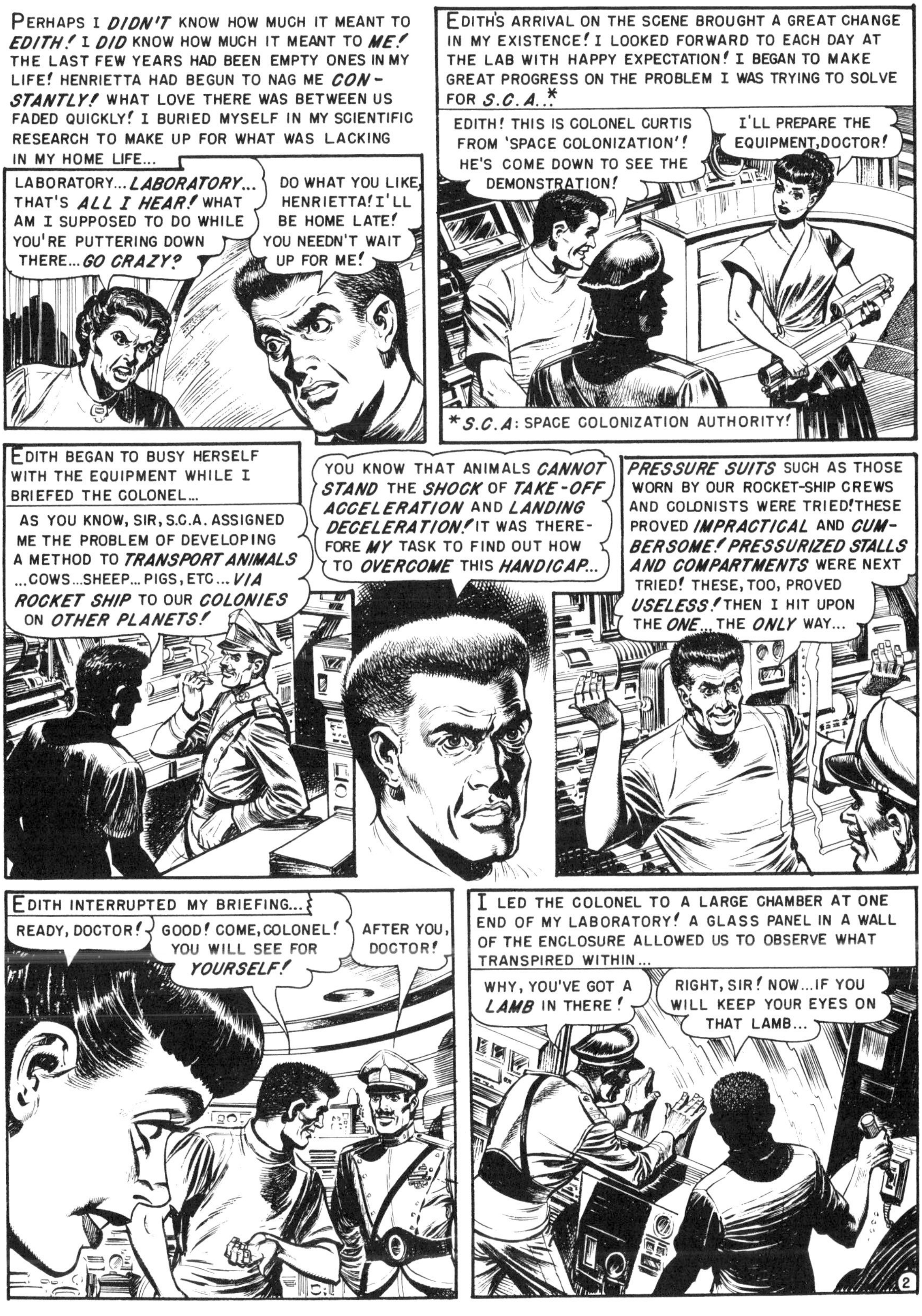
PERHAPS I DIDN'T KNOW HOW MUCH IT MEANT TO EDITH! I DID KNOW HOW MUCH IT MEANT TO ME! THE LAST FEW YEARS HAD BEEN EMPTY ONES IN MY LIFE! HENRIETTA HAD BEGUN TO NAG ME CONSTANTLY! WHAT LOVE THERE WAS BETWEEN US FADED QUICKLY! I BURIED MYSELF IN MY SCIENTIFIC RESEARCH TO MAKE UP FOR WHAT WAS LACKING IN MY HOME LIFE...
LABORATORY... LABORATORY... THAT'S ALL I HEAR! WHAT AM I SUPPOSED TO DO WHILE YOU'RE PUTTERING DOWN THERE... GO CRAZY?
DO WHAT YOU LIKE, HENRIETTA! I'LL BE HOME LATE! YOU NEEDN'T WAIT UP FOR ME!
EDITH'S ARRIVAL ON THE SCENE BROUGHT A GREAT CHANGE IN MY EXISTENCE! I LOOKED FORWARD TO EACH DAY AT THE LAB WITH HAPPY EXPECTATION! I BEGAN TO MAKE GREAT PROGRESS ON THE PROBLEM I WAS TRYING TO SOLVE FOR S.C.A...*
EDITH! THIS IS COLONEL CURTIS FROM 'SPACE COLONIZATION'! HE'S COME DOWN TO SEE THE DEMONSTRATION!
I'LL PREPARE THE EQUIPMENT, DOCTOR!
*S.C.A: SPACE COLONIZATION AUTHORITY!
EDITH BEGAN TO BUSY HERSELF WITH THE EQUIPMENT WHILE I BRIEFED THE COLONEL...
AS YOU KNOW, SIR, S.C.A. ASSIGNED ME THE PROBLEM OF DEVELOPING A METHOD TO TRANSPORT ANIMALS ...COWS...SHEEP...PIGS, ETC... VIA ROCKET SHIP TO OUR COLONIES ON OTHER PLANETS!
YOU KNOW THAT ANIMALS CANNOT STAND THE SHOCK OF TAKE-OFF ACCELERATION AND LANDING DECELERATION! IT WAS THEREFORE MY TASK TO FIND OUT HOW TO OVERCOME THIS HANDICAP...
PRESSURE SUITS SUCH AS THOSE WORN BY OUR ROCKET-SHIP CREWS AND COLONISTS WERE TRIED! THESE PROVED IMPRACTICAL AND CUMBERSOME! PRESSURIZED STALLS AND COMPARTMENTS WERE NEXT TRIED! THESE, TOO, PROVED USELESS! THEN I HIT UPON THE ONE... THE ONLY WAY...
EDITH INTERRUPTED MY BRIEFING...
READY, DOCTOR!
GOOD! COME, COLONEL! YOU WILL SEE FOR YOURSELF!
AFTER YOU, DOCTOR!
I LED THE COLONEL TO A LARGE CHAMBER AT ONE END OF MY LABORATORY! A GLASS PANEL IN A WALL OF THE ENCLOSURE ALLOWED US TO OBSERVE WHAT TRANSPIRED WITHIN...
WHY, YOU'VE GOT A LAMB IN THERE!
RIGHT, SIR! NOW...IF YOU WILL KEEP YOUR EYES ON THAT LAMB...
2

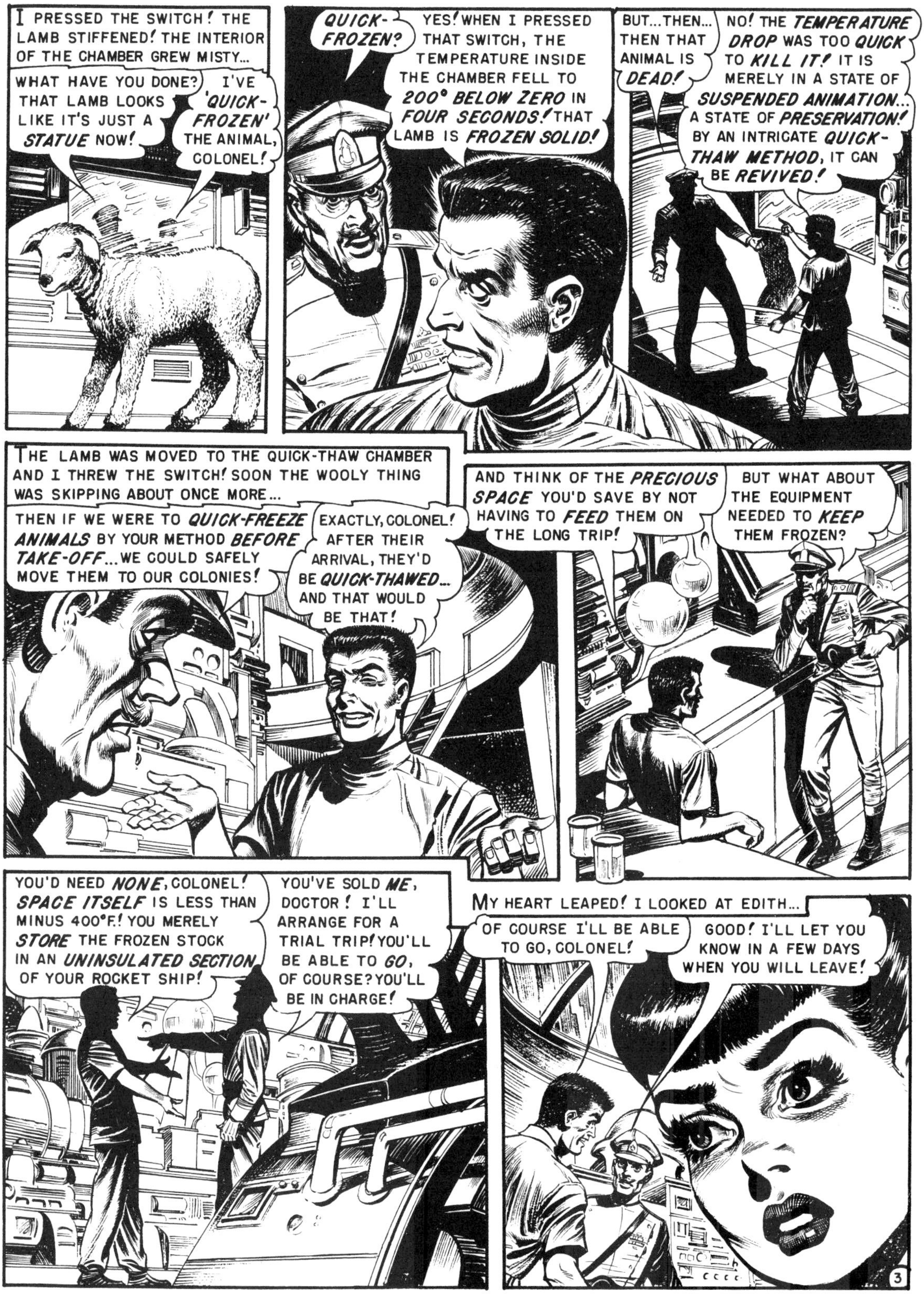
I PRESSED THE SWITCH! THE LAMB STIFFENED! THE INTERIOR OF THE CHAMBER GREW MISTY...
WHAT HAVE YOU DONE? THAT LAMB LOOKS LIKE IT'S JUST A STATUE NOW!
I'VE 'QUICK-FROZEN' THE ANIMAL, COLONEL!
QUICK-FROZEN?
YES! WHEN I PRESSED THAT SWITCH, THE TEMPERATURE INSIDE THE CHAMBER FELL TO 200° BELOW ZERO IN FOUR SECONDS! THAT LAMB IS FROZEN SOLID!
BUT...THEN... THEN THAT ANIMAL IS DEAD!
NO! THE TEMPERATURE DROP WAS TOO QUICK TO KILL IT! IT IS MERELY IN A STATE OF SUSPENDED ANIMATION... A STATE OF PRESERVATION! BY AN INTRICATE QUICK-THAW METHOD, IT CAN BE REVIVED!
THE LAMB WAS MOVED TO THE QUICK-THAW CHAMBER AND I THREW THE SWITCH! SOON THE WOOLY THING WAS SKIPPING ABOUT ONCE MORE...
THEN IF WE WERE TO QUICK-FREEZE ANIMALS BY YOUR METHOD BEFORE TAKE-OFF... WE COULD SAFELY MOVE THEM TO OUR COLONIES!
EXACTLY, COLONEL! AFTER THEIR ARRIVAL, THEY'D BE QUICK-THAWED... AND THAT WOULD BE THAT!
AND THINK OF THE PRECIOUS SPACE YOU'D SAVE BY NOT HAVING TO FEED THEM ON THE LONG TRIP!
BUT WHAT ABOUT THE EQUIPMENT NEEDED TO KEEP THEM FROZEN?
YOU'D NEED NONE, COLONEL! SPACE ITSELF IS LESS THAN MINUS 400°F.! YOU MERELY STORE THE FROZEN STOCK IN AN UNINSULATED SECTION OF YOUR ROCKET SHIP!
YOU'VE SOLD ME, DOCTOR! I'LL ARRANGE FOR A TRIAL TRIP! YOU'LL BE ABLE TO GO, OF COURSE? YOU'LL BE IN CHARGE!
MY HEART LEAPED! I LOOKED AT EDITH...
OF COURSE I'LL BE ABLE TO GO, COLONEL!
GOOD! I'LL LET YOU KNOW IN A FEW DAYS WHEN YOU WILL LEAVE!
3

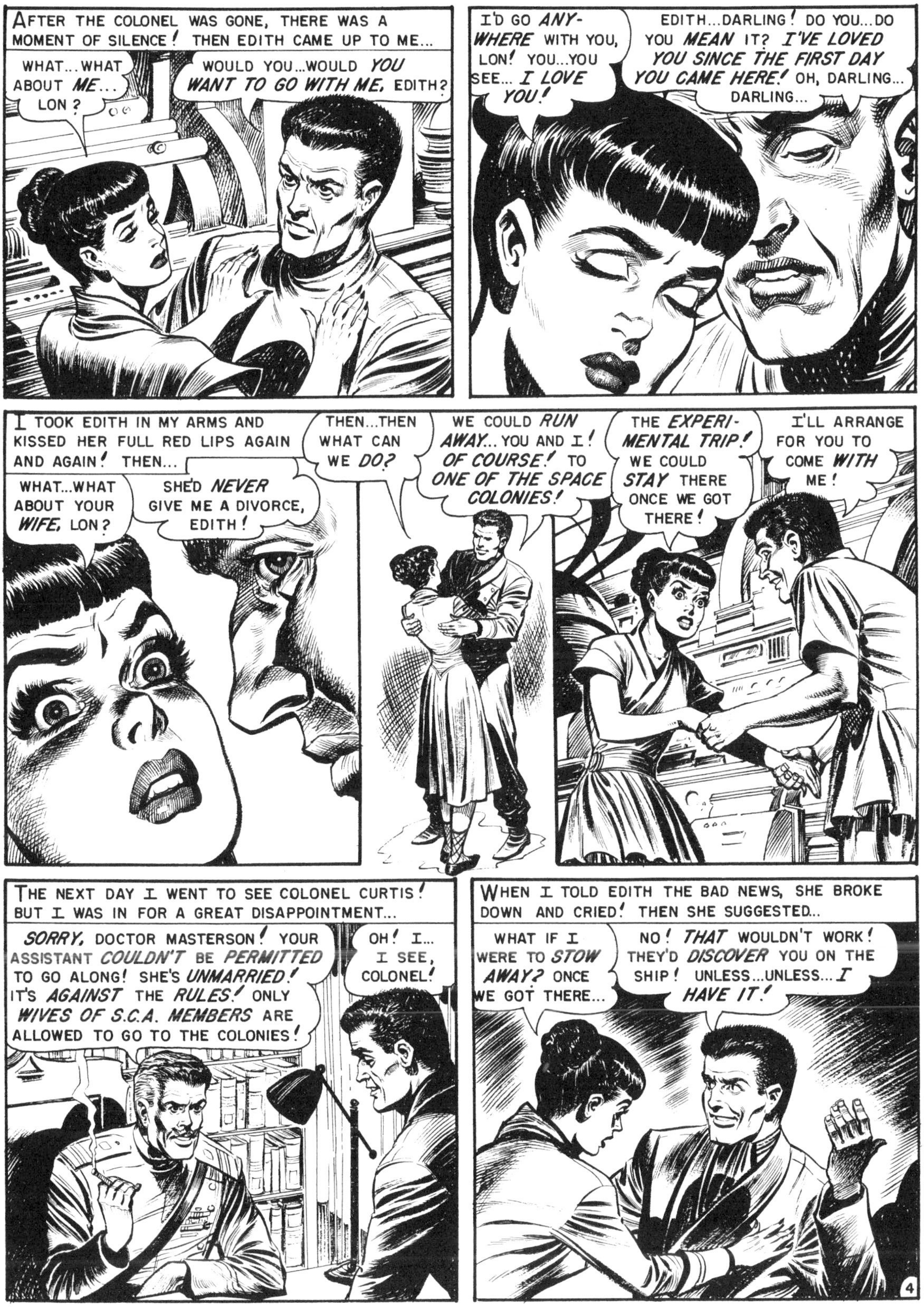
AFTER THE COLONEL WAS GONE, THERE WAS A MOMENT OF SILENCE! THEN EDITH CAME UP TO ME...
WHAT...WHAT ABOUT ME... LON?
WOULD YOU...WOULD YOU WANT TO GO WITH ME, EDITH?
I'D GO ANYWHERE WITH YOU, LON! YOU...YOU SEE... I LOVE YOU!
EDITH...DARLING! DO YOU...DO YOU MEAN IT? I'VE LOVED YOU SINCE THE FIRST DAY YOU CAME HERE! OH, DARLING... DARLING...
I TOOK EDITH IN MY ARMS AND KISSED HER FULL RED LIPS AGAIN AND AGAIN! THEN...
WHAT...WHAT ABOUT YOUR WIFE, LON?
SHE'D NEVER GIVE ME A DIVORCE, EDITH!
THEN...THEN WHAT CAN WE DO?
WE COULD RUN AWAY... YOU AND I! OF COURSE! TO ONE OF THE SPACE COLONIES!
THE EXPERIMENTAL TRIP! WE COULD STAY THERE ONCE WE GOT THERE!
I'LL ARRANGE FOR YOU TO COME WITH ME!
THE NEXT DAY I WENT TO SEE COLONEL CURTIS! BUT I WAS IN FOR A GREAT DISAPPOINTMENT...
SORRY, DOCTOR MASTERSON! YOUR ASSISTANT COULDN'T BE PERMITTED TO GO ALONG! SHE'S UNMARRIED! IT'S AGAINST THE RULES! ONLY WIVES OF S.C.A. MEMBERS ARE ALLOWED TO GO TO THE COLONIES!
OH! I... I SEE, COLONEL!
WHEN I TOLD EDITH THE BAD NEWS, SHE BROKE DOWN AND CRIED! THEN SHE SUGGESTED...
WHAT IF I WERE TO STOW AWAY? ONCE WE GOT THERE...
NO! THAT WOULDN'T WORK! THEY'D DISCOVER YOU ON THE SHIP! UNLESS...UNLESS... I HAVE IT!
4

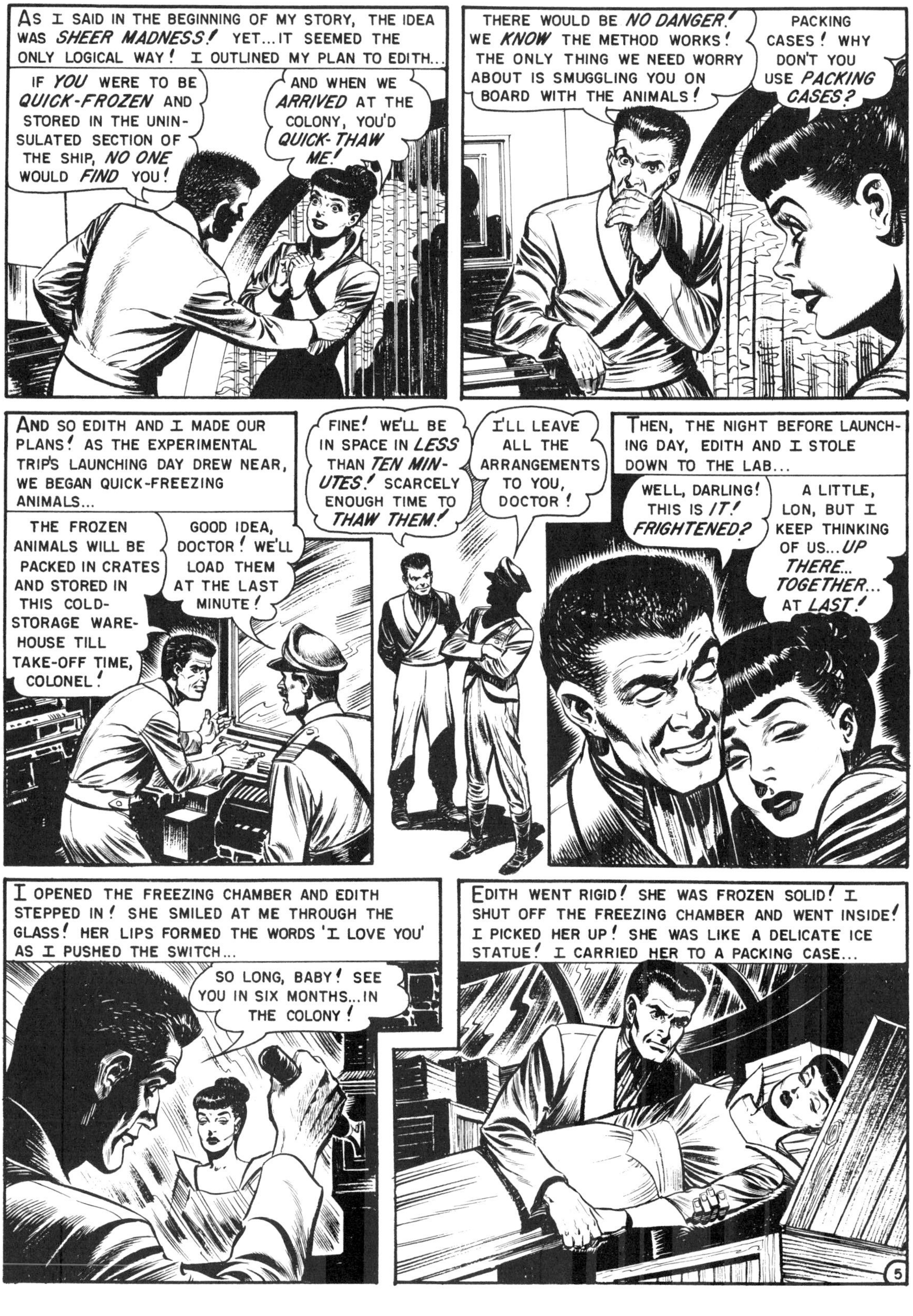
AS I SAID IN THE BEGINNING OF MY STORY, THE IDEA WAS SHEER MADNESS! YET...IT SEEMED THE ONLY LOGICAL WAY! I OUTLINED MY PLAN TO EDITH...
IF YOU WERE TO BE QUICK-FROZEN AND STORED IN THE UNINSULATED SECTION OF THE SHIP, NO ONE WOULD FIND YOU!
AND WHEN WE ARRIVED AT THE COLONY, YOU'D QUICK-THAW ME!
THERE WOULD BE NO DANGER! WE KNOW THE METHOD WORKS! THE ONLY THING WE NEED WORRY ABOUT IS SMUGGLING YOU ON BOARD WITH THE ANIMALS!
PACKING CASES! WHY DON'T YOU USE PACKING CASES?
AND SO EDITH AND I MADE OUR PLANS! AS THE EXPERIMENTAL TRIP'S LAUNCHING DAY DREW NEAR, WE BEGAN QUICK-FREEZING ANIMALS...
THE FROZEN ANIMALS WILL BE PACKED IN CRATES AND STORED IN THIS COLD-STORAGE WAREHOUSE TILL TAKE-OFF TIME, COLONEL!
GOOD IDEA, DOCTOR! WE'LL LOAD THEM AT THE LAST MINUTE!
FINE! WE'LL BE IN SPACE IN LESS THAN TEN MINUTES! SCARCELY ENOUGH TIME TO THAW THEM!
I'LL LEAVE ALL THE ARRANGEMENTS TO YOU, DOCTOR!
THEN, THE NIGHT BEFORE LAUNCHING DAY, EDITH AND I STOLE DOWN TO THE LAB...
WELL, DARLING! THIS IS IT! FRIGHTENED?
A LITTLE, LON, BUT I KEEP THINKING OF US...UP THERE... TOGETHER... AT LAST!
I OPENED THE FREEZING CHAMBER AND EDITH STEPPED IN! SHE SMILED AT ME THROUGH THE GLASS! HER LIPS FORMED THE WORDS 'I LOVE YOU' AS I PUSHED THE SWITCH...
SO LONG, BABY! SEE YOU IN SIX MONTHS...IN THE COLONY!
EDITH WENT RIGID! SHE WAS FROZEN SOLID! I SHUT OFF THE FREEZING CHAMBER AND WENT INSIDE! I PICKED HER UP! SHE WAS LIKE A DELICATE ICE STATUE! I CARRIED HER TO A PACKING CASE...
5

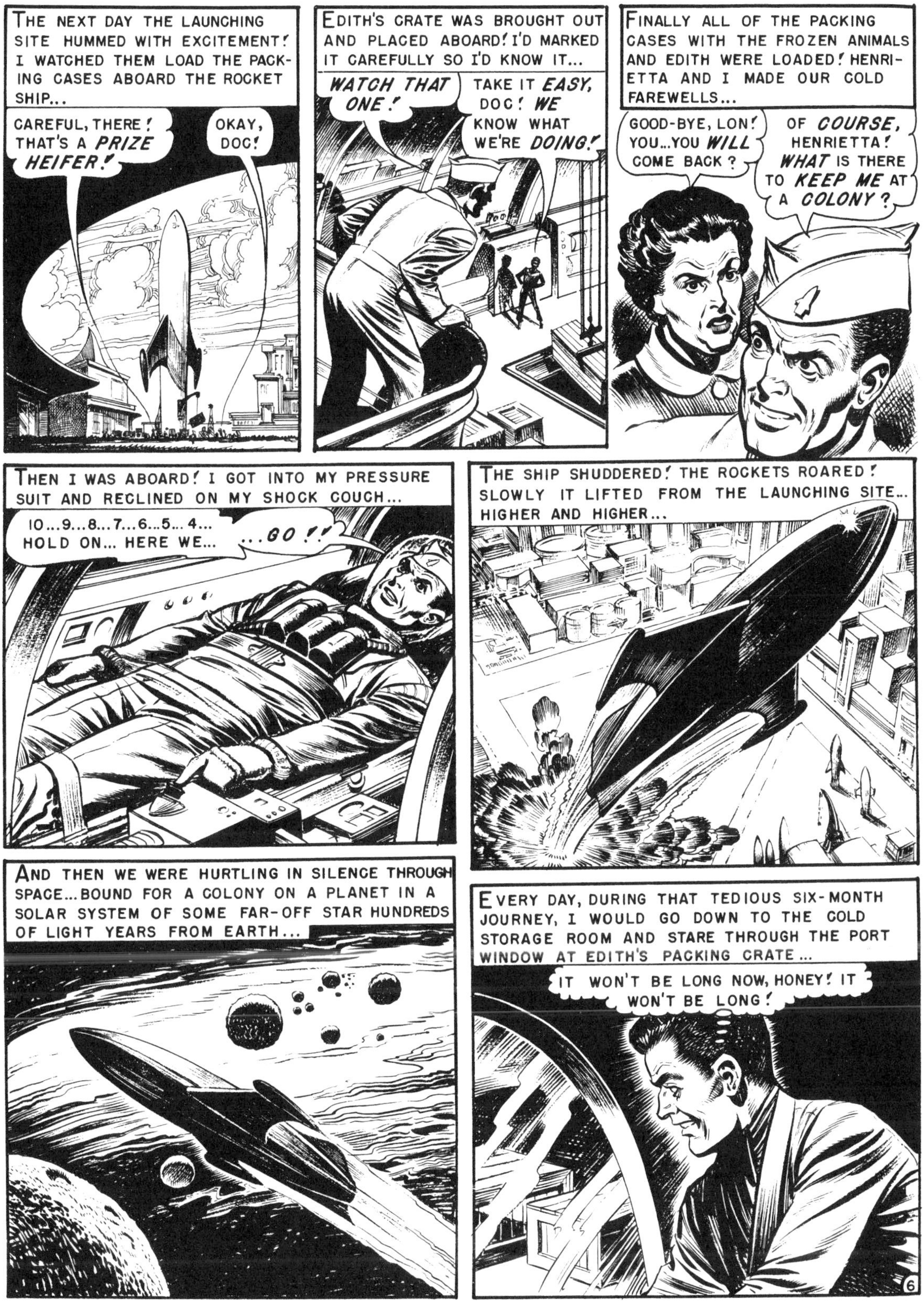
THE NEXT DAY THE LAUNCHING SITE HUMMED WITH EXCITEMENT! I WATCHED THEM LOAD THE PACKING CASES ABOARD THE ROCKET SHIP...
CAREFUL, THERE! THAT'S A PRIZE HEIFER!
OKAY, DOC!
EDITH'S CRATE WAS BROUGHT OUT AND PLACED ABOARD! I'D MARKED IT CAREFULLY SO I'D KNOW IT...
WATCH THAT ONE!
TAKE IT EASY, DOC! WE KNOW WHAT WE'RE DOING!
FINALLY ALL OF THE PACKING CASES WITH THE FROZEN ANIMALS AND EDITH WERE LOADED! HENRIETTA AND I MADE OUR COLD FAREWELLS...
GOOD-BYE, LON! YOU...YOU WILL COME BACK?
OF COURSE, HENRIETTA! WHAT IS THERE TO KEEP ME AT A COLONY?
THEN I WAS ABOARD! I GOT INTO MY PRESSURE SUIT AND RECLINED ON MY SHOCK COUCH...
10...9...8...7...6...5...4... HOLD ON... HERE WE...
...GO!!
THE SHIP SHUDDERED! THE ROCKETS ROARED! SLOWLY IT LIFTED FROM THE LAUNCHING SITE... HIGHER AND HIGHER...
AND THEN WE WERE HURTLING IN SILENCE THROUGH SPACE...BOUND FOR A COLONY ON A PLANET IN A SOLAR SYSTEM OF SOME FAR-OFF STAR HUNDREDS OF LIGHT YEARS FROM EARTH...
EVERY DAY, DURING THAT TEDIOUS SIX-MONTH JOURNEY, I WOULD GO DOWN TO THE COLD STORAGE ROOM AND STARE THROUGH THE PORT WINDOW AT EDITH'S PACKING CRATE...
IT WON'T BE LONG NOW, HONEY! IT WON'T BE LONG!
6

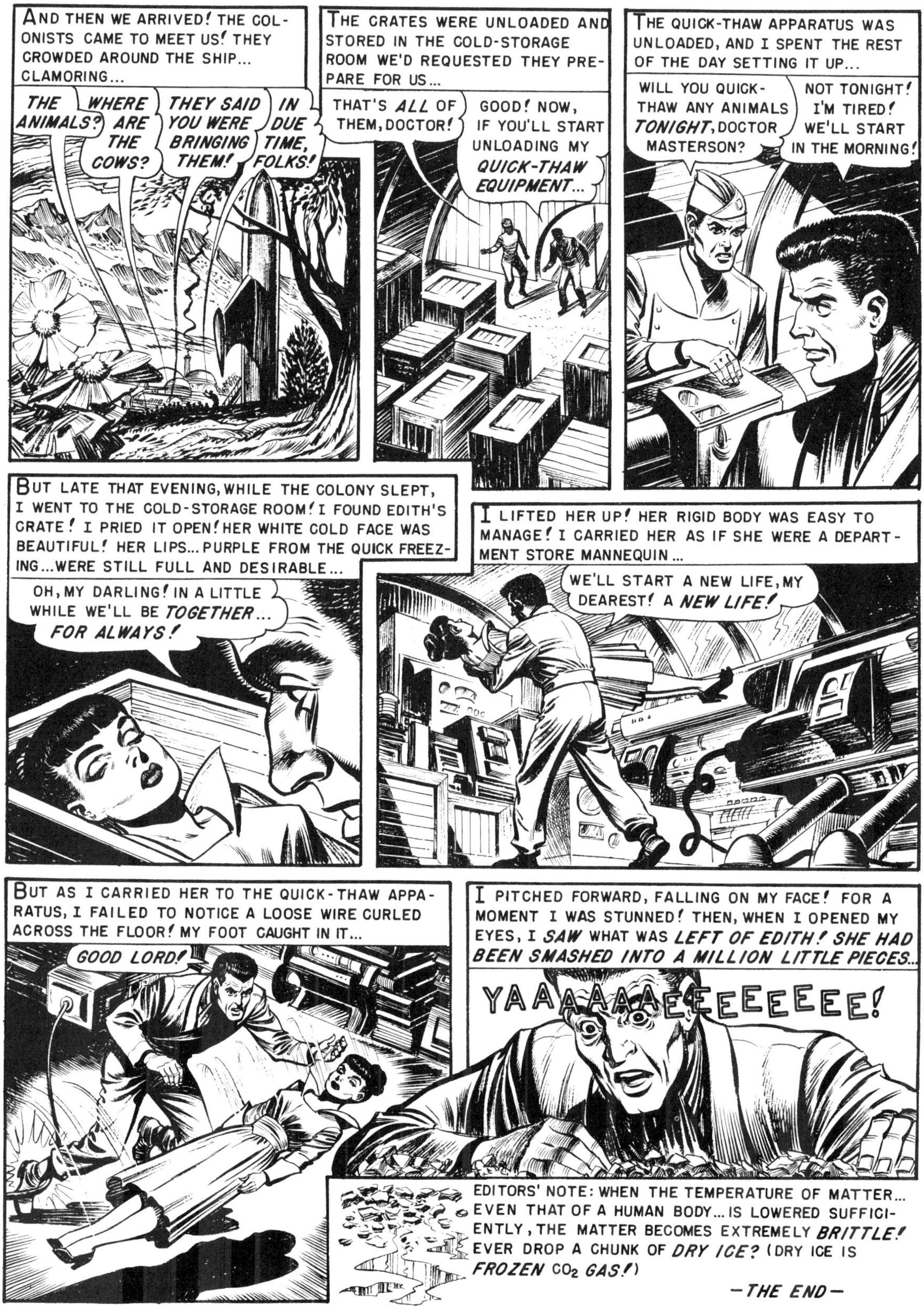
AND THEN WE ARRIVED! THE COLONISTS CAME TO MEET US! THEY CROWDED AROUND THE SHIP... CLAMORING...
THE ANIMALS?
WHERE ARE THE COWS?
THEY SAID YOU WERE BRINGING THEM!
IN DUE TIME, FOLKS!
THE CRATES WERE UNLOADED AND STORED IN THE COLD-STORAGE ROOM WE'D REQUESTED THEY PREPARE FOR US...
THAT'S ALL OF THEM, DOCTOR!
GOOD! NOW, IF YOU'LL START UNLOADING MY QUICK-THAW EQUIPMENT...
THE QUICK-THAW APPARATUS WAS UNLOADED, AND I SPENT THE REST OF THE DAY SETTING IT UP...
WILL YOU QUICK-THAW ANY ANIMALS TONIGHT, DOCTOR MASTERSON?
NOT TONIGHT! I'M TIRED! WE'LL START IN THE MORNING!
BUT LATE THAT EVENING, WHILE THE COLONY SLEPT, I WENT TO THE COLD-STORAGE ROOM! I FOUND EDITH'S CRATE! I PRIED IT OPEN! HER WHITE COLD FACE WAS BEAUTIFUL! HER LIPS... PURPLE FROM THE QUICK FREEZING... WERE STILL FULL AND DESIRABLE...
OH, MY DARLING! IN A LITTLE WHILE WE'LL BE TOGETHER... FOR ALWAYS!
I LIFTED HER UP! HER RIGID BODY WAS EASY TO MANAGE! I CARRIED HER AS IF SHE WERE A DEPARTMENT STORE MANNEQUIN...
WE'LL START A NEW LIFE, MY DEAREST! A NEW LIFE!
BUT AS I CARRIED HER TO THE QUICK-THAW APPARATUS, I FAILED TO NOTICE A LOOSE WIRE CURLED ACROSS THE FLOOR! MY FOOT CAUGHT IN IT...
GOOD LORD!
I PITCHED FORWARD, FALLING ON MY FACE! FOR A MOMENT I WAS STUNNED! THEN, WHEN I OPENED MY EYES, I SAW WHAT WAS LEFT OF EDITH! SHE HAD BEEN SMASHED INTO A MILLION LITTLE PIECES...
YAAAAAAEEEEEEEE!
EDITORS' NOTE: WHEN THE TEMPERATURE OF MATTER... EVEN THAT OF A HUMAN BODY... IS LOWERED SUFFICIENTLY, THE MATTER BECOMES EXTREMELY BRITTLE! EVER DROP A CHUNK OF DRY ICE? (DRY ICE IS FROZEN CO_2 GAS!)
—THE END—

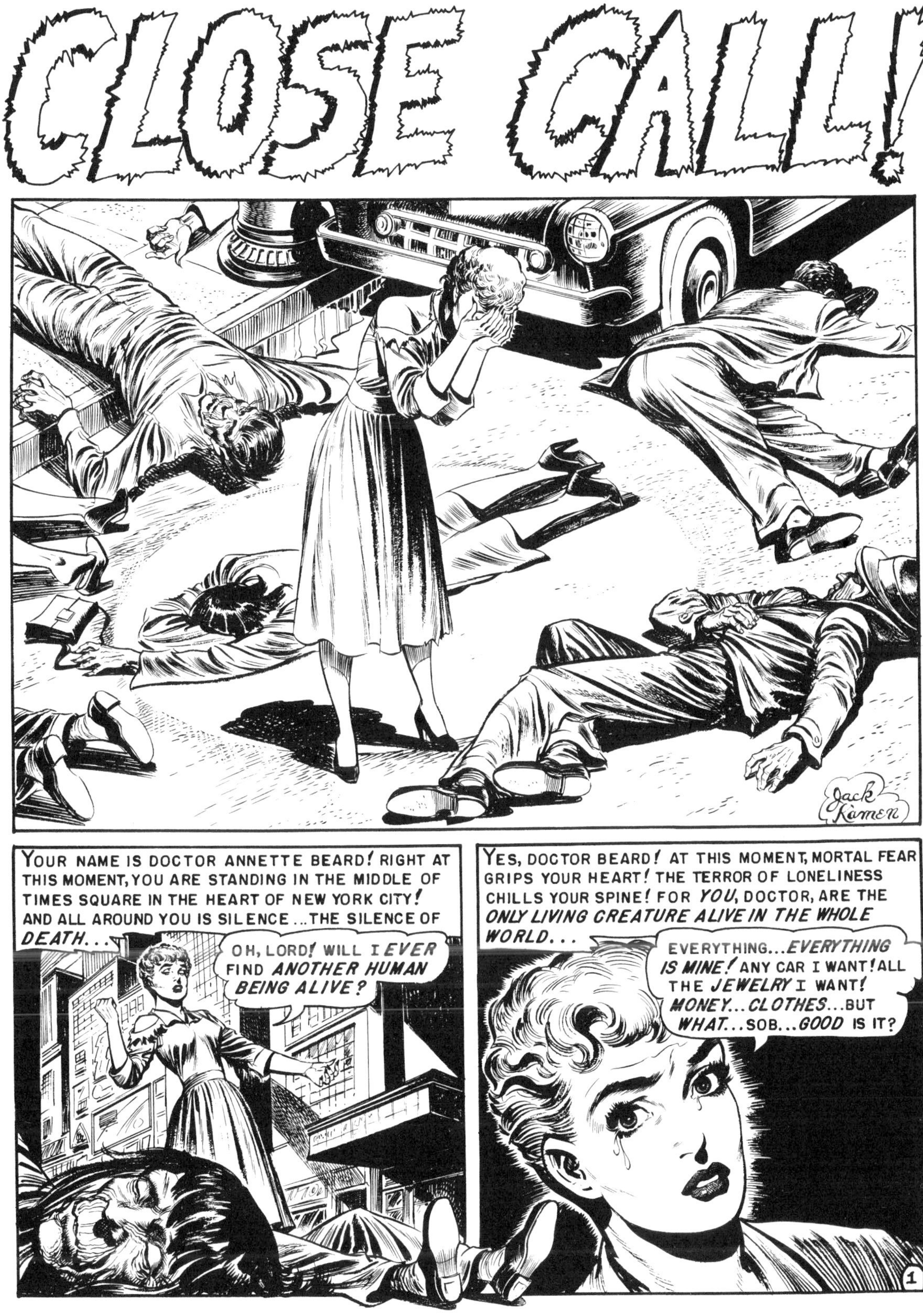
CLOSE CALL!
Jack Kamen
YOUR NAME IS DOCTOR ANNETTE BEARD! RIGHT AT THIS MOMENT, YOU ARE STANDING IN THE MIDDLE OF TIMES SQUARE IN THE HEART OF NEW YORK CITY! AND ALL AROUND YOU IS SILENCE...THE SILENCE OF DEATH...
OH, LORD! WILL I EVER FIND ANOTHER HUMAN BEING ALIVE?
YES, DOCTOR BEARD! AT THIS MOMENT, MORTAL FEAR GRIPS YOUR HEART! THE TERROR OF LONELINESS CHILLS YOUR SPINE! FOR YOU, DOCTOR, ARE THE ONLY LIVING CREATURE ALIVE IN THE WHOLE WORLD...
EVERYTHING...EVERYTHING IS MINE! ANY CAR I WANT! ALL THE JEWELRY I WANT! MONEY...CLOTHES...BUT WHAT...SOB...GOOD IS IT?
1

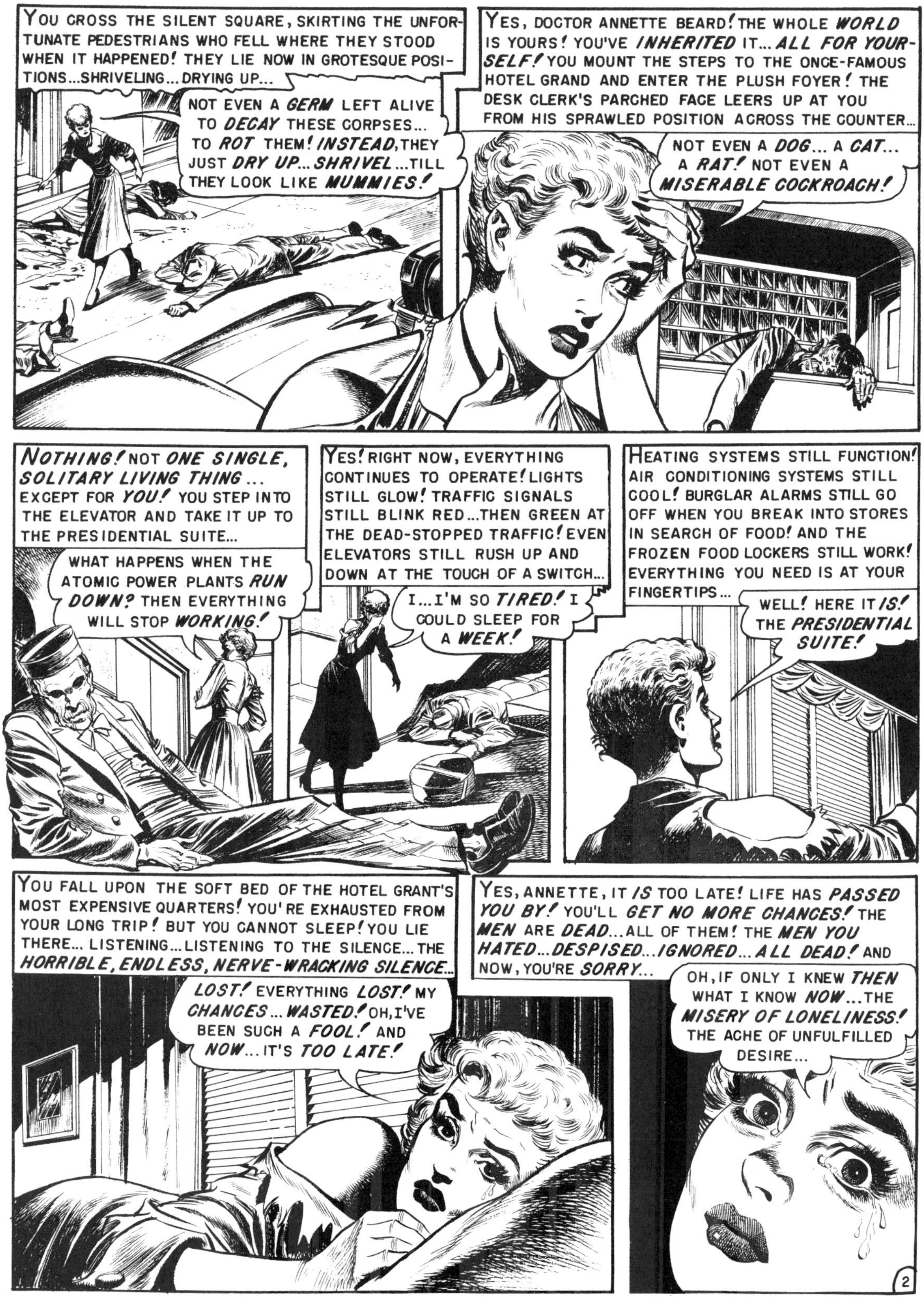
YOU CROSS THE SILENT SQUARE, SKIRTING THE UNFORTUNATE PEDESTRIANS WHO FELL WHERE THEY STOOD WHEN IT HAPPENED! THEY LIE NOW IN GROTESQUE POSITIONS...SHRIVELING...DRYING UP...
NOT EVEN A GERM LEFT ALIVE TO DECAY THESE CORPSES... TO ROT THEM! INSTEAD, THEY JUST DRY UP...SHRIVEL...TILL THEY LOOK LIKE MUMMIES!
YES, DOCTOR ANNETTE BEARD! THE WHOLE WORLD IS YOURS! YOU'VE INHERITED IT... ALL FOR YOURSELF! YOU MOUNT THE STEPS TO THE ONCE-FAMOUS HOTEL GRAND AND ENTER THE PLUSH FOYER! THE DESK CLERK'S PARCHED FACE LEERS UP AT YOU FROM HIS SPRAWLED POSITION ACROSS THE COUNTER...
NOT EVEN A DOG... A CAT... A RAT! NOT EVEN A MISERABLE COCKROACH!
NOTHING! NOT ONE SINGLE, SOLITARY LIVING THING... EXCEPT FOR YOU! YOU STEP INTO THE ELEVATOR AND TAKE IT UP TO THE PRESIDENTIAL SUITE...
WHAT HAPPENS WHEN THE ATOMIC POWER PLANTS RUN DOWN? THEN EVERYTHING WILL STOP WORKING!
YES! RIGHT NOW, EVERYTHING CONTINUES TO OPERATE! LIGHTS STILL GLOW! TRAFFIC SIGNALS STILL BLINK RED...THEN GREEN AT THE DEAD-STOPPED TRAFFIC! EVEN ELEVATORS STILL RUSH UP AND DOWN AT THE TOUCH OF A SWITCH...
I...I'M SO TIRED! I COULD SLEEP FOR A WEEK!
HEATING SYSTEMS STILL FUNCTION! AIR CONDITIONING SYSTEMS STILL COOL! BURGLAR ALARMS STILL GO OFF WHEN YOU BREAK INTO STORES IN SEARCH OF FOOD! AND THE FROZEN FOOD LOCKERS STILL WORK! EVERYTHING YOU NEED IS AT YOUR FINGERTIPS...
WELL! HERE IT IS! THE PRESIDENTIAL SUITE!
YOU FALL UPON THE SOFT BED OF THE HOTEL GRANT'S MOST EXPENSIVE QUARTERS! YOU'RE EXHAUSTED FROM YOUR LONG TRIP! BUT YOU CANNOT SLEEP! YOU LIE THERE... LISTENING...LISTENING TO THE SILENCE... THE HORRIBLE, ENDLESS, NERVE-WRACKING SILENCE...
LOST! EVERYTHING LOST! MY CHANCES... WASTED! OH, I'VE BEEN SUCH A FOOL! AND NOW... IT'S TOO LATE!
YES, ANNETTE, IT IS TOO LATE! LIFE HAS PASSED YOU BY! YOU'LL GET NO MORE CHANCES! THE MEN ARE DEAD...ALL OF THEM! THE MEN YOU HATED...DESPISED...IGNORED... ALL DEAD! AND NOW, YOU'RE SORRY...
OH, IF ONLY I KNEW THEN WHAT I KNOW NOW...THE MISERY OF LONELINESS! THE ACHE OF UNFULFILLED DESIRE...
2

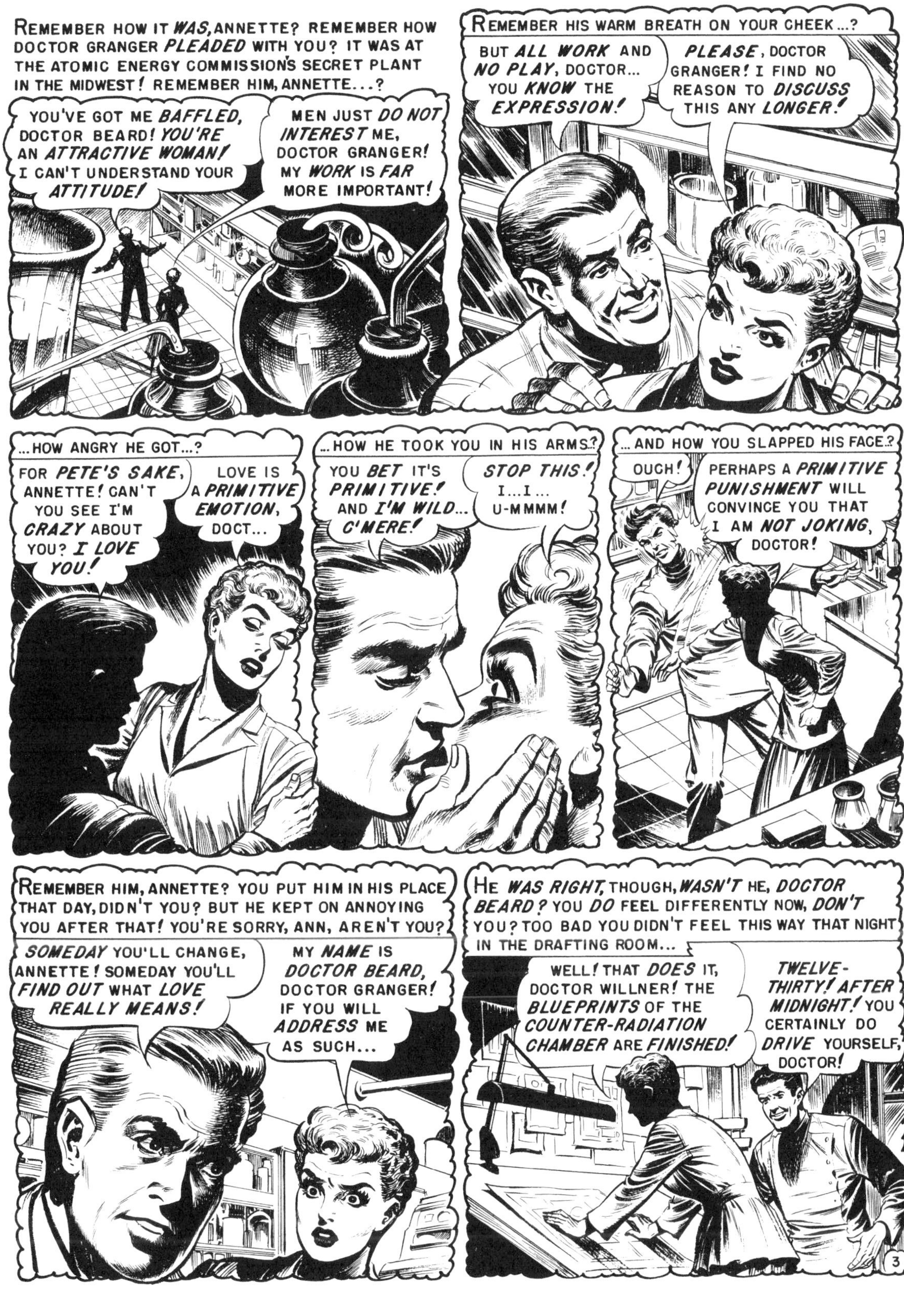
REMEMBER HOW IT WAS, ANNETTE? REMEMBER HOW DOCTOR GRANGER PLEADED WITH YOU? IT WAS AT THE ATOMIC ENERGY COMMISSION'S SECRET PLANT IN THE MIDWEST! REMEMBER HIM, ANNETTE...?
YOU'VE GOT ME BAFFLED, DOCTOR BEARD! YOU'RE AN ATTRACTIVE WOMAN! I CAN'T UNDERSTAND YOUR ATTITUDE!
MEN JUST DO NOT INTEREST ME, DOCTOR GRANGER! MY WORK IS FAR MORE IMPORTANT!
REMEMBER HIS WARM BREATH ON YOUR CHEEK...?
BUT ALL WORK AND NO PLAY, DOCTOR... YOU KNOW THE EXPRESSION!
PLEASE, DOCTOR GRANGER! I FIND NO REASON TO DISCUSS THIS ANY LONGER!
...HOW ANGRY HE GOT...?
FOR PETE'S SAKE, ANNETTE! CAN'T YOU SEE I'M CRAZY ABOUT YOU? I LOVE YOU!
LOVE IS A PRIMITIVE EMOTION, DOCT...
...HOW HE TOOK YOU IN HIS ARMS...?
YOU BET IT'S PRIMITIVE! AND I'M WILD... C'MERE!
STOP THIS! I...I... U-MMMM!
...AND HOW YOU SLAPPED HIS FACE...?
OUCH!
PERHAPS A PRIMITIVE PUNISHMENT WILL CONVINCE YOU THAT I AM NOT JOKING, DOCTOR!
REMEMBER HIM, ANNETTE? YOU PUT HIM IN HIS PLACE THAT DAY, DIDN'T YOU? BUT HE KEPT ON ANNOYING YOU AFTER THAT! YOU'RE SORRY, ANN, AREN'T YOU?
SOMEDAY YOU'LL CHANGE, ANNETTE! SOMEDAY YOU'LL FIND OUT WHAT LOVE REALLY MEANS!
MY NAME IS DOCTOR BEARD, DOCTOR GRANGER! IF YOU WILL ADDRESS ME AS SUCH...
HE WAS RIGHT, THOUGH, WASN'T HE, DOCTOR BEARD? YOU DO FEEL DIFFERENTLY NOW, DON'T YOU? TOO BAD YOU DIDN'T FEEL THIS WAY THAT NIGHT IN THE DRAFTING ROOM...
WELL! THAT DOES IT, DOCTOR WILLNER! THE BLUEPRINTS OF THE COUNTER-RADIATION CHAMBER ARE FINISHED!
TWELVE-THIRTY! AFTER MIDNIGHT! YOU CERTAINLY DO DRIVE YOURSELF, DOCTOR!
3

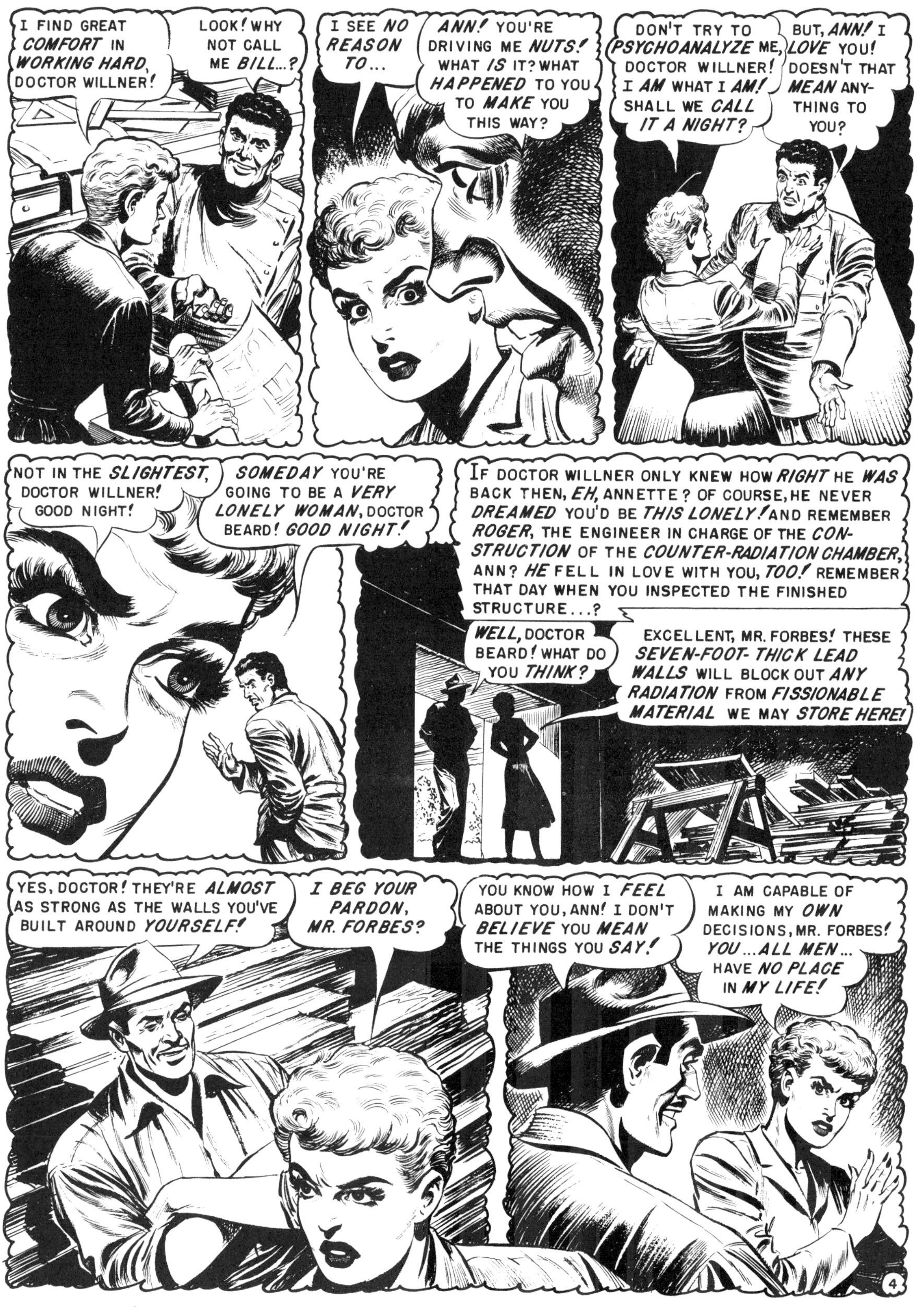

I FIND GREAT COMFORT IN WORKING HARD, DOCTOR WILLNER!
LOOK! WHY NOT CALL ME BILL...?
I SEE NO REASON TO...
ANN! YOU'RE DRIVING ME NUTS! WHAT IS IT? WHAT HAPPENED TO YOU TO MAKE YOU THIS WAY?
DON'T TRY TO PSYCHOANALYZE ME, DOCTOR WILLNER! I AM WHAT I AM! SHALL WE CALL IT A NIGHT?
BUT, ANN! I LOVE YOU! DOESN'T THAT MEAN ANYTHING TO YOU?
NOT IN THE SLIGHTEST, DOCTOR WILLNER! GOOD NIGHT!
SOMEDAY YOU'RE GOING TO BE A VERY LONELY WOMAN, DOCTOR BEARD! GOOD NIGHT!
IF DOCTOR WILLNER ONLY KNEW HOW RIGHT HE WAS BACK THEN, EH, ANNETTE? OF COURSE, HE NEVER DREAMED YOU'D BE THIS LONELY! AND REMEMBER ROGER, THE ENGINEER IN CHARGE OF THE CONSTRUCTION OF THE COUNTER-RADIATION CHAMBER, ANN? HE FELL IN LOVE WITH YOU, TOO! REMEMBER THAT DAY WHEN YOU INSPECTED THE FINISHED STRUCTURE...?
WELL, DOCTOR BEARD! WHAT DO YOU THINK?
EXCELLENT, MR. FORBES! THESE SEVEN-FOOT-THICK LEAD WALLS WILL BLOCK OUT ANY RADIATION FROM FISSIONABLE MATERIAL WE MAY STORE HERE!
YES, DOCTOR! THEY'RE ALMOST AS STRONG AS THE WALLS YOU'VE BUILT AROUND YOURSELF!
I BEG YOUR PARDON, MR. FORBES?
YOU KNOW HOW I FEEL ABOUT YOU, ANN! I DON'T BELIEVE YOU MEAN THE THINGS YOU SAY!
I AM CAPABLE OF MAKING MY OWN DECISIONS, MR. FORBES! YOU...ALL MEN... HAVE NO PLACE IN MY LIFE!
4

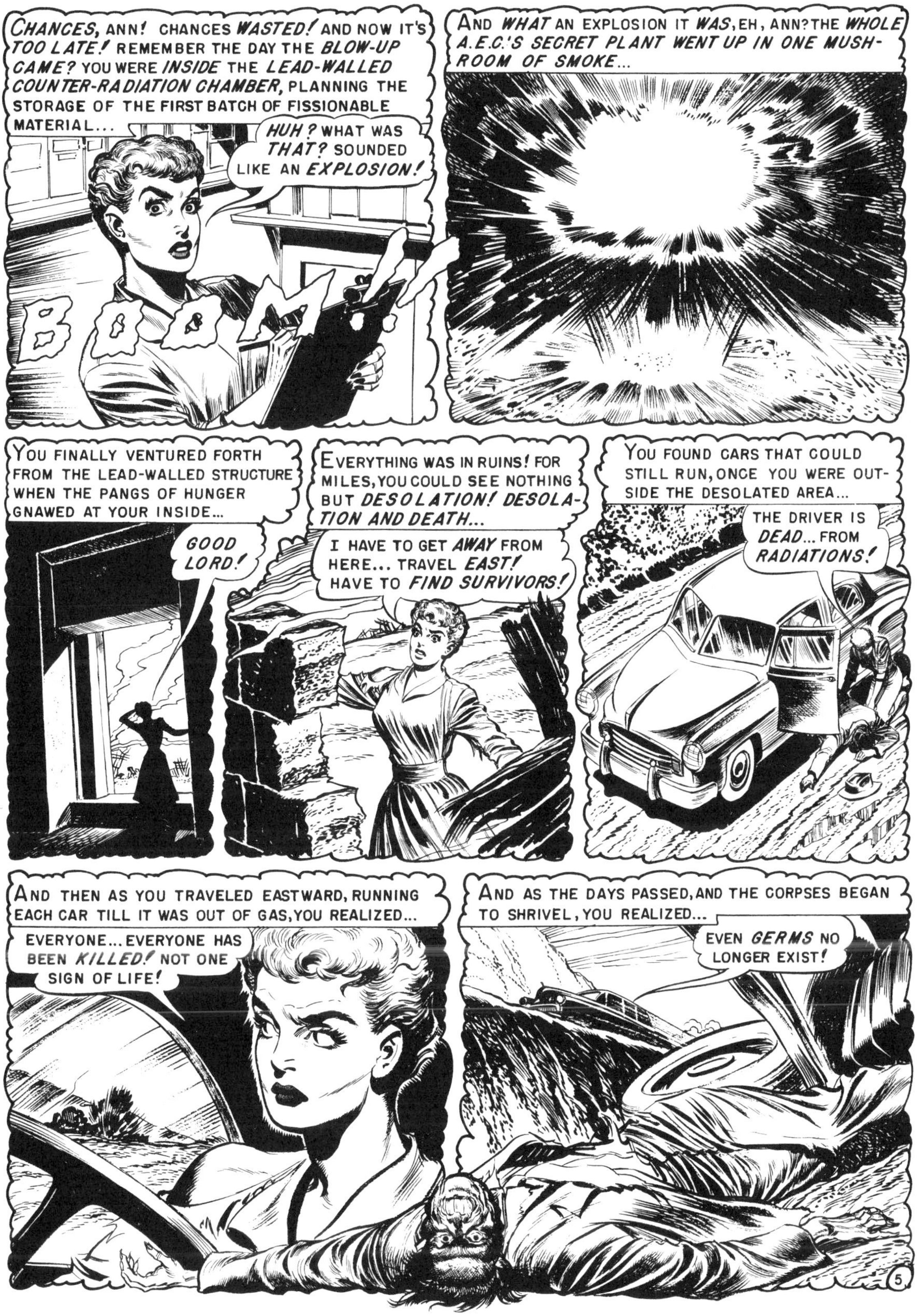
CHANCES, ANN! CHANCES WASTED! AND NOW IT'S TOO LATE! REMEMBER THE DAY THE BLOW-UP CAME? YOU WERE INSIDE THE LEAD-WALLED COUNTER-RADIATION CHAMBER, PLANNING THE STORAGE OF THE FIRST BATCH OF FISSIONABLE MATERIAL...
HUH? WHAT WAS THAT? SOUNDED LIKE AN EXPLOSION!
BOOM
AND WHAT AN EXPLOSION IT WAS, EH, ANN? THE WHOLE A.E.C.'S SECRET PLANT WENT UP IN ONE MUSH-ROOM OF SMOKE...
YOU FINALLY VENTURED FORTH FROM THE LEAD-WALLED STRUCTURE WHEN THE PANGS OF HUNGER GNAWED AT YOUR INSIDE...
GOOD LORD!
EVERYTHING WAS IN RUINS! FOR MILES, YOU COULD SEE NOTHING BUT DESOLATION! DESOLA-TION AND DEATH...
I HAVE TO GET AWAY FROM HERE... TRAVEL EAST! HAVE TO FIND SURVIVORS!
YOU FOUND CARS THAT COULD STILL RUN, ONCE YOU WERE OUT-SIDE THE DESOLATED AREA...
THE DRIVER IS DEAD... FROM RADIATIONS!
AND THEN AS YOU TRAVELED EASTWARD, RUNNING EACH CAR TILL IT WAS OUT OF GAS, YOU REALIZED...
EVERYONE... EVERYONE HAS BEEN KILLED! NOT ONE SIGN OF LIFE!
AND AS THE DAYS PASSED, AND THE CORPSES BEGAN TO SHRIVEL, YOU REALIZED...
EVEN GERMS NO LONGER EXIST!
5

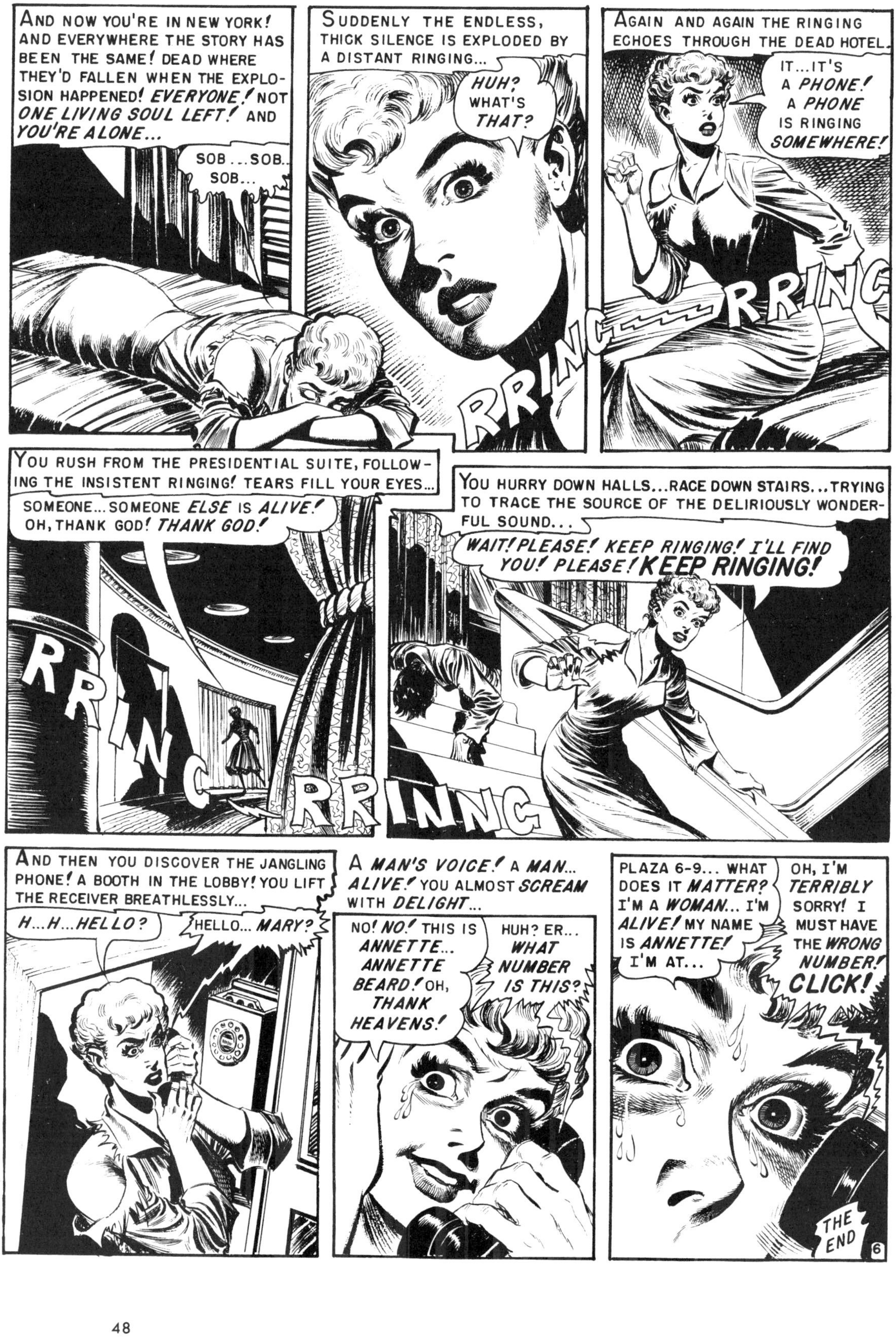
AND NOW YOU'RE IN NEW YORK! AND EVERYWHERE THE STORY HAS BEEN THE SAME! DEAD WHERE THEY'D FALLEN WHEN THE EXPLOSION HAPPENED! EVERYONE! NOT ONE LIVING SOUL LEFT! AND YOU'RE ALONE...
SOB...SOB.. SOB...
SUDDENLY THE ENDLESS, THICK SILENCE IS EXPLODED BY A DISTANT RINGING...
HUH? WHAT'S THAT?
RRING
AGAIN AND AGAIN THE RINGING ECHOES THROUGH THE DEAD HOTEL.
IT...IT'S A PHONE! A PHONE IS RINGING SOMEWHERE!
RRING
YOU RUSH FROM THE PRESIDENTIAL SUITE, FOLLOWING THE INSISTENT RINGING! TEARS FILL YOUR EYES...
SOMEONE...SOMEONE ELSE IS ALIVE! OH, THANK GOD! THANK GOD!
RRING
YOU HURRY DOWN HALLS...RACE DOWN STAIRS...TRYING TO TRACE THE SOURCE OF THE DELIRIOUSLY WONDERFUL SOUND...
WAIT! PLEASE! KEEP RINGING! I'LL FIND YOU! PLEASE! KEEP RINGING!
RRINNG
AND THEN YOU DISCOVER THE JANGLING PHONE! A BOOTH IN THE LOBBY! YOU LIFT THE RECEIVER BREATHLESSLY...
H...H...HELLO?
HELLO... MARY?
A MAN'S VOICE! A MAN... ALIVE! YOU ALMOST SCREAM WITH DELIGHT...
NO! NO! THIS IS ANNETTE... ANNETTE BEARD! OH, THANK HEAVENS!
HUH? ER... WHAT NUMBER IS THIS?
PLAZA 6-9... WHAT DOES IT MATTER? I'M A WOMAN... I'M ALIVE! MY NAME IS ANNETTE! I'M AT...
OH, I'M TERRIBLY SORRY! I MUST HAVE THE WRONG NUMBER! CLICK!
THE END
6

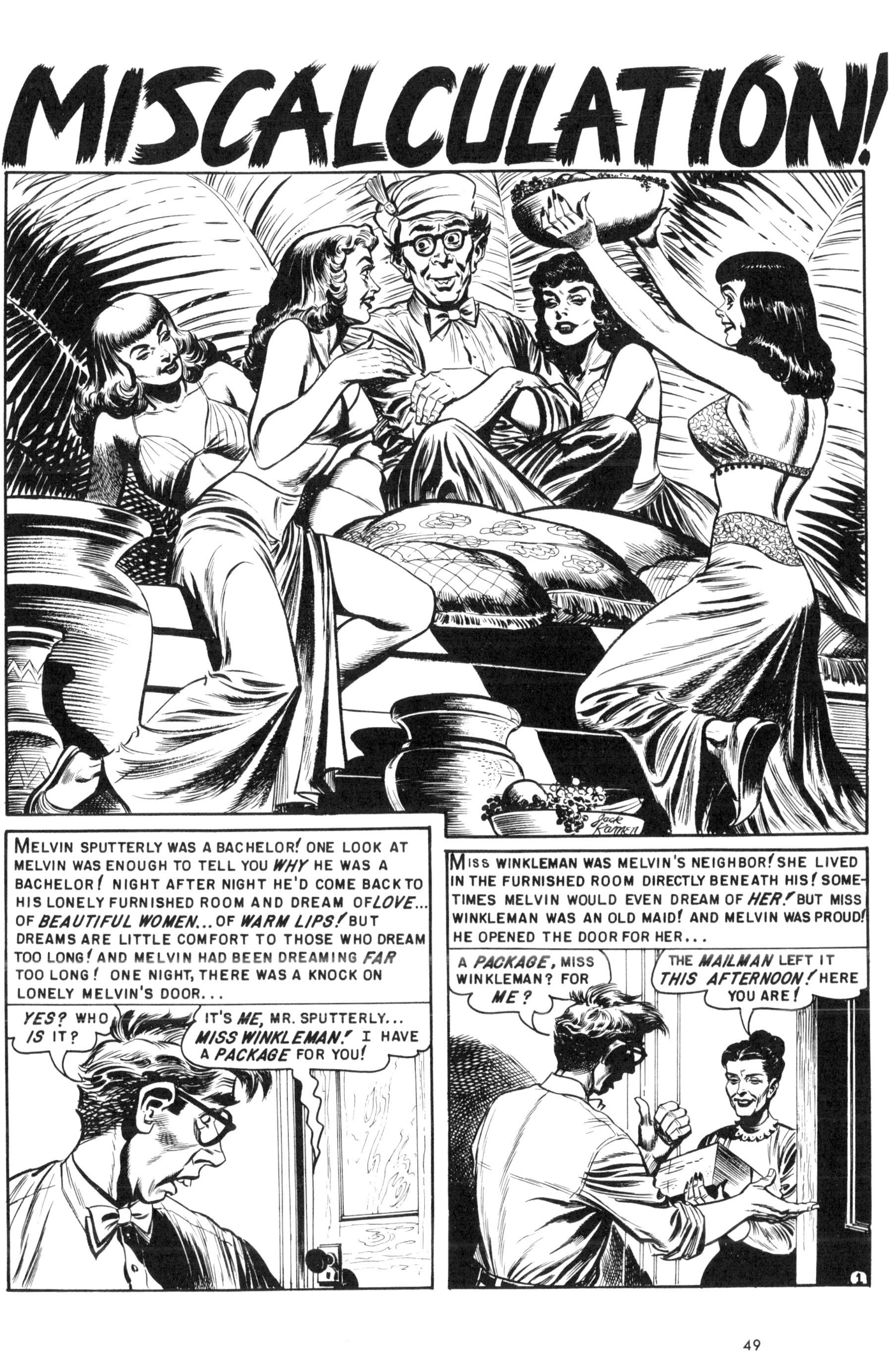
MISCALCULATION!
Jack Kamen
MELVIN SPUTTERLY WAS A BACHELOR! ONE LOOK AT MELVIN WAS ENOUGH TO TELL YOU WHY HE WAS A BACHELOR! NIGHT AFTER NIGHT HE'D COME BACK TO HIS LONELY FURNISHED ROOM AND DREAM OF LOVE... OF BEAUTIFUL WOMEN... OF WARM LIPS! BUT DREAMS ARE LITTLE COMFORT TO THOSE WHO DREAM TOO LONG! AND MELVIN HAD BEEN DREAMING FAR TOO LONG! ONE NIGHT, THERE WAS A KNOCK ON LONELY MELVIN'S DOOR...
YES? WHO IS IT?
IT'S ME, MR. SPUTTERLY... MISS WINKLEMAN! I HAVE A PACKAGE FOR YOU!
MISS WINKLEMAN WAS MELVIN'S NEIGHBOR! SHE LIVED IN THE FURNISHED ROOM DIRECTLY BENEATH HIS! SOMETIMES MELVIN WOULD EVEN DREAM OF HER! BUT MISS WINKLEMAN WAS AN OLD MAID! AND MELVIN WAS PROUD! HE OPENED THE DOOR FOR HER...
A PACKAGE, MISS WINKLEMAN? FOR ME?
THE MAILMAN LEFT IT THIS AFTERNOON! HERE YOU ARE!
1

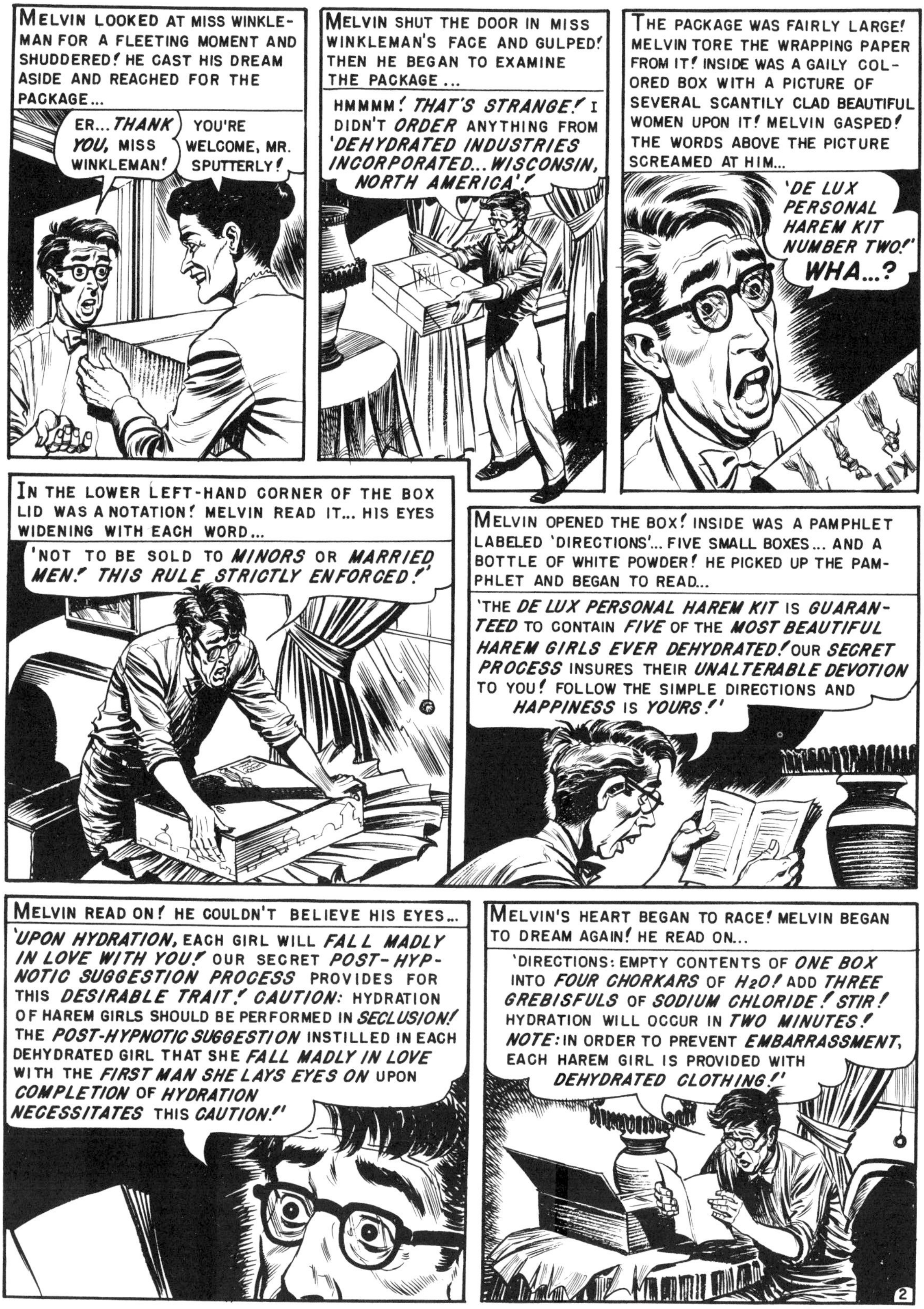
MELVIN LOOKED AT MISS WINKLEMAN FOR A FLEETING MOMENT AND SHUDDERED! HE CAST HIS DREAM ASIDE AND REACHED FOR THE PACKAGE...
ER... THANK YOU, MISS WINKLEMAN!
YOU'RE WELCOME, MR. SPUTTERLY!
MELVIN SHUT THE DOOR IN MISS WINKLEMAN'S FACE AND GULPED! THEN HE BEGAN TO EXAMINE THE PACKAGE...
HMMMM! THAT'S STRANGE! I DIDN'T ORDER ANYTHING FROM 'DEHYDRATED INDUSTRIES INCORPORATED... WISCONSIN, NORTH AMERICA'!
THE PACKAGE WAS FAIRLY LARGE! MELVIN TORE THE WRAPPING PAPER FROM IT! INSIDE WAS A GAILY COLORED BOX WITH A PICTURE OF SEVERAL SCANTILY CLAD BEAUTIFUL WOMEN UPON IT! MELVIN GASPED! THE WORDS ABOVE THE PICTURE SCREAMED AT HIM...
'DE LUX PERSONAL HAREM KIT NUMBER TWO!' WHA...?
IN THE LOWER LEFT-HAND CORNER OF THE BOX LID WAS A NOTATION! MELVIN READ IT... HIS EYES WIDENING WITH EACH WORD...
'NOT TO BE SOLD TO MINORS OR MARRIED MEN!' THIS RULE STRICTLY ENFORCED!'
MELVIN OPENED THE BOX! INSIDE WAS A PAMPHLET LABELED 'DIRECTIONS'... FIVE SMALL BOXES... AND A BOTTLE OF WHITE POWDER! HE PICKED UP THE PAMPHLET AND BEGAN TO READ...
'THE DE LUX PERSONAL HAREM KIT IS GUARANTEED TO CONTAIN FIVE OF THE MOST BEAUTIFUL HAREM GIRLS EVER DEHYDRATED! OUR SECRET PROCESS INSURES THEIR UNALTERABLE DEVOTION TO YOU! FOLLOW THE SIMPLE DIRECTIONS AND HAPPINESS IS YOURS!'
MELVIN READ ON! HE COULDN'T BELIEVE HIS EYES...
'UPON HYDRATION, EACH GIRL WILL FALL MADLY IN LOVE WITH YOU! OUR SECRET POST-HYPNOTIC SUGGESTION PROCESS PROVIDES FOR THIS DESIRABLE TRAIT! CAUTION: HYDRATION OF HAREM GIRLS SHOULD BE PERFORMED IN SECLUSION! THE POST-HYPNOTIC SUGGESTION INSTILLED IN EACH DEHYDRATED GIRL THAT SHE FALL MADLY IN LOVE WITH THE FIRST MAN SHE LAYS EYES ON UPON COMPLETION OF HYDRATION NECESSITATES THIS CAUTION!'
MELVIN'S HEART BEGAN TO RACE! MELVIN BEGAN TO DREAM AGAIN! HE READ ON...
'DIRECTIONS: EMPTY CONTENTS OF ONE BOX INTO FOUR CHORKARS OF H2O! ADD THREE GREBISFULS OF SODIUM CHLORIDE! STIR! HYDRATION WILL OCCUR IN TWO MINUTES! NOTE: IN ORDER TO PREVENT EMBARRASSMENT, EACH HAREM GIRL IS PROVIDED WITH DEHYDRATED CLOTHING!'
2

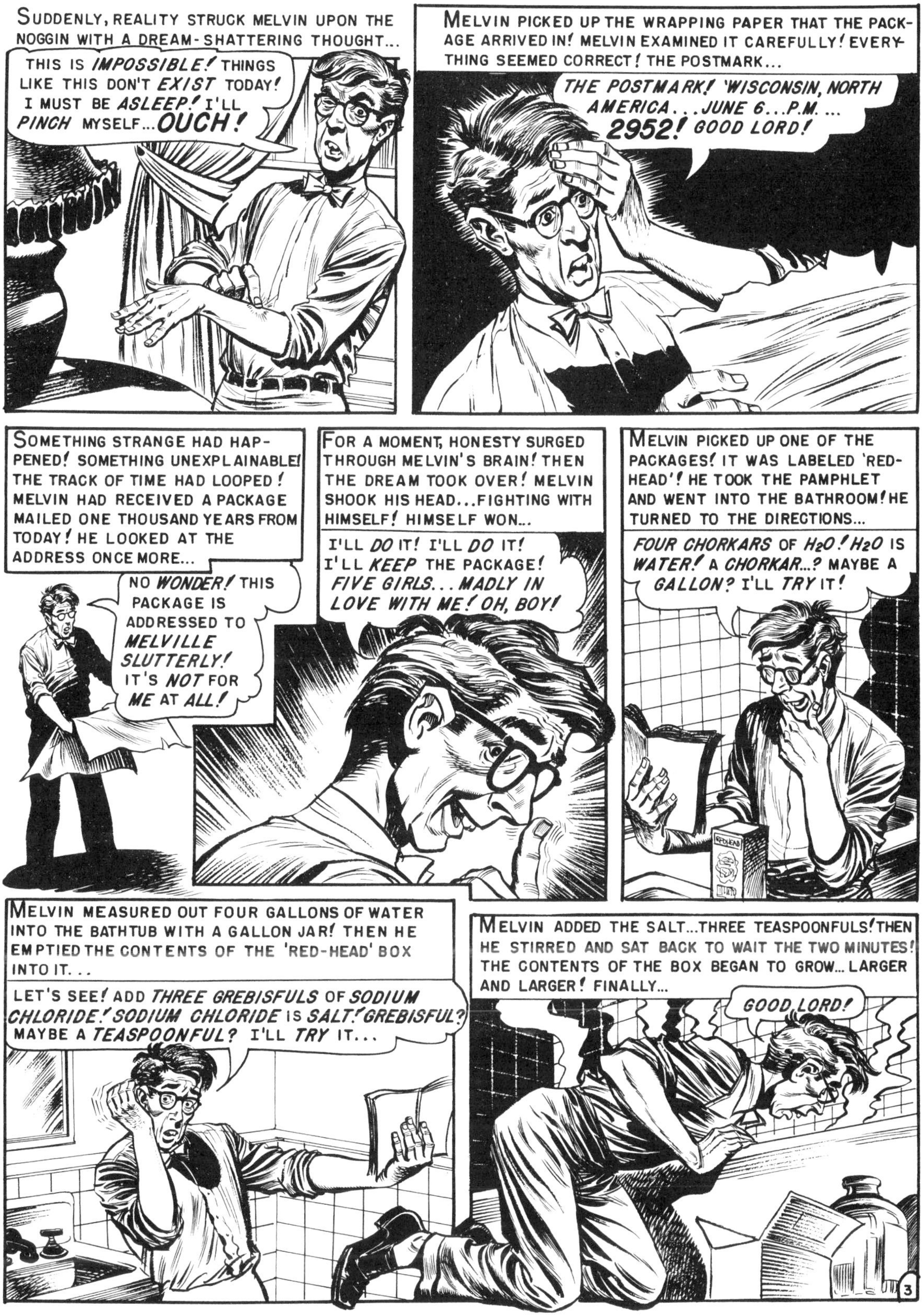

SUDDENLY, REALITY STRUCK MELVIN UPON THE NOGGIN WITH A DREAM-SHATTERING THOUGHT...
THIS IS IMPOSSIBLE! THINGS LIKE THIS DON'T EXIST TODAY! I MUST BE ASLEEP! I'LL PINCH MYSELF...OUCH!
MELVIN PICKED UP THE WRAPPING PAPER THAT THE PACKAGE ARRIVED IN! MELVIN EXAMINED IT CAREFULLY! EVERYTHING SEEMED CORRECT! THE POSTMARK...
THE POSTMARK! 'WISCONSIN, NORTH AMERICA...JUNE 6...P.M. ... 2952! GOOD LORD!
SOMETHING STRANGE HAD HAPPENED! SOMETHING UNEXPLAINABLE! THE TRACK OF TIME HAD LOOPED! MELVIN HAD RECEIVED A PACKAGE MAILED ONE THOUSAND YEARS FROM TODAY! HE LOOKED AT THE ADDRESS ONCE MORE...
NO WONDER! THIS PACKAGE IS ADDRESSED TO MELVILLE SLUTTERLY! IT'S NOT FOR ME AT ALL!
FOR A MOMENT, HONESTY SURGED THROUGH MELVIN'S BRAIN! THEN THE DREAM TOOK OVER! MELVIN SHOOK HIS HEAD...FIGHTING WITH HIMSELF! HIMSELF WON...
I'LL DO IT! I'LL DO IT! I'LL KEEP THE PACKAGE! FIVE GIRLS... MADLY IN LOVE WITH ME! OH, BOY!
MELVIN PICKED UP ONE OF THE PACKAGES! IT WAS LABELED 'RED-HEAD'! HE TOOK THE PAMPHLET AND WENT INTO THE BATHROOM! HE TURNED TO THE DIRECTIONS...
FOUR CHORKARS OF H2O! H2O IS WATER! A CHORKAR...? MAYBE A GALLON? I'LL TRY IT!
MELVIN MEASURED OUT FOUR GALLONS OF WATER INTO THE BATHTUB WITH A GALLON JAR! THEN HE EMPTIED THE CONTENTS OF THE 'RED-HEAD' BOX INTO IT...
LET'S SEE! ADD THREE GREBISFULS OF SODIUM CHLORIDE! SODIUM CHLORIDE IS SALT! GREBISFUL? MAYBE A TEASPOONFUL? I'LL TRY IT...
MELVIN ADDED THE SALT...THREE TEASPOONFULS! THEN HE STIRRED AND SAT BACK TO WAIT THE TWO MINUTES! THE CONTENTS OF THE BOX BEGAN TO GROW... LARGER AND LARGER! FINALLY...
GOOD LORD!
3

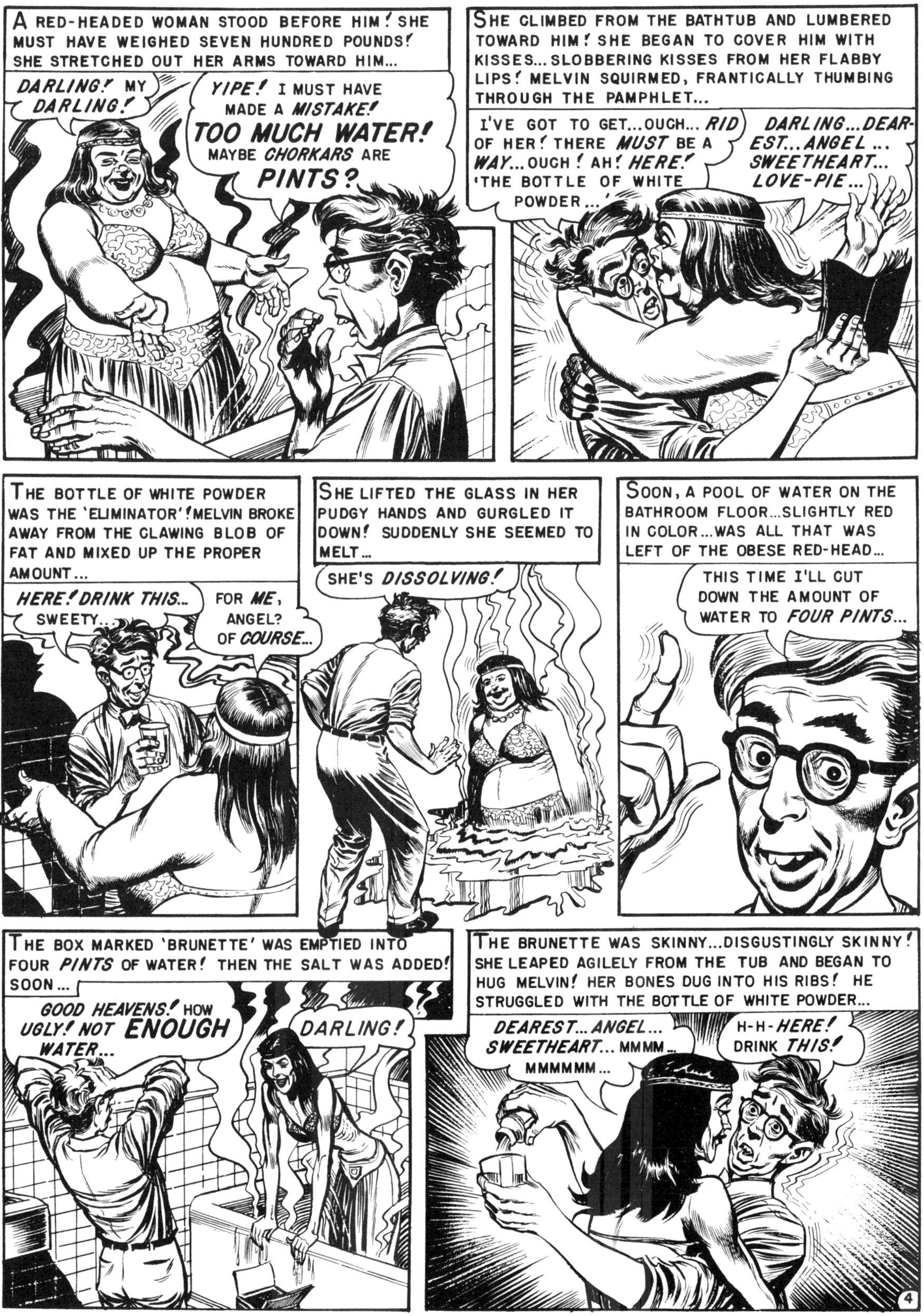
A RED-HEADED WOMAN STOOD BEFORE HIM! SHE MUST HAVE WEIGHED SEVEN HUNDRED POUNDS! SHE STRETCHED OUT HER ARMS TOWARD HIM...
DARLING! MY DARLING!
YIPE! I MUST HAVE MADE A MISTAKE! TOO MUCH WATER! MAYBE CHORKARS ARE PINTS?
SHE CLIMBED FROM THE BATHTUB AND LUMBERED TOWARD HIM! SHE BEGAN TO COVER HIM WITH KISSES... SLOBBERING KISSES FROM HER FLABBY LIPS! MELVIN SQUIRMED, FRANTICALLY THUMBING THROUGH THE PAMPHLET...
I'VE GOT TO GET... OUCH... RID OF HER! THERE MUST BE A WAY... OUCH! AH! HERE! 'THE BOTTLE OF WHITE POWDER...'
DARLING... DEAREST... ANGEL... SWEETHEART... LOVE-PIE...
THE BOTTLE OF WHITE POWDER WAS THE 'ELIMINATOR'! MELVIN BROKE AWAY FROM THE CLAWING BLOB OF FAT AND MIXED UP THE PROPER AMOUNT...
HERE! DRINK THIS... SWEETY...
FOR ME, ANGEL? OF COURSE...
SHE LIFTED THE GLASS IN HER PUDGY HANDS AND GURGLED IT DOWN! SUDDENLY SHE SEEMED TO MELT...
SHE'S DISSOLVING!
SOON, A POOL OF WATER ON THE BATHROOM FLOOR... SLIGHTLY RED IN COLOR... WAS ALL THAT WAS LEFT OF THE OBESE RED-HEAD...
THIS TIME I'LL CUT DOWN THE AMOUNT OF WATER TO FOUR PINTS...
THE BOX MARKED 'BRUNETTE' WAS EMPTIED INTO FOUR PINTS OF WATER! THEN THE SALT WAS ADDED! SOON...
GOOD HEAVENS! HOW UGLY! NOT ENOUGH WATER...
DARLING!
THE BRUNETTE WAS SKINNY... DISGUSTINGLY SKINNY! SHE LEAPED AGILELY FROM THE TUB AND BEGAN TO HUG MELVIN! HER BONES DUG INTO HIS RIBS! HE STRUGGLED WITH THE BOTTLE OF WHITE POWDER...
DEAREST... ANGEL... SWEETHEART... MMMM... MMMMMM...
H-H-HERE! DRINK THIS!
4

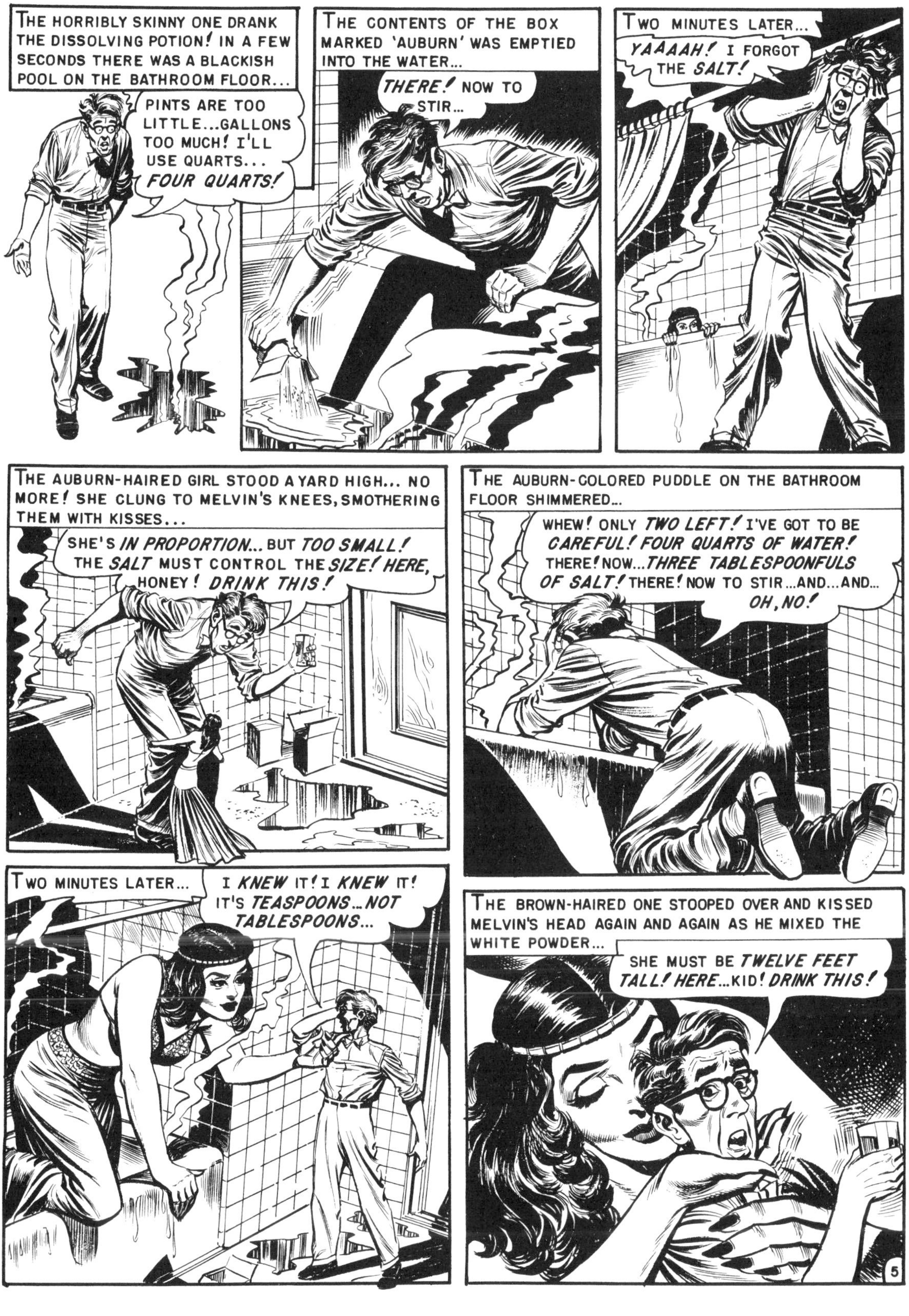
THE HORRIBLY SKINNY ONE DRANK THE DISSOLVING POTION! IN A FEW SECONDS THERE WAS A BLACKISH POOL ON THE BATHROOM FLOOR...
PINTS ARE TOO LITTLE...GALLONS TOO MUCH! I'LL USE QUARTS... FOUR QUARTS!
THE CONTENTS OF THE BOX MARKED 'AUBURN' WAS EMPTIED INTO THE WATER...
THERE! NOW TO STIR...
TWO MINUTES LATER...
YAAAAH! I FORGOT THE SALT!
THE AUBURN-HAIRED GIRL STOOD A YARD HIGH... NO MORE! SHE CLUNG TO MELVIN'S KNEES, SMOTHERING THEM WITH KISSES...
SHE'S IN PROPORTION... BUT TOO SMALL! THE SALT MUST CONTROL THE SIZE! HERE, HONEY! DRINK THIS!
THE AUBURN-COLORED PUDDLE ON THE BATHROOM FLOOR SHIMMERED...
WHEW! ONLY TWO LEFT! I'VE GOT TO BE CAREFUL! FOUR QUARTS OF WATER! THERE! NOW...THREE TABLESPOONFULS OF SALT! THERE! NOW TO STIR...AND...AND... OH, NO!
TWO MINUTES LATER...
I KNEW IT! I KNEW IT! IT'S TEASPOONS...NOT TABLESPOONS...
THE BROWN-HAIRED ONE STOOPED OVER AND KISSED MELVIN'S HEAD AGAIN AND AGAIN AS HE MIXED THE WHITE POWDER...
SHE MUST BE TWELVE FEET TALL! HERE...KID! DRINK THIS!
5

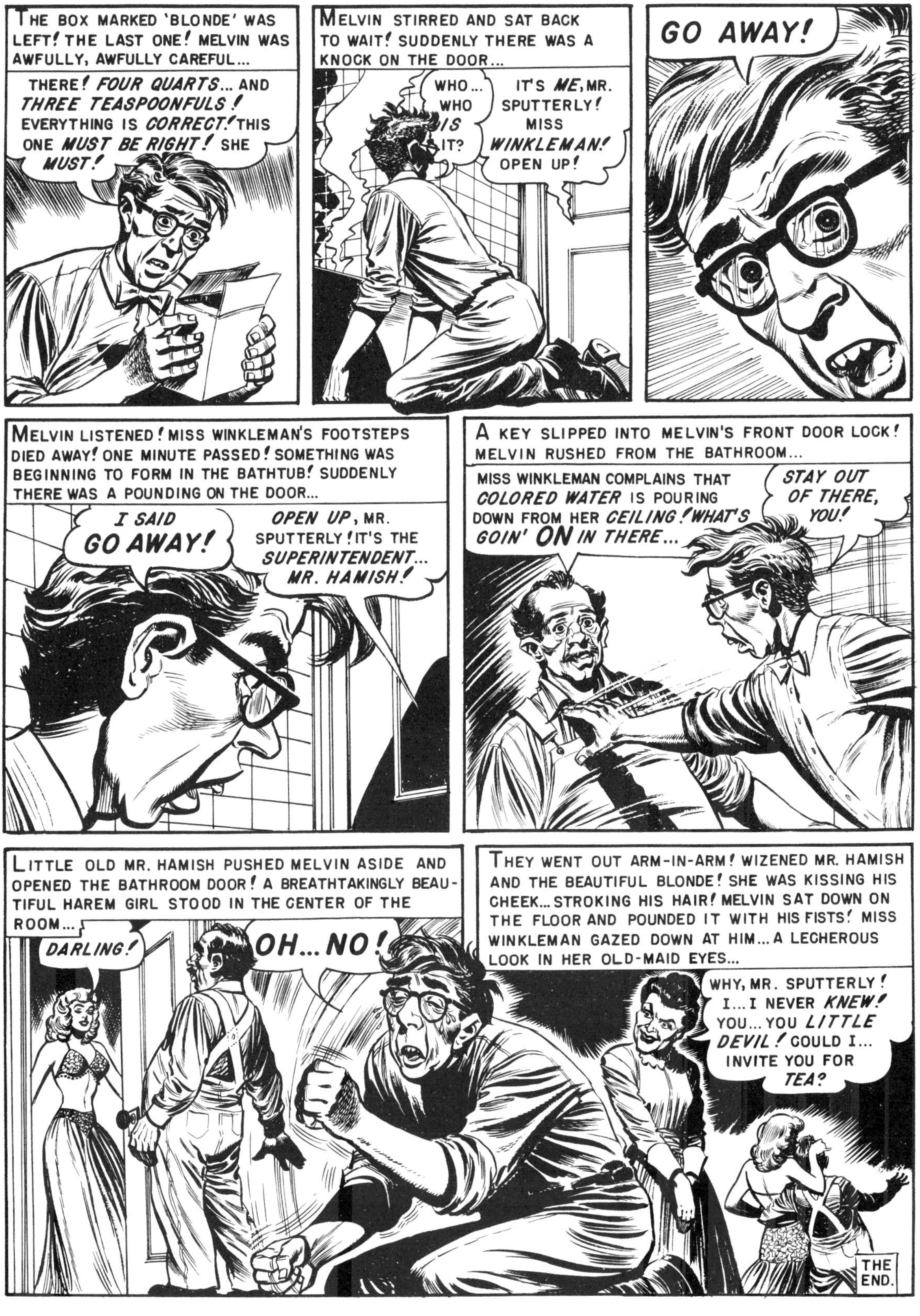
THE BOX MARKED 'BLONDE' WAS LEFT! THE LAST ONE! MELVIN WAS AWFULLY, AWFULLY CAREFUL...
THERE! FOUR QUARTS... AND THREE TEASPOONFULS! EVERYTHING IS CORRECT! THIS ONE MUST BE RIGHT! SHE MUST!
MELVIN STIRRED AND SAT BACK TO WAIT! SUDDENLY THERE WAS A KNOCK ON THE DOOR...
WHO... WHO IS IT?
IT'S ME, MR. SPUTTERLY! MISS WINKLEMAN! OPEN UP!
GO AWAY!
MELVIN LISTENED! MISS WINKLEMAN'S FOOTSTEPS DIED AWAY! ONE MINUTE PASSED! SOMETHING WAS BEGINNING TO FORM IN THE BATHTUB! SUDDENLY THERE WAS A POUNDING ON THE DOOR...
I SAID GO AWAY!
OPEN UP, MR. SPUTTERLY! IT'S THE SUPERINTENDENT... MR. HAMISH!
A KEY SLIPPED INTO MELVIN'S FRONT DOOR LOCK! MELVIN RUSHED FROM THE BATHROOM...
MISS WINKLEMAN COMPLAINS THAT COLORED WATER IS POURING DOWN FROM HER CEILING! WHAT'S GOIN' ON IN THERE...
STAY OUT OF THERE, YOU!
LITTLE OLD MR. HAMISH PUSHED MELVIN ASIDE AND OPENED THE BATHROOM DOOR! A BREATHTAKINGLY BEAUTIFUL HAREM GIRL STOOD IN THE CENTER OF THE ROOM...
DARLING!
OH... NO!
THEY WENT OUT ARM-IN-ARM! WIZENED MR. HAMISH AND THE BEAUTIFUL BLONDE! SHE WAS KISSING HIS CHEEK... STROKING HIS HAIR! MELVIN SAT DOWN ON THE FLOOR AND POUNDED IT WITH HIS FISTS! MISS WINKLEMAN GAZED DOWN AT HIM... A LECHEROUS LOOK IN HER OLD-MAID EYES...
WHY, MR. SPUTTERLY! I... I NEVER KNEW! YOU... YOU LITTLE DEVIL! COULD I... INVITE YOU FOR TEA?
THE END.

HE WHO WAITS!

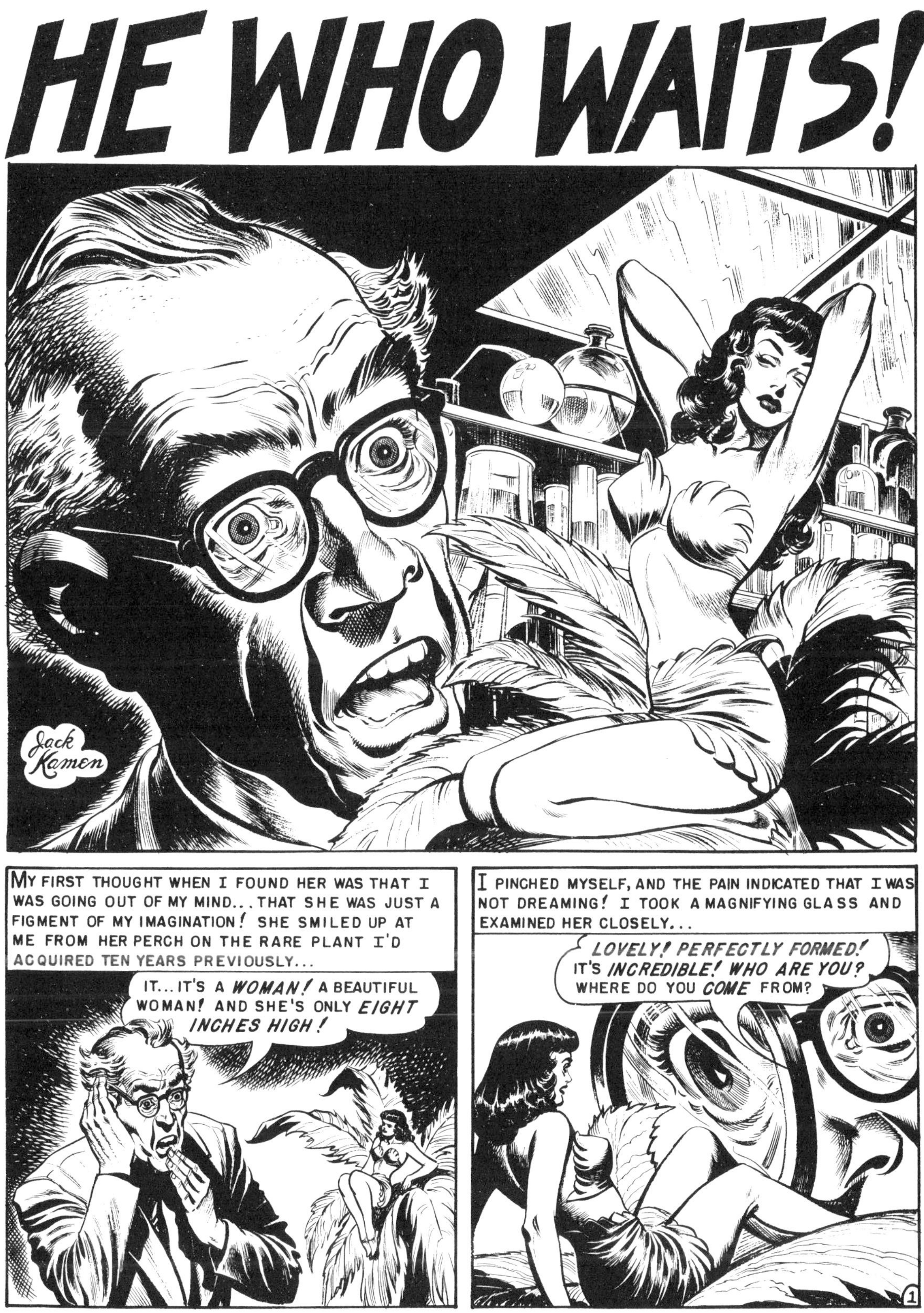

Jack Kamen
MY FIRST THOUGHT WHEN I FOUND HER WAS THAT I WAS GOING OUT OF MY MIND... THAT SHE WAS JUST A FIGMENT OF MY IMAGINATION! SHE SMILED UP AT ME FROM HER PERCH ON THE RARE PLANT I'D ACQUIRED TEN YEARS PREVIOUSLY...
IT... IT'S A WOMAN! A BEAUTIFUL WOMAN! AND SHE'S ONLY EIGHT INCHES HIGH!
I PINCHED MYSELF, AND THE PAIN INDICATED THAT I WAS NOT DREAMING! I TOOK A MAGNIFYING GLASS AND EXAMINED HER CLOSELY...
LOVELY! PERFECTLY FORMED! IT'S INCREDIBLE! WHO ARE YOU? WHERE DO YOU COME FROM?
1

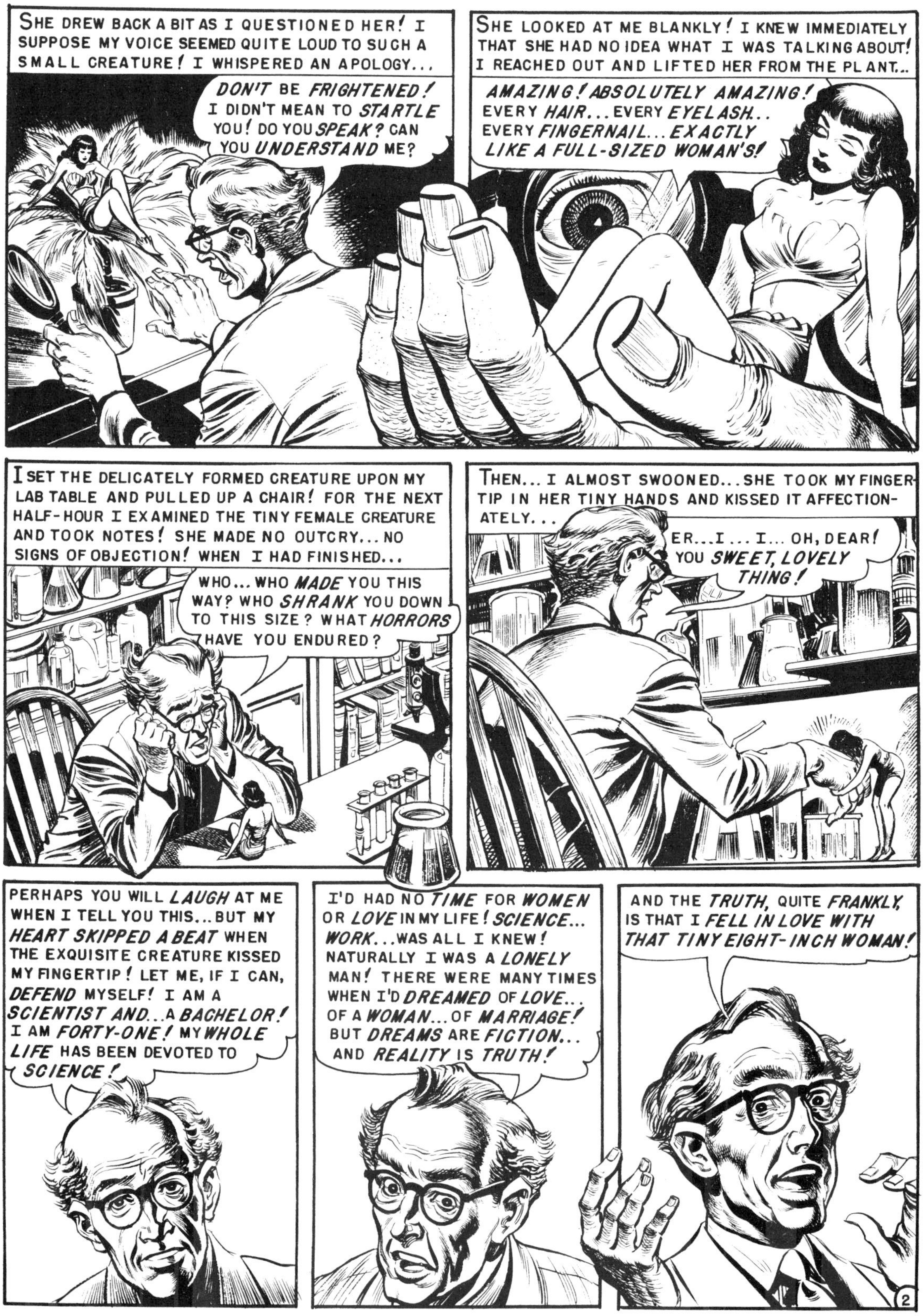
SHE DREW BACK A BIT AS I QUESTIONED HER! I SUPPOSE MY VOICE SEEMED QUITE LOUD TO SUCH A SMALL CREATURE! I WHISPERED AN APOLOGY...
DON'T BE FRIGHTENED! I DIDN'T MEAN TO STARTLE YOU! DO YOU SPEAK? CAN YOU UNDERSTAND ME?
SHE LOOKED AT ME BLANKLY! I KNEW IMMEDIATELY THAT SHE HAD NO IDEA WHAT I WAS TALKING ABOUT! I REACHED OUT AND LIFTED HER FROM THE PLANT...
AMAZING! ABSOLUTELY AMAZING! EVERY HAIR... EVERY EYELASH.. EVERY FINGERNAIL... EXACTLY LIKE A FULL-SIZED WOMAN'S!
I SET THE DELICATELY FORMED CREATURE UPON MY LAB TABLE AND PULLED UP A CHAIR! FOR THE NEXT HALF-HOUR I EXAMINED THE TINY FEMALE CREATURE AND TOOK NOTES! SHE MADE NO OUTCRY... NO SIGNS OF OBJECTION! WHEN I HAD FINISHED...
WHO... WHO MADE YOU THIS WAY? WHO SHRANK YOU DOWN TO THIS SIZE? WHAT HORRORS HAVE YOU ENDURED?
THEN... I ALMOST SWOONED... SHE TOOK MY FINGERTIP IN HER TINY HANDS AND KISSED IT AFFECTIONATELY...
ER... I... I... OH, DEAR! YOU SWEET, LOVELY THING!
PERHAPS YOU WILL LAUGH AT ME WHEN I TELL YOU THIS... BUT MY HEART SKIPPED A BEAT WHEN THE EXQUISITE CREATURE KISSED MY FINGERTIP! LET ME, IF I CAN, DEFEND MYSELF! I AM A SCIENTIST AND... A BACHELOR! I AM FORTY-ONE! MY WHOLE LIFE HAS BEEN DEVOTED TO SCIENCE!
I'D HAD NO TIME FOR WOMEN OR LOVE IN MY LIFE! SCIENCE... WORK... WAS ALL I KNEW! NATURALLY I WAS A LONELY MAN! THERE WERE MANY TIMES WHEN I'D DREAMED OF LOVE... OF A WOMAN... OF MARRIAGE! BUT DREAMS ARE FICTION... AND REALITY IS TRUTH!
AND THE TRUTH, QUITE FRANKLY, IS THAT I FELL IN LOVE WITH THAT TINY EIGHT-INCH WOMAN!
2

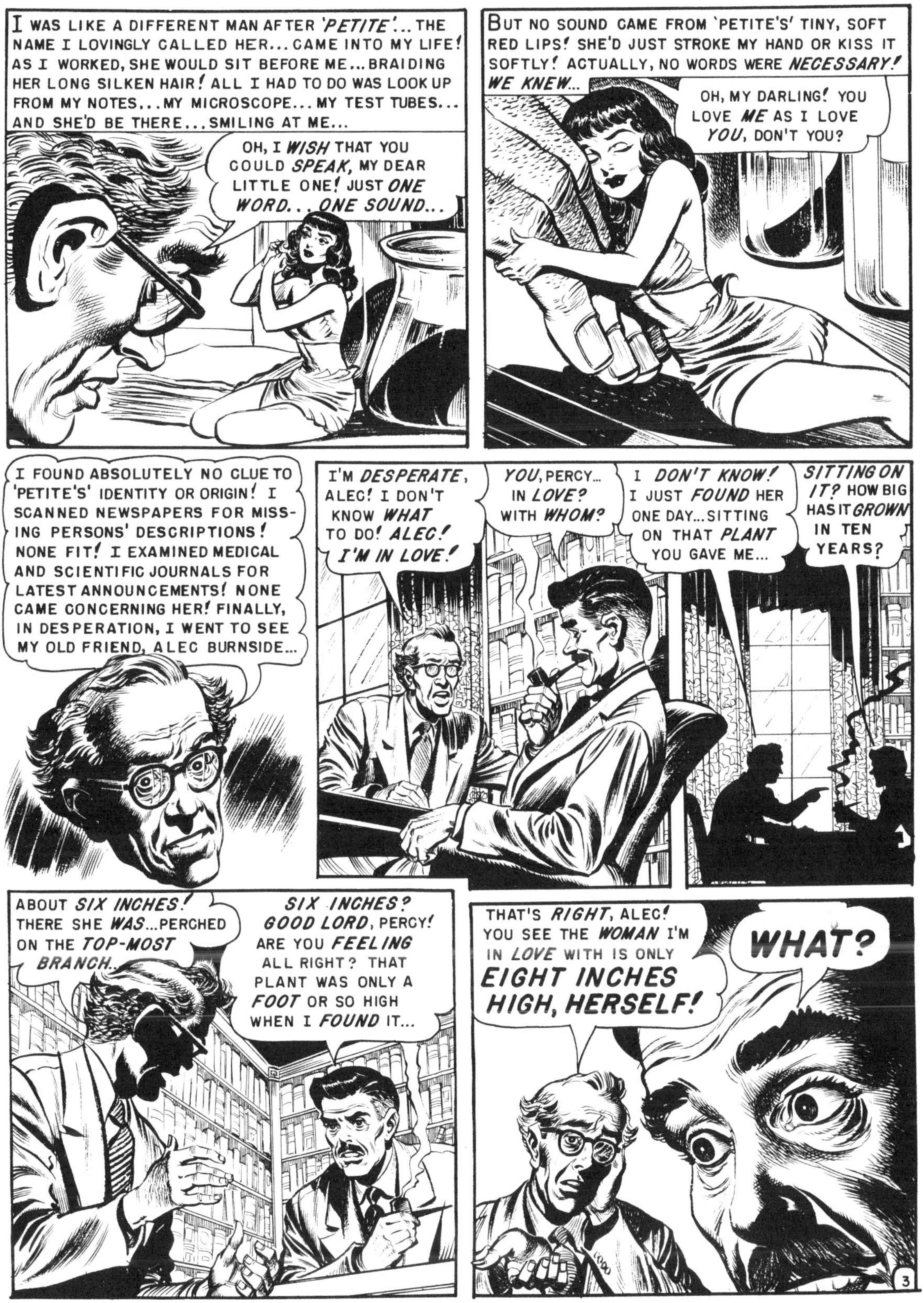
I WAS LIKE A DIFFERENT MAN AFTER 'PETITE'... THE NAME I LOVINGLY CALLED HER... CAME INTO MY LIFE! AS I WORKED, SHE WOULD SIT BEFORE ME... BRAIDING HER LONG SILKEN HAIR! ALL I HAD TO DO WAS LOOK UP FROM MY NOTES... MY MICROSCOPE... MY TEST TUBES... AND SHE'D BE THERE... SMILING AT ME...
OH, I WISH THAT YOU COULD SPEAK, MY DEAR LITTLE ONE! JUST ONE WORD... ONE SOUND...
BUT NO SOUND CAME FROM 'PETITE'S' TINY, SOFT RED LIPS! SHE'D JUST STROKE MY HAND OR KISS IT SOFTLY! ACTUALLY, NO WORDS WERE NECESSARY! WE KNEW...
OH, MY DARLING! YOU LOVE ME AS I LOVE YOU, DON'T YOU?
I FOUND ABSOLUTELY NO CLUE TO 'PETITE'S' IDENTITY OR ORIGIN! I SCANNED NEWSPAPERS FOR MISSING PERSONS' DESCRIPTIONS! NONE FIT! I EXAMINED MEDICAL AND SCIENTIFIC JOURNALS FOR LATEST ANNOUNCEMENTS! NONE CAME CONCERNING HER! FINALLY, IN DESPERATION, I WENT TO SEE MY OLD FRIEND, ALEC BURNSIDE...
I'M DESPERATE, ALEC! I DON'T KNOW WHAT TO DO! ALEC! I'M IN LOVE!
YOU, PERCY... IN LOVE? WITH WHOM?
I DON'T KNOW! I JUST FOUND HER ONE DAY... SITTING ON THAT PLANT YOU GAVE ME...
SITTING ON IT? HOW BIG HAS IT GROWN IN TEN YEARS?
ABOUT SIX INCHES! THERE SHE WAS... PERCHED ON THE TOP-MOST BRANCH...
SIX INCHES? GOOD LORD, PERCY! ARE YOU FEELING ALL RIGHT? THAT PLANT WAS ONLY A FOOT OR SO HIGH WHEN I FOUND IT...
THAT'S RIGHT, ALEC! YOU SEE THE WOMAN I'M IN LOVE WITH IS ONLY EIGHT INCHES HIGH, HERSELF!
WHAT?
3

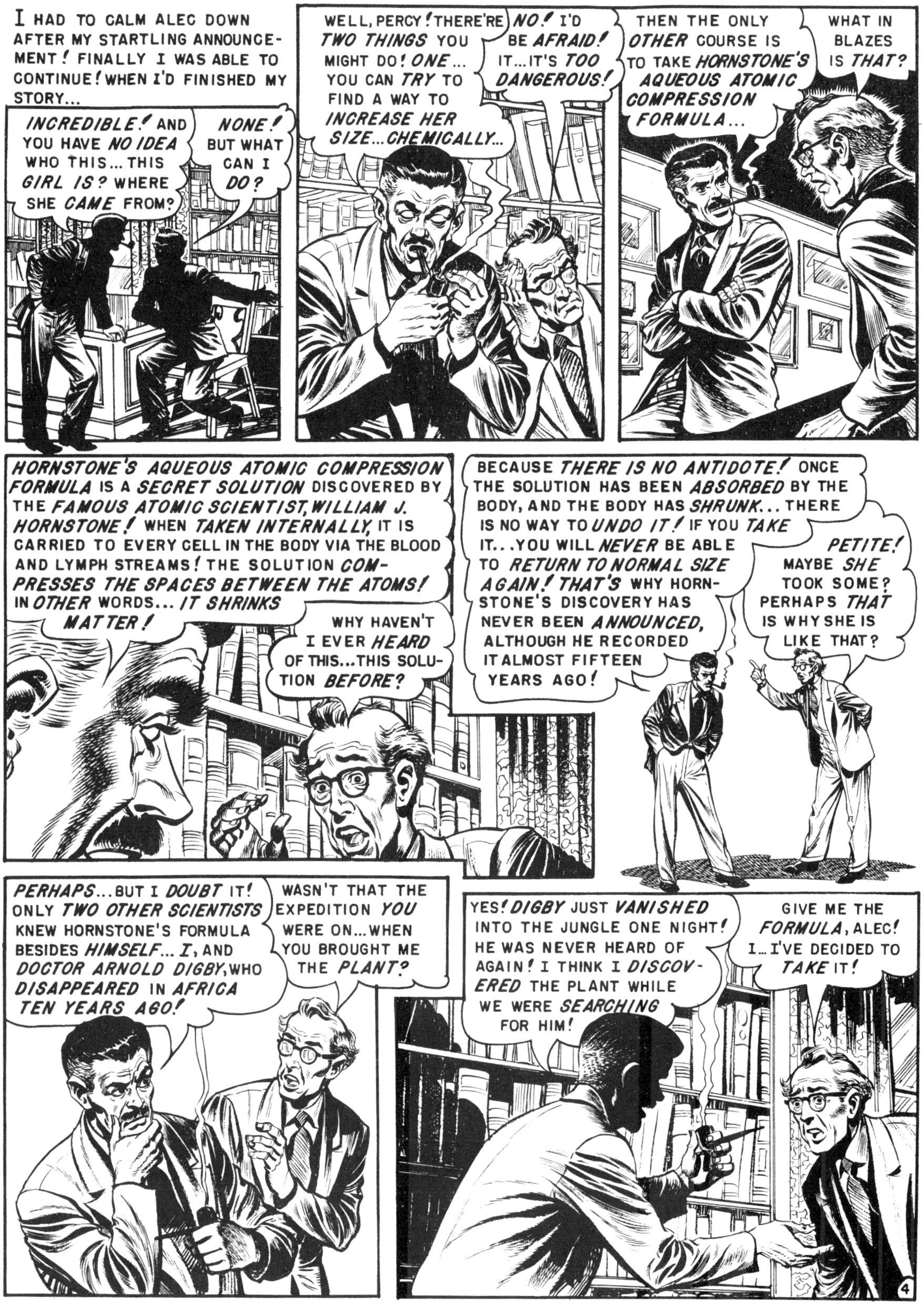
I HAD TO CALM ALEC DOWN AFTER MY STARTLING ANNOUNCEMENT! FINALLY I WAS ABLE TO CONTINUE! WHEN I'D FINISHED MY STORY...
INCREDIBLE! AND YOU HAVE NO IDEA WHO THIS... THIS GIRL IS? WHERE SHE CAME FROM?
NONE! BUT WHAT CAN I DO?
WELL, PERCY! THERE'RE TWO THINGS YOU MIGHT DO! ONE... YOU CAN TRY TO FIND A WAY TO INCREASE HER SIZE...CHEMICALLY...
NO! I'D BE AFRAID! IT...IT'S TOO DANGEROUS!
THEN THE ONLY OTHER COURSE IS TO TAKE HORNSTONE'S AQUEOUS ATOMIC COMPRESSION FORMULA...
WHAT IN BLAZES IS THAT?
HORNSTONE'S AQUEOUS ATOMIC COMPRESSION FORMULA IS A SECRET SOLUTION DISCOVERED BY THE FAMOUS ATOMIC SCIENTIST, WILLIAM J. HORNSTONE! WHEN TAKEN INTERNALLY, IT IS CARRIED TO EVERY CELL IN THE BODY VIA THE BLOOD AND LYMPH STREAMS! THE SOLUTION COMPRESSES THE SPACES BETWEEN THE ATOMS! IN OTHER WORDS... IT SHRINKS MATTER!
WHY HAVEN'T I EVER HEARD OF THIS...THIS SOLUTION BEFORE?
BECAUSE THERE IS NO ANTIDOTE! ONCE THE SOLUTION HAS BEEN ABSORBED BY THE BODY, AND THE BODY HAS SHRUNK... THERE IS NO WAY TO UNDO IT! IF YOU TAKE IT...YOU WILL NEVER BE ABLE TO RETURN TO NORMAL SIZE AGAIN! THAT'S WHY HORNSTONE'S DISCOVERY HAS NEVER BEEN ANNOUNCED, ALTHOUGH HE RECORDED IT ALMOST FIFTEEN YEARS AGO!
PETITE! MAYBE SHE TOOK SOME? PERHAPS THAT IS WHY SHE IS LIKE THAT?
PERHAPS...BUT I DOUBT IT! ONLY TWO OTHER SCIENTISTS KNEW HORNSTONE'S FORMULA BESIDES HIMSELF... I, AND DOCTOR ARNOLD DIGBY, WHO DISAPPEARED IN AFRICA TEN YEARS AGO!
WASN'T THAT THE EXPEDITION YOU WERE ON...WHEN YOU BROUGHT ME THE PLANT?
YES! DIGBY JUST VANISHED INTO THE JUNGLE ONE NIGHT! HE WAS NEVER HEARD OF AGAIN! I THINK I DISCOVERED THE PLANT WHILE WE WERE SEARCHING FOR HIM!
GIVE ME THE FORMULA, ALEC! I... I'VE DECIDED TO TAKE IT!
4

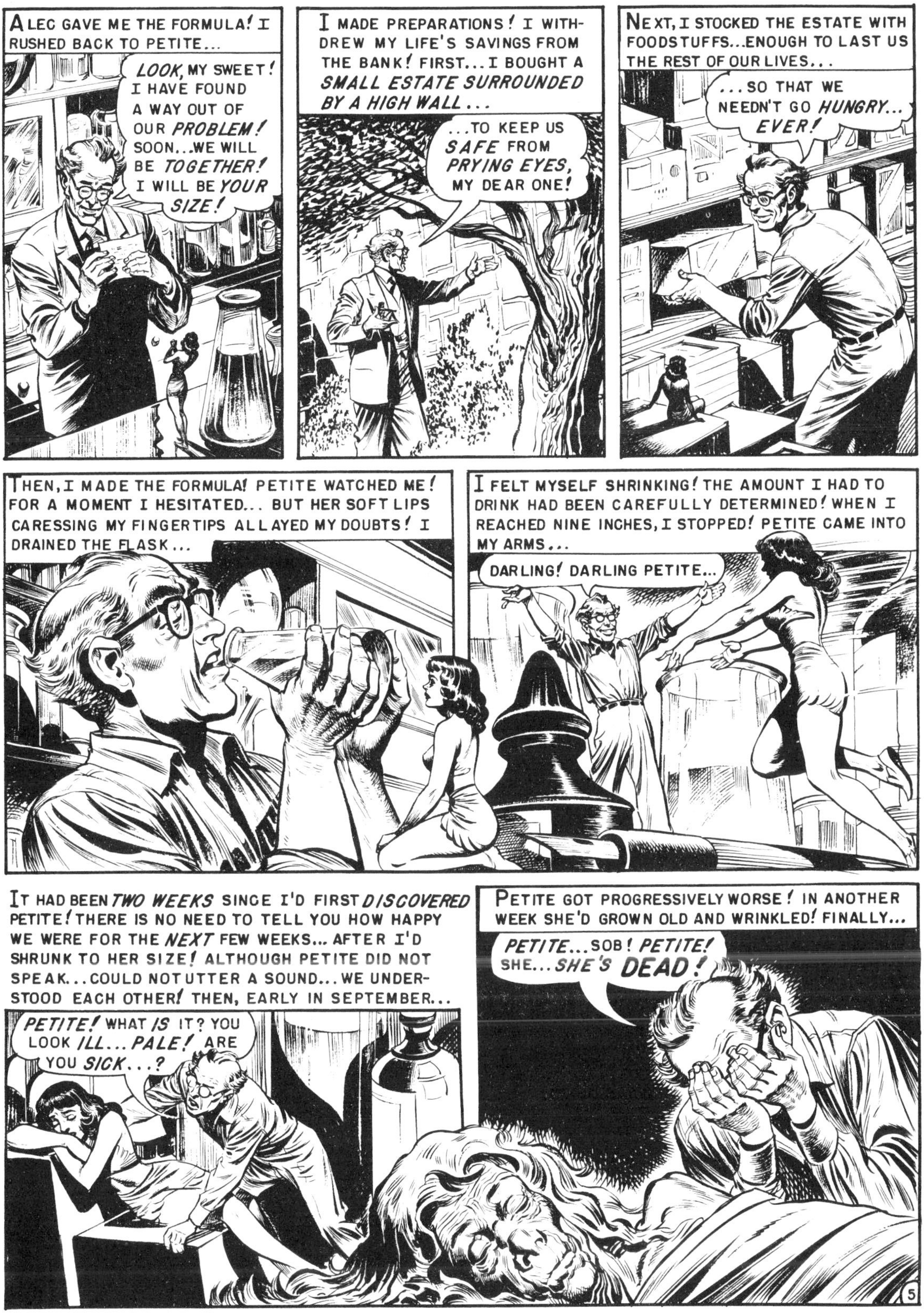
ALEC GAVE ME THE FORMULA! I RUSHED BACK TO PETITE...
LOOK, MY SWEET! I HAVE FOUND A WAY OUT OF OUR PROBLEM! SOON...WE WILL BE TOGETHER! I WILL BE YOUR SIZE!
I MADE PREPARATIONS! I WITH-DREW MY LIFE'S SAVINGS FROM THE BANK! FIRST... I BOUGHT A SMALL ESTATE SURROUNDED BY A HIGH WALL...
...TO KEEP US SAFE FROM PRYING EYES, MY DEAR ONE!
NEXT, I STOCKED THE ESTATE WITH FOODSTUFFS...ENOUGH TO LAST US THE REST OF OUR LIVES...
...SO THAT WE NEEDN'T GO HUNGRY... EVER!
THEN, I MADE THE FORMULA! PETITE WATCHED ME! FOR A MOMENT I HESITATED... BUT HER SOFT LIPS CARESSING MY FINGERTIPS ALLAYED MY DOUBTS! I DRAINED THE FLASK...
I FELT MYSELF SHRINKING! THE AMOUNT I HAD TO DRINK HAD BEEN CAREFULLY DETERMINED! WHEN I REACHED NINE INCHES, I STOPPED! PETITE CAME INTO MY ARMS...
DARLING! DARLING PETITE...
IT HAD BEEN TWO WEEKS SINCE I'D FIRST DISCOVERED PETITE! THERE IS NO NEED TO TELL YOU HOW HAPPY WE WERE FOR THE NEXT FEW WEEKS... AFTER I'D SHRUNK TO HER SIZE! ALTHOUGH PETITE DID NOT SPEAK...COULD NOT UTTER A SOUND...WE UNDER-STOOD EACH OTHER! THEN, EARLY IN SEPTEMBER...
PETITE! WHAT IS IT? YOU LOOK ILL... PALE! ARE YOU SICK...?
PETITE GOT PROGRESSIVELY WORSE! IN ANOTHER WEEK SHE'D GROWN OLD AND WRINKLED! FINALLY...
PETITE...SOB! PETITE! SHE...SHE'S DEAD!
5

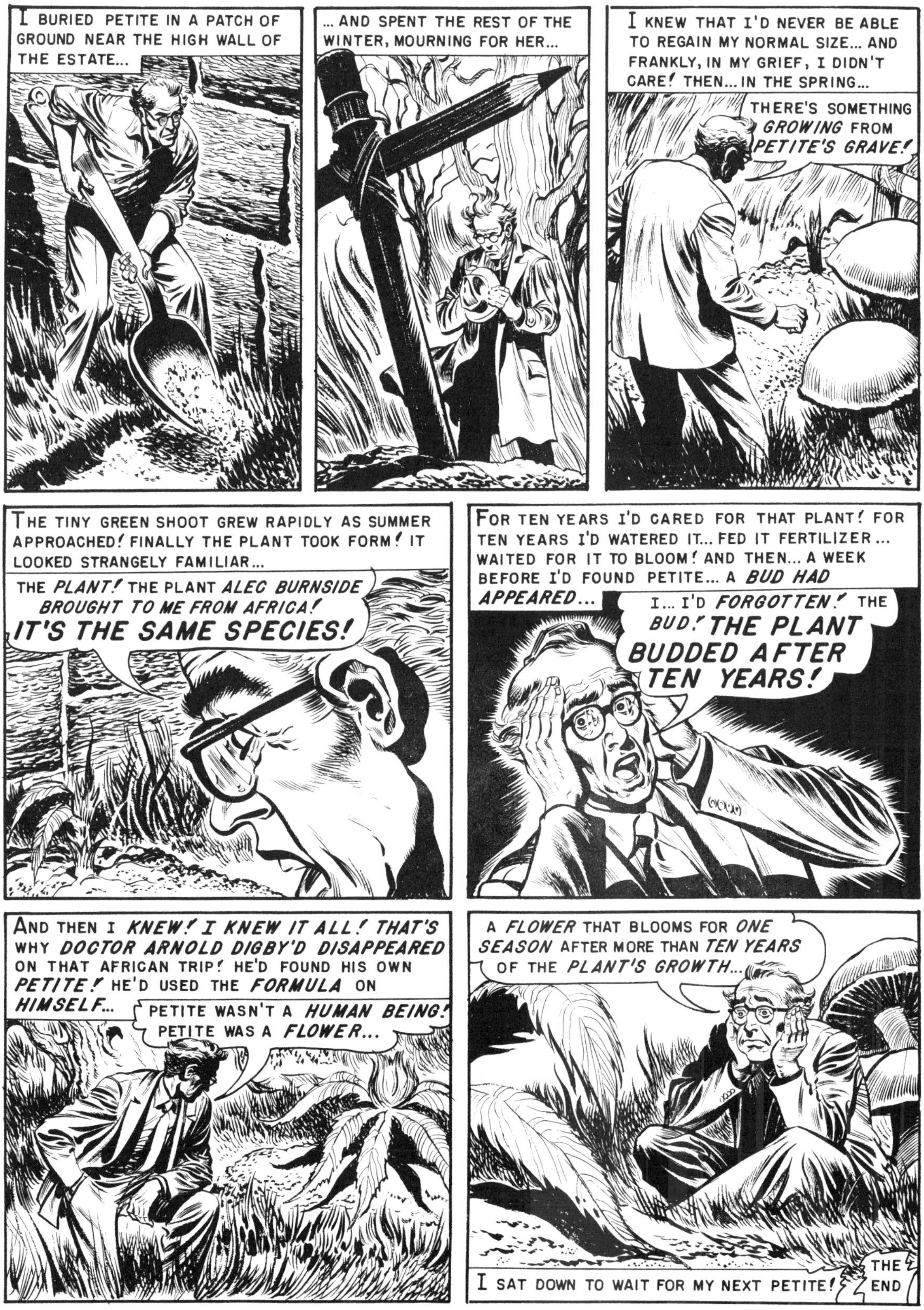
I BURIED PETITE IN A PATCH OF GROUND NEAR THE HIGH WALL OF THE ESTATE...
... AND SPENT THE REST OF THE WINTER, MOURNING FOR HER...
I KNEW THAT I'D NEVER BE ABLE TO REGAIN MY NORMAL SIZE... AND FRANKLY, IN MY GRIEF, I DIDN'T CARE! THEN... IN THE SPRING...
THERE'S SOMETHING GROWING FROM PETITE'S GRAVE!
THE TINY GREEN SHOOT GREW RAPIDLY AS SUMMER APPROACHED! FINALLY THE PLANT TOOK FORM! IT LOOKED STRANGELY FAMILIAR...
THE PLANT! THE PLANT ALEC BURNSIDE BROUGHT TO ME FROM AFRICA! IT'S THE SAME SPECIES!
FOR TEN YEARS I'D CARED FOR THAT PLANT! FOR TEN YEARS I'D WATERED IT... FED IT FERTILIZER... WAITED FOR IT TO BLOOM! AND THEN... A WEEK BEFORE I'D FOUND PETITE... A BUD HAD APPEARED...
I... I'D FORGOTTEN! THE BUD! THE PLANT BUDDED AFTER TEN YEARS!
AND THEN I KNEW! I KNEW IT ALL! THAT'S WHY DOCTOR ARNOLD DIGBY'D DISAPPEARED ON THAT AFRICAN TRIP! HE'D FOUND HIS OWN PETITE! HE'D USED THE FORMULA ON HIMSELF...
PETITE WASN'T A HUMAN BEING! PETITE WAS A FLOWER...
A FLOWER THAT BLOOMS FOR ONE SEASON AFTER MORE THAN TEN YEARS OF THE PLANT'S GROWTH...
I SAT DOWN TO WAIT FOR MY NEXT PETITE!
THE END

GIVEN THE HEIR!

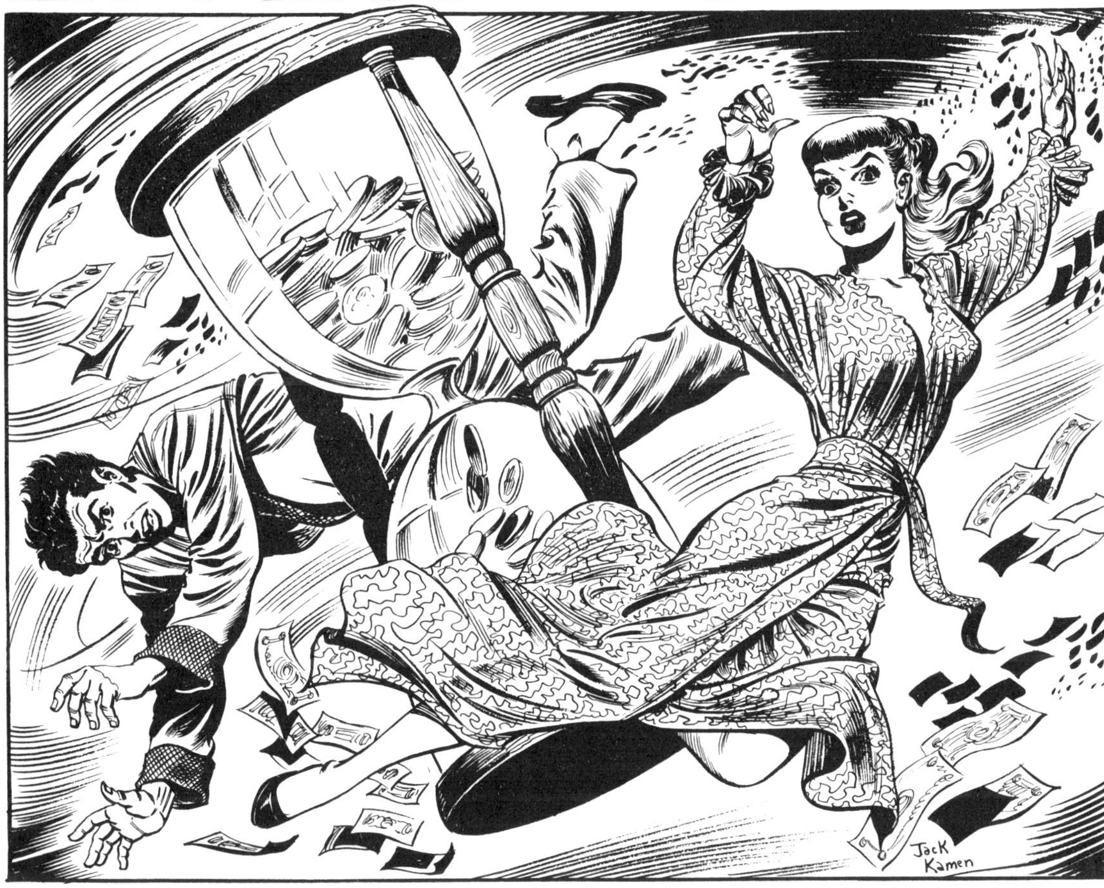

Jack Kamen

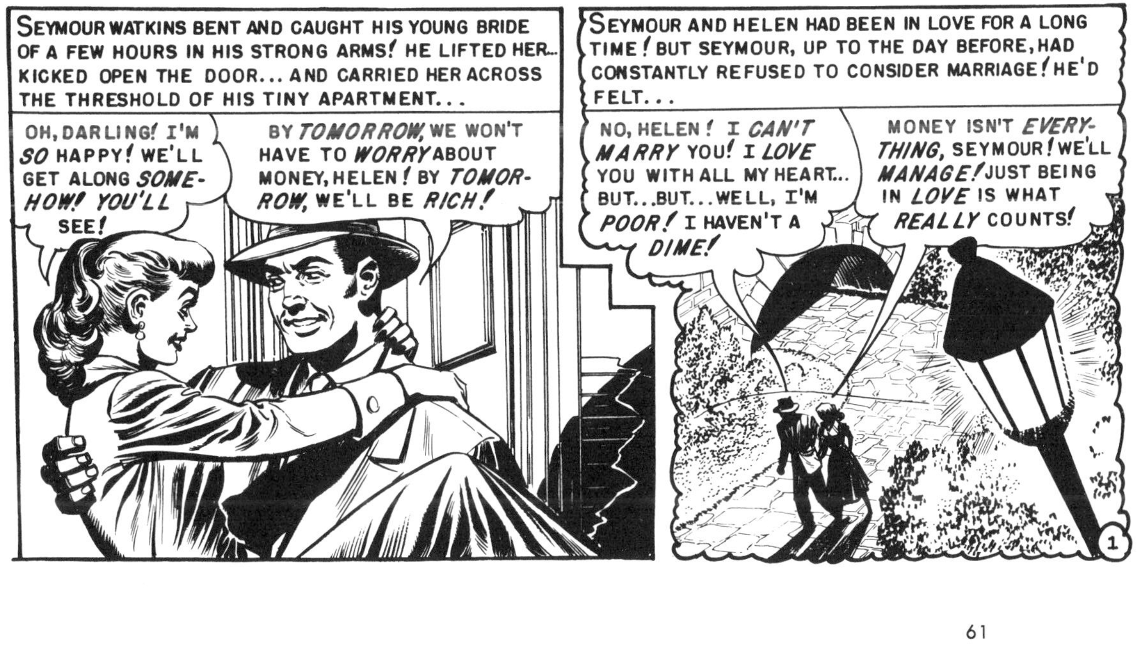

SEYMOUR WATKINS BENT AND CAUGHT HIS YOUNG BRIDE OF A FEW HOURS IN HIS STRONG ARMS! HE LIFTED HER... KICKED OPEN THE DOOR... AND CARRIED HER ACROSS THE THRESHOLD OF HIS TINY APARTMENT...
OH, DARLING! I'M SO HAPPY! WE'LL GET ALONG SOMEHOW! YOU'LL SEE!
BY TOMORROW, WE WON'T HAVE TO WORRY ABOUT MONEY, HELEN! BY TOMORROW, WE'LL BE RICH!
SEYMOUR AND HELEN HAD BEEN IN LOVE FOR A LONG TIME! BUT SEYMOUR, UP TO THE DAY BEFORE, HAD CONSTANTLY REFUSED TO CONSIDER MARRIAGE! HE'D FELT...
NO, HELEN! I CAN'T MARRY YOU! I LOVE YOU WITH ALL MY HEART... BUT...BUT...WELL, I'M POOR! I HAVEN'T A DIME!
MONEY ISN'T EVERYTHING, SEYMOUR! WE'LL MANAGE! JUST BEING IN LOVE IS WHAT REALLY COUNTS!
1

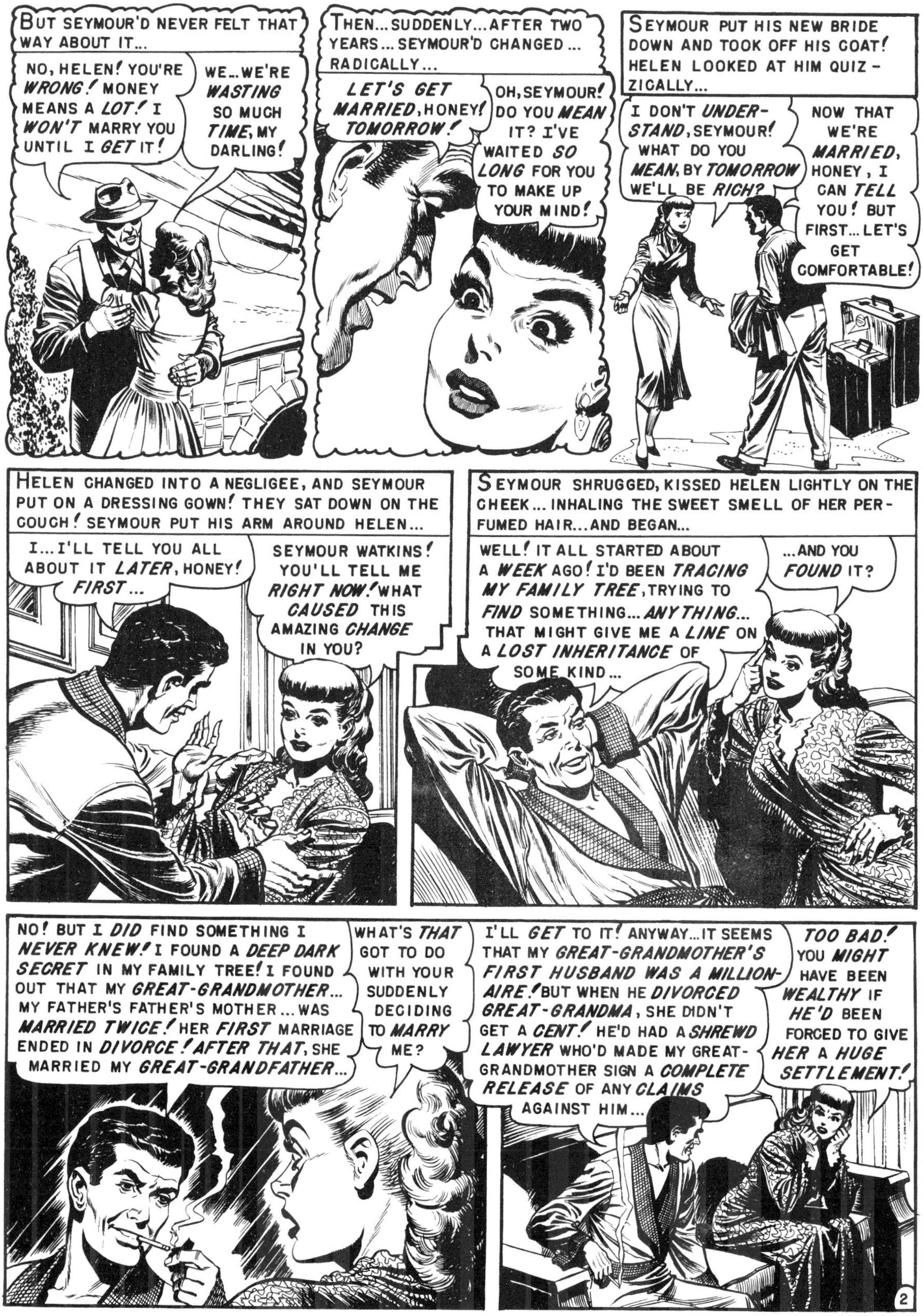
BUT SEYMOUR'D NEVER FELT THAT WAY ABOUT IT...
NO, HELEN! YOU'RE WRONG! MONEY MEANS A LOT! I WON'T MARRY YOU UNTIL I GET IT!
WE...WE'RE WASTING SO MUCH TIME, MY DARLING!
THEN...SUDDENLY...AFTER TWO YEARS... SEYMOUR'D CHANGED... RADICALLY...
LET'S GET MARRIED, HONEY! TOMORROW!
OH, SEYMOUR! DO YOU MEAN IT? I'VE WAITED SO LONG FOR YOU TO MAKE UP YOUR MIND!
SEYMOUR PUT HIS NEW BRIDE DOWN AND TOOK OFF HIS COAT! HELEN LOOKED AT HIM QUIZ-ZICALLY...
I DON'T UNDERSTAND, SEYMOUR! WHAT DO YOU MEAN, BY TOMORROW WE'LL BE RICH?
NOW THAT WE'RE MARRIED, HONEY, I CAN TELL YOU! BUT FIRST... LET'S GET COMFORTABLE!
HELEN CHANGED INTO A NEGLIGEE, AND SEYMOUR PUT ON A DRESSING GOWN! THEY SAT DOWN ON THE COUCH! SEYMOUR PUT HIS ARM AROUND HELEN...
I... I'LL TELL YOU ALL ABOUT IT LATER, HONEY! FIRST...
SEYMOUR WATKINS! YOU'LL TELL ME RIGHT NOW! WHAT CAUSED THIS AMAZING CHANGE IN YOU?
SEYMOUR SHRUGGED, KISSED HELEN LIGHTLY ON THE CHEEK... INHALING THE SWEET SMELL OF HER PER-FUMED HAIR...AND BEGAN...
WELL! IT ALL STARTED ABOUT A WEEK AGO! I'D BEEN TRACING MY FAMILY TREE, TRYING TO FIND SOMETHING... ANYTHING... THAT MIGHT GIVE ME A LINE ON A LOST INHERITANCE OF SOME KIND...
...AND YOU FOUND IT?
NO! BUT I DID FIND SOMETHING I NEVER KNEW! I FOUND A DEEP DARK SECRET IN MY FAMILY TREE! I FOUND OUT THAT MY GREAT-GRANDMOTHER... MY FATHER'S FATHER'S MOTHER... WAS MARRIED TWICE! HER FIRST MARRIAGE ENDED IN DIVORCE! AFTER THAT, SHE MARRIED MY GREAT-GRANDFATHER...
WHAT'S THAT GOT TO DO WITH YOUR SUDDENLY DECIDING TO MARRY ME?
I'LL GET TO IT! ANYWAY... IT SEEMS THAT MY GREAT-GRANDMOTHER'S FIRST HUSBAND WAS A MILLION-AIRE! BUT WHEN HE DIVORCED GREAT-GRANDMA, SHE DIDN'T GET A CENT! HE'D HAD A SHREWD LAWYER WHO'D MADE MY GREAT-GRANDMOTHER SIGN A COMPLETE RELEASE OF ANY CLAIMS AGAINST HIM...
TOO BAD! YOU MIGHT HAVE BEEN WEALTHY IF HE'D BEEN FORCED TO GIVE HER A HUGE SETTLEMENT!
2

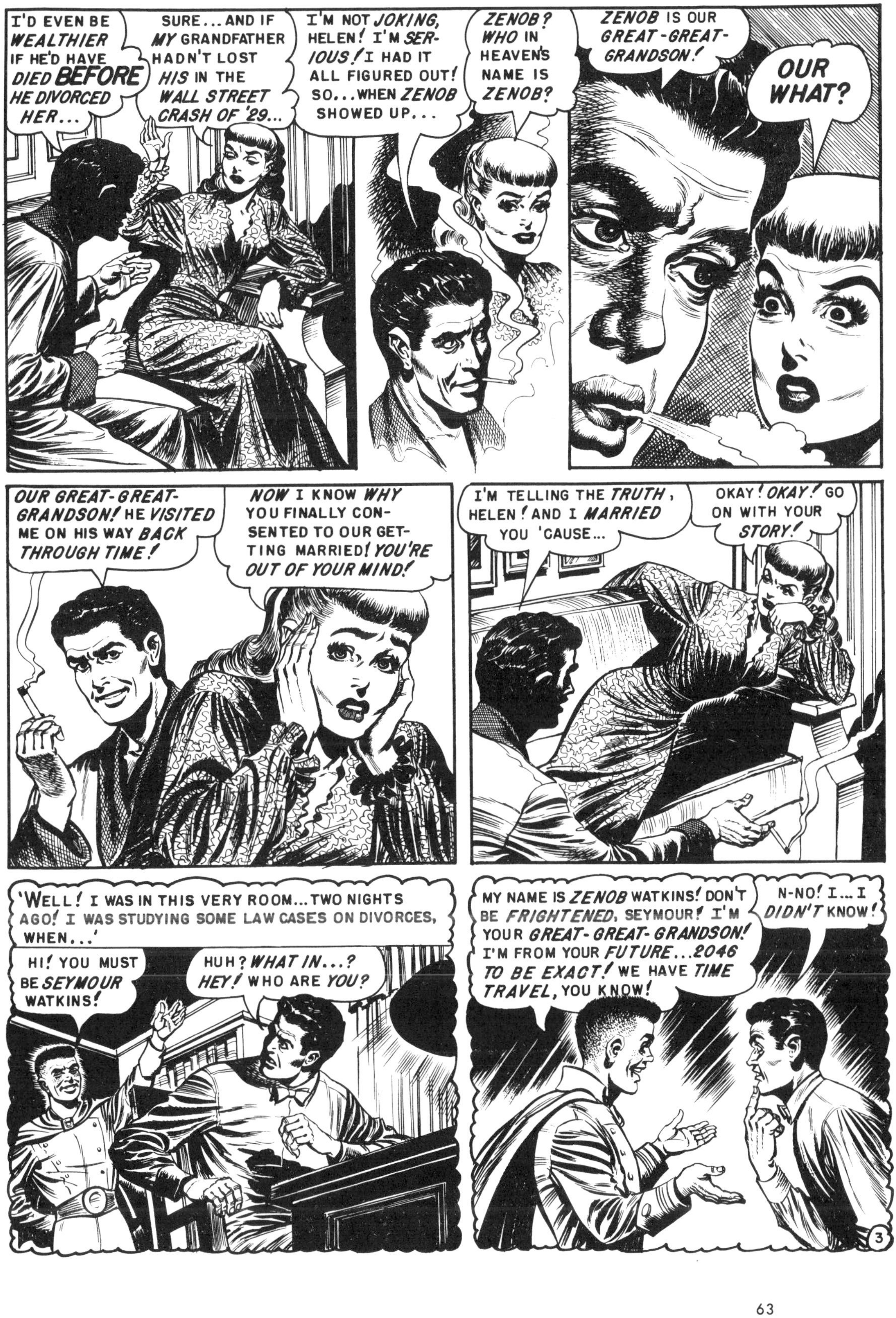
I'D EVEN BE WEALTHIER IF HE'D HAVE DIED BEFORE HE DIVORCED HER...
SURE... AND IF MY GRANDFATHER HADN'T LOST HIS IN THE WALL STREET CRASH OF '29...
I'M NOT JOKING, HELEN! I'M SERIOUS! I HAD IT ALL FIGURED OUT! SO... WHEN ZENOB SHOWED UP...
ZENOB? WHO IN HEAVEN'S NAME IS ZENOB?
ZENOB IS OUR GREAT-GREAT-GRANDSON!
OUR WHAT?
OUR GREAT-GREAT-GRANDSON! HE VISITED ME ON HIS WAY BACK THROUGH TIME!
NOW I KNOW WHY YOU FINALLY CONSENTED TO OUR GETTING MARRIED! YOU'RE OUT OF YOUR MIND!
I'M TELLING THE TRUTH, HELEN! AND I MARRIED YOU 'CAUSE...
OKAY! OKAY! GO ON WITH YOUR STORY!
'WELL! I WAS IN THIS VERY ROOM... TWO NIGHTS AGO! I WAS STUDYING SOME LAW CASES ON DIVORCES, WHEN...'
HI! YOU MUST BE SEYMOUR WATKINS!
HUH? WHAT IN...? HEY! WHO ARE YOU?
MY NAME IS ZENOB WATKINS! DON'T BE FRIGHTENED, SEYMOUR! I'M YOUR GREAT-GREAT-GRANDSON! I'M FROM YOUR FUTURE... 2046 TO BE EXACT! WE HAVE TIME TRAVEL, YOU KNOW!
N-NO! I... I DIDN'T KNOW!
3

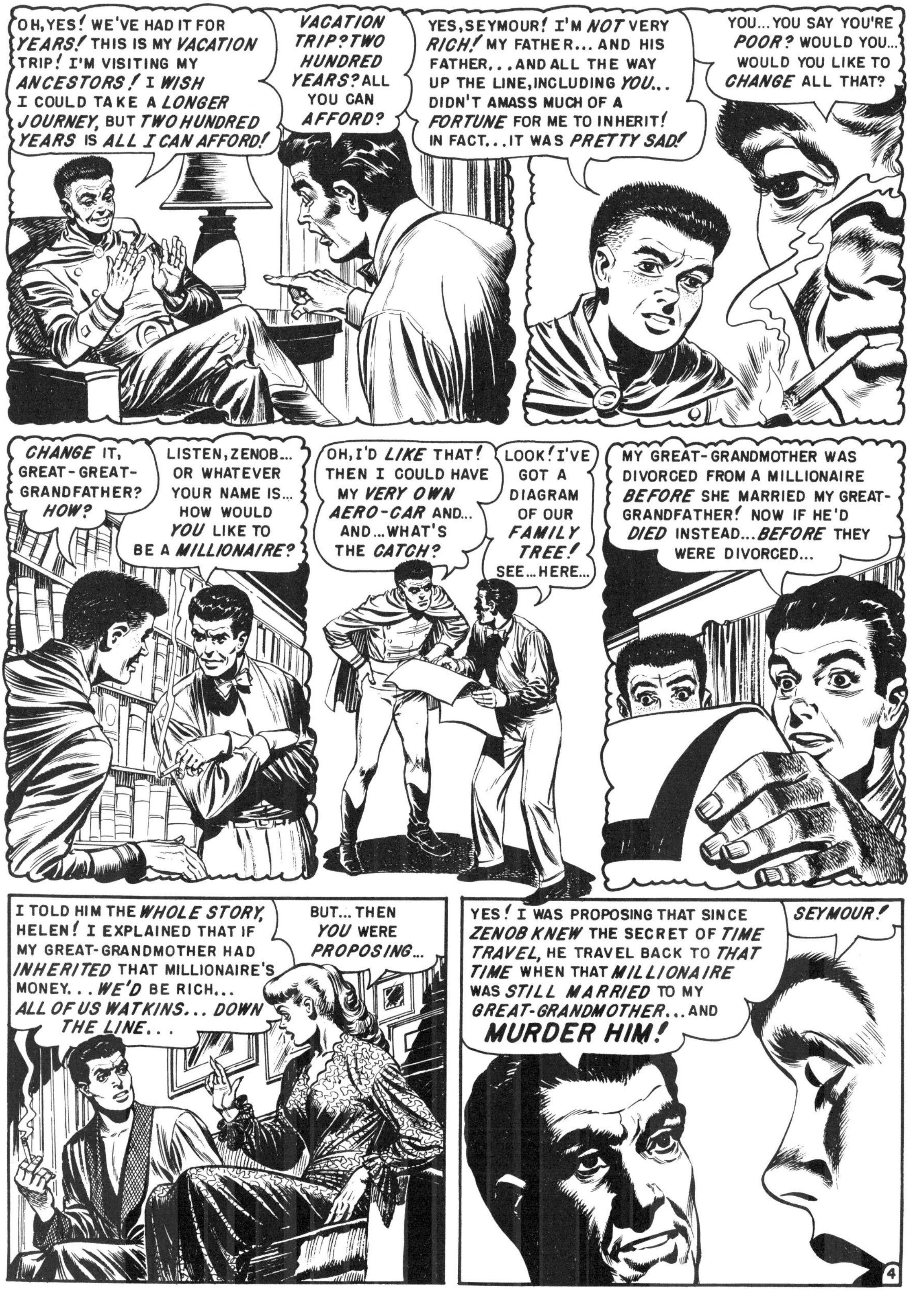
OH, YES! WE'VE HAD IT FOR YEARS! THIS IS MY VACATION TRIP! I'M VISITING MY ANCESTORS! I WISH I COULD TAKE A LONGER JOURNEY, BUT TWO HUNDRED YEARS IS ALL I CAN AFFORD!
VACATION TRIP? TWO HUNDRED YEARS? ALL YOU CAN AFFORD?
YES, SEYMOUR! I'M NOT VERY RICH! MY FATHER... AND HIS FATHER... AND ALL THE WAY UP THE LINE, INCLUDING YOU... DIDN'T AMASS MUCH OF A FORTUNE FOR ME TO INHERIT! IN FACT... IT WAS PRETTY SAD!
YOU... YOU SAY YOU'RE POOR? WOULD YOU... WOULD YOU LIKE TO CHANGE ALL THAT?
CHANGE IT, GREAT-GREAT-GRANDFATHER? HOW?
LISTEN, ZENOB... OR WHATEVER YOUR NAME IS... HOW WOULD YOU LIKE TO BE A MILLIONAIRE?
OH, I'D LIKE THAT! THEN I COULD HAVE MY VERY OWN AERO-CAR AND... AND... WHAT'S THE CATCH?
LOOK! I'VE GOT A DIAGRAM OF OUR FAMILY TREE! SEE... HERE...
MY GREAT-GRANDMOTHER WAS DIVORCED FROM A MILLIONAIRE BEFORE SHE MARRIED MY GREAT-GRANDFATHER! NOW IF HE'D DIED INSTEAD... BEFORE THEY WERE DIVORCED...
I TOLD HIM THE WHOLE STORY, HELEN! I EXPLAINED THAT IF MY GREAT-GRANDMOTHER HAD INHERITED THAT MILLIONAIRE'S MONEY... WE'D BE RICH... ALL OF US WATKINS... DOWN THE LINE...
BUT... THEN YOU WERE PROPOSING...
YES! I WAS PROPOSING THAT SINCE ZENOB KNEW THE SECRET OF TIME TRAVEL, HE TRAVEL BACK TO THAT TIME WHEN THAT MILLIONAIRE WAS STILL MARRIED TO MY GREAT-GRANDMOTHER... AND MURDER HIM!
SEYMOUR!
4

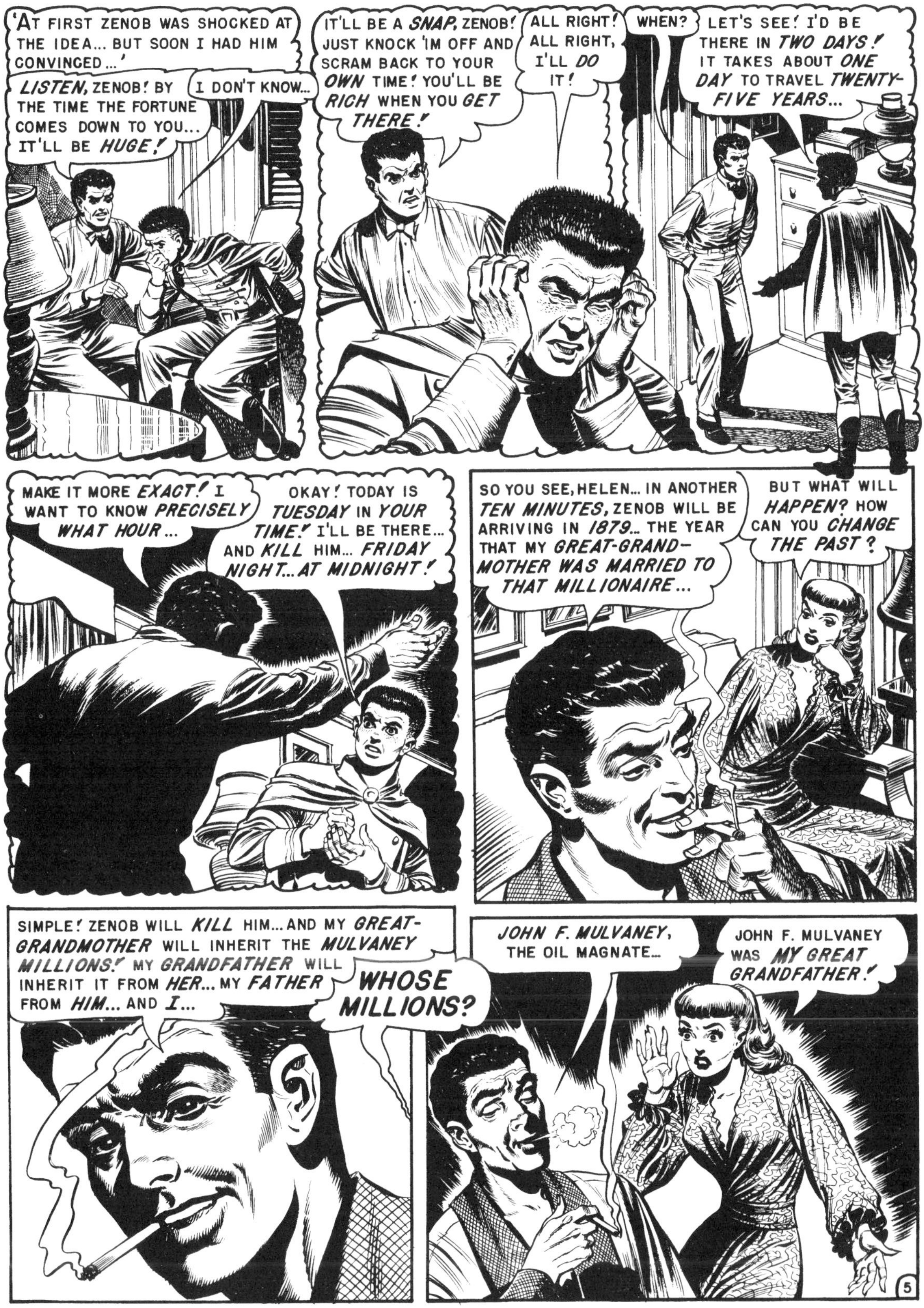
'AT FIRST ZENOB WAS SHOCKED AT THE IDEA... BUT SOON I HAD HIM CONVINCED...'
LISTEN, ZENOB! BY THE TIME THE FORTUNE COMES DOWN TO YOU... IT'LL BE HUGE!
I DON'T KNOW...
IT'LL BE A SNAP, ZENOB! JUST KNOCK 'IM OFF AND SCRAM BACK TO YOUR OWN TIME! YOU'LL BE RICH WHEN YOU GET THERE!
ALL RIGHT! ALL RIGHT, I'LL DO IT!
WHEN?
LET'S SEE! I'D BE THERE IN TWO DAYS! IT TAKES ABOUT ONE DAY TO TRAVEL TWENTY-FIVE YEARS...
MAKE IT MORE EXACT! I WANT TO KNOW PRECISELY WHAT HOUR...
OKAY! TODAY IS TUESDAY IN YOUR TIME! I'LL BE THERE... AND KILL HIM... FRIDAY NIGHT... AT MIDNIGHT!
SO YOU SEE, HELEN... IN ANOTHER TEN MINUTES, ZENOB WILL BE ARRIVING IN 1879... THE YEAR THAT MY GREAT-GRANDMOTHER WAS MARRIED TO THAT MILLIONAIRE...
BUT WHAT WILL HAPPEN? HOW CAN YOU CHANGE THE PAST?
SIMPLE! ZENOB WILL KILL HIM... AND MY GREAT-GRANDMOTHER WILL INHERIT THE MULVANEY MILLIONS! MY GRANDFATHER WILL INHERIT IT FROM HER... MY FATHER FROM HIM... AND I...
WHOSE MILLIONS?
JOHN F. MULVANEY, THE OIL MAGNATE...
JOHN F. MULVANEY WAS MY GREAT GRANDFATHER!
5

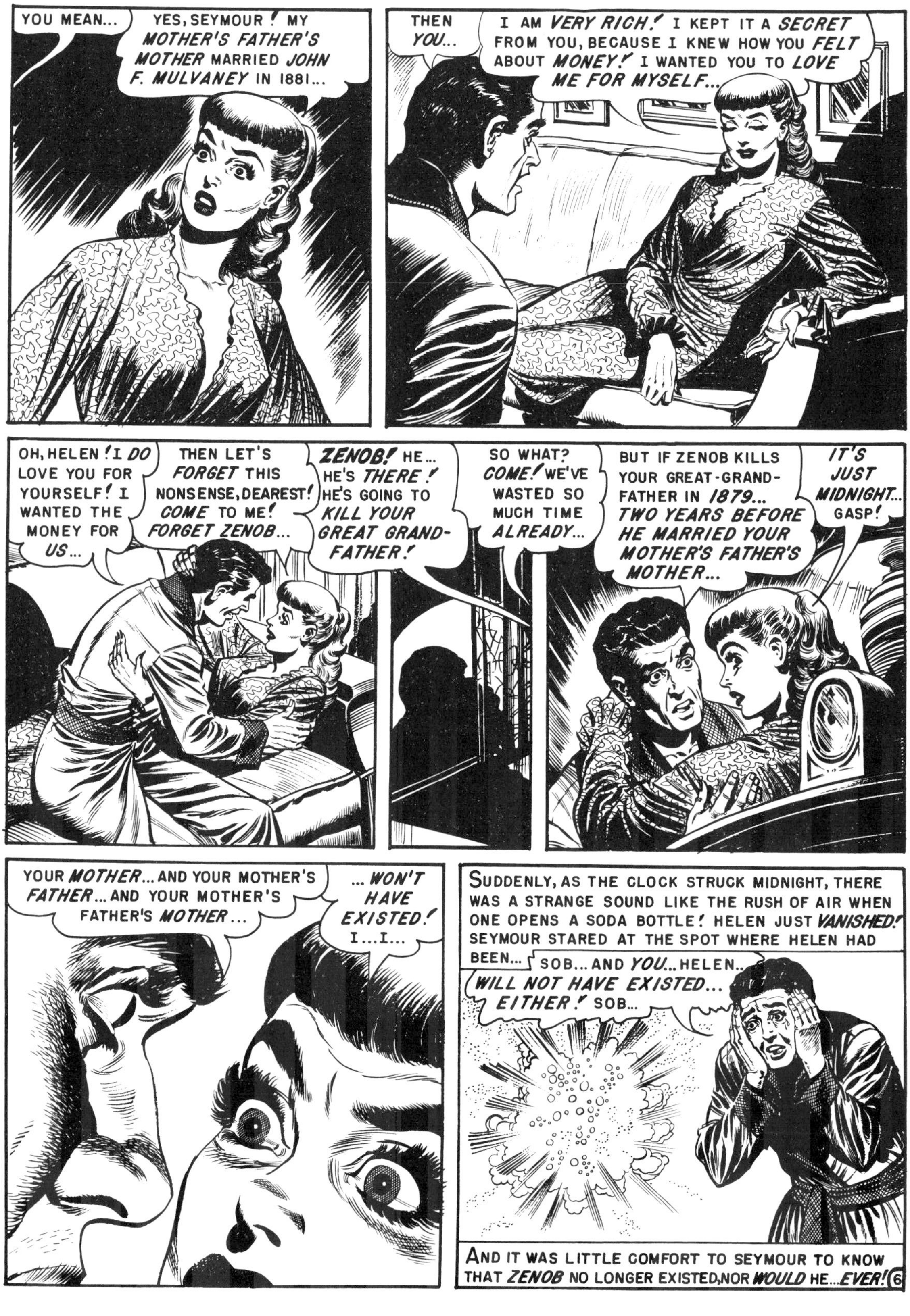
YOU MEAN...
YES, SEYMOUR! MY MOTHER'S FATHER'S MOTHER MARRIED JOHN F. MULVANEY IN 1881...
THEN YOU...
I AM VERY RICH! I KEPT IT A SECRET FROM YOU, BECAUSE I KNEW HOW YOU FELT ABOUT MONEY! I WANTED YOU TO LOVE ME FOR MYSELF...
OH, HELEN! I DO LOVE YOU FOR YOURSELF! I WANTED THE MONEY FOR US...
THEN LET'S FORGET THIS NONSENSE, DEAREST! COME TO ME! FORGET ZENOB...
ZENOB! HE... HE'S THERE! HE'S GOING TO KILL YOUR GREAT GRAND-FATHER!
SO WHAT? COME! WE'VE WASTED SO MUCH TIME ALREADY...
BUT IF ZENOB KILLS YOUR GREAT-GRAND-FATHER IN 1879... TWO YEARS BEFORE HE MARRIED YOUR MOTHER'S FATHER'S MOTHER...
IT'S JUST MIDNIGHT... GASP!
YOUR MOTHER... AND YOUR MOTHER'S FATHER... AND YOUR MOTHER'S FATHER'S MOTHER...
...WON'T HAVE EXISTED! I...I...
SUDDENLY, AS THE CLOCK STRUCK MIDNIGHT, THERE WAS A STRANGE SOUND LIKE THE RUSH OF AIR WHEN ONE OPENS A SODA BOTTLE! HELEN JUST VANISHED! SEYMOUR STARED AT THE SPOT WHERE HELEN HAD BEEN...
SOB... AND YOU... HELEN... WILL NOT HAVE EXISTED... EITHER! SOB...
AND IT WAS LITTLE COMFORT TO SEYMOUR TO KNOW THAT ZENOB NO LONGER EXISTED, NOR WOULD HE... EVER!
6

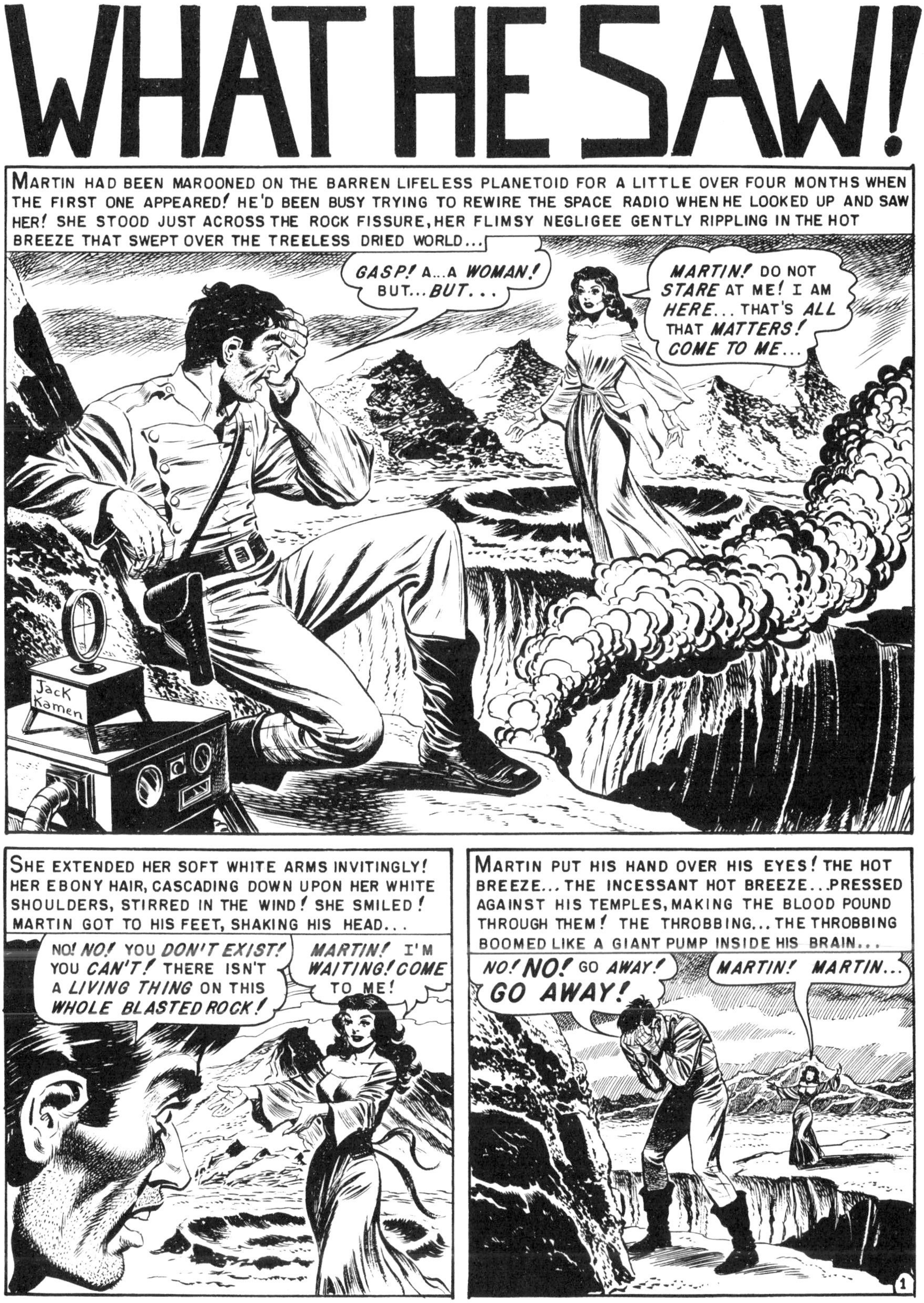
WHAT HE SAW!
MARTIN HAD BEEN MAROONED ON THE BARREN LIFELESS PLANETOID FOR A LITTLE OVER FOUR MONTHS WHEN THE FIRST ONE APPEARED! HE'D BEEN BUSY TRYING TO REWIRE THE SPACE RADIO WHEN HE LOOKED UP AND SAW HER! SHE STOOD JUST ACROSS THE ROCK FISSURE, HER FLIMSY NEGLIGEE GENTLY RIPPLING IN THE HOT BREEZE THAT SWEPT OVER THE TREELESS DRIED WORLD...
GASP! A...A WOMAN! BUT...BUT...
MARTIN! DO NOT STARE AT ME! I AM HERE... THAT'S ALL THAT MATTERS! COME TO ME...
Jack Kamen
SHE EXTENDED HER SOFT WHITE ARMS INVITINGLY! HER EBONY HAIR, CASCADING DOWN UPON HER WHITE SHOULDERS, STIRRED IN THE WIND! SHE SMILED! MARTIN GOT TO HIS FEET, SHAKING HIS HEAD...
NO! NO! YOU DON'T EXIST! YOU CAN'T! THERE ISN'T A LIVING THING ON THIS WHOLE BLASTED ROCK!
MARTIN! I'M WAITING! COME TO ME!
MARTIN PUT HIS HAND OVER HIS EYES! THE HOT BREEZE... THE INCESSANT HOT BREEZE...PRESSED AGAINST HIS TEMPLES, MAKING THE BLOOD POUND THROUGH THEM! THE THROBBING... THE THROBBING BOOMED LIKE A GIANT PUMP INSIDE HIS BRAIN...
NO! NO! GO AWAY! GO AWAY!
MARTIN! MARTIN...
1

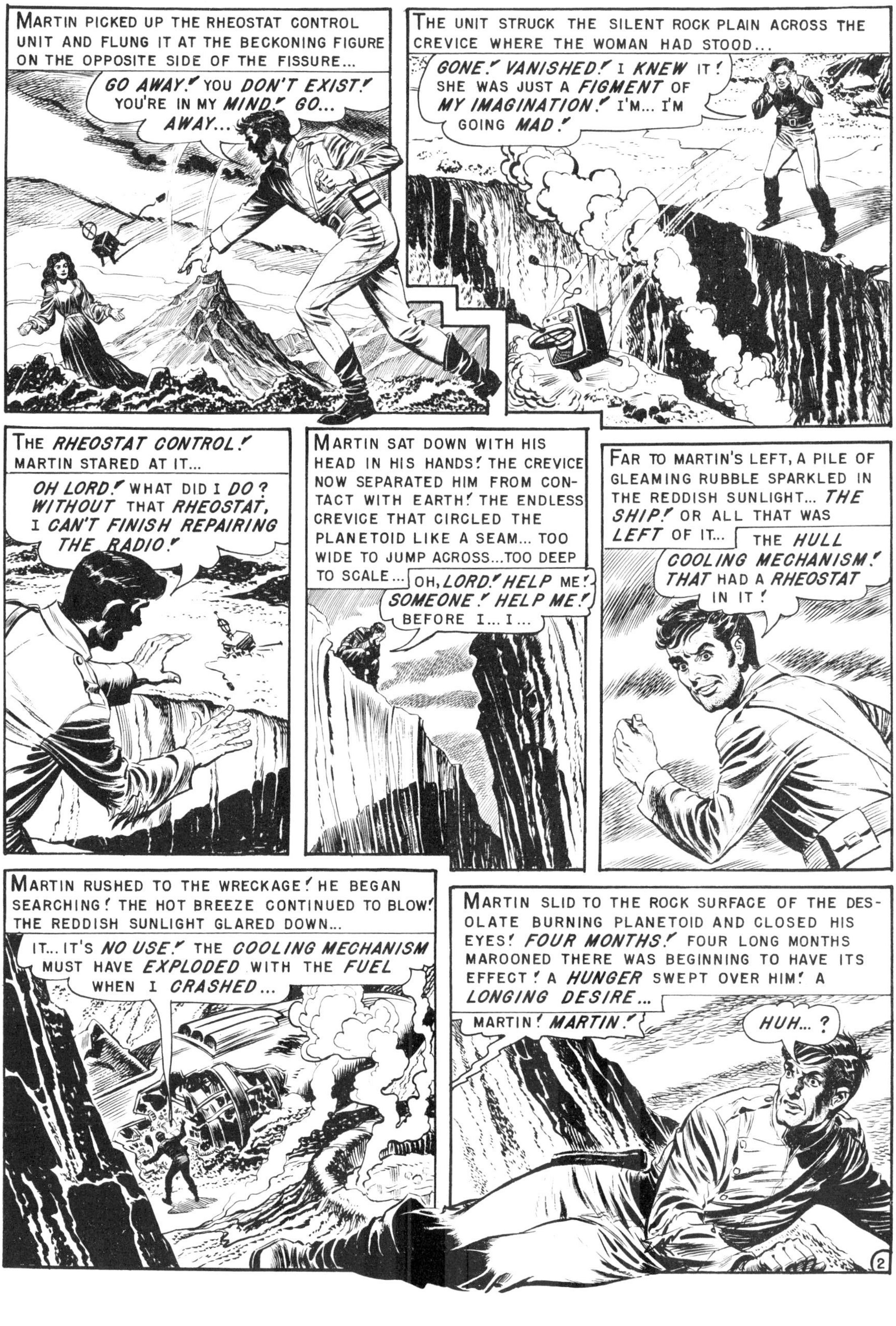
MARTIN PICKED UP THE RHEOSTAT CONTROL UNIT AND FLUNG IT AT THE BECKONING FIGURE ON THE OPPOSITE SIDE OF THE FISSURE...
GO AWAY! YOU DON'T EXIST! YOU'RE IN MY MIND! GO... AWAY...
THE UNIT STRUCK THE SILENT ROCK PLAIN ACROSS THE CREVICE WHERE THE WOMAN HAD STOOD...
GONE! VANISHED! I KNEW IT! SHE WAS JUST A FIGMENT OF MY IMAGINATION! I'M... I'M GOING MAD!
THE RHEOSTAT CONTROL! MARTIN STARED AT IT...
OH LORD! WHAT DID I DO? WITHOUT THAT RHEOSTAT, I CAN'T FINISH REPAIRING THE RADIO!
MARTIN SAT DOWN WITH HIS HEAD IN HIS HANDS! THE CREVICE NOW SEPARATED HIM FROM CONTACT WITH EARTH! THE ENDLESS CREVICE THAT CIRCLED THE PLANETOID LIKE A SEAM... TOO WIDE TO JUMP ACROSS...TOO DEEP TO SCALE...
OH, LORD! HELP ME! SOMEONE! HELP ME! BEFORE I... I...
FAR TO MARTIN'S LEFT, A PILE OF GLEAMING RUBBLE SPARKLED IN THE REDDISH SUNLIGHT... THE SHIP! OR ALL THAT WAS LEFT OF IT...
THE HULL COOLING MECHANISM! THAT HAD A RHEOSTAT IN IT!
MARTIN RUSHED TO THE WRECKAGE! HE BEGAN SEARCHING! THE HOT BREEZE CONTINUED TO BLOW! THE REDDISH SUNLIGHT GLARED DOWN...
IT... IT'S NO USE! THE COOLING MECHANISM MUST HAVE EXPLODED WITH THE FUEL WHEN I CRASHED...
MARTIN SLID TO THE ROCK SURFACE OF THE DESOLATE BURNING PLANETOID AND CLOSED HIS EYES! FOUR MONTHS! FOUR LONG MONTHS MAROONED THERE WAS BEGINNING TO HAVE ITS EFFECT! A HUNGER SWEPT OVER HIM! A LONGING DESIRE...
MARTIN! MARTIN!
HUH...?
2

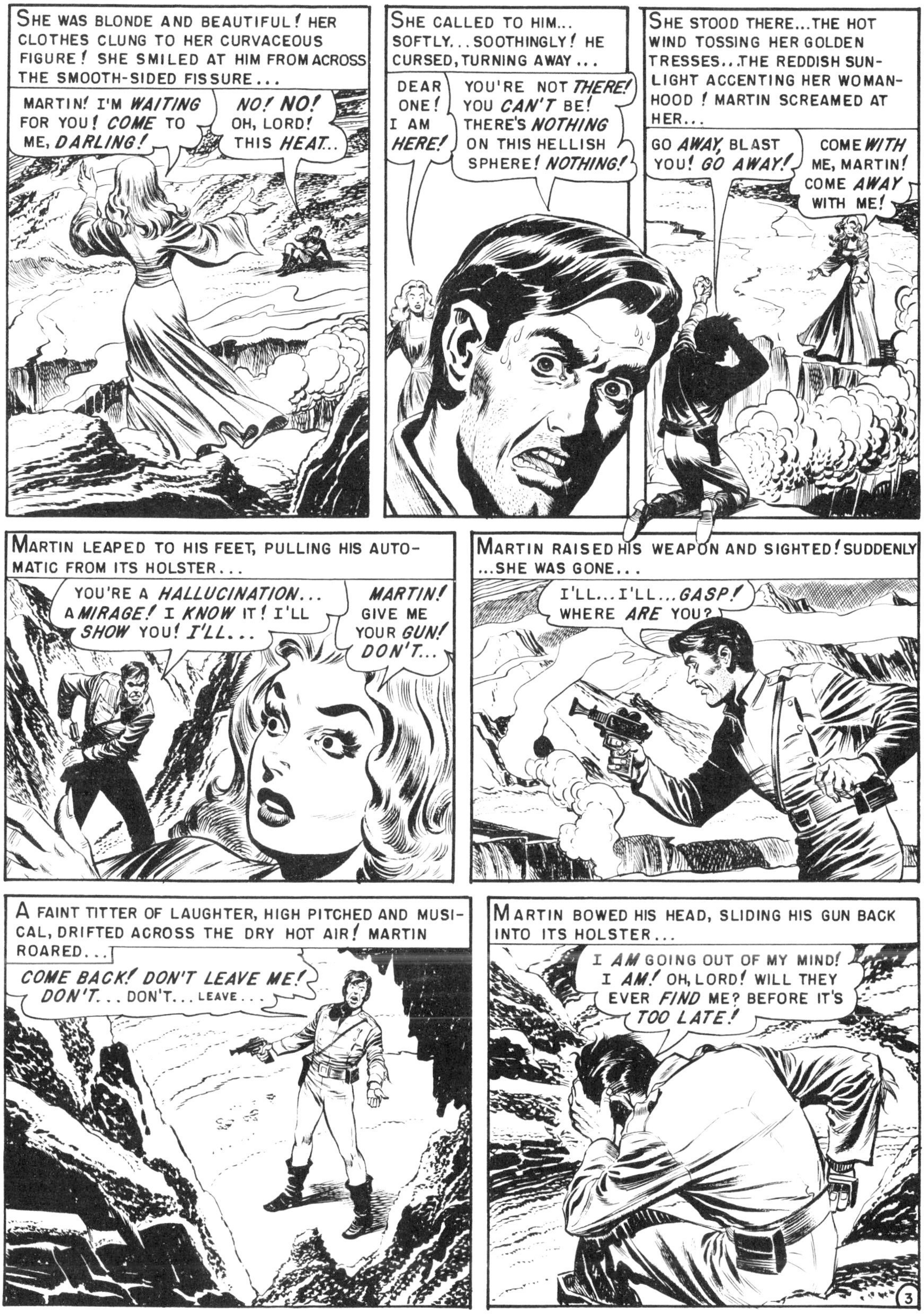
SHE WAS BLONDE AND BEAUTIFUL! HER CLOTHES CLUNG TO HER CURVACEOUS FIGURE! SHE SMILED AT HIM FROM ACROSS THE SMOOTH-SIDED FISSURE...
MARTIN! I'M WAITING FOR YOU! COME TO ME, DARLING!
NO! NO! OH, LORD! THIS HEAT...
SHE CALLED TO HIM... SOFTLY... SOOTHINGLY! HE CURSED, TURNING AWAY...
DEAR ONE! I AM HERE!
YOU'RE NOT THERE! YOU CAN'T BE! THERE'S NOTHING ON THIS HELLISH SPHERE! NOTHING!
SHE STOOD THERE... THE HOT WIND TOSSING HER GOLDEN TRESSES... THE REDDISH SUNLIGHT ACCENTING HER WOMANHOOD! MARTIN SCREAMED AT HER...
GO AWAY, BLAST YOU! GO AWAY!
COME WITH ME, MARTIN! COME AWAY WITH ME!
MARTIN LEAPED TO HIS FEET, PULLING HIS AUTOMATIC FROM ITS HOLSTER...
YOU'RE A HALLUCINATION... A MIRAGE! I KNOW IT! I'LL SHOW YOU! I'LL...
MARTIN! GIVE ME YOUR GUN! DON'T...
MARTIN RAISED HIS WEAPON AND SIGHTED! SUDDENLY ...SHE WAS GONE...
I'LL... I'LL... GASP! WHERE ARE YOU?
A FAINT TITTER OF LAUGHTER, HIGH PITCHED AND MUSICAL, DRIFTED ACROSS THE DRY HOT AIR! MARTIN ROARED...
COME BACK! DON'T LEAVE ME! DON'T... DON'T... LEAVE...
MARTIN BOWED HIS HEAD, SLIDING HIS GUN BACK INTO ITS HOLSTER...
I AM GOING OUT OF MY MIND! I AM! OH, LORD! WILL THEY EVER FIND ME? BEFORE IT'S TOO LATE!
3

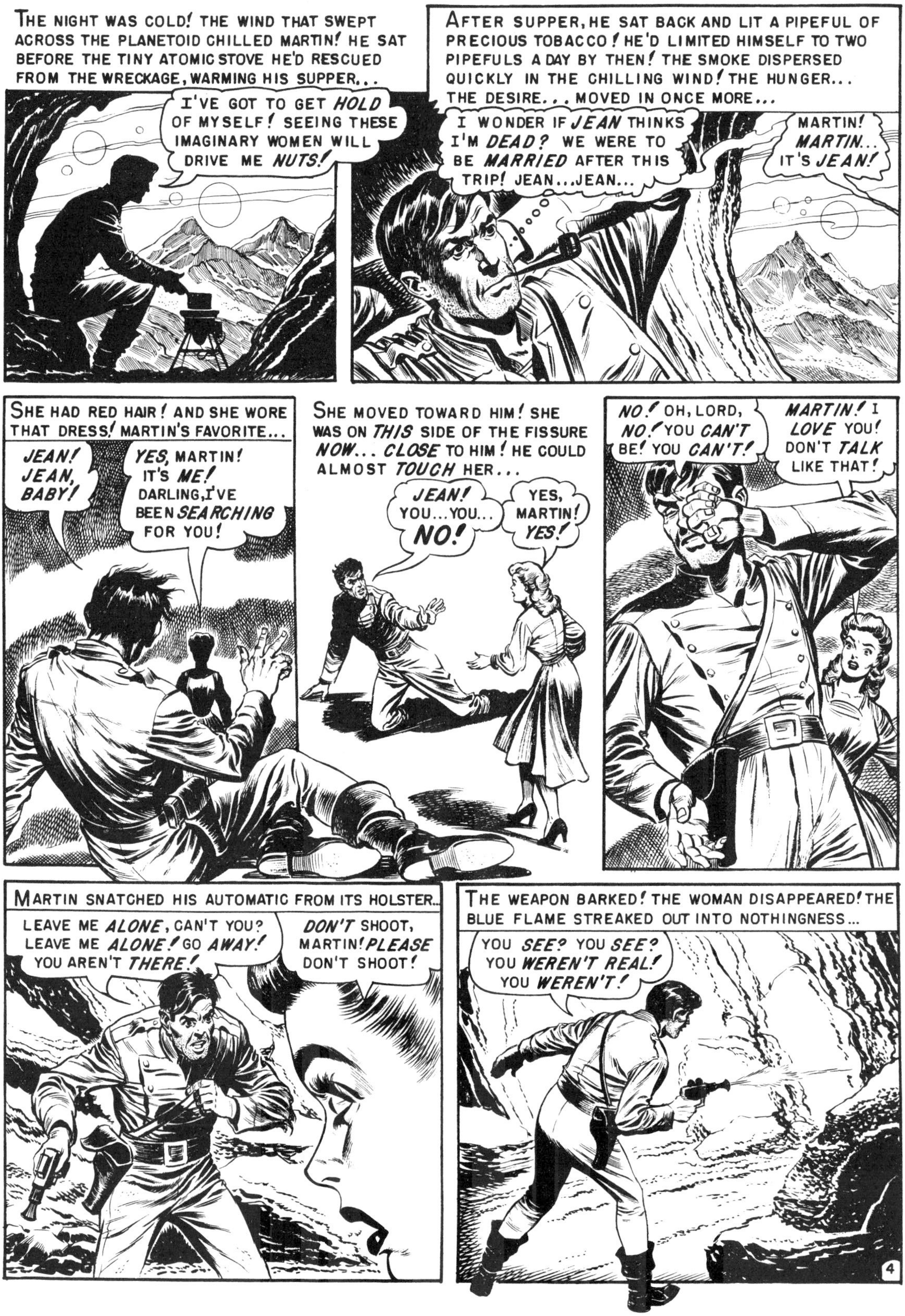
THE NIGHT WAS COLD! THE WIND THAT SWEPT ACROSS THE PLANETOID CHILLED MARTIN! HE SAT BEFORE THE TINY ATOMIC STOVE HE'D RESCUED FROM THE WRECKAGE, WARMING HIS SUPPER...
I'VE GOT TO GET HOLD OF MYSELF! SEEING THESE IMAGINARY WOMEN WILL DRIVE ME NUTS!
AFTER SUPPER, HE SAT BACK AND LIT A PIPEFUL OF PRECIOUS TOBACCO! HE'D LIMITED HIMSELF TO TWO PIPEFULS A DAY BY THEN! THE SMOKE DISPERSED QUICKLY IN THE CHILLING WIND! THE HUNGER... THE DESIRE... MOVED IN ONCE MORE...
I WONDER IF JEAN THINKS I'M DEAD? WE WERE TO BE MARRIED AFTER THIS TRIP! JEAN...JEAN...
MARTIN! MARTIN... IT'S JEAN!
SHE HAD RED HAIR! AND SHE WORE THAT DRESS! MARTIN'S FAVORITE...
JEAN! JEAN, BABY!
YES, MARTIN! IT'S ME! DARLING, I'VE BEEN SEARCHING FOR YOU!
SHE MOVED TOWARD HIM! SHE WAS ON THIS SIDE OF THE FISSURE NOW... CLOSE TO HIM! HE COULD ALMOST TOUCH HER...
JEAN! YOU...YOU... NO!
YES, MARTIN! YES!
NO! OH, LORD, NO! YOU CAN'T BE! YOU CAN'T!
MARTIN! I LOVE YOU! DON'T TALK LIKE THAT!
MARTIN SNATCHED HIS AUTOMATIC FROM ITS HOLSTER...
LEAVE ME ALONE, CAN'T YOU? LEAVE ME ALONE! GO AWAY! YOU AREN'T THERE!
DON'T SHOOT, MARTIN! PLEASE DON'T SHOOT!
THE WEAPON BARKED! THE WOMAN DISAPPEARED! THE BLUE FLAME STREAKED OUT INTO NOTHINGNESS...
YOU SEE? YOU SEE? YOU WEREN'T REAL! YOU WEREN'T!
4

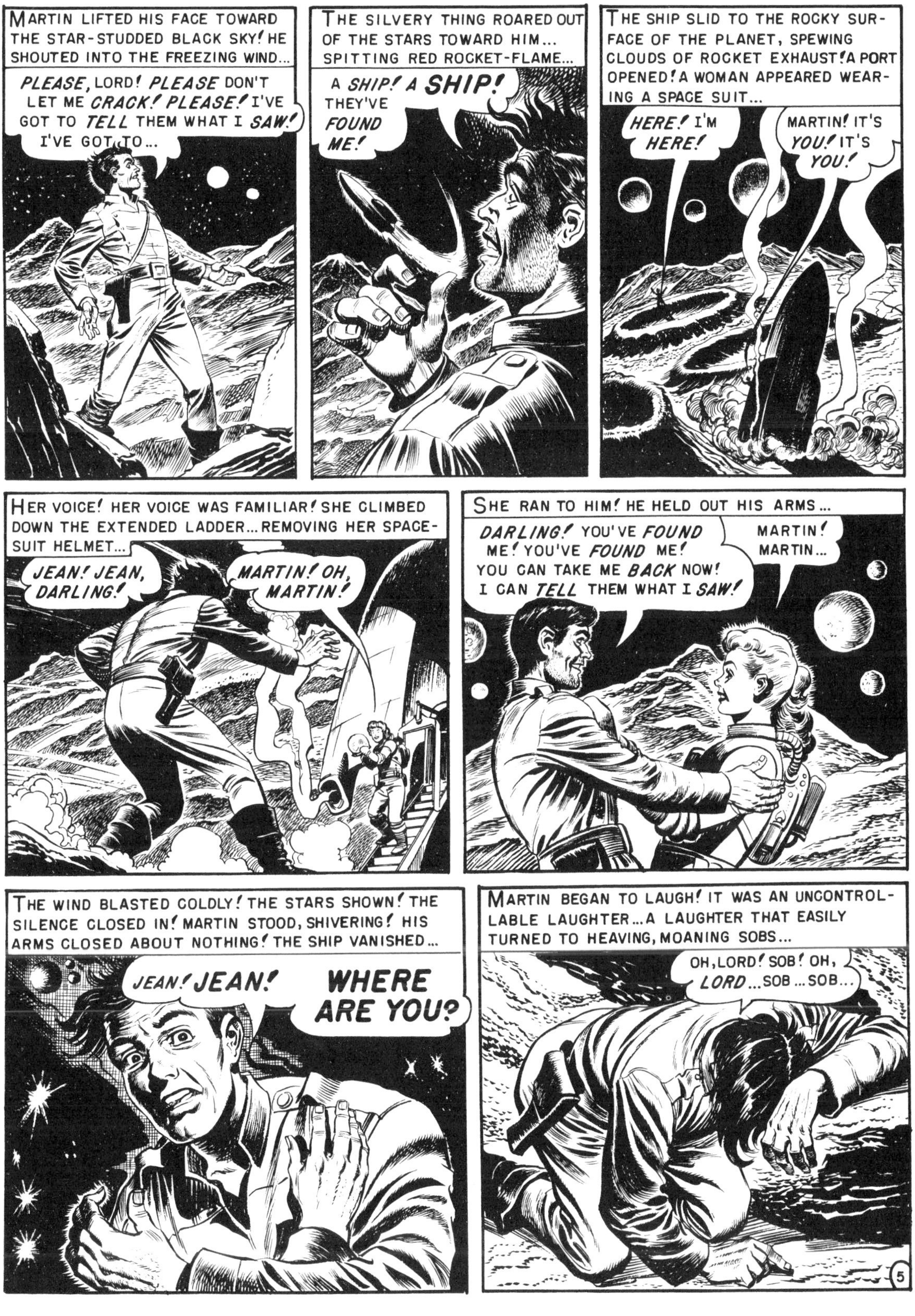
MARTIN LIFTED HIS FACE TOWARD THE STAR-STUDDED BLACK SKY! HE SHOUTED INTO THE FREEZING WIND...
PLEASE, LORD! PLEASE DON'T LET ME CRACK! PLEASE! I'VE GOT TO TELL THEM WHAT I SAW! I'VE GOT TO...
THE SILVERY THING ROARED OUT OF THE STARS TOWARD HIM... SPITTING RED ROCKET-FLAME...
A SHIP! A SHIP! THEY'VE FOUND ME!
THE SHIP SLID TO THE ROCKY SURFACE OF THE PLANET, SPEWING CLOUDS OF ROCKET EXHAUST! A PORT OPENED! A WOMAN APPEARED WEARING A SPACE SUIT...
HERE! I'M HERE!
MARTIN! IT'S YOU! IT'S YOU!
HER VOICE! HER VOICE WAS FAMILIAR! SHE CLIMBED DOWN THE EXTENDED LADDER... REMOVING HER SPACE-SUIT HELMET...
JEAN! JEAN, DARLING!
MARTIN! OH, MARTIN!
SHE RAN TO HIM! HE HELD OUT HIS ARMS...
DARLING! YOU'VE FOUND ME! YOU'VE FOUND ME! YOU CAN TAKE ME BACK NOW! I CAN TELL THEM WHAT I SAW!
MARTIN! MARTIN...
THE WIND BLASTED COLDLY! THE STARS SHOWN! THE SILENCE CLOSED IN! MARTIN STOOD, SHIVERING! HIS ARMS CLOSED ABOUT NOTHING! THE SHIP VANISHED...
JEAN! JEAN! WHERE ARE YOU?
MARTIN BEGAN TO LAUGH! IT WAS AN UNCONTROLLABLE LAUGHTER... A LAUGHTER THAT EASILY TURNED TO HEAVING, MOANING SOBS...
OH, LORD! SOB! OH, LORD... SOB... SOB...
5

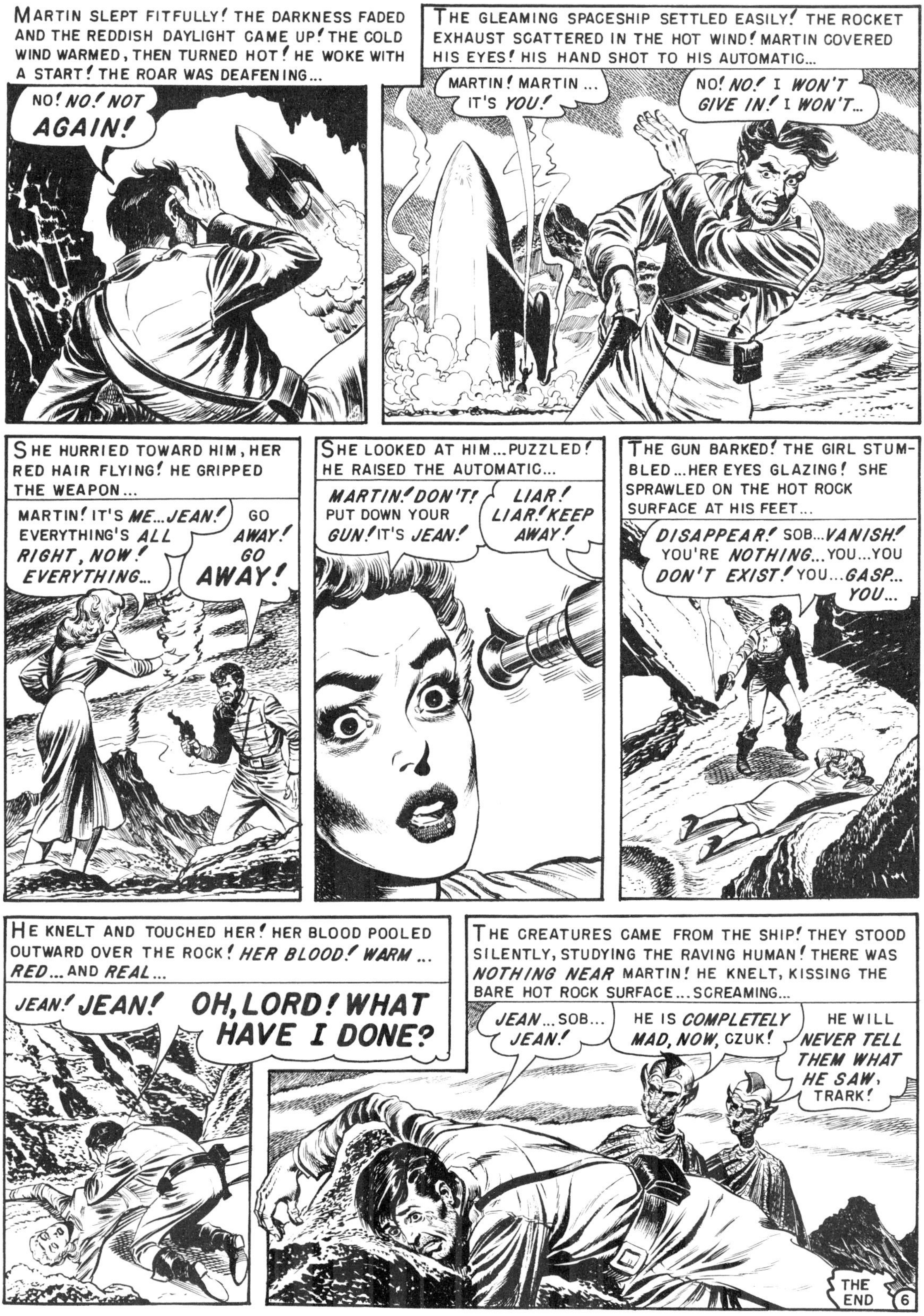
MARTIN SLEPT FITFULLY! THE DARKNESS FADED AND THE REDDISH DAYLIGHT CAME UP! THE COLD WIND WARMED, THEN TURNED HOT! HE WOKE WITH A START! THE ROAR WAS DEAFENING...
NO! NO! NOT AGAIN!
THE GLEAMING SPACESHIP SETTLED EASILY! THE ROCKET EXHAUST SCATTERED IN THE HOT WIND! MARTIN COVERED HIS EYES! HIS HAND SHOT TO HIS AUTOMATIC...
MARTIN! MARTIN ... IT'S YOU!
NO! NO! I WON'T GIVE IN! I WON'T...
SHE HURRIED TOWARD HIM, HER RED HAIR FLYING! HE GRIPPED THE WEAPON...
MARTIN! IT'S ME...JEAN! EVERYTHING'S ALL RIGHT, NOW! EVERYTHING...
GO AWAY! GO AWAY!
SHE LOOKED AT HIM...PUZZLED! HE RAISED THE AUTOMATIC...
MARTIN! DON'T! PUT DOWN YOUR GUN! IT'S JEAN!
LIAR! LIAR! KEEP AWAY!
THE GUN BARKED! THE GIRL STUMBLED...HER EYES GLAZING! SHE SPRAWLED ON THE HOT ROCK SURFACE AT HIS FEET...
DISAPPEAR! SOB...VANISH! YOU'RE NOTHING...YOU...YOU DON'T EXIST! YOU...GASP... YOU...
HE KNELT AND TOUCHED HER! HER BLOOD POOLED OUTWARD OVER THE ROCK! HER BLOOD! WARM ... RED... AND REAL...
JEAN! JEAN!
OH, LORD! WHAT HAVE I DONE?
THE CREATURES CAME FROM THE SHIP! THEY STOOD SILENTLY, STUDYING THE RAVING HUMAN! THERE WAS NOTHING NEAR MARTIN! HE KNELT, KISSING THE BARE HOT ROCK SURFACE...SCREAMING...
JEAN...SOB... JEAN!
HE IS COMPLETELY MAD, NOW, CZUK!
HE WILL NEVER TELL THEM WHAT HE SAW, TRARK!
THE END
6

OFF DAY!

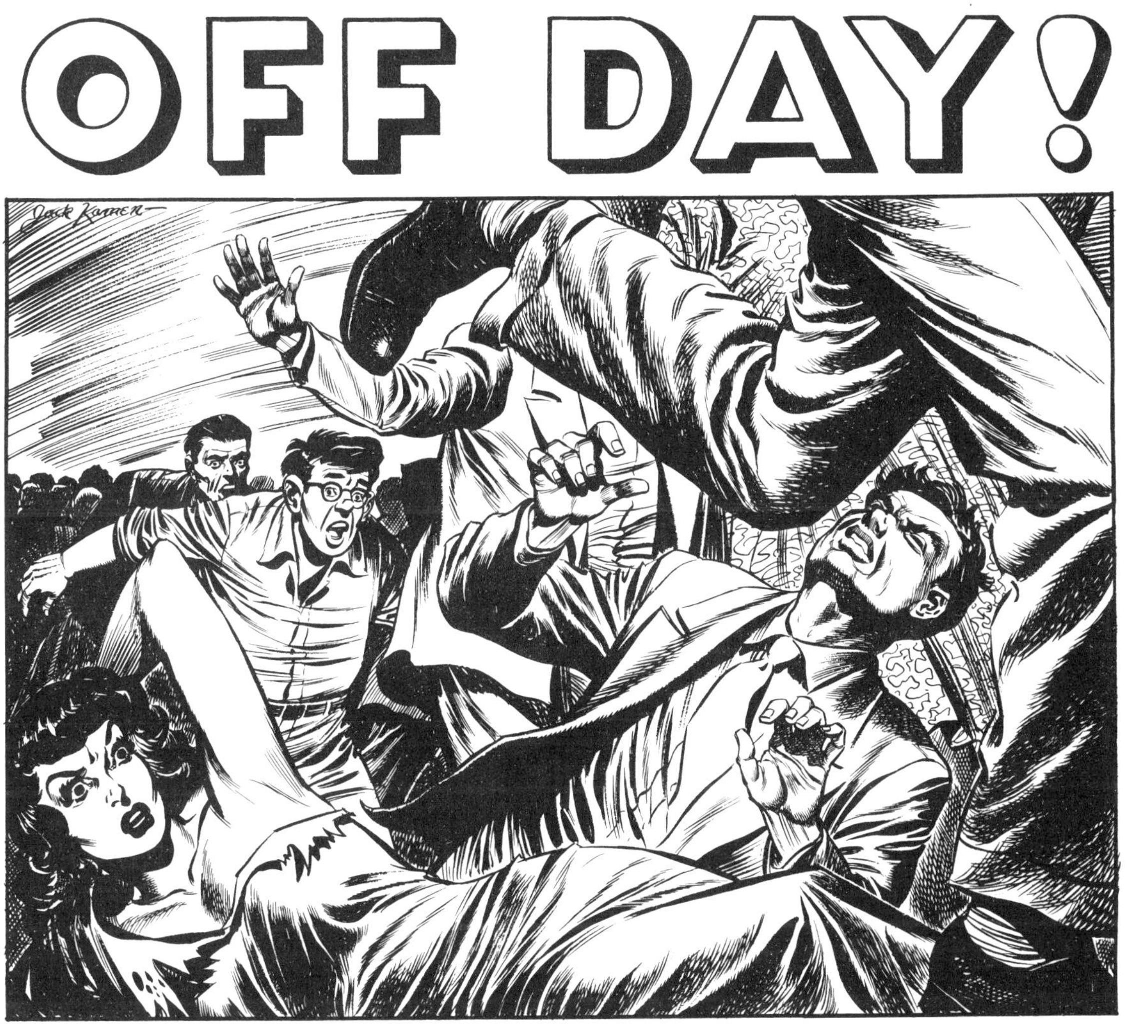
Jack Kamen

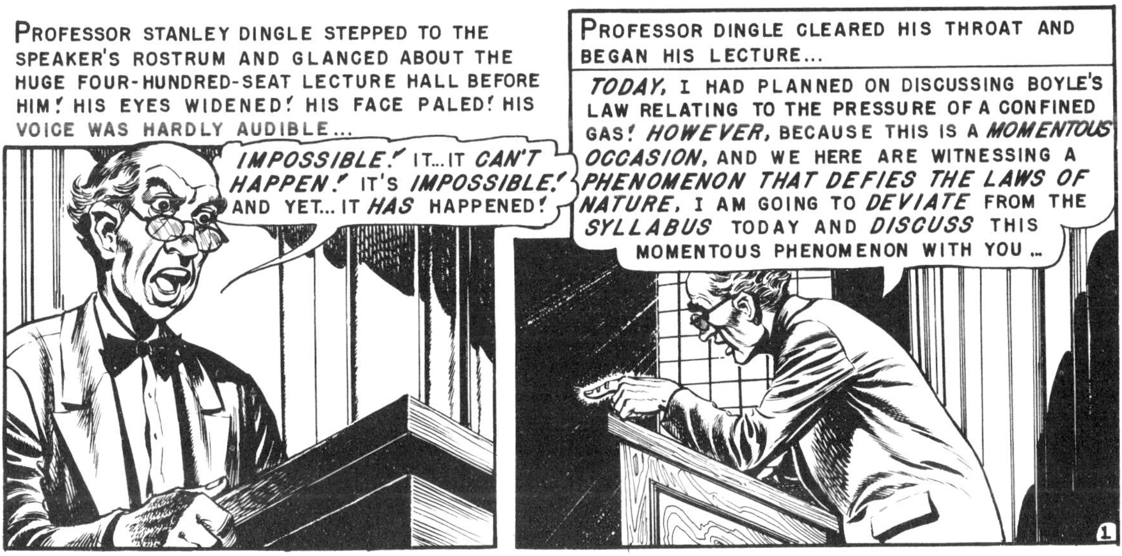
PROFESSOR STANLEY DINGLE STEPPED TO THE SPEAKER'S ROSTRUM AND GLANCED ABOUT THE HUGE FOUR-HUNDRED-SEAT LECTURE HALL BEFORE HIM! HIS EYES WIDENED! HIS FACE PALED! HIS VOICE WAS HARDLY AUDIBLE...
IMPOSSIBLE! IT...IT CAN'T HAPPEN! IT'S IMPOSSIBLE! AND YET... IT HAS HAPPENED!
PROFESSOR DINGLE CLEARED HIS THROAT AND BEGAN HIS LECTURE...
TODAY, I HAD PLANNED ON DISCUSSING BOYLE'S LAW RELATING TO THE PRESSURE OF A CONFINED GAS! HOWEVER, BECAUSE THIS IS A MOMENTOUS OCCASION, AND WE HERE ARE WITNESSING A PHENOMENON THAT DEFIES THE LAWS OF NATURE, I AM GOING TO DEVIATE FROM THE SYLLABUS TODAY AND DISCUSS THIS MOMENTOUS PHENOMENON WITH YOU...
1

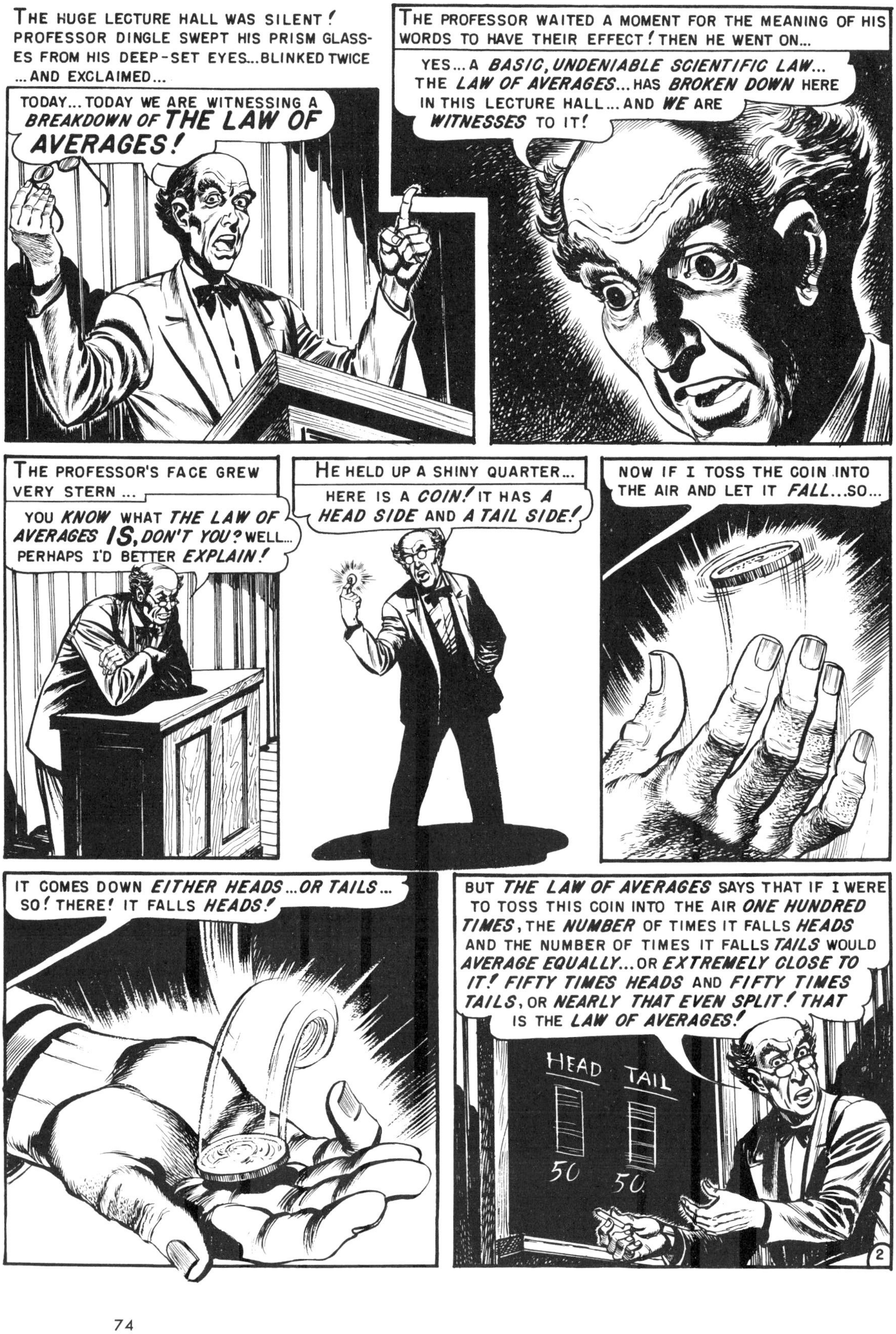
THE HUGE LECTURE HALL WAS SILENT! PROFESSOR DINGLE SWEPT HIS PRISM GLASSES FROM HIS DEEP-SET EYES...BLINKED TWICE ...AND EXCLAIMED...
TODAY...TODAY WE ARE WITNESSING A BREAKDOWN OF THE LAW OF AVERAGES!
THE PROFESSOR WAITED A MOMENT FOR THE MEANING OF HIS WORDS TO HAVE THEIR EFFECT! THEN HE WENT ON...
YES...A BASIC, UNDENIABLE SCIENTIFIC LAW... THE LAW OF AVERAGES...HAS BROKEN DOWN HERE IN THIS LECTURE HALL...AND WE ARE WITNESSES TO IT!
THE PROFESSOR'S FACE GREW VERY STERN...
YOU KNOW WHAT THE LAW OF AVERAGES IS, DON'T YOU? WELL... PERHAPS I'D BETTER EXPLAIN!
HE HELD UP A SHINY QUARTER...
HERE IS A COIN! IT HAS A HEAD SIDE AND A TAIL SIDE!
NOW IF I TOSS THE COIN INTO THE AIR AND LET IT FALL...SO...
IT COMES DOWN EITHER HEADS...OR TAILS... SO! THERE! IT FALLS HEADS!
BUT THE LAW OF AVERAGES SAYS THAT IF I WERE TO TOSS THIS COIN INTO THE AIR ONE HUNDRED TIMES, THE NUMBER OF TIMES IT FALLS HEADS AND THE NUMBER OF TIMES IT FALLS TAILS WOULD AVERAGE EQUALLY...OR EXTREMELY CLOSE TO IT! FIFTY TIMES HEADS AND FIFTY TIMES TAILS, OR NEARLY THAT EVEN SPLIT! THAT IS THE LAW OF AVERAGES!
HEAD TAIL
50 50
2

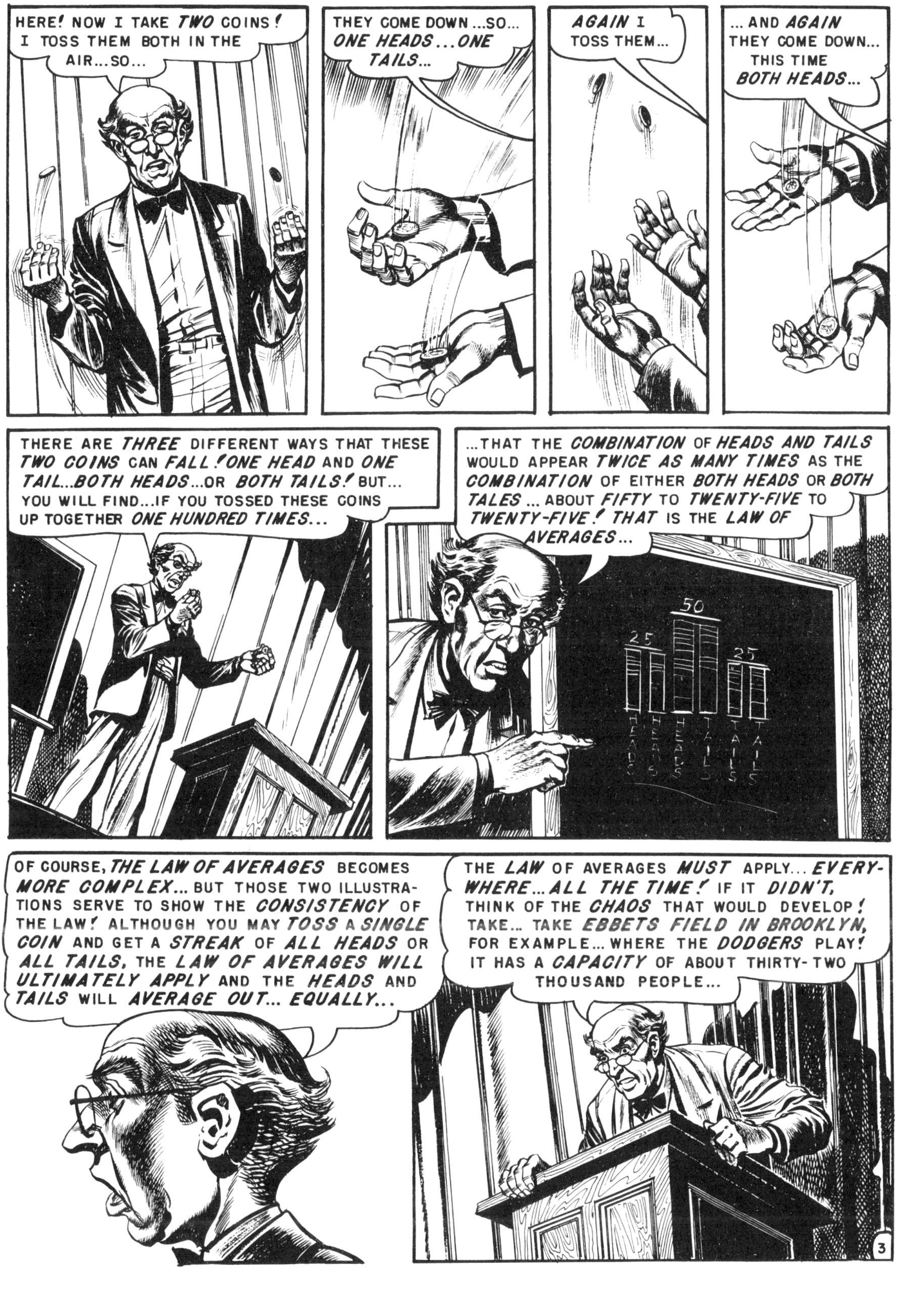
HERE! NOW I TAKE TWO COINS! I TOSS THEM BOTH IN THE AIR...SO...
THEY COME DOWN ...SO... ONE HEADS...ONE TAILS...
AGAIN I TOSS THEM...
...AND AGAIN THEY COME DOWN... THIS TIME BOTH HEADS...
THERE ARE THREE DIFFERENT WAYS THAT THESE TWO COINS CAN FALL! ONE HEAD AND ONE TAIL...BOTH HEADS...OR BOTH TAILS! BUT... YOU WILL FIND...IF YOU TOSSED THESE COINS UP TOGETHER ONE HUNDRED TIMES...
...THAT THE COMBINATION OF HEADS AND TAILS WOULD APPEAR TWICE AS MANY TIMES AS THE COMBINATION OF EITHER BOTH HEADS OR BOTH TALES ... ABOUT FIFTY TO TWENTY-FIVE TO TWENTY-FIVE! THAT IS THE LAW OF AVERAGES...
50
25
25
HEADS
HEADS
HEADS
TAILS
TAILS
TAILS
OF COURSE, THE LAW OF AVERAGES BECOMES MORE COMPLEX... BUT THOSE TWO ILLUSTRATIONS SERVE TO SHOW THE CONSISTENCY OF THE LAW! ALTHOUGH YOU MAY TOSS A SINGLE COIN AND GET A STREAK OF ALL HEADS OR ALL TAILS, THE LAW OF AVERAGES WILL ULTIMATELY APPLY AND THE HEADS AND TAILS WILL AVERAGE OUT... EQUALLY...
THE LAW OF AVERAGES MUST APPLY... EVERYWHERE... ALL THE TIME! IF IT DIDN'T, THINK OF THE CHAOS THAT WOULD DEVELOP! TAKE... TAKE EBBETS FIELD IN BROOKLYN, FOR EXAMPLE... WHERE THE DODGERS PLAY! IT HAS A CAPACITY OF ABOUT THIRTY-TWO THOUSAND PEOPLE...
3

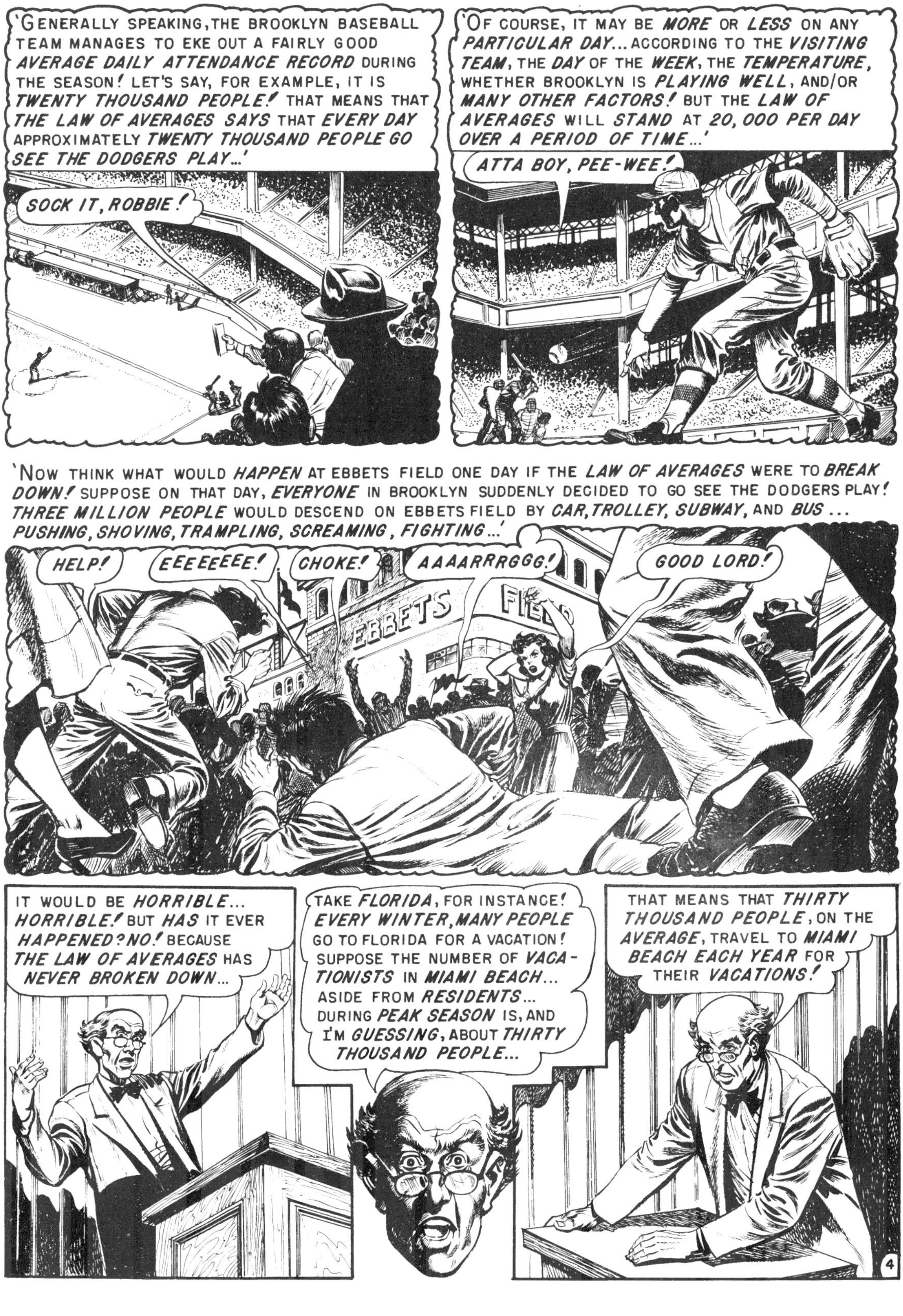
'GENERALLY SPEAKING, THE BROOKLYN BASEBALL TEAM MANAGES TO EKE OUT A FAIRLY GOOD AVERAGE DAILY ATTENDANCE RECORD DURING THE SEASON! LET'S SAY, FOR EXAMPLE, IT IS TWENTY THOUSAND PEOPLE! THAT MEANS THAT THE LAW OF AVERAGES SAYS THAT EVERY DAY APPROXIMATELY TWENTY THOUSAND PEOPLE GO SEE THE DODGERS PLAY...'
SOCK IT, ROBBIE!
'OF COURSE, IT MAY BE MORE OR LESS ON ANY PARTICULAR DAY... ACCORDING TO THE VISITING TEAM, THE DAY OF THE WEEK, THE TEMPERATURE, WHETHER BROOKLYN IS PLAYING WELL, AND/OR MANY OTHER FACTORS! BUT THE LAW OF AVERAGES WILL STAND AT 20,000 PER DAY OVER A PERIOD OF TIME...'
ATTA BOY, PEE-WEE!
'NOW THINK WHAT WOULD HAPPEN AT EBBETS FIELD ONE DAY IF THE LAW OF AVERAGES WERE TO BREAK DOWN! SUPPOSE ON THAT DAY, EVERYONE IN BROOKLYN SUDDENLY DECIDED TO GO SEE THE DODGERS PLAY! THREE MILLION PEOPLE WOULD DESCEND ON EBBETS FIELD BY CAR, TROLLEY, SUBWAY, AND BUS... PUSHING, SHOVING, TRAMPLING, SCREAMING, FIGHTING...'
HELP!
EEEEEEEE!
CHOKE!
AAAARRRGGG!
GOOD LORD!
EBBETS FIELD
IT WOULD BE HORRIBLE... HORRIBLE! BUT HAS IT EVER HAPPENED? NO! BECAUSE THE LAW OF AVERAGES HAS NEVER BROKEN DOWN...
TAKE FLORIDA, FOR INSTANCE! EVERY WINTER, MANY PEOPLE GO TO FLORIDA FOR A VACATION! SUPPOSE THE NUMBER OF VACATIONISTS IN MIAMI BEACH... ASIDE FROM RESIDENTS... DURING PEAK SEASON IS, AND I'M GUESSING, ABOUT THIRTY THOUSAND PEOPLE...
THAT MEANS THAT THIRTY THOUSAND PEOPLE, ON THE AVERAGE, TRAVEL TO MIAMI BEACH EACH YEAR FOR THEIR VACATIONS!
4

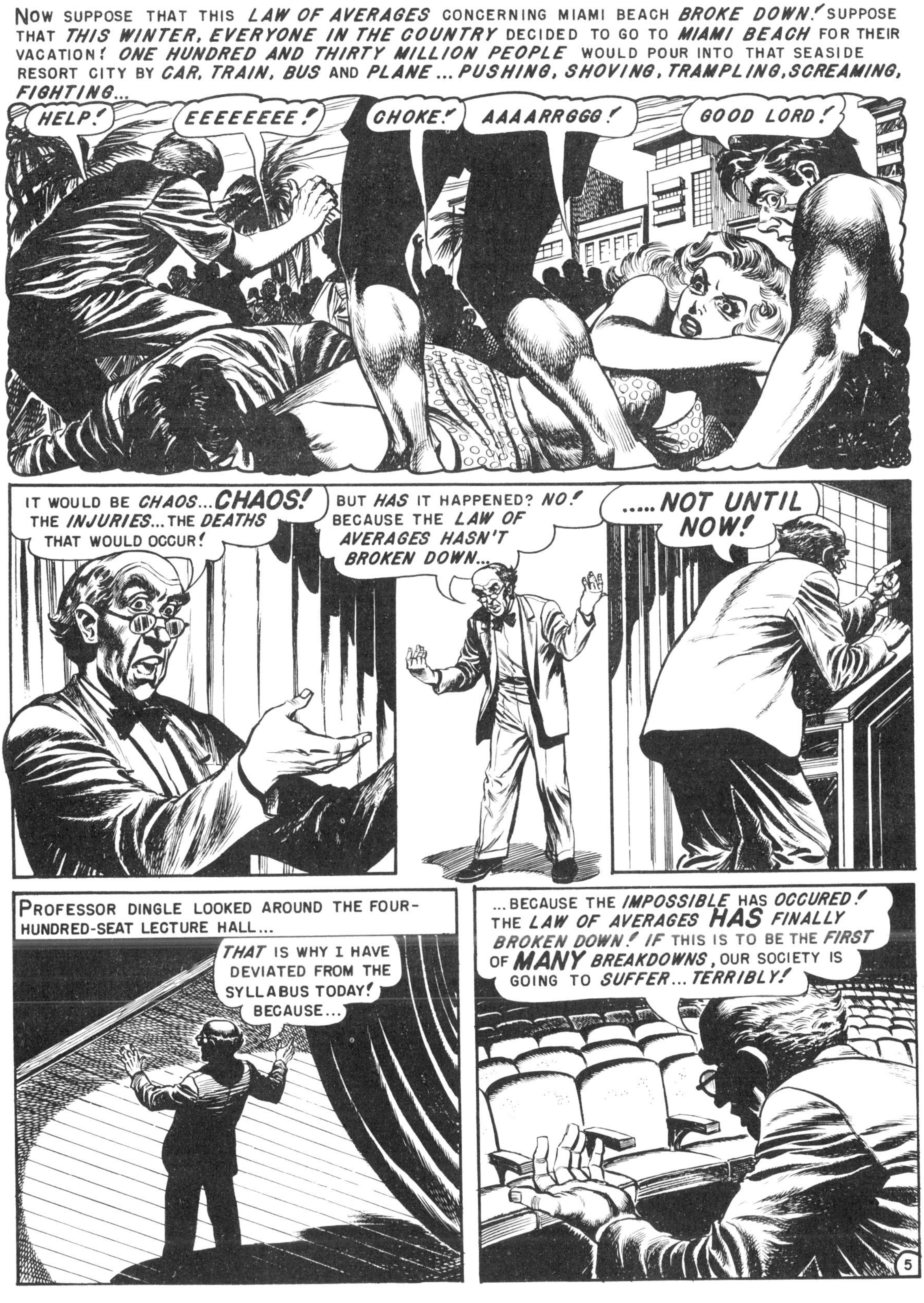
NOW SUPPOSE THAT THIS LAW OF AVERAGES CONCERNING MIAMI BEACH BROKE DOWN! SUPPOSE THAT THIS WINTER, EVERYONE IN THE COUNTRY DECIDED TO GO TO MIAMI BEACH FOR THEIR VACATION! ONE HUNDRED AND THIRTY MILLION PEOPLE WOULD POUR INTO THAT SEASIDE RESORT CITY BY CAR, TRAIN, BUS AND PLANE ... PUSHING, SHOVING, TRAMPLING, SCREAMING, FIGHTING...
HELP!
EEEEEEEE!
CHOKE!
AAAARRGGG!
GOOD LORD!
IT WOULD BE CHAOS... CHAOS! THE INJURIES... THE DEATHS THAT WOULD OCCUR!
BUT HAS IT HAPPENED? NO! BECAUSE THE LAW OF AVERAGES HASN'T BROKEN DOWN...
.....NOT UNTIL NOW!
PROFESSOR DINGLE LOOKED AROUND THE FOUR-HUNDRED-SEAT LECTURE HALL...
THAT IS WHY I HAVE DEVIATED FROM THE SYLLABUS TODAY! BECAUSE...
...BECAUSE THE IMPOSSIBLE HAS OCCURED! THE LAW OF AVERAGES HAS FINALLY BROKEN DOWN! IF THIS IS TO BE THE FIRST OF MANY BREAKDOWNS, OUR SOCIETY IS GOING TO SUFFER... TERRIBLY!
5

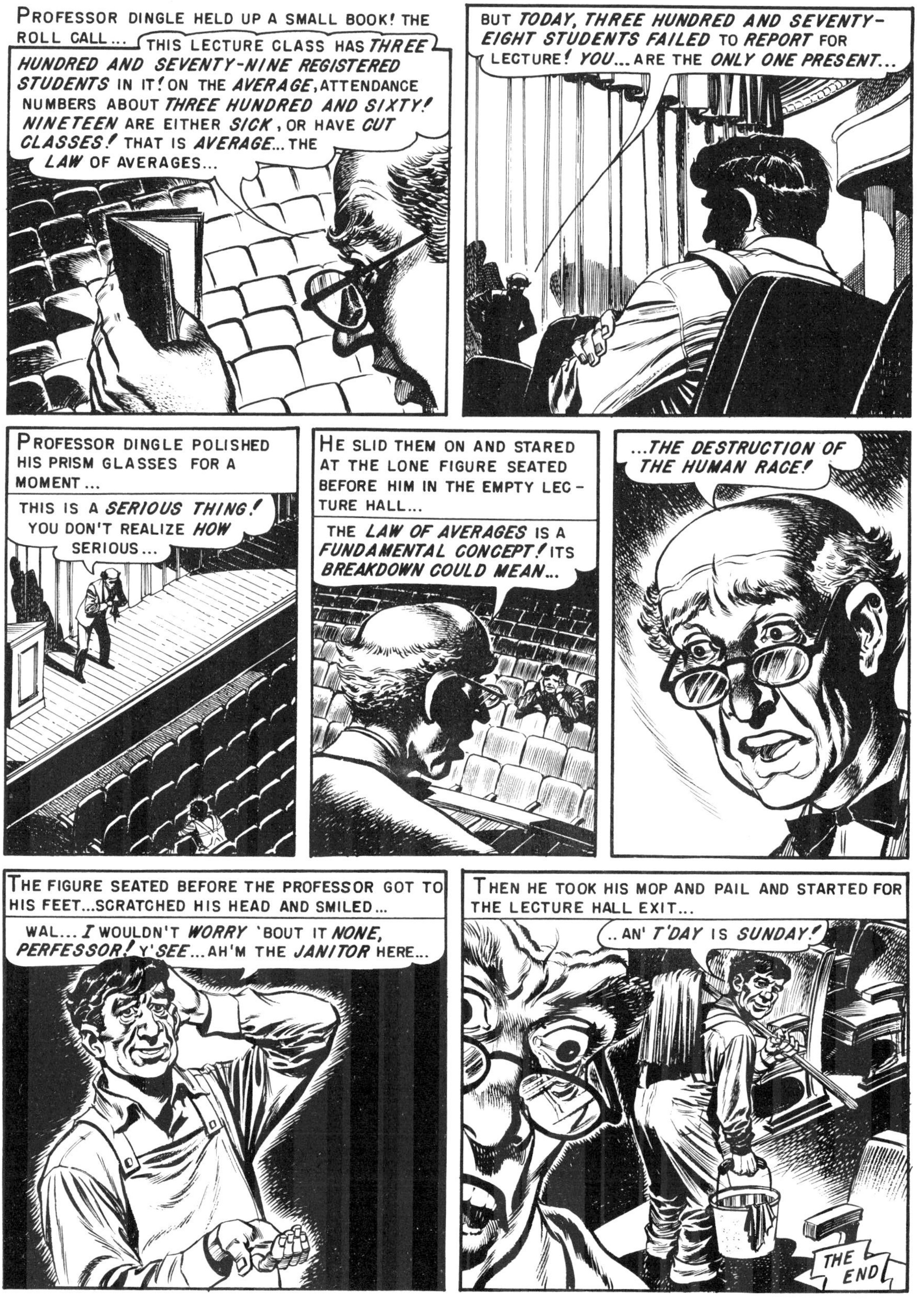
PROFESSOR DINGLE HELD UP A SMALL BOOK! THE ROLL CALL...
THIS LECTURE CLASS HAS THREE HUNDRED AND SEVENTY-NINE REGISTERED STUDENTS IN IT! ON THE AVERAGE, ATTENDANCE NUMBERS ABOUT THREE HUNDRED AND SIXTY! NINETEEN ARE EITHER SICK, OR HAVE CUT CLASSES! THAT IS AVERAGE... THE LAW OF AVERAGES...
BUT TODAY, THREE HUNDRED AND SEVENTY-EIGHT STUDENTS FAILED TO REPORT FOR LECTURE! YOU... ARE THE ONLY ONE PRESENT...
PROFESSOR DINGLE POLISHED HIS PRISM GLASSES FOR A MOMENT...
THIS IS A SERIOUS THING! YOU DON'T REALIZE HOW SERIOUS...
HE SLID THEM ON AND STARED AT THE LONE FIGURE SEATED BEFORE HIM IN THE EMPTY LECTURE HALL...
THE LAW OF AVERAGES IS A FUNDAMENTAL CONCEPT! ITS BREAKDOWN COULD MEAN...
...THE DESTRUCTION OF THE HUMAN RACE!
THE FIGURE SEATED BEFORE THE PROFESSOR GOT TO HIS FEET...SCRATCHED HIS HEAD AND SMILED...
WAL... I WOULDN'T WORRY 'BOUT IT NONE, PERFESSOR! Y'SEE... AH'M THE JANITOR HERE...
THEN HE TOOK HIS MOP AND PAIL AND STARTED FOR THE LECTURE HALL EXIT...
..AN' T'DAY IS SUNDAY!
THE END

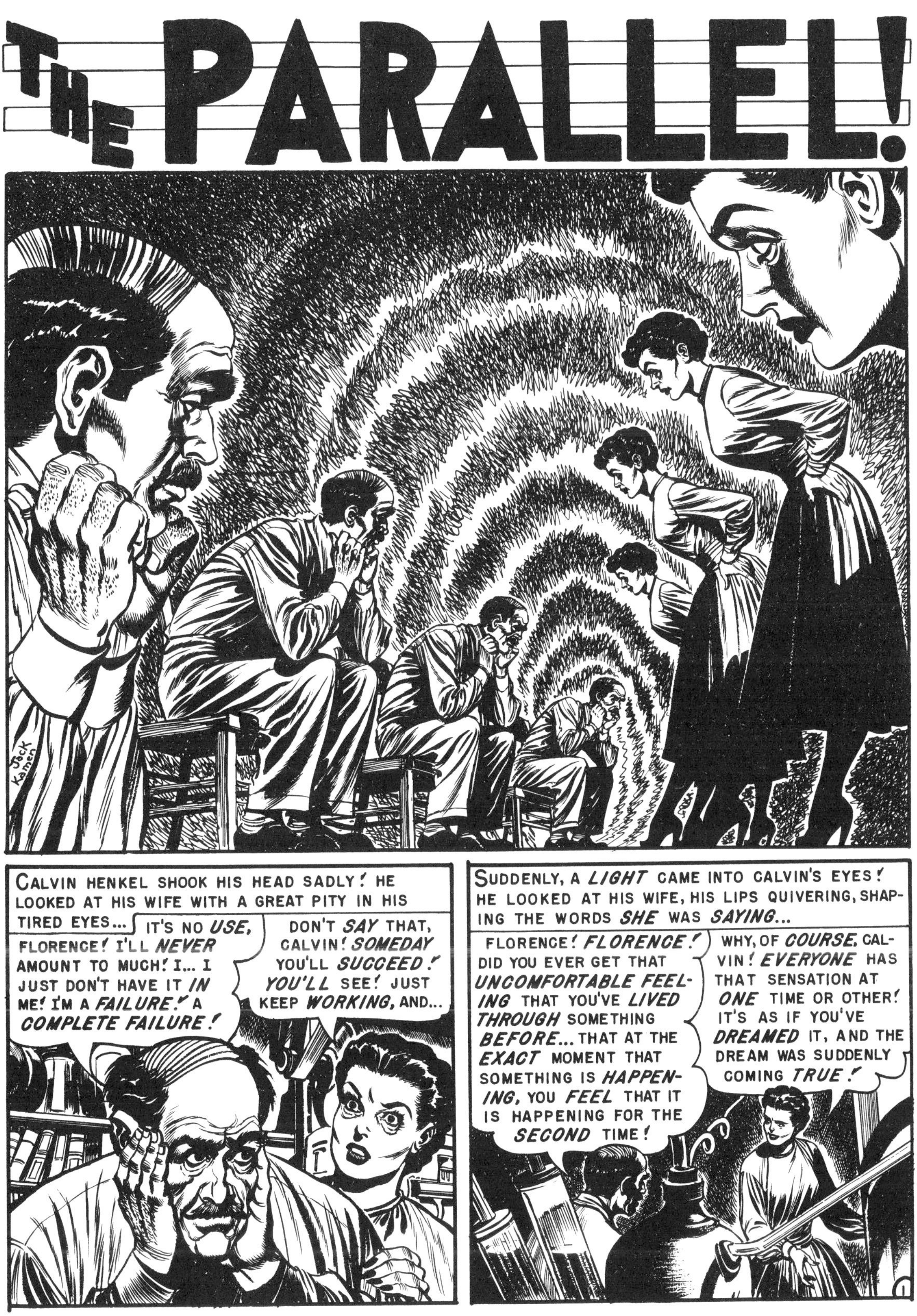
THE PARALLEL!
Jack Kamen
CALVIN HENKEL SHOOK HIS HEAD SADLY! HE LOOKED AT HIS WIFE WITH A GREAT PITY IN HIS TIRED EYES...
IT'S NO USE, FLORENCE! I'LL NEVER AMOUNT TO MUCH! I... I JUST DON'T HAVE IT IN ME! I'M A FAILURE! A COMPLETE FAILURE!
DON'T SAY THAT, CALVIN! SOMEDAY YOU'LL SUCCEED! YOU'LL SEE! JUST KEEP WORKING, AND...
SUDDENLY, A LIGHT CAME INTO CALVIN'S EYES! HE LOOKED AT HIS WIFE, HIS LIPS QUIVERING, SHAPING THE WORDS SHE WAS SAYING...
FLORENCE! FLORENCE! DID YOU EVER GET THAT UNCOMFORTABLE FEELING THAT YOU'VE LIVED THROUGH SOMETHING BEFORE... THAT AT THE EXACT MOMENT THAT SOMETHING IS HAPPENING, YOU FEEL THAT IT IS HAPPENING FOR THE SECOND TIME!
WHY, OF COURSE, CALVIN! EVERYONE HAS THAT SENSATION AT ONE TIME OR OTHER! IT'S AS IF YOU'VE DREAMED IT, AND THE DREAM WAS SUDDENLY COMING TRUE!
1

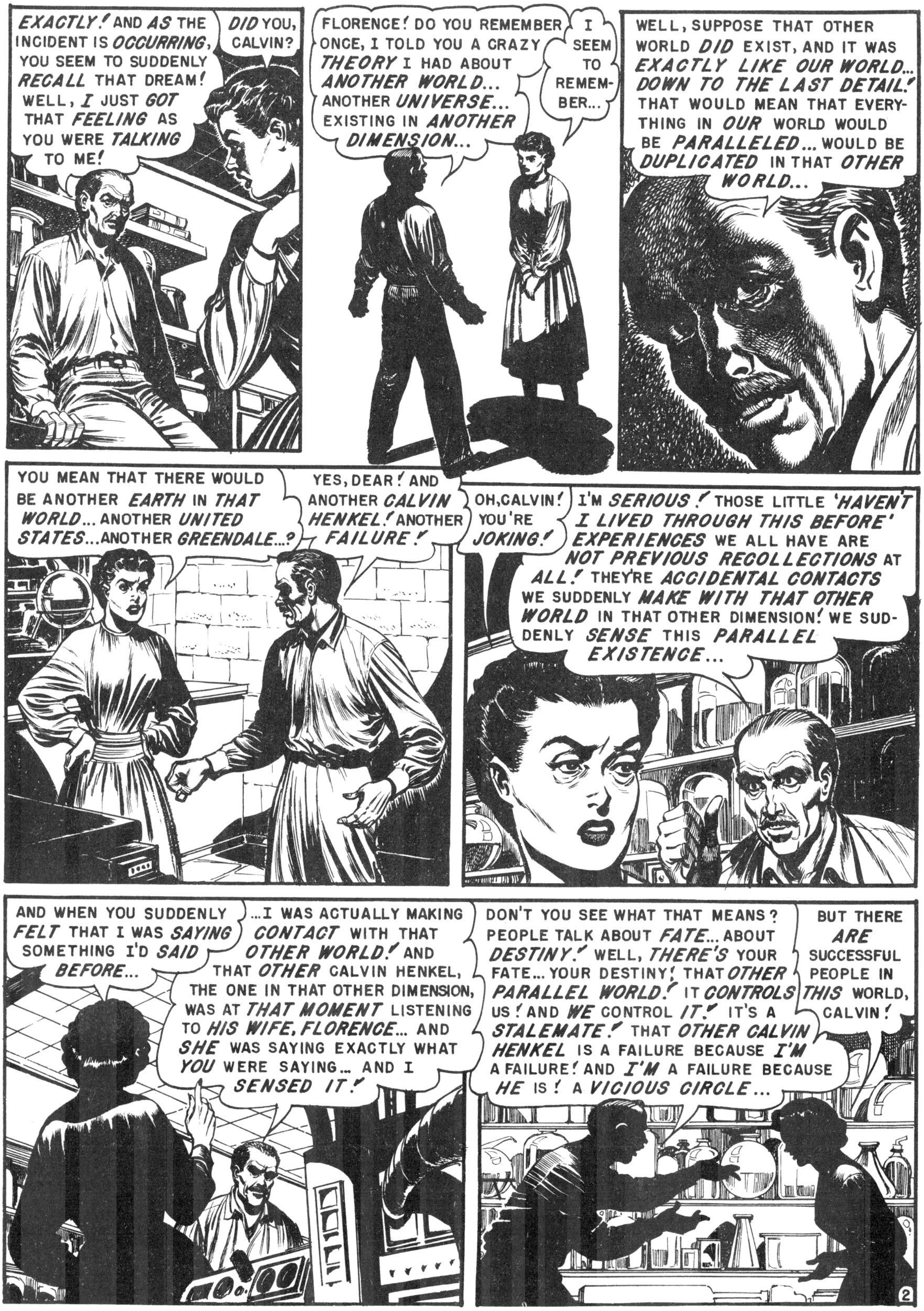
EXACTLY! AND AS THE INCIDENT IS OCCURRING, YOU SEEM TO SUDDENLY RECALL THAT DREAM! WELL, I JUST GOT THAT FEELING AS YOU WERE TALKING TO ME!
DID YOU, CALVIN?
FLORENCE! DO YOU REMEMBER ONCE, I TOLD YOU A CRAZY THEORY I HAD ABOUT ANOTHER WORLD... ANOTHER UNIVERSE... EXISTING IN ANOTHER DIMENSION...
I SEEM TO REMEMBER...
WELL, SUPPOSE THAT OTHER WORLD DID EXIST, AND IT WAS EXACTLY LIKE OUR WORLD... DOWN TO THE LAST DETAIL! THAT WOULD MEAN THAT EVERYTHING IN OUR WORLD WOULD BE PARALLELED... WOULD BE DUPLICATED IN THAT OTHER WORLD...
YOU MEAN THAT THERE WOULD BE ANOTHER EARTH IN THAT WORLD... ANOTHER UNITED STATES... ANOTHER GREENDALE...?
YES, DEAR! AND ANOTHER CALVIN HENKEL! ANOTHER FAILURE!
OH, CALVIN! YOU'RE JOKING!
I'M SERIOUS! THOSE LITTLE 'HAVEN'T I LIVED THROUGH THIS BEFORE' EXPERIENCES WE ALL HAVE ARE NOT PREVIOUS RECOLLECTIONS AT ALL! THEY'RE ACCIDENTAL CONTACTS WE SUDDENLY MAKE WITH THAT OTHER WORLD IN THAT OTHER DIMENSION! WE SUDDENLY SENSE THIS PARALLEL EXISTENCE...
AND WHEN YOU SUDDENLY FELT THAT I WAS SAYING SOMETHING I'D SAID BEFORE...
...I WAS ACTUALLY MAKING CONTACT WITH THAT OTHER WORLD! AND THAT OTHER CALVIN HENKEL, THE ONE IN THAT OTHER DIMENSION, WAS AT THAT MOMENT LISTENING TO HIS WIFE, FLORENCE... AND SHE WAS SAYING EXACTLY WHAT YOU WERE SAYING... AND I SENSED IT!
DON'T YOU SEE WHAT THAT MEANS? PEOPLE TALK ABOUT FATE... ABOUT DESTINY! WELL, THERE'S YOUR FATE... YOUR DESTINY! THAT OTHER PARALLEL WORLD! IT CONTROLS US! AND WE CONTROL IT! IT'S A STALEMATE! THAT OTHER CALVIN HENKEL IS A FAILURE BECAUSE I'M A FAILURE! AND I'M A FAILURE BECAUSE HE IS! A VICIOUS CIRCLE...
BUT THERE ARE SUCCESSFUL PEOPLE IN THIS WORLD, CALVIN!
2

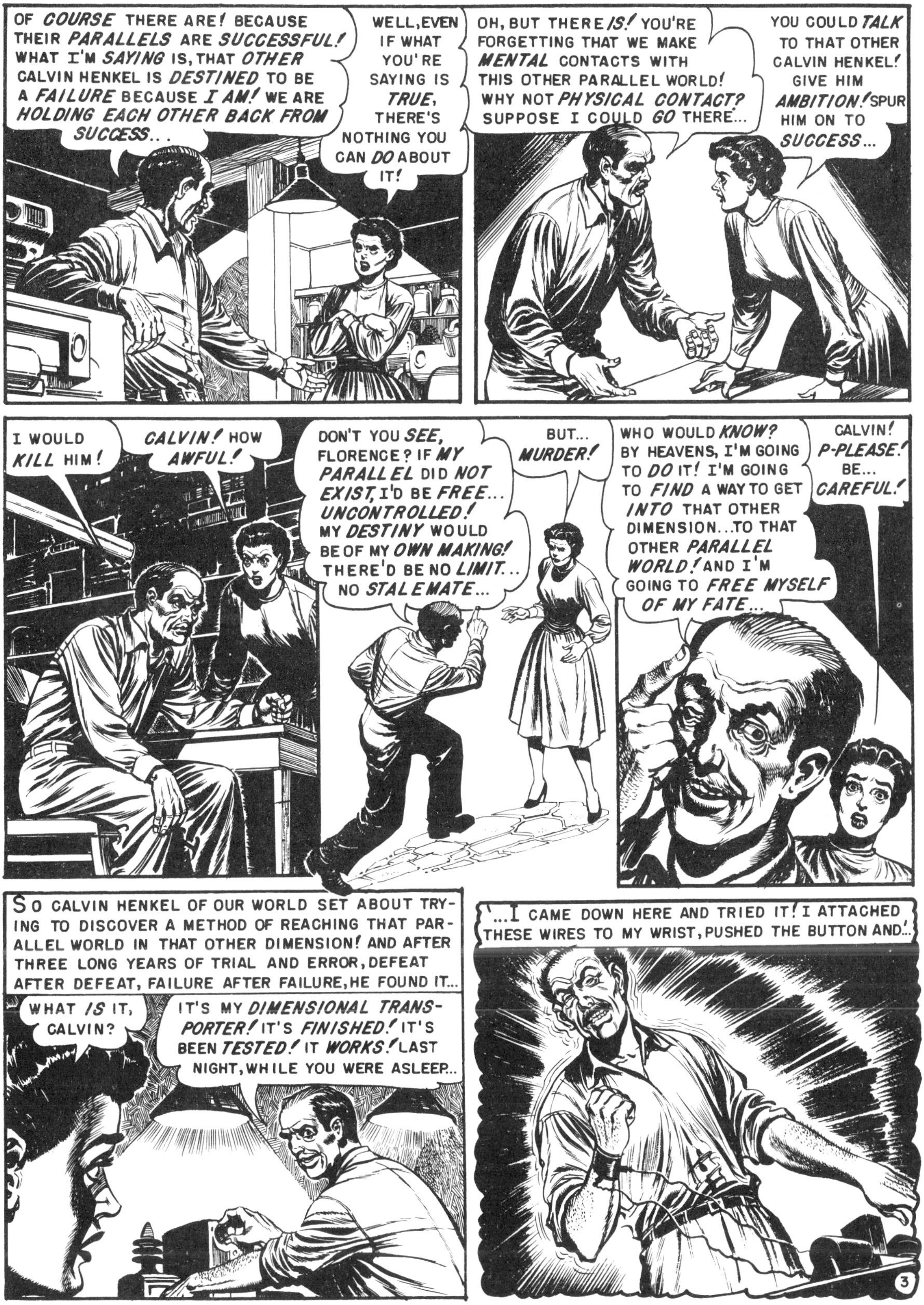
OF COURSE THERE ARE! BECAUSE THEIR PARALLELS ARE SUCCESSFUL! WHAT I'M SAYING IS, THAT OTHER CALVIN HENKEL IS DESTINED TO BE A FAILURE BECAUSE I AM! WE ARE HOLDING EACH OTHER BACK FROM SUCCESS...
WELL, EVEN IF WHAT YOU'RE SAYING IS TRUE, THERE'S NOTHING YOU CAN DO ABOUT IT!
OH, BUT THERE IS! YOU'RE FORGETTING THAT WE MAKE MENTAL CONTACTS WITH THIS OTHER PARALLEL WORLD! WHY NOT PHYSICAL CONTACT? SUPPOSE I COULD GO THERE...
YOU COULD TALK TO THAT OTHER CALVIN HENKEL! GIVE HIM AMBITION! SPUR HIM ON TO SUCCESS...
I WOULD KILL HIM!
CALVIN! HOW AWFUL!
DON'T YOU SEE, FLORENCE? IF MY PARALLEL DID NOT EXIST, I'D BE FREE... UNCONTROLLED! MY DESTINY WOULD BE OF MY OWN MAKING! THERE'D BE NO LIMIT... NO STALEMATE...
BUT... MURDER!
WHO WOULD KNOW? BY HEAVENS, I'M GOING TO DO IT! I'M GOING TO FIND A WAY TO GET INTO THAT OTHER DIMENSION... TO THAT OTHER PARALLEL WORLD! AND I'M GOING TO FREE MYSELF OF MY FATE...
CALVIN! P-PLEASE! BE... CAREFUL!
SO CALVIN HENKEL OF OUR WORLD SET ABOUT TRYING TO DISCOVER A METHOD OF REACHING THAT PARALLEL WORLD IN THAT OTHER DIMENSION! AND AFTER THREE LONG YEARS OF TRIAL AND ERROR, DEFEAT AFTER DEFEAT, FAILURE AFTER FAILURE, HE FOUND IT...
WHAT IS IT, CALVIN?
IT'S MY DIMENSIONAL TRANSPORTER! IT'S FINISHED! IT'S BEEN TESTED! IT WORKS! LAST NIGHT, WHILE YOU WERE ASLEEP...
'...I CAME DOWN HERE AND TRIED IT! I ATTACHED THESE WIRES TO MY WRIST, PUSHED THE BUTTON AND...'
3

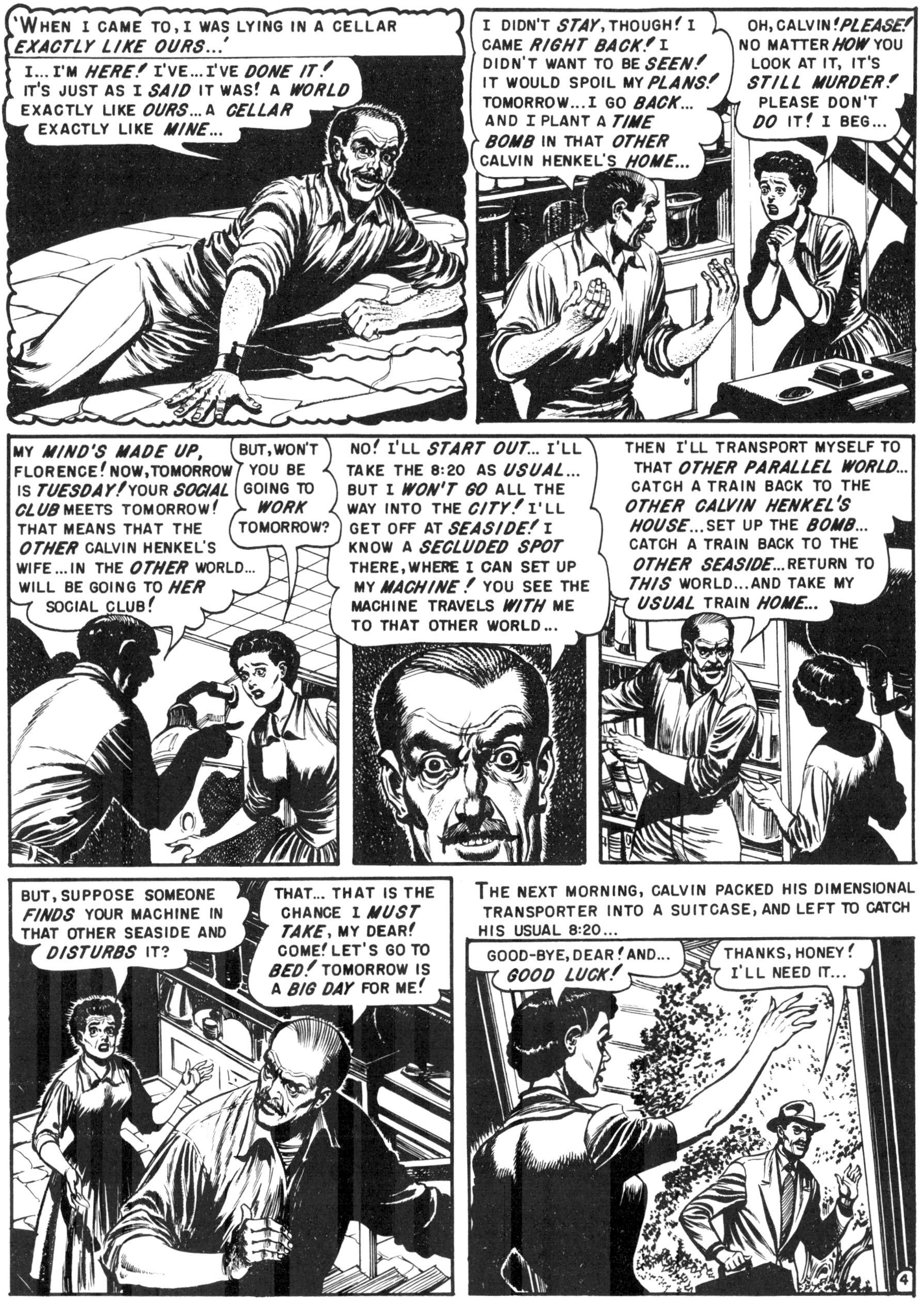
'WHEN I CAME TO, I WAS LYING IN A CELLAR EXACTLY LIKE OURS...'
I... I'M HERE! I'VE... I'VE DONE IT! IT'S JUST AS I SAID IT WAS! A WORLD EXACTLY LIKE OURS... A CELLAR EXACTLY LIKE MINE...
I DIDN'T STAY, THOUGH! I CAME RIGHT BACK! I DIDN'T WANT TO BE SEEN! IT WOULD SPOIL MY PLANS! TOMORROW... I GO BACK... AND I PLANT A TIME BOMB IN THAT OTHER CALVIN HENKEL'S HOME...
OH, CALVIN! PLEASE! NO MATTER HOW YOU LOOK AT IT, IT'S STILL MURDER! PLEASE DON'T DO IT! I BEG...
MY MIND'S MADE UP, FLORENCE! NOW, TOMORROW IS TUESDAY! YOUR SOCIAL CLUB MEETS TOMORROW! THAT MEANS THAT THE OTHER CALVIN HENKEL'S WIFE... IN THE OTHER WORLD... WILL BE GOING TO HER SOCIAL CLUB!
BUT, WON'T YOU BE GOING TO WORK TOMORROW?
NO! I'LL START OUT... I'LL TAKE THE 8:20 AS USUAL... BUT I WON'T GO ALL THE WAY INTO THE CITY! I'LL GET OFF AT SEASIDE! I KNOW A SECLUDED SPOT THERE, WHERE I CAN SET UP MY MACHINE! YOU SEE THE MACHINE TRAVELS WITH ME TO THAT OTHER WORLD...
THEN I'LL TRANSPORT MYSELF TO THAT OTHER PARALLEL WORLD... CATCH A TRAIN BACK TO THE OTHER CALVIN HENKEL'S HOUSE... SET UP THE BOMB... CATCH A TRAIN BACK TO THE OTHER SEASIDE... RETURN TO THIS WORLD... AND TAKE MY USUAL TRAIN HOME...
BUT, SUPPOSE SOMEONE FINDS YOUR MACHINE IN THAT OTHER SEASIDE AND DISTURBS IT?
THAT... THAT IS THE CHANCE I MUST TAKE, MY DEAR! COME! LET'S GO TO BED! TOMORROW IS A BIG DAY FOR ME!
THE NEXT MORNING, CALVIN PACKED HIS DIMENSIONAL TRANSPORTER INTO A SUITCASE, AND LEFT TO CATCH HIS USUAL 8:20...
GOOD-BYE, DEAR! AND... GOOD LUCK!
THANKS, HONEY! I'LL NEED IT...
4

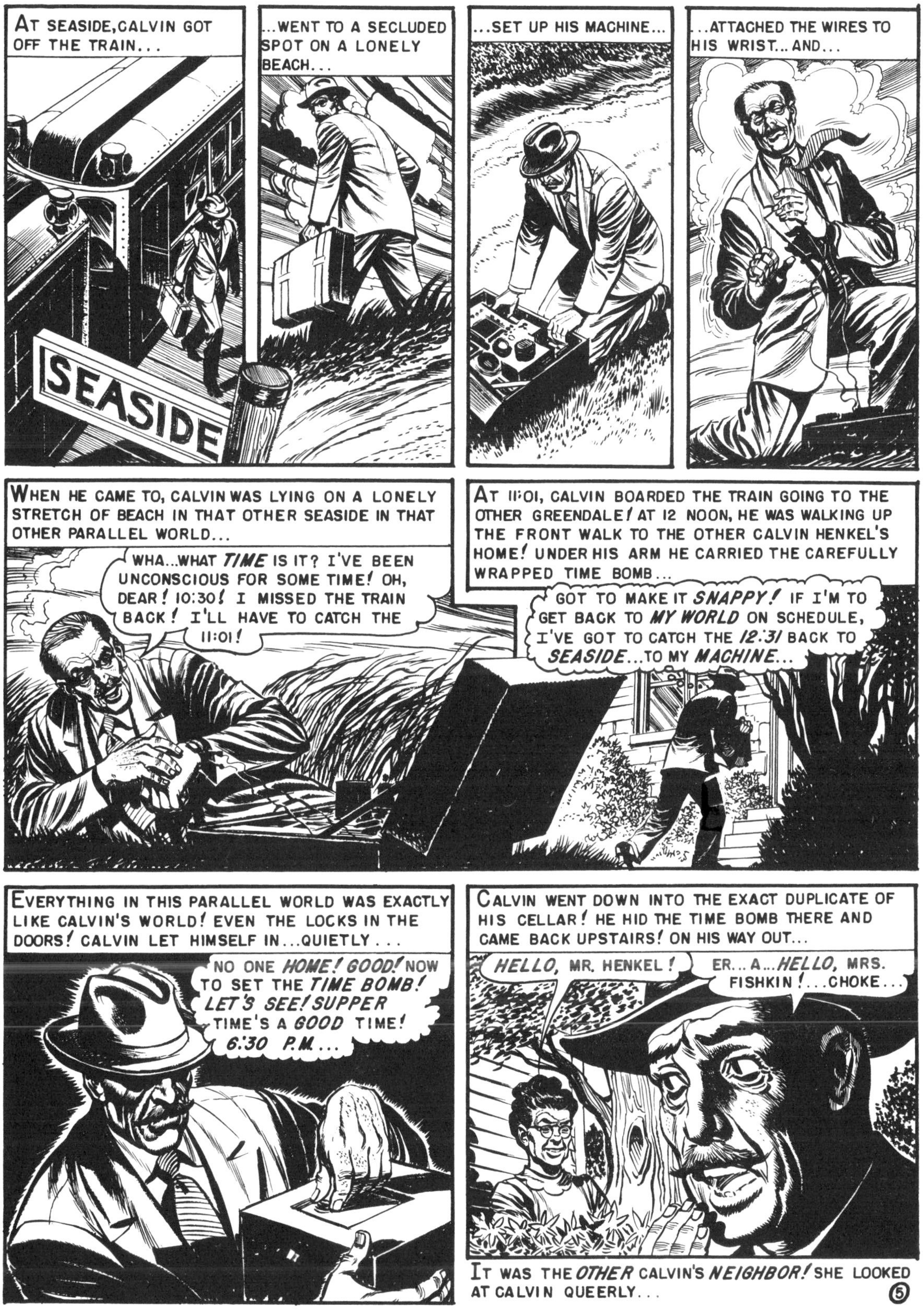
AT SEASIDE, CALVIN GOT OFF THE TRAIN...
SEASIDE
...WENT TO A SECLUDED SPOT ON A LONELY BEACH...
...SET UP HIS MACHINE...
..ATTACHED THE WIRES TO HIS WRIST... AND...
WHEN HE CAME TO, CALVIN WAS LYING ON A LONELY STRETCH OF BEACH IN THAT OTHER SEASIDE IN THAT OTHER PARALLEL WORLD...
WHA...WHAT TIME IS IT? I'VE BEEN UNCONSCIOUS FOR SOME TIME! OH, DEAR! 10:30! I MISSED THE TRAIN BACK! I'LL HAVE TO CATCH THE 11:01!
AT 11:01, CALVIN BOARDED THE TRAIN GOING TO THE OTHER GREENDALE! AT 12 NOON, HE WAS WALKING UP THE FRONT WALK TO THE OTHER CALVIN HENKEL'S HOME! UNDER HIS ARM HE CARRIED THE CAREFULLY WRAPPED TIME BOMB...
GOT TO MAKE IT SNAPPY! IF I'M TO GET BACK TO MY WORLD ON SCHEDULE, I'VE GOT TO CATCH THE 12:31 BACK TO SEASIDE...TO MY MACHINE...
EVERYTHING IN THIS PARALLEL WORLD WAS EXACTLY LIKE CALVIN'S WORLD! EVEN THE LOCKS IN THE DOORS! CALVIN LET HIMSELF IN...QUIETLY...
NO ONE HOME! GOOD! NOW TO SET THE TIME BOMB! LET'S SEE! SUPPER TIME'S A GOOD TIME! 6:30 P.M...
CALVIN WENT DOWN INTO THE EXACT DUPLICATE OF HIS CELLAR! HE HID THE TIME BOMB THERE AND CAME BACK UPSTAIRS! ON HIS WAY OUT...
HELLO, MR. HENKEL!
ER... A...HELLO, MRS. FISHKIN!...CHOKE...
IT WAS THE OTHER CALVIN'S NEIGHBOR! SHE LOOKED AT CALVIN QUEERLY...
5

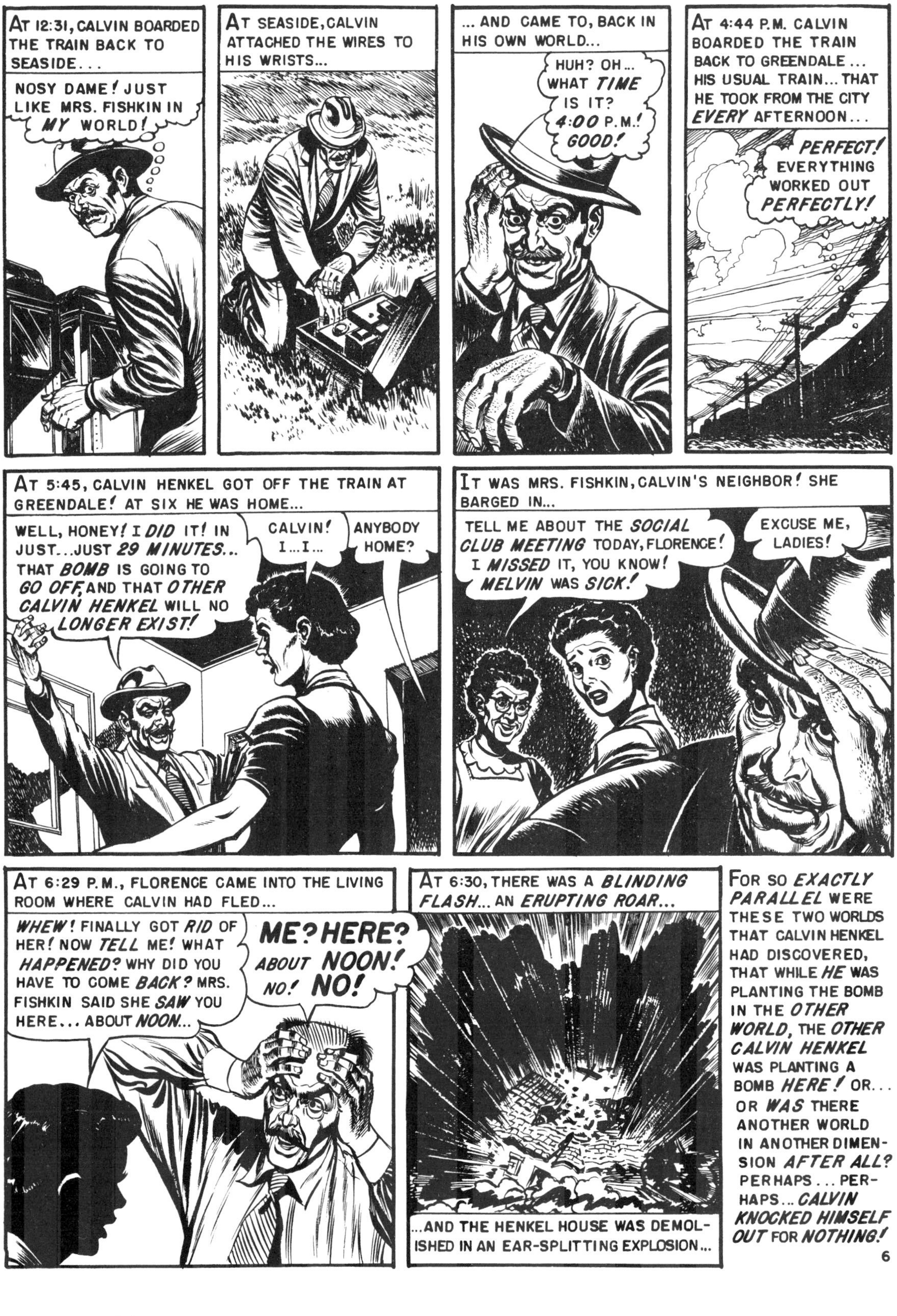
AT 12:31, CALVIN BOARDED THE TRAIN BACK TO SEASIDE...
NOSY DAME! JUST LIKE MRS. FISHKIN IN MY WORLD!
AT SEASIDE, CALVIN ATTACHED THE WIRES TO HIS WRISTS...
...AND CAME TO, BACK IN HIS OWN WORLD...
HUH? OH... WHAT TIME IS IT? 4:00 P.M.! GOOD!
AT 4:44 P.M. CALVIN BOARDED THE TRAIN BACK TO GREENDALE... HIS USUAL TRAIN... THAT HE TOOK FROM THE CITY EVERY AFTERNOON...
PERFECT! EVERYTHING WORKED OUT PERFECTLY!
AT 5:45, CALVIN HENKEL GOT OFF THE TRAIN AT GREENDALE! AT SIX HE WAS HOME...
ANYBODY HOME?
CALVIN! I...I...
WELL, HONEY! I DID IT! IN JUST...JUST 29 MINUTES... THAT BOMB IS GOING TO GO OFF, AND THAT OTHER CALVIN HENKEL WILL NO LONGER EXIST!
IT WAS MRS. FISHKIN, CALVIN'S NEIGHBOR! SHE BARGED IN...
TELL ME ABOUT THE SOCIAL CLUB MEETING TODAY, FLORENCE! I MISSED IT, YOU KNOW! MELVIN WAS SICK!
EXCUSE ME, LADIES!
AT 6:29 P.M., FLORENCE CAME INTO THE LIVING ROOM WHERE CALVIN HAD FLED...
WHEW! FINALLY GOT RID OF HER! NOW TELL ME! WHAT HAPPENED? WHY DID YOU HAVE TO COME BACK? MRS. FISHKIN SAID SHE SAW YOU HERE... ABOUT NOON...
ME? HERE? ABOUT NOON! NO! NO!
AT 6:30, THERE WAS A BLINDING FLASH... AN ERUPTING ROAR...
...AND THE HENKEL HOUSE WAS DEMOLISHED IN AN EAR-SPLITTING EXPLOSION...
FOR SO EXACTLY PARALLEL WERE THESE TWO WORLDS THAT CALVIN HENKEL HAD DISCOVERED, THAT WHILE HE WAS PLANTING THE BOMB IN THE OTHER WORLD, THE OTHER CALVIN HENKEL WAS PLANTING A BOMB HERE! OR... OR WAS THERE ANOTHER WORLD IN ANOTHER DIMENSION AFTER ALL? PERHAPS... PERHAPS... CALVIN KNOCKED HIMSELF OUT FOR NOTHING!
6

ZERO HOUR

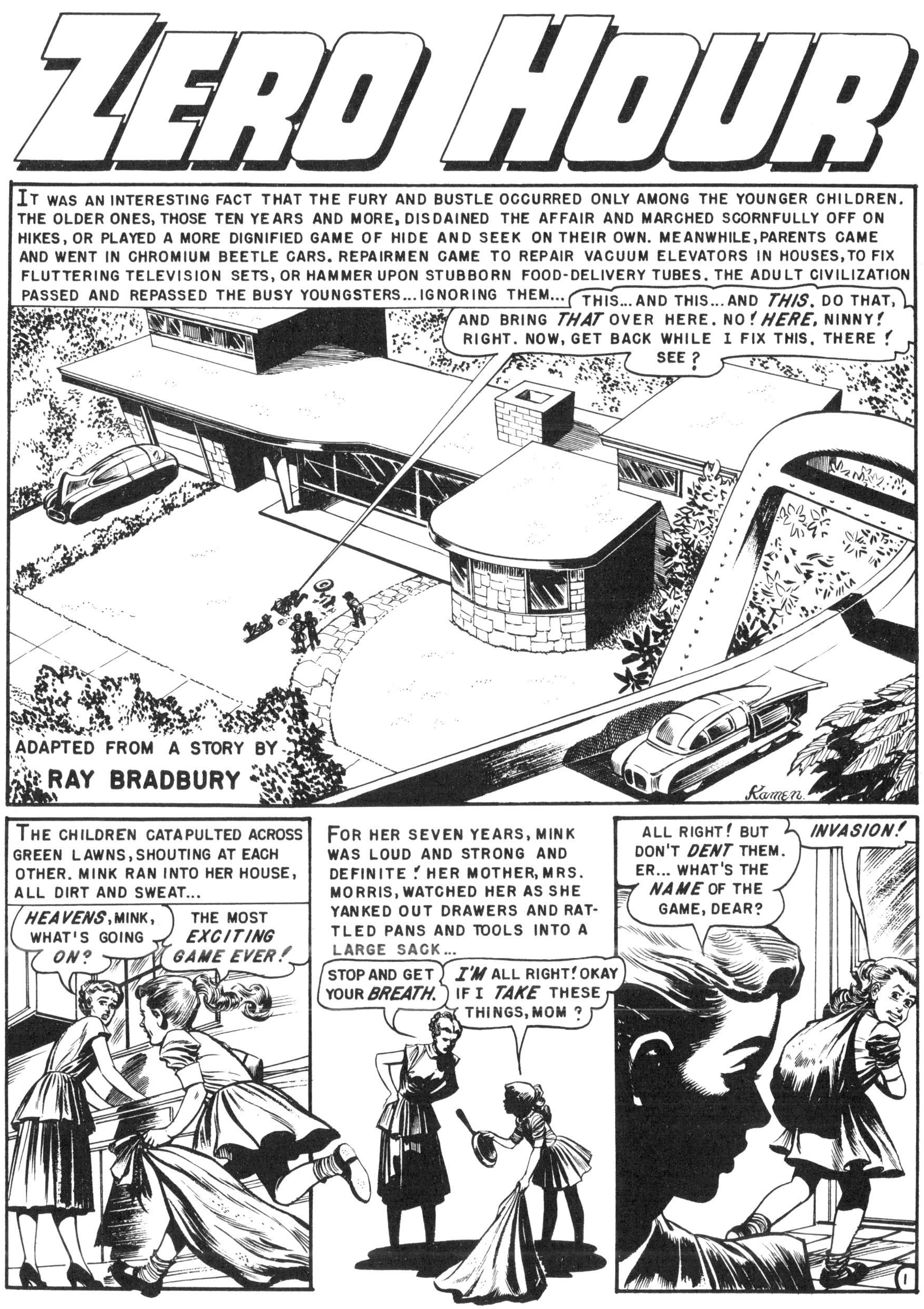
IT WAS AN INTERESTING FACT THAT THE FURY AND BUSTLE OCCURRED ONLY AMONG THE YOUNGER CHILDREN. THE OLDER ONES, THOSE TEN YEARS AND MORE, DISDAINED THE AFFAIR AND MARCHED SCORNFULLY OFF ON HIKES, OR PLAYED A MORE DIGNIFIED GAME OF HIDE AND SEEK ON THEIR OWN. MEANWHILE, PARENTS CAME AND WENT IN CHROMIUM BEETLE CARS. REPAIRMEN CAME TO REPAIR VACUUM ELEVATORS IN HOUSES, TO FIX FLUTTERING TELEVISION SETS, OR HAMMER UPON STUBBORN FOOD-DELIVERY TUBES. THE ADULT CIVILIZATION PASSED AND REPASSED THE BUSY YOUNGSTERS... IGNORING THEM...
THIS... AND THIS... AND THIS. DO THAT, AND BRING THAT OVER HERE. NO! HERE, NINNY! RIGHT. NOW, GET BACK WHILE I FIX THIS. THERE! SEE?
ADAPTED FROM A STORY BY
RAY BRADBURY
Kamen
THE CHILDREN CATAPULTED ACROSS GREEN LAWNS, SHOUTING AT EACH OTHER. MINK RAN INTO HER HOUSE, ALL DIRT AND SWEAT...
HEAVENS, MINK, WHAT'S GOING ON?
THE MOST EXCITING GAME EVER!
FOR HER SEVEN YEARS, MINK WAS LOUD AND STRONG AND DEFINITE! HER MOTHER, MRS. MORRIS, WATCHED HER AS SHE YANKED OUT DRAWERS AND RATTLED PANS AND TOOLS INTO A LARGE SACK...
STOP AND GET YOUR BREATH.
I'M ALL RIGHT! OKAY IF I TAKE THESE THINGS, MOM?
ALL RIGHT! BUT DON'T DENT THEM. ER... WHAT'S THE NAME OF THE GAME, DEAR?
INVASION!
1

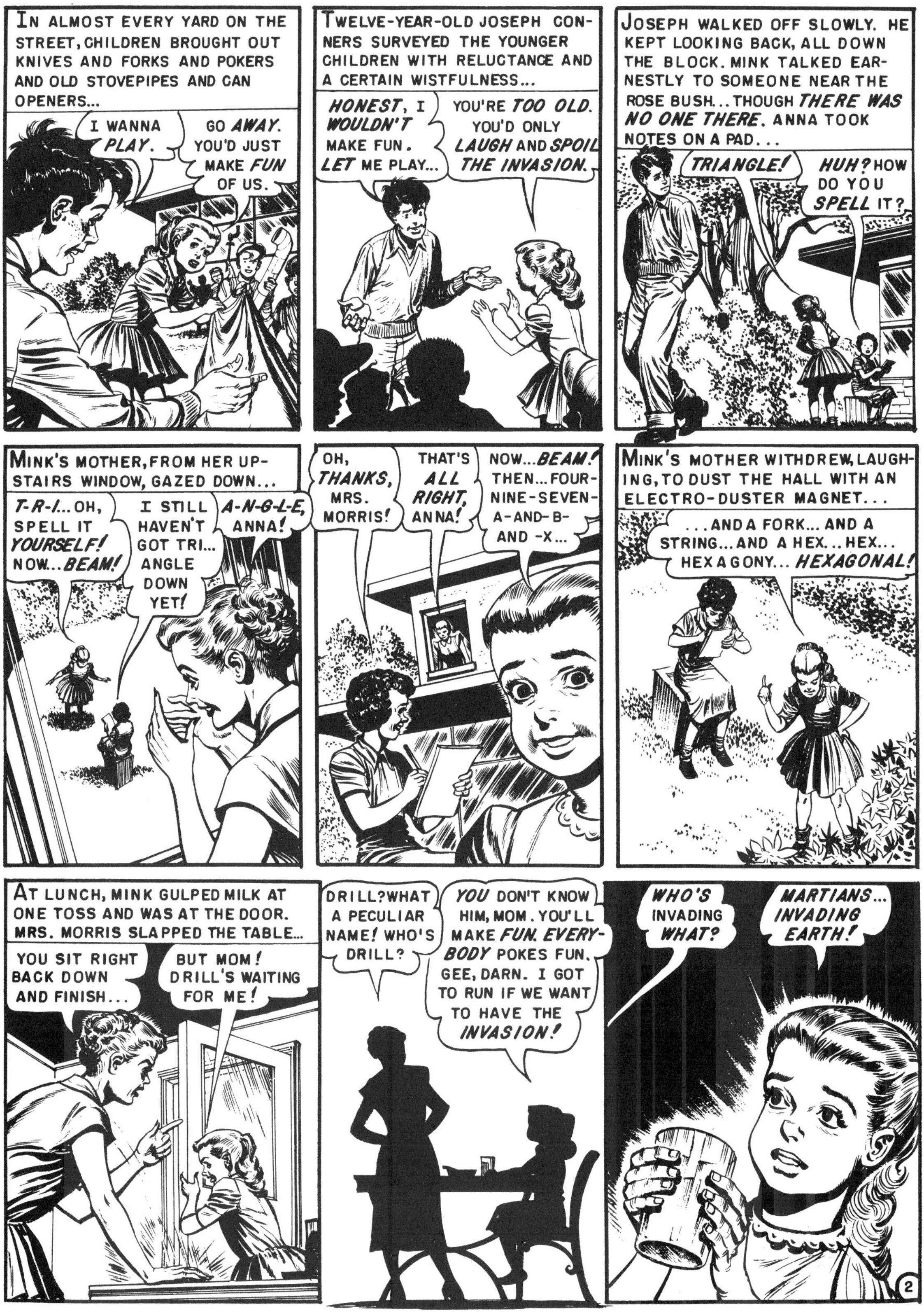
IN ALMOST EVERY YARD ON THE STREET, CHILDREN BROUGHT OUT KNIVES AND FORKS AND POKERS AND OLD STOVEPIPES AND CAN OPENERS...
I WANNA PLAY.
GO AWAY. YOU'D JUST MAKE FUN OF US.
TWELVE-YEAR-OLD JOSEPH CONNERS SURVEYED THE YOUNGER CHILDREN WITH RELUCTANCE AND A CERTAIN WISTFULNESS...
HONEST, I WOULDN'T MAKE FUN. LET ME PLAY...
YOU'RE TOO OLD. YOU'D ONLY LAUGH AND SPOIL THE INVASION.
JOSEPH WALKED OFF SLOWLY. HE KEPT LOOKING BACK, ALL DOWN THE BLOCK. MINK TALKED EARNESTLY TO SOMEONE NEAR THE ROSE BUSH... THOUGH THERE WAS NO ONE THERE. ANNA TOOK NOTES ON A PAD...
TRIANGLE!
HUH? HOW DO YOU SPELL IT?
MINK'S MOTHER, FROM HER UPSTAIRS WINDOW, GAZED DOWN...
T-R-I... OH, SPELL IT YOURSELF! NOW... BEAM!
I STILL HAVEN'T GOT TRI... ANGLE DOWN YET!
A-N-G-L-E, ANNA!
OH, THANKS, MRS. MORRIS!
THAT'S ALL RIGHT, ANNA!
NOW... BEAM! THEN... FOUR-NINE-SEVEN-A-AND-B-AND -X...
MINK'S MOTHER WITHDREW, LAUGHING, TO DUST THE HALL WITH AN ELECTRO-DUSTER MAGNET...
...AND A FORK... AND A STRING... AND A HEX... HEX... HEXAGONY... HEXAGONAL!
AT LUNCH, MINK GULPED MILK AT ONE TOSS AND WAS AT THE DOOR. MRS. MORRIS SLAPPED THE TABLE...
YOU SIT RIGHT BACK DOWN AND FINISH...
BUT MOM! DRILL'S WAITING FOR ME!
DRILL? WHAT A PECULIAR NAME! WHO'S DRILL?
YOU DON'T KNOW HIM, MOM. YOU'LL MAKE FUN. EVERYBODY POKES FUN. GEE, DARN. I GOT TO RUN IF WE WANT TO HAVE THE INVASION!
WHO'S INVADING WHAT?
MARTIANS... INVADING EARTH!
2

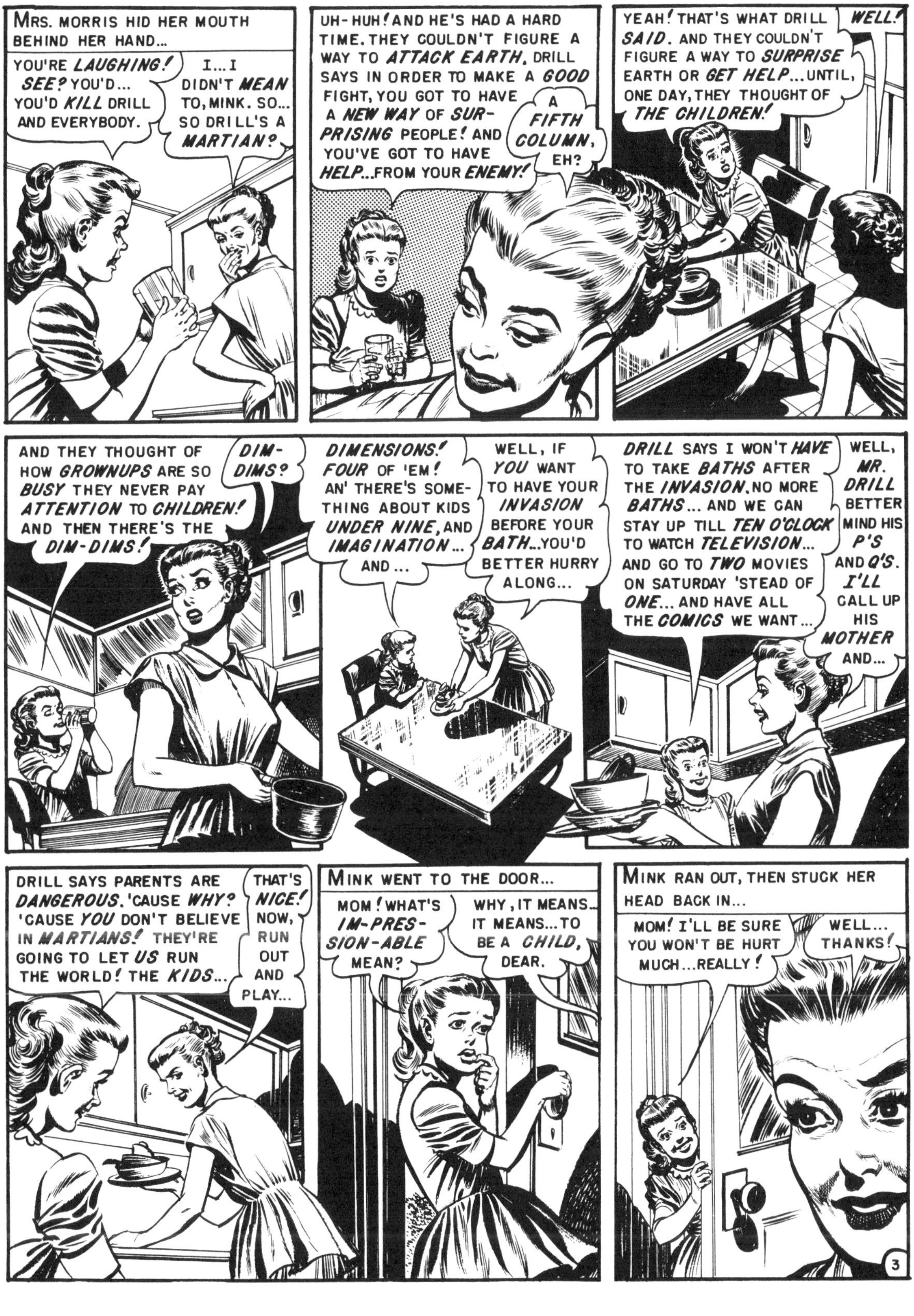

MRS. MORRIS HID HER MOUTH BEHIND HER HAND...
YOU'RE LAUGHING! SEE? YOU'D... YOU'D KILL DRILL AND EVERYBODY.
I...I DIDN'T MEAN TO, MINK. SO... SO DRILL'S A MARTIAN?
UH-HUH! AND HE'S HAD A HARD TIME. THEY COULDN'T FIGURE A WAY TO ATTACK EARTH. DRILL SAYS IN ORDER TO MAKE A GOOD FIGHT, YOU GOT TO HAVE A NEW WAY OF SUR-PRISING PEOPLE! AND YOU'VE GOT TO HAVE HELP...FROM YOUR ENEMY!
A FIFTH COLUMN, EH?
YEAH! THAT'S WHAT DRILL SAID. AND THEY COULDN'T FIGURE A WAY TO SURPRISE EARTH OR GET HELP... UNTIL, ONE DAY, THEY THOUGHT OF THE CHILDREN!
WELL!
AND THEY THOUGHT OF HOW GROWNUPS ARE SO BUSY THEY NEVER PAY ATTENTION TO CHILDREN! AND THEN THERE'S THE DIM-DIMS!
DIM-DIMS?
DIMENSIONS! FOUR OF 'EM! AN' THERE'S SOME-THING ABOUT KIDS UNDER NINE, AND IMAGINATION... AND...
WELL, IF YOU WANT TO HAVE YOUR INVASION BEFORE YOUR BATH...YOU'D BETTER HURRY ALONG...
DRILL SAYS I WON'T HAVE TO TAKE BATHS AFTER THE INVASION. NO MORE BATHS... AND WE CAN STAY UP TILL TEN O'CLOCK TO WATCH TELEVISION... AND GO TO TWO MOVIES ON SATURDAY 'STEAD OF ONE... AND HAVE ALL THE COMICS WE WANT...
WELL, MR. DRILL BETTER MIND HIS P'S AND Q'S. I'LL CALL UP HIS MOTHER AND...
DRILL SAYS PARENTS ARE DANGEROUS. 'CAUSE WHY? 'CAUSE YOU DON'T BELIEVE IN MARTIANS! THEY'RE GOING TO LET US RUN THE WORLD! THE KIDS...
THAT'S NICE! NOW, RUN OUT AND PLAY...
MINK WENT TO THE DOOR...
MOM! WHAT'S IM-PRES-SION-ABLE MEAN?
WHY, IT MEANS... IT MEANS... TO BE A CHILD, DEAR.
MINK RAN OUT, THEN STUCK HER HEAD BACK IN...
MOM! I'LL BE SURE YOU WON'T BE HURT MUCH...REALLY!
WELL... THANKS!
3

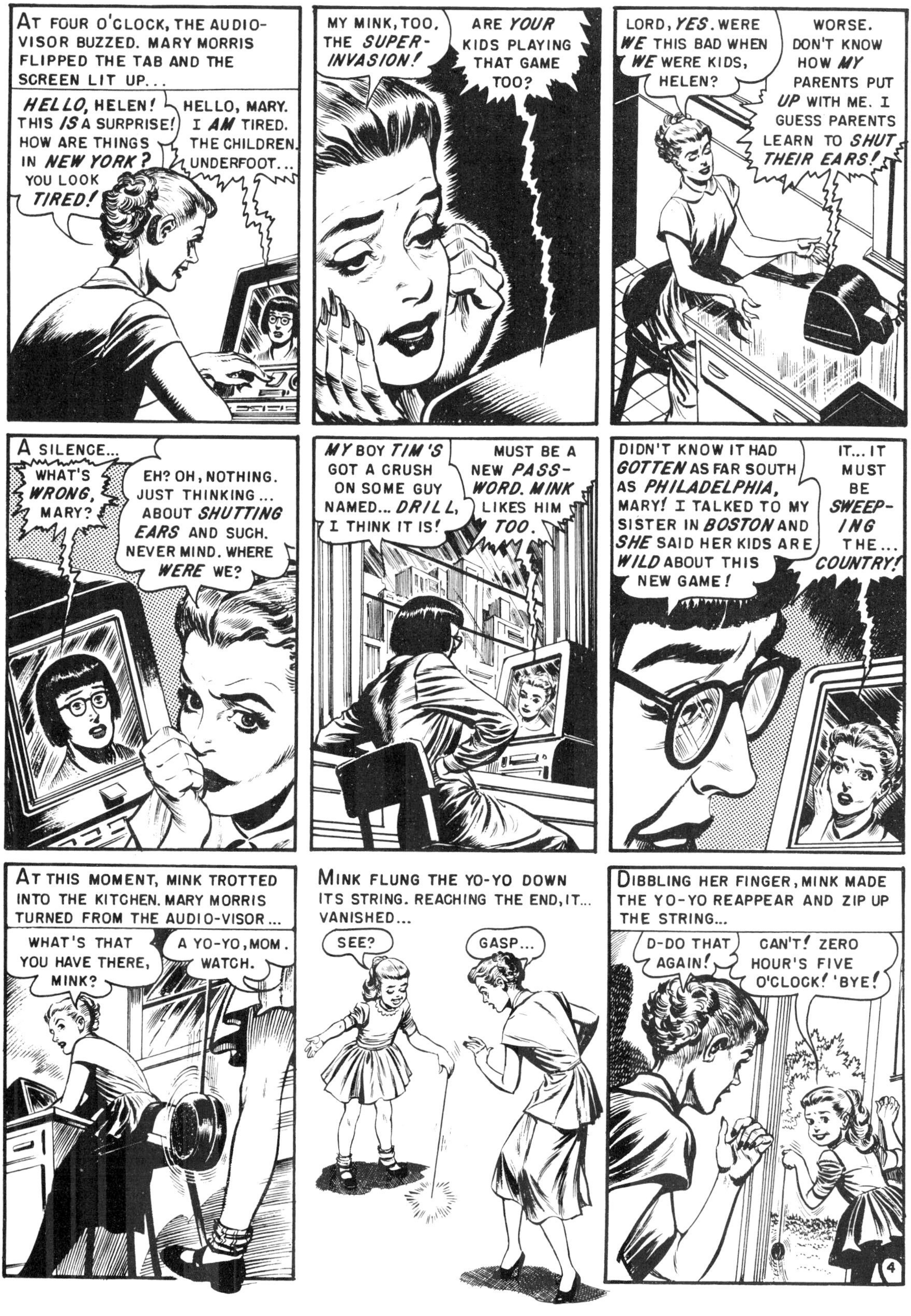
AT FOUR O'CLOCK, THE AUDIO-VISOR BUZZED. MARY MORRIS FLIPPED THE TAB AND THE SCREEN LIT UP...
HELLO, HELEN! THIS IS A SURPRISE! HOW ARE THINGS IN NEW YORK? YOU LOOK TIRED!
HELLO, MARY. I AM TIRED. THE CHILDREN. UNDERFOOT...
MY MINK, TOO. THE SUPER-INVASION!
ARE YOUR KIDS PLAYING THAT GAME TOO?
LORD, YES. WERE WE THIS BAD WHEN WE WERE KIDS, HELEN?
WORSE. DON'T KNOW HOW MY PARENTS PUT UP WITH ME. I GUESS PARENTS LEARN TO SHUT THEIR EARS!
A SILENCE...
WHAT'S WRONG, MARY?
EH? OH, NOTHING. JUST THINKING... ABOUT SHUTTING EARS AND SUCH. NEVER MIND. WHERE WERE WE?
MY BOY TIM'S GOT A CRUSH ON SOME GUY NAMED... DRILL, I THINK IT IS!
MUST BE A NEW PASS-WORD. MINK LIKES HIM TOO.
DIDN'T KNOW IT HAD GOTTEN AS FAR SOUTH AS PHILADELPHIA, MARY! I TALKED TO MY SISTER IN BOSTON AND SHE SAID HER KIDS ARE WILD ABOUT THIS NEW GAME!
IT... IT MUST BE SWEEP-ING THE... COUNTRY!
AT THIS MOMENT, MINK TROTTED INTO THE KITCHEN. MARY MORRIS TURNED FROM THE AUDIO-VISOR...
WHAT'S THAT YOU HAVE THERE, MINK?
A YO-YO, MOM. WATCH.
MINK FLUNG THE YO-YO DOWN ITS STRING. REACHING THE END, IT... VANISHED...
SEE?
GASP...
DIBBLING HER FINGER, MINK MADE THE YO-YO REAPPEAR AND ZIP UP THE STRING...
D-DO THAT AGAIN!
CAN'T! ZERO HOUR'S FIVE O'CLOCK! 'BYE!
4

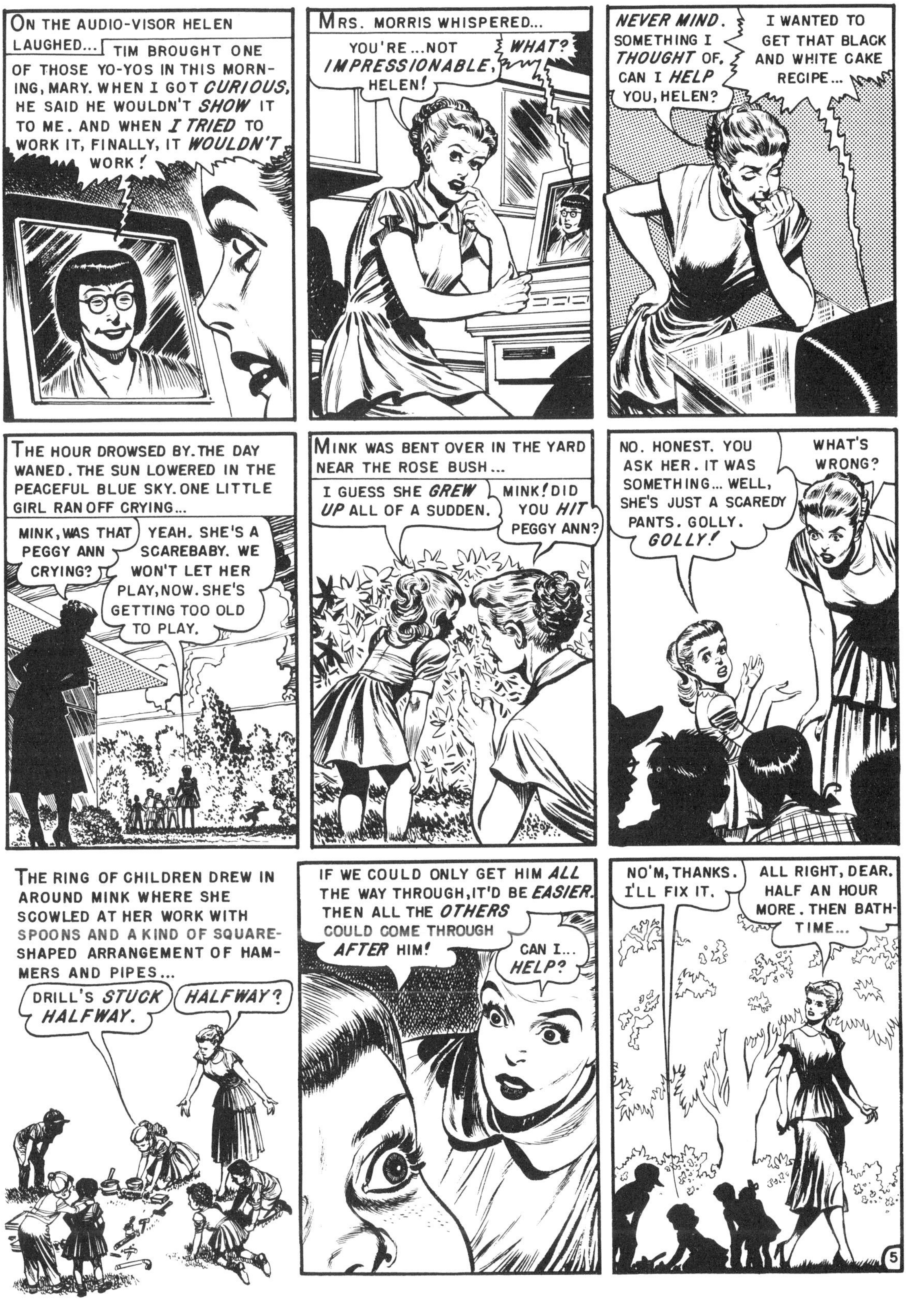

ON THE AUDIO-VISOR HELEN LAUGHED...
TIM BROUGHT ONE OF THOSE YO-YOS IN THIS MORNING, MARY. WHEN I GOT CURIOUS, HE SAID HE WOULDN'T SHOW IT TO ME. AND WHEN I TRIED TO WORK IT, FINALLY, IT WOULDN'T WORK!
MRS. MORRIS WHISPERED...
YOU'RE...NOT IMPRESSIONABLE, HELEN!
WHAT?
NEVER MIND. SOMETHING I THOUGHT OF. CAN I HELP YOU, HELEN?
I WANTED TO GET THAT BLACK AND WHITE CAKE RECIPE...
THE HOUR DROWSED BY. THE DAY WANED. THE SUN LOWERED IN THE PEACEFUL BLUE SKY. ONE LITTLE GIRL RAN OFF CRYING...
MINK, WAS THAT PEGGY ANN CRYING?
YEAH. SHE'S A SCAREBABY. WE WON'T LET HER PLAY, NOW. SHE'S GETTING TOO OLD TO PLAY.
MINK WAS BENT OVER IN THE YARD NEAR THE ROSE BUSH...
I GUESS SHE GREW UP ALL OF A SUDDEN.
MINK! DID YOU HIT PEGGY ANN?
NO. HONEST. YOU ASK HER. IT WAS SOMETHING... WELL, SHE'S JUST A SCAREDY PANTS. GOLLY. GOLLY!
WHAT'S WRONG?
THE RING OF CHILDREN DREW IN AROUND MINK WHERE SHE SCOWLED AT HER WORK WITH SPOONS AND A KIND OF SQUARE-SHAPED ARRANGEMENT OF HAMMERS AND PIPES...
DRILL'S STUCK HALFWAY.
HALFWAY?
IF WE COULD ONLY GET HIM ALL THE WAY THROUGH, IT'D BE EASIER. THEN ALL THE OTHERS COULD COME THROUGH AFTER HIM!
CAN I... HELP?
NO'M, THANKS. I'LL FIX IT.
ALL RIGHT, DEAR. HALF AN HOUR MORE. THEN BATH-TIME...
5

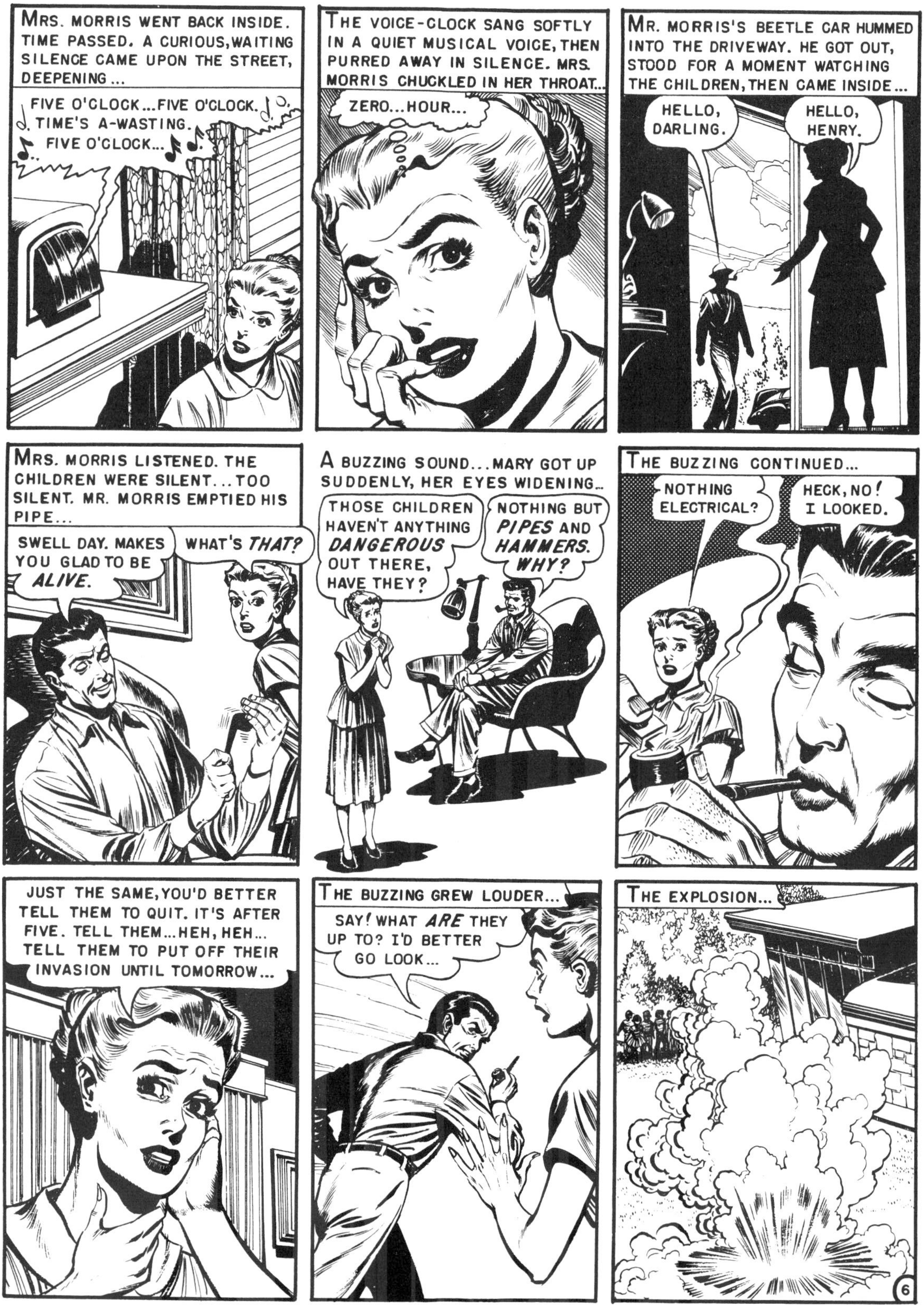
MRS. MORRIS WENT BACK INSIDE. TIME PASSED. A CURIOUS, WAITING SILENCE CAME UPON THE STREET, DEEPENING...
FIVE O'CLOCK... FIVE O'CLOCK. TIME'S A-WASTING. FIVE O'CLOCK...
THE VOICE-CLOCK SANG SOFTLY IN A QUIET MUSICAL VOICE, THEN PURRED AWAY IN SILENCE. MRS. MORRIS CHUCKLED IN HER THROAT...
ZERO... HOUR...
MR. MORRIS'S BEETLE CAR HUMMED INTO THE DRIVEWAY. HE GOT OUT, STOOD FOR A MOMENT WATCHING THE CHILDREN, THEN CAME INSIDE...
HELLO, DARLING.
HELLO, HENRY.
MRS. MORRIS LISTENED. THE CHILDREN WERE SILENT... TOO SILENT. MR. MORRIS EMPTIED HIS PIPE...
SWELL DAY. MAKES YOU GLAD TO BE ALIVE.
WHAT'S THAT?
A BUZZING SOUND... MARY GOT UP SUDDENLY, HER EYES WIDENING...
THOSE CHILDREN HAVEN'T ANYTHING DANGEROUS OUT THERE, HAVE THEY?
NOTHING BUT PIPES AND HAMMERS. WHY?
THE BUZZING CONTINUED...
NOTHING ELECTRICAL?
HECK, NO! I LOOKED.
JUST THE SAME, YOU'D BETTER TELL THEM TO QUIT. IT'S AFTER FIVE. TELL THEM... HEH, HEH... TELL THEM TO PUT OFF THEIR INVASION UNTIL TOMORROW...
THE BUZZING GREW LOUDER...
SAY! WHAT ARE THEY UP TO? I'D BETTER GO LOOK...
THE EXPLOSION...
6

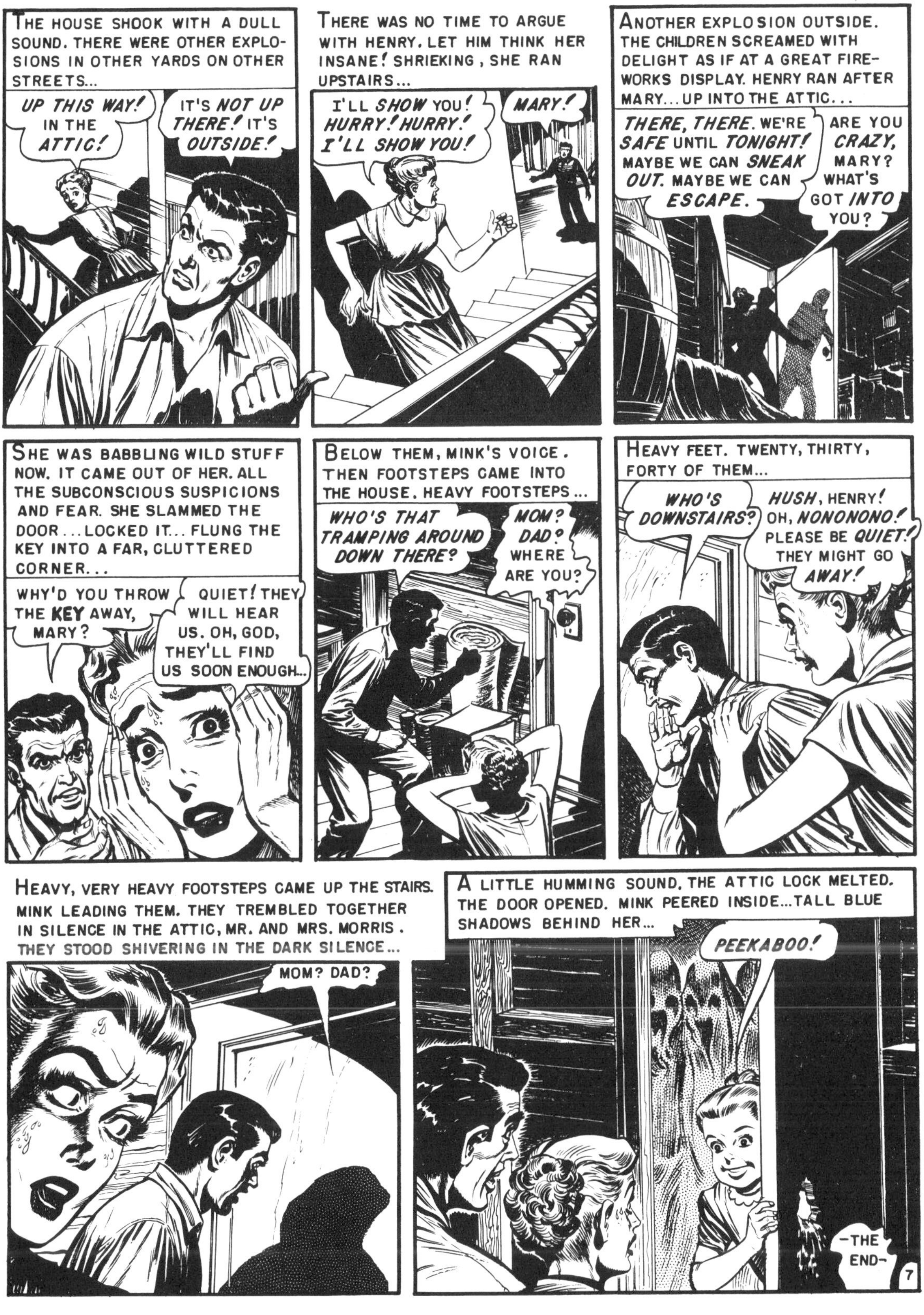
THE HOUSE SHOOK WITH A DULL SOUND. THERE WERE OTHER EXPLOSIONS IN OTHER YARDS ON OTHER STREETS...
UP THIS WAY! IN THE ATTIC!
IT'S NOT UP THERE! IT'S OUTSIDE!
THERE WAS NO TIME TO ARGUE WITH HENRY. LET HIM THINK HER INSANE! SHRIEKING, SHE RAN UPSTAIRS...
I'LL SHOW YOU! HURRY! HURRY! I'LL SHOW YOU!
MARY!
ANOTHER EXPLOSION OUTSIDE. THE CHILDREN SCREAMED WITH DELIGHT AS IF AT A GREAT FIRE-WORKS DISPLAY. HENRY RAN AFTER MARY... UP INTO THE ATTIC...
THERE, THERE. WE'RE SAFE UNTIL TONIGHT! MAYBE WE CAN SNEAK OUT. MAYBE WE CAN ESCAPE.
ARE YOU CRAZY, MARY? WHAT'S GOT INTO YOU?
SHE WAS BABBLING WILD STUFF NOW. IT CAME OUT OF HER. ALL THE SUBCONSCIOUS SUSPICIONS AND FEAR. SHE SLAMMED THE DOOR... LOCKED IT... FLUNG THE KEY INTO A FAR, CLUTTERED CORNER...
WHY'D YOU THROW THE KEY AWAY, MARY?
QUIET! THEY WILL HEAR US. OH, GOD, THEY'LL FIND US SOON ENOUGH...
BELOW THEM, MINK'S VOICE. THEN FOOTSTEPS CAME INTO THE HOUSE. HEAVY FOOTSTEPS...
WHO'S THAT TRAMPING AROUND DOWN THERE?
MOM? DAD? WHERE ARE YOU?
HEAVY FEET. TWENTY, THIRTY, FORTY OF THEM...
WHO'S DOWNSTAIRS?
HUSH, HENRY! OH, NONONONO! PLEASE BE QUIET! THEY MIGHT GO AWAY!
HEAVY, VERY HEAVY FOOTSTEPS CAME UP THE STAIRS. MINK LEADING THEM. THEY TREMBLED TOGETHER IN SILENCE IN THE ATTIC, MR. AND MRS. MORRIS. THEY STOOD SHIVERING IN THE DARK SILENCE...
MOM? DAD?
A LITTLE HUMMING SOUND. THE ATTIC LOCK MELTED. THE DOOR OPENED. MINK PEERED INSIDE... TALL BLUE SHADOWS BEHIND HER...
PEEKABOO!
-THE END-
7

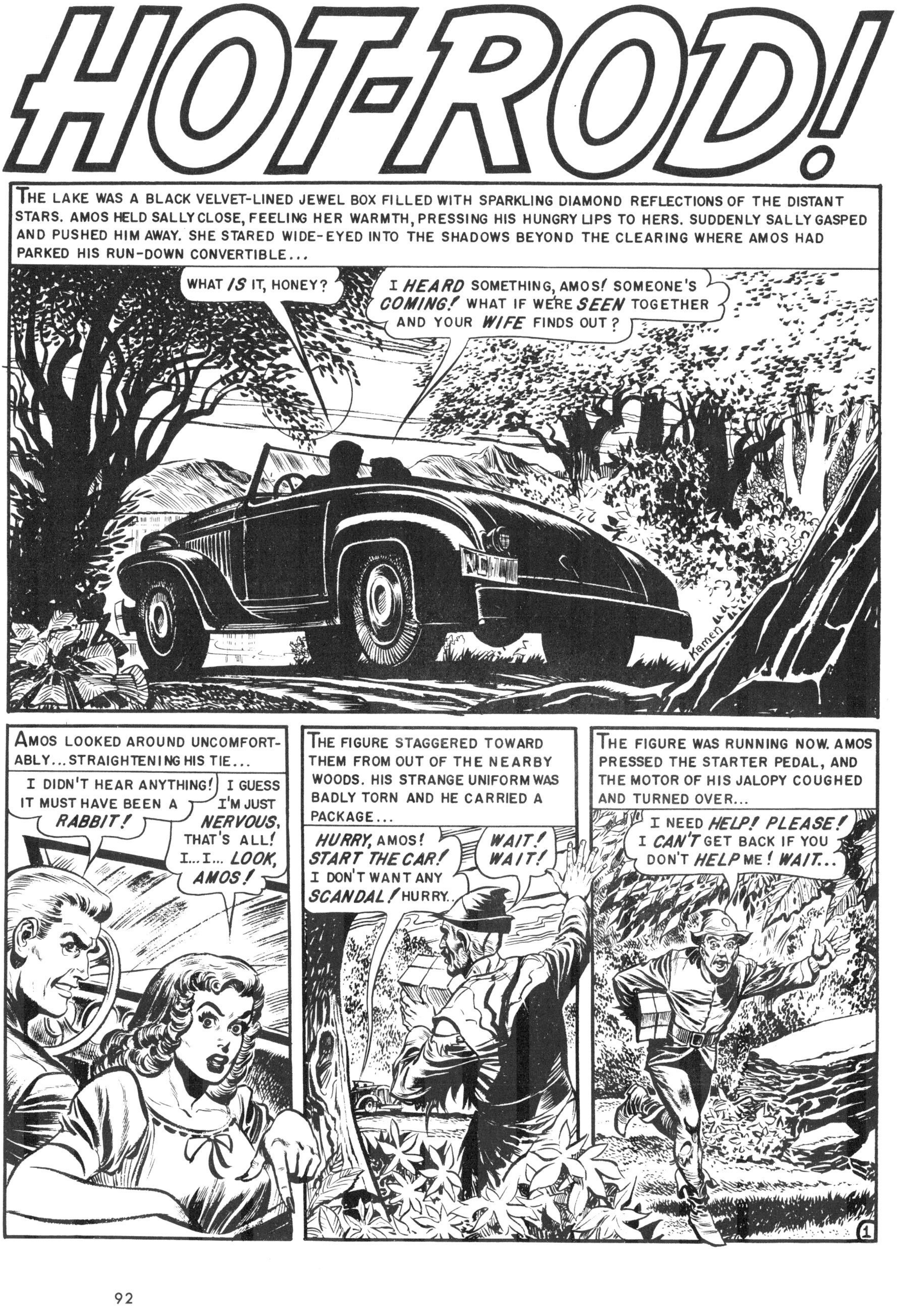
HOT-ROD!
THE LAKE WAS A BLACK VELVET-LINED JEWEL BOX FILLED WITH SPARKLING DIAMOND REFLECTIONS OF THE DISTANT STARS. AMOS HELD SALLY CLOSE, FEELING HER WARMTH, PRESSING HIS HUNGRY LIPS TO HERS. SUDDENLY SALLY GASPED AND PUSHED HIM AWAY. SHE STARED WIDE-EYED INTO THE SHADOWS BEYOND THE CLEARING WHERE AMOS HAD PARKED HIS RUN-DOWN CONVERTIBLE...
WHAT *IS* IT, HONEY?
I *HEARD* SOMETHING, AMOS! SOMEONE'S *COMING!* WHAT IF WE'RE *SEEN* TOGETHER AND YOUR *WIFE* FINDS OUT?
Kamen
AMOS LOOKED AROUND UNCOMFORTABLY... STRAIGHTENING HIS TIE...
I DIDN'T HEAR ANYTHING! IT MUST HAVE BEEN A *RABBIT!*
I GUESS I'M JUST *NERVOUS*, THAT'S ALL! I... I... *LOOK, AMOS!*
THE FIGURE STAGGERED TOWARD THEM FROM OUT OF THE NEARBY WOODS. HIS STRANGE UNIFORM WAS BADLY TORN AND HE CARRIED A PACKAGE...
HURRY, AMOS! *START THE CAR!* I DON'T WANT ANY *SCANDAL!* HURRY...
WAIT! WAIT!
THE FIGURE WAS RUNNING NOW. AMOS PRESSED THE STARTER PEDAL, AND THE MOTOR OF HIS JALOPY COUGHED AND TURNED OVER...
I NEED *HELP! PLEASE!* I *CAN'T* GET BACK IF YOU DON'T *HELP* ME! *WAIT...*
1

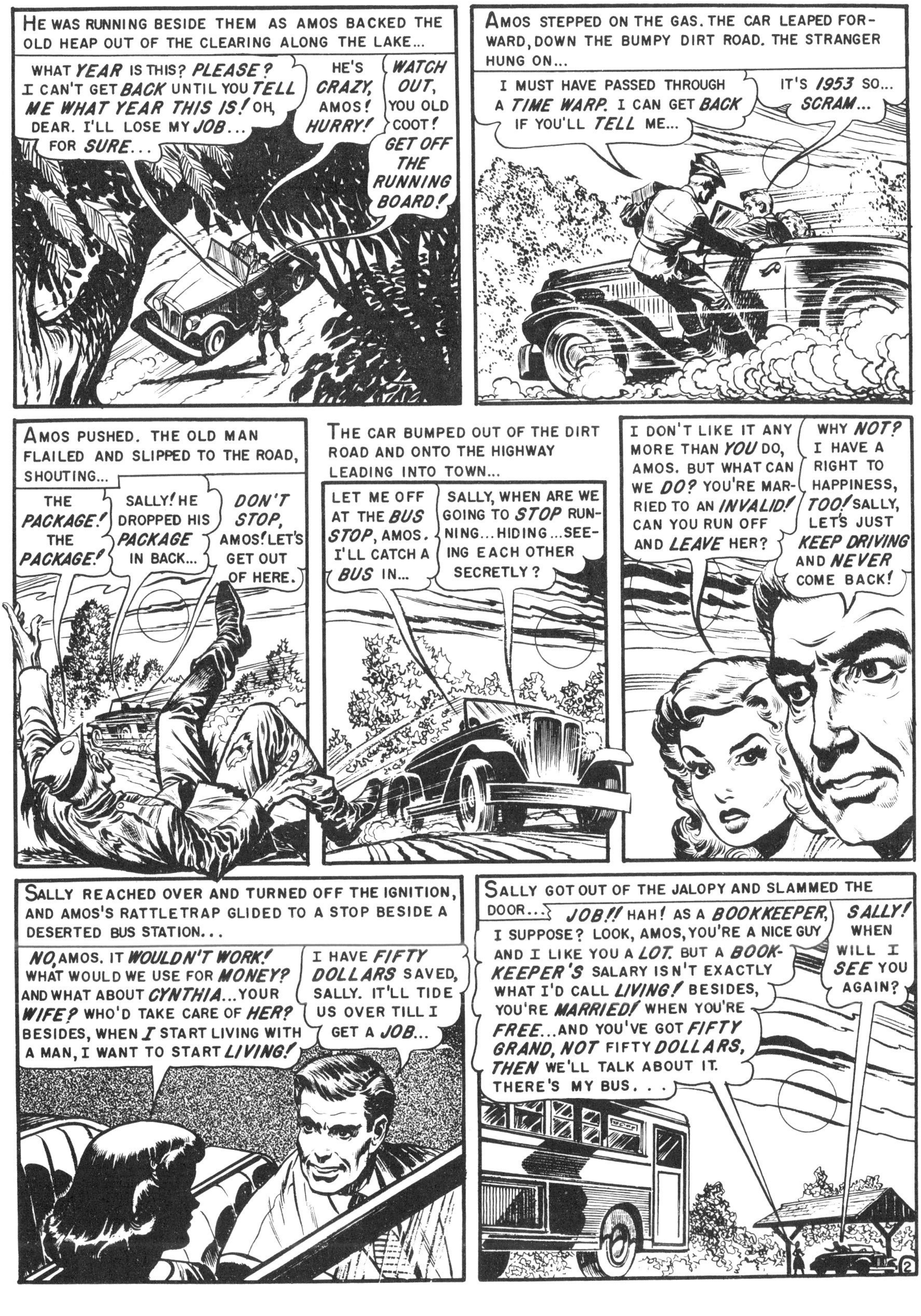
HE WAS RUNNING BESIDE THEM AS AMOS BACKED THE OLD HEAP OUT OF THE CLEARING ALONG THE LAKE...
WHAT YEAR IS THIS? PLEASE? I CAN'T GET BACK UNTIL YOU TELL ME WHAT YEAR THIS IS! OH, DEAR. I'LL LOSE MY JOB... FOR SURE...
HE'S CRAZY, AMOS! HURRY!
WATCH OUT, YOU OLD COOT! GET OFF THE RUNNING BOARD!
AMOS STEPPED ON THE GAS. THE CAR LEAPED FORWARD, DOWN THE BUMPY DIRT ROAD. THE STRANGER HUNG ON...
I MUST HAVE PASSED THROUGH A TIME WARP. I CAN GET BACK IF YOU'LL TELL ME...
IT'S 1953 SO... SCRAM...
AMOS PUSHED. THE OLD MAN FLAILED AND SLIPPED TO THE ROAD, SHOUTING...
THE PACKAGE! THE PACKAGE!
SALLY! HE DROPPED HIS PACKAGE IN BACK...
DON'T STOP, AMOS! LET'S GET OUT OF HERE.
THE CAR BUMPED OUT OF THE DIRT ROAD AND ONTO THE HIGHWAY LEADING INTO TOWN...
LET ME OFF AT THE BUS STOP, AMOS. I'LL CATCH A BUS IN...
SALLY, WHEN ARE WE GOING TO STOP RUNNING... HIDING... SEEING EACH OTHER SECRETLY?
I DON'T LIKE IT ANY MORE THAN YOU DO, AMOS. BUT WHAT CAN WE DO? YOU'RE MARRIED TO AN INVALID! CAN YOU RUN OFF AND LEAVE HER?
WHY NOT? I HAVE A RIGHT TO HAPPINESS, TOO! SALLY, LET'S JUST KEEP DRIVING AND NEVER COME BACK!
SALLY REACHED OVER AND TURNED OFF THE IGNITION, AND AMOS'S RATTLETRAP GLIDED TO A STOP BESIDE A DESERTED BUS STATION...
NO, AMOS. IT WOULDN'T WORK! WHAT WOULD WE USE FOR MONEY? AND WHAT ABOUT CYNTHIA... YOUR WIFE? WHO'D TAKE CARE OF HER? BESIDES, WHEN I START LIVING WITH A MAN, I WANT TO START LIVING!
I HAVE FIFTY DOLLARS SAVED, SALLY. IT'LL TIDE US OVER TILL I GET A JOB...
SALLY GOT OUT OF THE JALOPY AND SLAMMED THE DOOR...
JOB!! HAH! AS A BOOKKEEPER, I SUPPOSE? LOOK, AMOS, YOU'RE A NICE GUY AND I LIKE YOU A LOT. BUT A BOOKKEEPER'S SALARY ISN'T EXACTLY WHAT I'D CALL LIVING! BESIDES, YOU'RE MARRIED! WHEN YOU'RE FREE... AND YOU'VE GOT FIFTY GRAND, NOT FIFTY DOLLARS, THEN WE'LL TALK ABOUT IT. THERE'S MY BUS...
SALLY! WHEN WILL I SEE YOU AGAIN?
2

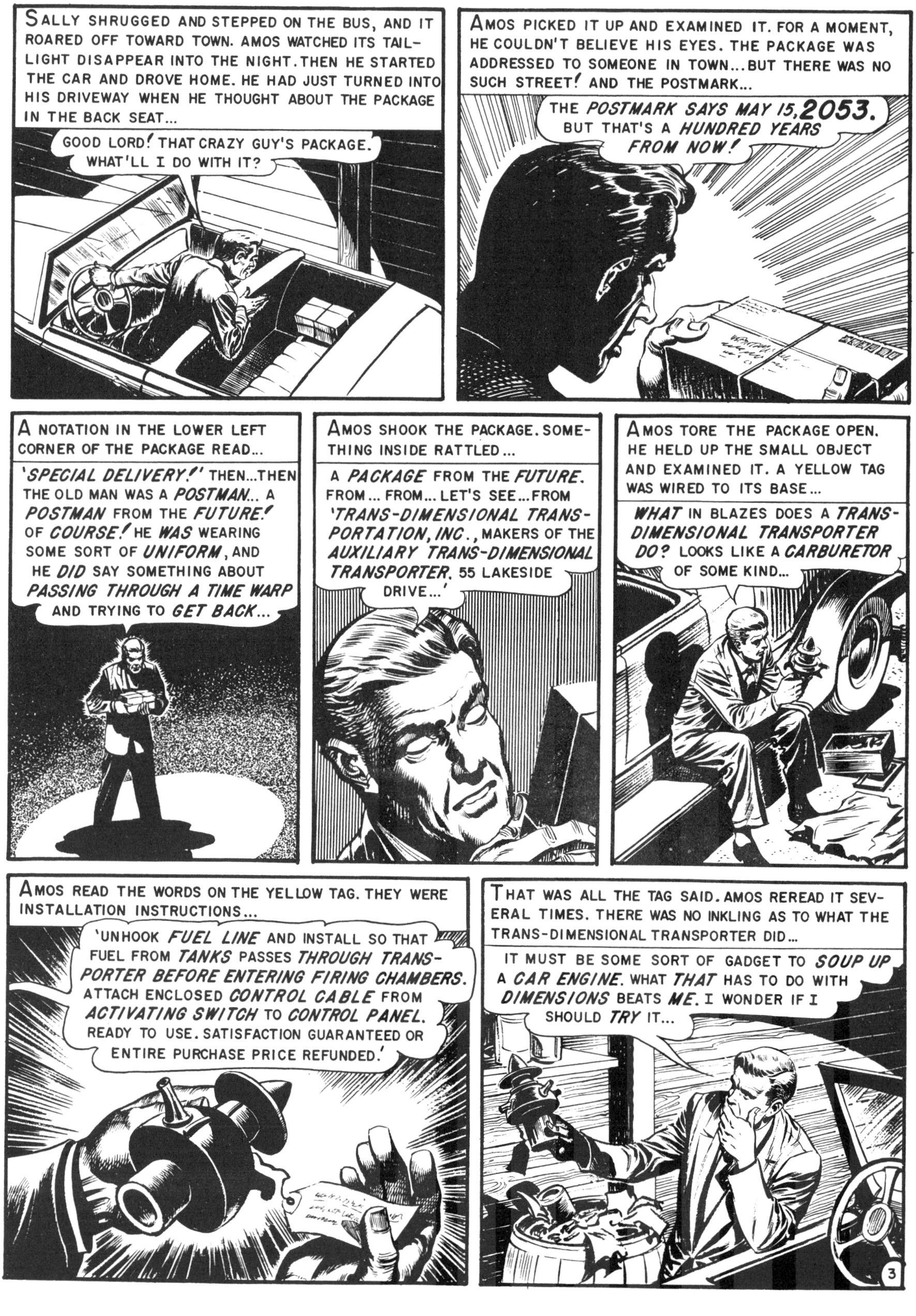
SALLY SHRUGGED AND STEPPED ON THE BUS, AND IT ROARED OFF TOWARD TOWN. AMOS WATCHED ITS TAIL-LIGHT DISAPPEAR INTO THE NIGHT. THEN HE STARTED THE CAR AND DROVE HOME. HE HAD JUST TURNED INTO HIS DRIVEWAY WHEN HE THOUGHT ABOUT THE PACKAGE IN THE BACK SEAT...
GOOD LORD! THAT CRAZY GUY'S PACKAGE. WHAT'LL I DO WITH IT?
AMOS PICKED IT UP AND EXAMINED IT. FOR A MOMENT, HE COULDN'T BELIEVE HIS EYES. THE PACKAGE WAS ADDRESSED TO SOMEONE IN TOWN... BUT THERE WAS NO SUCH STREET! AND THE POSTMARK...
THE POSTMARK SAYS MAY 15, 2053. BUT THAT'S A HUNDRED YEARS FROM NOW!
A NOTATION IN THE LOWER LEFT CORNER OF THE PACKAGE READ...
'SPECIAL DELIVERY!' THEN...THEN THE OLD MAN WAS A POSTMAN... A POSTMAN FROM THE FUTURE! OF COURSE! HE WAS WEARING SOME SORT OF UNIFORM, AND HE DID SAY SOMETHING ABOUT PASSING THROUGH A TIME WARP AND TRYING TO GET BACK...
AMOS SHOOK THE PACKAGE. SOMETHING INSIDE RATTLED...
A PACKAGE FROM THE FUTURE. FROM... FROM... LET'S SEE... FROM 'TRANS-DIMENSIONAL TRANSPORTATION, INC., MAKERS OF THE AUXILIARY TRANS-DIMENSIONAL TRANSPORTER, 55 LAKESIDE DRIVE...'
AMOS TORE THE PACKAGE OPEN. HE HELD UP THE SMALL OBJECT AND EXAMINED IT. A YELLOW TAG WAS WIRED TO ITS BASE...
WHAT IN BLAZES DOES A TRANS-DIMENSIONAL TRANSPORTER DO? LOOKS LIKE A CARBURETOR OF SOME KIND...
AMOS READ THE WORDS ON THE YELLOW TAG. THEY WERE INSTALLATION INSTRUCTIONS...
'UNHOOK FUEL LINE AND INSTALL SO THAT FUEL FROM TANKS PASSES THROUGH TRANSPORTER BEFORE ENTERING FIRING CHAMBERS. ATTACH ENCLOSED CONTROL CABLE FROM ACTIVATING SWITCH TO CONTROL PANEL. READY TO USE. SATISFACTION GUARANTEED OR ENTIRE PURCHASE PRICE REFUNDED.'
THAT WAS ALL THE TAG SAID. AMOS REREAD IT SEVERAL TIMES. THERE WAS NO INKLING AS TO WHAT THE TRANS-DIMENSIONAL TRANSPORTER DID...
IT MUST BE SOME SORT OF GADGET TO SOUP UP A CAR ENGINE. WHAT THAT HAS TO DO WITH DIMENSIONS BEATS ME. I WONDER IF I SHOULD TRY IT...
3

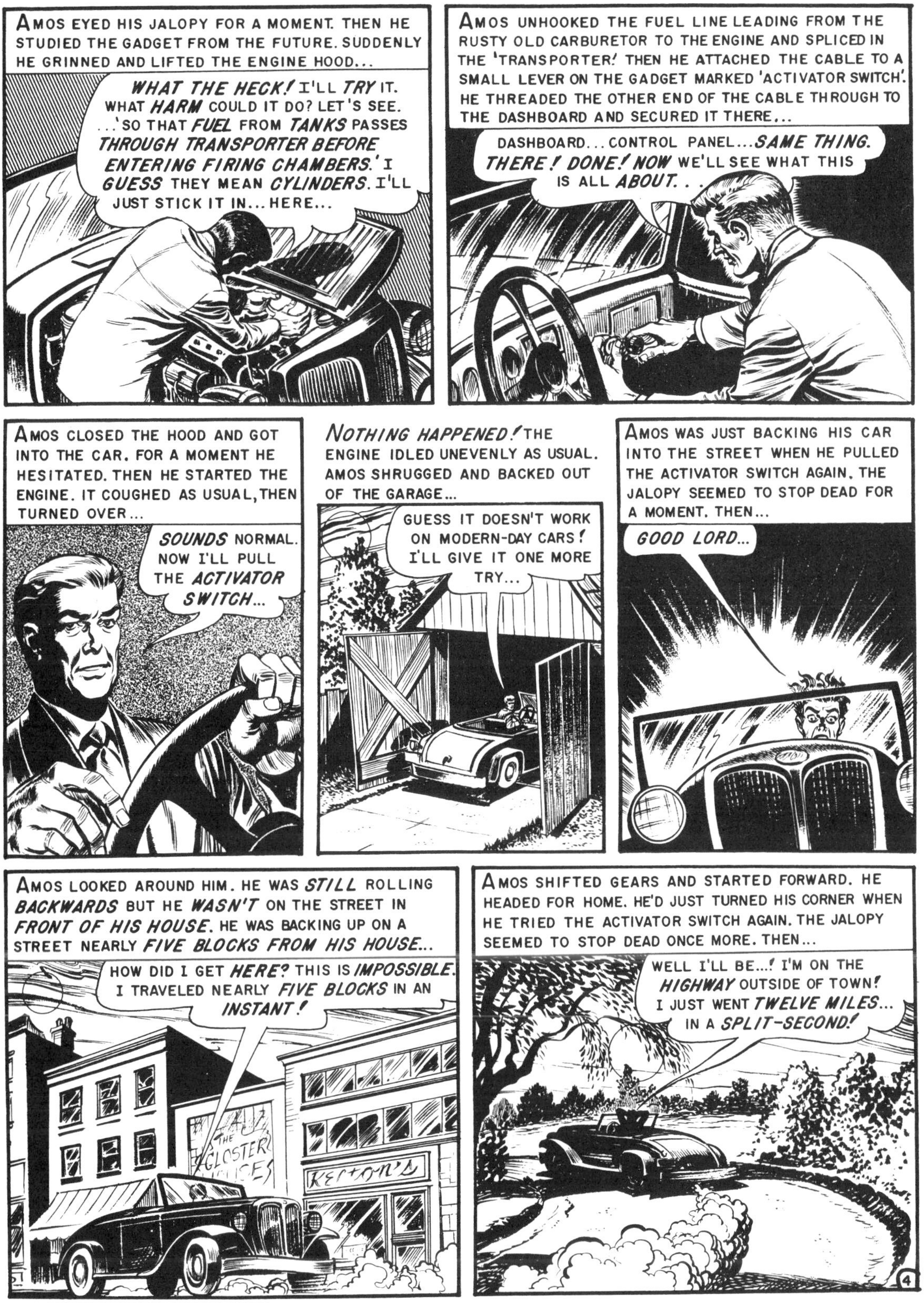
AMOS EYED HIS JALOPY FOR A MOMENT. THEN HE STUDIED THE GADGET FROM THE FUTURE. SUDDENLY HE GRINNED AND LIFTED THE ENGINE HOOD...
WHAT THE HECK! I'LL TRY IT. WHAT HARM COULD IT DO? LET'S SEE. ...'SO THAT FUEL FROM TANKS PASSES THROUGH TRANSPORTER BEFORE ENTERING FIRING CHAMBERS.' I GUESS THEY MEAN CYLINDERS. I'LL JUST STICK IT IN... HERE...
AMOS UNHOOKED THE FUEL LINE LEADING FROM THE RUSTY OLD CARBURETOR TO THE ENGINE AND SPLICED IN THE 'TRANSPORTER.' THEN HE ATTACHED THE CABLE TO A SMALL LEVER ON THE GADGET MARKED 'ACTIVATOR SWITCH'. HE THREADED THE OTHER END OF THE CABLE THROUGH TO THE DASHBOARD AND SECURED IT THERE...
DASHBOARD... CONTROL PANEL... SAME THING. THERE! DONE! NOW WE'LL SEE WHAT THIS IS ALL ABOUT...
AMOS CLOSED THE HOOD AND GOT INTO THE CAR. FOR A MOMENT HE HESITATED. THEN HE STARTED THE ENGINE. IT COUGHED AS USUAL, THEN TURNED OVER...
SOUNDS NORMAL. NOW I'LL PULL THE ACTIVATOR SWITCH...
NOTHING HAPPENED! THE ENGINE IDLED UNEVENLY AS USUAL. AMOS SHRUGGED AND BACKED OUT OF THE GARAGE...
GUESS IT DOESN'T WORK ON MODERN-DAY CARS! I'LL GIVE IT ONE MORE TRY...
AMOS WAS JUST BACKING HIS CAR INTO THE STREET WHEN HE PULLED THE ACTIVATOR SWITCH AGAIN. THE JALOPY SEEMED TO STOP DEAD FOR A MOMENT. THEN...
GOOD LORD...
AMOS LOOKED AROUND HIM. HE WAS STILL ROLLING BACKWARDS BUT HE WASN'T ON THE STREET IN FRONT OF HIS HOUSE. HE WAS BACKING UP ON A STREET NEARLY FIVE BLOCKS FROM HIS HOUSE...
HOW DID I GET HERE? THIS IS IMPOSSIBLE. I TRAVELED NEARLY FIVE BLOCKS IN AN INSTANT!
AMOS SHIFTED GEARS AND STARTED FORWARD. HE HEADED FOR HOME. HE'D JUST TURNED HIS CORNER WHEN HE TRIED THE ACTIVATOR SWITCH AGAIN. THE JALOPY SEEMED TO STOP DEAD ONCE MORE. THEN...
WELL I'LL BE...! I'M ON THE HIGHWAY OUTSIDE OF TOWN! I JUST WENT TWELVE MILES... IN A SPLIT-SECOND!
4

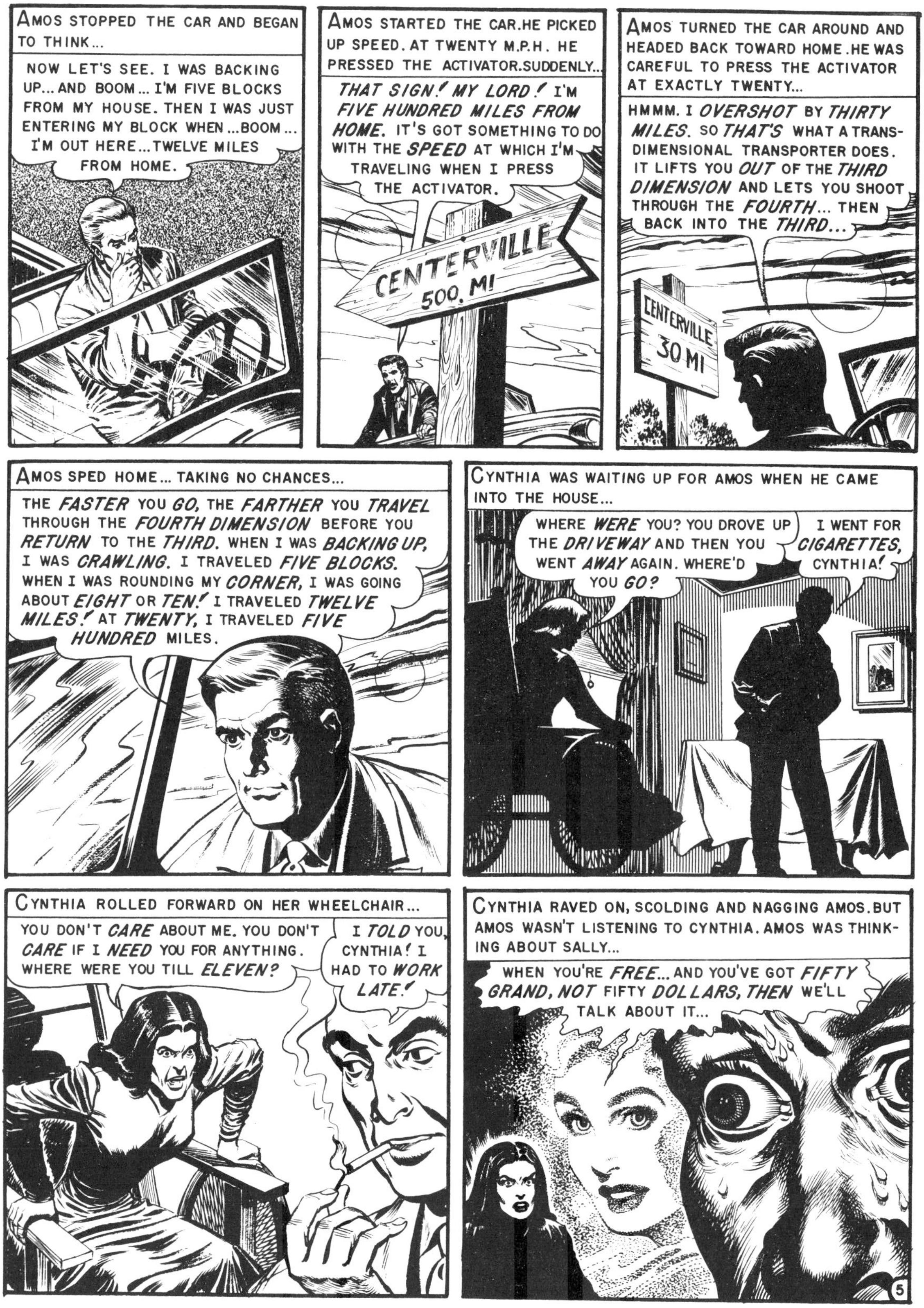
AMOS STOPPED THE CAR AND BEGAN TO THINK...
NOW LET'S SEE. I WAS BACKING UP... AND BOOM... I'M FIVE BLOCKS FROM MY HOUSE. THEN I WAS JUST ENTERING MY BLOCK WHEN ...BOOM... I'M OUT HERE...TWELVE MILES FROM HOME.
AMOS STARTED THE CAR. HE PICKED UP SPEED. AT TWENTY M.P.H. HE PRESSED THE ACTIVATOR. SUDDENLY...
THAT SIGN! MY LORD! I'M FIVE HUNDRED MILES FROM HOME. IT'S GOT SOMETHING TO DO WITH THE SPEED AT WHICH I'M TRAVELING WHEN I PRESS THE ACTIVATOR.
CENTERVILLE 500. MI
AMOS TURNED THE CAR AROUND AND HEADED BACK TOWARD HOME. HE WAS CAREFUL TO PRESS THE ACTIVATOR AT EXACTLY TWENTY...
HMMM. I OVERSHOT BY THIRTY MILES. SO THAT'S WHAT A TRANS-DIMENSIONAL TRANSPORTER DOES. IT LIFTS YOU OUT OF THE THIRD DIMENSION AND LETS YOU SHOOT THROUGH THE FOURTH... THEN BACK INTO THE THIRD...
CENTERVILLE 30 MI
AMOS SPED HOME... TAKING NO CHANCES...
THE FASTER YOU GO, THE FARTHER YOU TRAVEL THROUGH THE FOURTH DIMENSION BEFORE YOU RETURN TO THE THIRD. WHEN I WAS BACKING UP, I WAS CRAWLING. I TRAVELED FIVE BLOCKS. WHEN I WAS ROUNDING MY CORNER, I WAS GOING ABOUT EIGHT OR TEN! I TRAVELED TWELVE MILES! AT TWENTY, I TRAVELED FIVE HUNDRED MILES.
CYNTHIA WAS WAITING UP FOR AMOS WHEN HE CAME INTO THE HOUSE...
WHERE WERE YOU? YOU DROVE UP THE DRIVEWAY AND THEN YOU WENT AWAY AGAIN. WHERE'D YOU GO?
I WENT FOR CIGARETTES, CYNTHIA!
CYNTHIA ROLLED FORWARD ON HER WHEELCHAIR...
YOU DON'T CARE ABOUT ME. YOU DON'T CARE IF I NEED YOU FOR ANYTHING. WHERE WERE YOU TILL ELEVEN?
I TOLD YOU, CYNTHIA! I HAD TO WORK LATE!
CYNTHIA RAVED ON, SCOLDING AND NAGGING AMOS. BUT AMOS WASN'T LISTENING TO CYNTHIA. AMOS WAS THINKING ABOUT SALLY...
WHEN YOU'RE FREE... AND YOU'VE GOT FIFTY GRAND, NOT FIFTY DOLLARS, THEN WE'LL TALK ABOUT IT...
5

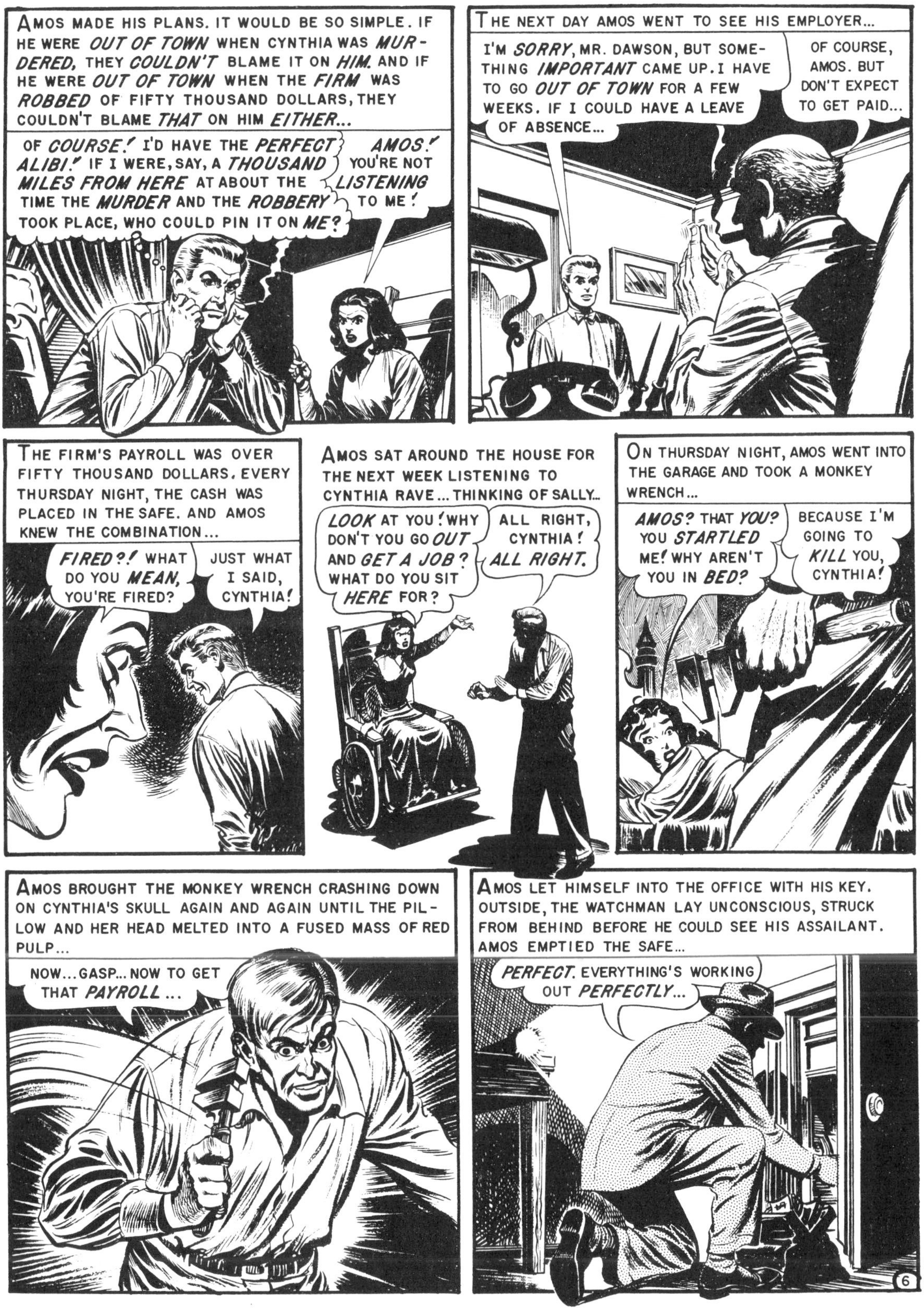
AMOS MADE HIS PLANS. IT WOULD BE SO SIMPLE. IF HE WERE OUT OF TOWN WHEN CYNTHIA WAS MURDERED, THEY COULDN'T BLAME IT ON HIM. AND IF HE WERE OUT OF TOWN WHEN THE FIRM WAS ROBBED OF FIFTY THOUSAND DOLLARS, THEY COULDN'T BLAME THAT ON HIM EITHER...
OF COURSE! I'D HAVE THE PERFECT ALIBI! IF I WERE, SAY, A THOUSAND MILES FROM HERE AT ABOUT THE TIME THE MURDER AND THE ROBBERY TOOK PLACE, WHO COULD PIN IT ON ME?
AMOS! YOU'RE NOT LISTENING TO ME!
THE NEXT DAY AMOS WENT TO SEE HIS EMPLOYER...
I'M SORRY, MR. DAWSON, BUT SOMETHING IMPORTANT CAME UP. I HAVE TO GO OUT OF TOWN FOR A FEW WEEKS. IF I COULD HAVE A LEAVE OF ABSENCE...
OF COURSE, AMOS. BUT DON'T EXPECT TO GET PAID...
THE FIRM'S PAYROLL WAS OVER FIFTY THOUSAND DOLLARS. EVERY THURSDAY NIGHT, THE CASH WAS PLACED IN THE SAFE. AND AMOS KNEW THE COMBINATION...
FIRED?! WHAT DO YOU MEAN, YOU'RE FIRED?
JUST WHAT I SAID, CYNTHIA!
AMOS SAT AROUND THE HOUSE FOR THE NEXT WEEK LISTENING TO CYNTHIA RAVE... THINKING OF SALLY...
LOOK AT YOU! WHY DON'T YOU GO OUT AND GET A JOB? WHAT DO YOU SIT HERE FOR?
ALL RIGHT, CYNTHIA! ALL RIGHT.
ON THURSDAY NIGHT, AMOS WENT INTO THE GARAGE AND TOOK A MONKEY WRENCH...
AMOS? THAT YOU? YOU STARTLED ME! WHY AREN'T YOU IN BED?
BECAUSE I'M GOING TO KILL YOU, CYNTHIA!
AMOS BROUGHT THE MONKEY WRENCH CRASHING DOWN ON CYNTHIA'S SKULL AGAIN AND AGAIN UNTIL THE PILLOW AND HER HEAD MELTED INTO A FUSED MASS OF RED PULP...
NOW... GASP... NOW TO GET THAT PAYROLL...
AMOS LET HIMSELF INTO THE OFFICE WITH HIS KEY. OUTSIDE, THE WATCHMAN LAY UNCONSCIOUS, STRUCK FROM BEHIND BEFORE HE COULD SEE HIS ASSAILANT. AMOS EMPTIED THE SAFE...
PERFECT. EVERYTHING'S WORKING OUT PERFECTLY...
6

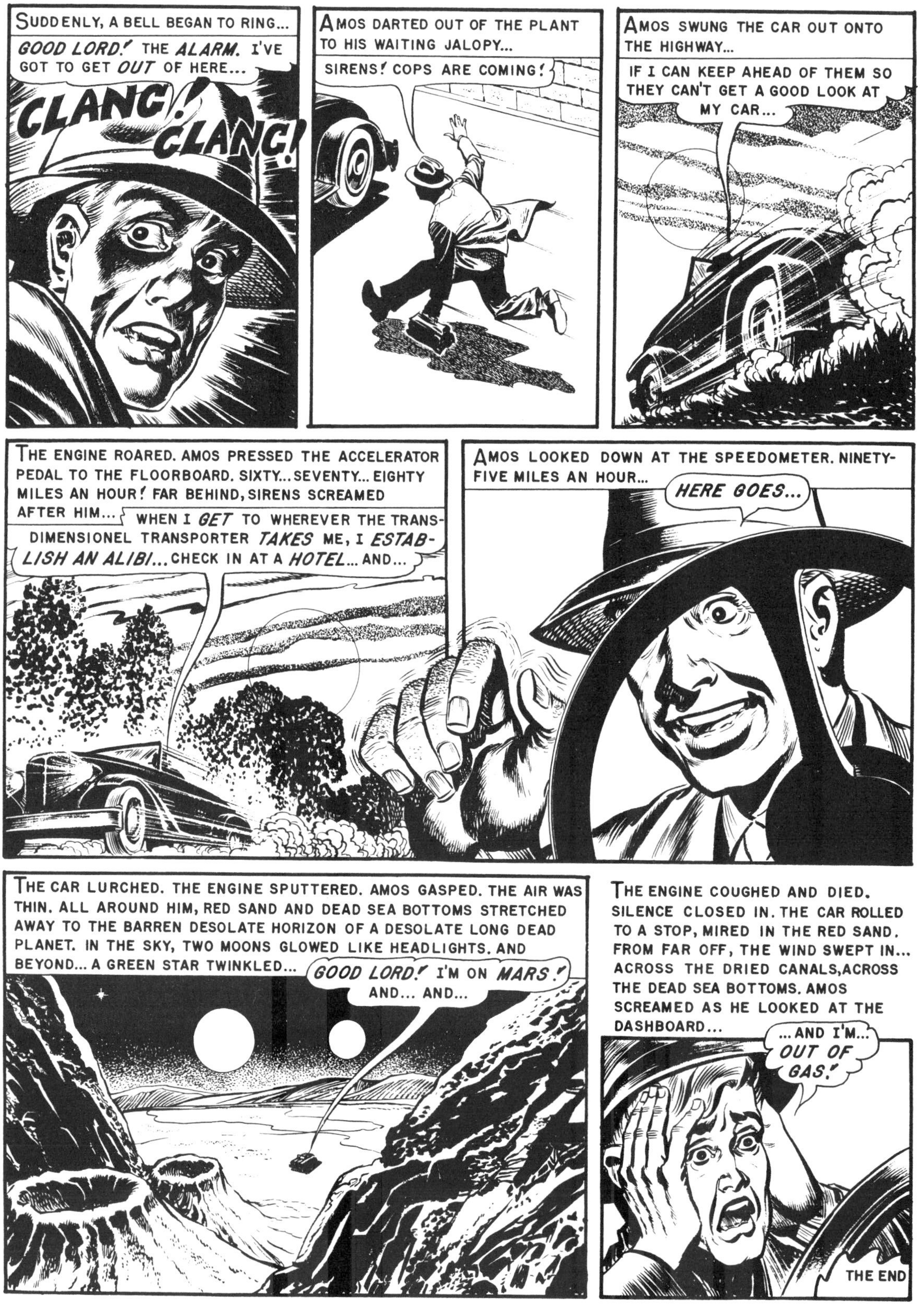
SUDDENLY, A BELL BEGAN TO RING...
GOOD LORD! THE ALARM. I'VE GOT TO GET OUT OF HERE...
CLANG! CLANG!
AMOS DARTED OUT OF THE PLANT TO HIS WAITING JALOPY...
SIRENS! COPS ARE COMING!
AMOS SWUNG THE CAR OUT ONTO THE HIGHWAY...
IF I CAN KEEP AHEAD OF THEM SO THEY CAN'T GET A GOOD LOOK AT MY CAR...
THE ENGINE ROARED. AMOS PRESSED THE ACCELERATOR PEDAL TO THE FLOORBOARD. SIXTY... SEVENTY... EIGHTY MILES AN HOUR! FAR BEHIND, SIRENS SCREAMED AFTER HIM...
WHEN I GET TO WHEREVER THE TRANS-DIMENSIONEL TRANSPORTER TAKES ME, I ESTABLISH AN ALIBI... CHECK IN AT A HOTEL... AND...
AMOS LOOKED DOWN AT THE SPEEDOMETER. NINETY-FIVE MILES AN HOUR...
HERE GOES...
THE CAR LURCHED. THE ENGINE SPUTTERED. AMOS GASPED. THE AIR WAS THIN. ALL AROUND HIM, RED SAND AND DEAD SEA BOTTOMS STRETCHED AWAY TO THE BARREN DESOLATE HORIZON OF A DESOLATE LONG DEAD PLANET. IN THE SKY, TWO MOONS GLOWED LIKE HEADLIGHTS. AND BEYOND... A GREEN STAR TWINKLED...
GOOD LORD! I'M ON MARS! AND... AND...
THE ENGINE COUGHED AND DIED. SILENCE CLOSED IN. THE CAR ROLLED TO A STOP, MIRED IN THE RED SAND. FROM FAR OFF, THE WIND SWEPT IN... ACROSS THE DRIED CANALS, ACROSS THE DEAD SEA BOTTOMS. AMOS SCREAMED AS HE LOOKED AT THE DASHBOARD...
...AND I'M... OUT OF GAS!
THE END

...CONQUERS ALL!

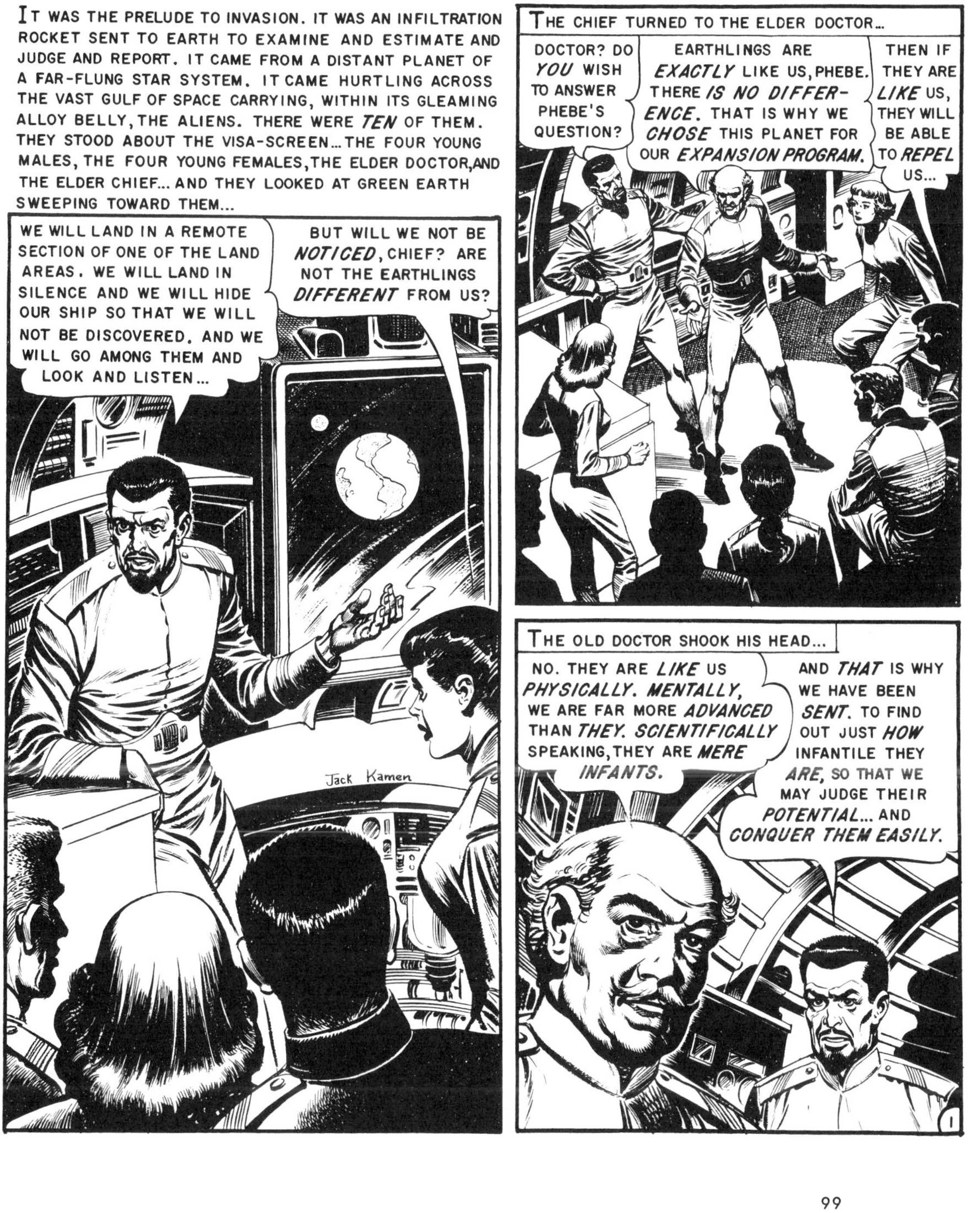

IT WAS THE PRELUDE TO INVASION. IT WAS AN INFILTRATION ROCKET SENT TO EARTH TO EXAMINE AND ESTIMATE AND JUDGE AND REPORT. IT CAME FROM A DISTANT PLANET OF A FAR-FLUNG STAR SYSTEM. IT CAME HURTLING ACROSS THE VAST GULF OF SPACE CARRYING, WITHIN ITS GLEAMING ALLOY BELLY, THE ALIENS. THERE WERE *TEN* OF THEM. THEY STOOD ABOUT THE VISA-SCREEN... THE FOUR YOUNG MALES, THE FOUR YOUNG FEMALES, THE ELDER DOCTOR, AND THE ELDER CHIEF... AND THEY LOOKED AT GREEN EARTH SWEEPING TOWARD THEM...
WE WILL LAND IN A REMOTE SECTION OF ONE OF THE LAND AREAS. WE WILL LAND IN SILENCE AND WE WILL HIDE OUR SHIP SO THAT WE WILL NOT BE DISCOVERED, AND WE WILL GO AMONG THEM AND LOOK AND LISTEN...
BUT WILL WE NOT BE *NOTICED*, CHIEF? ARE NOT THE EARTHLINGS *DIFFERENT* FROM US?
Jack Kamen
THE CHIEF TURNED TO THE ELDER DOCTOR...
DOCTOR? DO *YOU* WISH TO ANSWER PHEBE'S QUESTION?
EARTHLINGS ARE *EXACTLY* LIKE US, PHEBE. THERE *IS NO DIFFERENCE*. THAT IS WHY WE *CHOSE* THIS PLANET FOR OUR *EXPANSION PROGRAM*.
THEN IF THEY ARE *LIKE* US, THEY WILL BE ABLE TO *REPEL* US...
THE OLD DOCTOR SHOOK HIS HEAD...
NO. THEY ARE *LIKE* US *PHYSICALLY*. *MENTALLY*, WE ARE FAR MORE *ADVANCED* THAN *THEY*. *SCIENTIFICALLY* SPEAKING, THEY ARE *MERE INFANTS*.
AND *THAT* IS WHY WE HAVE BEEN *SENT*. TO FIND OUT JUST *HOW* INFANTILE THEY *ARE*, SO THAT WE MAY JUDGE THEIR *POTENTIAL*... AND *CONQUER THEM EASILY*.
1

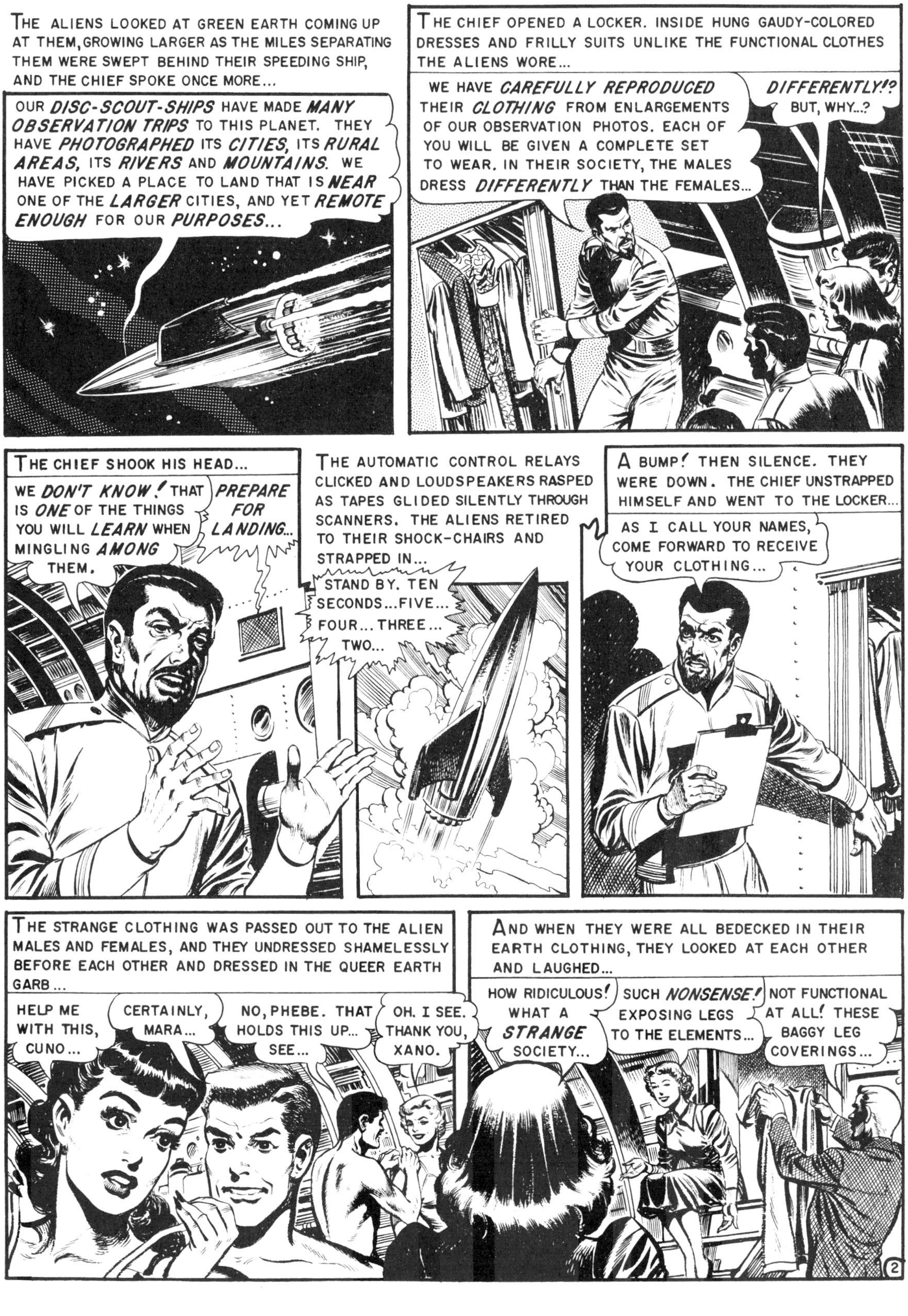
THE ALIENS LOOKED AT GREEN EARTH COMING UP AT THEM, GROWING LARGER AS THE MILES SEPARATING THEM WERE SWEPT BEHIND THEIR SPEEDING SHIP, AND THE CHIEF SPOKE ONCE MORE...
OUR DISC-SCOUT-SHIPS HAVE MADE MANY OBSERVATION TRIPS TO THIS PLANET. THEY HAVE PHOTOGRAPHED ITS CITIES, ITS RURAL AREAS, ITS RIVERS AND MOUNTAINS. WE HAVE PICKED A PLACE TO LAND THAT IS NEAR ONE OF THE LARGER CITIES, AND YET REMOTE ENOUGH FOR OUR PURPOSES...
THE CHIEF OPENED A LOCKER. INSIDE HUNG GAUDY-COLORED DRESSES AND FRILLY SUITS UNLIKE THE FUNCTIONAL CLOTHES THE ALIENS WORE...
WE HAVE CAREFULLY REPRODUCED THEIR CLOTHING FROM ENLARGEMENTS OF OUR OBSERVATION PHOTOS. EACH OF YOU WILL BE GIVEN A COMPLETE SET TO WEAR. IN THEIR SOCIETY, THE MALES DRESS DIFFERENTLY THAN THE FEMALES...
DIFFERENTLY!? BUT, WHY...?
THE CHIEF SHOOK HIS HEAD...
WE DON'T KNOW! THAT IS ONE OF THE THINGS YOU WILL LEARN WHEN MINGLING AMONG THEM.
PREPARE FOR LANDING...
THE AUTOMATIC CONTROL RELAYS CLICKED AND LOUDSPEAKERS RASPED AS TAPES GLIDED SILENTLY THROUGH SCANNERS. THE ALIENS RETIRED TO THEIR SHOCK-CHAIRS AND STRAPPED IN...
STAND BY. TEN SECONDS...FIVE... FOUR... THREE... TWO...
A BUMP! THEN SILENCE. THEY WERE DOWN. THE CHIEF UNSTRAPPED HIMSELF AND WENT TO THE LOCKER...
AS I CALL YOUR NAMES, COME FORWARD TO RECEIVE YOUR CLOTHING...
THE STRANGE CLOTHING WAS PASSED OUT TO THE ALIEN MALES AND FEMALES, AND THEY UNDRESSED SHAMELESSLY BEFORE EACH OTHER AND DRESSED IN THE QUEER EARTH GARB...
HELP ME WITH THIS, CUNO...
CERTAINLY, MARA...
NO, PHEBE. THAT HOLDS THIS UP... SEE...
OH. I SEE. THANK YOU, XANO.
AND WHEN THEY WERE ALL BEDECKED IN THEIR EARTH CLOTHING, THEY LOOKED AT EACH OTHER AND LAUGHED...
HOW RIDICULOUS! WHAT A STRANGE SOCIETY...
SUCH NONSENSE! EXPOSING LEGS TO THE ELEMENTS...
NOT FUNCTIONAL AT ALL! THESE BAGGY LEG COVERINGS...
2

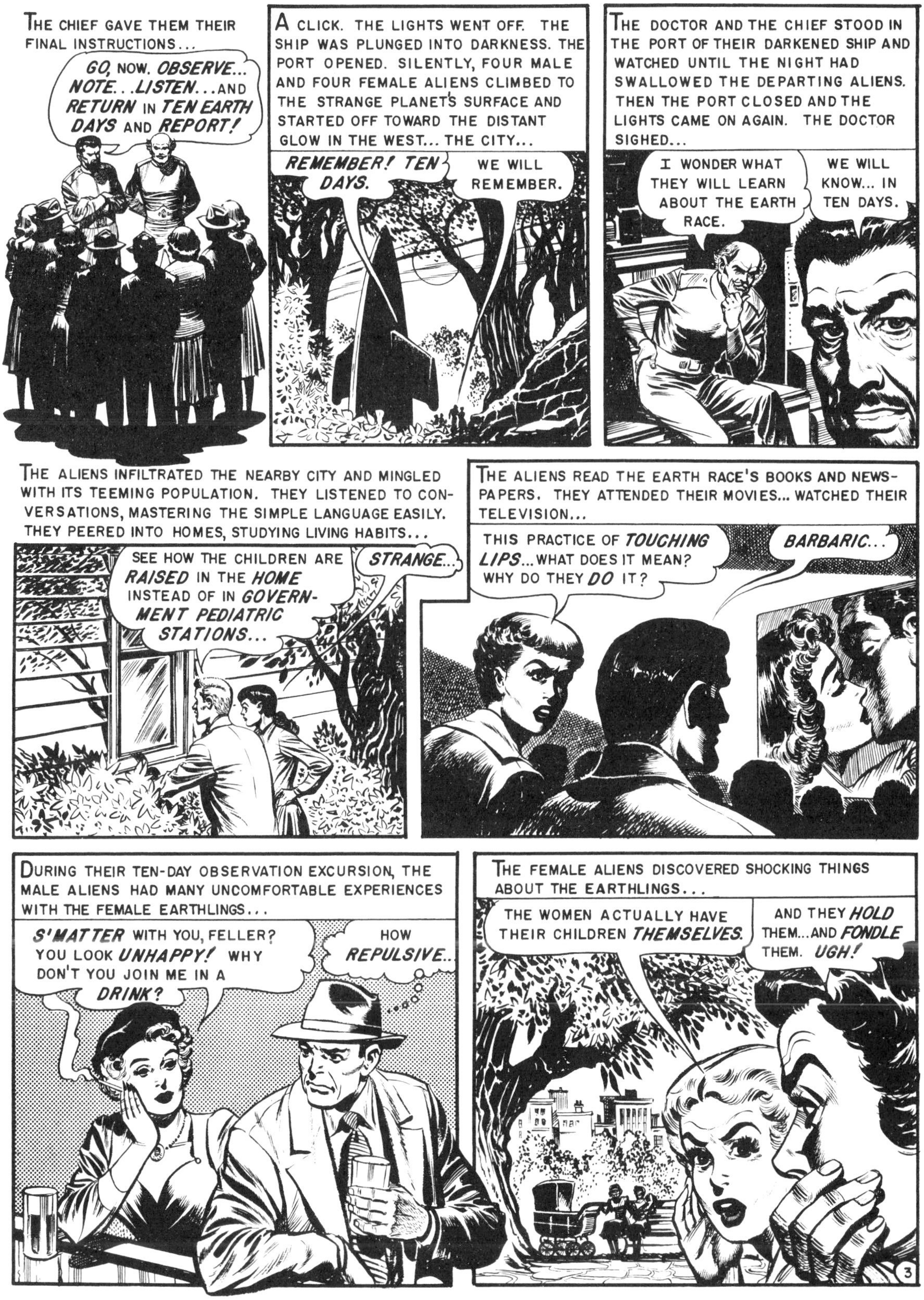
THE CHIEF GAVE THEM THEIR FINAL INSTRUCTIONS...
GO, NOW. OBSERVE... NOTE...LISTEN...AND RETURN IN TEN EARTH DAYS AND REPORT!
A CLICK. THE LIGHTS WENT OFF. THE SHIP WAS PLUNGED INTO DARKNESS. THE PORT OPENED. SILENTLY, FOUR MALE AND FOUR FEMALE ALIENS CLIMBED TO THE STRANGE PLANET'S SURFACE AND STARTED OFF TOWARD THE DISTANT GLOW IN THE WEST... THE CITY...
REMEMBER! TEN DAYS.
WE WILL REMEMBER.
THE DOCTOR AND THE CHIEF STOOD IN THE PORT OF THEIR DARKENED SHIP AND WATCHED UNTIL THE NIGHT HAD SWALLOWED THE DEPARTING ALIENS. THEN THE PORT CLOSED AND THE LIGHTS CAME ON AGAIN. THE DOCTOR SIGHED...
I WONDER WHAT THEY WILL LEARN ABOUT THE EARTH RACE.
WE WILL KNOW... IN TEN DAYS.
THE ALIENS INFILTRATED THE NEARBY CITY AND MINGLED WITH ITS TEEMING POPULATION. THEY LISTENED TO CONVERSATIONS, MASTERING THE SIMPLE LANGUAGE EASILY. THEY PEERED INTO HOMES, STUDYING LIVING HABITS...
SEE HOW THE CHILDREN ARE RAISED IN THE HOME INSTEAD OF IN GOVERNMENT PEDIATRIC STATIONS...
STRANGE...
THE ALIENS READ THE EARTH RACE'S BOOKS AND NEWSPAPERS. THEY ATTENDED THEIR MOVIES... WATCHED THEIR TELEVISION...
THIS PRACTICE OF TOUCHING LIPS...WHAT DOES IT MEAN? WHY DO THEY DO IT?
BARBARIC...
DURING THEIR TEN-DAY OBSERVATION EXCURSION, THE MALE ALIENS HAD MANY UNCOMFORTABLE EXPERIENCES WITH THE FEMALE EARTHLINGS...
S'MATTER WITH YOU, FELLER? YOU LOOK UNHAPPY! WHY DON'T YOU JOIN ME IN A DRINK?
HOW REPULSIVE...
THE FEMALE ALIENS DISCOVERED SHOCKING THINGS ABOUT THE EARTHLINGS...
THE WOMEN ACTUALLY HAVE THEIR CHILDREN THEMSELVES.
AND THEY HOLD THEM...AND FONDLE THEM. UGH!
3

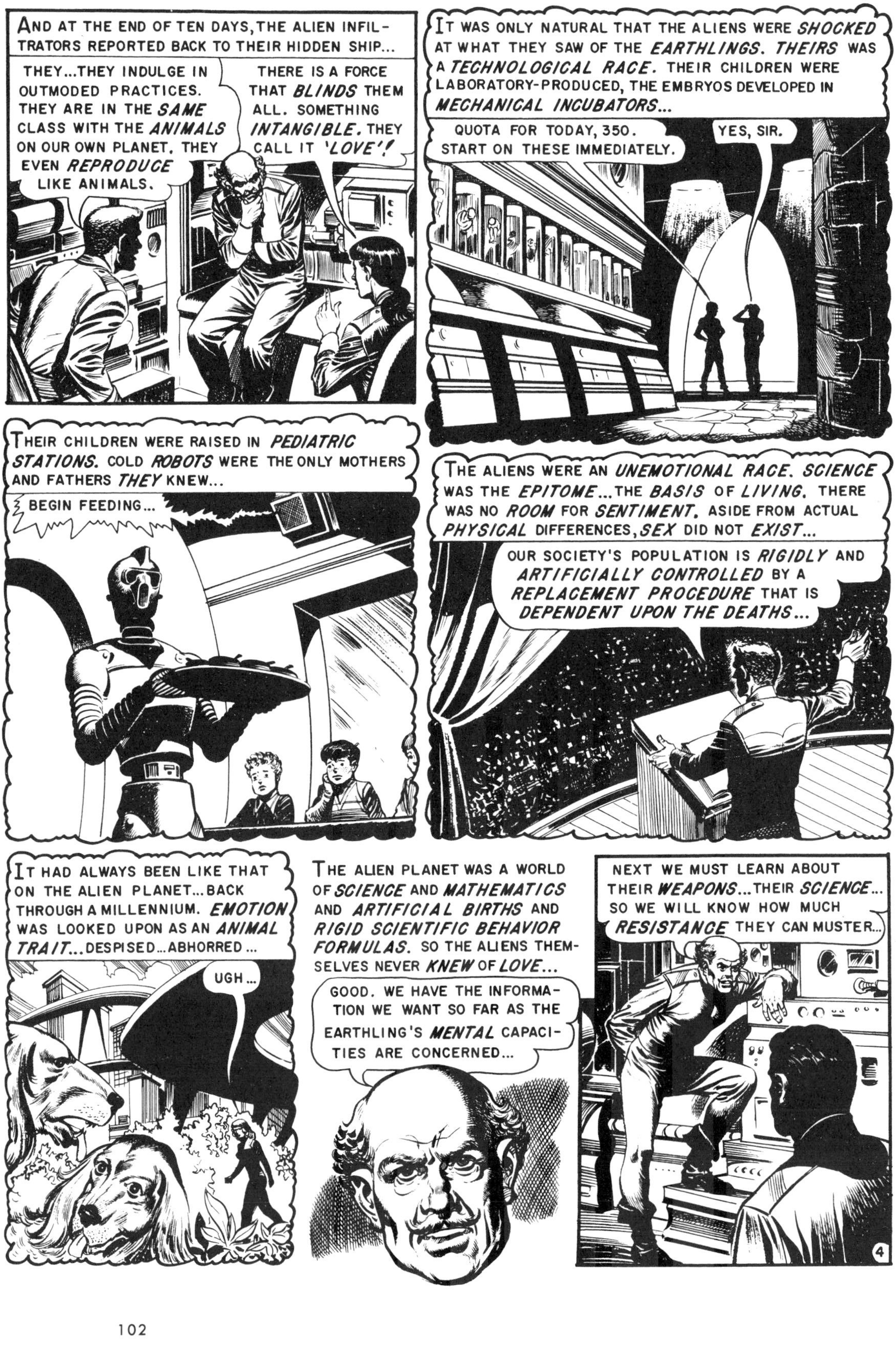
AND AT THE END OF TEN DAYS, THE ALIEN INFILTRATORS REPORTED BACK TO THEIR HIDDEN SHIP...
THEY...THEY INDULGE IN OUTMODED PRACTICES. THEY ARE IN THE SAME CLASS WITH THE ANIMALS ON OUR OWN PLANET. THEY EVEN REPRODUCE LIKE ANIMALS.
THERE IS A FORCE THAT BLINDS THEM ALL. SOMETHING INTANGIBLE. THEY CALL IT 'LOVE'!
IT WAS ONLY NATURAL THAT THE ALIENS WERE SHOCKED AT WHAT THEY SAW OF THE EARTHLINGS. THEIRS WAS A TECHNOLOGICAL RACE. THEIR CHILDREN WERE LABORATORY-PRODUCED, THE EMBRYOS DEVELOPED IN MECHANICAL INCUBATORS...
QUOTA FOR TODAY, 350. START ON THESE IMMEDIATELY.
YES, SIR.
THEIR CHILDREN WERE RAISED IN PEDIATRIC STATIONS. COLD ROBOTS WERE THE ONLY MOTHERS AND FATHERS THEY KNEW...
BEGIN FEEDING...
THE ALIENS WERE AN UNEMOTIONAL RACE. SCIENCE WAS THE EPITOME...THE BASIS OF LIVING. THERE WAS NO ROOM FOR SENTIMENT. ASIDE FROM ACTUAL PHYSICAL DIFFERENCES, SEX DID NOT EXIST...
OUR SOCIETY'S POPULATION IS RIGIDLY AND ARTIFICIALLY CONTROLLED BY A REPLACEMENT PROCEDURE THAT IS DEPENDENT UPON THE DEATHS...
IT HAD ALWAYS BEEN LIKE THAT ON THE ALIEN PLANET...BACK THROUGH A MILLENNIUM. EMOTION WAS LOOKED UPON AS AN ANIMAL TRAIT...DESPISED...ABHORRED...
UGH...
THE ALIEN PLANET WAS A WORLD OF SCIENCE AND MATHEMATICS AND ARTIFICIAL BIRTHS AND RIGID SCIENTIFIC BEHAVIOR FORMULAS. SO THE ALIENS THEMSELVES NEVER KNEW OF LOVE...
GOOD. WE HAVE THE INFORMATION WE WANT SO FAR AS THE EARTHLING'S MENTAL CAPACITIES ARE CONCERNED...
NEXT WE MUST LEARN ABOUT THEIR WEAPONS...THEIR SCIENCE... SO WE WILL KNOW HOW MUCH RESISTANCE THEY CAN MUSTER...
4

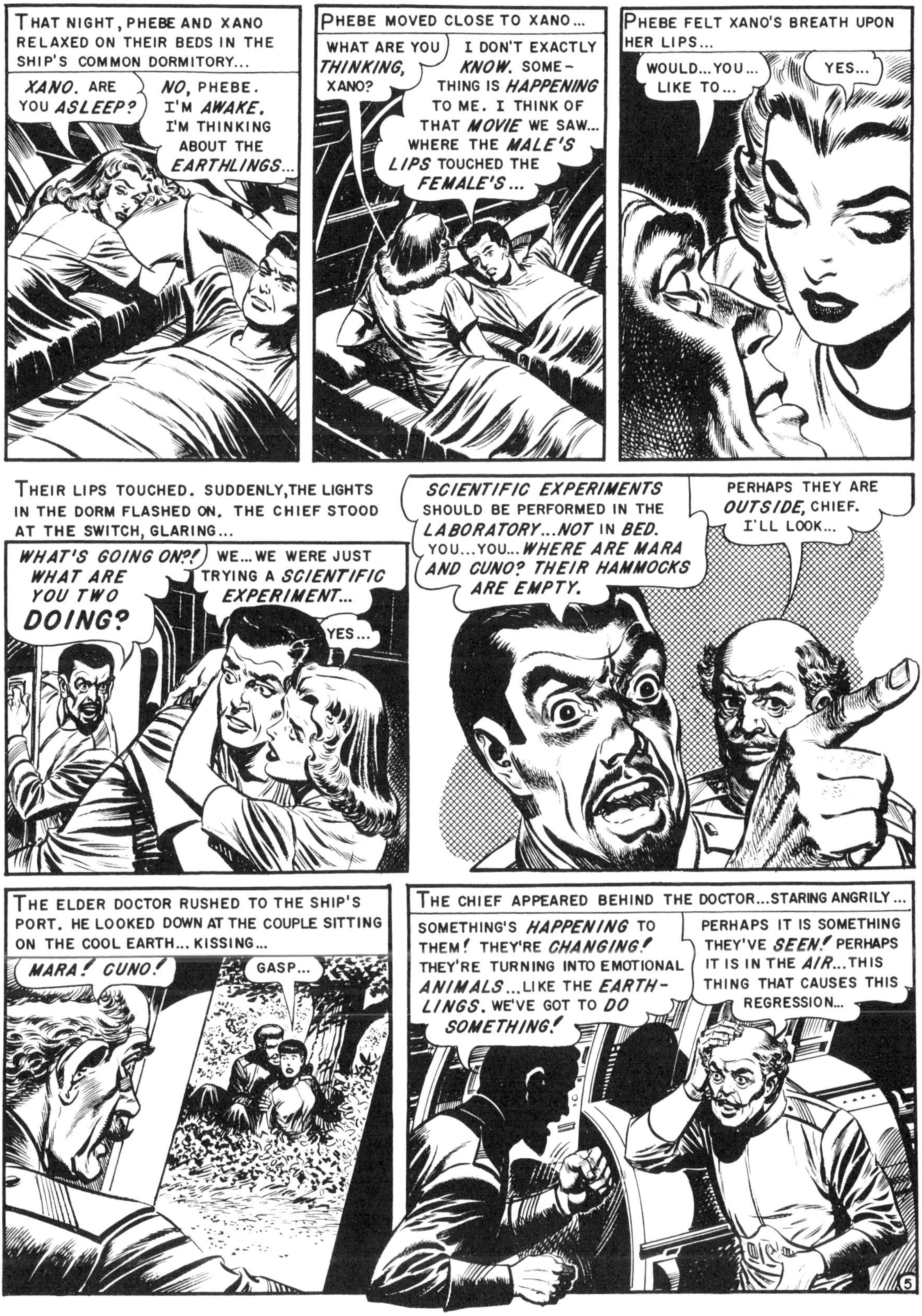
THAT NIGHT, PHEBE AND XANO RELAXED ON THEIR BEDS IN THE SHIP'S COMMON DORMITORY...
XANO. ARE YOU ASLEEP?
NO, PHEBE. I'M AWAKE. I'M THINKING ABOUT THE EARTHLINGS...
PHEBE MOVED CLOSE TO XANO...
WHAT ARE YOU THINKING, XANO?
I DON'T EXACTLY KNOW. SOME-THING IS HAPPENING TO ME. I THINK OF THAT MOVIE WE SAW... WHERE THE MALE'S LIPS TOUCHED THE FEMALE'S...
PHEBE FELT XANO'S BREATH UPON HER LIPS...
WOULD... YOU... LIKE TO...
YES...
THEIR LIPS TOUCHED. SUDDENLY, THE LIGHTS IN THE DORM FLASHED ON. THE CHIEF STOOD AT THE SWITCH, GLARING...
WHAT'S GOING ON?! WHAT ARE YOU TWO DOING?
WE... WE WERE JUST TRYING A SCIENTIFIC EXPERIMENT...
YES...
SCIENTIFIC EXPERIMENTS SHOULD BE PERFORMED IN THE LABORATORY... NOT IN BED. YOU... YOU... WHERE ARE MARA AND CUNO? THEIR HAMMOCKS ARE EMPTY.
PERHAPS THEY ARE OUTSIDE, CHIEF. I'LL LOOK...
THE ELDER DOCTOR RUSHED TO THE SHIP'S PORT. HE LOOKED DOWN AT THE COUPLE SITTING ON THE COOL EARTH... KISSING...
MARA! CUNO!
GASP...
THE CHIEF APPEARED BEHIND THE DOCTOR... STARING ANGRILY...
SOMETHING'S HAPPENING TO THEM! THEY'RE CHANGING! THEY'RE TURNING INTO EMOTIONAL ANIMALS... LIKE THE EARTH-LINGS. WE'VE GOT TO DO SOMETHING!
PERHAPS IT IS SOMETHING THEY'VE SEEN! PERHAPS IT IS IN THE AIR... THIS THING THAT CAUSES THIS REGRESSION...
5

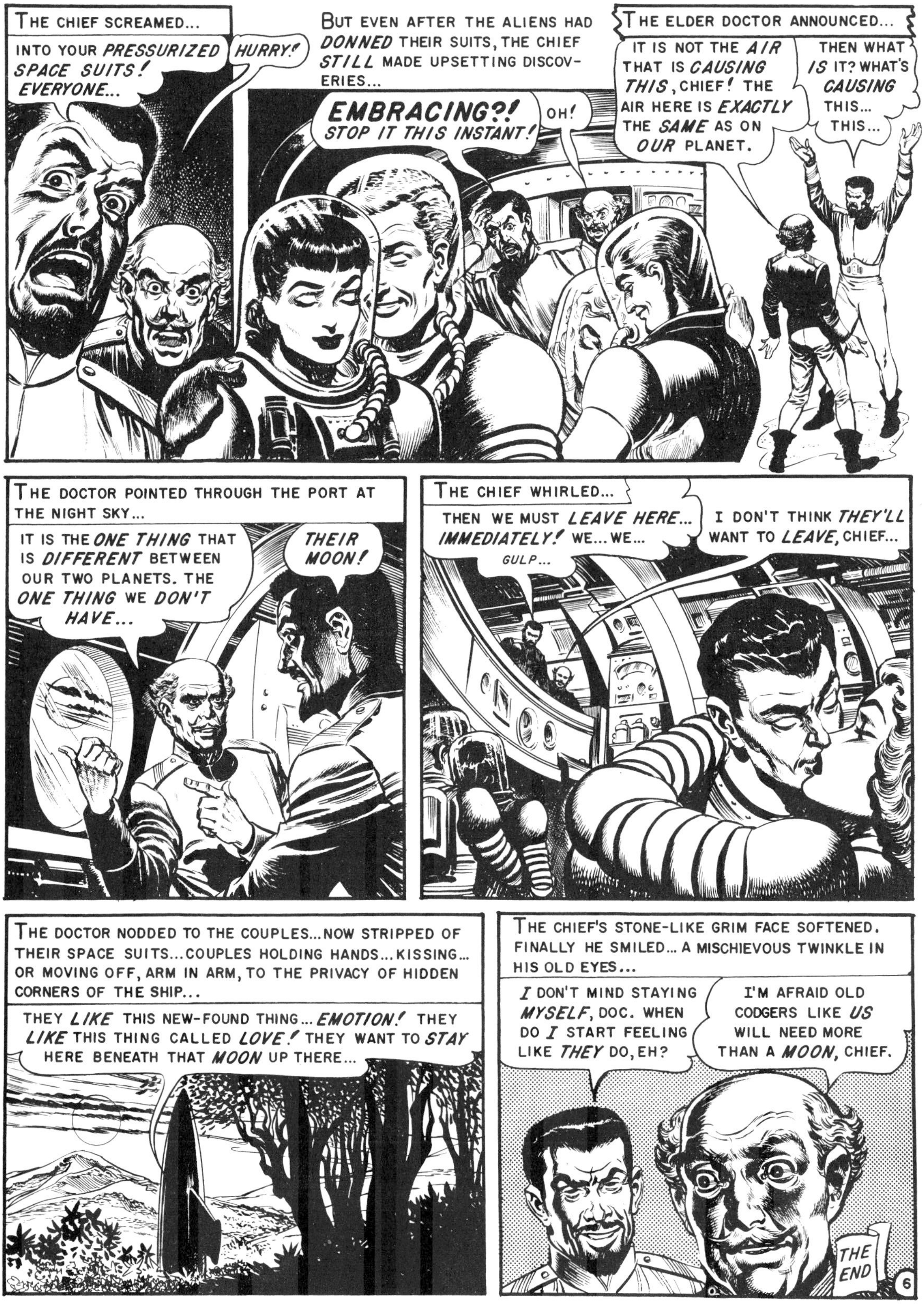
THE CHIEF SCREAMED...
INTO YOUR PRESSURIZED SPACE SUITS! EVERYONE...
HURRY!
BUT EVEN AFTER THE ALIENS HAD DONNED THEIR SUITS, THE CHIEF STILL MADE UPSETTING DISCOVERIES...
EMBRACING?! STOP IT THIS INSTANT!
OH!
THE ELDER DOCTOR ANNOUNCED...
IT IS NOT THE AIR THAT IS CAUSING THIS, CHIEF! THE AIR HERE IS EXACTLY THE SAME AS ON OUR PLANET.
THEN WHAT IS IT? WHAT'S CAUSING THIS... THIS...
THE DOCTOR POINTED THROUGH THE PORT AT THE NIGHT SKY...
IT IS THE ONE THING THAT IS DIFFERENT BETWEEN OUR TWO PLANETS. THE ONE THING WE DON'T HAVE...
THEIR MOON!
THE CHIEF WHIRLED...
THEN WE MUST LEAVE HERE... IMMEDIATELY! WE... WE... GULP...
I DON'T THINK THEY'LL WANT TO LEAVE, CHIEF...
THE DOCTOR NODDED TO THE COUPLES... NOW STRIPPED OF THEIR SPACE SUITS... COUPLES HOLDING HANDS... KISSING... OR MOVING OFF, ARM IN ARM, TO THE PRIVACY OF HIDDEN CORNERS OF THE SHIP...
THEY LIKE THIS NEW-FOUND THING... EMOTION! THEY LIKE THIS THING CALLED LOVE! THEY WANT TO STAY HERE BENEATH THAT MOON UP THERE...
THE CHIEF'S STONE-LIKE GRIM FACE SOFTENED. FINALLY HE SMILED... A MISCHIEVOUS TWINKLE IN HIS OLD EYES...
I DON'T MIND STAYING MYSELF, DOC. WHEN DO I START FEELING LIKE THEY DO, EH?
I'M AFRAID OLD CODGERS LIKE US WILL NEED MORE THAN A MOON, CHIEF.
THE END
6

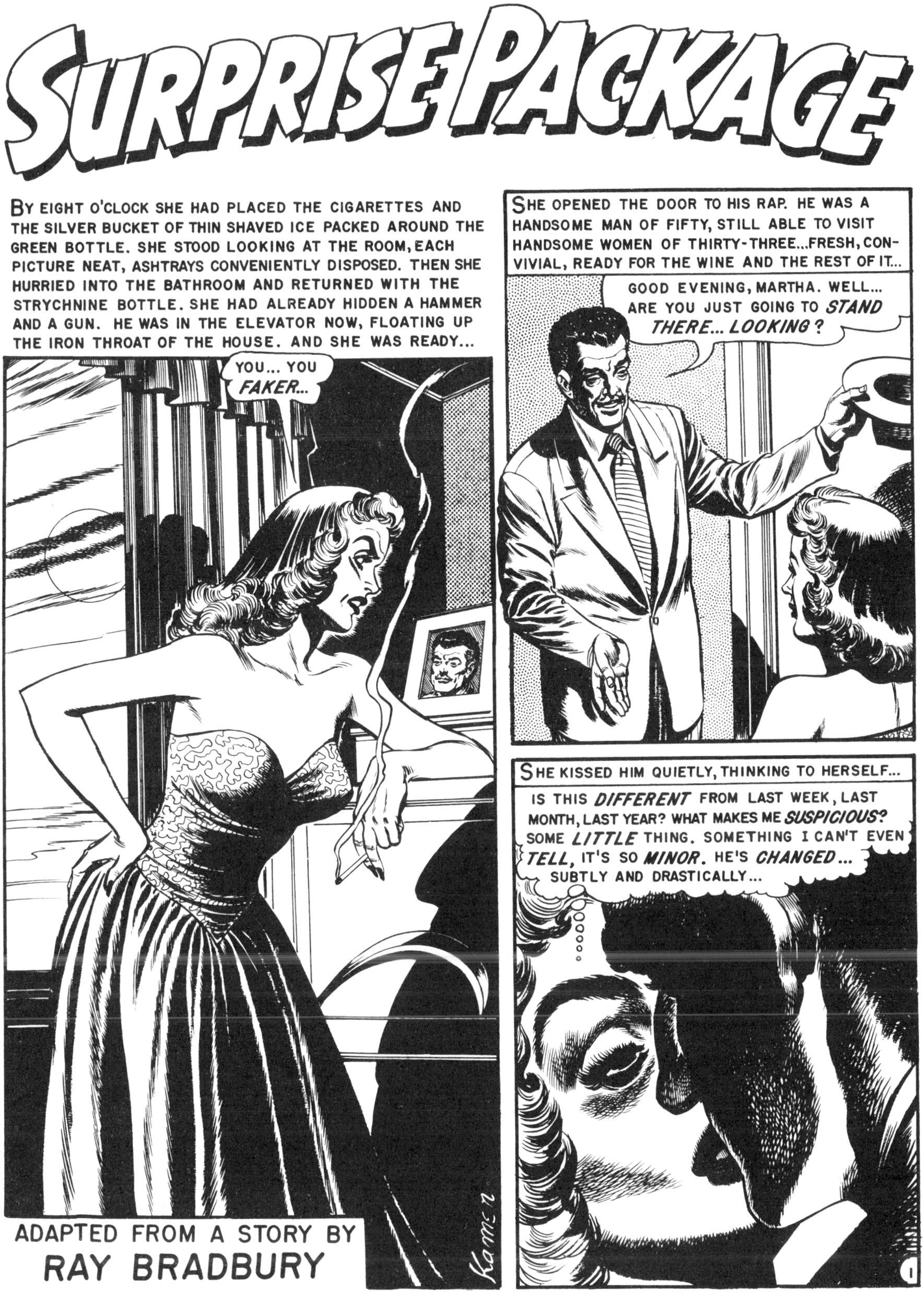
SURPRISE PACKAGE
BY EIGHT O'CLOCK SHE HAD PLACED THE CIGARETTES AND THE SILVER BUCKET OF THIN SHAVED ICE PACKED AROUND THE GREEN BOTTLE. SHE STOOD LOOKING AT THE ROOM, EACH PICTURE NEAT, ASHTRAYS CONVENIENTLY DISPOSED. THEN SHE HURRIED INTO THE BATHROOM AND RETURNED WITH THE STRYCHNINE BOTTLE. SHE HAD ALREADY HIDDEN A HAMMER AND A GUN. HE WAS IN THE ELEVATOR NOW, FLOATING UP THE IRON THROAT OF THE HOUSE. AND SHE WAS READY...
YOU... YOU *FAKER*...
ADAPTED FROM A STORY BY
RAY BRADBURY
Kamen
SHE OPENED THE DOOR TO HIS RAP. HE WAS A HANDSOME MAN OF FIFTY, STILL ABLE TO VISIT HANDSOME WOMEN OF THIRTY-THREE...FRESH, CONVIVIAL, READY FOR THE WINE AND THE REST OF IT...
GOOD EVENING, MARTHA. WELL... ARE YOU JUST GOING TO *STAND THERE... LOOKING*?
SHE KISSED HIM QUIETLY, THINKING TO HERSELF...
IS THIS *DIFFERENT* FROM LAST WEEK, LAST MONTH, LAST YEAR? WHAT MAKES ME *SUSPICIOUS*? SOME *LITTLE* THING. SOMETHING I CAN'T EVEN *TELL*, IT'S SO *MINOR*. HE'S *CHANGED*... SUBTLY AND DRASTICALLY...
1

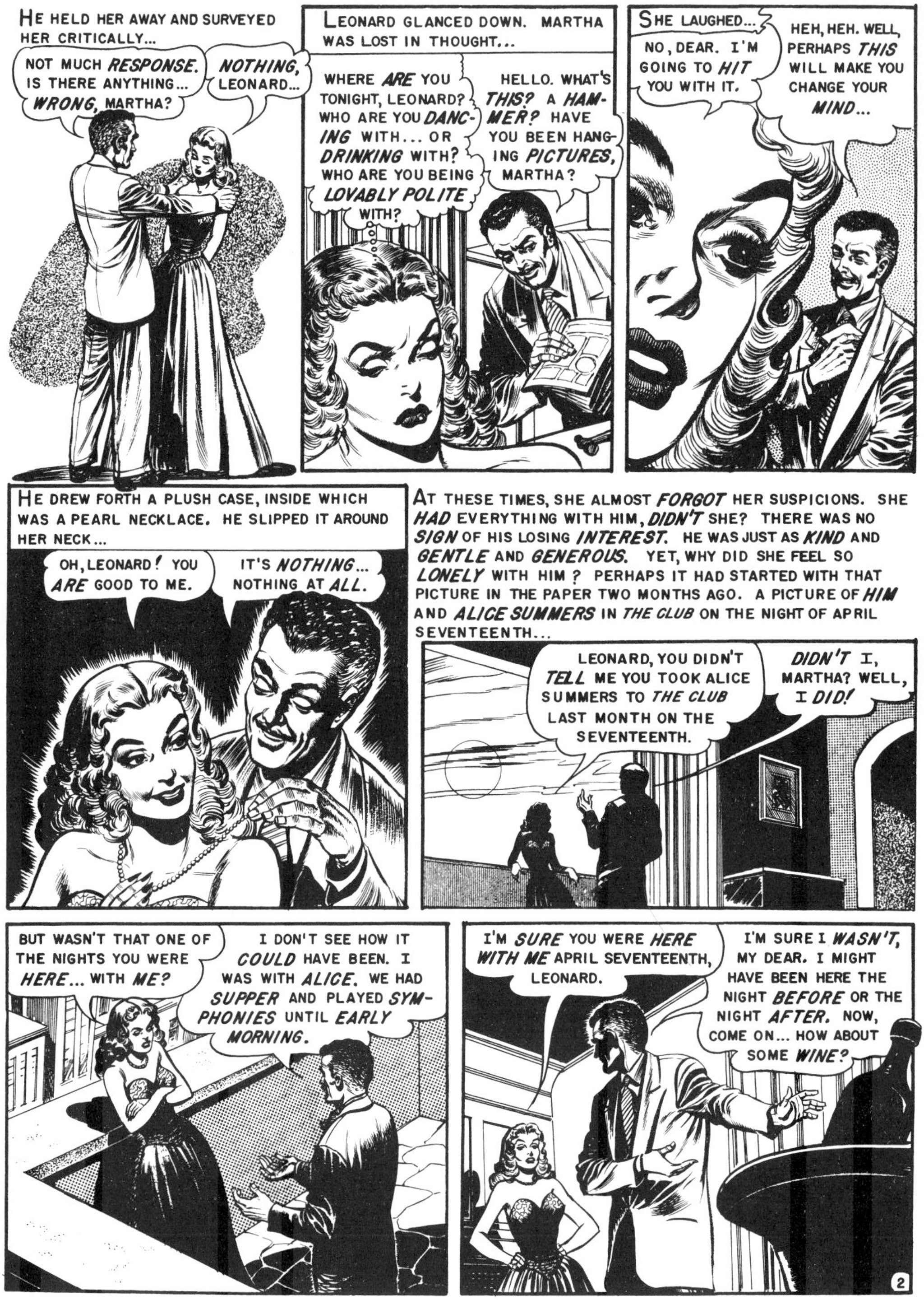
HE HELD HER AWAY AND SURVEYED HER CRITICALLY...
NOT MUCH RESPONSE. IS THERE ANYTHING... WRONG, MARTHA?
NOTHING, LEONARD...
LEONARD GLANCED DOWN. MARTHA WAS LOST IN THOUGHT...
WHERE ARE YOU TONIGHT, LEONARD? WHO ARE YOU DANCING WITH... OR DRINKING WITH? WHO ARE YOU BEING LOVABLY POLITE WITH?
HELLO. WHAT'S THIS? A HAMMER? HAVE YOU BEEN HANGING PICTURES, MARTHA?
SHE LAUGHED...
NO, DEAR. I'M GOING TO HIT YOU WITH IT.
HEH, HEH. WELL, PERHAPS THIS WILL MAKE YOU CHANGE YOUR MIND...
HE DREW FORTH A PLUSH CASE, INSIDE WHICH WAS A PEARL NECKLACE. HE SLIPPED IT AROUND HER NECK...
OH, LEONARD! YOU ARE GOOD TO ME.
IT'S NOTHING... NOTHING AT ALL.
AT THESE TIMES, SHE ALMOST FORGOT HER SUSPICIONS. SHE HAD EVERYTHING WITH HIM, DIDN'T SHE? THERE WAS NO SIGN OF HIS LOSING INTEREST. HE WAS JUST AS KIND AND GENTLE AND GENEROUS. YET, WHY DID SHE FEEL SO LONELY WITH HIM? PERHAPS IT HAD STARTED WITH THAT PICTURE IN THE PAPER TWO MONTHS AGO. A PICTURE OF HIM AND ALICE SUMMERS IN THE CLUB ON THE NIGHT OF APRIL SEVENTEENTH...
LEONARD, YOU DIDN'T TELL ME YOU TOOK ALICE SUMMERS TO THE CLUB LAST MONTH ON THE SEVENTEENTH.
DIDN'T I, MARTHA? WELL, I DID!
BUT WASN'T THAT ONE OF THE NIGHTS YOU WERE HERE... WITH ME?
I DON'T SEE HOW IT COULD HAVE BEEN. I WAS WITH ALICE. WE HAD SUPPER AND PLAYED SYMPHONIES UNTIL EARLY MORNING.
I'M SURE YOU WERE HERE WITH ME APRIL SEVENTEENTH, LEONARD.
I'M SURE I WASN'T, MY DEAR. I MIGHT HAVE BEEN HERE THE NIGHT BEFORE OR THE NIGHT AFTER. NOW, COME ON... HOW ABOUT SOME WINE?
2

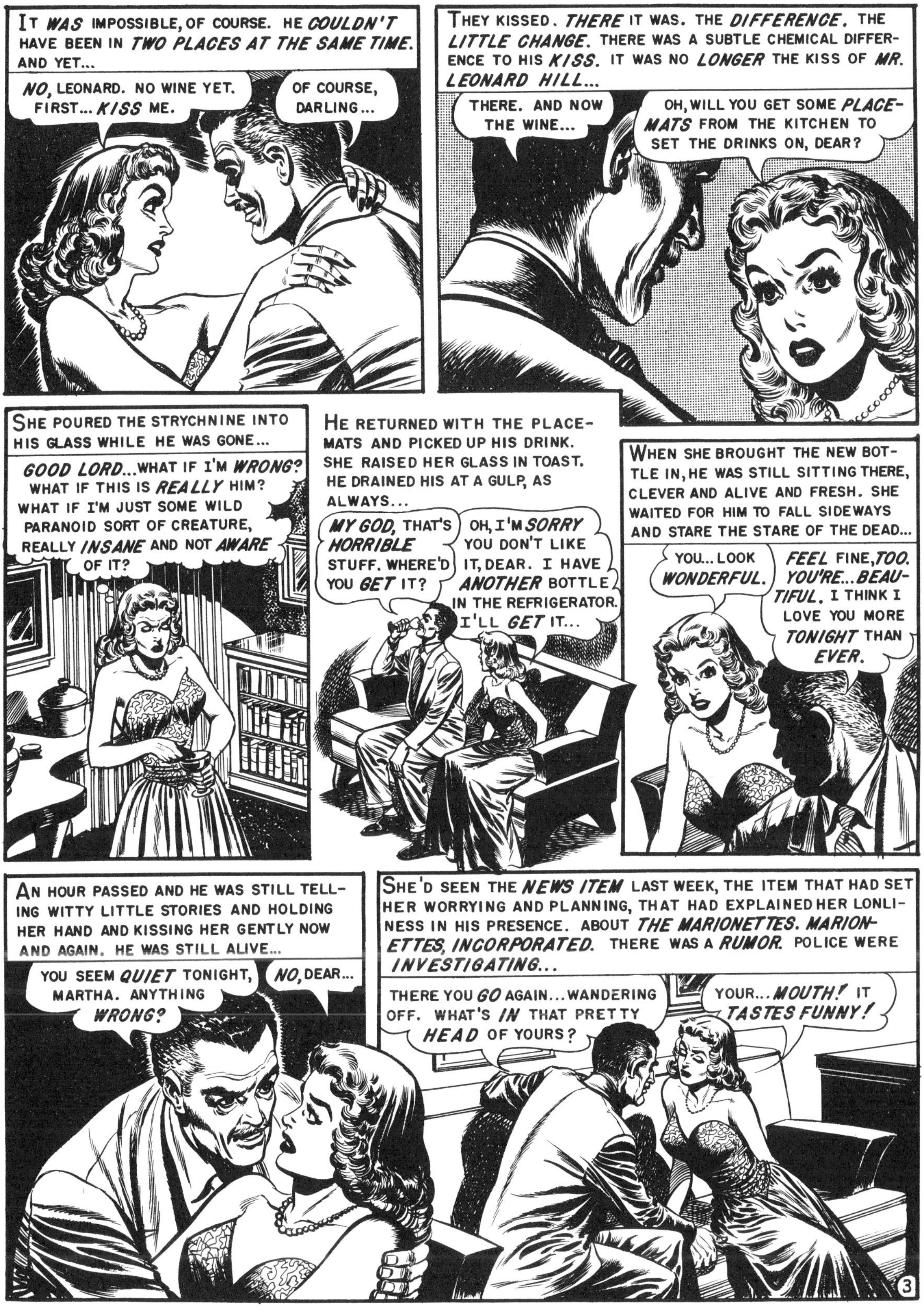
IT WAS IMPOSSIBLE, OF COURSE. HE COULDN'T HAVE BEEN IN TWO PLACES AT THE SAME TIME. AND YET...
NO, LEONARD. NO WINE YET. FIRST... KISS ME.
OF COURSE, DARLING...
THEY KISSED. THERE IT WAS. THE DIFFERENCE. THE LITTLE CHANGE. THERE WAS A SUBTLE CHEMICAL DIFFERENCE TO HIS KISS. IT WAS NO LONGER THE KISS OF MR. LEONARD HILL...
THERE. AND NOW THE WINE...
OH, WILL YOU GET SOME PLACE-MATS FROM THE KITCHEN TO SET THE DRINKS ON, DEAR?
SHE POURED THE STRYCHNINE INTO HIS GLASS WHILE HE WAS GONE...
GOOD LORD... WHAT IF I'M WRONG? WHAT IF THIS IS REALLY HIM? WHAT IF I'M JUST SOME WILD PARANOID SORT OF CREATURE, REALLY INSANE AND NOT AWARE OF IT?
HE RETURNED WITH THE PLACE-MATS AND PICKED UP HIS DRINK. SHE RAISED HER GLASS IN TOAST. HE DRAINED HIS AT A GULP, AS ALWAYS...
MY GOD, THAT'S HORRIBLE STUFF. WHERE'D YOU GET IT?
OH, I'M SORRY YOU DON'T LIKE IT, DEAR. I HAVE ANOTHER BOTTLE IN THE REFRIGERATOR. I'LL GET IT...
WHEN SHE BROUGHT THE NEW BOTTLE IN, HE WAS STILL SITTING THERE, CLEVER AND ALIVE AND FRESH. SHE WAITED FOR HIM TO FALL SIDEWAYS AND STARE THE STARE OF THE DEAD...
YOU... LOOK WONDERFUL.
FEEL FINE, TOO. YOU'RE... BEAUTIFUL. I THINK I LOVE YOU MORE TONIGHT THAN EVER.
AN HOUR PASSED AND HE WAS STILL TELLING WITTY LITTLE STORIES AND HOLDING HER HAND AND KISSING HER GENTLY NOW AND AGAIN. HE WAS STILL ALIVE...
YOU SEEM QUIET TONIGHT, MARTHA. ANYTHING WRONG?
NO, DEAR...
SHE'D SEEN THE NEWS ITEM LAST WEEK, THE ITEM THAT HAD SET HER WORRYING AND PLANNING, THAT HAD EXPLAINED HER LONLINESS IN HIS PRESENCE. ABOUT THE MARIONETTES. MARIONETTES, INCORPORATED. THERE WAS A RUMOR. POLICE WERE INVESTIGATING...
THERE YOU GO AGAIN... WANDERING OFF. WHAT'S IN THAT PRETTY HEAD OF YOURS?
YOUR... MOUTH! IT TASTES FUNNY!
3

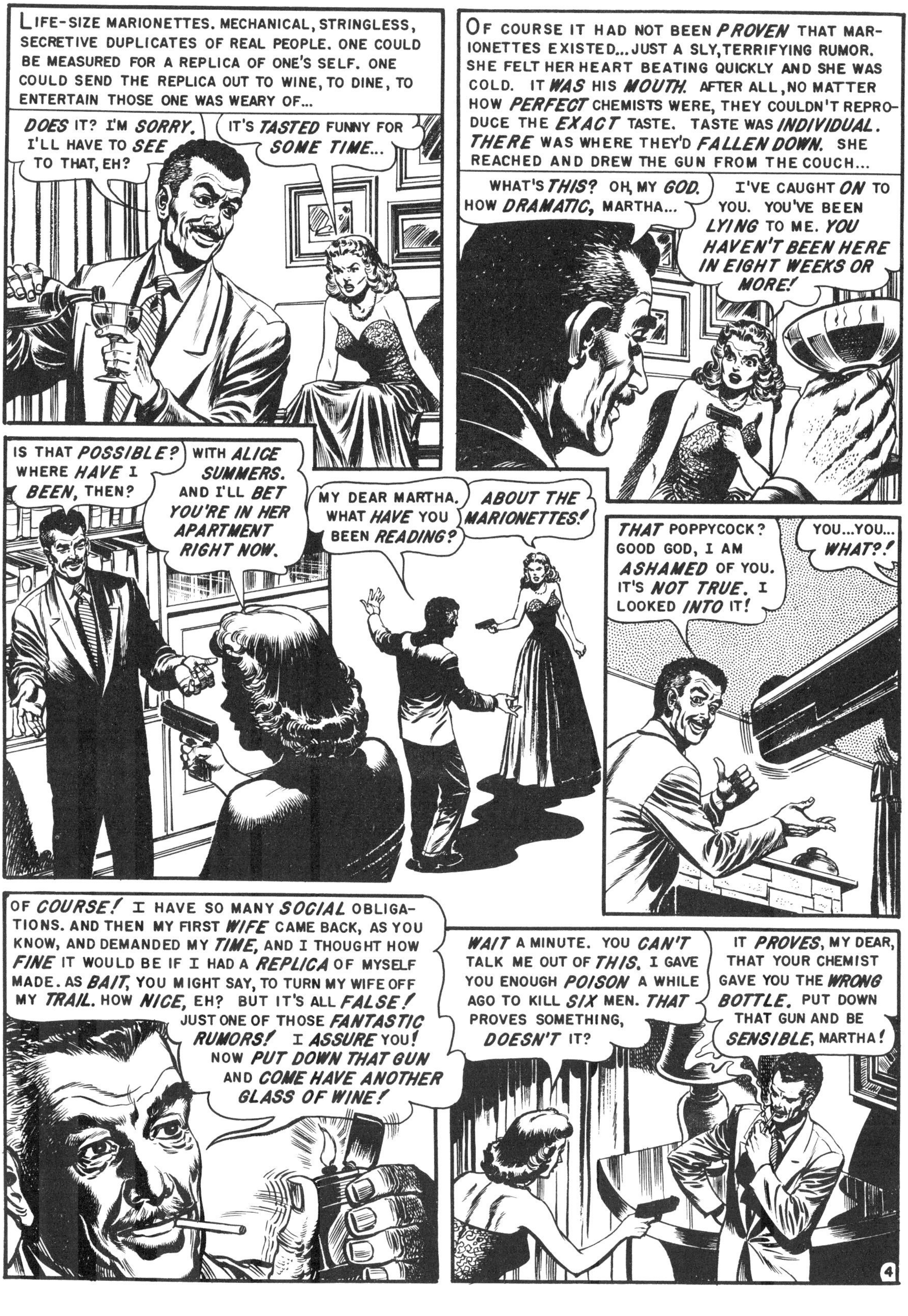
LIFE-SIZE MARIONETTES. MECHANICAL, STRINGLESS, SECRETIVE DUPLICATES OF REAL PEOPLE. ONE COULD BE MEASURED FOR A REPLICA OF ONE'S SELF. ONE COULD SEND THE REPLICA OUT TO WINE, TO DINE, TO ENTERTAIN THOSE ONE WAS WEARY OF...
IT'S TASTED FUNNY FOR SOME TIME...
DOES IT? I'M SORRY. I'LL HAVE TO SEE TO THAT, EH?
OF COURSE IT HAD NOT BEEN PROVEN THAT MARIONETTES EXISTED... JUST A SLY, TERRIFYING RUMOR. SHE FELT HER HEART BEATING QUICKLY AND SHE WAS COLD. IT WAS HIS MOUTH. AFTER ALL, NO MATTER HOW PERFECT CHEMISTS WERE, THEY COULDN'T REPRODUCE THE EXACT TASTE. TASTE WAS INDIVIDUAL. THERE WAS WHERE THEY'D FALLEN DOWN. SHE REACHED AND DREW THE GUN FROM THE COUCH...
I'VE CAUGHT ON TO YOU. YOU'VE BEEN LYING TO ME. YOU HAVEN'T BEEN HERE IN EIGHT WEEKS OR MORE!
WHAT'S THIS? OH, MY GOD. HOW DRAMATIC, MARTHA...
IS THAT POSSIBLE? WHERE HAVE I BEEN, THEN?
WITH ALICE SUMMERS. AND I'LL BET YOU'RE IN HER APARTMENT RIGHT NOW.
MY DEAR MARTHA. WHAT HAVE YOU BEEN READING?
ABOUT THE MARIONETTES!
THAT POPPYCOCK? GOOD GOD, I AM ASHAMED OF YOU. IT'S NOT TRUE. I LOOKED INTO IT!
YOU...YOU... WHAT?!
OF COURSE! I HAVE SO MANY SOCIAL OBLIGATIONS. AND THEN MY FIRST WIFE CAME BACK, AS YOU KNOW, AND DEMANDED MY TIME, AND I THOUGHT HOW FINE IT WOULD BE IF I HAD A REPLICA OF MYSELF MADE. AS BAIT, YOU MIGHT SAY, TO TURN MY WIFE OFF MY TRAIL. HOW NICE, EH? BUT IT'S ALL FALSE! JUST ONE OF THOSE FANTASTIC RUMORS! I ASSURE YOU! NOW PUT DOWN THAT GUN AND COME HAVE ANOTHER GLASS OF WINE!
WAIT A MINUTE. YOU CAN'T TALK ME OUT OF THIS. I GAVE YOU ENOUGH POISON A WHILE AGO TO KILL SIX MEN. THAT PROVES SOMETHING, DOESN'T IT?
IT PROVES, MY DEAR, THAT YOUR CHEMIST GAVE YOU THE WRONG BOTTLE. PUT DOWN THAT GUN AND BE SENSIBLE, MARTHA!
4

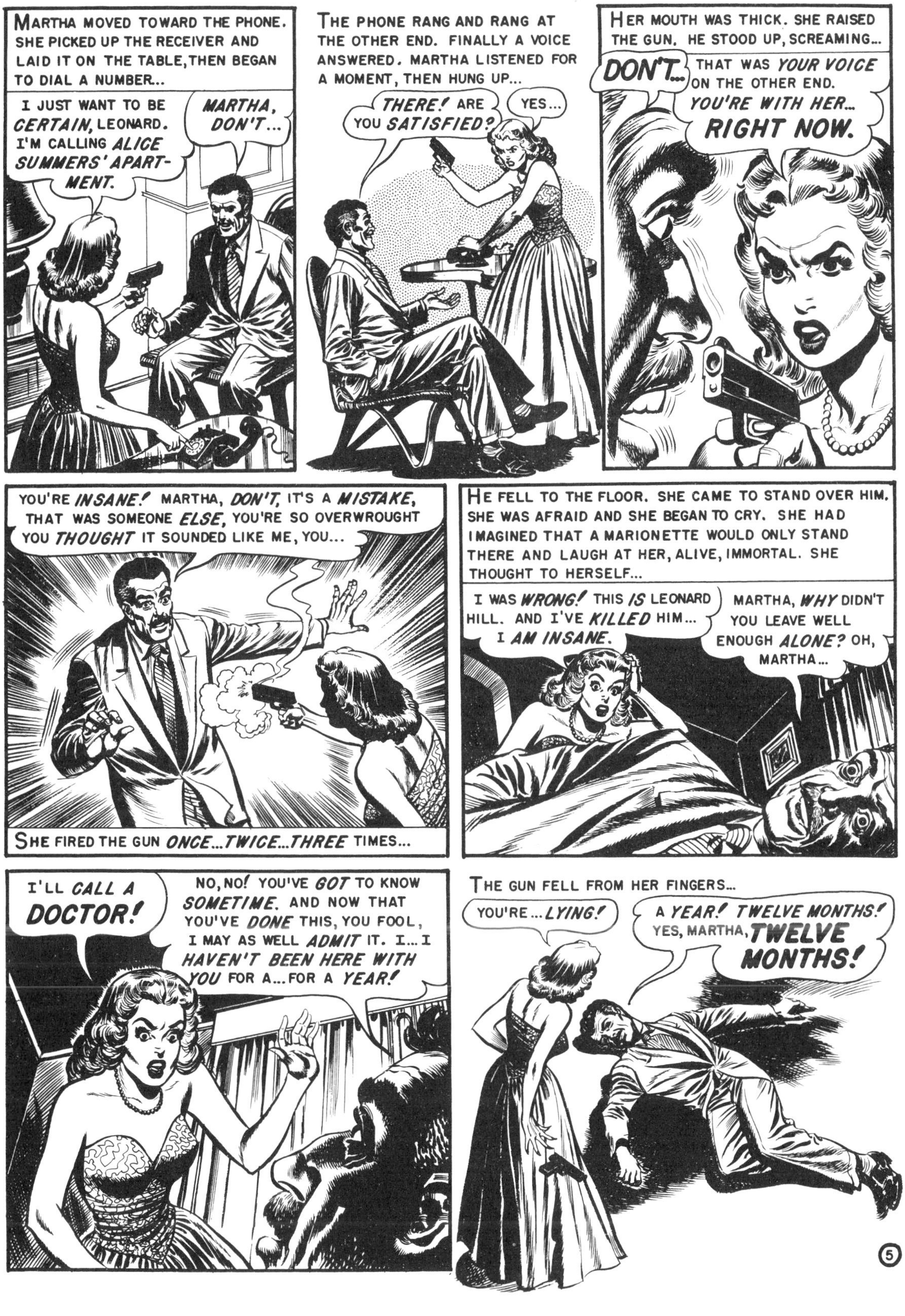
MARTHA MOVED TOWARD THE PHONE. SHE PICKED UP THE RECEIVER AND LAID IT ON THE TABLE, THEN BEGAN TO DIAL A NUMBER...
I JUST WANT TO BE CERTAIN, LEONARD. I'M CALLING ALICE SUMMERS' APARTMENT.
MARTHA, DON'T...
THE PHONE RANG AND RANG AT THE OTHER END. FINALLY A VOICE ANSWERED. MARTHA LISTENED FOR A MOMENT, THEN HUNG UP...
THERE! ARE YOU SATISFIED?
YES...
HER MOUTH WAS THICK. SHE RAISED THE GUN. HE STOOD UP, SCREAMING...
DON'T...
THAT WAS YOUR VOICE ON THE OTHER END. YOU'RE WITH HER... RIGHT NOW.
YOU'RE INSANE! MARTHA, DON'T, IT'S A MISTAKE, THAT WAS SOMEONE ELSE, YOU'RE SO OVERWROUGHT YOU THOUGHT IT SOUNDED LIKE ME, YOU...
SHE FIRED THE GUN ONCE...TWICE...THREE TIMES...
HE FELL TO THE FLOOR. SHE CAME TO STAND OVER HIM. SHE WAS AFRAID AND SHE BEGAN TO CRY. SHE HAD IMAGINED THAT A MARIONETTE WOULD ONLY STAND THERE AND LAUGH AT HER, ALIVE, IMMORTAL. SHE THOUGHT TO HERSELF...
I WAS WRONG! THIS IS LEONARD HILL. AND I'VE KILLED HIM... I AM INSANE.
MARTHA, WHY DIDN'T YOU LEAVE WELL ENOUGH ALONE? OH, MARTHA...
I'LL CALL A DOCTOR!
NO, NO! YOU'VE GOT TO KNOW SOMETIME. AND NOW THAT YOU'VE DONE THIS, YOU FOOL, I MAY AS WELL ADMIT IT. I...I HAVEN'T BEEN HERE WITH YOU FOR A...FOR A YEAR!
THE GUN FELL FROM HER FINGERS...
YOU'RE...LYING!
A YEAR! TWELVE MONTHS! YES, MARTHA, TWELVE MONTHS!
5

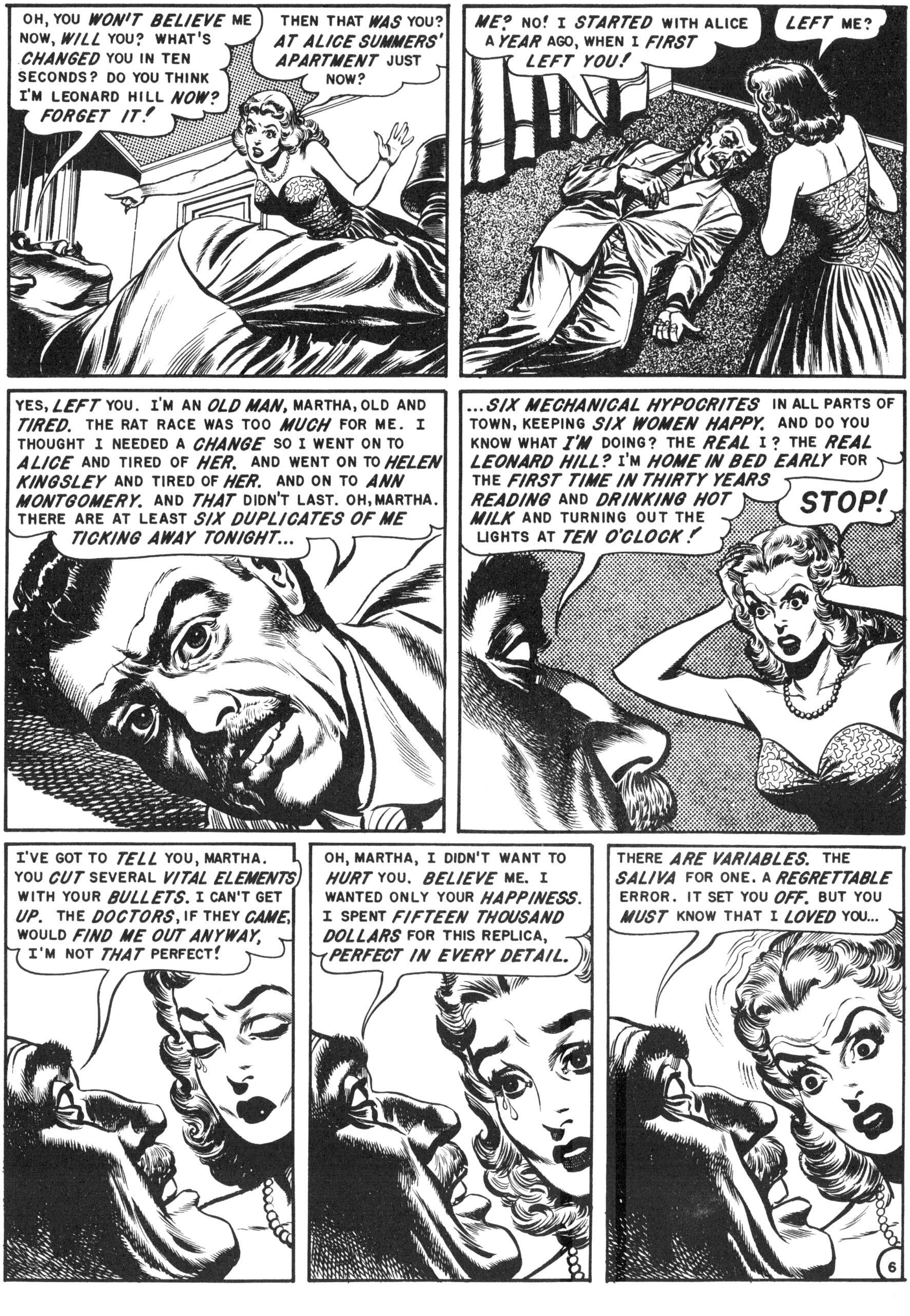
OH, YOU WON'T BELIEVE ME NOW, WILL YOU? WHAT'S CHANGED YOU IN TEN SECONDS? DO YOU THINK I'M LEONARD HILL NOW? FORGET IT!
THEN THAT WAS YOU? AT ALICE SUMMERS' APARTMENT JUST NOW?
ME? NO! I STARTED WITH ALICE A YEAR AGO, WHEN I FIRST LEFT YOU!
LEFT ME?
YES, LEFT YOU. I'M AN OLD MAN, MARTHA, OLD AND TIRED. THE RAT RACE WAS TOO MUCH FOR ME. I THOUGHT I NEEDED A CHANGE SO I WENT ON TO ALICE AND TIRED OF HER. AND WENT ON TO HELEN KINGSLEY AND TIRED OF HER. AND ON TO ANN MONTGOMERY. AND THAT DIDN'T LAST. OH, MARTHA. THERE ARE AT LEAST SIX DUPLICATES OF ME TICKING AWAY TONIGHT...
...SIX MECHANICAL HYPOCRITES IN ALL PARTS OF TOWN, KEEPING SIX WOMEN HAPPY. AND DO YOU KNOW WHAT I'M DOING? THE REAL I? THE REAL LEONARD HILL? I'M HOME IN BED EARLY FOR THE FIRST TIME IN THIRTY YEARS READING AND DRINKING HOT MILK AND TURNING OUT THE LIGHTS AT TEN O'CLOCK!
STOP!
I'VE GOT TO TELL YOU, MARTHA. YOU CUT SEVERAL VITAL ELEMENTS WITH YOUR BULLETS. I CAN'T GET UP. THE DOCTORS, IF THEY CAME, WOULD FIND ME OUT ANYWAY. I'M NOT THAT PERFECT!
OH, MARTHA, I DIDN'T WANT TO HURT YOU. BELIEVE ME. I WANTED ONLY YOUR HAPPINESS. I SPENT FIFTEEN THOUSAND DOLLARS FOR THIS REPLICA, PERFECT IN EVERY DETAIL.
THERE ARE VARIABLES. THE SALIVA FOR ONE. A REGRETTABLE ERROR. IT SET YOU OFF. BUT YOU MUST KNOW THAT I LOVED YOU...
6

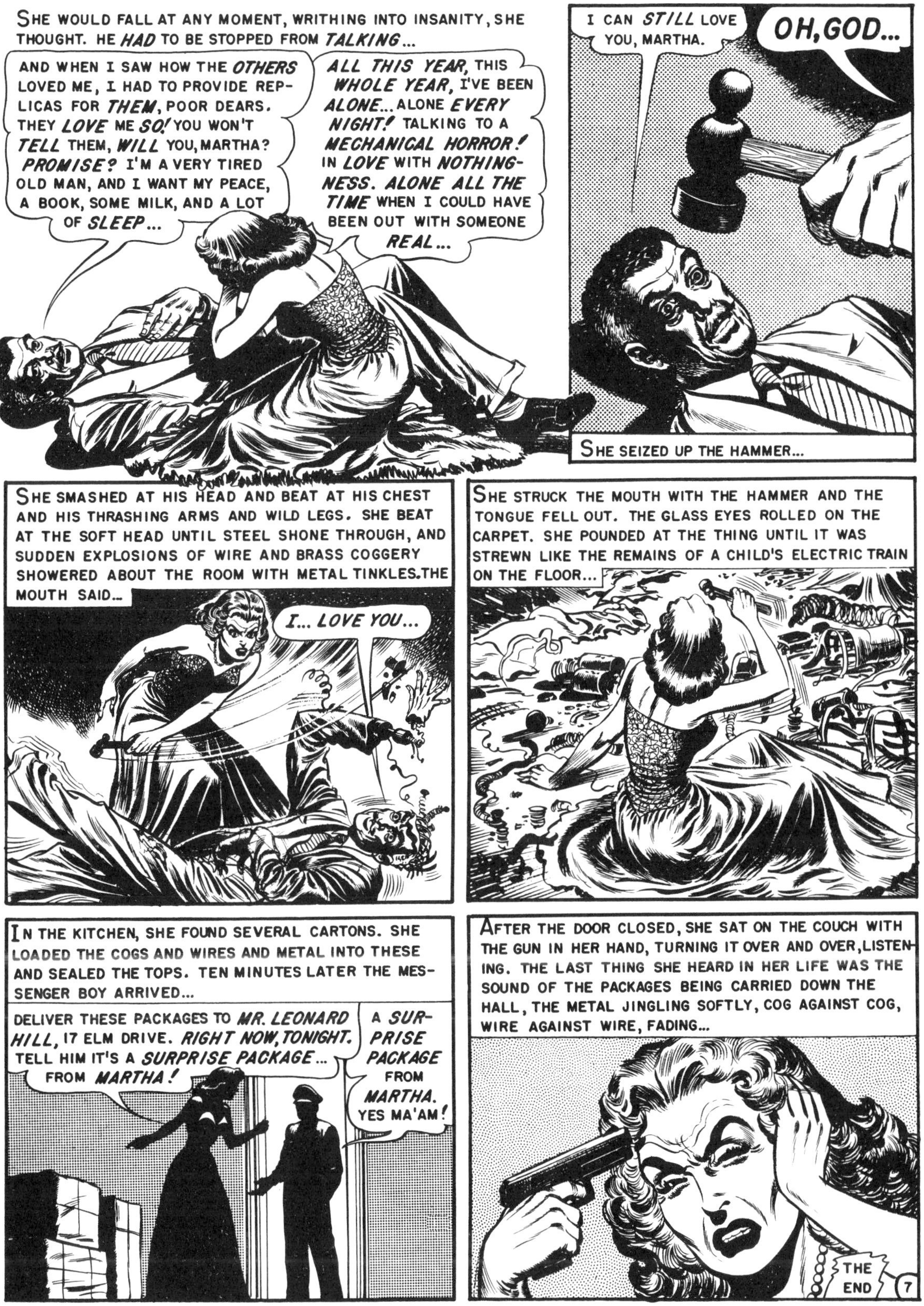
SHE WOULD FALL AT ANY MOMENT, WRITHING INTO INSANITY, SHE THOUGHT. HE HAD TO BE STOPPED FROM TALKING...
AND WHEN I SAW HOW THE OTHERS LOVED ME, I HAD TO PROVIDE REPLICAS FOR THEM, POOR DEARS. THEY LOVE ME SO! YOU WON'T TELL THEM, WILL YOU, MARTHA? PROMISE? I'M A VERY TIRED OLD MAN, AND I WANT MY PEACE, A BOOK, SOME MILK, AND A LOT OF SLEEP...
ALL THIS YEAR, THIS WHOLE YEAR, I'VE BEEN ALONE... ALONE EVERY NIGHT! TALKING TO A MECHANICAL HORROR! IN LOVE WITH NOTHINGNESS. ALONE ALL THE TIME WHEN I COULD HAVE BEEN OUT WITH SOMEONE REAL...
I CAN STILL LOVE YOU, MARTHA.
OH, GOD...
SHE SEIZED UP THE HAMMER...
SHE SMASHED AT HIS HEAD AND BEAT AT HIS CHEST AND HIS THRASHING ARMS AND WILD LEGS. SHE BEAT AT THE SOFT HEAD UNTIL STEEL SHONE THROUGH, AND SUDDEN EXPLOSIONS OF WIRE AND BRASS COGGERY SHOWERED ABOUT THE ROOM WITH METAL TINKLES. THE MOUTH SAID...
I... LOVE YOU...
SHE STRUCK THE MOUTH WITH THE HAMMER AND THE TONGUE FELL OUT. THE GLASS EYES ROLLED ON THE CARPET. SHE POUNDED AT THE THING UNTIL IT WAS STREWN LIKE THE REMAINS OF A CHILD'S ELECTRIC TRAIN ON THE FLOOR...
IN THE KITCHEN, SHE FOUND SEVERAL CARTONS. SHE LOADED THE COGS AND WIRES AND METAL INTO THESE AND SEALED THE TOPS. TEN MINUTES LATER THE MESSENGER BOY ARRIVED...
DELIVER THESE PACKAGES TO MR. LEONARD HILL, 17 ELM DRIVE. RIGHT NOW, TONIGHT. TELL HIM IT'S A SURPRISE PACKAGE... FROM MARTHA!
A SURPRISE PACKAGE FROM MARTHA. YES MA'AM!
AFTER THE DOOR CLOSED, SHE SAT ON THE COUCH WITH THE GUN IN HER HAND, TURNING IT OVER AND OVER, LISTENING. THE LAST THING SHE HEARD IN HER LIFE WAS THE SOUND OF THE PACKAGES BEING CARRIED DOWN THE HALL, THE METAL JINGLING SOFTLY, COG AGAINST COG, WIRE AGAINST WIRE, FADING...
THE END
7

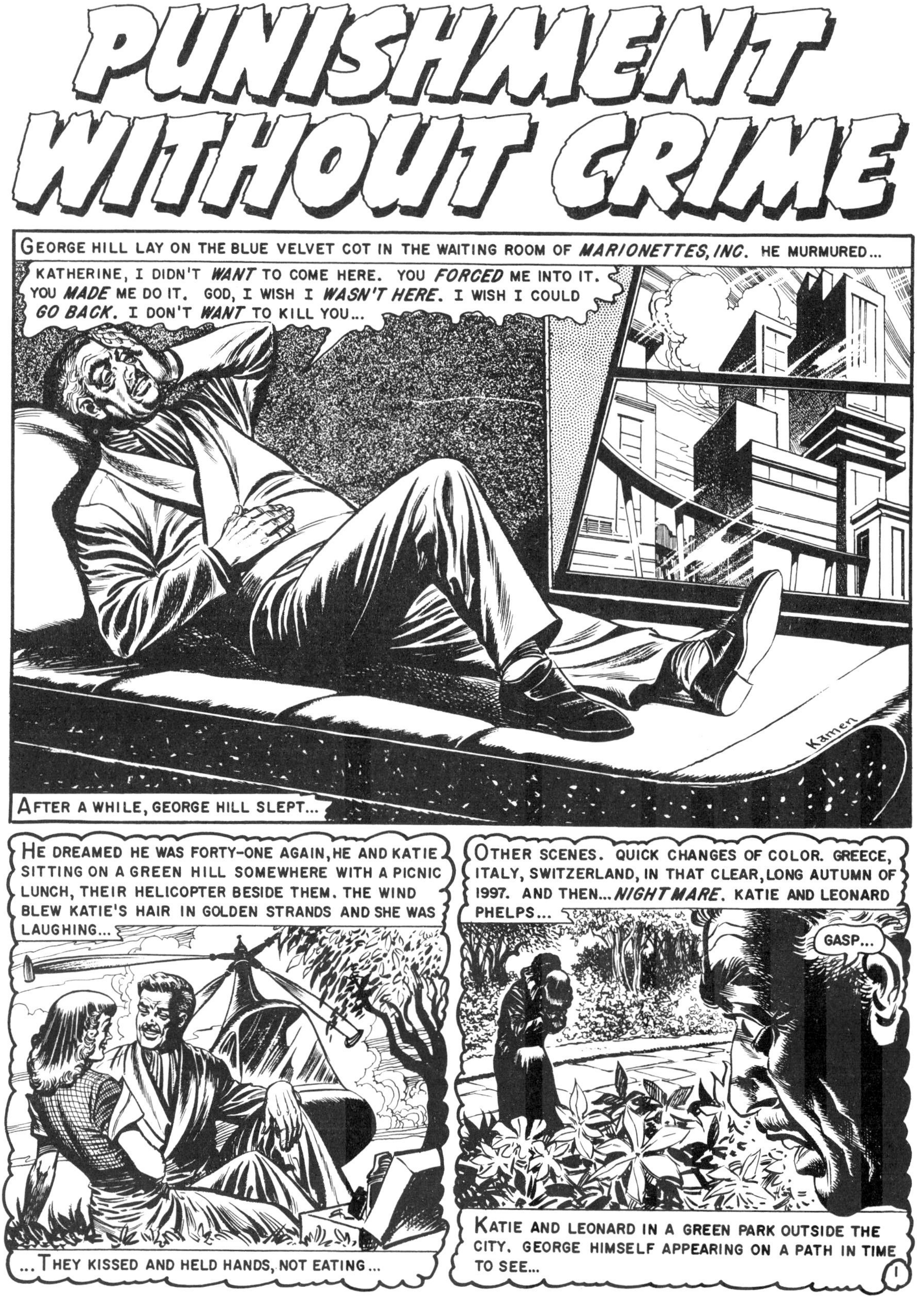
PUNISHMENT WITHOUT CRIME
GEORGE HILL LAY ON THE BLUE VELVET COT IN THE WAITING ROOM OF MARIONETTES, INC. HE MURMURED...
KATHERINE, I DIDN'T WANT TO COME HERE. YOU FORCED ME INTO IT. YOU MADE ME DO IT. GOD, I WISH I WASN'T HERE. I WISH I COULD GO BACK. I DON'T WANT TO KILL YOU...
Kamen
AFTER A WHILE, GEORGE HILL SLEPT...
HE DREAMED HE WAS FORTY-ONE AGAIN, HE AND KATIE SITTING ON A GREEN HILL SOMEWHERE WITH A PICNIC LUNCH, THEIR HELICOPTER BESIDE THEM. THE WIND BLEW KATIE'S HAIR IN GOLDEN STRANDS AND SHE WAS LAUGHING...
...THEY KISSED AND HELD HANDS, NOT EATING...
OTHER SCENES. QUICK CHANGES OF COLOR. GREECE, ITALY, SWITZERLAND, IN THAT CLEAR, LONG AUTUMN OF 1997. AND THEN... NIGHTMARE. KATIE AND LEONARD PHELPS...
GASP...
KATIE AND LEONARD IN A GREEN PARK OUTSIDE THE CITY. GEORGE HIMSELF APPEARING ON A PATH IN TIME TO SEE...
1

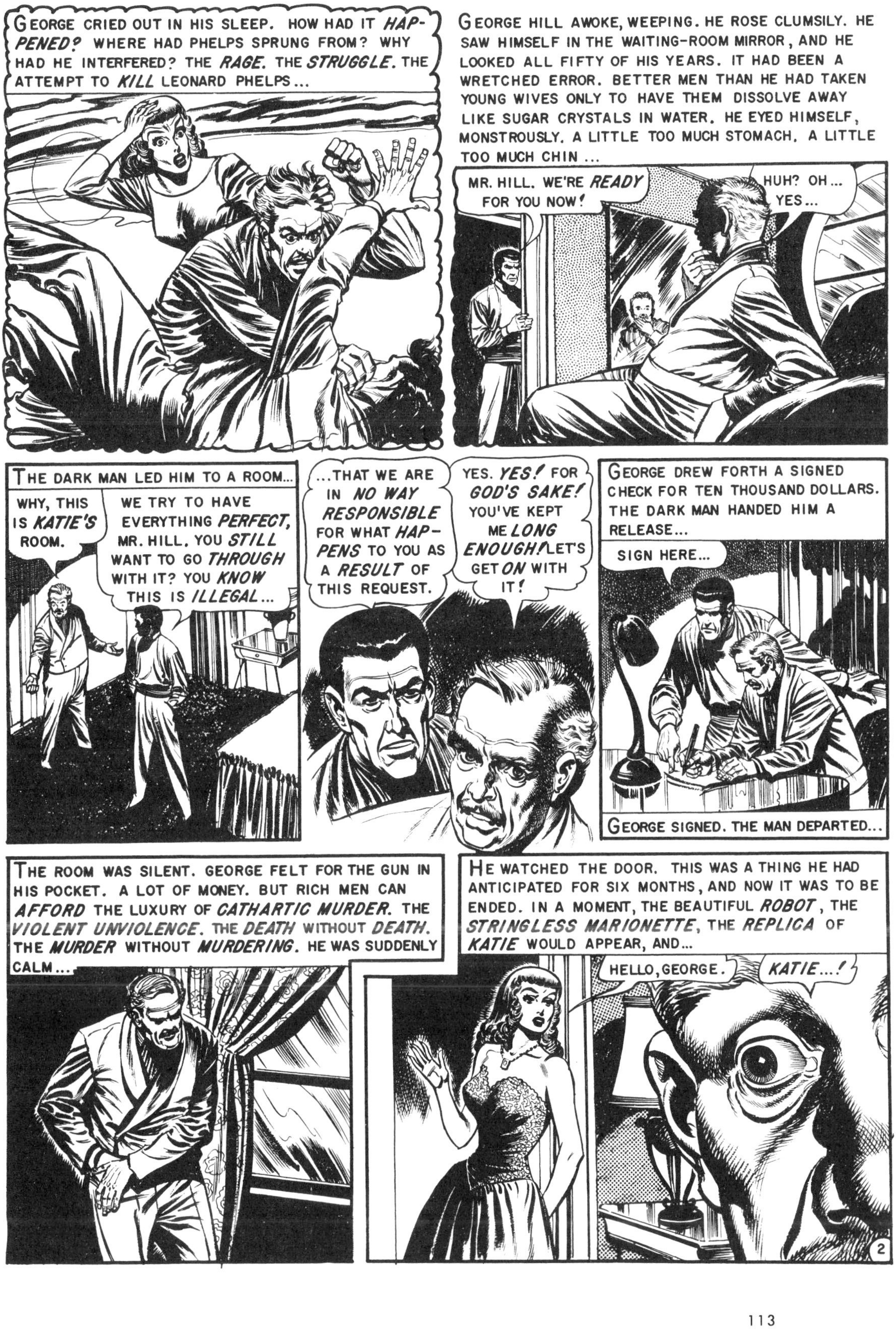
GEORGE CRIED OUT IN HIS SLEEP. HOW HAD IT HAPPENED? WHERE HAD PHELPS SPRUNG FROM? WHY HAD HE INTERFERED? THE RAGE. THE STRUGGLE. THE ATTEMPT TO KILL LEONARD PHELPS...
GEORGE HILL AWOKE, WEEPING. HE ROSE CLUMSILY. HE SAW HIMSELF IN THE WAITING-ROOM MIRROR, AND HE LOOKED ALL FIFTY OF HIS YEARS. IT HAD BEEN A WRETCHED ERROR. BETTER MEN THAN HE HAD TAKEN YOUNG WIVES ONLY TO HAVE THEM DISSOLVE AWAY LIKE SUGAR CRYSTALS IN WATER. HE EYED HIMSELF, MONSTROUSLY. A LITTLE TOO MUCH STOMACH. A LITTLE TOO MUCH CHIN...
MR. HILL. WE'RE READY FOR YOU NOW!
HUH? OH... YES...
THE DARK MAN LED HIM TO A ROOM...
WHY, THIS IS KATIE'S ROOM.
WE TRY TO HAVE EVERYTHING PERFECT, MR. HILL. YOU STILL WANT TO GO THROUGH WITH IT? YOU KNOW THIS IS ILLEGAL...
...THAT WE ARE IN NO WAY RESPONSIBLE FOR WHAT HAPPENS TO YOU AS A RESULT OF THIS REQUEST.
YES. YES! FOR GOD'S SAKE! YOU'VE KEPT ME LONG ENOUGH! LET'S GET ON WITH IT!
GEORGE DREW FORTH A SIGNED CHECK FOR TEN THOUSAND DOLLARS. THE DARK MAN HANDED HIM A RELEASE...
SIGN HERE...
GEORGE SIGNED. THE MAN DEPARTED...
THE ROOM WAS SILENT. GEORGE FELT FOR THE GUN IN HIS POCKET. A LOT OF MONEY. BUT RICH MEN CAN AFFORD THE LUXURY OF CATHARTIC MURDER. THE VIOLENT UNVIOLENCE. THE DEATH WITHOUT DEATH. THE MURDER WITHOUT MURDERING. HE WAS SUDDENLY CALM...
HE WATCHED THE DOOR. THIS WAS A THING HE HAD ANTICIPATED FOR SIX MONTHS, AND NOW IT WAS TO BE ENDED. IN A MOMENT, THE BEAUTIFUL ROBOT, THE STRINGLESS MARIONETTE, THE REPLICA OF KATIE WOULD APPEAR, AND...
HELLO, GEORGE.
KATIE...!
2

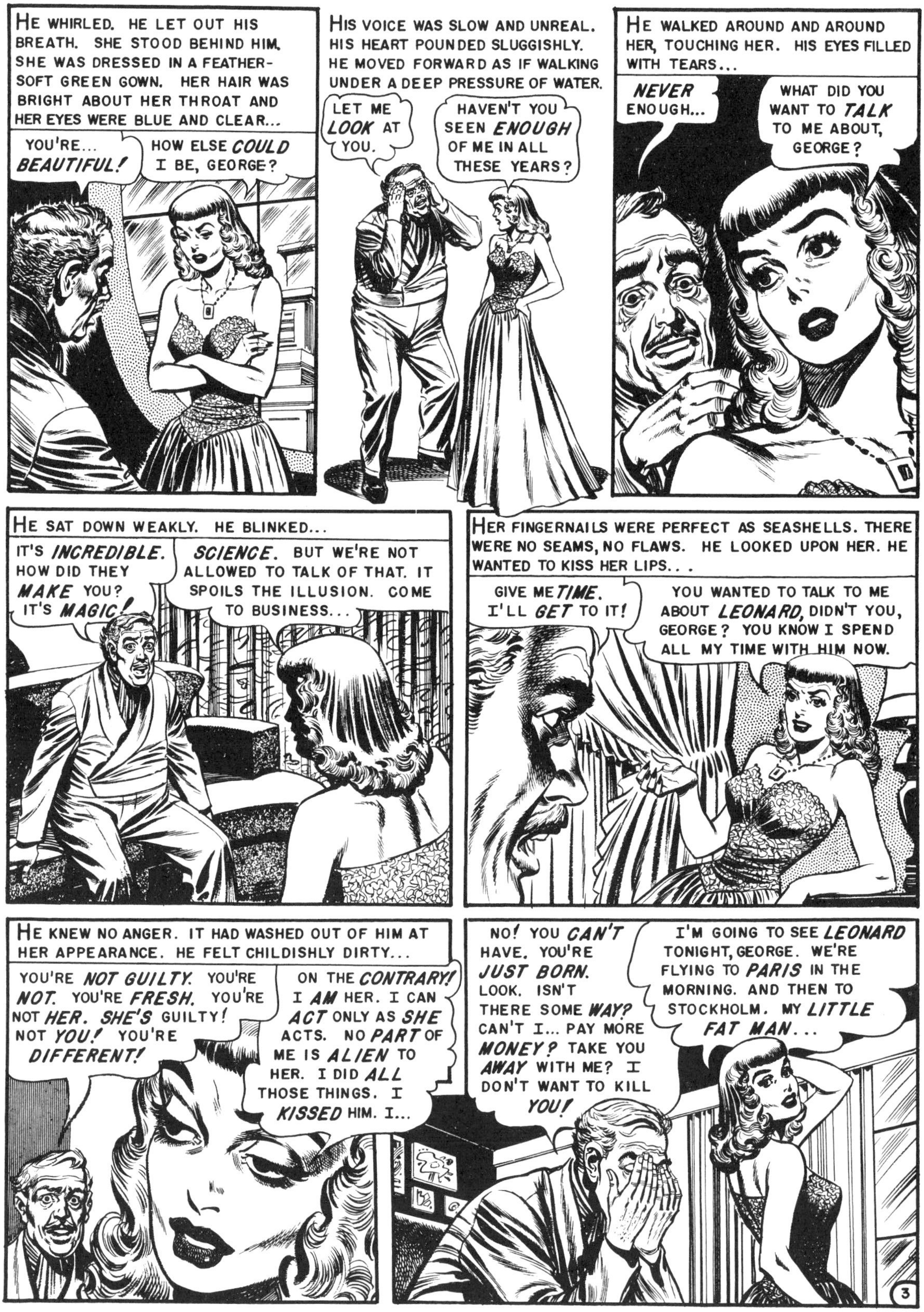
HE WHIRLED. HE LET OUT HIS BREATH. SHE STOOD BEHIND HIM. SHE WAS DRESSED IN A FEATHER-SOFT GREEN GOWN. HER HAIR WAS BRIGHT ABOUT HER THROAT AND HER EYES WERE BLUE AND CLEAR...
YOU'RE... BEAUTIFUL!
HOW ELSE COULD I BE, GEORGE?
HIS VOICE WAS SLOW AND UNREAL. HIS HEART POUNDED SLUGGISHLY. HE MOVED FORWARD AS IF WALKING UNDER A DEEP PRESSURE OF WATER.
LET ME LOOK AT YOU.
HAVEN'T YOU SEEN ENOUGH OF ME IN ALL THESE YEARS?
HE WALKED AROUND AND AROUND HER, TOUCHING HER. HIS EYES FILLED WITH TEARS...
NEVER ENOUGH...
WHAT DID YOU WANT TO TALK TO ME ABOUT, GEORGE?
HE SAT DOWN WEAKLY. HE BLINKED...
IT'S INCREDIBLE. HOW DID THEY MAKE YOU? IT'S MAGIC!
SCIENCE. BUT WE'RE NOT ALLOWED TO TALK OF THAT. IT SPOILS THE ILLUSION. COME TO BUSINESS...
HER FINGERNAILS WERE PERFECT AS SEASHELLS. THERE WERE NO SEAMS, NO FLAWS. HE LOOKED UPON HER. HE WANTED TO KISS HER LIPS...
GIVE ME TIME. I'LL GET TO IT!
YOU WANTED TO TALK TO ME ABOUT LEONARD, DIDN'T YOU, GEORGE? YOU KNOW I SPEND ALL MY TIME WITH HIM NOW.
HE KNEW NO ANGER. IT HAD WASHED OUT OF HIM AT HER APPEARANCE. HE FELT CHILDISHLY DIRTY...
YOU'RE NOT GUILTY. YOU'RE NOT. YOU'RE FRESH. YOU'RE NOT HER. SHE'S GUILTY! NOT YOU! YOU'RE DIFFERENT!
ON THE CONTRARY! I AM HER. I CAN ACT ONLY AS SHE ACTS. NO PART OF ME IS ALIEN TO HER. I DID ALL THOSE THINGS. I KISSED HIM. I...
NO! YOU CAN'T HAVE. YOU'RE JUST BORN. LOOK. ISN'T THERE SOME WAY? CAN'T I... PAY MORE MONEY? TAKE YOU AWAY WITH ME? I DON'T WANT TO KILL YOU!
I'M GOING TO SEE LEONARD TONIGHT, GEORGE. WE'RE FLYING TO PARIS IN THE MORNING. AND THEN TO STOCKHOLM. MY LITTLE FAT MAN...
3

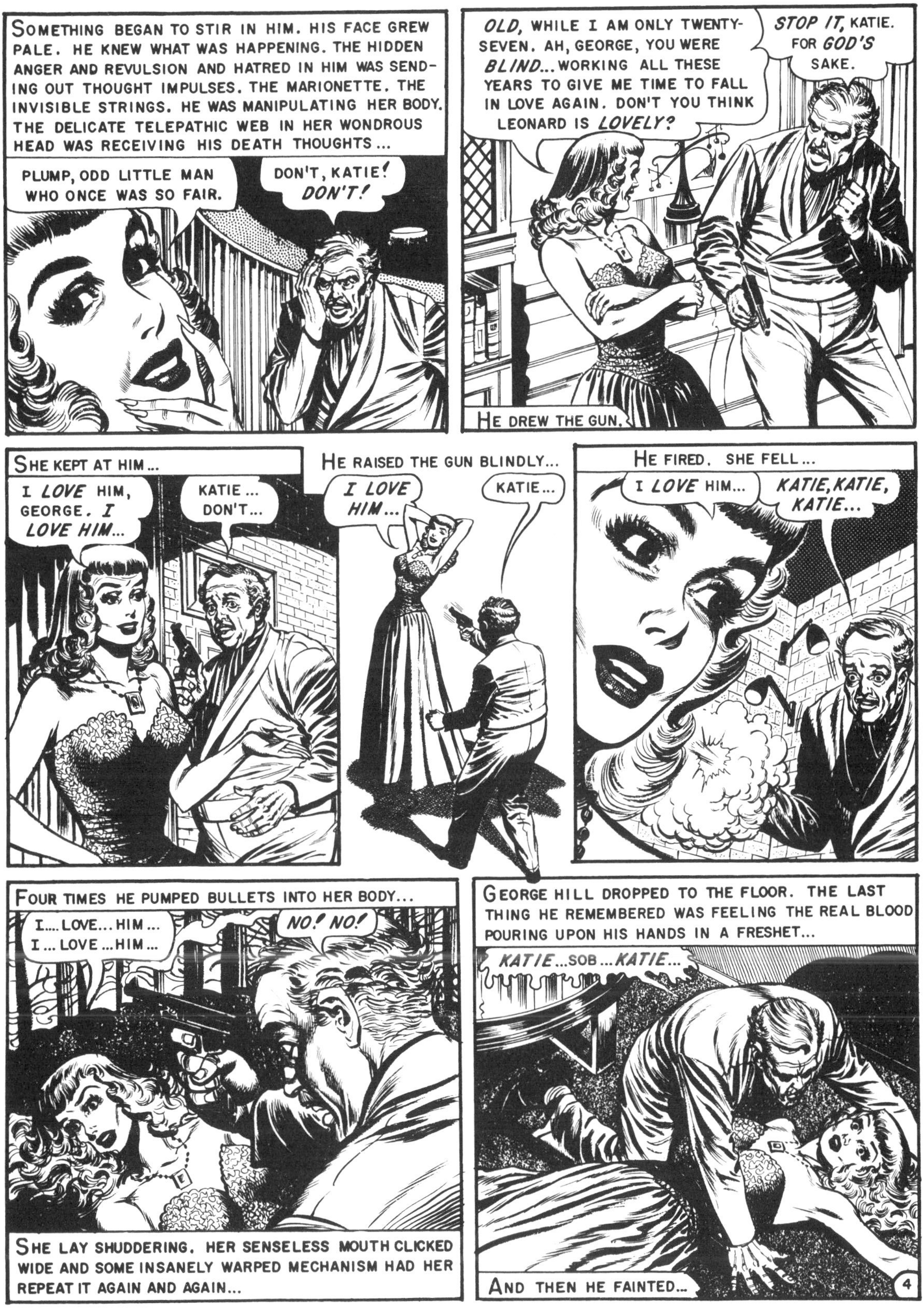
SOMETHING BEGAN TO STIR IN HIM. HIS FACE GREW PALE. HE KNEW WHAT WAS HAPPENING. THE HIDDEN ANGER AND REVULSION AND HATRED IN HIM WAS SENDING OUT THOUGHT IMPULSES. THE MARIONETTE. THE INVISIBLE STRINGS. HE WAS MANIPULATING HER BODY. THE DELICATE TELEPATHIC WEB IN HER WONDROUS HEAD WAS RECEIVING HIS DEATH THOUGHTS...
PLUMP, ODD LITTLE MAN WHO ONCE WAS SO FAIR.
DON'T, KATIE! DON'T!
OLD, WHILE I AM ONLY TWENTY-SEVEN. AH, GEORGE, YOU WERE BLIND... WORKING ALL THESE YEARS TO GIVE ME TIME TO FALL IN LOVE AGAIN. DON'T YOU THINK LEONARD IS LOVELY?
STOP IT, KATIE. FOR GOD'S SAKE.
HE DREW THE GUN.
SHE KEPT AT HIM...
I LOVE HIM, GEORGE. I LOVE HIM...
KATIE... DON'T...
HE RAISED THE GUN BLINDLY...
I LOVE HIM...
KATIE...
HE FIRED. SHE FELL...
I LOVE HIM...
KATIE, KATIE, KATIE...
FOUR TIMES HE PUMPED BULLETS INTO HER BODY...
I.... LOVE... HIM... I... LOVE ...HIM...
NO! NO!
SHE LAY SHUDDERING. HER SENSELESS MOUTH CLICKED WIDE AND SOME INSANELY WARPED MECHANISM HAD HER REPEAT IT AGAIN AND AGAIN...
GEORGE HILL DROPPED TO THE FLOOR. THE LAST THING HE REMEMBERED WAS FEELING THE REAL BLOOD POURING UPON HIS HANDS IN A FRESHET...
KATIE...SOB...KATIE...
AND THEN HE FAINTED...
4

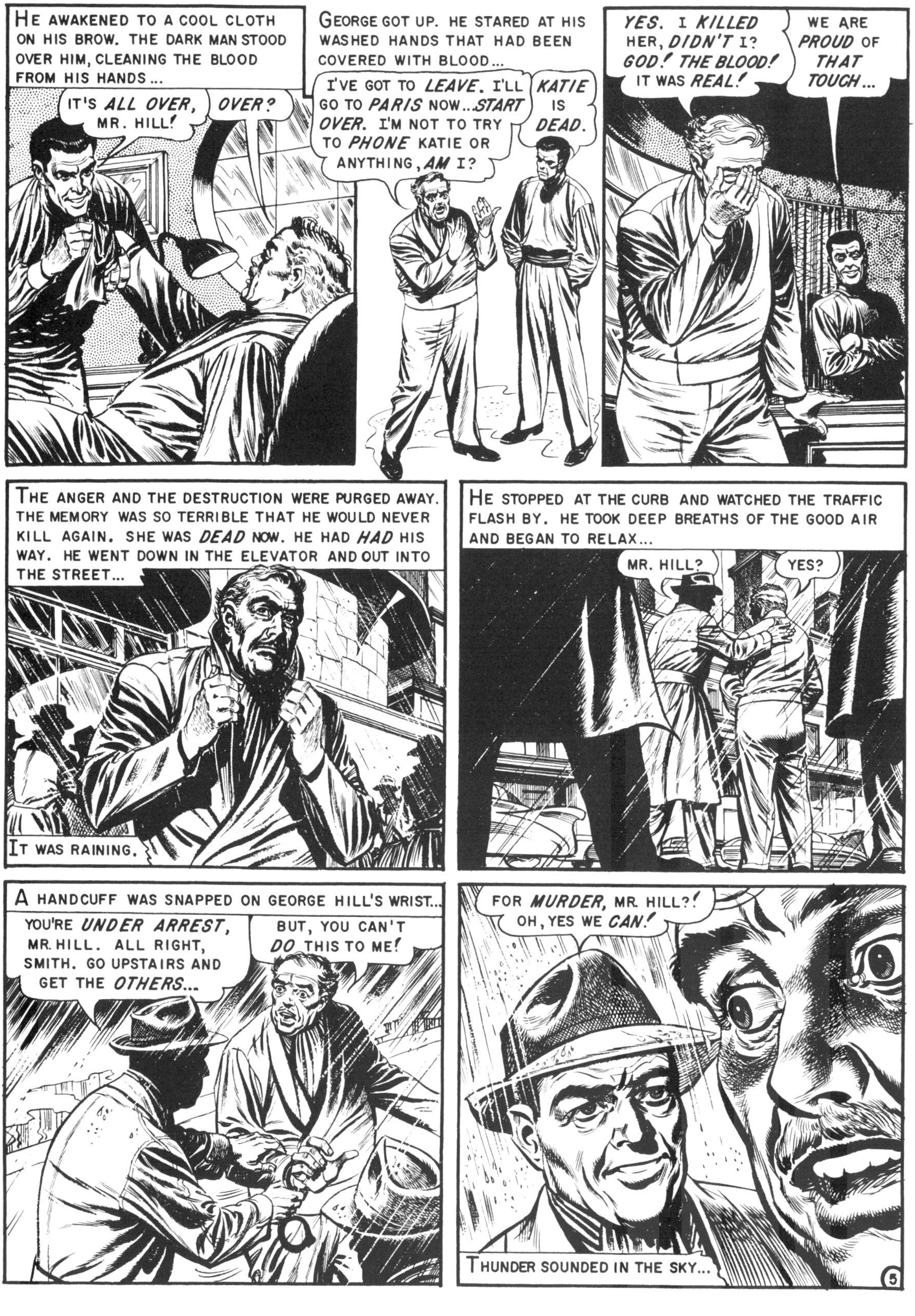
HE AWAKENED TO A COOL CLOTH ON HIS BROW. THE DARK MAN STOOD OVER HIM, CLEANING THE BLOOD FROM HIS HANDS...
IT'S ALL OVER, MR. HILL!
OVER?
GEORGE GOT UP. HE STARED AT HIS WASHED HANDS THAT HAD BEEN COVERED WITH BLOOD...
I'VE GOT TO LEAVE. I'LL GO TO PARIS NOW...START OVER. I'M NOT TO TRY TO PHONE KATIE OR ANYTHING, AM I?
KATIE IS DEAD.
YES. I KILLED HER, DIDN'T I? GOD! THE BLOOD! IT WAS REAL!
WE ARE PROUD OF THAT TOUCH...
THE ANGER AND THE DESTRUCTION WERE PURGED AWAY. THE MEMORY WAS SO TERRIBLE THAT HE WOULD NEVER KILL AGAIN. SHE WAS DEAD NOW. HE HAD HAD HIS WAY. HE WENT DOWN IN THE ELEVATOR AND OUT INTO THE STREET...
IT WAS RAINING.
HE STOPPED AT THE CURB AND WATCHED THE TRAFFIC FLASH BY. HE TOOK DEEP BREATHS OF THE GOOD AIR AND BEGAN TO RELAX...
MR. HILL?
YES?
A HANDCUFF WAS SNAPPED ON GEORGE HILL'S WRIST...
YOU'RE UNDER ARREST, MR. HILL. ALL RIGHT, SMITH. GO UPSTAIRS AND GET THE OTHERS...
BUT, YOU CAN'T DO THIS TO ME!
FOR MURDER, MR. HILL?! OH, YES WE CAN!
THUNDER SOUNDED IN THE SKY...
5

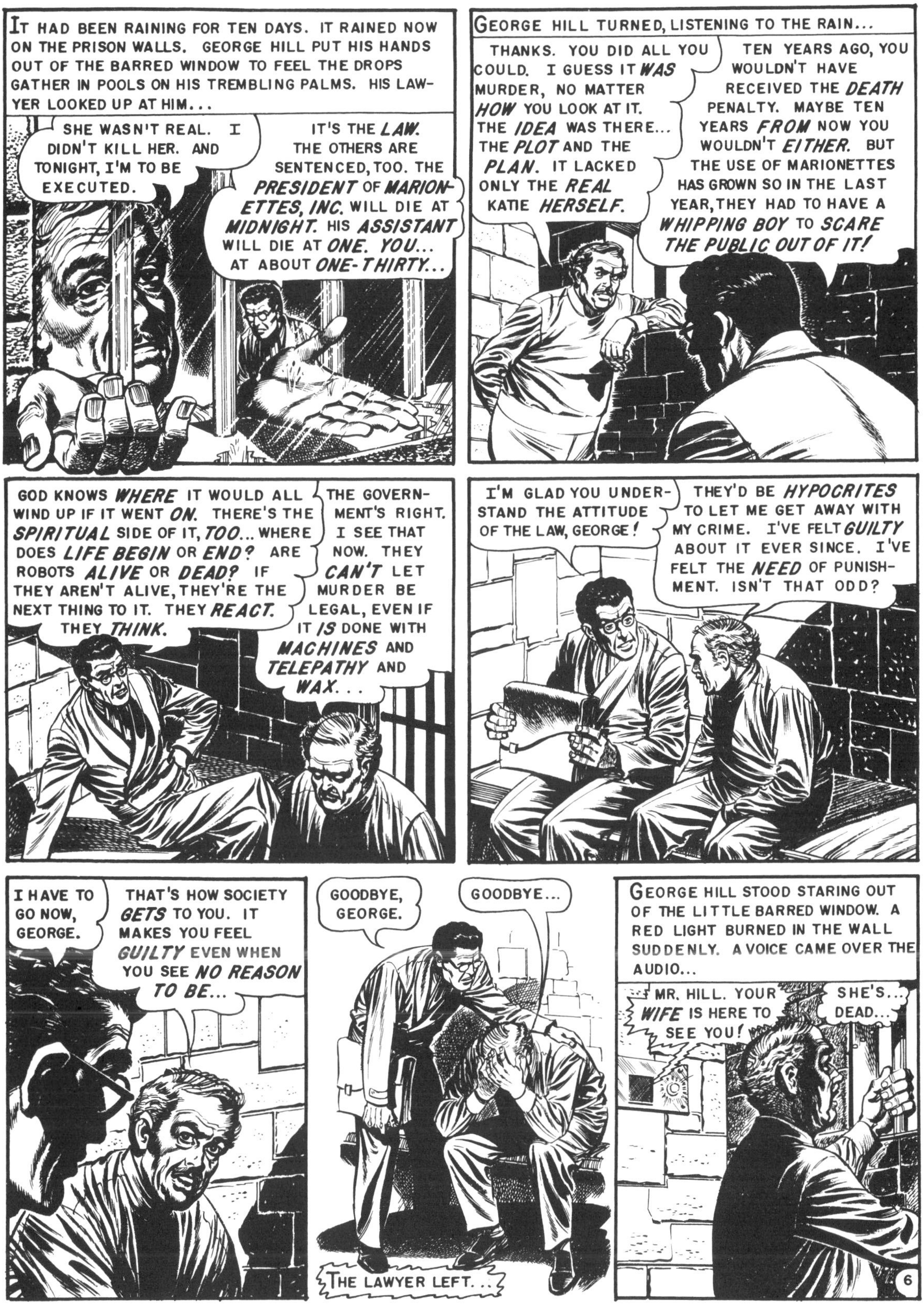
IT HAD BEEN RAINING FOR TEN DAYS. IT RAINED NOW ON THE PRISON WALLS. GEORGE HILL PUT HIS HANDS OUT OF THE BARRED WINDOW TO FEEL THE DROPS GATHER IN POOLS ON HIS TREMBLING PALMS. HIS LAWYER LOOKED UP AT HIM...
SHE WASN'T REAL. I DIDN'T KILL HER. AND TONIGHT, I'M TO BE EXECUTED.
IT'S THE LAW. THE OTHERS ARE SENTENCED, TOO. THE PRESIDENT OF MARIONETTES, INC. WILL DIE AT MIDNIGHT. HIS ASSISTANT WILL DIE AT ONE. YOU... AT ABOUT ONE-THIRTY...
GEORGE HILL TURNED, LISTENING TO THE RAIN...
THANKS. YOU DID ALL YOU COULD. I GUESS IT WAS MURDER, NO MATTER HOW YOU LOOK AT IT. THE IDEA WAS THERE... THE PLOT AND THE PLAN. IT LACKED ONLY THE REAL KATIE HERSELF.
TEN YEARS AGO, YOU WOULDN'T HAVE RECEIVED THE DEATH PENALTY. MAYBE TEN YEARS FROM NOW YOU WOULDN'T EITHER. BUT THE USE OF MARIONETTES HAS GROWN SO IN THE LAST YEAR, THEY HAD TO HAVE A WHIPPING BOY TO SCARE THE PUBLIC OUT OF IT!
GOD KNOWS WHERE IT WOULD ALL WIND UP IF IT WENT ON. THERE'S THE SPIRITUAL SIDE OF IT, TOO... WHERE DOES LIFE BEGIN OR END? ARE ROBOTS ALIVE OR DEAD? IF THEY AREN'T ALIVE, THEY'RE THE NEXT THING TO IT. THEY REACT. THEY THINK.
THE GOVERNMENT'S RIGHT. I SEE THAT NOW. THEY CAN'T LET MURDER BE LEGAL, EVEN IF IT IS DONE WITH MACHINES AND TELEPATHY AND WAX...
I'M GLAD YOU UNDERSTAND THE ATTITUDE OF THE LAW, GEORGE!
THEY'D BE HYPOCRITES TO LET ME GET AWAY WITH MY CRIME. I'VE FELT GUILTY ABOUT IT EVER SINCE. I'VE FELT THE NEED OF PUNISHMENT. ISN'T THAT ODD?
I HAVE TO GO NOW, GEORGE.
THAT'S HOW SOCIETY GETS TO YOU. IT MAKES YOU FEEL GUILTY EVEN WHEN YOU SEE NO REASON TO BE...
GOODBYE, GEORGE.
GOODBYE...
THE LAWYER LEFT...
GEORGE HILL STOOD STARING OUT OF THE LITTLE BARRED WINDOW. A RED LIGHT BURNED IN THE WALL SUDDENLY. A VOICE CAME OVER THE AUDIO...
MR. HILL. YOUR WIFE IS HERE TO SEE YOU!
SHE'S... DEAD...
6

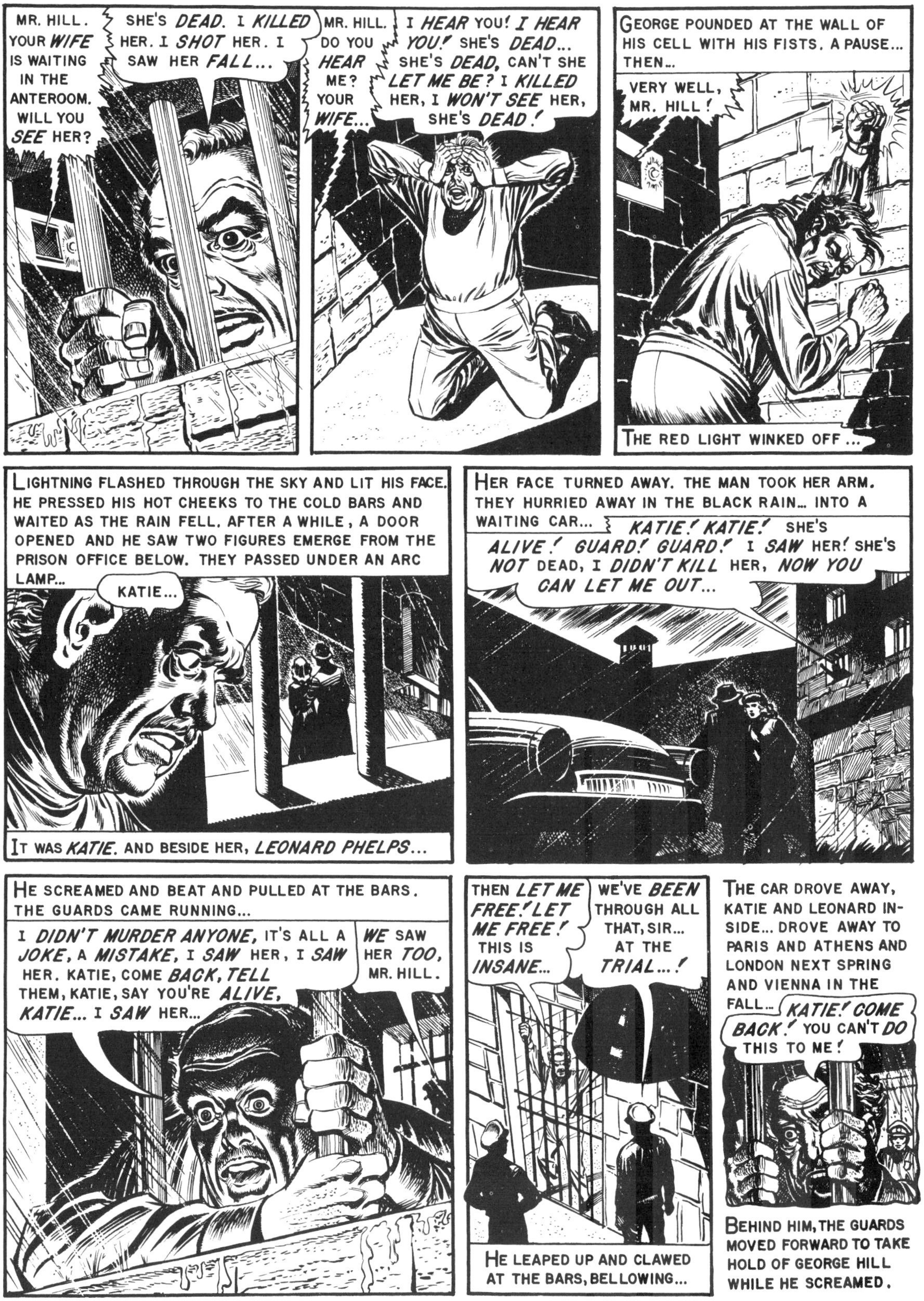
MR. HILL. YOUR WIFE IS WAITING IN THE ANTEROOM. WILL YOU SEE HER?
SHE'S DEAD. I KILLED HER. I SHOT HER. I SAW HER FALL...
MR. HILL. DO YOU HEAR ME? YOUR WIFE...
I HEAR YOU! I HEAR YOU! SHE'S DEAD... SHE'S DEAD, CAN'T SHE LET ME BE? I KILLED HER, I WON'T SEE HER, SHE'S DEAD!
GEORGE POUNDED AT THE WALL OF HIS CELL WITH HIS FISTS. A PAUSE... THEN...
VERY WELL, MR. HILL!
THE RED LIGHT WINKED OFF...
LIGHTNING FLASHED THROUGH THE SKY AND LIT HIS FACE. HE PRESSED HIS HOT CHEEKS TO THE COLD BARS AND WAITED AS THE RAIN FELL. AFTER A WHILE, A DOOR OPENED AND HE SAW TWO FIGURES EMERGE FROM THE PRISON OFFICE BELOW. THEY PASSED UNDER AN ARC LAMP...
KATIE...
IT WAS KATIE. AND BESIDE HER, LEONARD PHELPS...
HER FACE TURNED AWAY. THE MAN TOOK HER ARM. THEY HURRIED AWAY IN THE BLACK RAIN... INTO A WAITING CAR...
KATIE! KATIE! SHE'S ALIVE! GUARD! GUARD! I SAW HER! SHE'S NOT DEAD, I DIDN'T KILL HER, NOW YOU CAN LET ME OUT...
HE SCREAMED AND BEAT AND PULLED AT THE BARS. THE GUARDS CAME RUNNING...
I DIDN'T MURDER ANYONE, IT'S ALL A JOKE, A MISTAKE, I SAW HER, I SAW HER. KATIE, COME BACK, TELL THEM, KATIE, SAY YOU'RE ALIVE, KATIE... I SAW HER...
WE SAW HER TOO, MR. HILL.
THEN LET ME FREE! LET ME FREE! THIS IS INSANE...
WE'VE BEEN THROUGH ALL THAT, SIR... AT THE TRIAL...!
HE LEAPED UP AND CLAWED AT THE BARS, BELLOWING...
THE CAR DROVE AWAY, KATIE AND LEONARD INSIDE... DROVE AWAY TO PARIS AND ATHENS AND LONDON NEXT SPRING AND VIENNA IN THE FALL...
KATIE! COME BACK! YOU CAN'T DO THIS TO ME!
BEHIND HIM, THE GUARDS MOVED FORWARD TO TAKE HOLD OF GEORGE HILL WHILE HE SCREAMED.

PLANELY POSSIBLE

MY NAME IS WALTER THURMOND. THERE ARE ONLY A FEW MINUTES LEFT FOR ME TO TELL YOU MY STORY, SO I'LL MAKE IT SHORT. LISTEN CAREFULLY. YOU MAY NOT BELIEVE IT, BUT IT'S *TRUE*... EVERY WORD OF IT. IT BEGAN WHEN RUTH... THAT'S MY WIFE... AND I WERE DRIVING SOUTH ON THE FIRST LEG OF OUR LONG ANTICIPATED SUMMER VACATION. IT BEGAN WITH THE ROAR OF OUR CONVERTIBLE AS IT SPED ALONG THE WINDING HIGHWAY DOING BETTER THAN SEVENTY. IT BEGAN WITH THE SUDDEN LOOMING HULK OF THE TRAILER-TRUCK SWINGING WIDE AROUND A CURVE, BLOCKING THE ROAD. IT BEGAN WITH THE SCREAMING OF TIRES ON CONCRETE, THE BLOOD-CURDLING SHRIEK OF MY WIFE, RUTH, AND THE SICKENING IMPACT OF METAL AND GLASS SPLINTERING AGAINST METAL AND GLASS. . .

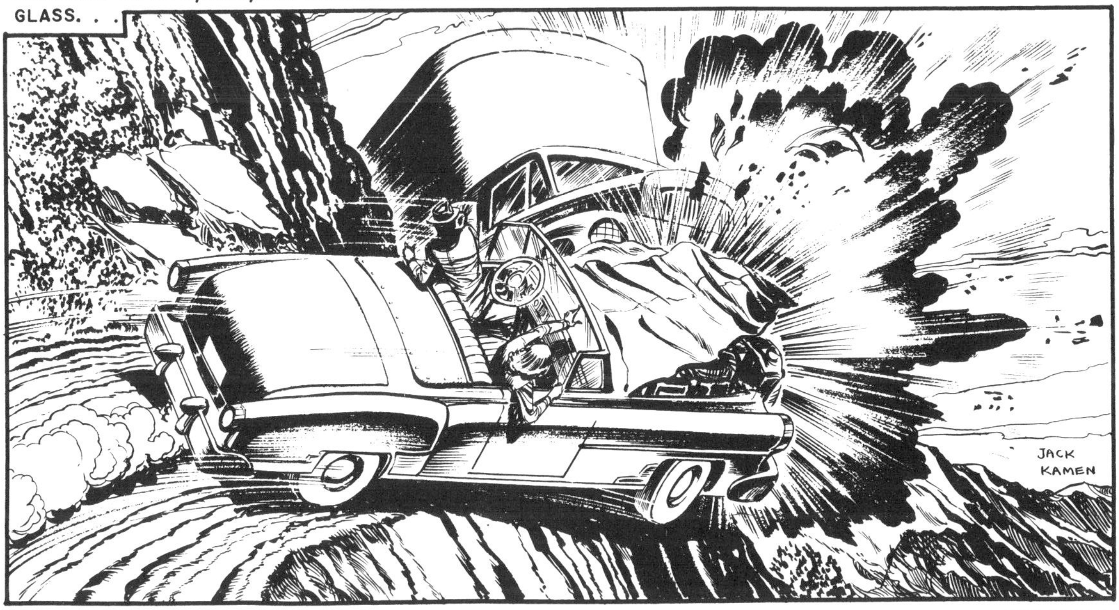
JACK KAMEN

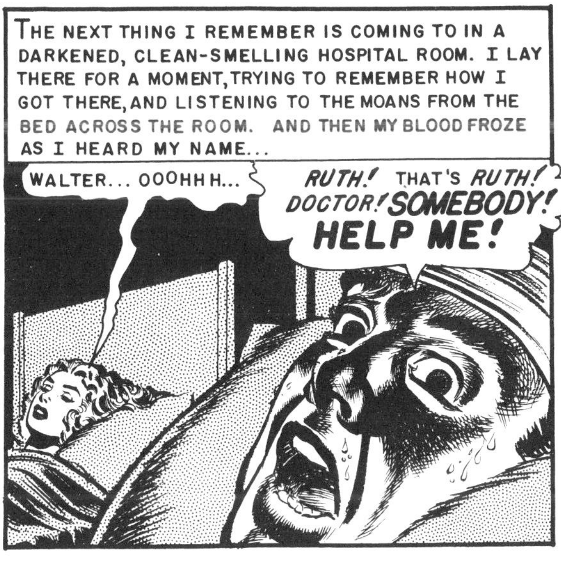
THE NEXT THING I REMEMBER IS COMING TO IN A DARKENED, CLEAN-SMELLING HOSPITAL ROOM. I LAY THERE FOR A MOMENT, TRYING TO REMEMBER HOW I GOT THERE, AND LISTENING TO THE MOANS FROM THE BED ACROSS THE ROOM. AND THEN MY BLOOD FROZE AS I HEARD MY NAME...
WALTER... OOOHHH...
RUTH! THAT'S RUTH! DOCTOR! SOMEBODY! HELP ME!

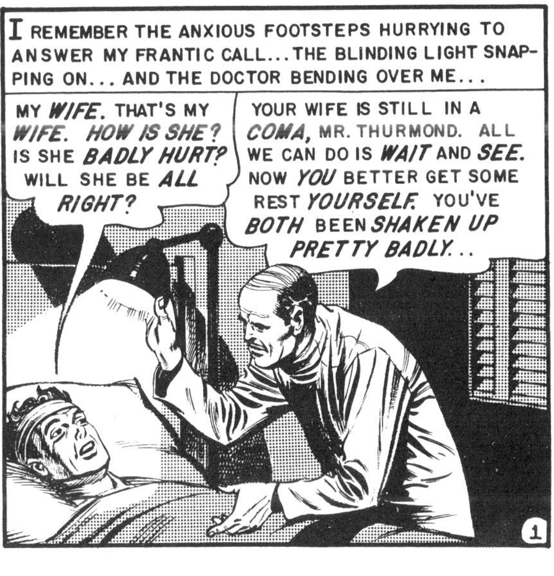
I REMEMBER THE ANXIOUS FOOTSTEPS HURRYING TO ANSWER MY FRANTIC CALL... THE BLINDING LIGHT SNAPPING ON... AND THE DOCTOR BENDING OVER ME...
MY WIFE. THAT'S MY WIFE. HOW IS SHE? IS SHE BADLY HURT? WILL SHE BE ALL RIGHT?
YOUR WIFE IS STILL IN A COMA, MR. THURMOND. ALL WE CAN DO IS WAIT AND SEE. NOW YOU BETTER GET SOME REST YOURSELF. YOU'VE BOTH BEEN SHAKEN UP PRETTY BADLY...
1

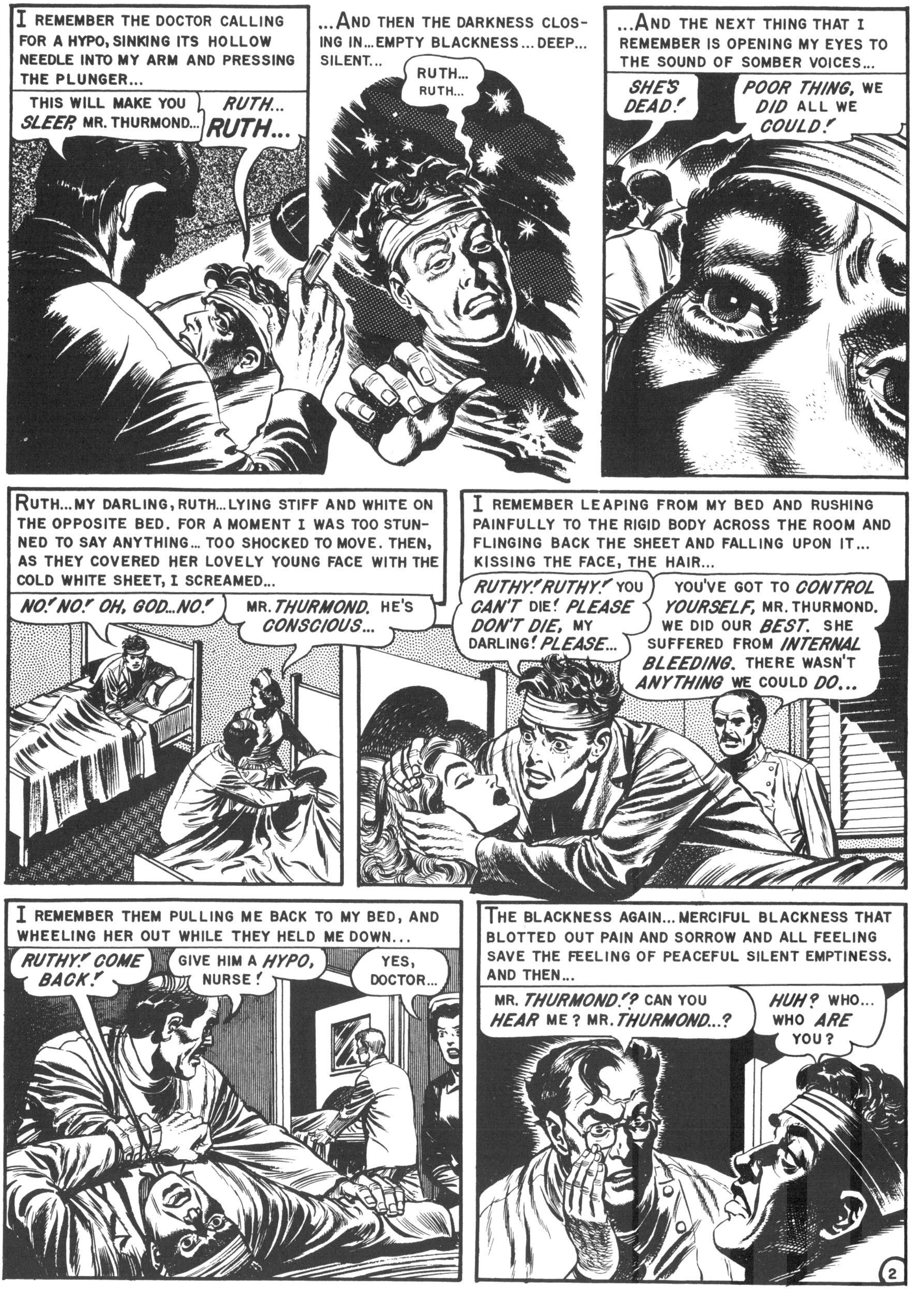
I REMEMBER THE DOCTOR CALLING FOR A HYPO, SINKING ITS HOLLOW NEEDLE INTO MY ARM AND PRESSING THE PLUNGER...
THIS WILL MAKE YOU SLEEP, MR. THURMOND...
RUTH... RUTH...
...AND THEN THE DARKNESS CLOSING IN... EMPTY BLACKNESS... DEEP... SILENT...
RUTH... RUTH...
...AND THE NEXT THING THAT I REMEMBER IS OPENING MY EYES TO THE SOUND OF SOMBER VOICES...
SHE'S DEAD!
POOR THING, WE DID ALL WE COULD!
RUTH... MY DARLING, RUTH... LYING STIFF AND WHITE ON THE OPPOSITE BED. FOR A MOMENT I WAS TOO STUNNED TO SAY ANYTHING... TOO SHOCKED TO MOVE. THEN, AS THEY COVERED HER LOVELY YOUNG FACE WITH THE COLD WHITE SHEET, I SCREAMED...
NO! NO! OH, GOD...NO!
MR. THURMOND. HE'S CONSCIOUS...
I REMEMBER LEAPING FROM MY BED AND RUSHING PAINFULLY TO THE RIGID BODY ACROSS THE ROOM AND FLINGING BACK THE SHEET AND FALLING UPON IT... KISSING THE FACE, THE HAIR...
RUTHY! RUTHY! YOU CAN'T DIE! PLEASE DON'T DIE, MY DARLING! PLEASE...
YOU'VE GOT TO CONTROL YOURSELF, MR. THURMOND. WE DID OUR BEST. SHE SUFFERED FROM INTERNAL BLEEDING. THERE WASN'T ANYTHING WE COULD DO...
I REMEMBER THEM PULLING ME BACK TO MY BED, AND WHEELING HER OUT WHILE THEY HELD ME DOWN...
RUTHY! COME BACK!
GIVE HIM A HYPO, NURSE!
YES, DOCTOR...
THE BLACKNESS AGAIN... MERCIFUL BLACKNESS THAT BLOTTED OUT PAIN AND SORROW AND ALL FEELING SAVE THE FEELING OF PEACEFUL SILENT EMPTINESS. AND THEN...
MR. THURMOND!? CAN YOU HEAR ME? MR. THURMOND...?
HUH? WHO... WHO ARE YOU?
2

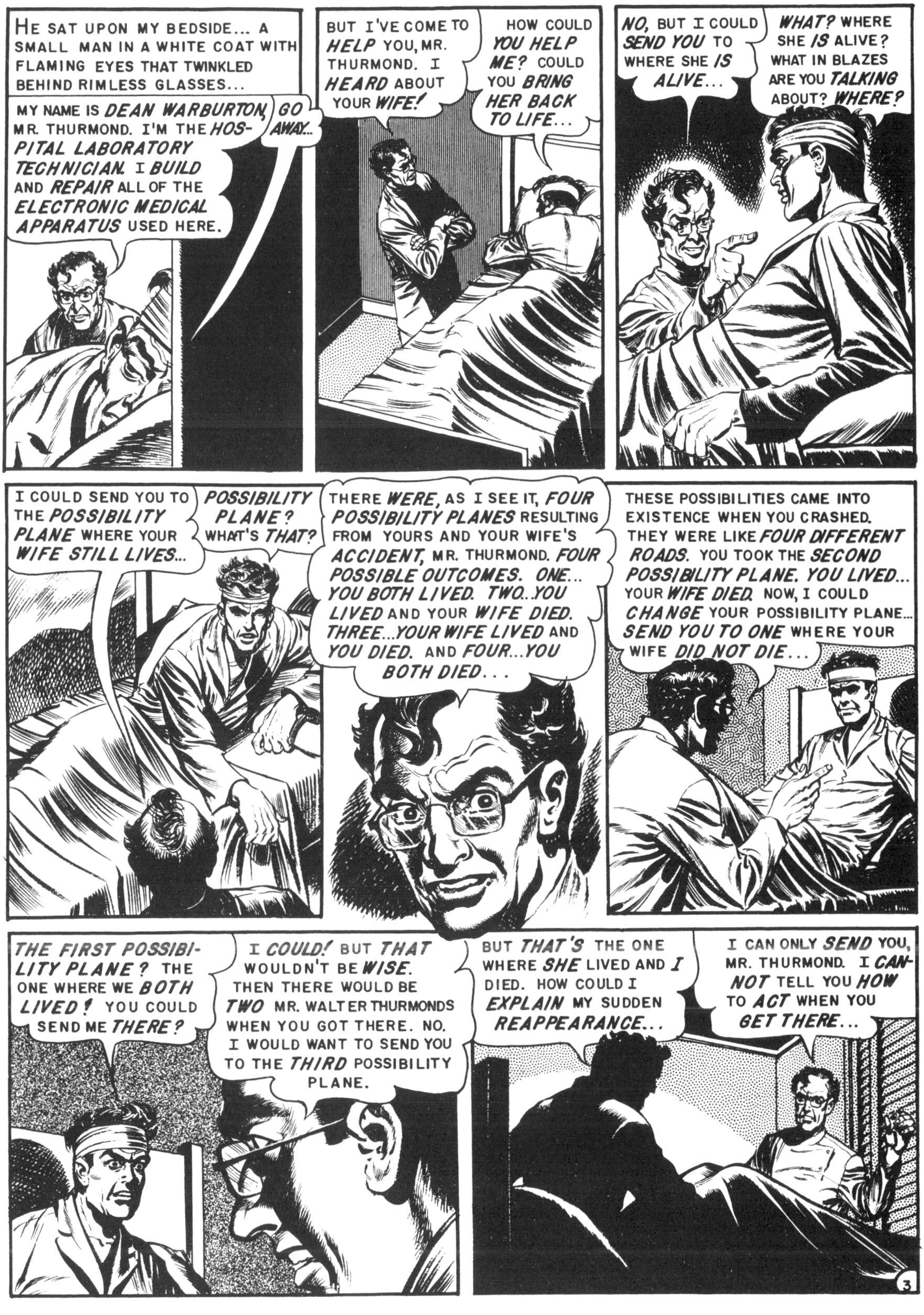
HE SAT UPON MY BEDSIDE... A SMALL MAN IN A WHITE COAT WITH FLAMING EYES THAT TWINKLED BEHIND RIMLESS GLASSES...
MY NAME IS DEAN WARBURTON, MR. THURMOND. I'M THE HOSPITAL LABORATORY TECHNICIAN. I BUILD AND REPAIR ALL OF THE ELECTRONIC MEDICAL APPARATUS USED HERE.
GO AWAY...
BUT I'VE COME TO HELP YOU, MR. THURMOND. I HEARD ABOUT YOUR WIFE!
HOW COULD YOU HELP ME? COULD YOU BRING HER BACK TO LIFE...
NO, BUT I COULD SEND YOU TO WHERE SHE IS ALIVE...
WHAT? WHERE SHE IS ALIVE? WHAT IN BLAZES ARE YOU TALKING ABOUT? WHERE?
I COULD SEND YOU TO THE POSSIBILITY PLANE WHERE YOUR WIFE STILL LIVES...
POSSIBILITY PLANE? WHAT'S THAT?
THERE WERE, AS I SEE IT, FOUR POSSIBILITY PLANES RESULTING FROM YOURS AND YOUR WIFE'S ACCIDENT, MR. THURMOND. FOUR POSSIBLE OUTCOMES. ONE... YOU BOTH LIVED. TWO...YOU LIVED AND YOUR WIFE DIED. THREE...YOUR WIFE LIVED AND YOU DIED. AND FOUR...YOU BOTH DIED...
THESE POSSIBILITIES CAME INTO EXISTENCE WHEN YOU CRASHED. THEY WERE LIKE FOUR DIFFERENT ROADS. YOU TOOK THE SECOND POSSIBILITY PLANE. YOU LIVED... YOUR WIFE DIED. NOW, I COULD CHANGE YOUR POSSIBILITY PLANE... SEND YOU TO ONE WHERE YOUR WIFE DID NOT DIE...
THE FIRST POSSIBILITY PLANE? THE ONE WHERE WE BOTH LIVED! YOU COULD SEND ME THERE?
I COULD! BUT THAT WOULDN'T BE WISE. THEN THERE WOULD BE TWO MR. WALTER THURMONDS WHEN YOU GOT THERE. NO. I WOULD WANT TO SEND YOU TO THE THIRD POSSIBILITY PLANE.
BUT THAT'S THE ONE WHERE SHE LIVED AND I DIED. HOW COULD I EXPLAIN MY SUDDEN REAPPEARANCE...
I CAN ONLY SEND YOU, MR. THURMOND. I CANNOT TELL YOU HOW TO ACT WHEN YOU GET THERE...
3

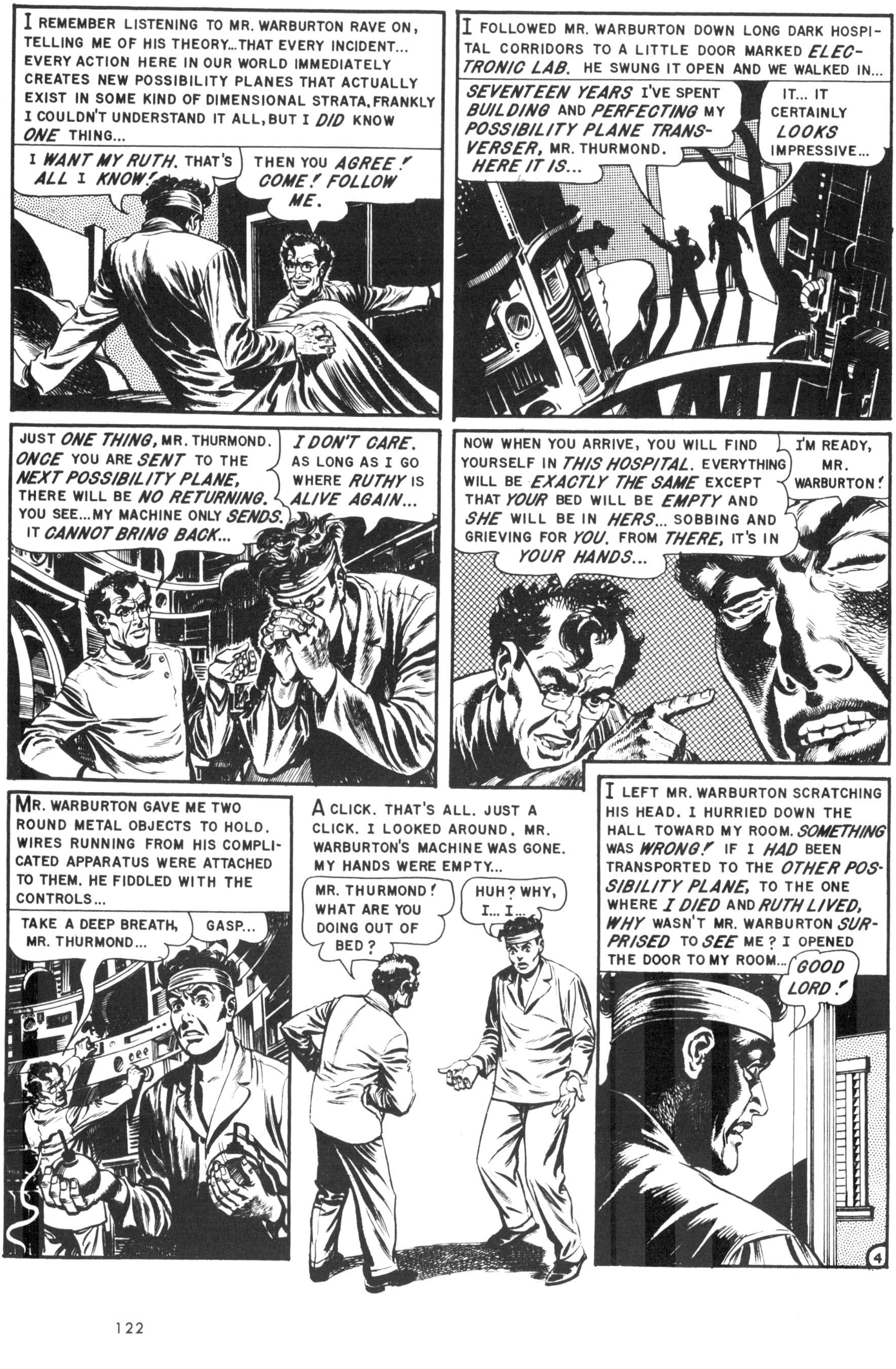
I REMEMBER LISTENING TO MR. WARBURTON RAVE ON, TELLING ME OF HIS THEORY... THAT EVERY INCIDENT... EVERY ACTION HERE IN OUR WORLD IMMEDIATELY CREATES NEW POSSIBILITY PLANES THAT ACTUALLY EXIST IN SOME KIND OF DIMENSIONAL STRATA. FRANKLY I COULDN'T UNDERSTAND IT ALL, BUT I DID KNOW ONE THING...
I WANT MY RUTH. THAT'S ALL I KNOW!
THEN YOU AGREE! COME! FOLLOW ME.
I FOLLOWED MR. WARBURTON DOWN LONG DARK HOSPITAL CORRIDORS TO A LITTLE DOOR MARKED ELECTRONIC LAB. HE SWUNG IT OPEN AND WE WALKED IN...
SEVENTEEN YEARS I'VE SPENT BUILDING AND PERFECTING MY POSSIBILITY PLANE TRANSVERSER, MR. THURMOND. HERE IT IS...
IT... IT CERTAINLY LOOKS IMPRESSIVE...
JUST ONE THING, MR. THURMOND. ONCE YOU ARE SENT TO THE NEXT POSSIBILITY PLANE, THERE WILL BE NO RETURNING. YOU SEE... MY MACHINE ONLY SENDS. IT CANNOT BRING BACK...
I DON'T CARE. AS LONG AS I GO WHERE RUTHY IS ALIVE AGAIN...
NOW WHEN YOU ARRIVE, YOU WILL FIND YOURSELF IN THIS HOSPITAL. EVERYTHING WILL BE EXACTLY THE SAME EXCEPT THAT YOUR BED WILL BE EMPTY AND SHE WILL BE IN HERS... SOBBING AND GRIEVING FOR YOU. FROM THERE, IT'S IN YOUR HANDS...
I'M READY, MR. WARBURTON!
MR. WARBURTON GAVE ME TWO ROUND METAL OBJECTS TO HOLD. WIRES RUNNING FROM HIS COMPLICATED APPARATUS WERE ATTACHED TO THEM. HE FIDDLED WITH THE CONTROLS...
TAKE A DEEP BREATH, MR. THURMOND...
GASP...
A CLICK. THAT'S ALL. JUST A CLICK. I LOOKED AROUND. MR. WARBURTON'S MACHINE WAS GONE. MY HANDS WERE EMPTY...
MR. THURMOND! WHAT ARE YOU DOING OUT OF BED?
HUH? WHY, I... I...
I LEFT MR. WARBURTON SCRATCHING HIS HEAD. I HURRIED DOWN THE HALL TOWARD MY ROOM. SOMETHING WAS WRONG! IF I HAD BEEN TRANSPORTED TO THE OTHER POSSIBILITY PLANE, TO THE ONE WHERE I DIED AND RUTH LIVED, WHY WASN'T MR. WARBURTON SURPRISED TO SEE ME? I OPENED THE DOOR TO MY ROOM...
GOOD LORD!
4

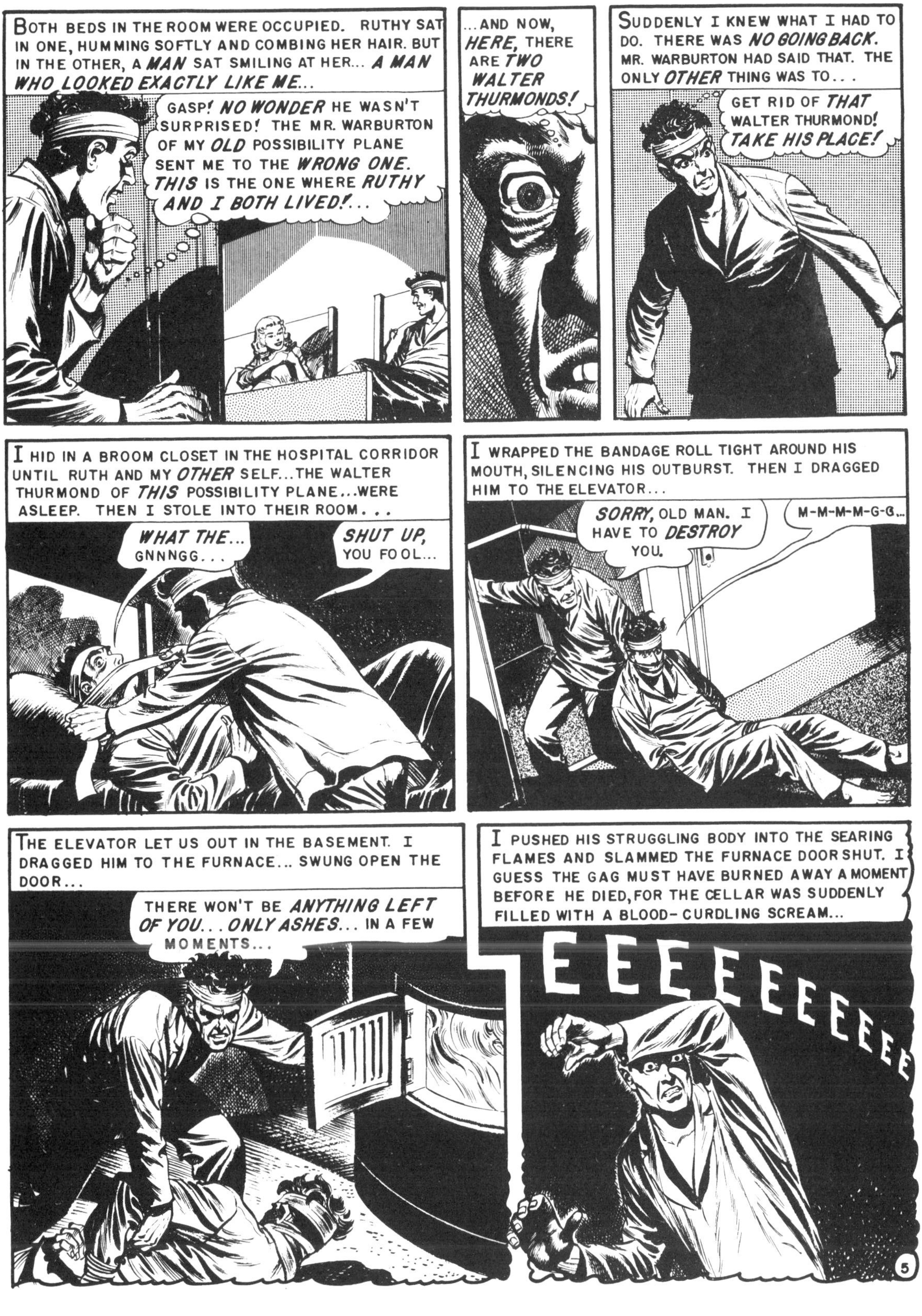
BOTH BEDS IN THE ROOM WERE OCCUPIED. RUTHY SAT IN ONE, HUMMING SOFTLY AND COMBING HER HAIR. BUT IN THE OTHER, A MAN SAT SMILING AT HER... A MAN WHO LOOKED EXACTLY LIKE ME...
GASP! NO WONDER HE WASN'T SURPRISED! THE MR. WARBURTON OF MY OLD POSSIBILITY PLANE SENT ME TO THE WRONG ONE. THIS IS THE ONE WHERE RUTHY AND I BOTH LIVED!...
...AND NOW, HERE, THERE ARE TWO WALTER THURMONDS!
SUDDENLY I KNEW WHAT I HAD TO DO. THERE WAS NO GOING BACK. MR. WARBURTON HAD SAID THAT. THE ONLY OTHER THING WAS TO . . .
GET RID OF THAT WALTER THURMOND! TAKE HIS PLACE!
I HID IN A BROOM CLOSET IN THE HOSPITAL CORRIDOR UNTIL RUTH AND MY OTHER SELF...THE WALTER THURMOND OF THIS POSSIBILITY PLANE...WERE ASLEEP. THEN I STOLE INTO THEIR ROOM. . .
WHAT THE... GNNNGG. . .
SHUT UP, YOU FOOL...
I WRAPPED THE BANDAGE ROLL TIGHT AROUND HIS MOUTH, SILENCING HIS OUTBURST. THEN I DRAGGED HIM TO THE ELEVATOR...
SORRY, OLD MAN. I HAVE TO DESTROY YOU.
M-M-M-M-G-G...
THE ELEVATOR LET US OUT IN THE BASEMENT. I DRAGGED HIM TO THE FURNACE... SWUNG OPEN THE DOOR...
THERE WON'T BE ANYTHING LEFT OF YOU...ONLY ASHES... IN A FEW MOMENTS...
I PUSHED HIS STRUGGLING BODY INTO THE SEARING FLAMES AND SLAMMED THE FURNACE DOOR SHUT. I GUESS THE GAG MUST HAVE BURNED AWAY A MOMENT BEFORE HE DIED, FOR THE CELLAR WAS SUDDENLY FILLED WITH A BLOOD-CURDLING SCREAM...
EEEEEEEEEEE
5

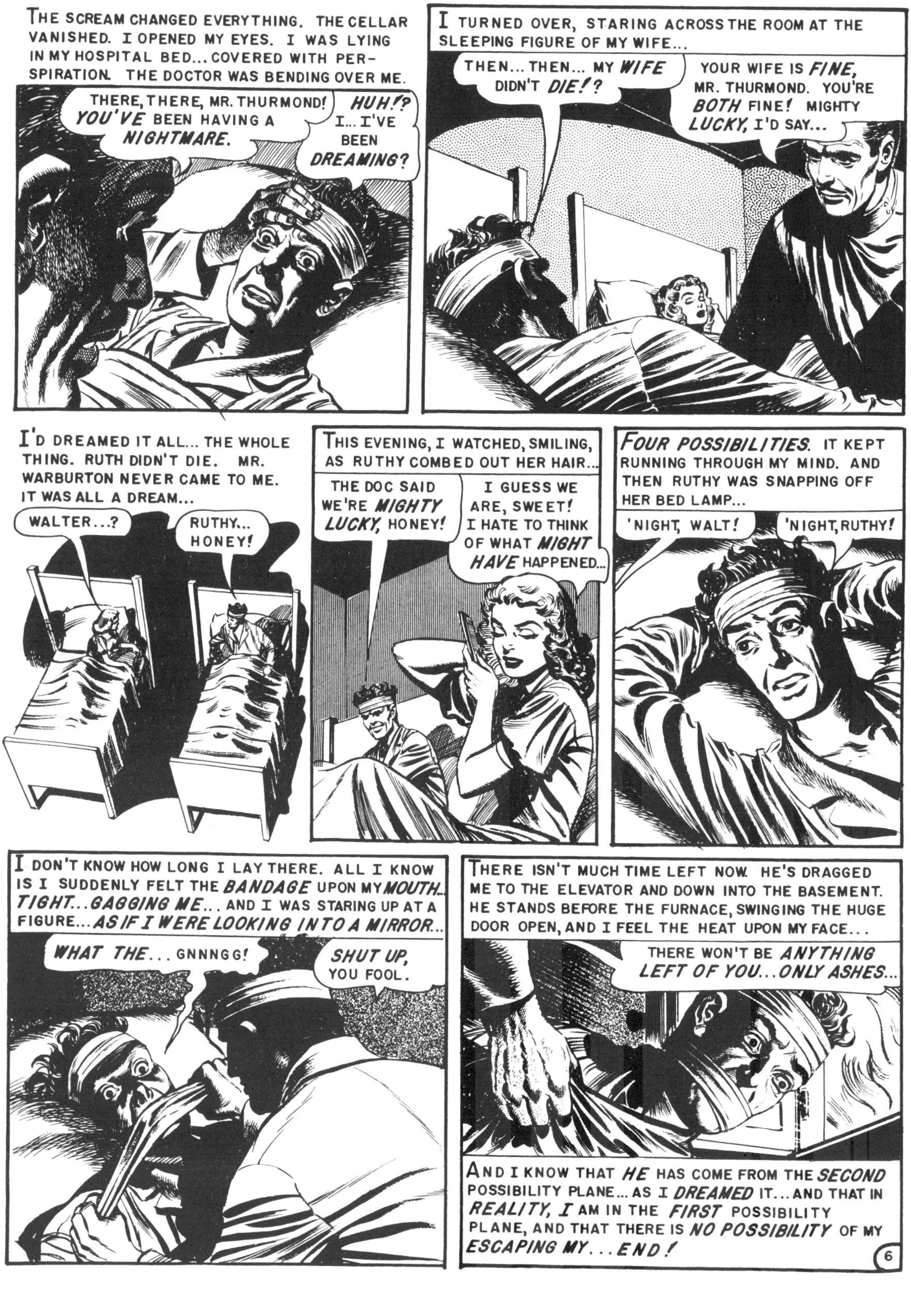
THE SCREAM CHANGED EVERYTHING. THE CELLAR VANISHED. I OPENED MY EYES. I WAS LYING IN MY HOSPITAL BED... COVERED WITH PERSPIRATION. THE DOCTOR WAS BENDING OVER ME.
THERE, THERE, MR. THURMOND! YOU'VE BEEN HAVING A NIGHTMARE.
HUH!? I... I'VE BEEN DREAMING?
I TURNED OVER, STARING ACROSS THE ROOM AT THE SLEEPING FIGURE OF MY WIFE...
THEN... THEN... MY WIFE DIDN'T DIE!?
YOUR WIFE IS FINE, MR. THURMOND. YOU'RE BOTH FINE! MIGHTY LUCKY, I'D SAY...
I'D DREAMED IT ALL... THE WHOLE THING. RUTH DIDN'T DIE. MR. WARBURTON NEVER CAME TO ME. IT WAS ALL A DREAM...
WALTER...?
RUTHY... HONEY!
THIS EVENING, I WATCHED, SMILING, AS RUTHY COMBED OUT HER HAIR...
THE DOC SAID WE'RE MIGHTY LUCKY, HONEY!
I GUESS WE ARE, SWEET! I HATE TO THINK OF WHAT MIGHT HAVE HAPPENED...
FOUR POSSIBILITIES. IT KEPT RUNNING THROUGH MY MIND. AND THEN RUTHY WAS SNAPPING OFF HER BED LAMP...
'NIGHT, WALT!
'NIGHT, RUTHY!
I DON'T KNOW HOW LONG I LAY THERE. ALL I KNOW IS I SUDDENLY FELT THE BANDAGE UPON MY MOUTH... TIGHT... GAGGING ME... AND I WAS STARING UP AT A FIGURE... AS IF I WERE LOOKING INTO A MIRROR...
WHAT THE... GNNNGG!
SHUT UP, YOU FOOL.
THERE ISN'T MUCH TIME LEFT NOW. HE'S DRAGGED ME TO THE ELEVATOR AND DOWN INTO THE BASEMENT. HE STANDS BEFORE THE FURNACE, SWINGING THE HUGE DOOR OPEN, AND I FEEL THE HEAT UPON MY FACE...
THERE WON'T BE ANYTHING LEFT OF YOU... ONLY ASHES...
AND I KNOW THAT HE HAS COME FROM THE SECOND POSSIBILITY PLANE... AS I DREAMED IT... AND THAT IN REALITY, I AM IN THE FIRST POSSIBILITY PLANE, AND THAT THERE IS NO POSSIBILITY OF MY ESCAPING MY... END!
6

The FREAKS

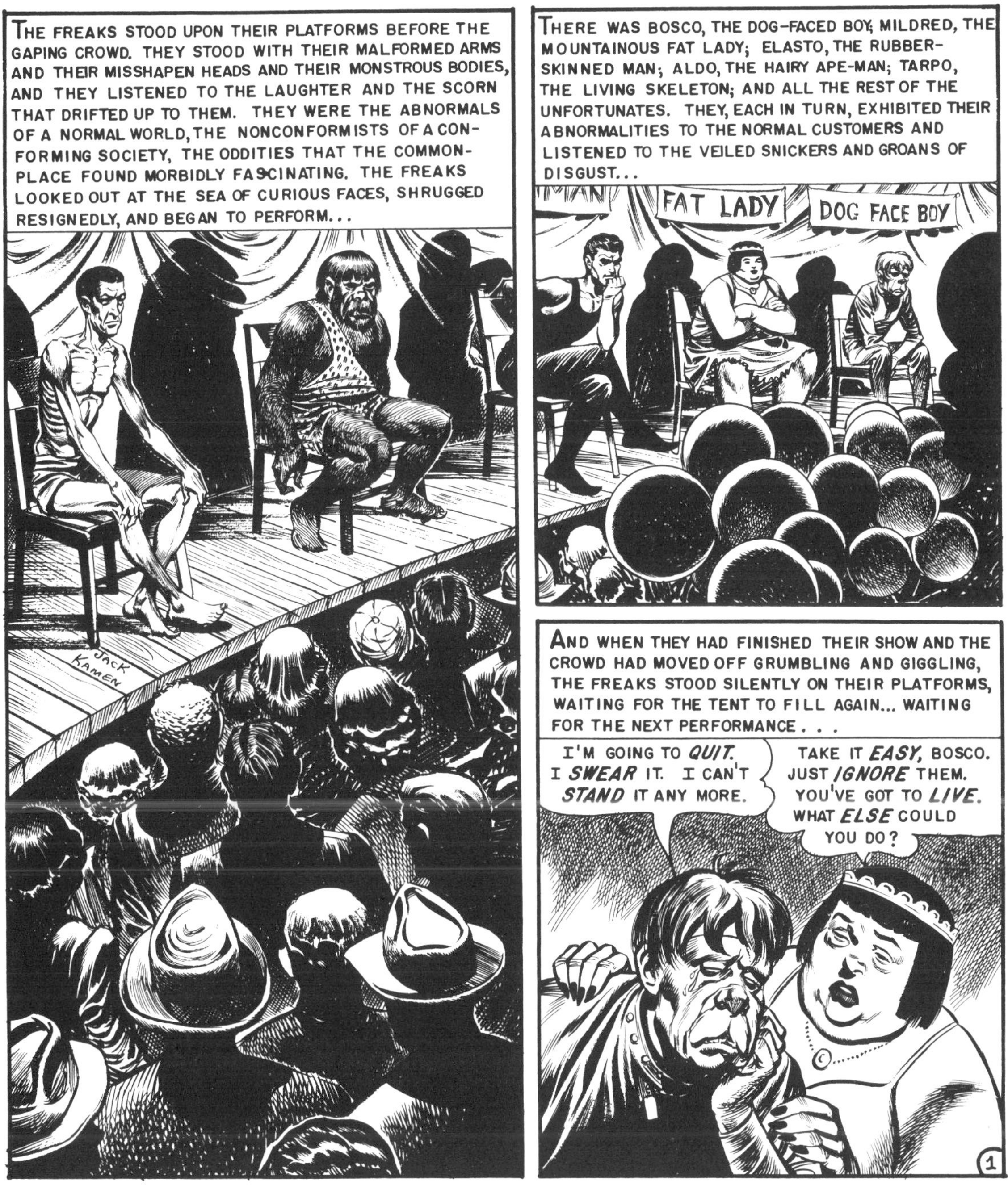

THE FREAKS STOOD UPON THEIR PLATFORMS BEFORE THE GAPING CROWD. THEY STOOD WITH THEIR MALFORMED ARMS AND THEIR MISSHAPEN HEADS AND THEIR MONSTROUS BODIES, AND THEY LISTENED TO THE LAUGHTER AND THE SCORN THAT DRIFTED UP TO THEM. THEY WERE THE ABNORMALS OF A NORMAL WORLD, THE NONCONFORMISTS OF A CONFORMING SOCIETY, THE ODDITIES THAT THE COMMONPLACE FOUND MORBIDLY FASCINATING. THE FREAKS LOOKED OUT AT THE SEA OF CURIOUS FACES, SHRUGGED RESIGNEDLY, AND BEGAN TO PERFORM...
JACK KAMEN
THERE WAS BOSCO, THE DOG-FACED BOY; MILDRED, THE MOUNTAINOUS FAT LADY; ELASTO, THE RUBBER-SKINNED MAN; ALDO, THE HAIRY APE-MAN; TARPO, THE LIVING SKELETON; AND ALL THE REST OF THE UNFORTUNATES. THEY, EACH IN TURN, EXHIBITED THEIR ABNORMALITIES TO THE NORMAL CUSTOMERS AND LISTENED TO THE VEILED SNICKERS AND GROANS OF DISGUST...
FAT LADY
DOG FACE BOY
AND WHEN THEY HAD FINISHED THEIR SHOW AND THE CROWD HAD MOVED OFF GRUMBLING AND GIGGLING, THE FREAKS STOOD SILENTLY ON THEIR PLATFORMS, WAITING FOR THE TENT TO FILL AGAIN... WAITING FOR THE NEXT PERFORMANCE...
I'M GOING TO *QUIT*. I *SWEAR* IT. I CAN'T *STAND* IT ANY MORE.
TAKE IT *EASY*, BOSCO. JUST *IGNORE* THEM. YOU'VE GOT TO *LIVE*. WHAT *ELSE* COULD YOU DO?
1

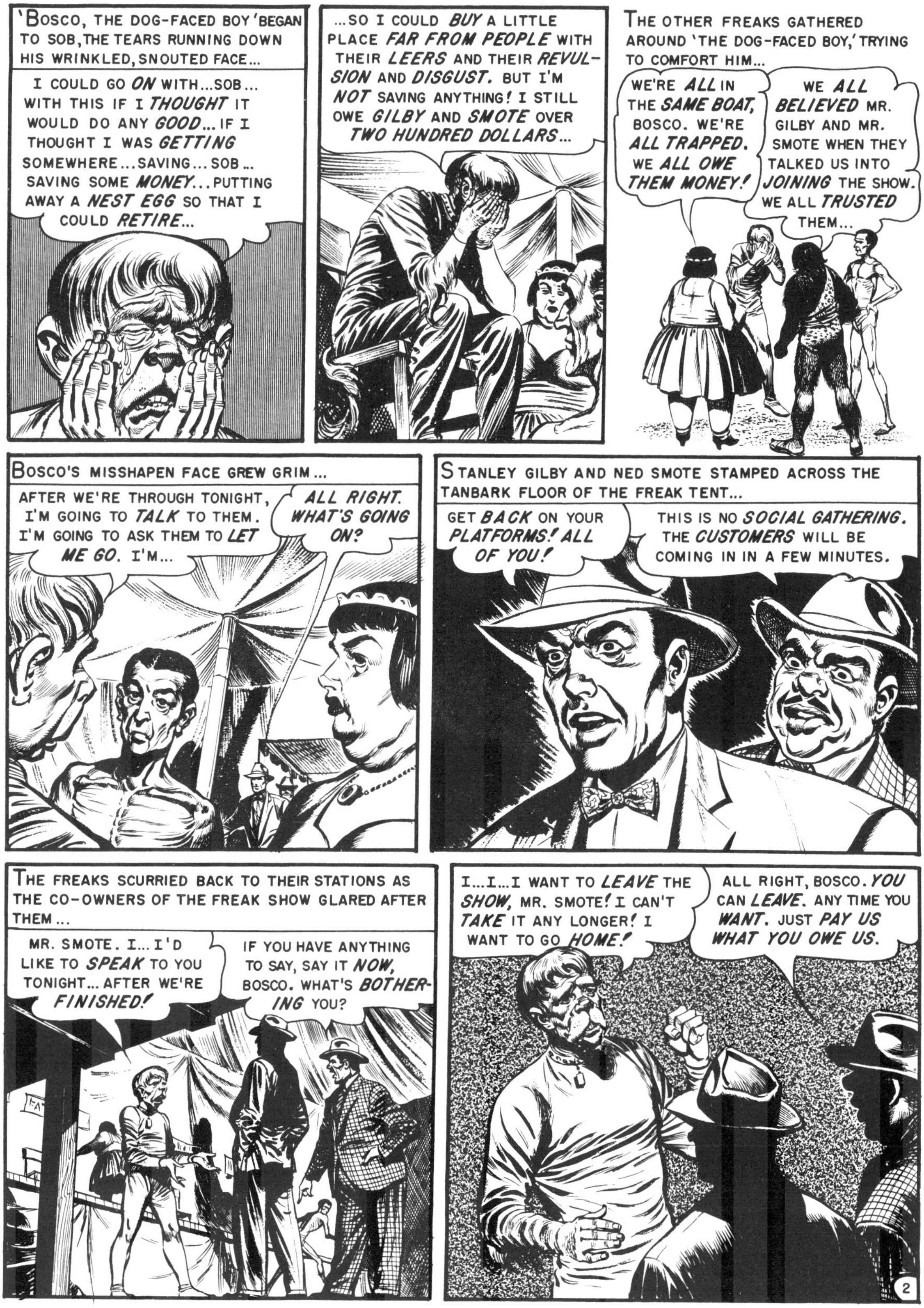
'BOSCO, THE DOG-FACED BOY' BEGAN TO SOB, THE TEARS RUNNING DOWN HIS WRINKLED, SNOUTED FACE...
I COULD GO ON WITH...SOB... WITH THIS IF I THOUGHT IT WOULD DO ANY GOOD... IF I THOUGHT I WAS GETTING SOMEWHERE...SAVING...SOB... SAVING SOME MONEY... PUTTING AWAY A NEST EGG SO THAT I COULD RETIRE...
...SO I COULD BUY A LITTLE PLACE FAR FROM PEOPLE WITH THEIR LEERS AND THEIR REVULSION AND DISGUST. BUT I'M NOT SAVING ANYTHING! I STILL OWE GILBY AND SMOTE OVER TWO HUNDRED DOLLARS...
THE OTHER FREAKS GATHERED AROUND 'THE DOG-FACED BOY,' TRYING TO COMFORT HIM...
WE'RE ALL IN THE SAME BOAT, BOSCO. WE'RE ALL TRAPPED. WE ALL OWE THEM MONEY!
WE ALL BELIEVED MR. GILBY AND MR. SMOTE WHEN THEY TALKED US INTO JOINING THE SHOW. WE ALL TRUSTED THEM...
BOSCO'S MISSHAPEN FACE GREW GRIM...
AFTER WE'RE THROUGH TONIGHT, I'M GOING TO TALK TO THEM. I'M GOING TO ASK THEM TO LET ME GO. I'M...
ALL RIGHT. WHAT'S GOING ON?
STANLEY GILBY AND NED SMOTE STAMPED ACROSS THE TANBARK FLOOR OF THE FREAK TENT...
GET BACK ON YOUR PLATFORMS! ALL OF YOU!
THIS IS NO SOCIAL GATHERING. THE CUSTOMERS WILL BE COMING IN IN A FEW MINUTES.
THE FREAKS SCURRIED BACK TO THEIR STATIONS AS THE CO-OWNERS OF THE FREAK SHOW GLARED AFTER THEM...
MR. SMOTE. I... I'D LIKE TO SPEAK TO YOU TONIGHT... AFTER WE'RE FINISHED!
IF YOU HAVE ANYTHING TO SAY, SAY IT NOW, BOSCO. WHAT'S BOTHERING YOU?
I...I...I WANT TO LEAVE THE SHOW, MR. SMOTE! I CAN'T TAKE IT ANY LONGER! I WANT TO GO HOME!
ALL RIGHT, BOSCO. YOU CAN LEAVE. ANY TIME YOU WANT. JUST PAY US WHAT YOU OWE US.
2

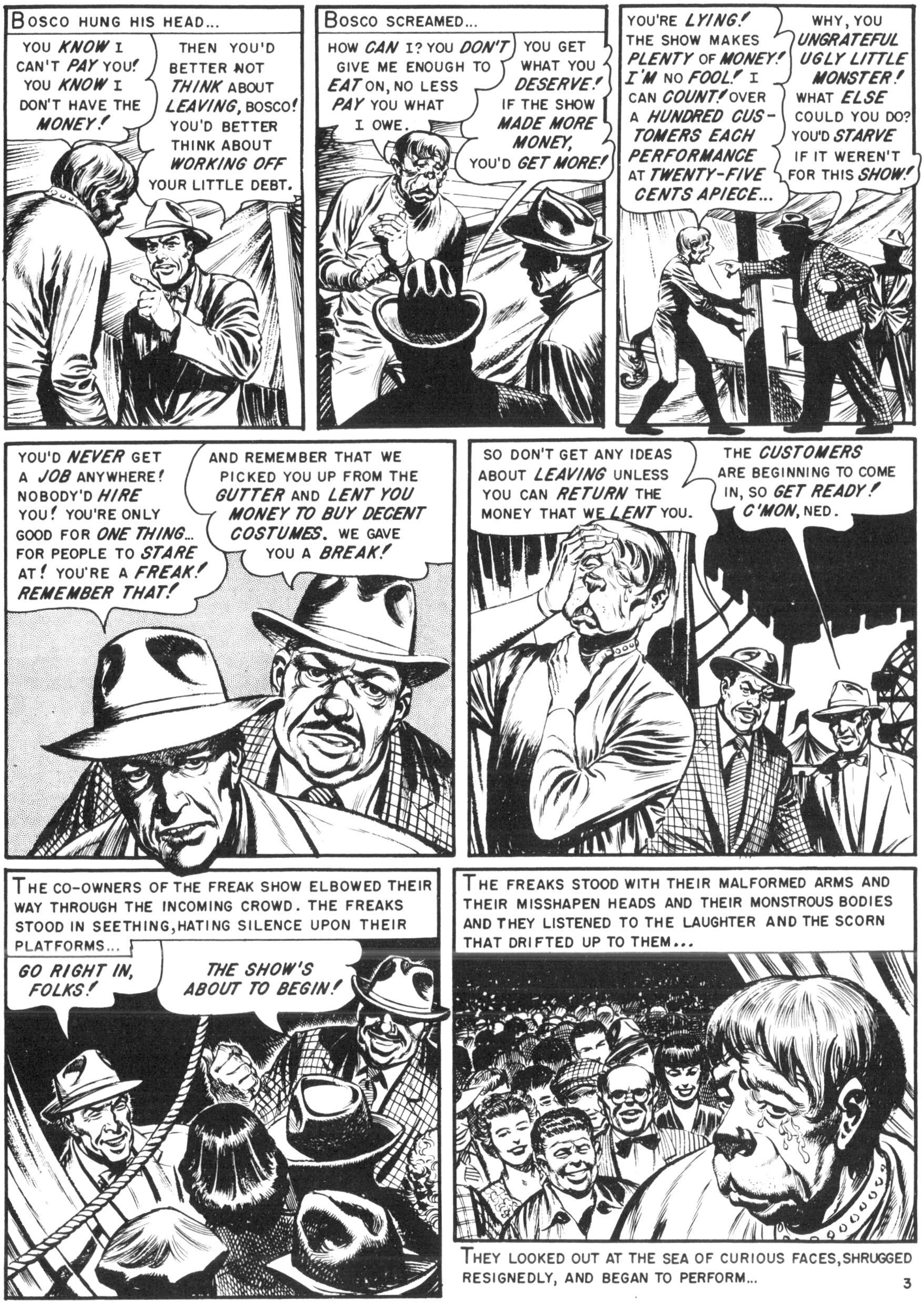
BOSCO HUNG HIS HEAD...
YOU KNOW I CAN'T PAY YOU! YOU KNOW I DON'T HAVE THE MONEY!
THEN YOU'D BETTER NOT THINK ABOUT LEAVING, BOSCO! YOU'D BETTER THINK ABOUT WORKING OFF YOUR LITTLE DEBT.
BOSCO SCREAMED...
HOW CAN I? YOU DON'T GIVE ME ENOUGH TO EAT ON, NO LESS PAY YOU WHAT I OWE.
YOU GET WHAT YOU DESERVE! IF THE SHOW MADE MORE MONEY, YOU'D GET MORE!
YOU'RE LYING! THE SHOW MAKES PLENTY OF MONEY! I'M NO FOOL! I CAN COUNT! OVER A HUNDRED CUS-TOMERS EACH PERFORMANCE AT TWENTY-FIVE CENTS APIECE...
WHY, YOU UNGRATEFUL UGLY LITTLE MONSTER! WHAT ELSE COULD YOU DO? YOU'D STARVE IF IT WEREN'T FOR THIS SHOW!
YOU'D NEVER GET A JOB ANYWHERE! NOBODY'D HIRE YOU! YOU'RE ONLY GOOD FOR ONE THING... FOR PEOPLE TO STARE AT! YOU'RE A FREAK! REMEMBER THAT!
AND REMEMBER THAT WE PICKED YOU UP FROM THE GUTTER AND LENT YOU MONEY TO BUY DECENT COSTUMES. WE GAVE YOU A BREAK!
SO DON'T GET ANY IDEAS ABOUT LEAVING UNLESS YOU CAN RETURN THE MONEY THAT WE LENT YOU.
THE CUSTOMERS ARE BEGINNING TO COME IN, SO GET READY! C'MON, NED.
THE CO-OWNERS OF THE FREAK SHOW ELBOWED THEIR WAY THROUGH THE INCOMING CROWD. THE FREAKS STOOD IN SEETHING, HATING SILENCE UPON THEIR PLATFORMS...
GO RIGHT IN, FOLKS!
THE SHOW'S ABOUT TO BEGIN!
THE FREAKS STOOD WITH THEIR MALFORMED ARMS AND THEIR MISSHAPEN HEADS AND THEIR MONSTROUS BODIES AND THEY LISTENED TO THE LAUGHTER AND THE SCORN THAT DRIFTED UP TO THEM...
THEY LOOKED OUT AT THE SEA OF CURIOUS FACES, SHRUGGED RESIGNEDLY, AND BEGAN TO PERFORM...
3

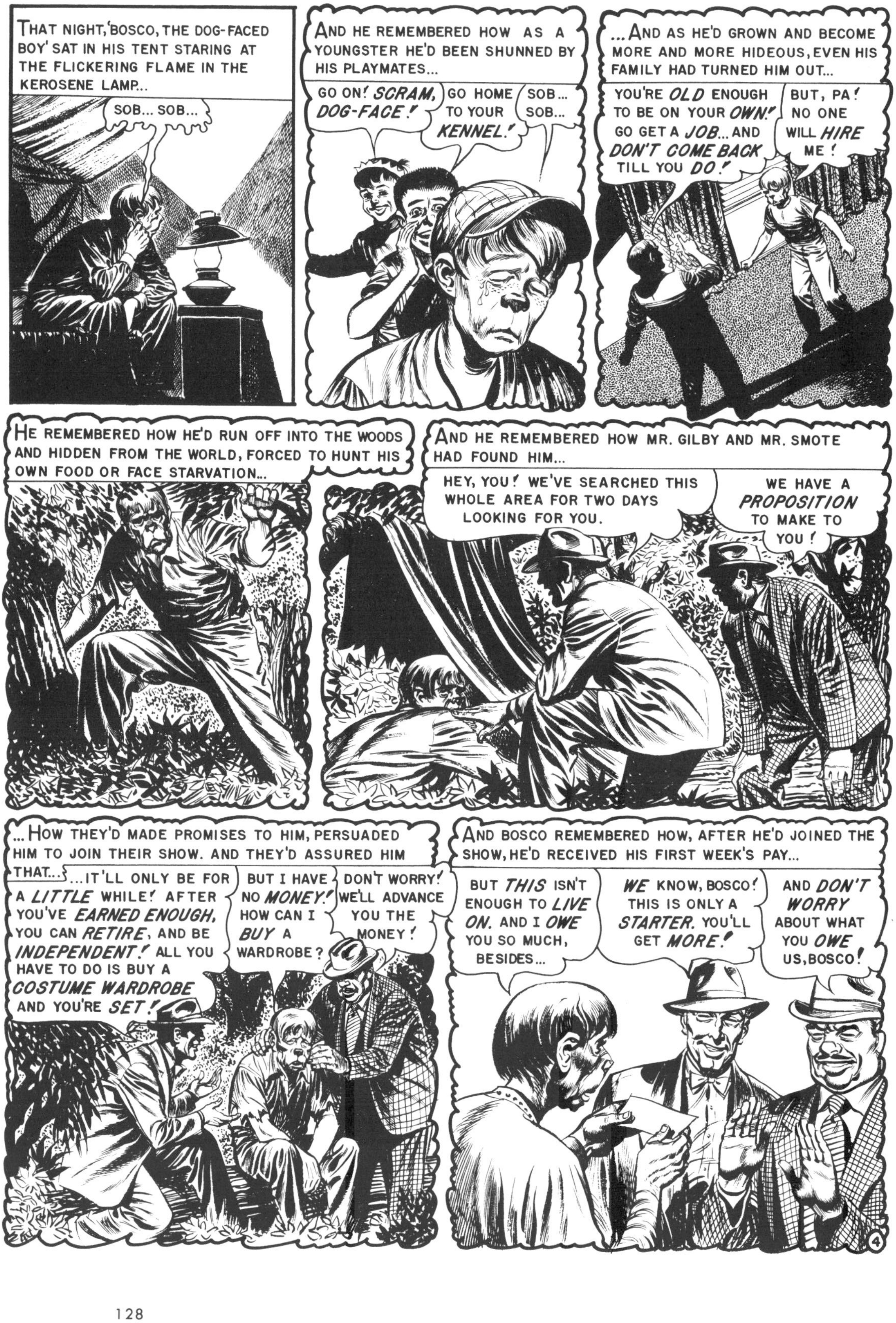
THAT NIGHT, 'BOSCO, THE DOG-FACED BOY' SAT IN HIS TENT STARING AT THE FLICKERING FLAME IN THE KEROSENE LAMP...
SOB... SOB...
AND HE REMEMBERED HOW AS A YOUNGSTER HE'D BEEN SHUNNED BY HIS PLAYMATES...
GO ON! SCRAM, DOG-FACE!
GO HOME TO YOUR KENNEL!
SOB... SOB...
...AND AS HE'D GROWN AND BECOME MORE AND MORE HIDEOUS, EVEN HIS FAMILY HAD TURNED HIM OUT...
YOU'RE OLD ENOUGH TO BE ON YOUR OWN! GO GET A JOB... AND DON'T COME BACK TILL YOU DO!
BUT, PA! NO ONE WILL HIRE ME!
HE REMEMBERED HOW HE'D RUN OFF INTO THE WOODS AND HIDDEN FROM THE WORLD, FORCED TO HUNT HIS OWN FOOD OR FACE STARVATION...
AND HE REMEMBERED HOW MR. GILBY AND MR. SMOTE HAD FOUND HIM...
HEY, YOU! WE'VE SEARCHED THIS WHOLE AREA FOR TWO DAYS LOOKING FOR YOU.
WE HAVE A PROPOSITION TO MAKE TO YOU!
...HOW THEY'D MADE PROMISES TO HIM, PERSUADED HIM TO JOIN THEIR SHOW. AND THEY'D ASSURED HIM THAT...
...IT'LL ONLY BE FOR A LITTLE WHILE! AFTER YOU'VE EARNED ENOUGH, YOU CAN RETIRE, AND BE INDEPENDENT! ALL YOU HAVE TO DO IS BUY A COSTUME WARDROBE AND YOU'RE SET!
BUT I HAVE NO MONEY! HOW CAN I BUY A WARDROBE?
DON'T WORRY! WE'LL ADVANCE YOU THE MONEY!
AND BOSCO REMEMBERED HOW, AFTER HE'D JOINED THE SHOW, HE'D RECEIVED HIS FIRST WEEK'S PAY...
BUT THIS ISN'T ENOUGH TO LIVE ON. AND I OWE YOU SO MUCH, BESIDES...
WE KNOW, BOSCO! THIS IS ONLY A STARTER. YOU'LL GET MORE!
AND DON'T WORRY ABOUT WHAT YOU OWE US, BOSCO!
4

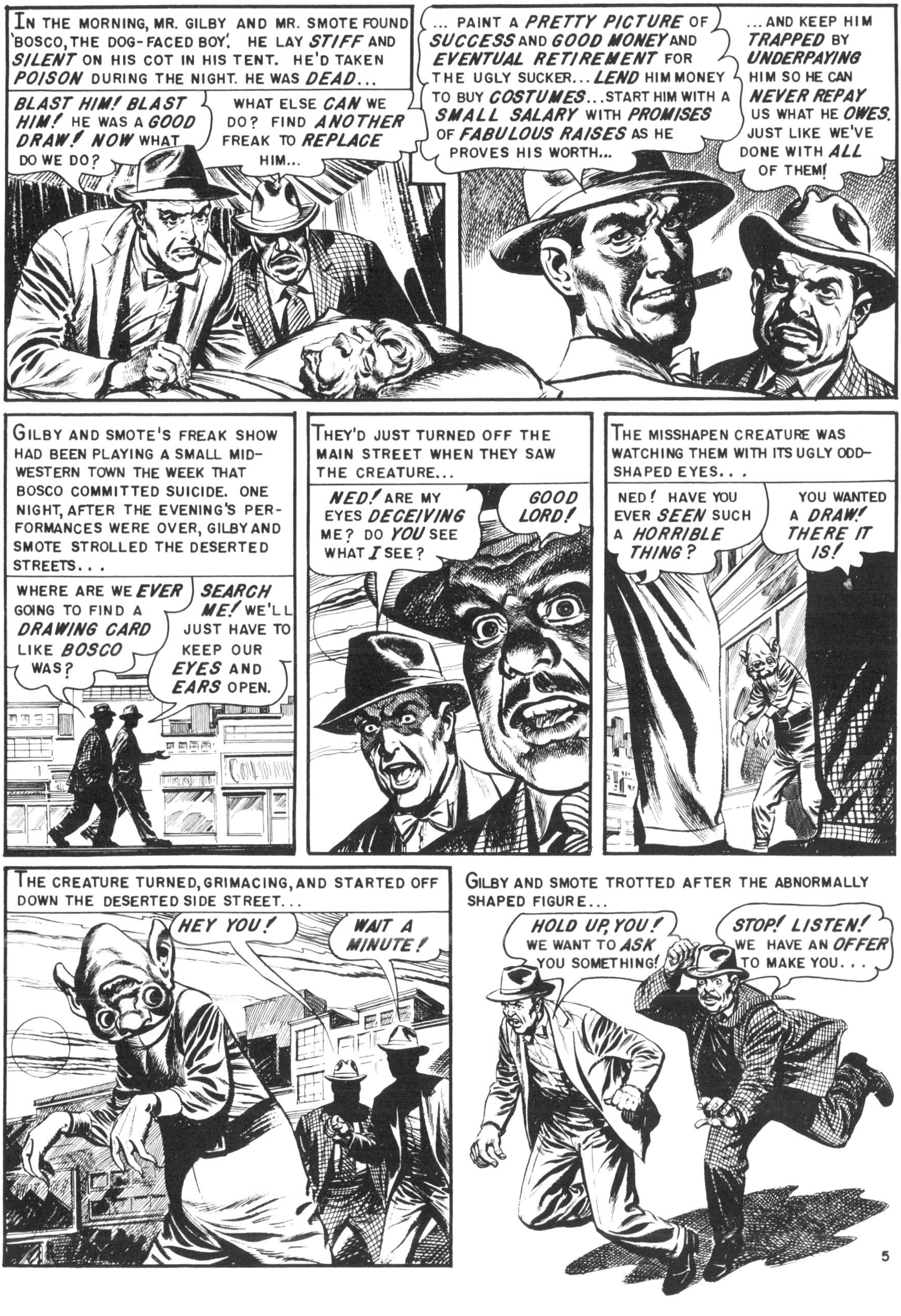

IN THE MORNING, MR. GILBY AND MR. SMOTE FOUND 'BOSCO, THE DOG-FACED BOY'. HE LAY STIFF AND SILENT ON HIS COT IN HIS TENT. HE'D TAKEN POISON DURING THE NIGHT. HE WAS DEAD...
BLAST HIM! BLAST HIM! HE WAS A GOOD DRAW! NOW WHAT DO WE DO?
WHAT ELSE CAN WE DO? FIND ANOTHER FREAK TO REPLACE HIM...
... PAINT A PRETTY PICTURE OF SUCCESS AND GOOD MONEY AND EVENTUAL RETIREMENT FOR THE UGLY SUCKER... LEND HIM MONEY TO BUY COSTUMES... START HIM WITH A SMALL SALARY WITH PROMISES OF FABULOUS RAISES AS HE PROVES HIS WORTH...
... AND KEEP HIM TRAPPED BY UNDERPAYING HIM SO HE CAN NEVER REPAY US WHAT HE OWES. JUST LIKE WE'VE DONE WITH ALL OF THEM!
GILBY AND SMOTE'S FREAK SHOW HAD BEEN PLAYING A SMALL MID-WESTERN TOWN THE WEEK THAT BOSCO COMMITTED SUICIDE. ONE NIGHT, AFTER THE EVENING'S PERFORMANCES WERE OVER, GILBY AND SMOTE STROLLED THE DESERTED STREETS...
WHERE ARE WE EVER GOING TO FIND A DRAWING CARD LIKE BOSCO WAS?
SEARCH ME! WE'LL JUST HAVE TO KEEP OUR EYES AND EARS OPEN.
THEY'D JUST TURNED OFF THE MAIN STREET WHEN THEY SAW THE CREATURE...
NED! ARE MY EYES DECEIVING ME? DO YOU SEE WHAT I SEE?
GOOD LORD!
THE MISSHAPEN CREATURE WAS WATCHING THEM WITH ITS UGLY ODD-SHAPED EYES...
NED! HAVE YOU EVER SEEN SUCH A HORRIBLE THING?
YOU WANTED A DRAW! THERE IT IS!
THE CREATURE TURNED, GRIMACING, AND STARTED OFF DOWN THE DESERTED SIDE STREET...
HEY YOU!
WAIT A MINUTE!
GILBY AND SMOTE TROTTED AFTER THE ABNORMALLY SHAPED FIGURE...
HOLD UP, YOU! WE WANT TO ASK YOU SOMETHING!
STOP! LISTEN! WE HAVE AN OFFER TO MAKE YOU...
5

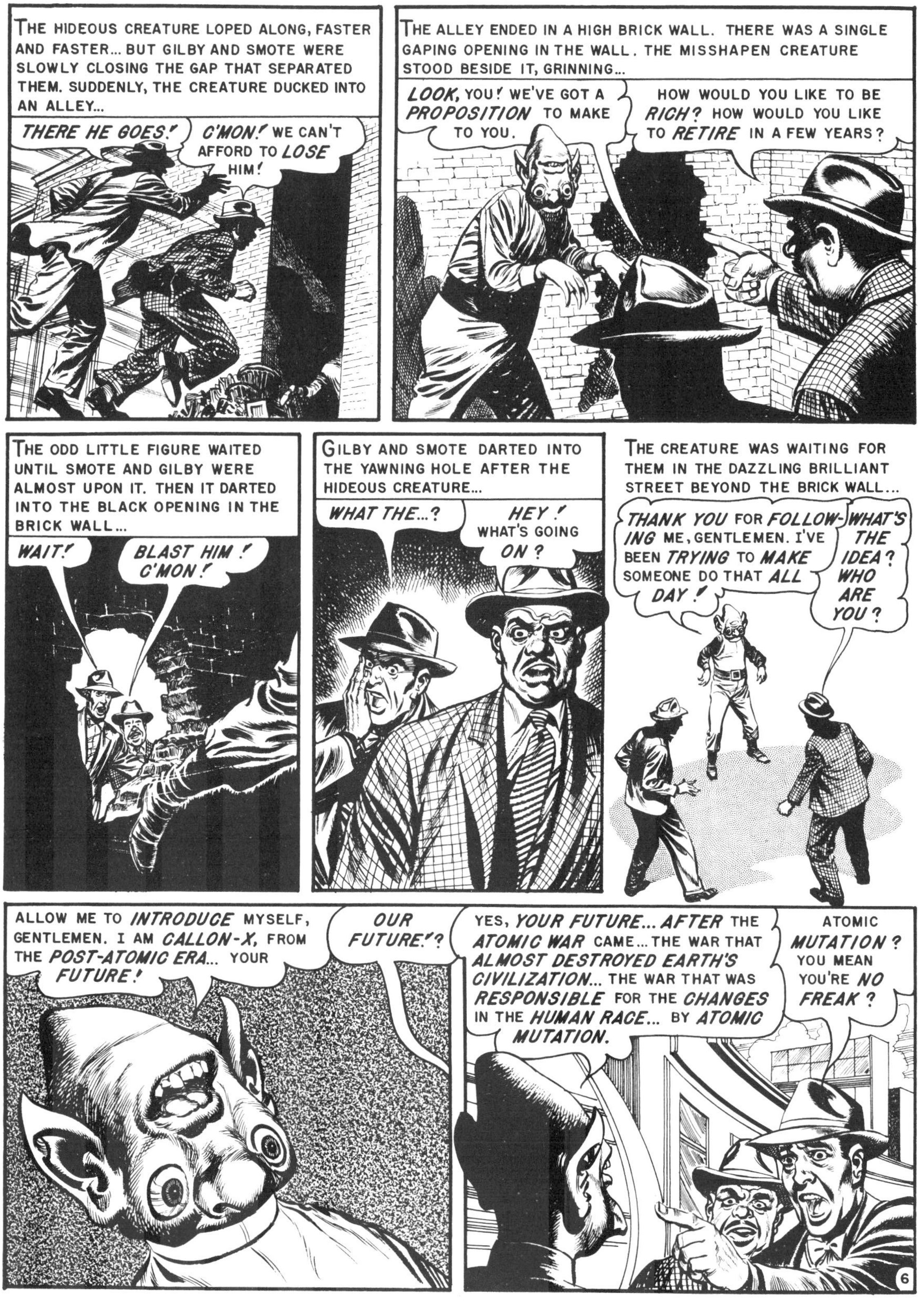
THE HIDEOUS CREATURE LOPED ALONG, FASTER AND FASTER... BUT GILBY AND SMOTE WERE SLOWLY CLOSING THE GAP THAT SEPARATED THEM. SUDDENLY, THE CREATURE DUCKED INTO AN ALLEY...
THERE HE GOES!
C'MON! WE CAN'T AFFORD TO LOSE HIM!
THE ALLEY ENDED IN A HIGH BRICK WALL. THERE WAS A SINGLE GAPING OPENING IN THE WALL. THE MISSHAPEN CREATURE STOOD BESIDE IT, GRINNING...
LOOK, YOU! WE'VE GOT A PROPOSITION TO MAKE TO YOU.
HOW WOULD YOU LIKE TO BE RICH? HOW WOULD YOU LIKE TO RETIRE IN A FEW YEARS?
THE ODD LITTLE FIGURE WAITED UNTIL SMOTE AND GILBY WERE ALMOST UPON IT. THEN IT DARTED INTO THE BLACK OPENING IN THE BRICK WALL...
WAIT!
BLAST HIM! C'MON!
GILBY AND SMOTE DARTED INTO THE YAWNING HOLE AFTER THE HIDEOUS CREATURE...
WHAT THE...?
HEY! WHAT'S GOING ON?
THE CREATURE WAS WAITING FOR THEM IN THE DAZZLING BRILLIANT STREET BEYOND THE BRICK WALL...
THANK YOU FOR FOLLOWING ME, GENTLEMEN. I'VE BEEN TRYING TO MAKE SOMEONE DO THAT ALL DAY!
WHAT'S THE IDEA? WHO ARE YOU?
ALLOW ME TO INTRODUCE MYSELF, GENTLEMEN. I AM CALLON-X, FROM THE POST-ATOMIC ERA... YOUR FUTURE!
OUR FUTURE!?
YES, YOUR FUTURE... AFTER THE ATOMIC WAR CAME... THE WAR THAT ALMOST DESTROYED EARTH'S CIVILIZATION... THE WAR THAT WAS RESPONSIBLE FOR THE CHANGES IN THE HUMAN RACE... BY ATOMIC MUTATION.
ATOMIC MUTATION? YOU MEAN YOU'RE NO FREAK?
6

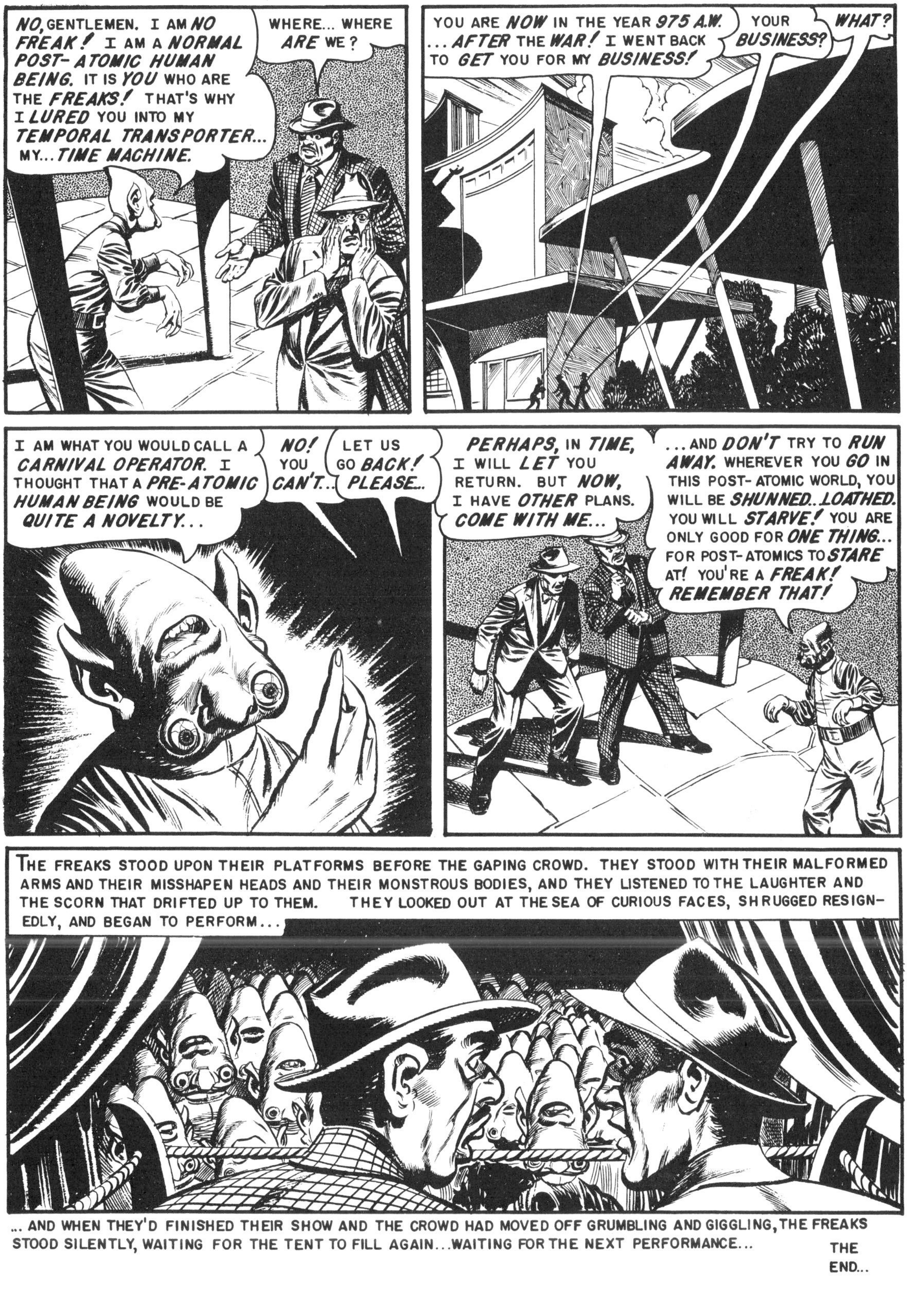
NO, GENTLEMEN. I AM NO FREAK! I AM A NORMAL POST-ATOMIC HUMAN BEING. IT IS YOU WHO ARE THE FREAKS! THAT'S WHY I LURED YOU INTO MY TEMPORAL TRANSPORTER... MY... TIME MACHINE.
WHERE... WHERE ARE WE?
YOU ARE NOW IN THE YEAR 975 A.W. ... AFTER THE WAR! I WENT BACK TO GET YOU FOR MY BUSINESS!
YOUR BUSINESS?
WHAT?
I AM WHAT YOU WOULD CALL A CARNIVAL OPERATOR. I THOUGHT THAT A PRE-ATOMIC HUMAN BEING WOULD BE QUITE A NOVELTY...
NO! YOU CAN'T...
LET US GO BACK! PLEASE...
PERHAPS, IN TIME, I WILL LET YOU RETURN. BUT NOW, I HAVE OTHER PLANS. COME WITH ME...
...AND DON'T TRY TO RUN AWAY. WHEREVER YOU GO IN THIS POST-ATOMIC WORLD, YOU WILL BE SHUNNED.. LOATHED. YOU WILL STARVE! YOU ARE ONLY GOOD FOR ONE THING... FOR POST-ATOMICS TO STARE AT! YOU'RE A FREAK! REMEMBER THAT!
THE FREAKS STOOD UPON THEIR PLATFORMS BEFORE THE GAPING CROWD. THEY STOOD WITH THEIR MALFORMED ARMS AND THEIR MISSHAPEN HEADS AND THEIR MONSTROUS BODIES, AND THEY LISTENED TO THE LAUGHTER AND THE SCORN THAT DRIFTED UP TO THEM. THEY LOOKED OUT AT THE SEA OF CURIOUS FACES, SHRUGGED RESIGNEDLY, AND BEGAN TO PERFORM...
... AND WHEN THEY'D FINISHED THEIR SHOW AND THE CROWD HAD MOVED OFF GRUMBLING AND GIGGLING, THE FREAKS STOOD SILENTLY, WAITING FOR THE TENT TO FILL AGAIN... WAITING FOR THE NEXT PERFORMANCE...
THE END...

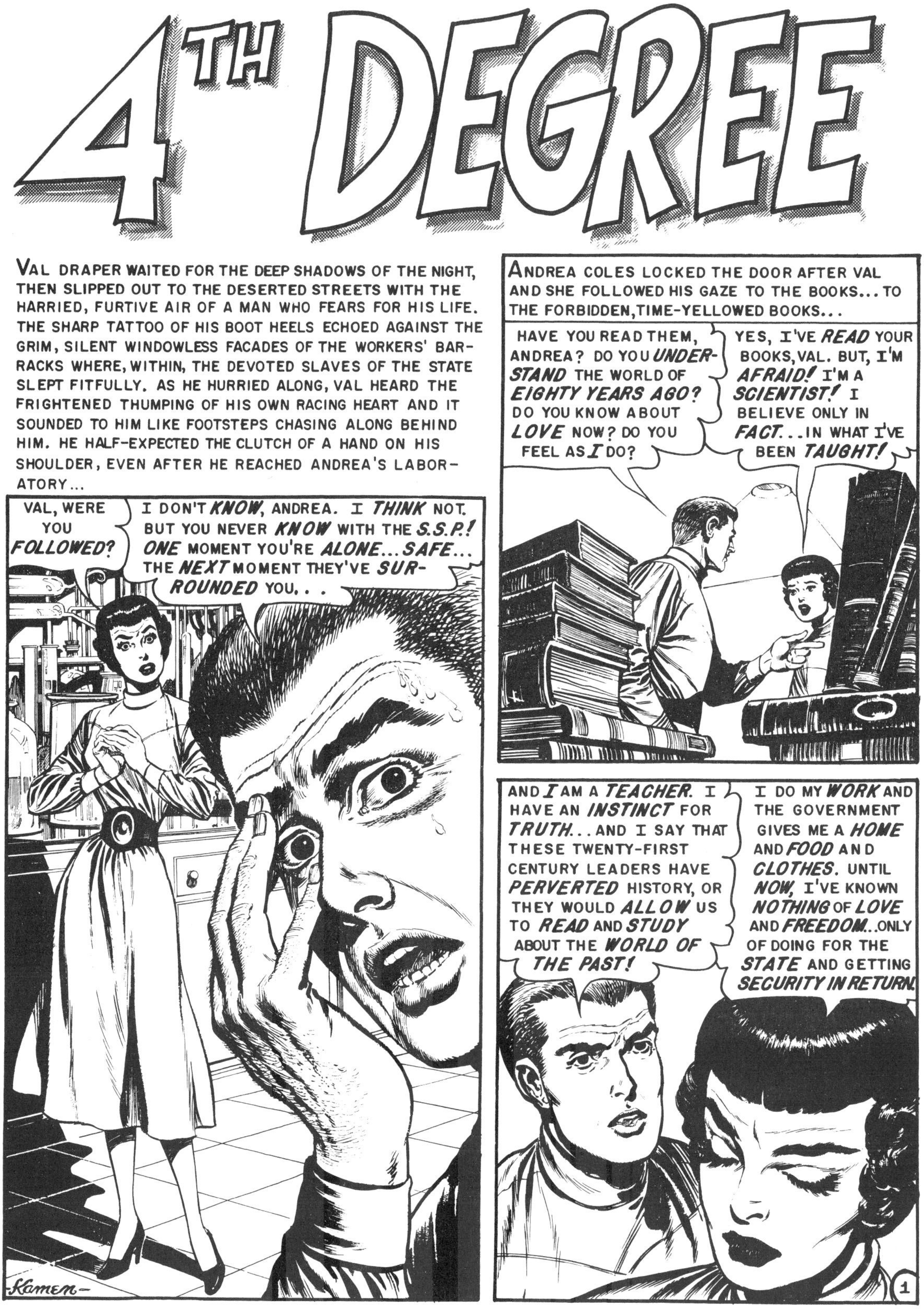
4TH DEGREE
VAL DRAPER WAITED FOR THE DEEP SHADOWS OF THE NIGHT, THEN SLIPPED OUT TO THE DESERTED STREETS WITH THE HARRIED, FURTIVE AIR OF A MAN WHO FEARS FOR HIS LIFE. THE SHARP TATTOO OF HIS BOOT HEELS ECHOED AGAINST THE GRIM, SILENT WINDOWLESS FACADES OF THE WORKERS' BARRACKS WHERE, WITHIN, THE DEVOTED SLAVES OF THE STATE SLEPT FITFULLY. AS HE HURRIED ALONG, VAL HEARD THE FRIGHTENED THUMPING OF HIS OWN RACING HEART AND IT SOUNDED TO HIM LIKE FOOTSTEPS CHASING ALONG BEHIND HIM. HE HALF-EXPECTED THE CLUTCH OF A HAND ON HIS SHOULDER, EVEN AFTER HE REACHED ANDREA'S LABORATORY...
VAL, WERE YOU FOLLOWED?
I DON'T KNOW, ANDREA. I THINK NOT. BUT YOU NEVER KNOW WITH THE S.S.P.! ONE MOMENT YOU'RE ALONE... SAFE... THE NEXT MOMENT THEY'VE SURROUNDED YOU. . .
-Kamen-
ANDREA COLES LOCKED THE DOOR AFTER VAL AND SHE FOLLOWED HIS GAZE TO THE BOOKS... TO THE FORBIDDEN, TIME-YELLOWED BOOKS...
HAVE YOU READ THEM, ANDREA? DO YOU UNDERSTAND THE WORLD OF EIGHTY YEARS AGO? DO YOU KNOW ABOUT LOVE NOW? DO YOU FEEL AS I DO?
YES, I'VE READ YOUR BOOKS, VAL. BUT, I'M AFRAID! I'M A SCIENTIST! I BELIEVE ONLY IN FACT... IN WHAT I'VE BEEN TAUGHT!
AND I AM A TEACHER. I HAVE AN INSTINCT FOR TRUTH... AND I SAY THAT THESE TWENTY-FIRST CENTURY LEADERS HAVE PERVERTED HISTORY, OR THEY WOULD ALLOW US TO READ AND STUDY ABOUT THE WORLD OF THE PAST!
I DO MY WORK AND THE GOVERNMENT GIVES ME A HOME AND FOOD AND CLOTHES. UNTIL NOW, I'VE KNOWN NOTHING OF LOVE AND FREEDOM... ONLY OF DOING FOR THE STATE AND GETTING SECURITY IN RETURN.
1

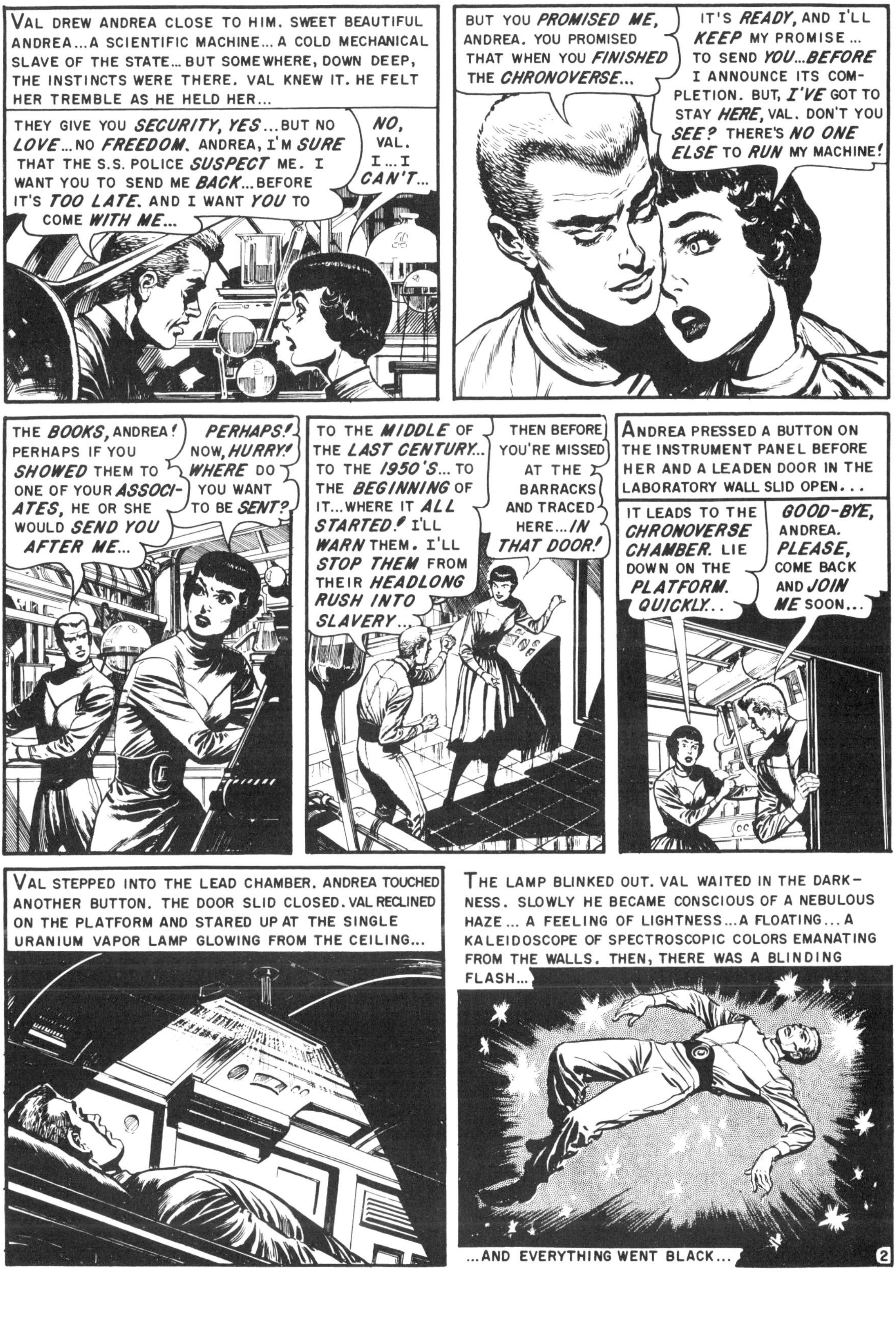
VAL DREW ANDREA CLOSE TO HIM. SWEET BEAUTIFUL ANDREA...A SCIENTIFIC MACHINE...A COLD MECHANICAL SLAVE OF THE STATE...BUT SOMEWHERE, DOWN DEEP, THE INSTINCTS WERE THERE. VAL KNEW IT. HE FELT HER TREMBLE AS HE HELD HER...
THEY GIVE YOU SECURITY, YES...BUT NO LOVE...NO FREEDOM. ANDREA, I'M SURE THAT THE S.S. POLICE SUSPECT ME. I WANT YOU TO SEND ME BACK...BEFORE IT'S TOO LATE. AND I WANT YOU TO COME WITH ME...
NO, VAL. I...I CAN'T...
BUT YOU PROMISED ME, ANDREA. YOU PROMISED THAT WHEN YOU FINISHED THE CHRONOVERSE...
IT'S READY, AND I'LL KEEP MY PROMISE... TO SEND YOU...BEFORE I ANNOUNCE ITS COMPLETION. BUT, I'VE GOT TO STAY HERE, VAL. DON'T YOU SEE? THERE'S NO ONE ELSE TO RUN MY MACHINE!
THE BOOKS, ANDREA! PERHAPS IF YOU SHOWED THEM TO ONE OF YOUR ASSOCIATES, HE OR SHE WOULD SEND YOU AFTER ME...
PERHAPS! NOW, HURRY! WHERE DO YOU WANT TO BE SENT?
TO THE MIDDLE OF THE LAST CENTURY... TO THE 1950'S... TO THE BEGINNING OF IT...WHERE IT ALL STARTED! I'LL WARN THEM. I'LL STOP THEM FROM THEIR HEADLONG RUSH INTO SLAVERY...
THEN BEFORE YOU'RE MISSED AT THE BARRACKS AND TRACED HERE...IN THAT DOOR!
ANDREA PRESSED A BUTTON ON THE INSTRUMENT PANEL BEFORE HER AND A LEADEN DOOR IN THE LABORATORY WALL SLID OPEN...
IT LEADS TO THE CHRONOVERSE CHAMBER. LIE DOWN ON THE PLATFORM. QUICKLY...
GOOD-BYE, ANDREA.
PLEASE, COME BACK AND JOIN ME SOON...
VAL STEPPED INTO THE LEAD CHAMBER. ANDREA TOUCHED ANOTHER BUTTON. THE DOOR SLID CLOSED. VAL RECLINED ON THE PLATFORM AND STARED UP AT THE SINGLE URANIUM VAPOR LAMP GLOWING FROM THE CEILING...
THE LAMP BLINKED OUT. VAL WAITED IN THE DARKNESS. SLOWLY HE BECAME CONSCIOUS OF A NEBULOUS HAZE... A FEELING OF LIGHTNESS...A FLOATING... A KALEIDOSCOPE OF SPECTROSCOPIC COLORS EMANATING FROM THE WALLS. THEN, THERE WAS A BLINDING FLASH...
...AND EVERYTHING WENT BLACK...
2

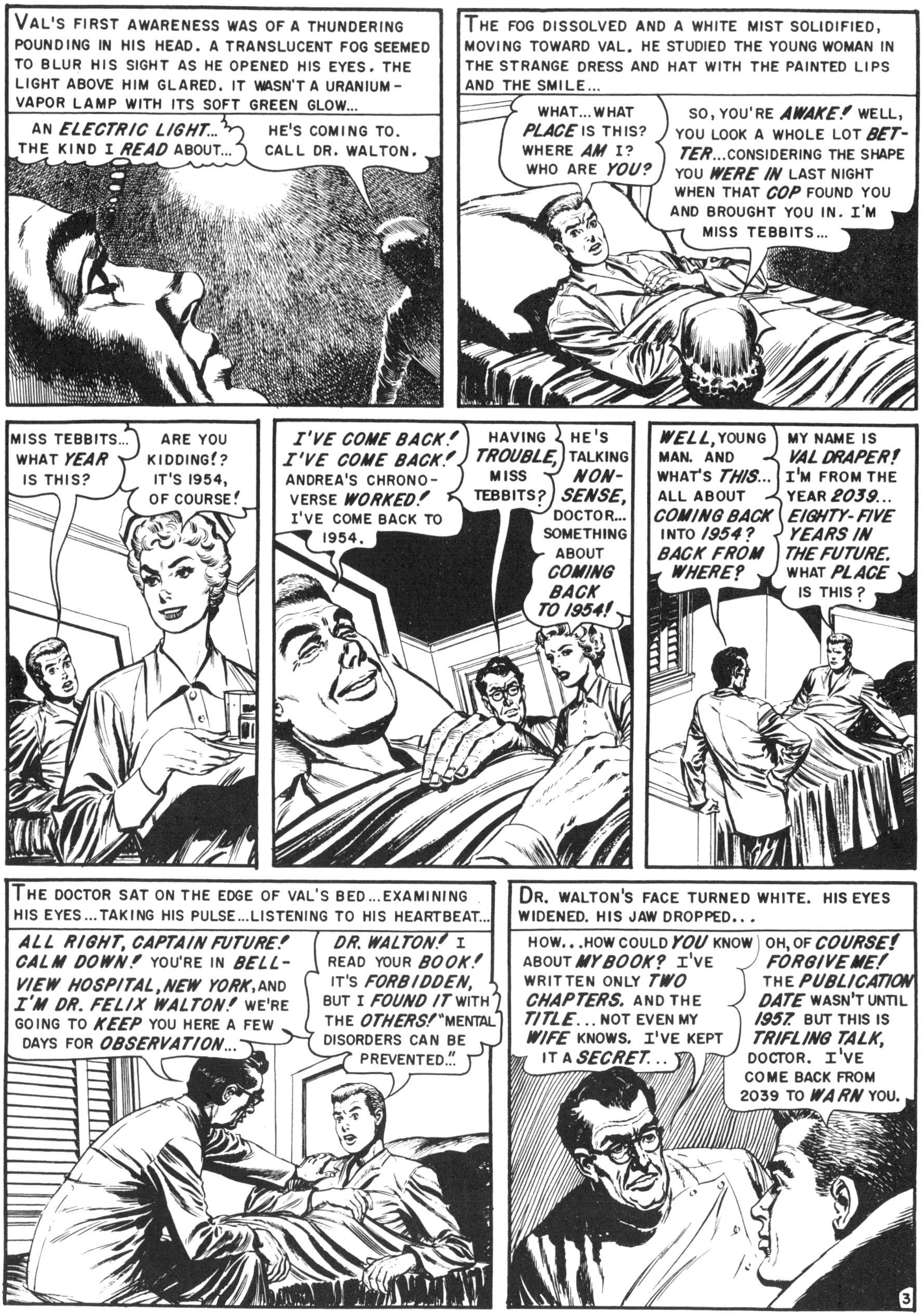
VAL'S FIRST AWARENESS WAS OF A THUNDERING POUNDING IN HIS HEAD. A TRANSLUCENT FOG SEEMED TO BLUR HIS SIGHT AS HE OPENED HIS EYES. THE LIGHT ABOVE HIM GLARED. IT WASN'T A URANIUM-VAPOR LAMP WITH ITS SOFT GREEN GLOW...
AN ELECTRIC LIGHT... THE KIND I READ ABOUT...
HE'S COMING TO. CALL DR. WALTON.
THE FOG DISSOLVED AND A WHITE MIST SOLIDIFIED, MOVING TOWARD VAL. HE STUDIED THE YOUNG WOMAN IN THE STRANGE DRESS AND HAT WITH THE PAINTED LIPS AND THE SMILE...
WHAT... WHAT PLACE IS THIS? WHERE AM I? WHO ARE YOU?
SO, YOU'RE AWAKE! WELL, YOU LOOK A WHOLE LOT BETTER...CONSIDERING THE SHAPE YOU WERE IN LAST NIGHT WHEN THAT COP FOUND YOU AND BROUGHT YOU IN. I'M MISS TEBBITS...
MISS TEBBITS... WHAT YEAR IS THIS?
ARE YOU KIDDING!? IT'S 1954, OF COURSE!
I'VE COME BACK! I'VE COME BACK! ANDREA'S CHRONOVERSE WORKED! I'VE COME BACK TO 1954.
HAVING TROUBLE, MISS TEBBITS?
HE'S TALKING NONSENSE, DOCTOR... SOMETHING ABOUT COMING BACK TO 1954!
WELL, YOUNG MAN. AND WHAT'S THIS... ALL ABOUT COMING BACK INTO 1954? BACK FROM WHERE?
MY NAME IS VAL DRAPER! I'M FROM THE YEAR 2039... EIGHTY-FIVE YEARS IN THE FUTURE. WHAT PLACE IS THIS?
THE DOCTOR SAT ON THE EDGE OF VAL'S BED...EXAMINING HIS EYES...TAKING HIS PULSE...LISTENING TO HIS HEARTBEAT...
ALL RIGHT, CAPTAIN FUTURE! CALM DOWN! YOU'RE IN BELLVIEW HOSPITAL, NEW YORK, AND I'M DR. FELIX WALTON! WE'RE GOING TO KEEP YOU HERE A FEW DAYS FOR OBSERVATION...
DR. WALTON! I READ YOUR BOOK! IT'S FORBIDDEN, BUT I FOUND IT WITH THE OTHERS! "MENTAL DISORDERS CAN BE PREVENTED."
DR. WALTON'S FACE TURNED WHITE. HIS EYES WIDENED. HIS JAW DROPPED...
HOW...HOW COULD YOU KNOW ABOUT MY BOOK? I'VE WRITTEN ONLY TWO CHAPTERS, AND THE TITLE... NOT EVEN MY WIFE KNOWS. I'VE KEPT IT A SECRET...
OH, OF COURSE! FORGIVE ME! THE PUBLICATION DATE WASN'T UNTIL 1957. BUT THIS IS TRIFLING TALK, DOCTOR. I'VE COME BACK FROM 2039 TO WARN YOU.
3

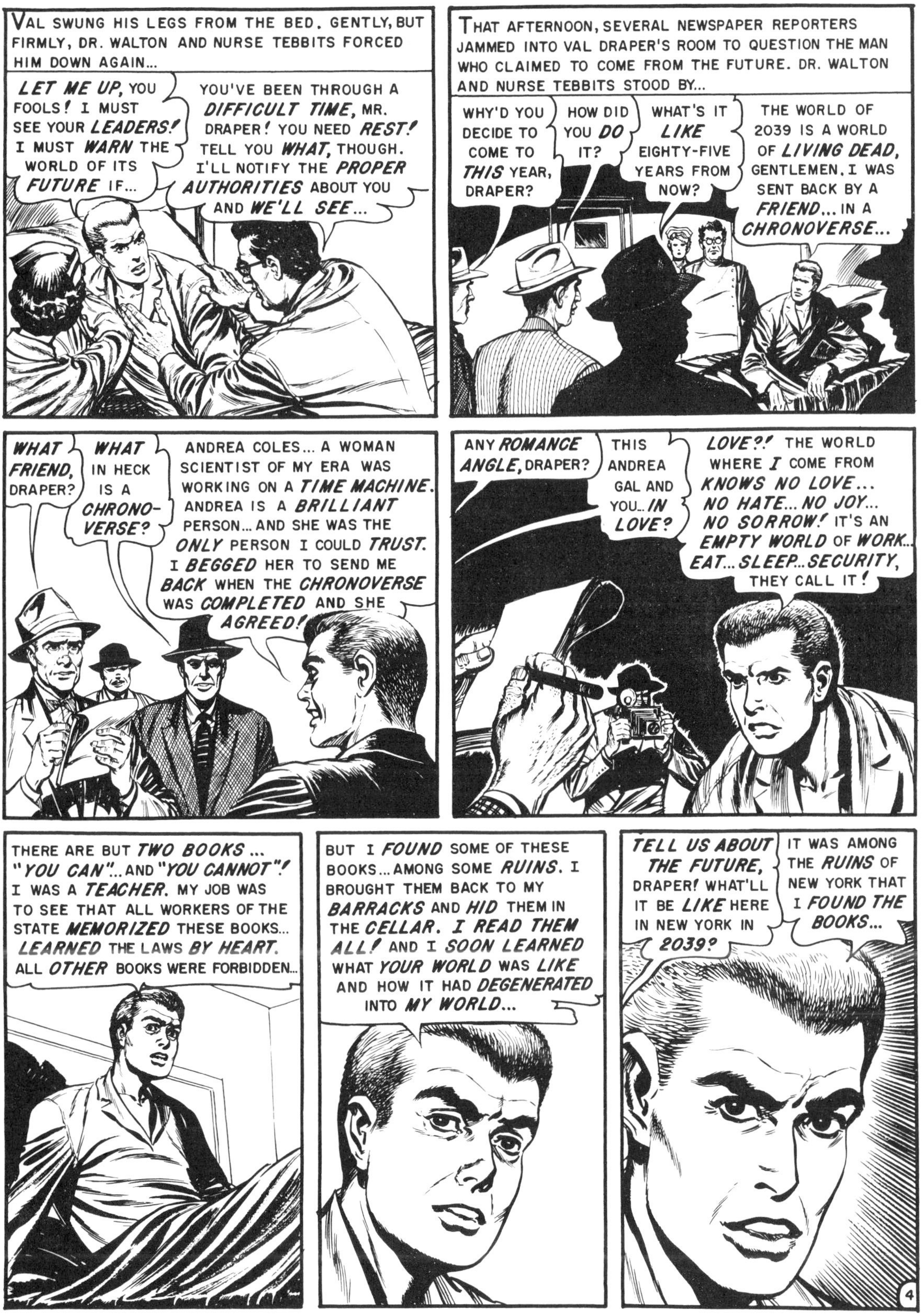
VAL SWUNG HIS LEGS FROM THE BED. GENTLY, BUT FIRMLY, DR. WALTON AND NURSE TEBBITS FORCED HIM DOWN AGAIN...
LET ME UP, YOU FOOLS! I MUST SEE YOUR LEADERS! I MUST WARN THE WORLD OF ITS FUTURE IF...
YOU'VE BEEN THROUGH A DIFFICULT TIME, MR. DRAPER! YOU NEED REST! TELL YOU WHAT, THOUGH. I'LL NOTIFY THE PROPER AUTHORITIES ABOUT YOU AND WE'LL SEE...
THAT AFTERNOON, SEVERAL NEWSPAPER REPORTERS JAMMED INTO VAL DRAPER'S ROOM TO QUESTION THE MAN WHO CLAIMED TO COME FROM THE FUTURE. DR. WALTON AND NURSE TEBBITS STOOD BY...
WHY'D YOU DECIDE TO COME TO THIS YEAR, DRAPER?
HOW DID YOU DO IT?
WHAT'S IT LIKE EIGHTY-FIVE YEARS FROM NOW?
THE WORLD OF 2039 IS A WORLD OF LIVING DEAD, GENTLEMEN. I WAS SENT BACK BY A FRIEND... IN A CHRONOVERSE...
WHAT FRIEND, DRAPER?
WHAT IN HECK IS A CHRONO-VERSE?
ANDREA COLES... A WOMAN SCIENTIST OF MY ERA WAS WORKING ON A TIME MACHINE. ANDREA IS A BRILLIANT PERSON... AND SHE WAS THE ONLY PERSON I COULD TRUST. I BEGGED HER TO SEND ME BACK WHEN THE CHRONOVERSE WAS COMPLETED AND SHE AGREED!
ANY ROMANCE ANGLE, DRAPER?
THIS ANDREA GAL AND YOU... IN LOVE?
LOVE?! THE WORLD WHERE I COME FROM KNOWS NO LOVE... NO HATE... NO JOY... NO SORROW! IT'S AN EMPTY WORLD OF WORK... EAT... SLEEP... SECURITY, THEY CALL IT!
THERE ARE BUT TWO BOOKS... "YOU CAN"... AND "YOU CANNOT"! I WAS A TEACHER. MY JOB WAS TO SEE THAT ALL WORKERS OF THE STATE MEMORIZED THESE BOOKS... LEARNED THE LAWS BY HEART. ALL OTHER BOOKS WERE FORBIDDEN...
BUT I FOUND SOME OF THESE BOOKS... AMONG SOME RUINS. I BROUGHT THEM BACK TO MY BARRACKS AND HID THEM IN THE CELLAR. I READ THEM ALL! AND I SOON LEARNED WHAT YOUR WORLD WAS LIKE AND HOW IT HAD DEGENERATED INTO MY WORLD...
TELL US ABOUT THE FUTURE, DRAPER! WHAT'LL IT BE LIKE HERE IN NEW YORK IN 2039?
IT WAS AMONG THE RUINS OF NEW YORK THAT I FOUND THE BOOKS...
4

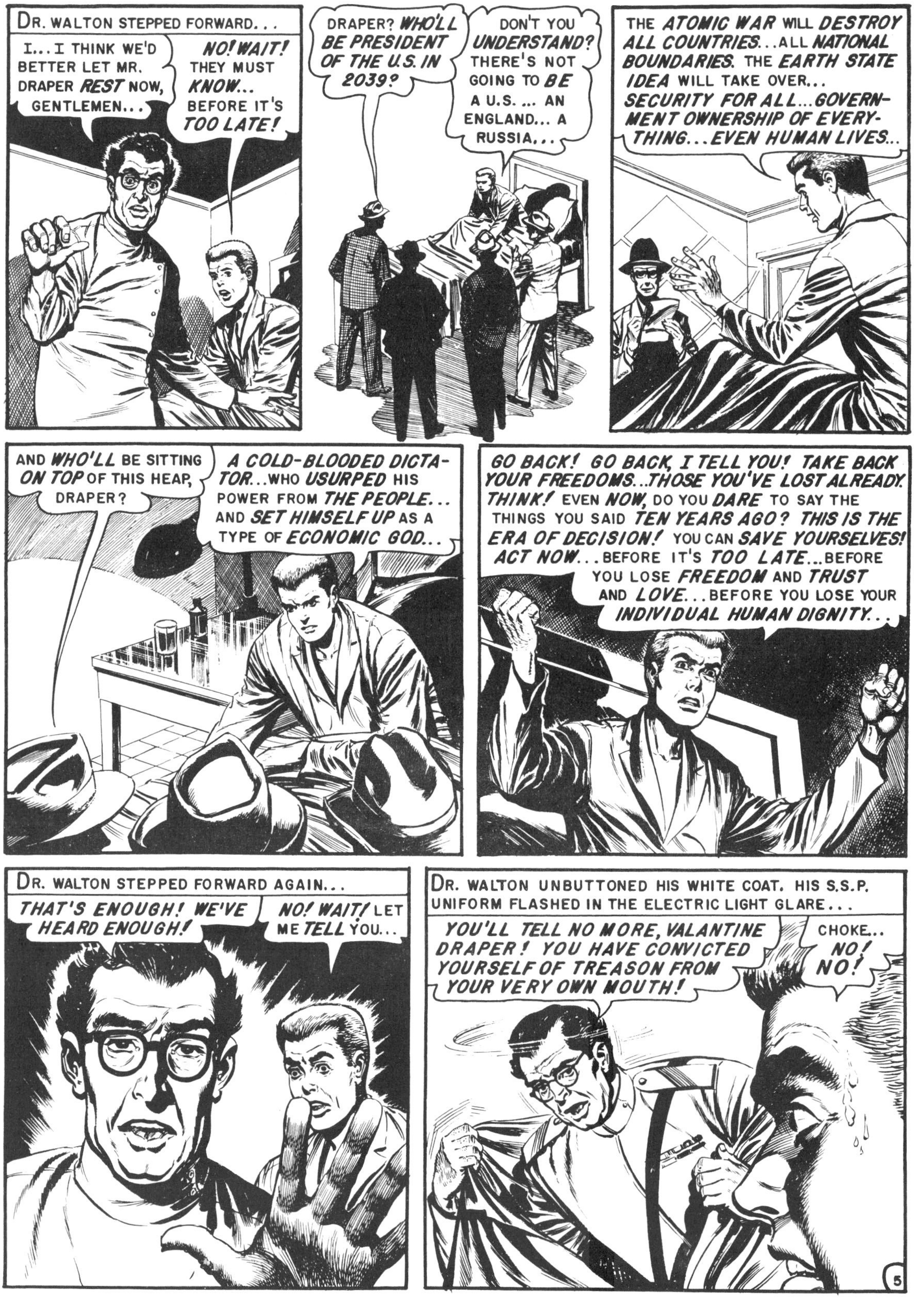
DR. WALTON STEPPED FORWARD...
I... I THINK WE'D BETTER LET MR. DRAPER REST NOW, GENTLEMEN...
NO! WAIT! THEY MUST KNOW... BEFORE IT'S TOO LATE!
DRAPER? WHO'LL BE PRESIDENT OF THE U.S. IN 2039?
DON'T YOU UNDERSTAND? THERE'S NOT GOING TO BE A U.S. ... AN ENGLAND... A RUSSIA...
THE ATOMIC WAR WILL DESTROY ALL COUNTRIES...ALL NATIONAL BOUNDARIES. THE EARTH STATE IDEA WILL TAKE OVER... SECURITY FOR ALL...GOVERNMENT OWNERSHIP OF EVERYTHING...EVEN HUMAN LIVES...
AND WHO'LL BE SITTING ON TOP OF THIS HEAP, DRAPER?
A COLD-BLOODED DICTATOR...WHO USURPED HIS POWER FROM THE PEOPLE... AND SET HIMSELF UP AS A TYPE OF ECONOMIC GOD...
GO BACK! GO BACK, I TELL YOU! TAKE BACK YOUR FREEDOMS...THOSE YOU'VE LOST ALREADY. THINK! EVEN NOW, DO YOU DARE TO SAY THE THINGS YOU SAID TEN YEARS AGO? THIS IS THE ERA OF DECISION! YOU CAN SAVE YOURSELVES! ACT NOW...BEFORE IT'S TOO LATE...BEFORE YOU LOSE FREEDOM AND TRUST AND LOVE...BEFORE YOU LOSE YOUR INDIVIDUAL HUMAN DIGNITY...
DR. WALTON STEPPED FORWARD AGAIN...
THAT'S ENOUGH! WE'VE HEARD ENOUGH!
NO! WAIT! LET ME TELL YOU...
DR. WALTON UNBUTTONED HIS WHITE COAT. HIS S.S.P. UNIFORM FLASHED IN THE ELECTRIC LIGHT GLARE...
YOU'LL TELL NO MORE, VALANTINE DRAPER! YOU HAVE CONVICTED YOURSELF OF TREASON FROM YOUR VERY OWN MOUTH!
CHOKE... NO! NO!
5

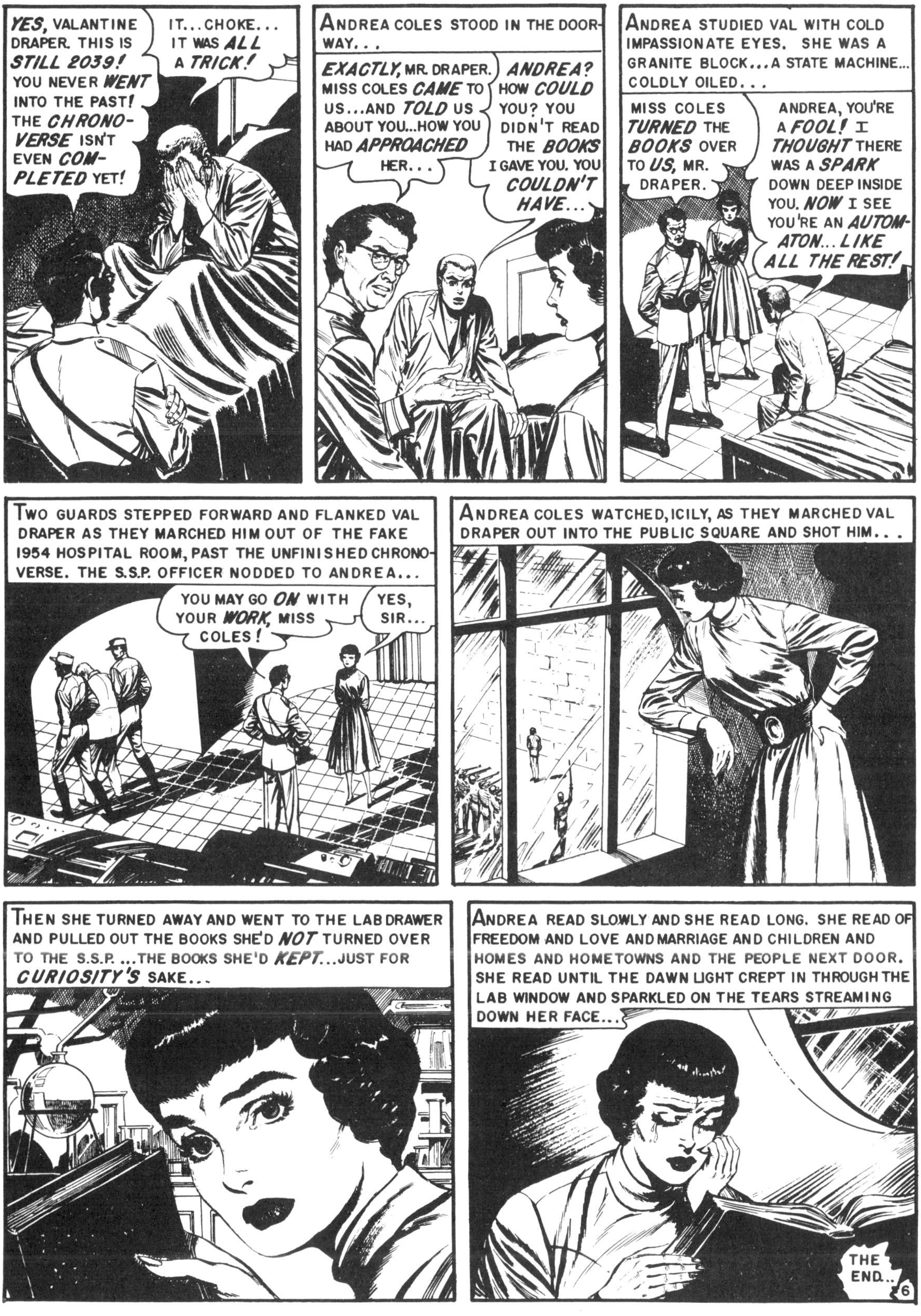
YES, VALANTINE DRAPER. THIS IS STILL 2039! YOU NEVER WENT INTO THE PAST! THE CHRONO-VERSE ISN'T EVEN COM-PLETED YET!
IT...CHOKE... IT WAS ALL A TRICK!
ANDREA COLES STOOD IN THE DOORWAY...
EXACTLY, MR. DRAPER. MISS COLES CAME TO US...AND TOLD US ABOUT YOU...HOW YOU HAD APPROACHED HER...
ANDREA? HOW COULD YOU? YOU DIDN'T READ THE BOOKS I GAVE YOU. YOU COULDN'T HAVE...
ANDREA STUDIED VAL WITH COLD IMPASSIONATE EYES. SHE WAS A GRANITE BLOCK...A STATE MACHINE... COLDLY OILED...
MISS COLES TURNED THE BOOKS OVER TO US, MR. DRAPER.
ANDREA, YOU'RE A FOOL! I THOUGHT THERE WAS A SPARK DOWN DEEP INSIDE YOU. NOW I SEE YOU'RE AN AUTOM-ATON... LIKE ALL THE REST!
TWO GUARDS STEPPED FORWARD AND FLANKED VAL DRAPER AS THEY MARCHED HIM OUT OF THE FAKE 1954 HOSPITAL ROOM, PAST THE UNFINISHED CHRONO-VERSE. THE S.S.P. OFFICER NODDED TO ANDREA...
YOU MAY GO ON WITH YOUR WORK, MISS COLES!
YES, SIR...
ANDREA COLES WATCHED, ICILY, AS THEY MARCHED VAL DRAPER OUT INTO THE PUBLIC SQUARE AND SHOT HIM...
THEN SHE TURNED AWAY AND WENT TO THE LAB DRAWER AND PULLED OUT THE BOOKS SHE'D NOT TURNED OVER TO THE S.S.P. ...THE BOOKS SHE'D KEPT...JUST FOR CURIOSITY'S SAKE...
ANDREA READ SLOWLY AND SHE READ LONG. SHE READ OF FREEDOM AND LOVE AND MARRIAGE AND CHILDREN AND HOMES AND HOMETOWNS AND THE PEOPLE NEXT DOOR. SHE READ UNTIL THE DAWN LIGHT CREPT IN THROUGH THE LAB WINDOW AND SPARKLED ON THE TEARS STREAMING DOWN HER FACE...
THE END...
6

ROUND TRIP

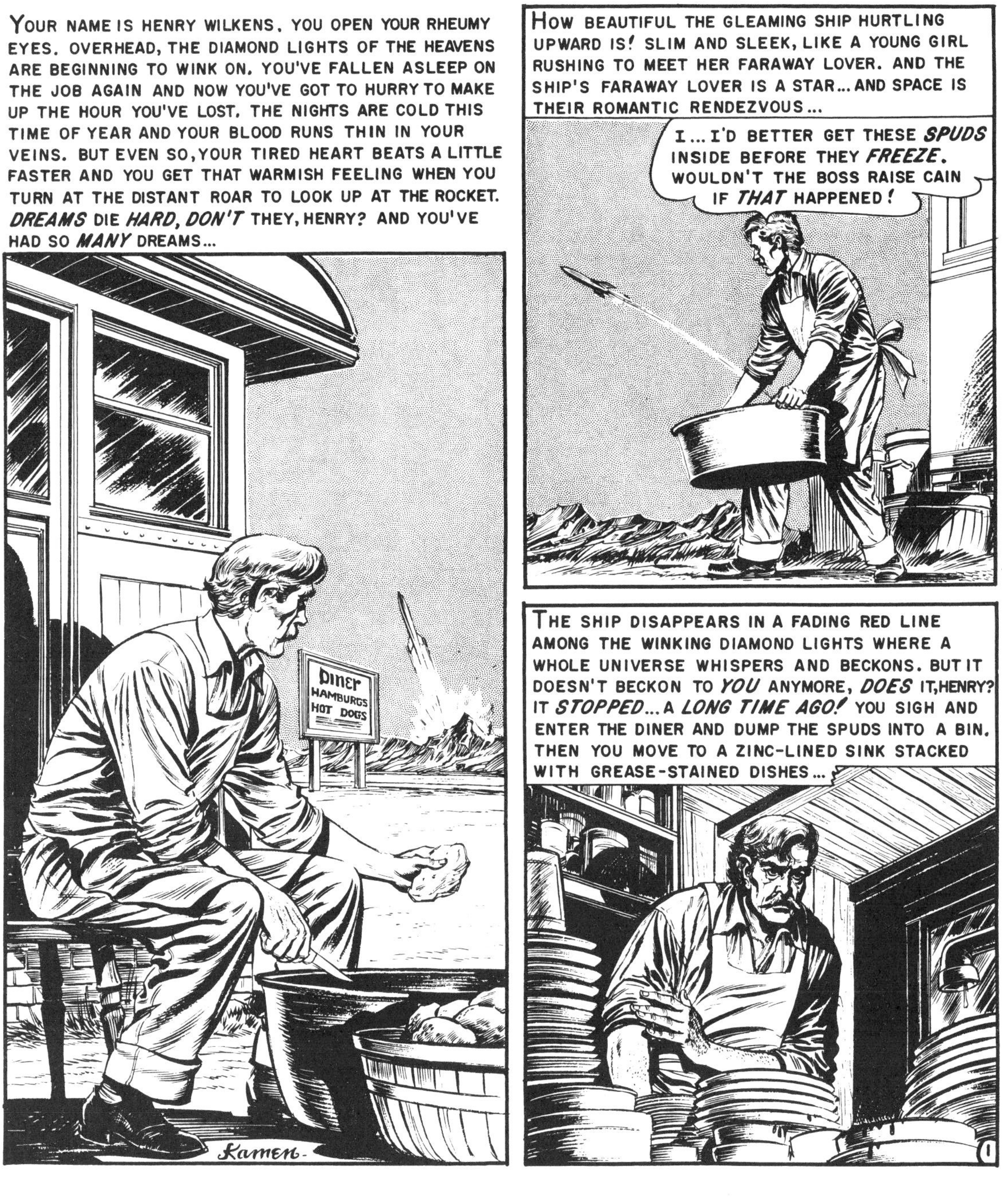
YOUR NAME IS HENRY WILKENS. YOU OPEN YOUR RHEUMY EYES. OVERHEAD, THE DIAMOND LIGHTS OF THE HEAVENS ARE BEGINNING TO WINK ON. YOU'VE FALLEN ASLEEP ON THE JOB AGAIN AND NOW YOU'VE GOT TO HURRY TO MAKE UP THE HOUR YOU'VE LOST. THE NIGHTS ARE COLD THIS TIME OF YEAR AND YOUR BLOOD RUNS THIN IN YOUR VEINS. BUT EVEN SO, YOUR TIRED HEART BEATS A LITTLE FASTER AND YOU GET THAT WARMISH FEELING WHEN YOU TURN AT THE DISTANT ROAR TO LOOK UP AT THE ROCKET. *DREAMS* DIE *HARD, DON'T* THEY, HENRY? AND YOU'VE HAD SO *MANY* DREAMS...
DINER
HAMBURGS
HOT DOGS
Kamen
HOW BEAUTIFUL THE GLEAMING SHIP HURTLING UPWARD IS! SLIM AND SLEEK, LIKE A YOUNG GIRL RUSHING TO MEET HER FARAWAY LOVER. AND THE SHIP'S FARAWAY LOVER IS A STAR... AND SPACE IS THEIR ROMANTIC RENDEZVOUS...
I... I'D BETTER GET THESE *SPUDS* INSIDE BEFORE THEY *FREEZE*. WOULDN'T THE BOSS RAISE CAIN IF *THAT* HAPPENED!
THE SHIP DISAPPEARS IN A FADING RED LINE AMONG THE WINKING DIAMOND LIGHTS WHERE A WHOLE UNIVERSE WHISPERS AND BECKONS. BUT IT DOESN'T BECKON TO *YOU* ANYMORE, *DOES* IT, HENRY? IT *STOPPED*... A *LONG TIME AGO!* YOU SIGH AND ENTER THE DINER AND DUMP THE SPUDS INTO A BIN. THEN YOU MOVE TO A ZINC-LINED SINK STACKED WITH GREASE-STAINED DISHES...

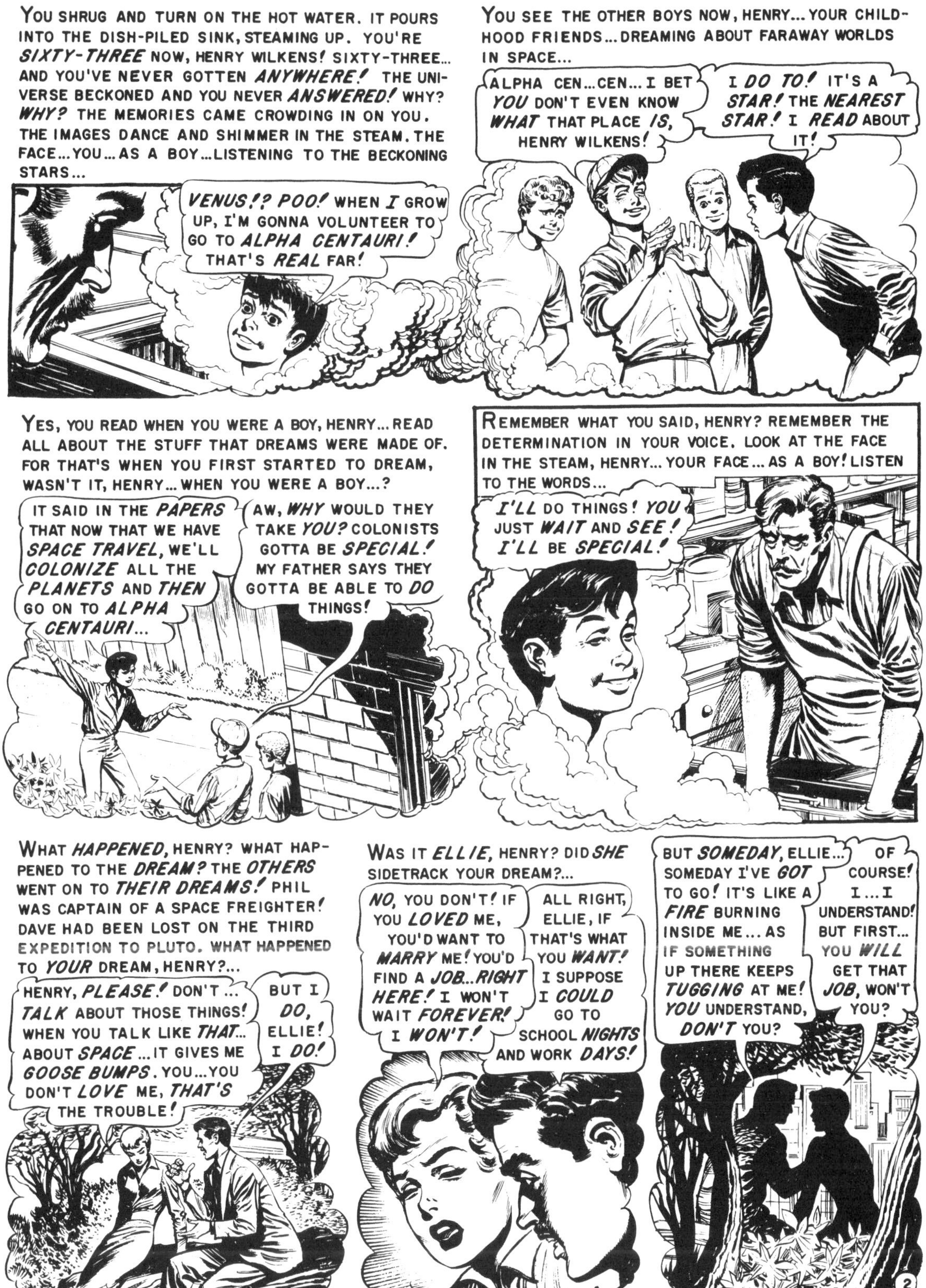
YOU SHRUG AND TURN ON THE HOT WATER. IT POURS INTO THE DISH-PILED SINK, STEAMING UP. YOU'RE SIXTY-THREE NOW, HENRY WILKENS! SIXTY-THREE... AND YOU'VE NEVER GOTTEN ANYWHERE! THE UNIVERSE BECKONED AND YOU NEVER ANSWERED! WHY? WHY? THE MEMORIES CAME CROWDING IN ON YOU. THE IMAGES DANCE AND SHIMMER IN THE STEAM. THE FACE... YOU... AS A BOY... LISTENING TO THE BECKONING STARS...
VENUS!? POO! WHEN I GROW UP, I'M GONNA VOLUNTEER TO GO TO ALPHA CENTAURI! THAT'S REAL FAR!
YOU SEE THE OTHER BOYS NOW, HENRY... YOUR CHILDHOOD FRIENDS... DREAMING ABOUT FARAWAY WORLDS IN SPACE...
ALPHA CEN...CEN... I BET YOU DON'T EVEN KNOW WHAT THAT PLACE IS, HENRY WILKENS!
I DO TO! IT'S A STAR! THE NEAREST STAR! I READ ABOUT IT!
YES, YOU READ WHEN YOU WERE A BOY, HENRY... READ ALL ABOUT THE STUFF THAT DREAMS WERE MADE OF. FOR THAT'S WHEN YOU FIRST STARTED TO DREAM, WASN'T IT, HENRY... WHEN YOU WERE A BOY...?
IT SAID IN THE PAPERS THAT NOW THAT WE HAVE SPACE TRAVEL, WE'LL COLONIZE ALL THE PLANETS AND THEN GO ON TO ALPHA CENTAURI...
AW, WHY WOULD THEY TAKE YOU? COLONISTS GOTTA BE SPECIAL! MY FATHER SAYS THEY GOTTA BE ABLE TO DO THINGS!
REMEMBER WHAT YOU SAID, HENRY? REMEMBER THE DETERMINATION IN YOUR VOICE. LOOK AT THE FACE IN THE STEAM, HENRY... YOUR FACE... AS A BOY! LISTEN TO THE WORDS...
I'LL DO THINGS! YOU JUST WAIT AND SEE! I'LL BE SPECIAL!
WHAT HAPPENED, HENRY? WHAT HAPPENED TO THE DREAM? THE OTHERS WENT ON TO THEIR DREAMS! PHIL WAS CAPTAIN OF A SPACE FREIGHTER! DAVE HAD BEEN LOST ON THE THIRD EXPEDITION TO PLUTO. WHAT HAPPENED TO YOUR DREAM, HENRY?...
HENRY, PLEASE! DON'T... TALK ABOUT THOSE THINGS! WHEN YOU TALK LIKE THAT... ABOUT SPACE... IT GIVES ME GOOSE BUMPS. YOU... YOU DON'T LOVE ME, THAT'S THE TROUBLE!
BUT I DO, ELLIE! I DO!
WAS IT ELLIE, HENRY? DID SHE SIDETRACK YOUR DREAM?...
NO, YOU DON'T! IF YOU LOVED ME, YOU'D WANT TO MARRY ME! YOU'D FIND A JOB... RIGHT HERE! I WON'T WAIT FOREVER! I WON'T!
ALL RIGHT, ELLIE, IF THAT'S WHAT YOU WANT! I SUPPOSE I COULD GO TO SCHOOL NIGHTS AND WORK DAYS!
BUT SOMEDAY, ELLIE... SOMEDAY I'VE GOT TO GO! IT'S LIKE A FIRE BURNING INSIDE ME... AS IF SOMETHING UP THERE KEEPS TUGGING AT ME! YOU UNDERSTAND, DON'T YOU?
OF COURSE! I... I UNDERSTAND! BUT FIRST... YOU WILL GET THAT JOB, WON'T YOU?
2

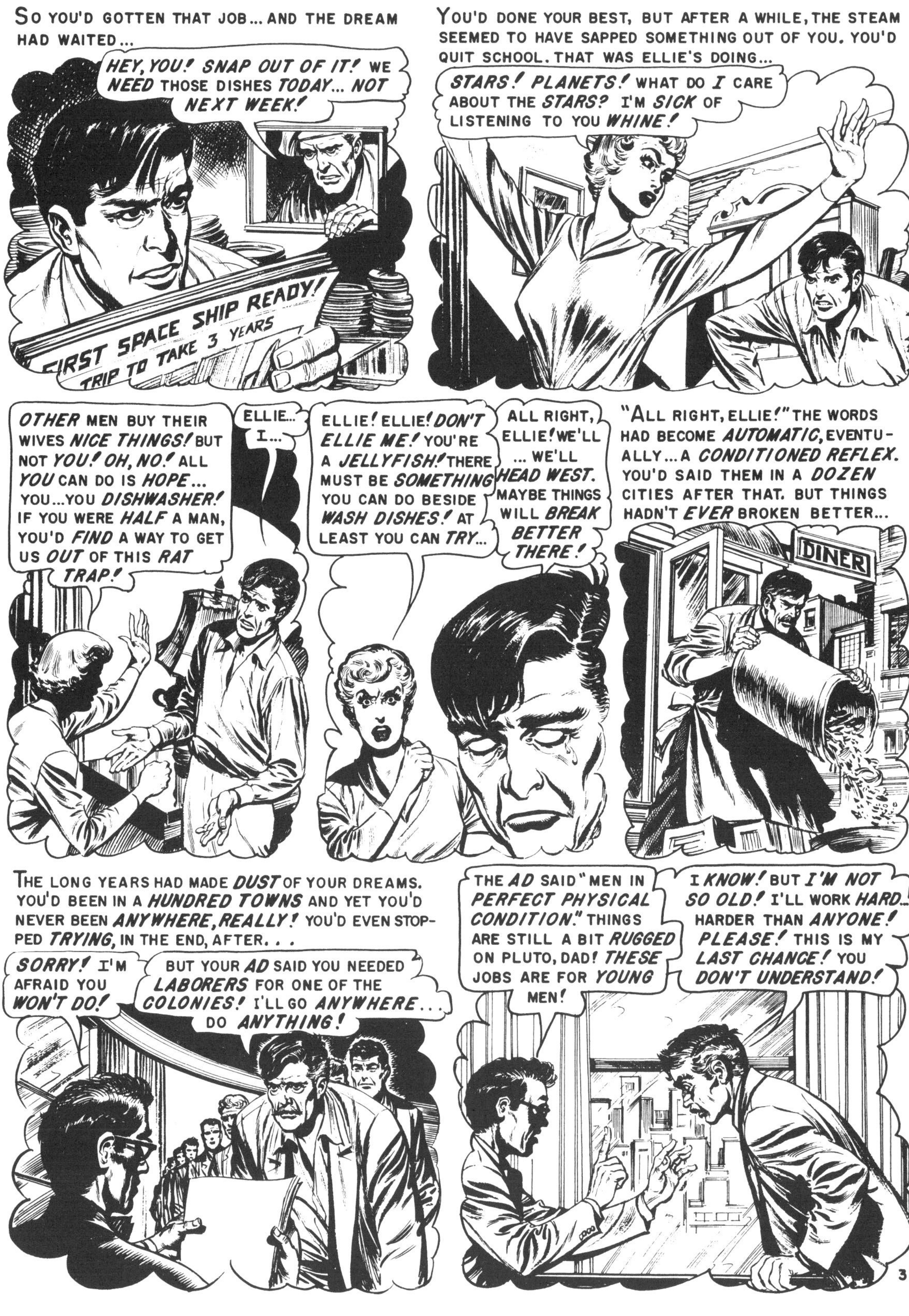
SO YOU'D GOTTEN THAT JOB... AND THE DREAM HAD WAITED...
HEY, YOU! SNAP OUT OF IT! WE NEED THOSE DISHES TODAY... NOT NEXT WEEK!
FIRST SPACE SHIP READY! TRIP TO TAKE 3 YEARS
YOU'D DONE YOUR BEST, BUT AFTER A WHILE, THE STEAM SEEMED TO HAVE SAPPED SOMETHING OUT OF YOU. YOU'D QUIT SCHOOL. THAT WAS ELLIE'S DOING...
STARS! PLANETS! WHAT DO I CARE ABOUT THE STARS? I'M SICK OF LISTENING TO YOU WHINE!
OTHER MEN BUY THEIR WIVES NICE THINGS! BUT NOT YOU! OH, NO! ALL YOU CAN DO IS HOPE... YOU...YOU DISHWASHER! IF YOU WERE HALF A MAN, YOU'D FIND A WAY TO GET US OUT OF THIS RAT TRAP!
ELLIE... I...
ELLIE! ELLIE! DON'T ELLIE ME! YOU'RE A JELLYFISH! THERE MUST BE SOMETHING YOU CAN DO BESIDE WASH DISHES! AT LEAST YOU CAN TRY...
ALL RIGHT, ELLIE! WE'LL ... WE'LL HEAD WEST. MAYBE THINGS WILL BREAK BETTER THERE!
"ALL RIGHT, ELLIE!" THE WORDS HAD BECOME AUTOMATIC, EVENTUALLY... A CONDITIONED REFLEX. YOU'D SAID THEM IN A DOZEN CITIES AFTER THAT. BUT THINGS HADN'T EVER BROKEN BETTER...
DINER
THE LONG YEARS HAD MADE DUST OF YOUR DREAMS. YOU'D BEEN IN A HUNDRED TOWNS AND YET YOU'D NEVER BEEN ANYWHERE, REALLY! YOU'D EVEN STOPPED TRYING, IN THE END, AFTER. . .
SORRY! I'M AFRAID YOU WON'T DO!
BUT YOUR AD SAID YOU NEEDED LABORERS FOR ONE OF THE COLONIES! I'LL GO ANYWHERE... DO ANYTHING!
THE AD SAID "MEN IN PERFECT PHYSICAL CONDITION." THINGS ARE STILL A BIT RUGGED ON PLUTO, DAD! THESE JOBS ARE FOR YOUNG MEN!
I KNOW! BUT I'M NOT SO OLD! I'LL WORK HARD... HARDER THAN ANYONE! PLEASE! THIS IS MY LAST CHANCE! YOU DON'T UNDERSTAND!
3

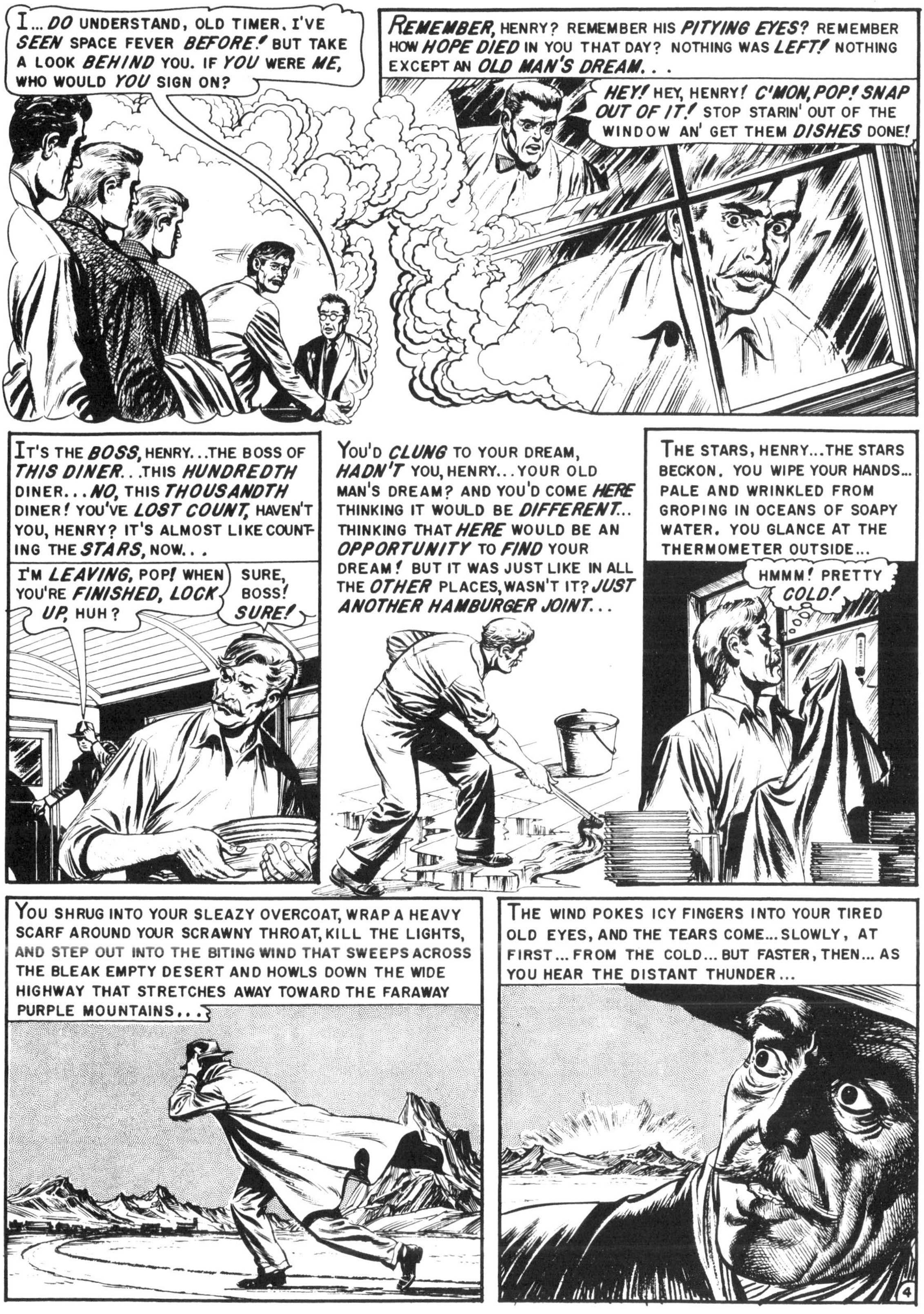
I... DO UNDERSTAND, OLD TIMER. I'VE SEEN SPACE FEVER BEFORE! BUT TAKE A LOOK BEHIND YOU. IF YOU WERE ME, WHO WOULD YOU SIGN ON?
REMEMBER, HENRY? REMEMBER HIS PITYING EYES? REMEMBER HOW HOPE DIED IN YOU THAT DAY? NOTHING WAS LEFT! NOTHING EXCEPT AN OLD MAN'S DREAM. . .
HEY! HEY, HENRY! C'MON, POP! SNAP OUT OF IT! STOP STARIN' OUT OF THE WINDOW AN' GET THEM DISHES DONE!
IT'S THE BOSS, HENRY...THE BOSS OF THIS DINER. . .THIS HUNDREDTH DINER. . . NO, THIS THOUSANDTH DINER! YOU'VE LOST COUNT, HAVEN'T YOU, HENRY? IT'S ALMOST LIKE COUNTING THE STARS, NOW. . .
I'M LEAVING, POP! WHEN YOU'RE FINISHED, LOCK UP, HUH?
SURE, BOSS! SURE!
YOU'D CLUNG TO YOUR DREAM, HADN'T YOU, HENRY... YOUR OLD MAN'S DREAM? AND YOU'D COME HERE THINKING IT WOULD BE DIFFERENT... THINKING THAT HERE WOULD BE AN OPPORTUNITY TO FIND YOUR DREAM! BUT IT WAS JUST LIKE IN ALL THE OTHER PLACES, WASN'T IT? JUST ANOTHER HAMBURGER JOINT...
THE STARS, HENRY...THE STARS BECKON. YOU WIPE YOUR HANDS... PALE AND WRINKLED FROM GROPING IN OCEANS OF SOAPY WATER. YOU GLANCE AT THE THERMOMETER OUTSIDE...
HMMM! PRETTY COLD!
YOU SHRUG INTO YOUR SLEAZY OVERCOAT, WRAP A HEAVY SCARF AROUND YOUR SCRAWNY THROAT, KILL THE LIGHTS, AND STEP OUT INTO THE BITING WIND THAT SWEEPS ACROSS THE BLEAK EMPTY DESERT AND HOWLS DOWN THE WIDE HIGHWAY THAT STRETCHES AWAY TOWARD THE FARAWAY PURPLE MOUNTAINS. . .
THE WIND POKES ICY FINGERS INTO YOUR TIRED OLD EYES, AND THE TEARS COME... SLOWLY, AT FIRST... FROM THE COLD... BUT FASTER, THEN... AS YOU HEAR THE DISTANT THUNDER...
4

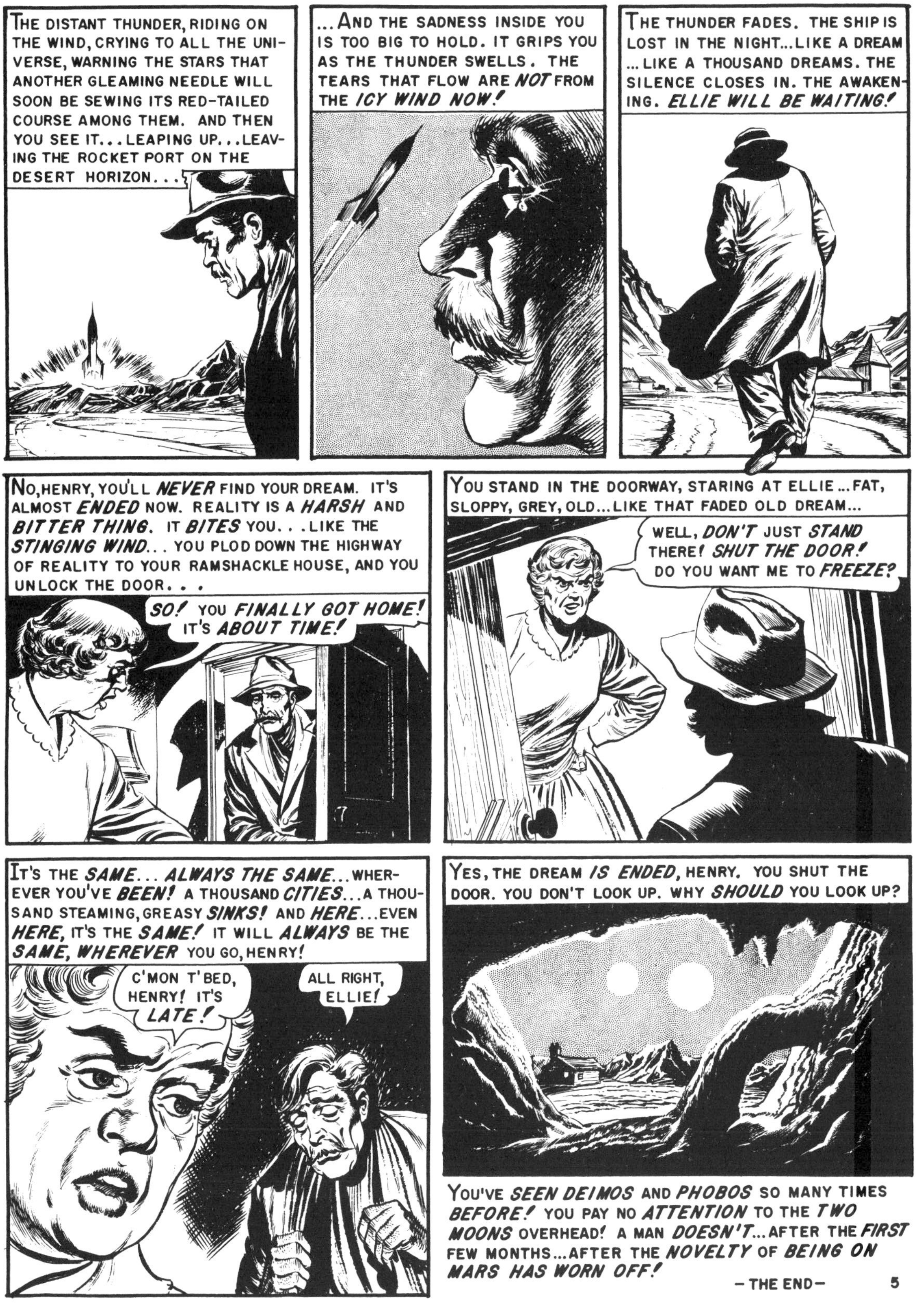
THE DISTANT THUNDER, RIDING ON THE WIND, CRYING TO ALL THE UNIVERSE, WARNING THE STARS THAT ANOTHER GLEAMING NEEDLE WILL SOON BE SEWING ITS RED-TAILED COURSE AMONG THEM. AND THEN YOU SEE IT... LEAPING UP... LEAVING THE ROCKET PORT ON THE DESERT HORIZON...
...AND THE SADNESS INSIDE YOU IS TOO BIG TO HOLD. IT GRIPS YOU AS THE THUNDER SWELLS. THE TEARS THAT FLOW ARE NOT FROM THE ICY WIND NOW!
THE THUNDER FADES. THE SHIP IS LOST IN THE NIGHT... LIKE A DREAM ... LIKE A THOUSAND DREAMS. THE SILENCE CLOSES IN. THE AWAKENING. ELLIE WILL BE WAITING!
NO, HENRY, YOU'LL NEVER FIND YOUR DREAM. IT'S ALMOST ENDED NOW. REALITY IS A HARSH AND BITTER THING. IT BITES YOU... LIKE THE STINGING WIND... YOU PLOD DOWN THE HIGHWAY OF REALITY TO YOUR RAMSHACKLE HOUSE, AND YOU UNLOCK THE DOOR...
SO! YOU FINALLY GOT HOME! IT'S ABOUT TIME!
YOU STAND IN THE DOORWAY, STARING AT ELLIE... FAT, SLOPPY, GREY, OLD... LIKE THAT FADED OLD DREAM...
WELL, DON'T JUST STAND THERE! SHUT THE DOOR! DO YOU WANT ME TO FREEZE?
IT'S THE SAME... ALWAYS THE SAME... WHEREVER YOU'VE BEEN! A THOUSAND CITIES... A THOUSAND STEAMING, GREASY SINKS! AND HERE... EVEN HERE, IT'S THE SAME! IT WILL ALWAYS BE THE SAME, WHEREVER YOU GO, HENRY!
C'MON T'BED, HENRY! IT'S LATE!
ALL RIGHT, ELLIE!
YES, THE DREAM IS ENDED, HENRY. YOU SHUT THE DOOR. YOU DON'T LOOK UP. WHY SHOULD YOU LOOK UP?
YOU'VE SEEN DEIMOS AND PHOBOS SO MANY TIMES BEFORE! YOU PAY NO ATTENTION TO THE TWO MOONS OVERHEAD! A MAN DOESN'T... AFTER THE FIRST FEW MONTHS... AFTER THE NOVELTY OF BEING ON MARS HAS WORN OFF!
—THE END—
5

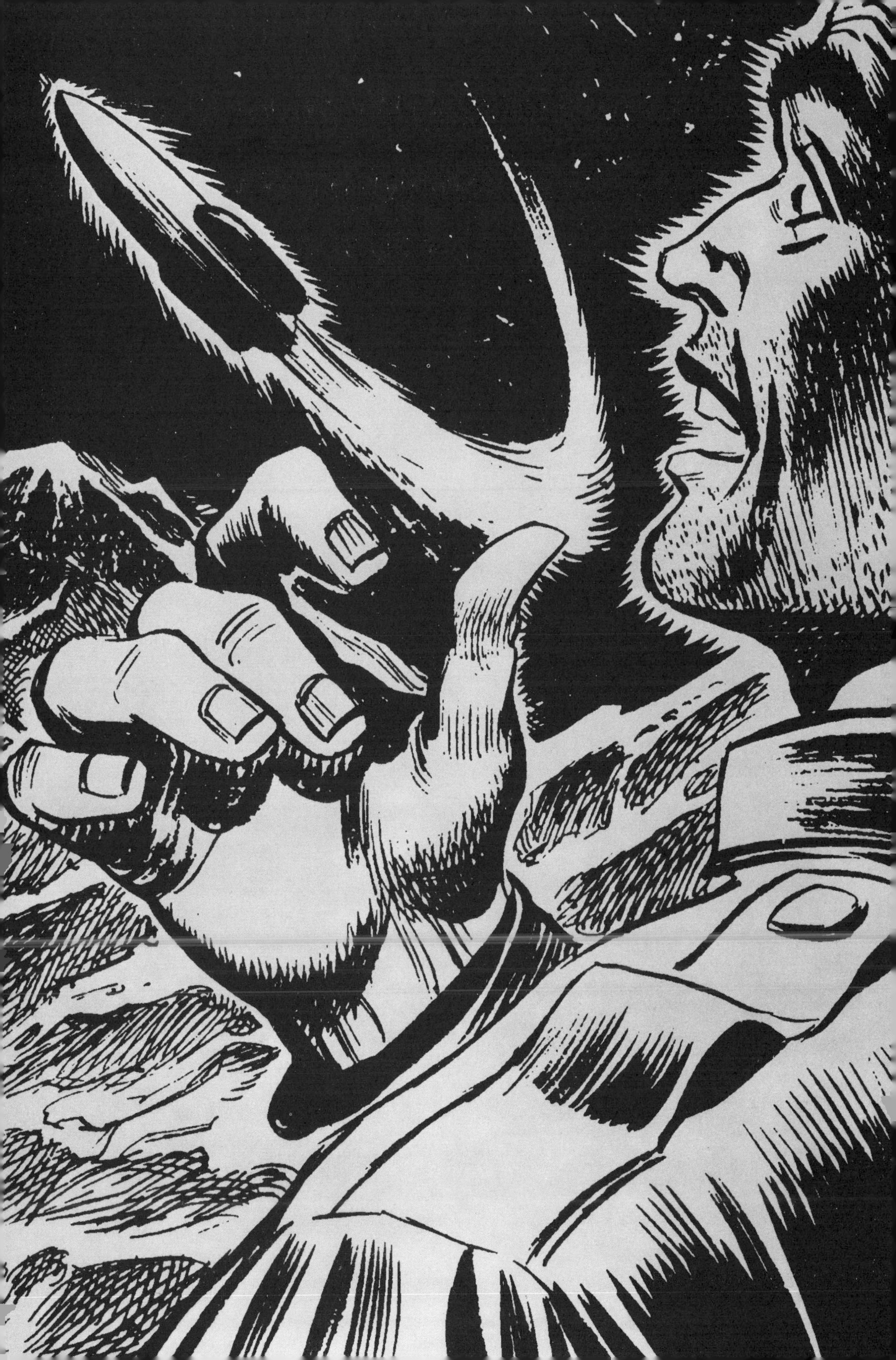

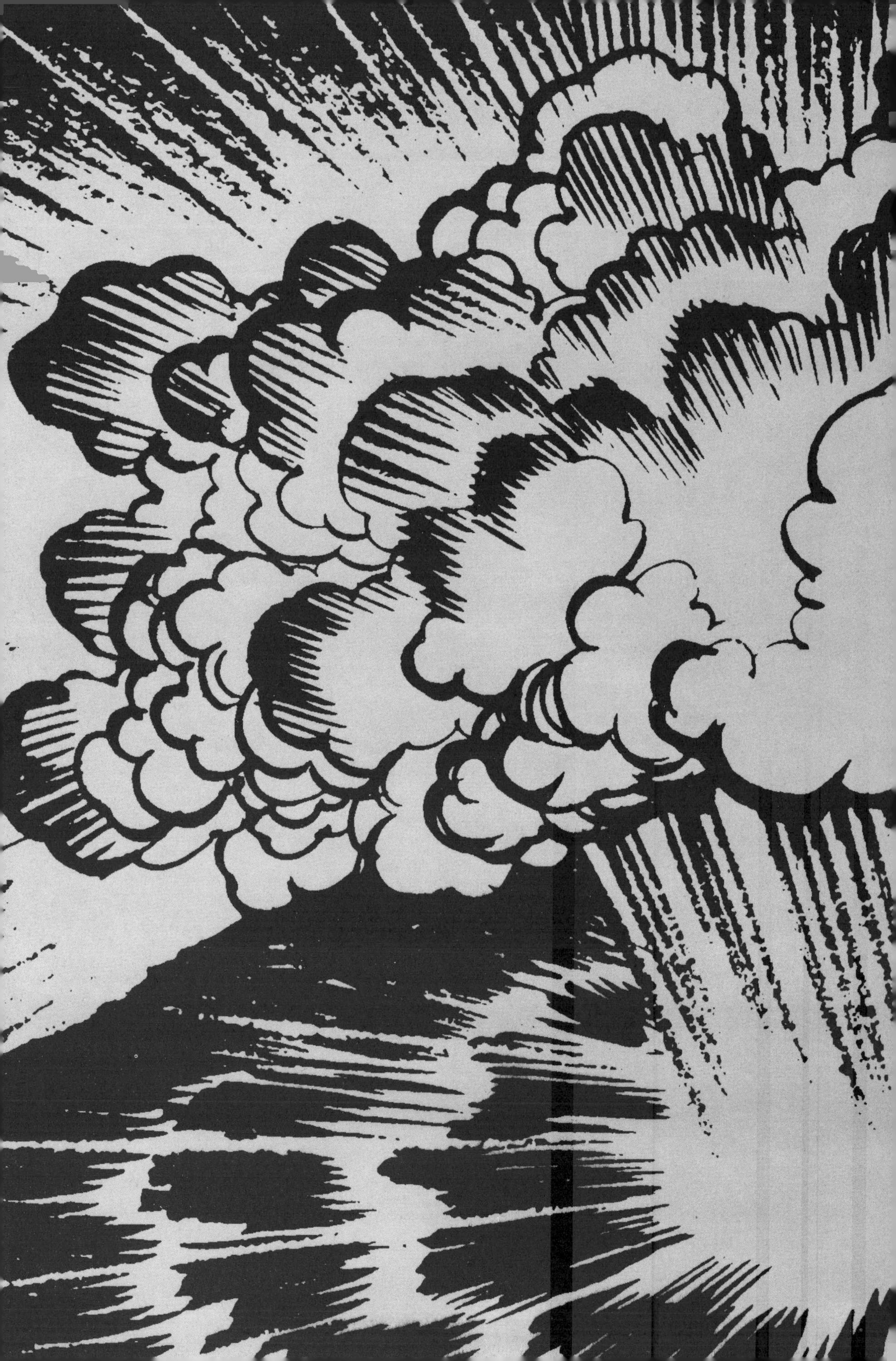

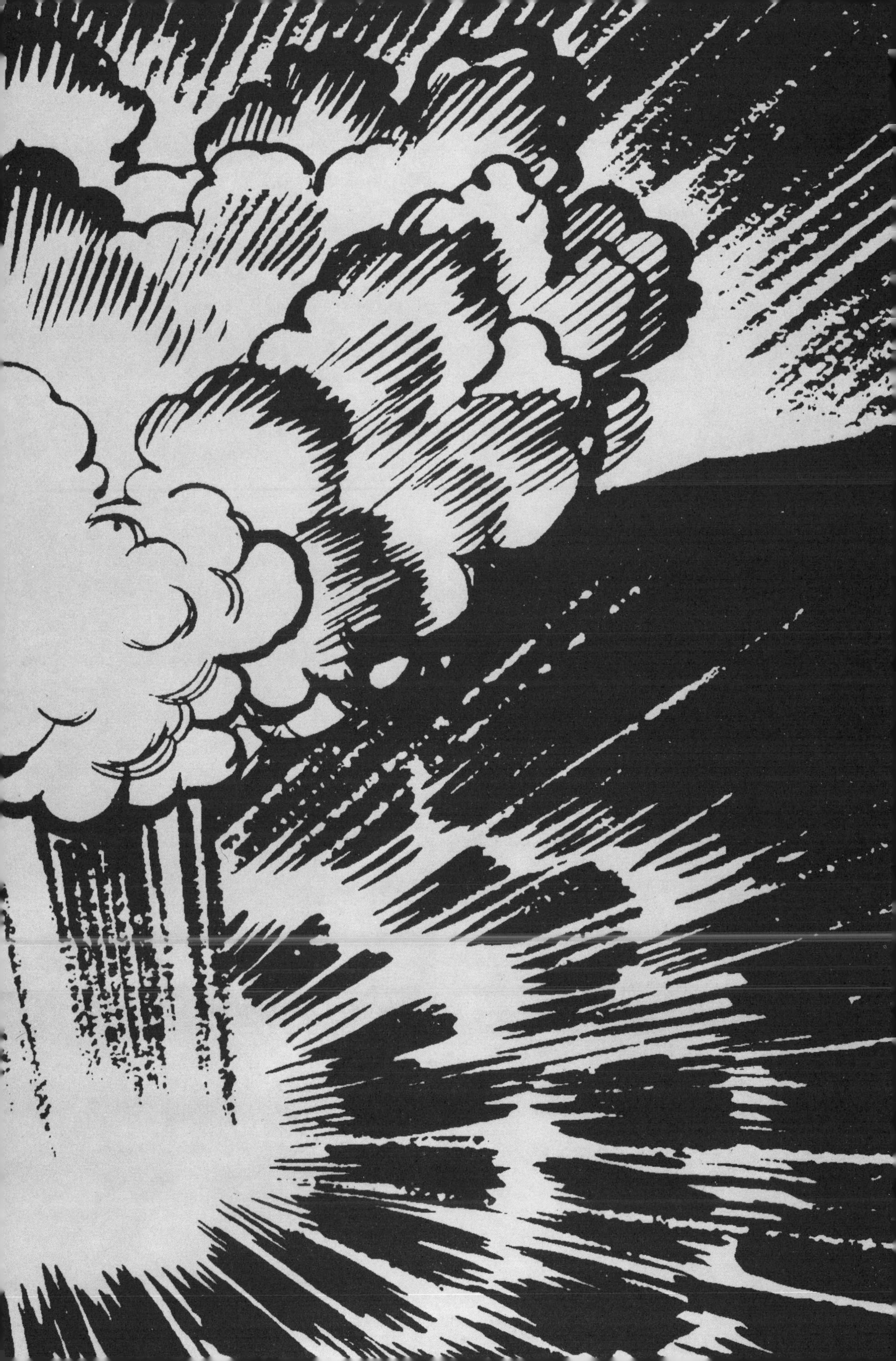

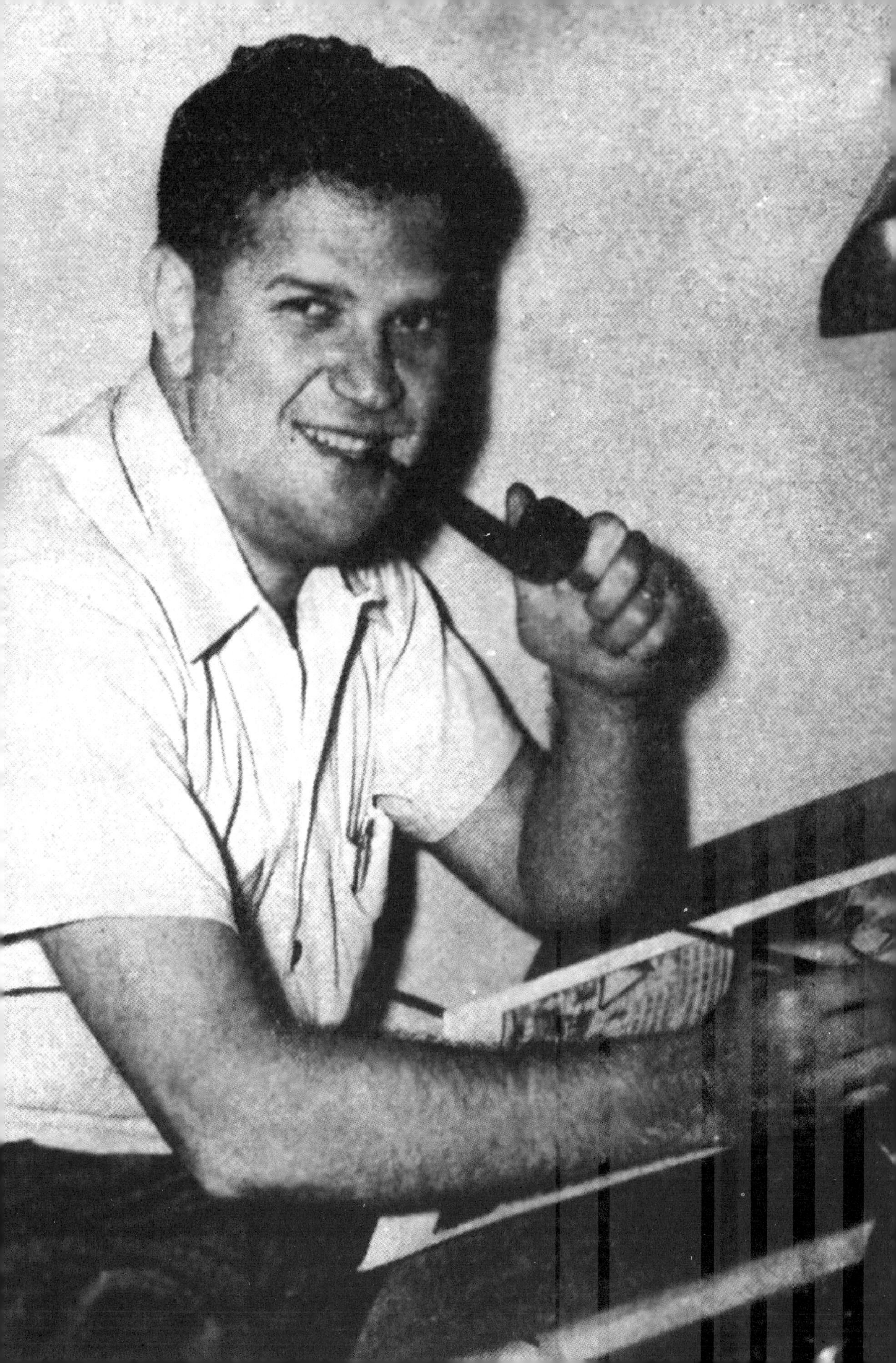

S.C. RINGGENBERG

JACK KAMEN

"Jack was one of the happiest guys around ... almost the prototype of the legendary salesman who comes in with six dirty jokes every time you see him. Every time he walked into the office it was with a good feeling that we greeted him. I personally always liked Jack's work."

— Bill Gaines, *EC Lives!*

During the heyday of EC Comics, the prolific Jack Kamen, who drew 160 stories (more than any other artist), and 11 covers was, perhaps, the *least* popular artist in the company's stable. That was then. History has not borne out that paltry assessment, and today he is highly regarded among contemporary EC fans not only for his talent but also for helping publisher Bill Gaines and editor Al Feldstein create their innovative, though short-lived, picto-fiction titles at the end of the EC era.

Kamen is also the father of Dean Kamen, the world-famous inventor of the Segway PT ("personal transporter"), the first portable drug infusion pump, the first portable kidney dialysis machine, and the holder of more than 440 U.S. and foreign patents.

Jack Kamen had a slick, easily accessible style and worked for various publishers in a variety of genres, including superhero and jungle adventure. Kamen's gift for drawing beautiful women (usually with icy hearts and murderous tendencies) was employed to maximum effect in EC's horror and shock titles, for which he is best known. He also drew a few romance stories for the company, along with a good number of generally overlooked science fiction stories, including adaptations of Ray Bradbury stories. Yet his talents were overshadowed in some fans' eyes by the bravura renderings of Wallace Wood and Al

OPPOSITE: This 1951 photo of Jack Kamen at his drawing board accompanied his "Artist of the Issue" feature that ran in EC Comics in early 1952.

Williamson, and the outrageously creepy approaches of Jack Davis and Graham Ingels.

Gaines and Feldstein used Kamen regularly on the science fiction titles, but they were careful to give him stories that played to another of his strengths: depicting contemporary 1950s urban and suburban milieus. They tended to avoid giving him stories involving rocketships, robots, and futuristic machinery — ironic because, when the imagined future gave way to real events, it was Jack Kamen who drew the detailed patent diagrams for some of son Dean's high tech inventions, including the Segway.

Born May 29, 1920, Kamen, like many pioneering comic book artists, gravitated to art early in life. Although he came from a family of artists, he received no art training until high school. The death of his father when Jack was 14 prompted him to go to work to help support the family. He had aspirations to become a fine artist, and so attended The Art Students League of New York, where he studied with famed illustrators George Bridgman and Harvey Dunn. Kamen paid for art school working as a sculptor, painting scenery for plays, dressing mannequins, and creating eye-catching window displays.

His first job in comics was at the Harry "A" Chesler shop (Kamen called him "the Chestnut"), where he stayed a few years, doing backgrounds on the Bulletman strip and on various filler stories for Fawcett. At about the age of 18, he began freelancing for Harvey and Fawcett, and he provided black-and-white illustrations for Better Publications' line of crime and Western pulps. From there, he joined the S.M. Iger shop and began cranking out comics pages for Iger's clients.

Kamen was drafted in 1942 and spent four years in the Army. The Army put his artistic talents to good use on training manuals and visual aids for GIs going abroad. He was later assigned to the Signal Corps, where he served in combat on New Guinea and in The Philippines.

With the end of the war, Iger welcomed him back with open arms. At the shop, Kamen worked alongside the highly regarded artists Matt Baker and Reed Crandall (the

latter a future EC colleague). He also met Al Feldstein, another returning veteran. He contributed to the jungle adventures of *Jo-Jo Congo King* and *Rulah, Jungle Goddess*. He drew *Ghost Gallery* and *ZX-5* for *Jumbo Comics* from Fiction House, *Blue Beetle* and romance comics for Victor Fox, and Leslie Charteris's *The Saint* for Avon. During this period, Kamen became well known for his ability to draw pretty women.

Kamen left Iger in 1950 to join EC on the recommendation of his friend Feldstein, who was by then assistant editor at EC. Publisher Gaines was happy to offer Kamen a higher page rate and within a year Gaines asked Kamen to work exclusively for him. Kamen's first EC work appeared in the final two issues of *Modern Love* and the first issues of the science fiction titles *Weird Science* and *Weird Fantasy*.

Aside from supplying him with a steady stream of assignments, EC offered Kamen another advantage: he rarely needed to make the long trek to the office in Manhattan from his home on Long Island. Since Feldstein lived nearby, Kamen would simply drive his finished pages over to Feldstein's house, where Feldstein would have the next assignment waiting for him.

Kamen proved to be fast and reliable, and he never missed a deadline. His work appeared regularly in all three horror titles, both science fiction titles, and in every issue of *Shock SuspenStories*. He drew most of the "Grim Fairy Tales" that ran in the horror titles. He did three covers for *Crime SuspenStories*, and drew what is arguably one of the most artistic covers on any EC comic: his nightmarish, Dali-esque cover to *Psychoanalysis* #3.

Psychoanalysis, a New Direction title and one of EC's last, was perfectly suited for his low-key, realistic style. Kamen drew all of the stories and covers for all four issues, which made him the only artist to draw the complete run of an EC title. In *Psychoanalysis*, the various characters explored their dreams, phobias, and mental health concerns with an unnamed psychiatrist. According to Kamen, he, Gaines, and Feldstein first tried to sell *Psychoanalysis* as a syndicated newspaper strip. But when that got nowhere, Kamen and his wife repasted the daily strips into comic book form and that became the basis for the first issue of *Psychoanalysis*.

Kamen's light, humorous touch was a perfect complement to Feldstein's often brutal and cynical scripts. Though he was known for his sense of humor around the EC offices and drew the hilariously autobiographical "Kamen's Kalamity" for an issue of *Tales From the Crypt* (#31, August-September 1952), Kamen's only work on an EC humor comic book story was "Little Red Riding Hood" in *Panic* #1 (February-March 1954).

The only EC titles Kamen didn't work for were Harvey Kurtzman's *Mad, Two-Fisted Tales,* and *Frontline Combat*. He did work for one issue of *Mad* magazine after Al Feldstein became editor ("Make Your Own Love-Story Comic," and a single panel in "Real Estate Ads," both in *Mad* #29, September-October 1956). By then, Kamen was doing advertising, which paid much better than comics.

One area where Kamen has been given short shrift by comics historians and fans is as an innovator in graphic fiction formats. It was Kamen, with his knowledge of production and printing techniques, who came up with the idea for the "picto-fiction" format and showed Bill Gaines how it should be done.

Fed up with the meddling from the Comics Code Authority and faced with the steadily declining sales of his color comics, Gaines switched to picto-fiction, which combined illustrations with narrative blocks of text in a magazine-size format. Kamen single-handedly produced the first picto-fiction magazine, *Shock Illustrated* #1 (September-October 1955). He illustrated the cover and all of the stories inside and even did all the paste-up and production (with the help of his wife, Evelyn). With his facility for drawing women, Kamen was naturally suited for another picto-fiction title, *Confessions Illustrated*, EC's return to the romance genre. With picto-fiction, Kamen was freed from the simple line art requirement of color comics, and he employed shading and toning methods, especially in *Confessions Illustrated*, to produce some of the best artwork of his comics career.

Kamen, who had wanted to be a fine artist and illustrator all along, really enjoyed working on the picto-fiction titles. As he recalled in an interview in the *Comics Journal* #240, "If you look at it, you'll see a lot of pen work and atmosphere. I could do that very quickly. To me, that was the most enjoyable time ... I was so sorry to see that go. ... if it had continued and caught on, I would have stayed with it because I loved doing that stuff."

Unfortunately, all four picto-fiction titles (the other two were *Terror Illustrated* and *Crime Illustrated* but did not carry work by Kamen) proved to be a bust with the reading public and were quickly cancelled. But the format Kamen suggested — a magazine with black-and-white interior art printed on cheap paper

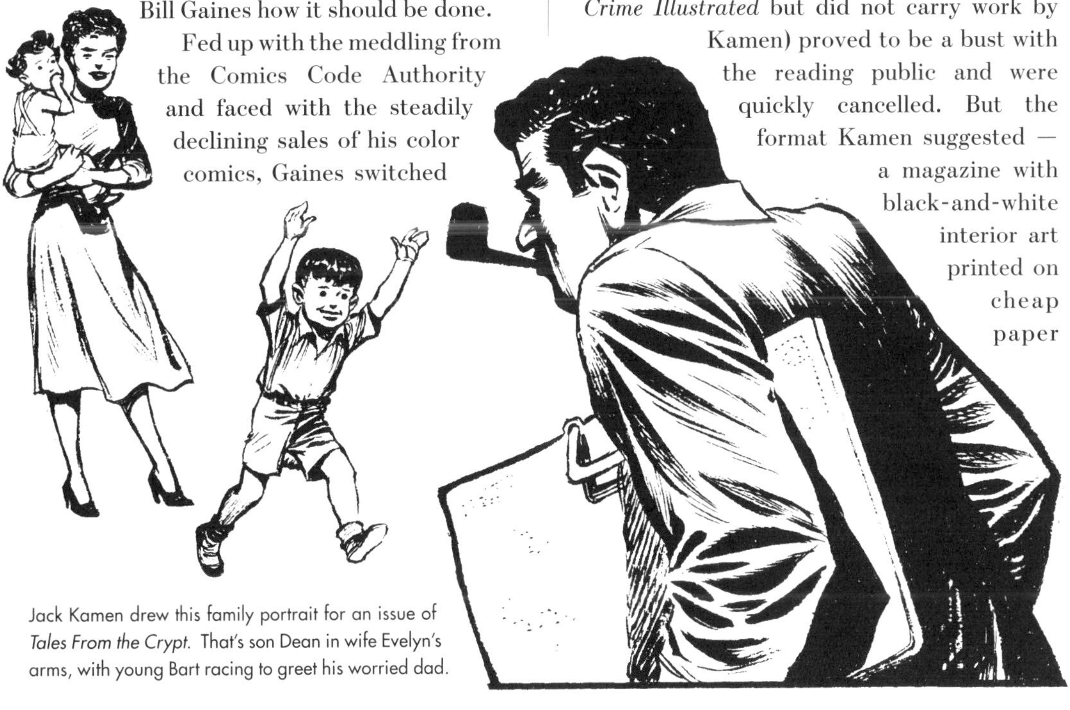

Jack Kamen drew this family portrait for an issue of *Tales From the Crypt*. That's son Dean in wife Evelyn's arms, with young Bart racing to greet his worried dad.

with glossy color covers — was a winner that Gaines employed for decades with *Mad*, though Kamen wasn't involved in the decision to transform *Mad* from its initial comic book format. *Mad*, of course, went on to become one of the most financially profitable and innovative humor magazines of the 20th century, and is still being published (albeit in a different, slicker format that employs full color throughout).

Kamen had seen the handwriting on the wall and he shifted from comics to the far more lucrative field of advertising illustration, producing black-and-white drawings and color paintings for a variety of prestigious clients, including Playtex, Smith-Corona, Reynolds Aluminum, Mack Truck, and U.S. Steel.

Among his most notable post-EC accomplishments was his work as art director for all 18 volumes of the *Harwyn Picture Encyclopedia* (1958), which utilized the talents of many of Kamen's EC Comics colleagues, including Reed Crandall, Wallace Wood, George Evans, Al Williamson, and Angelo Torres, and other talents, such as Bob Powell and Joe Sinnott. At a time when cartooning jobs were in short supply, most of them appreciated Kamen's thoughtfulness in giving them work, although the notoriously hard-to-get-along-with Wood later said, "I worked for Jack once. He was doing a comic book encyclopedia for some agency. I think everybody did panels for it. There would be a page on Ben Franklin, which would be set up like a splash page with a couple of boxes. It looked sort of like [Ripley's] *Believe-It-Or-Not*. There were thousands of these pages to do. And I quit."

Kamen stuck with advertising for several decades, but in later years, he also did technical drawings and advertising art for his son Dean's inventions, and for some of the other businesses his family owned. By the time he retired from commercial art in the late 1980s, Kamen was financially far more comfortable than most artists, not only from his own long and prolific career, but also because he had mortgaged his house to bankroll his son Dean's early inventions and had profited from that success.

"I'm pretty well off," Kamen noted in a 1995 interview. "[We have] a medical research company. We have a helicopter company, and we have real estate ... we were, at one time, the largest producer of portable medical equipment, the portable infusion pump, which actually started the whole business ..."

His only other comics-related work after EC was doing the movie poster for the 1982 EC-inspired film *Creepshow*. His poster also became the cover for the graphic novel adaptation of the film, which was drawn in its entirety by EC acolyte Bernie Wrightson. Kamen also drew some pages of comic art that were featured in the film. In 2000, Kamen was honored with an Inkpot Award at Comic-Con International: San Diego.

After a long, happy, and artistically fulfilled life, Jack Kamen died peacefully at his home in Boca Raton, Florida, August 5th, 2008, from causes related to cancer. He was survived by his wife Evelyn, his sons Barton, Dean, and Mitch, his daughter (and Mitch's twin) Terri, and one grandchild. Barton Kamen died in 2012.

S.C. "STEVE" RINGGENBERG *has been an EC Comics fan since his early teens and has had the good fortune to interview many EC contributors, including publisher William Gaines, editors Al Feldstein and Harvey Kurtzman, and artists John Severin, George Evans, Jack Davis, Jack Kamen, Al Williamson, Angelo Torres, and Frank Frazetta. He has written comics scripts for DC, Marvel, Bongo, Heavy Metal, Red Circle, and Americomics. He has authored six young adult novels and co-authored* Al Williamson: Hidden Lands.

FROM SCIENCE FICTION TO SCIENCE FORTUNE

When Jack Kamen decided to mortgage his house to invest in his son Dean's idea for a portable drug infusion pump, the younger Kamen had no idea that his dad had already designed a larger version of a comparable device 20 years earlier — in the story "Saving for the Future" (p. 29).

"Saving for the Future" was a story Bill Gaines and Al Feldstein cooked up for an issue of EC's *Weird Science* that was intended to demonstrate the power of compounding interest: a man invests $10 at 3 percent annually, waits "five hundred years," and becomes a multi-millionaire.

It was the "five hundred years" part that the two had to solve to make the story work.

Instead of a time machine, they chose to place the man (and his mistress) into a drug-induced state of suspended animation.

Feldstein wrote a description of a "foolproof" "revival mechanism" into the story, and Kamen designed the device that would inject the protagonists with the antidote at the appropriate time. (Those seeking to replicate that device might want to be cautious about suspending a chunk of radium over their pelvic region for half a millennium, however.)

As it turned out, Kamen didn't have to wait five centuries to realize his fortune and for the concept to become real. Some two decades later, his son asked him to design the look of a wearable drug infusion pump — a medical device that delivers a precise amount of a drug into the bloodstream of a patient at a specified time. The pump was patented, brought to market — and set Dean Kamen on the path to earning his own millions.

Science fiction predictions usually don't come true, but not only did this one come true — it came true in a personal way for the artist who imagined it!

RAY DOUGLAS BRADBURY (1920–2012, b. Waukegan, Illinois), one of the most well loved authors of the 20th century, was first published in 1938. He went on to write 26 more novels and more than 500 short stories and film and television scripts.

EC Comics began adapting Bradbury's stories in 1951 — without permission. Bradbury, a comics fan, caught on but instead of unleashing a lawyer, he wrote Bill Gaines, suggesting it had been an "oversight," adding, "You have not as yet sent on the check for $50.00 ...". Gaines promptly paid and that led to frequent, authorized adaptations of Bradbury's work.

Among many other honors, Bradbury was awarded the National Medal of Arts by President George W. Bush. And a real celestial object — 9766 Bradbury, a main-belt asteroid — was named for him.

Bradbury married in 1947 and had four daughters. When Bradbury died in June 2012, he was lauded by librarians, filmmakers, fellow authors, and President Barack Obama.

In August 2012, NASA named the site where the rover Curiosity landed on the surface of Mars "Bradbury Landing."

ALBERT B. FELDSTEIN (b. October 25, 1925, Brooklyn, New York) started in comics at 15 at the Eisner and Iger Studio. He graduated from the High School of Music and Art, then attended classes at Brooklyn College and the Art Students League before entering the Air Corps during World War II. After the war, he returned to Iger before moving to Fox Feature Syndicate.

Feldstein began at EC in 1947. Though initially hired as an artist, he is best known for his writing. He also served as editor for most of EC's comic book titles. With Bill Gaines, he created EC's famous line of horror comics, including *Tales From the Crypt*. He became editor of *Mad* in 1956, where he remained until 1984.

After moving to Wyoming, he fulfilled his lifelong dream of becoming a fine artist.

Feldstein was inducted into the Will Eisner Comic Book Hall of Fame in 2003. In 2011, he received the Bram Stoker Award for Lifetime Achievement from the Horror Writers Association. Feldstein lives in Livingston, Montana, with his wife, Michelle.

WILLIAM MAXWELL GAINES (1922–1992, b. New York City) was the son of M.C. Gaines, the founder and original publisher of EC Comics. Bill Gaines was studying chemistry at New York University when his father died in a boating accident in 1947, leaving him to run the family business.

Under Bill Gaines, EC became known for its popular horror, crime, war, and science fiction comics, such as *Tales From the Crypt, Crime SuspenStories, Two-Fisted Tales,* and *Weird Science* — and *Mad,* which created its own category.

In 1954, Gaines badly mishandled his appearance before a Senate subcommittee investigating the alleged link between juvenile delinquency and comic books. Shortly thereafter, EC fell victim to the Comics Code Authority, an organization hastily put together by a group of comic book publishers to head off Congressional pressure.

By 1956, EC had dropped all of its titles except *Mad.* Gaines remained publisher of *Mad* until his death in 1992. He was inducted into the Will Eisner Hall of Fame in 1993 and the Jack Kirby Hall of Fame in 1997.

JACK OLECK (1914–1981, b. Massapequa, New York) broke into comics, not once, but three times. In 1940, likely through his connection with brother-in-law Joe Simon, Oleck wrote one of the early *Silver Streak* stories for publisher Lev Gleason, only to have his career interrupted by World War II. After serving as a sergeant, he returned to become a prolific writer for the Simon and Kirby studio. He then established himself at EC Comics.

He worked on multiple titles at EC, but especially made his mark in the horror genre. After EC, Oleck became a successful publisher, editor, and acclaimed novelist. He returned to comics again in the 1970s, this time at DC Comics, where he became one of the premiere writers for DC's horror ("mystery") titles. He retired in 1979, just before his untimely death two years later at age 67.

TOM SPURGEON, JANICE LEE, *and* **ARTHUR LORTIE** *contributed to these profiles.*

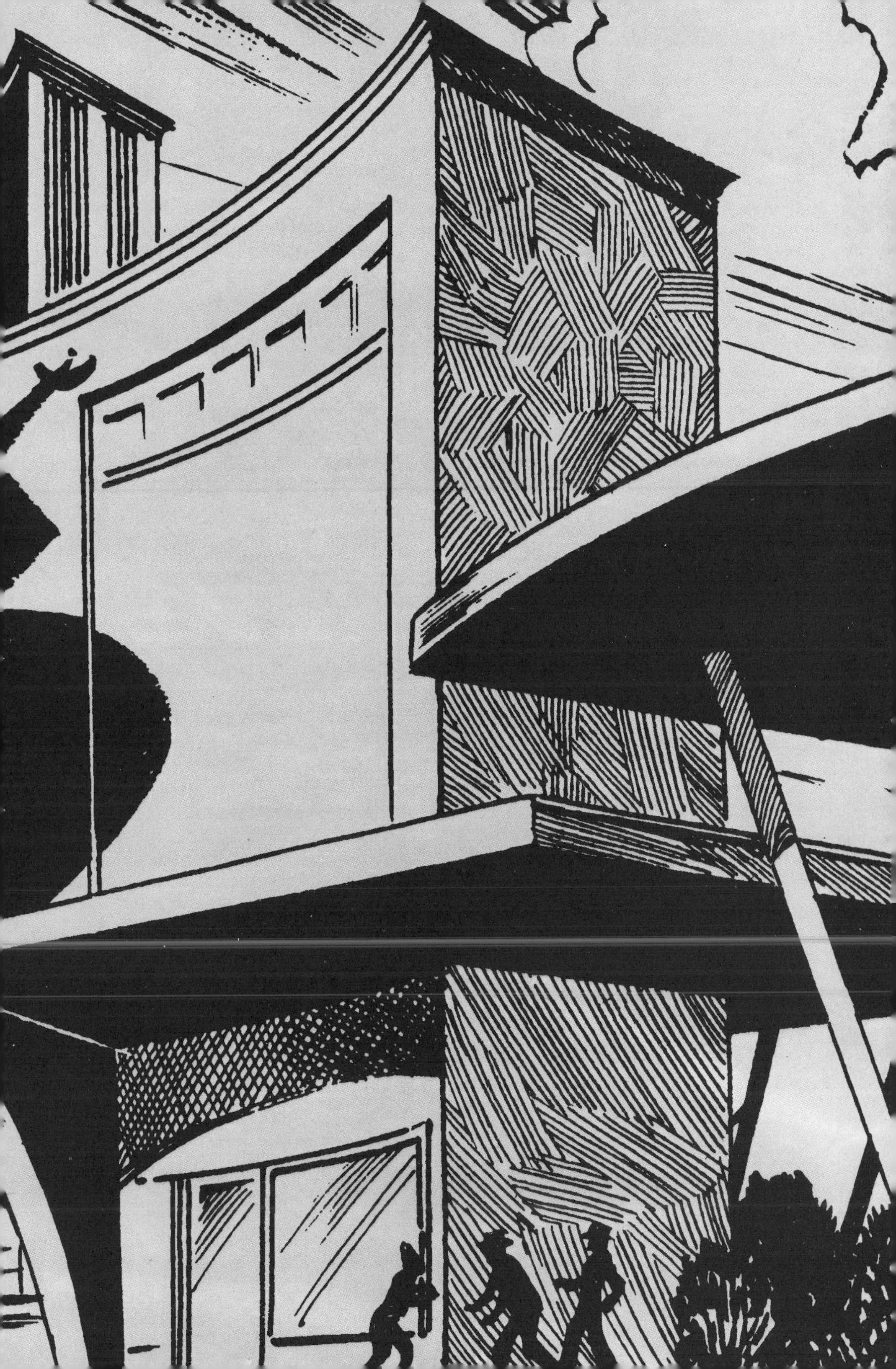

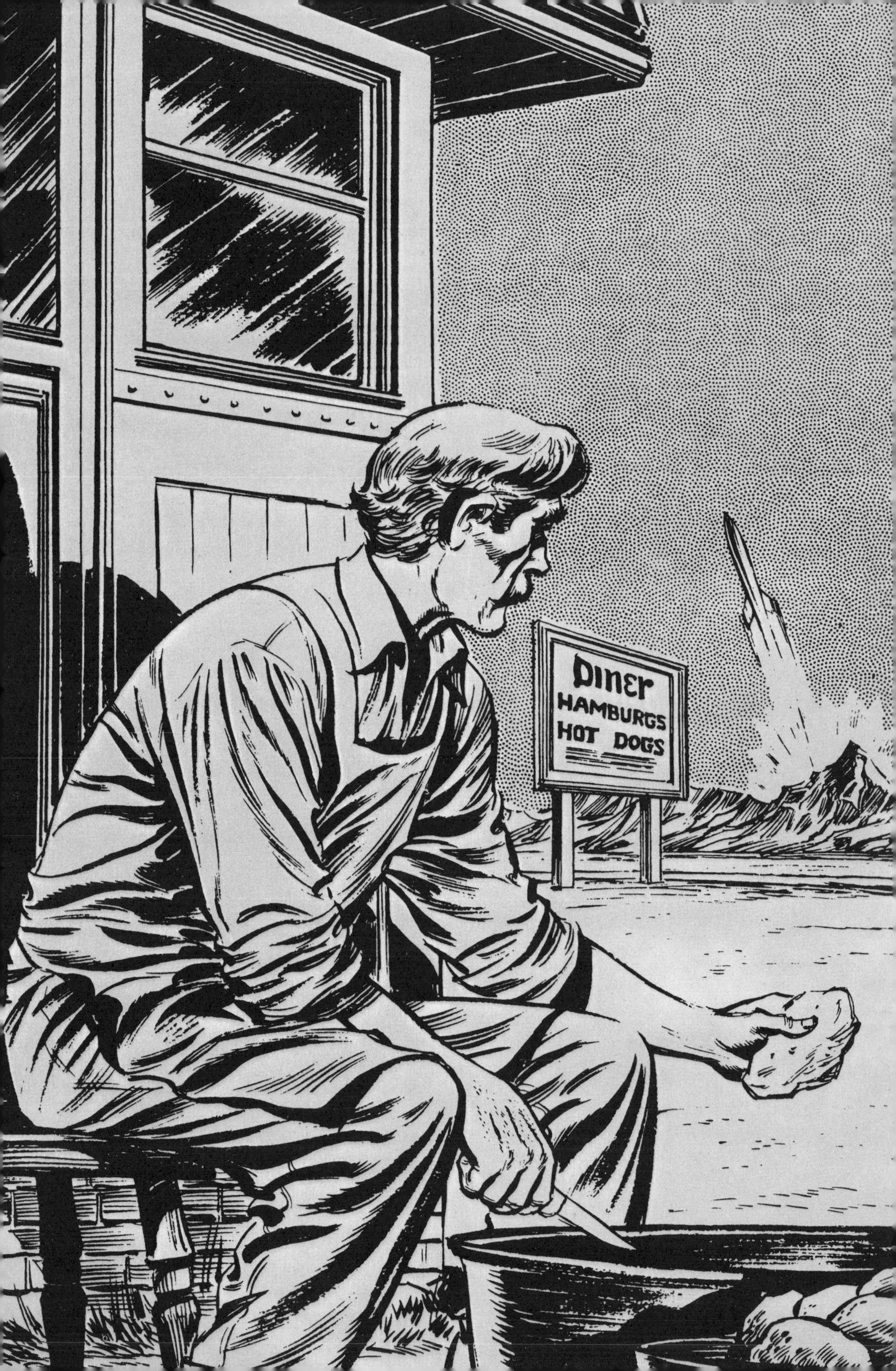
Diner
HAMBURGS
HOT DOGS